Greek Islands
by air

Introduction	vii
Travel	1
Practical A–Z	13
History, Mythology and Art	35
Athens	47
Crete	71
Direct from the UK	147
From Athens	311
Chronology and Glossary of Terms	416
Language	418
Further Reading	428
Index	429

Cadogan Guides
West End House, 11 Hills Place,
London W1R 1AG, UK
cadoganguides@morrispub.co.uk

The Globe Pequot Press
246 Goose Lane, PO Box 480, Guilford,
Connecticut 06437–0480

Copyright © Dana Facaros 1979, 1981, 1986, 1988,
1993, 1995, 1998, 2000
Updated by Catherine Weiss
Illustrations © Suzan Kentli 1995

Book and cover design by Animage
Cover photographs: front: Travel Ink/Stephen Psallidas
back: Catherine Weiss
Maps © Cadogan Guides, drawn by Map Creation Ltd

Editorial Director: Vicki Ingle
Series Editor: Linda McQueen
Editor: Christine Stroyan
Proofing: Martin Noble, Claudia Martin
Indexing: Isobel McLean
Production: Book Production Services

A catalogue record for this book is available from the British Library
ISBN 1-86011-943-3

Printed and bound in Italy by LEGOPRINT.

We have done our best to ensure that the information in this guide is correct at the time of going to press. But places and facilities are constantly changing, and standards and prices in hotels and restaurants fluctuate. We would be delighted to receive any comments concerning existing entries or omissions. Authors of the best letters will receive a copy of the Cadogan Guide of their choice.

About the Author

Dana Facaros lives in Ireland with her husband, writer Michael Pauls, and children Jackson and Lily. Her Greek father comes from Ikaría and her golfing mother has now shot six holes-in-one.

Acknowledgements

A big *efcháristo parapolí* to my ever-affable hosts extraordinaire and experts on the Greek condition, Michael and Brian; to my cousin Filia for everything, and Toula and Kosta and Anna and Theophilos on Ikaria; to Gina and Anita on Astypalaia, Elias and Argyro on Karpathos, Niko and Anna on Lipsi, Nokos on Folegandros, the new owners of the Ios Club, Petros on Kythnos, Sophia on Sífnos, Apostoli on Sikinos, Panyioti of Teamwork on Syros, and all the people on the various island tourist offices who lent a hand. Heartfelt thanks to Catherine for her fantastic updating work, and to Christine for her editing.

About the Updater

Catherine Weiss has crossed five continents and lived in the USA, Argentina, Portugal, Belgium and England. After dallying with City life, she left law to return to Greece, which she first visited 20 years ago. Catherine is now pursuing a future in human rights, yet more experimental cooking tested on unsuspecting friends and, of course, more travel.

Updater's Acknowledgements

A huge round of thanks to everyone who brought the islands alive and humoured me when the ferries failed, and especially to: EOT in London; the honorary Irish consul and his lovely wife, Mary, on Corfu, as well as Julia, for the boozy talks about life; Joanna, who organized me on Léfkada; the Alfacars duo in Herákleon, for the endless coffee, beers, melon, eggs and cinquecento; Rosario, Pepe and Ludovico in Chaniá; Alexis in Oía; Peter, for his invaluable advice and delightful company on Páros; Despina and Stavros of Náxos Information Centre; Tim on Rhodes; Alexis, who was so generous and ferried me around Kos; Giorgos and his sublime fare on Léros; Jocelyn, who was there when the boats weren't on Sámos; the Spordilises in Chíos; the vital Jan in Sígri and Barbara, fount of intriguing tales in Vaterá; Christine; and to Alex, without whom it wouldn't have happened.

Contents

Introduction   vii

Travel   1–12

Getting to Greece and the Islands	2	Getting Around Greece and the Islands	8
Entry Formalities	7	Specialist Holidays	10

Practical A–Z   13–34

Bugs and Pests	14	National Holidays	24
Climate, Measures and Time	14	The Per**í**ptero	24
Electricity	15	Post Offices	25
Embassies and Consulates	15	Shopping	25
Events and Cultural Attractions	15	Sports	25
		Telephones	26
Food and Drink	17	Toilets and Water	27
Health	22	Tourist Information	27
Money	23	Travelling with Children	28
Museums, Archaeological Sites and Opening Hours	23	Where to Stay	28
		Women Travellers	33

History, Mythology and Art   35–46

Modern Greece: An Outline of Recent History	36	A Brief Outline of Greek Art and Architecture	42
A Quick Who's Who in Greek Mythology	41		

Athens   47–70

History	48	Other Museums and Sites	60
Getting Around	51	Byzantine Churches and Monasteries	62
Tourist Information	52		
Orientation	53	Where to Stay	63
Major Museums and Sites	55	Eating Out	66
The Heart of Ancient Athens	58	Entertainment and Nightlife	69

Crete 71–146

History	75	Herákleon	103
Chaniá	80	Knossós	110
Nomós Chaniá	87	Nomós Herákleon	118
The Gorge of Samariá	90	Nomós Lassíthi	130
Réthymnon	95	Ag. Nikólaos	134
Nomós Réthymnon	98		

Direct from the UK 147–310

Corfu	148	Náxos	228
Kefaloniá	173	Rhodes	236
Kos	188	Sými	265
Psérimos	199	Sámos	271
Lefkáda	200	Skiáthos	280
Meganísi	210	Thássos	293
Lésbos	210	Zákynthos	299

From Athens 311–415

Astypálaia	312	Mílos	364
Chíos	315	Mýkonos	372
Ikaría	329	Délos	378
Foúrni	335	Páros	384
Kárpathos	336	Antíparos	391
Kýthera	344	Santoríni	392
Léros	351	Skýros	402
Límnos	357	Sýros	409
Ag. Efstrátios	363		

Chronology and Glossary of Terms 416–17

Language 418–27

Further Reading 428

Index 429–38

Maps

Greek Islands	*inside front cover*
Athens	*inside back cover*
Crete	72
Chaniá	81
Nomós Chaniá	88
Nomós Réthymnon	100
Herákleon	104–5
Knossós	114
Nomós Herákleon	120
Phaistós	125
Nomós Lassíthi	131
Zákros	145
Corfu	149
Corfu Town	156–7
Kefaloniá	175
Kos	189
Kos Town	193
Léfkada	201
Lésbos	213
Mytílini Town	216
Náxos	231
Rhodes	239
Rhodes Town	246–7
Sými	265
Sámos	273
Sámos/Váthi	276
Skiáthos	287
Thássos	295
Zákynthos	300
Astypálaia	313
Chíos	317
Chíos Town	319
Ikaría	329
Kárpathos	339
Kýthera	345
Léros	352
Límnos	359
Mílos	365
Mýkonos	373
Délos	380
Páros	384
Santoríni	393
Skýros	404
Sýros	410

Introduction

What weighs the bosom of Abraham and the immaterial spectres of Christian paradise against this Greek eternity made of water, rock and cooling winds?

Níkós Kazantzákis

There's nothing like the Greek islands to make the rest of the world seem blurred, hesitant and grey. Their frontiers are clearly defined by a sea that varies from emerald and turquoise to indigo blue, with none of the sloppiness of a changing tide; the clear sky and dry air cut their mountainous contours into sharp outline; the whiteness and simplicity of their architecture is both abstract and organic. Even the smells, be they fragrant (lemon blossoms, incense, wild thyme, grilling fish) or stinks (donkey flops, caique diesel engines, plastic melted cheese sandwiches) are pure and unforgettable. In such an environment, the islanders themselves have developed strong, open and often quirky characters; they have bright eyes and are quick to laugh or cry or scream in fury, or shamelessly enquire into the intimate details of your personal life ('Just how much do you weigh?'), or offer unsolicited lectures on politics, how to brush your teeth or find a good husband.

Since the 1970s this clarity and brightness have been magnets to the world beyond. After shipping, tourism is Greece's most important source of income, to the extent that migrants from the north have become a regular fixture in the seasonal calendar: first comes Lent and Greek Easter, then the tourists, followed by the grape harvest, and, in December, the olives. From June to September, flights and accommodation are packed with holidaymakers, both Greek and foreign. The popularity of the islands has meant that they have become increasingly easy to reach. It is now possible to fly inexpensively to Athens and pick up a flight to an island—or even fly direct to many islands from major European cities.

As each island has its own strong character, each has responded to the influx in a different way. On some islands, resort hotels have toadstooled up willy-nilly in search of the fast package-tour buck, while other islands cling stubbornly to their traditions and do all they can to keep outside interests from exploiting their coasts. Others still, including some of the most visited, are enjoying a renaissance of traditional arts and customs, often led by the young who are pained to see their centuries-old heritage eroding into Euro-blandness.

This book is geared towards the airborne traveller, but its scope extends far beyond package-tour resorts. Beautiful places don't have to be difficult to reach, and whether you seek all the mod-cons of home, sports facilities and dancing until dawn, or an island rich in ancient sites, Byzantine frescoes, landscapes and beautiful villages, or just an escape to a secluded shore where there's the luxury of doing nothing at all, this is the guide to help you find it. Or perhaps you want a bit of each. For, in spite of all the rush to join the 20th century, the Greek islands have retained the enchantment that inspired Homer and Byron—the 'wine-dark sea', the scent of jasmine at twilight and nights alive with shooting stars. The ancient Greeks dedicated the islands to the gods, and they have yet to surrender them entirely to us mortals.

The Islands at a Glance

There are 3,000 Greek islands, of which a mere 170 or so are inhabited. This book covers the 25 you can fly to from Athens; 12 also have direct connections from the UK. Picking an island is as personal as choosing a flavour in an ice-cream parlour. The following thumbnail sketches of the islands in this book start with the more touristy ones.

Mýkonos, as jet-setty as you can get, still retains an air of class, despite the hordes that it attracts. It has great beaches and the best nightlife (both gay and straight), and is only a short boat ride from holy Délos, now an outdoor archaeological museum. Cosmopolitan **Skiáthos**, lusher and greener, with some of the best beaches in the Mediterranean, matches Mýkonos in prices, if not in spirit. The lovely islands of **Kos** and **Zákynthos** have lost much of their original character under the strain of mass package tourism, but there's plenty going on to keep you amused, as on **Páros**, which paradoxically has retained its island charm, despite being a top destination for backpackers and the jet set alike. Volcanic, dramatically beautiful **Santoríni** is the number one spot for visiting cruise ships, honeymooners and practically every first-timer to Greece. The two queens of Greek tourism, **Corfu** and **Rhodes**, are both large enough to absorb huge numbers of tourists, but suffer from pockets of mass package tourism of the least attractive type. Both have stunning capitals and charming mountain villages.

Crete, 'the Big Island', has everything for everyone: the glories of Minoan civilization, the riviera around Ag. Nikólaos, the mighty mountain ranges and the Gorge of Samariá, the Venetian charms of Chaniá and Réthymnon, traditional villages, palm groves, superb beaches on every coast and a strong sense of island identity.

Arguably the best type of island holiday can be found on islands where there are enough tourists to ensure more than basic facilities—watersports, a choice of decent tavernas, a bar or two for an evening drink and, most important of all, a place to sit out and watch life idle by. **Léfkada, Mílos, Náxos, Límnos, Skýros, Kefaloniá, Léros** and **Sýros** fall happily into this category; all have a mixture of rugged island scenery, typical villages, good restaurants and swimming. Then there are special cases like **Kárpathos**, which has dramatic scenery and a strong folklore tradition and is popular with both Greek and foreign tourists. Off in the Northeastern Aegean, the large, lush and lovely islands of **Sámos, Chíos** and **Lésbos** (all with growing package trade, especially Sámos) and smaller **Thássos** provide everything required for the perfect island holiday, as well as plenty of places to explore. Greek tourists have always preferred them to the barren, whitewashed Cyclades.

Lastly, there are islands that come under the heading of 'almost away from it all'—not quite your desert island but not a lot to do after a two or three days unless you are resourceful—**Astypálaia, Ikaría** and **Kýthera** fall more or less into this category, each with its own individual charms.

Timing is important. From mid-July to 20 August the footloose independent traveller can expect nothing but frustration trying to find an unbooked room on the more popular islands or on the smaller ones with a limited number of beds. Also, don't assume that the more isolated the island, the cheaper the rooms. Out of season you can pick and choose; islands with a high percentage of Greek tourists (Límnos, Lésbos, Ikaría, Kýthera) tend to be especially good value, although expect to see fewer signs in English. The vast majority of hotels and restaurants close in November and reopen in April; Rhodes and Crete open the earliest and are the last to shut.

A Guide to the Guide

The **Travel** and **Practical A–Z** chapters are packed with information to help you plan your holiday, covering everything from tour operators to toilets. The next chapter contains a rapid rundown of modern Greek **history** and some background on **art and architecture**, as well as a brief who's who in **mythology**.

The main part of the guide comprises four chapters. Many of you will pass through **Athens** on your way to or from the Greek islands and may well spend at least one night, so highlights of that city are covered in a chapter of its own. **Crete**, too, as the largest of the islands, has a chapter to itself. The rest of the isles are divided into two chapters, reflecting visitors' most likely mode of airborne arrival: **Direct from the UK** or **From Athens**. There's practical advice on getting there and, once there, away from the airport and the main resorts to the most charming corners of each island. Five satellite islets—**Psérimos, Meganísi, Sými, Délos** and **Antíparos**—which make good excursions by boat from the main islands are also covered in this guide.

The book concludes with a **Chronology and Glossary of Terms,** a chapter on **Language** which supplies essential phrases and useful vocabulary, and suggestions for **Further Reading**.

A Note on Pronunciation

There is no general agreement within Greece on a standard method of transliterating the Greek alphabet into Roman letters. This means that you will constantly come across many variations in the spellings of place names and words, on maps, in books and on road signs. To help you, this book includes island names and those of major towns in the Greek alphabet. When transcribing, we have used D for the Greek *delta* (Δ), which you may see elsewhere as DH or TH, CH for *chi* (X), which is pronounced like the 'ch' in 'loch' and which you may see written as H, e.g. in Chaniá or Chóra; F for *fi* (Φ), which you may see elsewhere as PH; and G for the Greek *gamma* (Γ), which sounds more like a guttural GH verging on a Y, e.g. with *agios* (saint), pronounced more like 'ayios'. Exceptions to this are made where there is a very common ancient name or modern English spelling such as Phaistos or Rhodes.

Stressing the right syllable is vital to the correct pronunciation of Greek; in this book the stressed letter of each word or name is accented with an acute (´) accent.

See also **Language** pp.418–27.

Flying to Greece and the Islands	2
Entry Formalities	7
Getting Around the Islands	8
Specialist Holidays	10

Travel

Flying to Greece and the Islands

The bible of travel to and around Greece is the *Greek Travel Pages*, updated monthly. Consult a copy at the Greek National Tourist Organization or a travel agency specializing in Greece, or check out the websites at *www.gogreece.com* and *www.gtpnet.com*.

'The air and sky are free,' Daedalus told his son Icarus as he planned their ill-fated winged escape from Crete. They aren't free any more, but you can fly fairly inexpensively if you look around. As competition increases in Europe, don't automatically assume that charter flights, with their restrictions, are your best buy; flying with the Greek national carrier Olympic opens up very reasonable onward prices to island airports. Students or anyone under 26 will find the most bargains (*see* pp.4–5). The good news is that you can get 'open jaw' tickets flying into one Greek airport and out of another (e.g. UK–Athens, Athens–Santoríni, Santoríni–UK). The bad news is that a Greek airport tax (£20 at the time of writing) is added on to some ticket prices. Anyone arriving from Cyprus with Turkish Cypriot stamps in their passport will automatically be refused entry to Greece.

Charter Flights

Charter flights **to Athens** are frequent in the summer from Europe, less frequent from North America and non-existent from Australasia. Europeans also have the luxury of charter flights **direct to many islands** (notably, from London Gatwick, Luton, Glasgow, Cardiff, Newcastle, Manchester and Belfast in the UK, and Dublin). Check the travel sections in the major weekend papers, *Time Out* or the London *Evening Standard* for last-minute discounts on unsold seats, or get advice from your local travel agent or the specialists listed below. Most UK charters run from May to mid-October, but some firms feature early specials in March and April, depending on when Greek Easter falls, usually from London Gatwick and Manchester.

Charter tickets have fixed outward and return dates, usually for one- or two-week periods with, as often as not, departure and arrival times in the wee hours. Nowadays the Greek authorities have completely relaxed their previously strict rules on visiting Turkey from Greece if you have flown in on a charter flight (however, this does not apply to Northern Cyprus; *see* above); if you want to hop over to Turkey, Sámos, Rhodes or Kos are the easiest island departure points. Returning from Greece, make sure you confirm your return flight three days prior to departure.

Scheduled Flights from the UK and Ireland

There are scheduled flights direct to Athens several times daily from London with **Olympic**, **British Airways**, **easyJet**, **Virgin Atlantic** and **Cronus Air** (a private, well-run Greek company). In the peak season Olympic flies three times daily from Heathrow and twice daily from Manchester (remember, if you book an international flight on Olympic through a travel agent you should be able to obtain massive discounts on onward flights to domestic destinations in Greece; fares can be as low as £20.) Olympic also offers direct flights from London Gatwick to Thessaloníki (and on to Athens), convenient if you plan to visit the more northerly islands. Cronus offers flights to Athens (and from Athens on Aegean Airlines to Corfu and Santoríni), and also has direct connections from Heathrow to Crete and Rhodes. Eastern European companies such as **Czech Airlines** also fly to Athens and can work out slightly cheaper in season, but you may have to wait for hours for connections in Prague. Apex and

SuperApex flights and easyJet offer substantially reduced fares, with flights from London to Athens ranging from £70–80 low season to £220 high season. They must, however, be paid for instantly and are not refundable or flexible.

Scheduled flights from Ireland to Athens on Olympic and Aer Lingus fly via Heathrow and tend to be considerably pricier than charters.

Aer Lingus	Belfast ✆ (0845) 973 7747; Dublin ✆ (01) 705 3333
British Airways	London and Belfast ✆ (0345) 222 111; Dublin ✆ (1 800) 626 747, *www.britishairways.com*
Cronus Airlines	UK ✆ (020) 7580 3500
Czech Airlines	London ✆ (020) 7255 1898, *www.czech-airways.com*
easyJet	UK ✆ (0870) 6000 000, *www.easyjet.com*
Olympic Airways	London ✆ (0870) 660 460; Dublin ✆ (01) 608 0090, *www.olympicairways.co.uk*
Virgin Atlantic	London ✆ (01293) 747 747, *www.virgin.com*

discounts and special deals

Avro, charter flights to Athens, Corfu and Crete from London Gatwick ✆ (020) 8715 0000.

Balkan Tours, ✆ (01232) 246 795. Charter flights to Crete and Rhodes from Belfast.

Delta Travel, ✆ (0161) 272 8455; ✆ (0151) 708 7955; ✆ (0121) 471 2282, *www.deltatravel.co.uk*. Manchester-based agents for scheduled flights from Heathrow to Athens; and from Manchester and Birmingham to Athens and Thessaloníki; also island charters flying direct to a wide range of islands including Rhodes, Crete and Corfu.

Eclipse Direct, reservations ✆ (0870) 501 0203; ✆ (01293) 554400; ✆ (0161) 742 2277. Charter flights from London Gatwick, Manchester and Birmingham direct to Corfu, Crete and Rhodes, as well as Athens.

Island Wandering, ✆ (01580) 860733. Helpful company offering very reasonably priced accommodation and/or island-hopping package holidays on 54 Greek islands. Good advice on flight booking and routes etc.

Trailfinders, London, ✆ (020) 7738 3939; Bristol ✆ (0117) 929 9000; Birmingham ✆ (0121) 236 1234; Manchester ✆ (0161) 839 6969; Glasgow ✆ (0141) 353 2224. One of the best for finding affordable flights.

Virgin Sun, ✆ (01293) 616261, *www.virginholidays.co.uk*. Charter flights and 7–14-day package holidays from Gatwick/Manchester via Athens to Rhodes, Crete, Corfu and Kos. They can offer a few flight-only tickets, but you will be restricted to 7- or 14-day time spans.

Scheduled Flights from North America

Olympic, TWA and **Delta** offer daily nonstop flights from New York to Athens in the summer. Olympic also flies direct to Athens from Boston, and from Toronto and Montreal in Canada. American economy fares (Apex and SuperApex/Eurosavers, booked at least three weeks in advance) range from $750 return New York–Athens in low season to $1,200 high season. Canadian economy fares to Athens from Toronto or Montreal range from $1,000 low season to $1,400–1,900 high season. When ringing around, take into consideration the hefty discount offered by travel agents on domestic flights within Greece for travellers on Olympic Airlines. From many cities in the USA and Canada, European airlines such as **KLM** or **Czech Airlines** offer the best deals to Greece. Finally, if you have more time than money, get a cheap or standby flight to London and once there hunt down a cheap ticket to an island (*see* above), although this may be a headache in July and August.

Air Canada	Canada ✆ (888) 247 2262; *www.aircanada.ca*
British Airways	USA and Canada ✆ (800) AIRWAYS/247 9297
Czech Airlines	USA ✆ (800) 223 2365. All flights via Prague.
Delta	USA ✆ (800) 241 414, *www.delta-air.com*
KLM	USA ✆ (800) 374 7747; Canada ✆ (800) 361 5330
Olympic Airways	USA ✆ (800) 223 1226; New York ✆ (212) 735 0200 or 838 3600 (reservations); Canada: Montreal ✆ (514) 878 9691; Toronto ✆ (416) 964 2720; *www.olympicairways.gr*
TWA	USA ✆ (800) 892 4141
Virgin	USA ✆ (800) 862 8621

discounts and special deals

Air Brokers International, USA (800) 883 3273. Discount agency.

Encore Travel Club, USA (800) 444 9800. Scheduled flight discount club.

Homeric Tours, USA ✆ (800) 223 5570, @ 753 0319. Charter flights and custom tours.

Last Minute Travel Club, USA (800) 527 8646. Annual membership fee gets you cheap standby deals.

New Frontiers, USA ✆ (800) 366 6387.

Travel Avenue, USA ✆ (800) 333 3335.

Scheduled Flights from Australasia

Olympic flies at least twice a week direct to Athens from Melbourne and Sydney,and, though their fares aren't the cheapest, consider the discounts the Greek carrier offers international passengers on its domestic flights. Other carriers include Quntas, KLM, British Airways and Singapore Airlines. If you can pick up a bargain flight to London, it may work out cheaper to take that and find a discount flight from there (*see* above).

Air New Zealand	Auckland ✆ (09) 357 3000; Sydney ✆ (09) 937 5299
British Airways	Sydney ✆ (02) 8904 8800; Auckland ✆ (09) 356 8690
KLM	Australia ✆ (1 300) 303 747
Olympic Airlines	Sydney and Brisbane toll free ✆ (008) 221 663; Melbourne ✆ (008) 933 1448; Adelaide toll free ✆ (1 800) 331 448; no office in New Zealand
Qantas	Sydney ✆ (02) 9691 3636; Auckland ✆ (09) 357 8700

Student and Youth Travel

If you're under 26 or a full-time student under 32 with an **International Student Identity Card** to prove it, you are eligible for **student/youth charters**. These are often sold as one-way tickets, enabling you to stay in Greece longer than is possible with a regular charter flight. Students under 26 are sometimes eligible for discounts on scheduled flights as well, especially with Olympic Airways, who currently offer excellent discounts to ISIC card holders on connecting flights from Athens to the islands. Young people of Greek origin (age 10–15) may be eligible for Gold Card discounts (contact your country's Greek National Tourist Organization). Specialists in youth and student travel include:

Council Travel, 205 E. 42nd St, New York, NY 10017, ✆ (800) 822 2700. Major specialist in student and charter flights; branches all over the **USA**.

STA Travel, 74 & 86 Old Brompton Rd, London SW7 and 84 Shaftesbury Ave, London W1V 7AD, ✆ (020) 7361 6161; Bristol ✆ (0117) 929 4399; Cambridge ✆ (01223) 366966; Leeds ✆ (0113) 244 9212; Manchester ✆ (0161) 834 0668; Oxford ✆ (01865) 792800; and many other branches in the UK. In the **USA**, New York City ✆ (212) 627 3111; outside New York ✆ (800) 777 0112.

Travel Cuts, 187 College St, Toronto, Ontario M5T 1P7, ✆ (416) 979 2406. **Canada**'s largest student travel specialists; branches in most provinces.

usit, Aston Quay, Dublin 2, ✆ (01) 679 8833; Cork ✆ (021) 270 900; Belfast ✆ (01232) 324 073; Galway (091) 565 177; Limerick (061) 415 064; Waterford (051) 72601. **Ireland**'s largest student travel agents.

usit Campus Travel, 52 Grosvenor Gardens, London SW1W OAG, ✆ (020) 7730 3402; *www.usitcampus.co.uk*. Branches at most UK universities: Bristol ✆ (0117) 929 2494; Cambridge ✆ (01223) 324283; Edinburgh ✆ (0131) 668 3303; Leeds ✆ (0113) 246 1155; Manchester ✆ (0161) 833 2046; Oxford ✆ (01865) 242067. Runs its own youth charters to Athens in summer.

Children and Pregnancy

Free child places on package holidays and discount air fares for tiny travellers vary from company to company. Get a good travel agent, trawl through the brochures and read all the small print. The big package operators geared to family holidays, such as Thomson, offer a wide range of child discounts and seasonal savers with in-resort amusements, kiddie clubs and baby-sitting, as well as deals for children under 12 in hotels and teenagers up to 17 in self-catering accommodation. On some UK charter flights, infants under two travel free on a full fare-paying adult's lap, while on others you may be charged £15–£20 for the baby, or 10% of the adult fare. Children from two to 12 cost from 25%–65%, and over 12 you'll have to fork out full fare. On international Olympic flights, you'll pay 67% of the adult fare for children aged two to 12 and 10% for infants under two, while under-12s go for half-fare on all domestic flights. Watch out for birthdays; if your toddler has crossed the magic two-year-old age barrier by the return journey you'll have to pay for another seat. Note that many airlines won't let single mothers travel with two infants, although you may get around the restriction by having one on your lap and one in a car seat; explain your position when you book in case they are adamant on the one child per adult rule or turn you away at check-in.

If you're pregnant, think before you fly. Although Greek hospitals have improved in recent years, you should make sure your insurance covers repatriation. Most airlines will carry women up to 34 weeks of pregnancy—Olympic even later—but you will have to provide a doctor's certificate after 28 weeks to prove you are well enough to fly. Again, check when you book.

Getting to and from Ellinikon Airport, Athens

Athens' Ellinikon Airport is divided into three terminals: East Terminal (used by some charters, all non-Olympic international airlines and Air Greece/Aegean), West Terminal, or Olympiki (used for all Olympic Airlines flights, both international and domestic) and the Charter Terminal; if you're on a charter, double-check to make sure you go to the right one. Express bus 091 connects all three terminals to central Athens, stopping in front of the post office in Sýntagma Square and leaving from Stadíou Street by Omónia Square every 20 minutes between 5.21am and midnight and every hour at night from 1.12am to 4.12am. Fares are 160dr from 7am to 11.30pm, 200dr otherwise. From Karaiskaki Square in Piraeus, express bus no.19 goes to the airport's three terminals every hour from 6am to midnight, and at 2.30am and 5am. The same buses will take you from terminal to terminal, or catch a taxi (under 1,500dr). For more on taxis and getting around Athens, see p.51.

There's a **left luggage** facility in the Olympic terminal, and another at the international terminal, down at the far end beyond the charters' hall.

essential airport numbers (℡ 01–)

East Terminal	℡ 969 4111
West Terminal	℡ 926 9111
Charter Terminal	℡ 997 2581

airlines in Athens (℡ 01–)

Aegean Airlines	572 Vouliágmenis, Glyfáda, ℡ 998 8300, ✆ 995 7598; airport ℡ 995 0953
Aeroflot	14 Xenofóndos, ℡ 322 0986, ✆ 323 6375
Air Canada	10 Óthonos, ℡ 322 3206, ✆ 323 1057
Air France	18 Vouliágmenis, Glyfáda, ℡ 960 1100, ✆ 960 1457; airport ℡ 969 9334
Air Greece	22 Filellínon, ℡ 324 4457, ✆ 324 4479; airport ℡ 960 0646
Air Zimbabwe	22 Filellínon, ℡ 324 5415, ✆ 324 5446
Alitalia	577 Vouliágmenis, Argyroupoulis, ℡ 995 9200, ✆ 995 9214; airport ℡ 961 3621
American Airlines	15 Panepistímiou, ℡ 331 1045
British Airways	10 Óthonos, ℡ 325 0601, ✆ 325 5171; airport ℡ 961 0402
Continental Airlines	25 Filellínon, ℡ 324 9300
Cronus Airlines	517 Vouliágmenis, ℡ 995 6400, ✆ 995 6405; airport ℡ 960 1205
Cyprus Airways	10 Filellínon, ℡ 324 7801, ✆ 324 4935; airport ℡ 961 0325
Czech Airlines	15 Panepistímiou, ℡ 323 0174
Delta	4 Óthonos, ℡ 331 1668, ✆ 325 0451; airport ℡ 964 8800
Iberia	8 Xenofóndos, ℡ 323 4523; ✆ 324 0655; airport ℡ 969 9813
KLM	22 Voúlis, ℡ 988 0177; airport ℡ 969 9733
Lufthansa	East Terminal, ℡ 369 2200, ✆ 363 6881

Malev	15 Papepistímiou, ✆ 324 1116
Olympic	96 Syngroú, among many branches; reservations ✆ 966 6666, 🖷 966 6111; information ✆ 936 3363
Qantas	East Terminal, ✆ 969 9323
Sabena	41c Vouliágmenis, Glyfáda, ✆ 960 0021, 🖷 960 0219; airport ✆ 961 3903
SAS	E. Terminal, ✆ 960 1003, 🖷 960 1306; airport ✆ 961 4201
Singapore Airlines	9 Xenofóndos, ✆ 323 9111, 🖷 325 4326
South African Airways	8 Merlin, ✆ 361 7278, 🖷 362 7433
Swissair	4 Óthonos, ✆ 323 5813, 🖷 322 5548; airport ✆ 961 0203
Thai Airlines	1 Sekeri, ✆ 364 7610, 🖷 364 7680; airport ✆ 960 0607
TWA	8 Xenofóndos, ✆ 322 6451, 🖷 322 8973; airport ✆ 961 0012
United Airlines	5 Syngrou, ✆ 924 2645, 🖷 922 9268
Virgin Atlantic	8–10 Tzireon, Makrigianni, ✆ 924 9100, 🖷 924 9144; airport ✆ 960 1461

Athens to the Islands

Flights from Athens to the islands can be booked in advance through **Olympic**, notorious for the approximate nature of their plane times; as many planes are small, do this as far in advance as possible. Some only have 18 seats and are good fun; they seem to just skim over the mountain tops (but note: they can't take off or land in high winds and you could end up back where you started). Because planes are small, baggage allowances (15kg) tend to be enforced—unless you've bought your ticket abroad, when you're allowed all 23kg. Children under 12 go half-price. **Air Greece** has recently merged with Aegean and is preferable if you arrive on a non-Olympic flight since there'll be no scurrying between terminals; its flights are also cheaper. From Athens they fly to Crete, Corfu, Lésbos, Rhodes and Thessaloníki, as well as Crete and Rhodes to Thessaloníki. **Cronus** flies the same routes bar Lésbos and Corfu.

Island-to-Island Flights

Olympic Airways also offer island-to-island flights in season, which precludes the need to go to Athens. Although these have a habit of changing from year to year, flights between Crete and Santoríni/Rhodes; Lésbos and Límnos/Chíos; Rhodes and Santoríni/Mýkonos/Kárpathos; and Santoríni and Mýkonos are well-established. It's also possible to get a scheduled 'open-jaws' ticket to Athens and on to any permutation of islands, but you have to return home from Athens.

Entry Formalities

All **European Union** members can stay indefinitely. The only reason you would need special permission to stay would be for working or if complicated banking procedures were involved requiring proof of residence; contact the Aliens Bureau at 173 Leof. Alexandrás, 11522 Athens,

℗ (01) 646 8103. The formalities for **non-EU tourists** entering Greece are very simple: American, Australian and Canadian citizens can stay for up to three months in Greece on presentation of a valid passport; South Africans are permitted two months. If you want to stay longer, 20 days before your time in Greece expires take your passport to the Aliens Bureau or your local police station, and be prepared to prove you can support yourself with bank statements and the like. If you overstay your three months, be prepared to pay a fine of 22,200dr.

Getting Around the Islands

Tourist Excursion Boats

These are generally slick and clean, and have become quite numerous in recent years. They are usually more expensive than the regular ferries or steamers, but often have schedules that allow visitors to make day trips to nearby islands (though you can also take them one-way), and are very convenient, having largely taken the place of the little caique operators, many of whom now specialize in excursions to remote beaches. Hydrofoils may well allow for day trips to neighbouring islands too, but beware: all water transport is delightfully at the mercy of those Greek gales.

By Car

There are countless rent-a-car firms on the islands; most are family-run and fairly reliable (asking around a bit will usually reveal who the stinkers are). If an island has a lot of unpaved roads and not a lot of competition, prices tend to be higher; at the time of writing, hiring a small car varies between 10–15,000dr a day in the summer, and open-air Jeeps at least one-third more. Most require that you be at least 21, some 25. Most cars offer unlimited mileage and third-party insurance; check the small print of your contract with care and don't be surprised if you have to leave your driving licence as security. In the off season, negiotiate. Arriving at a car hire agent's with a handful of brochures from the competition has been known to strengthen one's bargaining position. Fuel at the time of writing cost around 280–300dr a litre; unleaded (*amólivdi*) a wee bit less.

An **International Driving Licence** is not required for EU citizens to drive in Greece, although if you hire a car some car hire companies require one anyway. EU citizens and other nationals can obtain an international licence at home, or from one of the Automobile Club offices in Greece (ELPA), by presenting a national driving licence, passport and photograph. The minimum age is 18 years.

AA	General enquiries, ℗ (0800) 88 77 66; advice on international driving permits, motorway tolls and travel abroad, ℗ 0990 500 600
RAC	General enquiries, ℗ (0800) 550 055; advice on routes and international driving permits, ℗ (0906) 470 1740 (60p a minute)
AAA	General enquiries, ℗ (1 800) JOIN AAA

While driving in the centre of Athens may be a hair-raising experience, the rest of Greece is fairly easy and pleasant. There are few cars on most roads, even in summer, and most signs, when you're lucky enough to find one, have their Latin equivalents. Traffic regulations and signalling comply with standard practice on the European Continent (i.e. driving on the right).

Crossroads, tipsy tourists, Greeks arguing and gesticulating while driving, and low visibility in the mountains are probably the greatest hazards. Where there are no right-of-way signs at a crossroads, give priority to traffic coming from the right, and always beep your horn on blind corners. If you're exploring, you may want to take a spare container of petrol along, as stations can be scarce on the ground (especially on the islands) and only open shop hours. There is a speed limit of 50km per hour (30mph) in inhabited areas.

By Motorbike and Moped

Motorbikes and even more popular mopeds are ideal for the islands in the summer. It almost never rains, and what could be more pleasant than a gentle, thyme-scented breeze freshening your journey? Scooters (the Greeks call them *papákia*, 'little ducks', supposedly for the noise they make) are both more economical and more practical than cars. They can fit into almost any boat and travel paths where cars fear to tread. Rental is not expensive, and includes third-party insurance coverage in most cases. You will have to have a valid driving licence (for Americans, this means an international one) For larger motorbikes (anything over 75cc) you may be asked to show a motorcycle driver's licence. The down-sides: many of the bikes are poorly maintained, the same goes for many of the roads, and everyone takes too many risks— hospital beds in Greece fill up each summer with casualties, both foreign and Greek (check your insurance to see if you're covered). Most islands have laws about using motorbikes after midnight (the 'little ducks', often stripped of their mufflers, tend to howl like a flock of Daffys and Donalds on amphetamines), but they are enforced as often as the helmet requirement. Actually, you do see Greeks wearing helmets, but only on their elbows, which, judging by the way they drive their machines, must be where they keep their brains. Literally hundreds of people, nearly all young, are killed every year in Greece. Be careful.

By Bicycle

Cycling has not caught on in mountainous Greece, either as a sport or as a means of transport, though you can usually hire an old bike in most major resorts. Planes carry bicycles for a small fee, and Greek boats generally take them along for nothing. Rugged Crete is one of the best islands for cycling. You will find fresh water, places to camp, and a warm and surprised welcome in the villages.

Hitch-hiking

Greek taxi drivers have recently convinced the government to pass a law forbidding other Greeks from picking up hitch-hikers. As with the aforementioned helmet-wearing law, this is regarded as optional, but it is true that you may find hitching slow going; perhaps because of the law, motorized holiday-makers now seem to stop and offer more rides than the locals. The Greek double standard produces the following percentages for hopeful hitch-hikers:

Single woman: 99% of cars will stop. You hardly have to stick out your thumb.

Two women: 75% of cars will find room for you.

Woman and man: 50%; more if the woman is pretty.

Single man: 25% if you are well dressed with little luggage; less otherwise.

Two men: start walking.

A complete list is available from the **National Tourist Organization of Greece** (*see* p.27).

in the UK

British Museum Tours, 46 Bloomsbury Street, London WC1B 3QQ, ✆ (020) 7323 8895. Different archaeological guided tours every year; annual tour to Greece.

Cox & Kings, Gordon House, 10 Greencoat Lane, London SW1P 1PH, ✆ (020) 7873 5000, ✉ 7630 6038, *Cox.Kings@coxkings.sprint.com*, *www.coxandkings.co.uk*. Botanic holidays on Corfu, Crete and Rhodes.

Explore Worldwide, 1 Frederick Street, Aldershot, Hants GUII ILQ, ✆ (01252) 344161, *www.explore.co.uk*. Rambles in western Crete, Náxos and Santoríni; Ionian island treks; mini cruises.

Filoxenia, Sourdock Hill, Barkisland, Halifax, West Yorkshire, HX4 0AG, ✆ (01422) 371796, ✉ 310340, *www.filoxenia.co.uk*. Archaeological, walking, spring flowers, wine and cookery tours in Crete; cookery on Corfu and Léros; and painting in Kýthera. Expert advice on where to go, flights and 'tailor-made' holidays to unusual islands for the discerning traveller.

Greek Islands Club, 10–12 Upper Square, Old Isleworth, Middx TW7 7BJ, ✆ (020) 8232 9780, ✉ 8568 8330; US and Canada ✆ 800 394 5577; *www.greekislandsclub.com*. Helpful and friendly, with choice villas and a range of holidays on the Ionian islands.

Island Holidays, Drummond Street, Comrie, Perthshire PH6 2DS, ✆ (01764) 670107. Natural history holidays on Crete and Lésbos.

Laskarina Holidays, St Mary's Gate, Wirksworth, Matlock, Derbyshire DE4 4DQ, ✆ (01629) 824884, ✉ 822 205, *www.laskarina.co.uk*. Painting holidays on islands including Sými and Sámos, led by Muriel Owen.

Norfolk and Suffolk Wildlife Holidays, Dudwick House, Buxton, Norwich NR10 5HX, ✆ (01603) 278296. Join members of the Norfolk and Suffolk Wildlife Trust on botany and bird-watching trips to Crete, Rhodes, Lésbos and Corfu.

Peligoni Club, PO Box 88, Chichester, West Sussex PO20 7DP, ✆ (01243) 511499, *www.peligoni.com*. A one-off, friendly, English-run sailing and windsurfing club on the northeast coast of Zákynthos. *See* p.309.

Peng Travel, 86 Station Road, Gidea Park, Romford, Essex RM2 6DB, ✆ (01708) 471832. Naturist holidays on Crete.

Peregrine Holidays, 40–41 South Parade, Summertown, Oxford OX2 7JP, ✆ (01865) 559988, *www.peregrineholidays.co.uk*. Natural history and walking tours on Crete and other islands.

Ramblers Holidays, Box 43, Welwyn Garden City, Hertfordshire AL8 6PQ, ✆ (01707) 331133, *www.ramblersholidays.co.uk*. Huge range of walking tours on Crete, Sámos, Kefaloniá, Léros, Sámos and Náxos.

Skyros Centre, 92 Prince of Wales Road, London NW5 3NE, ✆ (020) 7284 3065, *www.skyros.com*. Wide range of personal development courses (artists' workshops, holistic bodywork workshops in Alexander technique, dance and massage, and creative writing courses led by the likes of Sue Townsend, Andrew Davies, Nell Dunn and Wendy Cope) and outdoor pursuits holidays (watersports, windsurfing, abseiling and watsu—a kind of water-based shiatsu).

Solos Holidays Ltd, 41 Watford Way, London NW4 3JH, ✆ (020) 8951 2800, *www.soloshol-idays.co.uk*. Singles group holidays in four-star hotels on Zákynthos, Rhodes, Corfu, Kefaloniá and Crete for independent people in the 25–55 and 45–69 age brackets. Also spring and autumn rambling on Corfu, Zákynthos, Rhodes and Crete.

First Choice Astral Tower, Betts Way, Crawley, West Sussex RH10 2GX, ✆ (0161) 745 7000 or (01293) 599966. Villa parties for single travellers in traditional houses on Sými.

Swan Hellenic Ltd, 77 New Oxford Street, London WC1A 1PP, ✆ (020) 7800 2200. Cultural, archaeological and art history tours and cruises.

Travel Companions, 110 High Mount, Station Road, London NW4 3ST, ✆ (020) 8202 8478. Vera Coppard can match you up with a kindred spirit, for a moderate fee, if you don't want to travel alone.

Waymark Holidays, 44 Windsor Road, Slough SL1 2EJ, ✆ (01753) 516477, *www.waymarkholidays.com*. Guided hiking groups on Mílos, Crete and Sámos; spring and autumn breaks.

in the USA/Canada

Aegean Workshops, 148 Old Black Point Road, Niantic, CT 06357, ✆ (860) 739 0378. Harry J. Danos, a university art teacher, offers excellent water colour, drawing and design workshops of 15 to 21 days on Mýkonos, Sámos or Santoríni.

Avenir Adventures, Box 2730, 2029 Sidewinder Drive, Park City, UT 84060, ✆ (800) 367 3230. Expeditions by land and sea for small groups.

Central Holiday Tours, Inc., 120 Sylvan Ave, Anglewood Cliff, NJ 07632, ✆ (201) 798 5777, toll free ✆ (800) 935 5000, 🖷 228 5355. Tours in ancient history and archaeology, 'In the Steps of St Paul', mythology and theatre.

Classic Adventures, PO Box 143, Hamlin, NY 14464, ✆ (716) 964 8488, toll free ✆ (800) 777 8090, 🖷 964 7297, *www.classicadventures.com*. Bicycling and walking holidays on Crete and Zákynthos.

Cloud Tours, 31–09 New Town Ave, Long Island City, NY 11102, ✆ (212) 753 6104, toll free ✆ (800) 223 7880, 🖷 980 6941. Scuba-diving, biking, honeymoon tours, women's groups, religious history tours and many others.

IST Cultural Tours, 225 West 34th Street, Suite 1020, New York, NY 10122, ✆ (212) 563 1202, toll free ✆ (800) 833 2111, 🖷 594 6953, *www.ist-tours.com*. Customized tours including yacht cruises and lectures on archaeology.

Metro Tours, 484 Lowell Street, Peabody, MA 01960, ✆ (978) 535 4000, toll free ✆ (800) 221 2810, 🖷 535 8830. Weddings and honeymoons on Santoríni.

Our Family Abroad, 40 W. 57th St, Suite 430, New York, NY 10019, ✆ (212) 459 1800, toll free ✆ (800) 999 5500, 🖷 581 3756. Gay and lesbian tours.

Peddlers Destination & Adventures International, 8489 Crescent Drive, Los Angeles, CA 90046, (800) 695 4599, 🖷 (213) 650 6902. Island cycling tours.

The Greek Island Connection, 38–01 23rd Ave, Long Island City, NY 11105, ✆ (718) 204 8060, toll free ✆ (800) 241 2417, ✉ 674 4582. Archaeology, cooking, hiking, biking, gay and lesbian, religion.

in Greece

Amethyst, Skiáthos, Sporades, ✆ (00 30) 427 22 520. Therapy centre dealing with a wide range of disorders from drugs, alcohol and sex abuse, to stress and emotional problems.

Hellenic Culture Centre, Ikária, ✆ (00 30) 275 61482, ✉ 275 31 978 or ✉ 167 47 465. Greek language courses.

Hellenic Society for the Study and Protection of Dolphins and Whales, 201 Thessalias St, 13231 Petroúpolis, Athens. Study cruises in the Ionian sea, keeping tabs on the dolphin population.

The Path of Avatar, Corfu, ✆ (00 30) 663 51 845. Consciousness-raising (in English) with Nayana Gabriele Keller Jutta Weyck.

Disabled Travellers

Many of the Greek islands, with their ubiquitous steps and absence of suitable transport, would put severe constraints on visitors in wheelchairs, and ferry and hydrofoil access is difficult. Major islands, such as Corfu and Rhodes, and many smaller ones that receive lots of visitors (such as Skíathos, Zákynthos and Kos) have hotels with special facilities—the Greek National Tourist Organization has a list.

In the UK, Filoxenia's **Opus 23** (*see* p.31) offer special-needs holidays and accommodation on the islands, and several of the big package holiday companies, such as **Thomson**, have suitable tours. Contact **RADAR**, 12 City Forum, 250 City Road, London EC1V 8AS, ✆ (020) 7250 3222 for advice and referrals.

In the USA, a similar service is provided by the **Travel Disability Information Service**, Moss Rehabilitation Hospital, 1200 W. Tabor Rd, Philadelphia, PA 19141, ✆ (215) 456 9600; the **Society for the Advancement of Travel for the Handicapped**, 347 Fifth Avenue, Suite 610, New York, NY 10016, ✆ (212) 725 8253; and **New Directions**, 5276 Hollister Ave, Suite 207, Santa Barbara CA 93111, ✆ (805) 967 2841, ✉ 964 7344. In Canada, the **Jewish Rehabilitation Hospital**, 3205 Place Alton Goldbloom, Montréal PQ H7V 1R2 is a good source of travel info. In Greece, contact **The Panhellenic Association for the Blind**, 31 Veranzérou St, 10432 Athens, ✆ (01) 522 8333, ✉ 522 2112, or **Association Hermes**, Patriárchou 13, Grigouiou E, 16542 Argyroúpolis, ✆ (01) 996 1887.

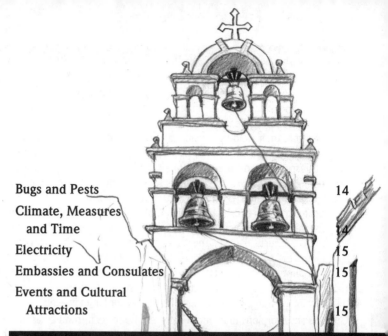

Bugs and Pests 14

Climate, Measures
and Time 14

Electricity 15

Embassies and Consulates 15

Events and Cultural
Attractions 15

Practical A–Z

Food and Drink 17

Health 22

Money 23

Museums, Archaeological Sites
and Opening Hours 23

National Holidays 24

The Periptero 24

Post Offices 25

Shopping 25

Sports 25

Telephones 26

Toilets and Water 27

Tourist Information 27

Travelling with Children 28

Where to Stay 28

Women Travellers 33

Bugs and Pests

Greece is home to various species of rare and protected flora and fauna. As for creatures unfortunately *not* on the endangered list, the wily mosquito tops the list for pure incivility. Most shops stock the usual defences: lotions, sprays and insect coils or, best of all, those inexpensive electric mosquito repellents that plug into a wall socket. Greek skeeters don't spread malaria, but bites from their sand-fly cousins can occasionally cause a nasty parasite infection. Wasps have a habit of appearing out of nowhere to nibble that honey-oozing baklava you've just ordered (especially on the lush Ionian islands). Pests lurk in the sea as well: harmless pale brown jellyfish (*méduses*) may drift in anywhere depending on winds and currents, but the oval transparent model (*tsoúchtres*) are stinging devils that can leave scars on tender parts of your anatomy if you brush against them; pharmacies sell soothing ungents. Pincushiony sea urchins live by rocky beaches, and if you're too cool to wear rubber swimming shoes and you step on one, it hurts like hell. The spines may break and embed themselves even deeper if you try to force them out; the Greeks recommend olive oil, a big pin and a lot of patience. Less common but more dangerous, the *drákena*, dragon (or weever) fish, with a poisonous spine, hides in the sand waiting for its lunch. If you step on one (rare, but it happens), you'll feel a mix of pain and numbness and should go the doctor for an injection.

Greece's shy scorpions hide out in between the rocks in rural areas; unless you're especially sensitive, their sting is no more or less painful than a bee's. Avoid the back legs of mules, unless you've been properly introduced. The really lethal creatures are rare: there are several species of small viper that lives in the nooks and crannies of stone walls, where it is well camouflaged, and only comes out occasionally to sun itself. Vipers will flee if possible, but if they feel cornered they will make a hissing sound like radio static before attacking. Since the time of Homer, mountain sheepdogs have been a more immediate danger in outer rural areas; by stooping as if to pick up a stone to throw, you might keep a dog at bay.

Climate, Measures and Time

average daily temperatures F°/C°

	Athens	Crete (HERAK'N)	Cyclades (MYKONOS)	Dodecs (RHODES)	Ionian (CORFU)	N.E.Aeg (MYTILINI)	Spor'des (SKYROS)
Jan	48/9	54/12	54/12	54/12	50/10	50/10	51/11
Feb	49/9	54/12	54/12	54/12	51/11	48/9	51/11
Mar	54/12	58/14	56/13	58/14	52/11	52/11	52/11
April	60/16	62/17	60/16	60/16	60/16	60/16	58/14
May	68/20	68/20	68/20	66/19	66/19	68/20	66/19
June	76/24	74/23	74/23	73/23	71/22	74/23	74/23
July	82/28	78/25	76/24	78/25	78/25	80/27	77/25
Aug	82/28	78/25	76/24	79/26	78/25	80/27	78/25
Sept	76/24	76/24	74/23	78/25	74/23	74/23	71/22
Oct	66/19	70/21	68/20	72/22	66/19	66/19	65/18
Nov	58/14	64/18	62/17	66/19	58/14	58/14	58/14
Dec	52/11	58/14	58/14	58/14	54/12	52/11	51/11

Greece enjoys hot, dry, clear and bright Mediterranean summers, cooled by winds, of which the *meltémi* from the northeast is the most notorious and most likely to upset Aegean sailing schedules. Winters are mild, and in general the wet season begins at the end of October or beginning of November, when it can rain 'tables and chairs' as the Greeks say. It begins to feel springlike in February, especially in Crete and Rhodes, when the first wild flowers appear.

Two uniquely Greek **measurements** you may come across are the *strémma*, a Greek land measurement (1 *strémma* = ¼ acre), and the *oká*, an old-fashioned weight standard, divided into 400 drams (1 *oká* = 3lb; 35 drams = ¼lb, 140 drams = 1lb).

'God gave watches to the Europeans and time to the Greeks,' they say, but if you need more precision, **Greek time** is Eastern European, 2 hours ahead of Greenwich Mean Time, 7 hours ahead of Eastern Standard Time in North America.

Electricity

The **electric current** in Greece is mainly 220 volts, 50Hz; plugs are continental two-pin. Buy an adaptor in the UK before you leave, as they are rare in Greece; North Americans will need adaptors and transformers.

Embassies and Consulates

Australia	37 D. Soútsou, 115 21 Athens, ✆ 645 0404, ✉ 644 3633.
Canada	4 I. Gennadíou, 115 21 Athens, ✆ 727 3400, ✉ 727 3460.
Ireland	7 Vas. Konstantínou, 106 74 Athens, ✆ 723 2771, ✉ 724 0217. Also *see* Corfu.
Netherlands	5–7 Vas. Konstantínou, Athens, ✆ 723 9701. Also *see* Corfu.
New Zealand	24 Xenia, 115 28 Athens, ✆ 771 0112.
South Africa	60 Kifissías, 151 25 Maroússi, ✆ 680 6459, ✉ 689 5320.
United Kingdom	1 Ploutárchou Street, 106 75 Athens, ✆ 723 6211, ✉ 724 1872. Also *see* Corfu, Rhodes and Heráklion (Crete).
USA	91 Vassilías Soffás, 115 21 Athens, ✆ 721 2951, ✉ 645 6282.

Events and Cultural Attractions

Besides the big religious and national holidays, the Greek islands offer a wide range of other events in the summer. Each island has a section on its own particular feast days; below is a list of more ambitious annual events. Dates squirm around a lot; ring the Greek National Tourist Organization a month or two before the event to pin them down.

May

> **Three Days of Jazz**, Réthymnon, Crete.

May–June

> **Homer Cultural Centre events**, on Chíos, with traditional dancing, songs, handicrafts, drama.

June–September

> **Athens Festival**. Festival of international culture: modern and ancient theatre, jazz, classical music and dance, often with visiting British companies, in the stunning

setting of the Herodus Atticus Odeon beneath the Acropolis. Also a wide range of performances at the Lycabettus Theatre, Likavitós Hill, including the **International Jazz and Blues Festival** in late June.

Epídávros Festival in the Peloponnese. Ancient Greek drama under the stars in the authentic setting, so take a cushion or something to sit on. Special buses from Athens. The festivals Box Office is at 4 Stadíou Street (in the arcade), Athens, ✆ 322 1459.

June–August

Ermoupouleia, on Sýros, with theatre, music, art and folk music in the main square.

Hippocrateia, Kos. Music in the castle.

Pallimniaka, Límnos. Musical evenings, shadow theatre, painting and photography.

Sými Festival, big name cultural events, dance, music, theatre, workshops and more.

Lésbos summer, cultural events in the castle; also the **Festival of Ouzo**, with plenty of dancing and free samples.

July

International Festival of Music, Rhodes.

Ikaría Eleuthería. Celebrating the island's liberation from the Turks on the 17th.

Kyrvia Festival. Festivities in Ierápetra, Crete.

Kornareia, in Sitía, Crete. Wide range of cultural events in the birthplace of 15th-century Cretan poet Kornáros.

Dáphní Wine Festival near Athens; Cretan wine festival, Réthymnon.

July–August

Skýros Festival, cultural events, theatre, traditional dances.

Lato Festival, Crete. Artistic events in Ag. Nikólaos and the ancient city of Lato.

Irákleio Summer, Herákleon, Crete. Highbrow festival of ballet, opera, classical music, theatre, symposia, lectures, etc.

Renaissance Festival, Réthymnon, Crete.

August

Zákyntheia, Zákynthos, cultural events.

Sultanina Grape Festival. Sitía, Crete.

International Folklore Festival, Lefkáda, with groups from around the world.

Theológos summer,Thássos, first 10 days of August. Music, folklore, dancing and re-enactment of a traditional wedding.

Violin Days, Skiáthos.

Koukania, Astypálaia, with sports and traditional games; also feasts with traditional music on 15 August.

Wine Festivals, Rhodes, with music and celebrities. Also takes place at Léros, Zákynthos and Sámos.

August–September

International Music Festival, Santoríni. Classical music concerts.

Kefaloniá International Choral Music Festival, Lixoúri. Gathering of Greek and foreign choirs, symphony orchestras and folk dance groups.

Summer Festival, Chaniá, Crete. Greek and foreign dance troupes, classical music, exhibitions, puppets and local celebrations.

August–October

Rhodes Festival, with a wide programme of arts activities, but the cork has been pulled on the wine tastings in Rodíni Park.

September

Robolo Festival, wine festival at Omala, Kefaloniá.

Chestnut Festival, Crete. Merry-making and old songs in the village of Élos, near Kíssamou, where sweets made from chestnuts are offered to visitors.

Food and Drink

Life's fundamental principle is the satisfaction of the needs and wants of the stomach. All important and trivial matters depend on this principle and cannot be differentiated from it.

Epicurus, 3rd century BC

Epicurus may have given his name to gourmets, but in reality his philosophy was an economical one that advocated maximizing the simple pleasures of life: rather than continually seek novelty and delight in ever more extreme ways, Epicurus suggests, make a plate of bread and olives taste sublime by fasting for a couple of days. In this way modern Greeks are all epicureans: centuries of occupation and extreme poverty have taught them to relish food more than cuisine, and they eat with great zest and conviviality. Meals are not about scaling gastronomic heights, but a daily reminder to the Greeks of who they are and what their country has to offer—fish from the seas; lamb from the valleys; fresh herbs and honey from the mountains; wild young greens from the hills; olives, fruits and nuts from the groves. The method of cooking these things is often quite simple, and Turkish and Italian influences remain strong, just as they do in the language. What's more, recent studies show that Greek food not only tastes good, but is remarkably good for you, too (*see* pp.77–8).

For all that, Greece has acquired a poor reputation for food. In the 1970s, the relatively few restaurants that existed, especially on the islands, were overrun. Standards fell as they tried to cope with the influx of people; standards fell even lower when making as much money as possible in a few short months became the overriding consideration. Nor did the first generation of taverna-owners in the tourist age see any reason to improve; the masses, mostly travelling on a shoestring, seemed content with cheap village salads, reheated moussaká, kebabs, taramosaláta and more kebabs, often served in a kind of caricature of Greekness (plastic grapes and Zorba, Zorba, Zorba). Others, like the hotel owner in Páxos who dished out tinned brussels sprouts with everything, struggled haplessly to please middle-aged customers from the pale north who swore that they couldn't abide garlic or even olive oil, which in Greece is close to nectar (guide books used to train their readers to say WHORE-is LA-thi, parakaLO—'without oil, please').

While too many tourist tavernas still grind out greasy grub, advertised with plastic idiot photos of food sun-blasted over the years into greenish plates of flaking scabs (no wonder they have to hire obnoxious touts to drag in clients from the street!), their days seem to be numbered, as diners have come to know and expect better. The new generation of taverna-owners is making a concerted effort to offer real Greek cooking, reviving recipes handed down from mother to daughter, recipes very much based on what's in season: vegetables like butter beans, green beans and okra in rich tomato and olive oil sauces; *briáms* of aubergines and courgettes; beetroot with hot garlic *skordaliá* dip; stuffed, lightly battered courgette flowers; prawns in filo parcels; octopus *stifádo*; beef stew with baby onions; lamb grazed on mountain herbs baked with fresh dill, yoghurt and lemon; ragout of snails; and whitebait so fresh they're almost wriggling. A simple, sun-ripened Greek tomato in August, sprinkled with fresh oregano and anointed with olive oil from the family grove, is enough to jump start the old taste buds. Just try to reproduce the same sensation back home.

One criticism levelled at Greek food is that it's served cold. It usually is, and that's because Greeks believe tepid food is better for the digestion than hot in the summer (once you get used to it, you realize that many dishes are actually tastier once they're left to cool in their own juices). The pace of life is different as well—there's no rush. Lunches begin late and stretch long into the afternoon, and dinners into the small hours. While we tend to shovel down quick dinners in front of the TV, the gregarious Greeks eat to enjoy, to relax, to talk. A night out with friends in a taverna is the best entertainment going.

vegetarians

Of all the people in the European Union, the Greeks now eat the most meat per capita, but they also eat most cheese, more even than the French, and follow only the Italians in eating pasta. Basically, they just eat a lot, which means there are plenty of dishes for vegetarians—a wide range of pulses and *ladera* (fresh vegetable main courses cooked with olive oil, invented for the many Orthodox fasts), and salads from artichokes to aubergines, as well as okra, beetroot leaves, spinach-style greens with lemon and, in some places, *cápari*, or pickled caper plant, which looks like prunings from a rose bush but tastes delicious. There are delicate cheese and spinach pies in flaky filo pastry; pasta dishes and pizzas up to Italian standards, thanks to the influx of those pickiest of all diners; stuffed peppers and tomatoes; deep-fried courgettes; *dolmádes*, sometimes using cabbage leaves instead of vines; and, in Crete especially, *oftés patátes*, or potatoes roasted in their jackets.

If you're a vegetarian or used to buying pre-packed, sanitized meat, it's worth pointing out that in many parts of Greece, especially the remoter islands, food comes on the hoof, on the wing or in the net. It's not uncommon to see a kid or sheep despatched near a taverna by day and then turn up on the menu at night. Bunnies hopping around the village also hop into the pot, the family pig turns into sausages, free-range chickens end up being barbecued and after a while the washing line of drying octopus becomes part of the scenery.

Eating Out

So, how can you find a good place to eat? As always, follow the locals. Greek families aren't going to throw away hard-earned cash on tourist food. If you're hungry for something a cut above taverna fare, keep an eye open for restaurants that have made an effort to revive traditional Greek decor, austere but colourful with handpainted signs, painted chairs, weaving and so on—their owners usually prove to be just as serious about reviving traditional recipes in the kitchen.

Greek eating places are divided into five categories. **Tavernas** and *estiatória* (restaurants) are found everywhere and the differences between them tend to get a bit blurred. But you'll generally find that the *estiatório* has a wider menu and is a bit more upmarket. Tavernas are more like family-run bistros and can range from shacks on the beach to barn-like affairs called *kéntrikos* that provide music in the evening. There may not be a menu as such. The waiter will reel off what's on or even invite you to have a look for yourself. Homemade English translations may leave you more baffled than ever; the **menu decoder** on pp.424–7 may help.

A typical Greek meal begins with a basket of bread and a range of starters that everyone shares: *taramosaláta*, *tzatzíki* (cucumbers and yoghurt), prawns, feta cheese, little cheese or spinach pies, *saganáki* (fried cheese sprinkled with lemon), greens in olive oil and lemon sauces, green beans, okra or butter beans in sauce, or fried courgettes and aubergines. These are followed by a shared salad and potatoes, and a main course that you eat on your own— fish, a pasta, an oven dish ('ready dishes', such as moussaká and stuffed vegetables) or else meat. This can be lamb, pork, beef or kid, either stewed, baked in a casserole (*stifádo*, *kokinistó*, veal *youvétsi* with tear-drop pasta are typical) or freshly grilled (*tis óras*, the 'on times')—chops (*brizóles*) lamb cutlets (*paidhákia*), souvláki (kebabs), meatballs (*keftédes* or *sousoukákia*), sausages (*lukániko*), or chicken (*koutópolou*, usually free-range). Greeks eat very little duck; if offered 'quacker', you'll get rolled oats. Desserts are rare outside tourist places, although you may find some fresh watermelon or yoghurt; the Greeks make lovely sweets, puddings, cakes and ice creams (just look at the displays in any *zacharoplasteío* or pastry shop), but tend to eat them in the late afternoon with a coffee after the siesta, or in the early evening, hours before dinner.

At the seaside you'll find the fish tavernas, *psarotavérnes*, specializing in all kinds of seafood from freshly fried calamari, shrimps and giant prawns, to red mullet, swordfish, bream and sardines. Ironically, fish is expensive because of depletion of stocks in the Med, but you can find cheapies like fresh whitebait (*marídes*), cuttlefish stew (*soupiá*) and small shrimps (*garídes*), sometimes cooked in feta cheese, and fish soups like *psarósoupa* or spicy *kakavia* are a meal in themselves with hunks of fresh bread and a bottle of wine. When eating fish soup it's customary to remove the fish, put it on a plate, drink the broth then tuck into the fish. Note that each type of fish has its own price and portions are priced by weight.

If you're a red-blooded **meat eater**, then head for the nearest *hasapotavérna*, which is a grill room attached to a local butcher's shop. Not that common, they offer fresh meat of all kinds, kebabs, home-made sausages and sometimes delicious stews, usually served by the butcher's assistant in a bloodstained apron for added carnivorous effect. The *psistariá* is another version of the theme, specializing in chicken, lamb, pork or *kokorétsi*, a kind of lamb's offal doner. You may even find a *mageiría*, simple old-fashioned pots simmering on the stove in home-cooking places, often only open for lunch. Other kinds of eateries in Greece need no introduction: the pizzeria (often spelled *pitsaria*) and, in big towns and major resorts, American fast fooderies, along with Goody's, the main Greek clone, and mom-and-pop attempts at the same.

A pitcher or bottle of tap water comes with each meal, and most Greeks order wine or beer. Note that when dining with Greeks it's customary to pour wine for each other—always guests first—and drink constant toasts, glasses chinking—*steen yámass*, good health to us; *steen yássou* or *yássas*, good health to you; or, in Crete, *Avíva* or *Áspro Páto*, bottoms up. By all means clink glasses, but on no account bring your glass down on another person's (unless your intentions for the evening are entirely dishonourable). If a man does it to your glass, it's best to say *'yámass'* and act dumb, unless you want to take him up on it.

Eating out in Greece has always been something of a movable feast. Because of the intense heat in summer, Greek families tend to eat late lunch at home, followed by their siesta or *mesiméri*. Then it's back to work, and around 8 or 9pm, it's time for the evening *vólta*, or stroll to see and be seen, catch up on the news and decide where to go. Greeks eat late, rarely before 10pm, and meals can go on into the small hours. The children are there (they too nap in the afternoon) and are more than welcome—babies are rocked, toddlers crawl under the table and the older children get up to goodness knows what. Dinner is often boisterous, punctuated with fiery discussions, and maybe bursts of song or dance. The more company round the table the merrier, and the more likely your meal to turn into a spontaneous cabaret that no tour operator's organized 'Greek Night' can match. You may even get your table whipped away from under you in a dancer's jaws. *Kalí órexi! Bon appetit!*

prices

A **Greek menu**, *katálogos*, may have two-tier prices—with and without tax; you pay the highest. **Prices** are fixed according to category of restaurant, although there can be seasonal fluctuations when they jump, especially at Easter and in August. If you suspect you're being ripped off, the system makes it easy to complain. If you eat with the Greeks, there's no Western nit-picking over who's had what. You share the food, drink, company and the bill, *to logariasmó*, although hosts will seldom let foreign guests part with a drachma. A new law designed to catch tax evaders insists that you take a receipt (*apóthexi*); the police make periodic checks.

An average taverna meal—if you don't order a major fish—usually comes in at around 3,000–3,500dr a head with generous carafes of house wine (*see* below). Prices at sophisticated restaurants or blatantly touristy places tend to be a bit higher, and places on remote islands can be just as costly because of extra transport prices. Quite a few eateries now offer set-price meals with a glass of wine (often for under 3,000dr), some for two people, some better than others. In the 'Eating Out' sections of this book, any price given is per person with house wine.

kafeneíons and cafés

Every one-mule village will have at least one **kafeneíon**, a social institution where men (and increasingly women, although they're still outnumbered) gather to discuss the latest news, read the papers, nap in hard wooden chairs, play cards or backgammon and incidentally drink coffee. Some men seem to live in them. They are so essential to Greek identity that in at least one instance, on Skópelos, when real estate interests threatened the last old *kafeneíon* with extinction, the town hall opened one for its citizens. The bill of fare features Greek coffee (*café hellinikó*), which is the same stuff as Turkish coffee, prepared to order in 40 different ways, although *glykó* (sweet), *métrio* (medium) and *skéto* (no sugar) are the basic orders. It is always served with a glass of water. *'Nes'*, aka Nescafé, with condensed Dutch milk has by popular tourist demand become available everywhere, though Greeks prefer their instant coffee whipped and iced (*frappé*)—and it's lovely on a hot day. Tea will be a pot of hot water and a bag. Soft drinks, *tsikoúdia* (rakí), brandy and ouzo round out the old-style *kafeneíon* fare.

Newer cafés (those with the cushy soft plastic chairs under awnings) usually open much earlier and close much later than *kafeneíons*. They are good places to find various kinds of breakfast, from simple to complete English, with rashers, baked beans and eggs, and attempts at cappuccinos. They also serve mineral water (try the sparkling IOΛH), ice cream concoctions, milkshakes, fruit juices, cocktails, pastries, and thick Greek yoghurt (cow, sheep or goat milk) and honey. They are also a traditional place to stop for a late-night Metaxa; the more stars on the label (from three to seven), the smoother and the higher the price.

bars (barákia) and ouzeriés

Nearly every island has at least one trendy music bar, usually playing the latest hit records and serving fancy cocktails as well as standard drinks. These establishments come to life at cocktail hour, then again around midnight, when everyone has spent the day on the beach and the earlier part of the evening in a taverna. Bars used to close at dawn, but in 1994 the Greek government decreed a 2am weekday closing, claiming that the nation was nodding off at work after a night on the tiles. In general, bars are not cheap, sometimes outrageously dear by Greek standards, and it can be disconcerting to realize that you have paid the same for your Harvey Wallbanger as you paid for your entire meal half an hour before in the taverna next door. Cocktails have now risen to beyond the 1,000dr mark in many bars, but before you complain remember that the measures are triples by British standards. If in doubt, stick to beer (Greece has a new brand to try, Mythos), ouzo, *suma* (like ouzo, but often sweeter—each island makes its own), wine and Metaxá (Metaxá and Coke, if you can stomach it, is generally about half the price of a rum and coke). One unfortunate practice on the islands is the doctoring of bottles, whereby some bar owners buy cheaper versions of spirits and use them to refill brand-name bottles.

Just when it seemed time to write the obituary on a grand old Greek institution, the **ouzeríe**, it has come back with a vengeance. The national aperitif, ouzo—the *rakí* drunk by the Byzantines and Venetians, inexplicably renamed ouzo in the 18th century from the Latin *usere*, 'usable'— is clear and anise-flavoured, and served in small glasses or a *karafáki* holding about three or four doses which many drinkers dilute and cloud with water. It is cheap and famous for making its imbibers optimistic. As the Greeks look askance at drunkenness—as they did in ancient times, when they cut their wine with water and honey—ouzo is traditionally served with a little plate of snacks called *mezédes*, which can range from grilled octopus, nuts, olives, chunks of cheese and tomatoes to elaborate seafood platters; for an assortment, ask for a *pikilía* (usually translated as '*seafood various*'). Similar to *ouzeríes* are **mezedopoieíons**, specializing in these Greek tapas, where you can build up an entire meal, sometimes from a hundred choices on the menu, and wash them down with wine or beer.

Wine

The country's best-known wine, **retsina**, has a very distinctive taste of pine resin. In ancient times, the Greeks stored their wine in clay amphorae sealed airtight with resin; the disintegration of the resin helped prevent oxidation in the wine and lent it its distinctive flavour. It is an acquired taste, and many people can be put off by the pungent odour and sharp taste of some bottled varieties. Modern retsinas show increasingly restrained use of resin; all retsinas are best appreciated well chilled. Draught retsína (*retsína varelísio*) can be found only on some islands, but in Athens it is the accepted, delicious accompaniment to meals. Retsina is admirably suited to Greek food, and after a while you may find non-resinated wines a rather bland alternative. Traditionally, it comes to the table in chilled copper-anodized jugs, by the kilo (about a litre), or *mesó kiló* (half-litre) or *tétarto* (250ml), and is served in small tumblers. Etiquette requires that these are never filled to the brim or drained empty; you keep topping up your companions' glasses as best you can.

Ordinary red and white **house wines** are often locally produced bargains—ask for *krasí varelísio* (barrelled wine) or *krasí chíma* (loose wine). These wines are nearly always better than fine, though you may be unlucky and get one that's a stinker; if you're suspicious, order a *tétarto kiló*. Greece also produces an ample selection of medium-priced red and white wines in bottles. They tend to be highly regionalized, each island and village offering their own varieties made from indigenous grapes; forget the tyranny of Cabernet Sauvignon and Chardonnay. All the principal wine companies—Boutari, Achaia-Clauss, Carras, Tsantali—have made strides to improve the quality in the past decade, investing heavily in new equipment and foreign expertise, and it shows; even that humblest of bottles (and Greece's best-seller), **Deméstika**, has become very acceptable of late, and bears little resemblance to the rough stuff that earned it some unflattering sound-alike nicknames. Look out for the nobler labels. Boutari Náoussa is an old-style, slightly astringent red, while Boutari's Grande Réserve is their best red; Lac des Roches is their most popular white on the islands, while Santoríni is their finest island white. Peloponnesiakos from Achaia-Clauss is an easy-drinking, light white wine which is faddishly popular at the moment anywhere within exportable distance of the Peloponnese. From Carras, Château Carras is a Bordeaux-style red wine made from the Cabernet Sauvignon and Merlot grapes; if you're lucky you might find Carras Limnio, one of Greece's most distinct red wines. In Rhodes, CAIR supplies Greece with its sparkling *méthode traditionelle* white, Caïr. Emery produces some good whites, including Villare. The best red wines come from Nemea, and are superb with roast lamb.

In recent years, small producers have become very fashionable with the wine-drinking élite. Some are superb, others deserve obscurity, but for the most part you are unlikely to come across them in the average taverna. If you're a wine buff, it's worth seeking out local recommendations in wine shops (*kávas*) and high-class restaurants.

Health

At the bare minimum, there is at least one doctor (*iatrós*) on every island with more than a couple of hundred people; office hours are from 9 to 1 and from 5 to 7. On bigger islands there are hospitals which are open all day, and outpatient clinics, open in the mornings. EU citizens are entitled to free medical care; British travellers are often urged to carry a Form E111, available from DSS offices (apply well in advance on a form CM1 from post offices), which will admit them to the most basic IKA (Greek NHS) hospitals for treatment; however, this doesn't cover medicines or nursing care. In any case, the E111 seems to be looked on with total disregard outside Athens; expect to pay up front, and get receipts so you can be reimbursed back home. As private doctors and hospital stays can be very expensive, you should take out a travel insurance policy. Make sure your holiday insurance has adequate repatriation cover; Greek hospitals have improved by leaps and bounds, but as it's still common for families to supply food and help with the nursing, you may feel neglected. Non-Europeans should check their own health policies to see if they're covered while abroad.

Greek general practitioners' fees are usually reasonable. Most doctors pride themselves on their English, as do the pharmacists (found in the *farmakeío*), whose advice on minor ailments is good, although their medicine is not particularly cheap.

If you forgot to bring your own condoms and are caught short, they are widely available from *farmakeío* and kiosks, with lusty brand names such as 'Squirrel' or 'Rabbit'. If you can't see them on display, the word *kapótes* (condom) gets results. You can also get the Pill (*chápi antisiliptikó*), morning-after Pill and HRT over the pharmacy counter without a prescription. Be sure to take your old packet to show them the brand you use.

For some reason Greeks buy more medicines than anyone else in Europe (is it hypochondria? the old hoarding instinct?), but you shouldn't have to. The sun is the most likely cause of grief, so be careful, hatted and sunscreened. If you find the olive oil too much, Coca Cola or retsina will help cut it. Fresh parsley is good for stomach upsets. See p.14 for possibly unkind wildlife. If anything else goes wrong, do what the islanders have done for centuries: pee on it.

Money

The word for **bank** in Greek is *trápeza*, derived from the word *trapézi*, or table, used back in the days of money-changers. On all the islands there is some sort of banking establishment or, increasingly, as least an automatic teller machine. If there's no bank, travel agents, tourist offices or post offices will change cash, traveller's cheques and Eurocheques. Beware that small but popular islands often have only one bank, where exchanging money can take forever: beat the crowds by going at 8am, when the banks open; normal banking hours are 8–2 (8–1.30 on Fridays).

The number of 24-hour **automatic cash-tellers** on the islands grows every year: some accept one kind of credit card and not another (VISA is perhaps the most widely accepted). You can also use these to withdraw cash at banks. Major hotels, luxury shops and resort restaurants take cards (look for the little signs), but smaller hotels and tavernas certainly won't.

Traveller's cheques are always useful, even though commission rates are lower for cash. The major brands (Thomas Cook and American Express) are accepted in all banks and post offices; take your passport as ID and shop around for commission rates.

Running out? Athens and Piraeus, with offices of many British and American banks, are the easiest places to have money sent by cash transfer from someone at home—though it may take a few days. **American Express** may be helpful here; their office in Athens is 2 Ermoú St, right by Sýntagma Square, © 324 4975 (*open Mon–Fri 8.30–4, Sat 8.30–1.30*), and there are branches on Corfu, Mýkonos, Pátras, Rhodes, Santoríni, Skiáthos and Thessaloníki.

The Greek drachma (abbreviated dr, in Greek δρχ) is circulated in coins of 100, 50, 20, 10, and 5 drachma and in notes of 100, 500, 1,000, 5,000 and 10,000 drachma.

Museums, Archaeological Sites and Opening Hours

Significant archaeological sites and museums have regular admission hours. Nearly all are closed on Mondays, and open other weekdays from 8 or 9 to around 2, although more important sites now tend to stay open later—until 4 or 5pm. Hours tend to be shorter in the winter. On the other hand, churches are often open only in the late afternoon (from 6 to 7pm), when they're being cleaned. Students with valid ID often get a discount on admission fees. These are usually between 400 and1,000dr; more expensive places are indicated as such in the text.

National Holidays

Note that most businesses and shops close down for the afternoon before and the morning after a religious holiday. If a national holiday falls on a Sunday, the following Monday is observed. The Orthodox Easter is generally a week or so after the Roman Easter.

1 January	New Year's Day	*Protochroniá*; also *Ag. Vassílios* (Greek Father Christmas)
6 January	Epiphany	*Ta Fóta/ Theofánia*
February–March	'Clean Monday' (precedes Shrove Tuesday and follows a three-week carnival)	*Katharí Deftéra*
25 March	Annunciation/ Greek Independence Day	*Evangelismós*
late March–April	Good Friday	*Megáli Paraskeví*
	Easter Sunday	*Páscha*
	Easter Monday	*Theftéra tou Páscha*
1 May	Labour Day	*Protomayá*
40 days after Easter	Pentacost (Whit Monday)	*Pentikostí*
15 August	Assumption of the Virgin	*Koímisis tis Theotókou*
28 October	'*Ochí*' Day (in celebration of Metaxás' 'no' to Mussolini)	
25 December	Christmas	*Christoúyena*
26 December	Gathering of the Virgin	*Sináxi Theotókou*

In Greece, Easter is equivalent in significance to Christmas and New Year in northern climes, the time when far-flung relatives return to see their families back home; it's a good time of year to visit for the atmosphere, feasts and fireworks. After Easter and May 1, spring (*ánixi*—the opening) has officially come, and the tourist season begins. Festival dates for saints' days listed in the text vary over a period of several given days, or even weeks, owing to the Greek liturgical calendar's calculations for Easter; check these locally. It's also worth remembering that the main partying often happens the night *before* the saint's day.

The Períptero

In Greece you'll see it everywhere, the greatest of modern Greek inventions, the indispensable *períptero*. It is the best-equipped kiosk in the world, where people gather to chat, make phone calls or grab a few minutes' shade under the little projecting roof. The *períptero* is a substitute bar, selling everything from water to ice-cream to cold beer; an emergency pharmacy stocked with aspirin, mosquito killers, condoms and Band Aids; a convenient newsagent for publications from *Ta Néa* to *Die Zeit*; a tourist shop offering maps, guides, postcards and stamps; a toy shop for balloons and plastic swords; a general store for shoelaces, cigarettes, batteries and rolls of film—recently one in Póros produced an instant breakfast. In Athens they're at most traffic lights. On the islands, they are a more common sight than a donkey. You'll wonder how you ever survived before *períptera* and the treasures they contain.

Post Offices

Signs for post offices (*tachidromío*) as well as postboxes (*grammatokivótio*) are bright yellow and easy to find. Post offices (which are also useful for changing money) are open Monday to Saturday from 7.30am to 8pm, although on quite a few islands they close at 2pm. Stamps (*grammatósima*) can also be bought at kiosks and in some tourist shops, although they may charge a small commission. Be warned that postcards can take up to three weeks to arrive at their destinations, while anything in an envelope will usually get there in a week or so, depending on the route. If you're in a hurry, pay extra for an express service. To send a package, always go to an island's main post office. If you do not have an address, mail can be sent to you poste restante at any post office in Greece, and picked up with proof of identity (you'll find the postal codes for all the islands in the text, which will get your letters there faster). After one month all unretrieved letters are returned to sender. In small villages, particularly on the islands, mail is not delivered to the house but to the village centre, either a *kafeneíon* or bakery.

Shopping

Official shopping hours in Greece are: Mon, Wed, 9–5; Tues, Thurs and Fri, 10–7; Sat, 8.30–3.30; and Sun closed; in practice, tourist-orientated shops stay open as late as 1am in season. Leather goods, gold and jewellery, traditional handicrafts, embroideries and weavings, onyx, ceramics, alabaster, herbs and spices, and tacky knick-knacks are favourite purchases; also check the text for island specialities. Duty-free Rhodes has some of the biggest bargains.

Non-EU citizens tempted by Greek jewellery, carpets, perfumes and other costly items can perhaps justify their indulgences by having the sales tax (VAT) reimbursed—this is 18% of the purchase price (or 13%, on Aegean islands). Make sure the shop has a TAX FREE FOR TOURISTS sticker in the window, spend at least 40,000dr inside, and pick up a tax-free shopping cheque for your purchases. When you leave Greece, you must show your purchases and get the customs official to stamp your cheques (allow an extra hour for this, especially at the airport), and cash them in at the refund point as you leave. If you are flying out of another EU country, hold on to the cheques, get them stamped again by the other EU country's customs and use their refund point. You can also post your tax-free cheques back to Greece for refund (10 Nikis St, 10563 Athens, ✆ (01) 325 4995, ✉ 322 4701), but they skim off 20% of the amount as commission.

Sports

watersports

Greece was made for watersports and, by law, all the beaches, no matter how private they might look, are public. All but a fraction meet European guidelines for water cleanliness, although a few could stand to have less litter on the sand. Beaches near built-up areas often have umbrellas and sunbed concessions and snack bars, and if there's a breeze you'll probably find a windsurfer to rent at affordable prices (favourite windy spots are Páros—which holds world championships in August—Léfkas, Rhodes and Lésbos). Bigger beaches have paragliding and jet skis, and waterskiing is available on most islands and large hotel complexes; on Kos you can bungee jump over the sea. The Ministry of Tourism allocated huge sums to build up marinas on the islands, which may improve chances of finding a small sail or motor boat to hire by the day.

Nudism is forbidden by law in Greece, but tolerated in numerous designated or out-of-the-way areas. On the other hand, topless sunbathing is now legal on the majority of popular beaches as long as they're not smack in the middle of a village; exercise discretion. Even young Greek women are shedding their tops, but nearly always on someone else's island.

Scuba diving, once strictly banned to keep divers from snatching antiquities and to protect Greece's much-harassed marine life, is permitted between dawn and sunset in specially defined coastal areas; local diving excursions will take you there. The areas are within striking distance of the cities of Chanía, Herákleon, Réthymnon and Ag. Níkolaos, all on **Crete**; **Mýkonos, Kos, Rhodes** (at Kallithéa), **Léros, Sýros, Mílos, Corfu** (around Cape Róda, Paleokastrítsa and Cape Kountoúri), Meganíssi island by **Léfkas**, and **Zákynthos**. For information contact the Hellenic Federation of Underwater Activities, Post Office of the West Air Terminal, 16604 Elliniko, Athens, ✆ (01) 981 9961.

average sea temperatures

Jan	Feb	Mar	April	May	June	July	Aug	Sept	Oct	Nov	Dec
59°F	59°F	59°F	61°F	64°F	72°F	75°F	77°F	75°F	72°F	64°F	63°F
15°C	15°C	15°C	16°C	18°C	22°C	24°C	25°C	24°C	22°C	18°C	17°C

land sports

Walking is the favourite activity on every island, but especially on Crete, with its superb natural scenery, gorges, wild flowers and wide open spaces; *see* **Travel** for guided walking tours. Increasingly, locals are arranging treks, and small, often locally produced, maps and guides are a big help for finding the most interesting country paths. Never set out without a hat and water; island shops have begun to sell handy water-bottle shoulder slings. If you like altitudes, Crete has seven mountain shelters, all belonging to the **Greek Mountain Club** (15 Evans St, Herákleon, Crete, ✆ (081) 280 610.

Tennis is very popular in Athens, with numerous clubs from Glyfáda to Kifissiá, and at all major resort hotels (many are lit up at night so you can beat the heat); often non-residents are allowed to play in the off season. **Golf courses** are rare, but four new ones are planned on Crete as part of efforts to attract more upmarket tourists. On Rhodes, the **Afandou Golf Club**, 19km from Rhodes town, ✆ (0241) 51 255, has 18 holes, par 70, equipment hire and shop, lounges, changing rooms and a restaurant. Fees are from 4,000dr per round, or 22,000dr for seven rounds in one week (cheaper out of season). The **Corfu Golf Club**, Rópa Valley, PO Box 71, ✆ (0663) 94 220, has 18 holes, par 72, a practice range and similar facilities. Green fees are 7,000dr daily in May, Sept and Oct, and less in other months. Many small stables offer **horse-riding** on the islands. For details, call the **Riding Club of Greece**, Parádissos, ✆ 682 6128 and Riding Club of Athens, Gerakos, ✆ 661 1088.

Telephones

The new improved Organismós Telefikoinonía Elládos, or OTE, has replaced most of its old phone offices with new card phones, which work a treat, although many on the islands, for some reason, seem to be set up for basketball players only. If you can reach the buttons, you can dial abroad direct (dial 00 before the country code). Cards for 100 units cost 1,000dr. For a decent long-distance chat you may need more, although the 500 unit and 1,000 unit *telekártas* are hard to find outside of big resort areas. As a last resort, find a telephone *me métriki* (with a meter), which is often more costly and usually located in kiosks (*períptera*), *kafeneíons*, some travel agents, hotels and shops. As a general rule, international calls are cheaper after 10pm, but this may change. **Telegrams** can be sent from one of the surviving OTE offices in big cities or from the post office. When **phoning Greece** from overseas, the country code is 30; drop the first '0' of the local area code.

Toilets and Water

Greek plumbing has improved dramatically in the past few years, and in the newer hotels you can flush everything away as merrily as you do at home (at least, as often as your conscience lets you on arid islands strapped for water). Tavernas, *kafeneíons* and sweet shops almost always have facilities (it's good manners to buy something), and there are often public pay toilets in strategic area of the towns.

In older pensions and tavernas, the plumbing often makes up in inventiveness for what it lacks in efficiency. Do not tempt fate by disobeying the little notices 'the papers they please to throw in the basket'—or it's bound to lead to trouble (a popular new sticker has Poseidon himself bursting out of the toilet bowl and pricking an offender with his trident). Old *kafeneíons* and bus stations tend to have only a ceramic hole squatter. Always have paper of some sort handy.

If you stay in a private room or pension, you may have to have the electric water heater turned on for about 20 minutes before you take a shower. In most smaller pensions, water is heated by a solar panel on the roof, so the best time to take a shower is in the late afternoon or the early evening (before other residents use up the finite supply of hot water). In larger hotels there is often hot water in the mornings and evenings, but not in the afternoons. Actually 'cold' showers in the summer aren't all that bad, because the tap water itself is generally luke-warm, especially after noon. A good many showers are of the hand-held variety, which is potentially dangerous (especially if you have kids) because Greeks don't believe in shower curtains and one careless moment means your towel or toilet paper is soaked.

Greek tap water is perfectly safe to drink, but on some islands it tastes less than delicious. On the other hand, inexpensive plastic bottles of spring water are widely available (and responsible for for untold pollution, taking up half the available room in landfill sites). On dry islands, remember to ask what time the water is turned off.

Tourist Information

If the Greek National Tourist Organization (in Greek the initials are **EOT**) can't answer your questions about Greece, at least they can refer you to someone who can.

Canada

 1300 Bay Street, Toronto, Ontario, M5R 3K8, ✆ (416) 968 2220, 🖷 968 6533

 c/o Greek Consulate, 1170 Place de Frère André, 3rd Floor, Montreal 83B 3C6, ✆ (514) 871 1535, 🖷 871 1498

Great Britain and Ireland

 4 Conduit Street, London W1R 0DJ, ✆ (020) 7734 5997, 🖷 287 1369

Netherlands

Leidsestraat 13, NS 1017 Amsterdam, ℂ 625 4212/3/4, ✉ 620 7031

USA

Head Office: Olympic Tower, 645 Fifth Avenue, 5th Floor, New York, NY 10022, ℂ (212) 421 5777, ✉ 826 6940, *gnto@orama.com, www.gnto.gr*

in Greece

The most popular islands have EOT offices, while the others often have some form of local tourist office; if not, most have tourist police (usually located in an office in the regular police station, although nine times out of ten they're the only people on the island who don't speak any foreign language). If nothing else, they have listings of rooms on the island. **Legal Assistance for Tourists** is available free, but in July and Aug only: in Athens at 43–45 Valtetsiou St, ℂ (01) 330 0673, ✉ 330 1137; in Vólos, 51 Hatziargiri St, ℂ/✉ (0421) 33 589; in Kavála, 3 Ydras St, ℂ/✉ (051) 221 159; and in Pátras, 213B Kointhou St, ℂ (061) 272481.

Travelling with Children

Greece is a great country for children, who are not barely tolerated but generally enjoyed and encouraged. Depending on their age, they go free or receive discounts on ships and buses. However, if they're babies, don't count on island pharmacies stocking your brand of milk powder or baby foods—they may have some, but it's safest to bring your own supply. Disposable nappies (diapers), especially Pampers, are widely available, even on small islands.

Travelling with a tot is like having a special passport. Greeks adore them and spoil them rotten, so don't be surprised if your infant is passed round like a parcel. Greek children usually have an afternoon nap (as do their parents), so it's quite normal for Greeks to eat *en famille* until the small hours. Finding a babysitter is rarely a problem: some of the larger hotels even offer special supervised kiddie campgrounds and activity areas for some real time off.

Superstitions are still given more credit than you might expect; you'll see babies with amulets pinned to their clothes or wearing blue beads to ward off the evil eye before their baptism. Beware of commenting on a Greek child's intelligence, beauty or whatever, as this may call down the jealous interest of the old gods and some of the nastier saints. The response in the old days was to spit in the admired child's face, but these days superstitious grannies are usually content with a ritual 'phtew-phtew-phtew' dry spit, to protect the child from harm.

Where to Stay

Hotels

All hotels in Greece are classed into six categories: Luxury, A, B, C, D and E. This grading system bears little relationship to the quality of service, charm, views, etc., but everything to do with how the building is constructed, size of bedrooms, lifts, and so on; i.e. if the hotel has a marble-clad bathroom it gets a higher rating. **Pensions**, most without restaurants, are a confusing subdivision in Greek hotel classifications, especially as many call themselves hotels. They are family-run and more modest (an A-class pension is roughly equivalent to a C- or D-class hotel and is priced accordingly). A few islands still have their government-built hotels from the 1960s, the Xenias, many of which resemble barracks, the fashion in those junta-ruled days. On the Internet, *www.greekhotel.com* lists, with musical accompaniment, 8,000 hotels and villas in Greece, with forms for more information about prices and availability and booking.

prices

Prices are set and strictly controlled by the tourist police. Off season (i.e. mid-September to July) you can generally get a discount, sometimes as much as 40%. Other charges include an 8% government tax, a 4.5% community bed tax, a 12% stamp tax, an optional 10% surcharge for stays of only one or two days, an air-conditioning surcharge and a 20% surcharge for an extra bed. All these prices are listed on the door of every room and authorized and checked at regular intervals. If your hotelier fails to abide by the posted prices, or if you have any other reason to believe all is not on the level, take your complaint to the tourist police.

approximate hotel rates (drachma) for high season (mid-July–mid-Sept)

	L	A	B	C	D
Single with bath	20,000–70,000	15,000–40,000	15,000–23,000	9,000–20,000	6,000–9,000
Double with bath	30,000–200,000	25,000–50,000	20,000–35,000	11,000–28,000	9,000–14,000

Prices for E-class hotels are about 20% less than D rates.

During the summer, hotels with restaurants may require guests to take their meals in the hotel, either full pension or half pension, and there is no refund for an uneaten dinner. Twelve noon is the official check-out time, although on the islands it is usually geared to the arrival of the next boat. Most Luxury and class A, if not B, hotels situated far from the town or port supply buses or cars to pick up guests. Hotels down to class B all have private en-suite bathrooms. In C most do, as do most Ds. E will have a shower down the hall; in these hotels don't always expect to find a towel or soap, although the bedding is clean.

In the 'Where to Stay' sections of this book, accommodation is listed according to the following price categories:

luxury	29,000 to astronomical
expensive	17,000–30,000
moderate	11,000–18,000
inexpensive	up to 12,000

Prices quoted in the book are approximate and for **double rooms in high season**.

booking a hotel

The importance of reserving a room in advance, especially during July and August, cannot be over-emphasized. Reservations can be made through the individual hotel, through travel agents, through the Hellenic Chamber of Hotels by writing, at least two months in advance, to 24 Stadíou St, 105 61 Athens, ☎ (01) 322 5449, or in person in Athens, at the Hotels Desk in the National Bank of Greece building, 2 Karageorgi Servias, ℗ 323 7193 (open Mon–Thurs, 8.30–2; Fri, 8.30–1.30; and Sat, 9–12.30).

Rooms and Studios

These are, for the most part, cheaper than hotels and sometimes more pleasant. Although you can still find a few rooms (ΔOMATIA, *domátia*) in private houses, on the whole rooms to rent are found off a family's living quarters, sometimes upstairs or in a separate annexe; an increasing number have en-suite baths. One advantage rooms hold over hotels is that nearly all will provide a place to handwash your clothes and a line to hang them on. Another is the widespread availability of basic kitchen facilities (sink, table and chairs, at least a couple of gas rings, fridge, utensils and dishes), which immediately turns a room into a **studio**; these obviously cost a bit more, but out of season the difference is often negligible. Depending on facilities, a double room in high season will cost between 5,000–8,000dr with bath, a studio from 6,000–12,000. Until June and after August prices are always negotiable. Owners will nearly always drop the price per day the longer you stay.

Prices also depend a lot on how much competition exists between owners on each island. On some it's good-natured dog eat dog (you can, for instance, get a very good deal on Santoríni, because the locals have overbuilt); when you step off the ferry you will be courted with all kinds of interesting proposals, photos of the rooms and even guidebook reviews of their establishments. On others, room and hotel owners have co-operated to organize accommodation booths by the port to sort out customers; if the room is not within walking distance, they'll collect you in a car or minivan. If you still can't find a room, most travel agencies will be able to dig one up (although these always cost more).

Youth Hostels

Some of these are official and require a membership card from the Association of Youth Hostels, or alternatively an International Membership Card (about 2,600dr) from the Greek Association of Youth Hostels, 4 Dragatsaníou Street, Athens, ℗ 323 4107; other hostels are informal, have no irksome regulations, and admit anyone. Most charge extra for a shower, sometimes for sheets. Expect to pay around 2,000–4,000dr a night, depending on the quality of facilities and services offered. The official ones have a curfew, which in Greece means you miss the fun.

Camping Out

The climate of summertime Greece is perfect for sleeping out of doors, especially close to the sea, where the breezes keep the the worst of the mosquitoes at bay. Unauthorized camping is illegal (the law was enacted to displace gypsy camps, and is still used for this purpose), although each village on each island enforces the ban as it sees fit. Some couldn't care less if you put up a tent at the edge of their beach; in others the police may pull up your tent pegs and fine you. All you can do is ask around to see what other tourists or friendly locals advise. Naturally, the more remote the beach, the less likely you are to be disturbed. Most islands have at least one privately operated camping ground, though some have only minimal facilities. Islands with no campsites at all usually have a beach where free camping is tolerated. If the police are in some places lackadaisical about enforcing the camping regulations, they come down hard on anyone lighting any kind of fire in a forest, and may very well put you in jail for two months; every year fires damage huge swathes of land.

Camping prices are not fixed by law but these are the approximate guidelines, per day:

Adult	1,300dr
Child (4–12)	700dr
Caravan	1,800dr
Small tent	800dr
Large tent	1,000dr
Car	700dr
Sleeping bag	350dr

Self-catering Holidays

On most islands it is possible to rent cottages or villas, generally for a week or more at a time. Villas can often be reserved from abroad: contact a travel agent or the National Tourist Organization (EOT) for names and addresses of rental agents, or see the list below. In the off season, villas may be found on the spot with a little enquiry, and, depending on the facilities, can work out quite reasonably per person. Generally, the longer you stay, the more economical it becomes. If you book from abroad, packages generally include flights and transfers by coach, ferry, hydrofoil or domestic planes.

in the UK

Catherine Secker (Crete), 102A Burnt Ash Lane, Bromley, Kent BR1 4DD, ✆ (020) 8460 8022. Superb home-run business with the personal touch, featuring superior luxury villas with swimming pools on the Akrotíri Peninsula near Chaniá. Catherine Secker offers all mod cons in quiet beachside villas, with everything from hairdriers to high chairs and toyboxes. Removal of noisy dogs and cockerels guaranteed.

CV Travel, The Manor Stables, Great Somerford, Chippenham, Wilts SN15 5EH, ✆ (01249) 721485. Upmarket villas at fair prices on Corfu, Páxos, Crete and Santoríni. Most villas have 6-day-a-week maid service; cooks provided on request. The friendly staff are very knowledgeable and really care about the islands.

Direct Greece, Granite House, 31–33 Stockwell Street, Glasgow G1 4RY, ✆ (020) 8785 4000 or (0141) 559 7111, *www.direct-greece.co.uk*. Particularly good for Líndos on Rhodes, with a wealth of traditional Lindian houses. Jenny May is uncrowned queen of Líndos. Also villas and flats on Crete, Corfu, Lésbos, Lefkáda, Kos, Kefaloniá and Zákynthos, plus low-season specials. Reps are extremely helpful and knowledgeable; most have lived in Greece for a long time.

Elysian Holidays, 16A High Street, Tenterden, Kent TN30 6AP, ✆ (01580) 766599, *www.elysianholidays.co.uk*. Specialists in restored houses in Kámbos, Chíos and other pretty spots.

Filoxenia Ltd, Sourdock Hill, Barkisland, Halifax, West Yorkshire HX4 0AG, ✆ (01422) 371796, ✆ 310340, *www.filoxenia.co.uk*. Discerning holidays to Athens and a select range of islands, including Chíos and quiet parts of Corfu. Suzi Stembridge and family have scoured Greece for unusual holiday places and pass on their favourites to fellow Grecophiles. Houses, villas, tavernas, pensions, fly-drive. Also **Opus 23**, for travellers with disabilities.

Greek Islands Club, 10-12 Upper Square, Old Isleworth, Middx TW7 7BJ, ✆ (020) 8232 9780, ✉ 8568 8330; USA and Canada, ✆ (800) 394 5577; *www.greek islandsclub.com*. Well-run, established specialists of the Sporades and Ionian Islands (including Kýthera), with helpful yet unobtrusive reps. They also offer an unusually wide choice of personalized activity holidays (*see* p.10). Their new Private Collection features hideaway hotels and exclusive villas on Santoríni, Mýkonos, Páros, Sýros and Crete.

Greek Sun Holidays, 1 Bank Street, Sevenoaks, Kent TN13 1UW, ✆ (01732) 740317, *www.greeksun.co.uk*. Helpful and family-run, offering Athens and a range of unusual islands like Ikaría, Mílos, Chíos, Sámos, Náxos, Páros, Santoríni and Límnos. Tailor-made holidays and two-centre breaks.

Island Wandering, 51A London Road, Hurst Green, Sussex TN19 7QP, ✆ (01580) 860733, ✉ 860282, *www.islandwandering.com*. Excellent tour operator: island-hopping without tears, tailor-made or self-catering holidays in hotels or studios on over 50 isles on all the island groups, pre-booked before you go or with a wandering voucher system.

Kosmar Villa Holidays plc, The Grange, 100 High Street, Southgate, London N14 6FS, ✆ (0870) 7000 747, ✉ 7000 717, *www.kosmar.co.uk*. Self-catering villas, studios and apartments on most of the islands: Crete, Corfu, Rhodes, Sými and Kos. Two-centre holidays, flights from all over the UK, and family savers.

Laskarina Holidays, St Mary's Gate, Wirksworth, Derbyshire, ✆ (01629) 822203/4 and 824881, ✉ 822 205, *www.laskarina.co.uk*. Named after the heroine of Spétses, Laskarina has the largest independent programme in Greece, specializing in the Sporades, the lesser-known islands of the Dodecanese and Spétses, sometimes featuring restored traditional accommodation selected by directors Kate and Ian Murdoch. The Murdochs were made citizens of Sými for services rendered and Kate Murdoch shares honorary citizenship of Chálki, the former UNESCO island of Peace and Friendship, with Lady Thatcher. Two-centre holidays; long stays are available out of season.

Manos Holidays, Panorama House, Vale Road, Portslade, Sussex BM41 1HP, ✆ (01273) 427333, *www.manos.co.uk*. Good value holidays to the major resorts and lesser-known islands, island-hopping and two-centres. Ideal for children; low-season specials and singles deals.

Pure Crete, 79 George Street, Croydon, Surrey CR0 1LD, ✆ (020) 8760 0879, ✉ 8688 9951, *info@purecrete.com*. Anglo-Cretan company with traditional village accommo-dation in western Crete.

Skiathos Travel, 4 Holmedale Road, Kew Gardens, Richmond, Surrey GU13 8AA, ✆ (020) 8940 5157. Packages to Skiáthos, Páros, Náxos, Mýkonos, Páros and Santoríni.

Sunvil, Sunvil House, Upper Square, Isleworth TW7 7BJ ✆ (020) 8568 4499. Very friendly, well-run company offering good-value self-catering and hotel accommodation on Límnos, Chíos and Crete, plus most of the Sporades, Cyclades and Ionian islands.

Amphitriton Holidays, 1506 21st St, NW, Suite 100A, Washington DC, 20036, ✆ (800) 424 2471, ✉ (202) 872 8210. Houses, villas and apartments.

Apollo Tours, 1701 Lake Avenue, Suite 260, Glenview, IL 69925, ✆ (800) 228 4367, ✉ (847) 724 3277. Upmarket villas and apartments.

CTI Carriers, 65 Overlea Blvd, Suite 201, Toronto, Ontario M4H 1P1, ✆ (800) 363 8181, ✉ (429) 7159. One of the biggest Canadian operators with villas.

The Greek Island Connection, 38–01 23rd Ave, Long Island City, NY 11105, ✆ (718) 204 8060, toll free ✆ (800) 241 2417, ✉ 674 4582. Customized seaside villas and condos.

Omega Travel, 3220 West Broadway, Vancouver, British Columbia, ✆ (800) 663 2669, ✉ (604) 738 7101. Villas and apartments.

Triaena Tours, 1 World Trade Center, New York, NY 10001, ✆ (800) 223 1273, ✉ (212) 582 8815. Long-established operator.

Zeus Tours, 551 5th Avenue, Suite 1001, New York, NY 10176, ✆ (800) 447 5667, ✉ (212) 687 9758, *www.zeustours.com.*

in Greece

On Lésbos and Chíos there are women's agro-tourist cooperatives that offer accommodation and a taste of Greek rural life. Bookings are made directly with the cooperative; someone will speak English: **Women's Agricultural Cooperative of Chíos,** Pyrgí, Chíos, ✆ (0271) 72 496 (*see* p.324); and **Women's Agricultural Cooperative of Pétra,** Lésbos, ✆ (0253) 41 238, ✉ 34 1309.

The Greek National Tourist Organization runs a programme to restore village houses into guesthouses fitted out in traditional furnishings. Three of these settlements are on islands: Oía on **Santoríni** (houses sleeping two to seven, reservations from Paradosiakos Ikismos Oias, Oia Santoríni, ✆ (0286) 71 234; **Psára**, where an old parliament building has been converted into a guest house, Xenonas Psaron, ✆ (0272) 61 293 or (0251) 27 908; and Mestá on **Chíos**, a 14th-century mastic village, each room sleeping three, Paradosiakos Ikismos, EOT Box 25, Mesta, Chíos 81199, ✆ (0271) 76 319 or (0251) 27 908.

Four of the five annexes of the **Athenian School of Fine Arts** are located on the islands, at Rhodes, Lésbos, Hýdra and Mýkonos. These provide inexpensive accommodation for foreign artists (for up to 20 days in the summer and 30 in the winter), as well as studios, etc. One requirement is a recommendation from the Greek embassy in the artist's home country. Contact the School of Fine Arts, 42 Patission St, Athens, ✆ (01) 361 6930 for further information.

Women Travellers

Greece is a choice destination for women travellers, but going it alone can be viewed as an oddity. Be prepared for a fusillade of questions. Greeks tend to do everything in groups or pairs and can't understand people who want to go solo. The good news for women, however, is the dying out of that old pest, the *kamáki* (harpoon). These 'harpoons'—Romeos in tight trousers and gold jewellery who used to roar about on motorbikes, hang out in the bars and cafés, and strut about jangling their keys, hunting in pairs or packs—would try to 'spear' as many women as possible, notching up points for different nationalities. A few professional *kamákia* still haunt piano bars in the big resorts, gathering as many hearts, gold chains and parting gifts as they can; they winter all over the world with members of their harem.

Thank young Greek women for the decline in *kamáki* swagger. Watching the example set by foreign tourists, as well as the torrid soaps and dross that dominate Greek TV, they have decided they've had enough of 'traditional values'. Gone are the days when families used the evening promenade, or *vólta*, as a bridal market for their carefully sheltered unmarried daughters; now the girls hold jobs, go out drinking with their friends and move in with their lovers. They laughed at the old *kamákia* so much that ridicule, like bug spray, has killed them dead.

Modern Greece:
  An Outline of Recent History   36

A Quick Who's Who in
  Greek Mythology   41

A Brief Outline of
  Greek Art and Architecture   42

History, Mythology and Art

Modern Greece: An Outline of Recent History

Greece has been undergoing a political crisis for the past 3,000 years.

Politician during a recent election campaign

Aristotle declared man to be a political animal, and to this day no animal is as political as a Greek. If there are two *kafeneíons* in a village, inevitably one will be the haunt of the Socialists, the other of the Conservatives. Even barber shops have their political affiliations. On average, over 50 parties crowd the ballot in the national elections, among them five different flavours of communists and exotica like the Self-Respect Party, the Fatalist Party (this one is quite popular) and the Party of Parents of Many Children. If you visit during an election, all means of transport to the islands will be swamped with Athenians returning to their native villages to vote. To understand current Greek views and attitudes, a bit of recent history under your belt is essential; ancient and Byzantine history, which touches Greece less closely today, is dealt with under Athens and the individual islands.

The Spirit of Independence

Greeks have always lived beyond the boundaries of modern-day Greece: Asia Minor in particular, southern Italy, Egypt and the Middle East. Being Greek, like being Jewish, had nothing to do with geography, but everything with parents and religion. To this day, for instance, the new Rome founded by Constantine, Constantinople, is the Greeks' spiritual capital, *The City* (*stin pólis*, hence its currunt name, Istanbul) and seat of the Greek Orthodox Patriarch; in the Middle Ages, Athens was a backwater. The Greeks held on to their identity and religion, both during the lengthy Venetian occupation and during the 400-year Turkish occupation that followed—and the Venetians and Turks, for the most part, were content to let them be Greek as long as they paid their taxes.

The revolutionary spirit that swept through Europe at the end of the 18th and beginning of the 19th centuries did not fail to catch hold in Greece, which was by now more than weary of the lethargic inactivity and sporadic cruelties of the Ottomans. The Greek War of Independence began in the Peloponnese in 1821, and continued for more than six years in a series of bloody atrocities, intrigues and in-fighting.

In the end the Great Powers, namely Britain, Russia and France, came to assist the Greek cause, and, in the decisive battle of Navarino (20 October 1827), gave the newly formed Greek government of President Count John Capodístria of Corfu control of the Peloponnese and the mainland peninsula up to a line between the cities of Árta and Vólos. While the Great Powers searched about for a spare member of some inoffensive royal family to make king of the new state, Capodístria (ex-secretary to the Tsar of Russia) affronted the pro-British and pro-French factions in Greece—and also the powerful Mavromikális family, who had him assassinated in 1831. Before the subsequent anarchy spread too far, the Great Powers produced a King of the Greeks in Otho, a high-handed son of Ludwig I of Bavaria, who immediately offended Greek sensibilities by giving Bavarians all the official posts.

The Birth of the Great Idea, and the Great Debacle

The fledgling Greek state was born with what was known as the *Megáli Idéa*, or 'Great Idea', of liberating and uniting all the Greeks into a kind of Byzantium Revisited, although at first Athens lacked the muscle to do anything about it. Otho's arrogant inadequacies led to revolts and his dethronement in 1862, but the Great Powers found a replacement in William George, son of the King of Denmark (who, as a young naval cadet, learned of his new job in a newspaper wrapped around his sardine sandwich). In 1864, the National Assembly made Greece a constitutional monarchy, a system that began to work practically under Prime Minister Trikoúpis in 1875. During the long reign of George I, Greece began to develop, with shipping as its economic base.

In 1910, Elefthérios Venizélos became Prime Minister of Greece for the first time. He deftly used the two Balkan Wars of 1912–13 to further the Great Idea, annexing his native Crete, the Northeastern Aegean islands, Macedonia and southern Epirus to Greece. In the meantime, King George was assassinated by a madman and Constantine I ascended to the throne. Constantine was married to Kaiser Wilhelm's sister, and when the First World War broke out he supported the Central Powers while remaining officially neutral, while Venizélos set up his own government, with volunteers in support of the Allies in northern Greece. Things turned out Venizélos' way when the Allies forced Constantine to mobilize the Greek army.

The 'War to End all Wars' hardly extinguished the Great Idea. During the signing of the Treaty of Versailles after the war, Venizélos took advantage of the anarchy in Turkey by claiming Smyrna (Izmir), which at the time had a huge Greek population. Believing the claim had the backing of the Great Powers, especially Britain's Lloyd George, Venizélos' successors ordered Greek forces to occupy Smyrna and advance on Ankara. It was, as the Greeks call it, a catastrophe. The Turks, under nationalist leader Mustapha Kemal (later Atatürk), had grown formidable after their defeats in the Balkans, and in August 1922 the invading Greek army was forced back and routed at Smyrna, with enough atrocities committed on both sides to embitter relations for decades. Constantine immediately abdicated in favour of his son George II; the government fell and Colonel Plastiras took over with his officers, ignobly executing the ministers of the previous government. Relations between Greece and Turkey had reached such an impasse that massive population exchanges seemed to be the only solution, leaving Greece, then with a population of 4,800,000, with the difficulties of finding housing and work for over a million Anatolian refugees.

In 1924 a republic was proclaimed which lasted for 10 shaky years. Trade unions and the Greek Communist Party, or KKE, were formed and gained strength. Venizélos was re-elected as President and set the present borders of Greece (except for the Dodecanese Islands, which Italy snapped up at Versailles as part of its war prizes). His term also saw the start of another ongoing headache: the first uprising by Greek Cypriots, four-fifths of the population of what was then a British Crown Colony, who desired union with Greece.

Another Catastrophe: The Second World War and the Greek Civil War

The republic, beset with economic difficulties, collapsed in 1935, and King George II returned to Greece, with General Metaxás as his Prime Minister. Metaxás assumed dictatorial control under the regime of 4 August, exiled the opposition, instituted rigorous censorship and crushed the trade unions and all leftist activities. Although a sympathizer with Fascism, Metaxás had sufficient foreboding to prepare the Greek army in advance against occupation, and on 28 October 1940, as the apocryphal story goes, he responded with a laconic '*Óchi!*' (No!) to Mussolini's demands that his troops massed on the Albanian border be allowed passage through Greece. The first Allied country voluntarily to join Britain against the Axis, Greece's moment of glory came when it not only stopped the Italians, but pushed them back into Albania.

But by May 1941, after the Battle of Crete, all Greece was in the hands of the Nazis, and George II was in exile in Egypt. The miseries and horrors of the Occupation (more civilians died in Greece than in any other occupied country; an estimated 500,000 people starved to death) were compounded by political strife and uncertainty over the status of the monarchy in exile. The Communist-organized EAM, the National Liberation Front, and its army, ELAS, led the resistance and had vast popular support, but its politics were hardly palatable to Churchill, who was keen to restore the monarchy and keep Greece out of communist hands. The proud Greeks saw his manoeuvring as another example of outside interference, and the Greek Civil War—in retrospect the very first campaign of the Cold War—broke out three short months after the liberation of Greece, beginning in Athens, with British troops and a Greek monarchist minority fighting ELAS and their allies Yugoslavia and Bulgaria, followed by long-drawn-out guerrilla campaigns in the mountains, with more of the usual horrific atrocities. At the end of the Second World War, Britain's communist containment policy was taken over by the Truman Doctrine. American money and advisors poured into Greece. The Civil War dragged on until 1949; leftists who were not shot or imprisoned went into exile.

Recovery and Cyprus

Recovery was very slow, even if orchestrated by America, and the Greek diaspora that began in the early 20th century accelerated so fast that entire villages, especially on the islands, became ghost towns. In 1951, Greece and Turkey became full members of NATO, an uncomfortable arrangement from the start because of the unresolved issue of Cyprus, still ruled by Britain. General Papagos of the American-backed Greek Rally party won the elections of 1952. Two years later Greek Cypriots, led by Archbishop Makários, clamoured and rioted for union with Greece; the Americans and British turned a deaf ear. Meanwhile Papagos died, and the more liberal Konstantínos Karamanlís replaced him as Prime Minister, inaugurating eight years of stability and prosperity as agriculture and tourism began to make their contributions to the economy, although the opposition criticized his pro-Western policy and inability to resolve the worsening situation in Cyprus. Because one-fifth of Cypriots were Turkish, Turkey refused to let Cyprus join Greece—the independence or partitioning of the island was as far as Ankara would go. In 1960, a British-brokered compromise was reached, although it had little appeal for the Greeks: Cyprus became an independent republic and elected Makários president. Britain took care to retain sovereignty over its military bases.

To add to the unhappiness over Cyprus, Greece was rocked with record unemployment. The royal family, especially the neo-Fascist Queen Frederíka, were unpopular; there were strikes and powerful anti-American feelings. In 1963 came the assassination of left-wing Deputy Lambrákis (see Costa Gravas' film *Z*), for which police officers were tried and convicted. Karamanlís resigned and lost the next elections in 1965 to George Papandréou of the centre-left opposition. At the same time, King Paul, son of George II, died and was succeeded by his son, the 23-year-old conservative Constantine II. The combination did not bode well; a quarrel with the king over reforming the tradition-bound military led to Papandréou's resignation in 1966. Constantine was meant to call for new elections but, fearing Papandréou's re-election, he tried instead to organize a coalition around Konstantínos Misotákis, the future Néa Demokratikí leader. Massive discontent finally forced Constantine to call for elections in May, but on 21 April 1967 a coup by an obscure group of colonels established a military dictatorship and imprisoned George Papandréou and his son Andréas (an economics professor at Harvard and Adlai Stevenson's campaign manager), charging the latter with treason. Colonel George Papadópoulos became dictator of the junta. Constantine II attempted a ridiculous counter-coup and then fled to Rome.

A Vicious 'Moral Cleansing'

The proclaimed aim of the colonels' junta—propped up disgracefully by the CIA—was a 'moral cleansing of Orthodox Christian Greece'. Human rights were suppressed, strict and often absurd censorship undermined the nation's cultural life, and the secret police imprisoned and tortured thousands of dissidents—or their children. The internal situation went from bad to worse, and on 17 November 1973 students of the Polytechnic school in Athens went on strike. Tanks were brought in and many students were killed. After this incident, popular feeling rose to such a pitch that Papadópoulos was arrested, only to be replaced by his arrester, the head of the secret military police, Ioannídes. Greece was in turmoil. Attempting to save the situation by rallying the nation around the Great Idea, Ioannídes tried to launch a coup in Cyprus, to assassinate Makários and replace him with a president who would declare the long-desired union of Cyprus with Greece. It was a fiasco. Makários fled and the Turkish army invaded Cyprus, occupying 40% of the island. The Greek military rebelled, the dictatorship resigned and Karamanlís hurriedly returned from his exile in Paris to form a new government, release the political prisoners, order a ceasefire in Cyprus and legalize the Communist Party.

A New Greek Alphabet: ND, EEC, PASOK

Karamanlís and his conservative Néa Demokratikí (ND) easily won the November 1974 elections; the monarchy did less well in the subsequent plebiscite, and Greece became a republic. In the same year, Karamanlís realized his fondest dream when the country was anchored to the European Community. Karamanlís brought stability, but neglected the economic and social reforms Greece so badly needed; these reforms, along with a desire for national integrity and an independent foreign policy, were to be the ticket to populist Andréas Papandréou's victories, beginning in 1981. His party, PASOK (the Pan-Hellenic Socialist Movement, with a rising-green-sun symbol), promised much, beginning with withdrawal from NATO and the EEC, and the removal of US air bases; understandably, Papandréou's anti-USA and Europe rhetoric was music to Greek ears. PASOK's sun shone over some long-awaited reforms, especially women's rights, and a heady and hedonistic liberalization swept the land. PASOK easily triumphed again in the 1985 elections, in spite of Papandréou's failure to deliver Greece from the snares of NATO, the USA or the European Community, or even keep any of his promises on the economic front. Inflation soared and after the election Greece had to be bailed out by a huge EC loan, accompanied by an unpopular belt-tightening programme. In the end, however, it was scandals and corruption that brought Papandréou down: the old man's open affair and later marriage to a much younger woman—Dímitri (Mimi) Liáni—and the Bank of Crete corruption scandal didn't go down well in an essentially conservative country.

In 1990, Misotákis and the Néa Demokratikí conservatives won by a slim majority in the elections, promising to grapple with Greece's severe economic problems. ND immediately launched a wave of austerity measures which proved even more unpopular than Papandréou—a crackdown on tax evasion, a wage freeze for civil servants, privatization of most state-run companies, including Olympic Airways, and steep increases in charges for public services. This sparked off a wave of strikes in 1991 and 1992. By late 1992 Mitsotákis had also had his share of political scandals, and in October 1993 his party fell in the general election, returning rascally old Andréas Papandréou to office, a package that included wife Liáni as chief of staff.

Third time did prove lucky when it came to closing down the US bases in Greece (1994). Otherwise Papandréou kept Greece in his thrall by pushing all the Balkan nationalist buttons—rallying the country around the hallowed name of Macedonia when the new little landlocked country on Greece's border tried to snatch it (as punishment, Greece cut off its links to the sea until November 1995) and siding (verbally, mostly) with the Serbs in Bosnia because they too were Orthodox and that was all that mattered. As Papandréou played the gadfly, the once-reviled EU poured funds into the country, resulting in new roads, schools, sewers and agricultural subsidies. The once-low prices that fuelled the Greek tourist boom of the 1970s and 80s inched up to match the rest of Europe, but after 1994 (a record year for tourism, with 11.3 million arrivals), the strong drachma brought a steep decline.

In late 1995, Papandréou declined as well, and went into hospital. Seriously ill with kidney failure, he refused to resign as Prime Minister, while his wife's faction manoeuvred for power—thwarted in the end by a revolt led by former trade minister Kósta Simítis, a respected but 'bland' technocrat who toughed it out to get the party's nod to finish out the old man's term. Simítis' first weeks at the helm were severely tested when a dispute with Turkey erupted over an uninhabited rock pile in the Dodecanese, nearly bringing the two countries to a shooting war. Nationalists blamed Simítis for being soft on agreeing to an American-brokered mutual withdrawal pending mediation, but the feeling after all the rhetoric was that it was not an issue to send young men to die for.

Non-dogmatic, low-key, efficient and untainted by scandal, Simítis has proved to be a hard worker for pragmatic common sense, something all too rare in recent Greek politics. Even before Papandréou's death in June 1996 he broke with the shrill nationalism of his former boss (while keeping old PASOK hands happy by appointing Papandréou's intelligent and sensible son George as deputy Foreign Minister) and has since patched up relations with Greece's neighbours. Under Simítis, Greece has become a regional leader and prime investor in the Balkans; he has encouraged talks led by Richard Holbrook to come to an agreement over Cyprus; the paranoia index has plummeted, and a truce of sorts has kept Greek-Turkish relations from flying off the handle, in spite of political instability in Turkey. Although economically still sharing the European Union cellar along with Portugal, Simítis' Greece is doggedly trying to better itself: improving the country's infrastructure, providing a climate for capital investments, building new ties with Eastern Europe and Russia, and, in 1997, letting the drachma slide to make Greece more attractive to tourism, which today represents 15% of the annual income, by far the biggest foreign currency earner. The choice of Athens for the 2004 Olympics has boosted Greek pride tremendously—94% of the population were in favour of 'bringing the games home'.

A Quick Who's Who in Greek Mythology

Like all good polytheists, the ancient Greeks filled their pantheon with a colourful assortment of divinities, divinities perhaps more anthropomorphic than most, full of fathomless contradictions, subtleties and regional nuances. Nearly every island has stories about their doings; some have become part of the familiar baggage of Western civilization, while others read like strange collective dreams, or nightmares. But as classical Greek society grew more advanced and rational-minded, these gods were rounded up and made to live on the sanitized heights of Mount Olympos as idols of state religion, defined (and already ridiculed) in Homer. The meatier matters of birth, sex, death and hopes for an afterlife—i.e. the real religion—went underground in the mysteries and chthonic cults, surviving in such places as Eleusis (Elefsína) near Athens, and at the Sanctuary of the Great Gods on Samothráki.

The big cheese on Olympos was **Zeus** (Jupiter, to the Romans), a native of Crete, the great Indo-European sky god, lord of the thunderbolt with a libido to match, whose unenviable task was to keep the other gods in line. He was married to his sister **Hera** (Juno), the goddess of marriage, whose special role in myth is that of the wronged, jealous wife, and who periodically returned to her special island of Sámos to renew her virginity. Zeus' two younger brothers were given their own realms: **Poseidon** (Neptune) ruled the sea with his wife Amphytron (they had special sanctuaries on Póros and Tínos, and the famous 'Heliotrope' on Sýros), while **Hades** (Pluto) ruled the underworld and dead, and rarely left his dismal realm. Their sister was **Demeter** (Ceres), goddess of corn and growing things, who was worshipped in the mysteries of Eleusis. **Aphrodite** (Venus), the goddess of love, is nearly as old as these gods, born when Zeus overthrew their father Cronus (Saturn) by castrating him and tossed the bloody member in the sea foam. She first landed at Kýthera but later preferred Cyprus.

The second generation of Olympians were the offspring of Zeus: **Athena**, the urbane virgin goddess of wisdom, born full grown straight out of Zeus' brain and always associated with Athens, her special city; **Ares** (Mars), the whining bully god of war, disliked by the Greeks and associated with barbarian Thrace; **Hermes** (Mercury), the messenger, occasional trickster, and god of commerce; **Hephaistos** (Vulcan), the god of fire, the forge and metal working, married to Aphrodite and worshipped on Límnos; **Apollo**, the god of light, music, reason, poetry and prophesy, often identified with the sun; and his twin sister **Artemis** (Diana), the tomboy virgin moon goddess of the hunt, both born and worshipped on the little island of Délos. Their cross-dressing half-brother **Dionysos** (Bacchus), the god of wine, orgies and theatre, was the favourite on Náxos. In addition to the twelve Olympians, the Greeks had an assorted array of other gods, nymphs, satyrs and heroes, the greatest of whom was **Herakles** (Hercules), the mighty hero who earned himself a place on Olympos, and gods such as **Helios** (Sol), the unassuming sun god, whose special island has always been Rhodes.

A Brief Outline of Greek Art and Architecture

The oldest known settlements on the Greek islands date back to approximately 6000 BC—Knossós and Phaistós on **Crete**, obsidian-exporting Fylokopí on **Mílos** and sophisticated Paleóchnoe on **Límnos**. Artistic finds are typical of the era elsewhere—dark burnished pottery decorated with spirals and wavy lines, and statuettes of the fertility goddess in stone or terracotta.

Bronze Age: Cycladic and Minoan styles (3000–1100 BC)

Early contacts with Anatolia and the Near East brought Crete and the Cyclades to the cutting edge of not only Greek but European civilization. By 2600 BC Cycladic dead were being buried with their trademark—almost abstract white marble figurines, rubbed smoothly into shape with emery and ranging in size from a fly to a human (the best collections are in Náxos and Athens). At the same time, the people who would be dubbed the Minoans by Sir Arthur Evans were already demonstrating a precocious talent on Crete in polychrome pottery, elegant stone vases and gold jewellery. During the next period (Middle Minoan, 2000–1700 BC), when Crete's fleet ruled the seas, the Minoans felt sufficiently secure from external and internal threats to build themselves unfortified palaces and cities, always centred around a large rectangular courtyard, which may have been used for bull-leaping games. They installed a complex system of canals and drains, and, judging by the translations of the Linear A and Linear B tablets they left behind, they were bureaucrats extraordinaire who kept very careful accounts of the magazines of oil, honey, wine and grain stored in their huge characteristic *pithoi*. Crete's civilization reached its apogee between 1700 and 1450 BC. Minoan colonies stretched across the Aegean as far as Sicily and their elegant ambassadors figured in the tomb paintings of the Pharaohs; their own palaces at **Knossós, Phaistós, Zákros, Mália** and at their outpost of **Akrotíri**, on the island of Santoríni, were adorned with elegant frescoes and other remarkable treasures now on show in the archaeology museums of **Herákleon** and **Athens**.

Built mostly of wood and unbaked brick, the Minoan palaces collapsed like card castles in the earthquakes and dramatic fires that marked the end of their civilization. The Achaeans of Mycenae (who used the same Linear A script) rushed in to fill the vacuum of power and trade in the Aegean, taking over the Minoan colonies and carrying on much of their artistic traditions. Little of this ever reached the islands, although many have vestiges of the Achaeans' impressive stone walls, known as **cyclopean** after their gigantic blocks. Impressive as they are, they failed to keep out the Dorian invaders from the north, who destroyed what remained of Aegean unity in the confusing aftermath of the Trojan War and ushered in one of history's perennial Dark Ages.

Geometric (1000–700 BC) and Archaic (700–500 BC)

The splintering of the Minoan and Mycenaean world saw less trade and art and more agriculture, and the evolution of the *pólis*, or city-state. In art, Geometric refers to simple, abstract pottery designs; traces of Geometric temples, made of brick and wood, are much rarer. The temple of Apollo at Dréros on Crete and the first Temple of Hera on **Sámos** were built around the 8th century BC, although the discovery in 1981 of the huge sanctuary at **Lefkándi** on Évia, believed to date from *c.* 900 BC, has called previous chronological assumptions into question.

The Archaic Period is marked by the change to stone, especially limestone, for the building of temples, and a return to figurative art. It was an exceptionally fertile and imaginative period: the first known stone temple—and a prototype of the Classical temple with its columns, pediments and metopes—was **Corfu**'s stout-columned Doric Temple of Artemis (580 BC), its pediment decorated with a formidable 3½m relief of Medusa (now in Corfu's museum). The excavations at Embório, on **Chíos**, are among the best extant records we have of an Archaic town, while the 6th-century Efplinion tunnel at Pythagório, **Sámos**, was the engineering feat of the age.

This era also saw the beginning of life-size—and larger—figure sculpture, inspired by the Egyptians; poses are stiff, formal and rigid, one foot carefully placed before the other. Unlike Egyptian models, however, Greek statues are marked by their easy, confident Archaic smiles, as if they were all in on a secret joke. The male version is a *kouros*, or young man (see the giants of **Sámos** and **Náxos**); the female a *kore*, or maiden, dressed in graceful drapery.

The 7th century BC also saw the development of regional schools of pottery, influenced by the black-figured techniques of Corinth: **Rhodes** and the Cyclades produced some of the best.

Classical (500–380 BC)

As Athens became the dominant power in the Aegean, it sucked up most of the artistic talent in Greece and concentrated its most refined skills on its showpiece Acropolis, culminating with the extraordinary mathematical perfection of the Parthenon, the greatest of all Doric temples, built without a single straight line in the entire building. Nothing on the islands comes anywhere near, although there are a few classical era sites to visit: Liménas on **Thássos** and Líndos, Kámiros and Iálysos on **Rhodes**. In ceramics, there was a change over to more naturalistic red-figured black vases around 500 BC; again, the best collection is in the National Archaeology Museum, **Athens**.

Hellenistic (380–30 BC)

This era brought new stylistic influences from the eastern lands conquered and Hellenized by Alexander the Great and his lieutenants. Compared to the cool, aloof perfection of the classical era, Hellenistic sculpture is characterized by a more emotional, Baroque approach, all windswept drapery, violence and passion, revealed in the Louvre's showpiece *Victory of Samothrace* found in **Samothráki**'s Hellenistic Sanctuary of the Great Gods. Rhodes was at the height of its powers; besides its long-

DORIC

IONIC

CORINTHIAN

gone Colossus, it produced the writhing *Laocoön* (now in the Vatican museum) and the Aphrodites (including Durrell's *Marine Venus*) in the **Rhodes** museum. Houses became decidedly more plush, many decorated with mosaics and frescoes, as in the commercial town of **Délos** and in the suburbs of **Kos**.

Roman (30 BC–AD 527)

The Pax Romana not only ended the rivalries between the Greek city-states but pretty much dried up the sources of their inspiration, although sculptors, architects and other talents found a ready market for their skills in Rome, cranking out fair copies of classical and Hellenistic masterpieces.

The Romans themselves built little in Greece: the stoa and theatre of Herodes Atticus (AD 160) were the last large monuments erected in ancient Athens. On the islands, the largest site of the period is Górtyna, **Crete**, the Roman capital of the island and Libya.

Byzantine (527–1460)

The art and architecture of the Byzantines began to show its stylistic distinction under the reign of Justinian (527–565), while the immediate post-Justinian period saw a golden age in the splendour of Ag. Sofia in Istanbul and the churches of Ravenna, Italy. On the islands, you'll find only the remains of simple three-naved basilicas—with two exceptions: the 6th-century Ekatontapylianí of **Páros** and 7th-century Ag. Títos at Górtyna, **Crete**.

After the austere art purge of the Iconoclasm (726–843), the Macedonian style in painting (named after the Macedonian emperors then in power) slowly infiltrated the Greek provinces. The old Roman basilica plan was jettisoned in favour of a central Greek-cross crowned by a dome, elongated in front by a vestibule (narthex) and outer porch (exonarthex), and at the back by a choir and three apses. **Dafní**, just outside Athens, and Néa Moní on **Chíos**, with its massive cupola, are superb examples; both are decorated with superb mosaics from the second golden age of Byzantine art, under the dynasty of the Comnenes (12th–14th centuries). As in Italy, this period marked a renewed interest in antique models: the stiff, elongated hieratic figures with staring eyes are given more natural-istic proportions in graceful, rhythmic compositions. The age of the Comnenes also produced some fine painting, with at least a hundred frescoes on **Crete**, culminating in the early 13th-century church of Kerá Panagía at Kritsá, near Ag. Nikólaos. Crete's occupation by Venice after 1204 marked the beginning of an artistic cross-fertilization that developed into the highly esteemed Cretan school of painting—fine examples are to be seen in the Byzantine museums in **Herákleon** and **Athens**.

What never changed was the intent of Byzantine art, which is worth a small digression because in the 15th century Western art went off in an entirely different direction—so much so that everything before is disparagingly labelled 'primitive' in most art books. The most obvious difference is the strict iconography in Byzantine painting: if you know the code you can instantly identify each saint by the cut of beard, the key or pen in their hand, or other attributes. Their appeal to the viewer, even in the 13th century when the figures were given more naturalistic proportions, is equally purely symbolic: a Byzantine Christ on the Cross, the Virgin *Panagía* (the 'all-holy'), angels, saints and martyrs never make an emotional play for the heartstrings, but reside on a purely spiritual and intellectual plane, miles away from Western art invented in the Renaissance, 'based on horror, physical charm, infant-worship and easy weeping' as Patrick Leigh Fermor put it. Icons and Byzantine frescoes never ask the viewer to relive the passion of Christ or coo over Baby Jesus; Byzantine angels never lift their draperies to reveal a little leg; the stiff, wide-eyed *Panagía*, dressed like an Orthodox nun, has none of the fashionable charms of the Madonna. The figures never stray from their remote otherworldliness.

And yet, in the last gasp of Byzantine art under the Paleologos emperors (14th–early 15th centuries), humanist and naturalistic influences combined to produce the Byzantine equivalent of the late Gothic/early Renaissance painting in Italy, in Mistras in the Peloponnese. It is the great might-have-been of Byzantine art: after the Turkish conquest the best painters took refuge on Mount Áthos, or on **Zákynthos** (where there's a good museum) and **Corfu**, but none of their work radiates the same charm or confidence in the temporal world.

Turkish Occupation to the Present

The Turks left few important monuments in Greece, and much of what they did build was wrecked or neglected to death by the Greeks after independence. **Rhodes** town, followed by **Kos**, has the best surviving mosques, hammams, houses and public buildings, not only because the Turks loved it well, but because the Dodecanese only became Greek in 1945. **Crete** and **Corfu** especially remained Venetian longer than most places and have fine architectural souvenirs: impressive fortifications and gates, fountains, public buildings and town houses. Elsewhere, independent-minded islands that had their own fleets, for instance **Sými**, have impressive mansions built by sea captains and ship owners, while other islands continued traditional architectural styles: the whitewashed asymmetry of the Cyclades, the patterned *sgraffito* in the mastic villages of Chíos, the Macedonian wooden upper floors and balconies of the northernmost islands, and so on.

In the 19th century, Athens and Ermioúpolos on **Sýros** (briefly Greece's chief port) were built up in the neoclassical style, their buildings often restrained and elegantly simple; after years of neglect many are finally being restored to their former grandeur. A host of grandiose neo-Byzantine churches went up, while many older ones were unfortunately tarted up with tired bastard painting, Byzantine in iconography but most of it no better than the contents of a third-rate provincial museum in Italy.

On the whole, the less said about 20th-century architecture on the islands, the better: the Mussolini palazzi on the Dodecanese islands at least have a sense of style, which is more than can be said of the cheap concrete slabs that have gone up elsewhere. Prosperity in the 1980s has brought an increased interest in local architecture and historic preservation, and following the lead of the National Tourist Organization's traditional settlement programme, private individuals have begun to restore monasteries, abandoned villages and captains' mansions. Most new developments at least make an effort to harmonize with traditional styles—the island's own or the Costa del Sol's. One individual who won't be restoring any palaces is ex-King Constantine of Greece, whose property was expropriated by the Papandréou Government in 1994.

History: From Cradle to Grave
   and Back Again   48

Getting Around   51

Tourist Information   52

Orientation: Athens in a Nutshell   53

Major Museums and Sites   55

The Heart of Ancient Athens:
    The Agora, Thissío and Stoa of Attalus   58

Other Museums and Sites   60

Byzantine Churches and Monasteries   62

Where to Stay   63

Eating Out   66

Entertainment and Nightlife   69

Athens

Love for Athens, a city once famous, wrote these words; a love that plays with shadows, that gives a little comfort to burning desire... Though I live in Athens I see Athens nowhere: only sad, empty, and blessed dust.

Michael Akominátos, 12th century

Travellers to the Greek islands often find themselves in Athens, and although it has perked up considerably since the days of Michael Akominátos, it's rarely love at first sight. Look closely behind the ugly architecture and congestion, however, and you may be won over by this urban crazy quilt—small oases of green parks hidden amidst the hustle and bustle; tiny family-run tavernas tucked away in the most unexpected places; the feverish pace of its nightlife and summer festivals; and, best of all, the Athenians themselves, whose friendliness belies the reputation of most city dwellers. Another plus: Athens is the least expensive capital in the European Union.

History: From Cradle to Grave and Back Again

Athens had its share of inhabitants by the end of Neolithic Age (*c.* 3500 BC), but its significant début on history's stage occurred in the second millennium BC, when invaders, probably from Asia Minor, entered Attica and established small fortified enclaves. Their descendants would claim they were '**the children of Kecrops**', a half-man half-snake who united them into 12 villages and founded Kecropia on the rock that would later become the Acropolis. Kecrops gave them laws and taught them the cultivation and uses of the all-important crop of dry Attica, the olive. The owl was his sacred bird.

The next step in the process was the birth of **King Erechtheos**, 'the earth-born', raised up to the surface by Gaia (Earth) herself. Snake from the waist down himself, Erechtheos was the official founding father of Athens. According to the myth as it developed in historical times, Erechtheos introduced the worship of **Athena**, whose religion and name gradually came to preside in the city.

Athens was a significant centre in the **Mycenaean** period, as graves on the Acropolis hill show. Her great hero **Theseus**, best known for killing the Minotaur in Crete (no doubt a memory of the Mycenaeans' successful invasion there), dates from this era. Athens managed to escape the **Dorian invasions** after 1200 BC (although her culture declined during the Dark Ages). This escape was a great point of pride with Athenians who, as a result, considered themselves even more Greek, somehow more legitimate and certainly more refined than their Dorian counterparts. All of this together helped to create the amazing self-confidence that would produce the great Athenian city-state and democracy.

Some time during the 8th century BC all the towns of Attica were peaceably united under the leadership of Athens. The city was ruled by a king (who doubled as the chief priest), a *pole-march* (general) and an *archon* (civil ruler), positions that by the 6th century BC were annually elective. Eventually it was conflict between the landed aristocracy and the rising commercial classes that brought about the momentous invention of democratic government, beginning with the reforms and laws of **Solon** in 594 BC. However, Solon's good start didn't stop his relative **Pisístratos** from making himself a 'popular' dictator in 560 BC. He began the naval build-up that for the first time made Athens a threat to the other Greek city-states.

Pisístratos' son was followed in 510 BC by another democratic reformer, **Kleisthénes**, who attempted to make aristocratic takeovers harder by dividing the population (the free and male members, at any rate) into 10 political tribes. Lots were drawn to choose 50 members of the people's assembly, from which a further lot was drawn to select 10 *archons*, one from each tribe. The head *archon* gave his name to the Athenian year.

Meanwhile, as **Persian** strength grew in the east, Ionian intellectuals and artists took refuge in Athens, bringing with them philosophy, science and the roots of Attic tragedy. They prodded Athens to aid Ionia against the Persians, an unsuccessful adventure that landed the city in the soup when **Darius**, the Persian King of Kings, decided in turn to subdue Greece and, in particular, that upstart Athens. In 490 BC, Darius' vast army landed at **Marathon**, only to be defeated by a much smaller Athenian force under Miltiades.

Although powerful Sparta and the other Greek states woke up to the eastern threat, they continued to leave 'national' defence primarily to Athens and, in particular, the Athenian fleet, which grew ever mightier under **Themistocles**. However, it failed to keep the Persians from having another go at Greece. In 480 BC the new King of Kings, Xerxes, showed up with the greatest fleet and army the ancient world had ever seen. An oracle had told Themistocles that Athens would be saved by 'wooden walls'. He interpreted that to mean the navy and he persuaded the Athenian army to abandon the Acropolis for the safety of **Salamis**, where the fleet was anchored. One compelling reason why they did, according to contemporary gossip, was that the Acropolis snake was seen beating a fast retreat, a sure sign that the rock would fall. Athens and the Acropolis were razed by the Persians, but their navy was neatly outmanoeuvred by the Athenian ships at Salamis. The Persian army was finally repelled by the Athenians and Spartans at the Battle of **Plateía**.

With her undisputed superiority at sea, Athens set about creating a maritime empire, not only to increase her power but also to stabilize her combustible internal politics. She ruled the confederacy at Delos, demanding contributions from the islands in return for protection from the Persians. Sea trade became essential as the city's population grew, while new colonies were founded around the Mediterranean, not only to release the pressure but also to ensure a continual food supply for Athens. Athenian democracy became truly imperialistic under **Pericles**, who brought the treasure of Delos to Athens to 'protect it'—and to skim off funds to rebuild and beautify the city and build the **Parthenon**. It was the golden age of Athens, of Phidias, Herodotus, Sophocles, Aristophanes and Socrates.

It couldn't last. The devastating **Peloponnesian War** (431–404 BC) began over Athenian expansion in the west. Back and forth the struggle went, Sparta with superiority on land, Athens on the seas, until both city-states were near exhaustion. Finally, Lysander and the Spartans captured Athens, razed the walls and set up the brief rule of the Thirty Tyrants.

Although democracy and imperialism made quick recoveries (by 378 BC the city had set up its second Maritime League), the Peloponnesian War had struck a blow from which ancient Athens would never totally recover. The war-weary population grew dissatisfied with public life and refused to tolerate innovators and critics; **Socrates** was put to death. Economically, Athens had trouble maintaining the trade she needed. Yet her intellectual tradition held true in the 4th century BC, bringing forth the likes of Demosthenes, Praxiteles, Menander, Plato and Aristotle.

Philip II of Macedon took advantage of the general discontent to bully the city-states into joining the Macedonians (Hellenized barbarians, according to the haughty Athenians of the time) for an expedition against Greece's eternal rival, Persia. Athenian patriotism and indepen-dence were kept alive by the orator Demosthenes until Philip subdued the city (338 BC). Philip was assassinated shortly before beginning the Persian campaign, leaving his son Alexander, the pupil of Aristotle, to conquer the East. When Alexander died, Athens was a prize fought over by his generals, beginning with Dimitrios Poliorketes (the Besieger), who captured the city in 294 BC. Alexandria, Rhodes and Pergamon became Athens' intellectual rivals, although Athens continued to be honoured by them.

In 168 BC, **Rome** captured Athens, but granted her many privileges. However, 80 years later, when Athens betrayed Roman favour by siding with Mithridates of Pontus, Sulla destroyed Piraeus, the Agora and the walls of the city. But Rome always remembered her cultural debt; leading Romans attended Athens' academies and endowed the city with monuments. **St Paul** started the Athenians on the road to Christianity in AD 44. In the 3rd century, **Goths** and barbarians sacked Athens, and after they were driven away the city became a less and less important part of the growing Byzantine Empire. In 529, **Emperor Justinian** closed the philosophy schools, and converted the temples to churches and the Parthenon into a cathe-dral. It was a largely symbolic act; by then Athens had lost her position in the world.

She next enters history as the plaything of the **Franks** after they pillaged Constantinople in 1204. St Louis made Guy de la Roche the Duke of Athens, a dukedom which passed through many outstretched hands: the Catalans, Neapolitans and Venetians all controlled the city at various times. In 1456 it was the turn of the **Ottomans**, who converted the Parthenon into a mosque and the Erechtheion into a harem. The Venetians made several attempts to wrench it away; in Morosini's siege of 1687, a shell struck the Parthenon, where the Turks had stored their gunpowder. In 1800, **Lord Elgin** began the large-scale removal of the Parthenon's marbles to Britain.

In 1834, after the War of Independence, Athens—at the time a clutch of war-scarred houses rotting below the Acropolis, with a population of 200—was declared the **capital** of the new Greek state. Otto of Bavaria, the first King of the Greeks, brought his own architects with him to lay out a new city, based on the lines of Stadíou and El. Venezélou Streets, which still boast many of Athens' neoclassical public buildings. Much of the rest of the city was built on the quick and cheap in order to accommodate the flood of people from the countryside and the Anatolian Greeks who arrived after the population exchange with Turkey in 1922. As a result, Athens has become a dense domino game stacked over the hills of Attica.

Today, Greater Athens squeezes in four million lively, opinionated inhabitants—a full third of the population of Greece—who, thanks to native ingenuity and EU-membership, are now more prosperous than they have been since the age of Pericles. Unfortunately, this translates into a million cars, creating the worst smog problem east of Mexico City and one that threatens to choke this unique city. The word for smog is *néfos*, and if you happened to arrive on a brown day you'll soon know too much about it. The metro system is being improved and extended, which should make things better in the near future.

Modern Athens may never win any beauty prizes, but it's as alive as it is ugly—the opposite of its old master Venice, which is stunningly beautiful, and stunningly dead. Of late Athens is undergoing a quiet renaissance under Mayor Dimitris Avramópoulos. Neoclassical buildings are being restored, trees planted and car-less oases created in the centre. Construction of a new airport has begun at Spata, 20km away, and fresh immigrants from Eastern Europe and the Balkans are giving the city a new cosmopolitan buzz. Losing the 1996 Olympics to Atlanta may have been a kick in the *fustanella*, but it also focused Athens' attention on its problems like nothing before—hard work that has been rewarded by the selection of Athens to 'bring the Olympics home', at long last, in 2004.

Athens © (01–)   **Getting Around**

by bus

The excellent free map of Athens distributed by EOT (*see* below) marks the main city bus (the blue ones) and trolley routes. Purchase tickets (120dr) before boarding and punch them in the orange machines on board; if you're caught without a ticket, the fine is currently 4,500dr—paid on the spot. Tickets are sold in kiosks by the main bus stops, and often in shops near the stops. Ask for *eseeteério yia to leoforeéo*. Note that all trolleys except nos.1, 10 and 12 pass in front of the National Archaeology Museum; for the Acropolis and Thissío catch bus no.230 from the top of Sýntagma Square (Amalías and Óthonas Streets). For info, call © 185 between 7am and 9pm.

by metro

The metro (tickets sold in the stations) is an important means of getting across Athens, especially from Piraeus. The existing line runs as far as Kifissiá, stopping in the centre at Thissío (Theseum), Monastiráki (near Pláka) and Omónia. A $2.8 billion extension with two new lines is under way and some new stations are already operating. Tickets for the new part of the metro cost 250dr and can also be used for connecting buses. Everything has to be completed by 2004, and may be finished earlier if all the quibbling over financing gets settled. The new line should make crossing the city and getting to the Acropolis easier, so check on its progress when you arrive.

by taxi

Compared to other Western cities, Athenian taxis are dirt cheap. There are taxi stands in some squares, at the port, train station, airport and bus station, but most cabs cruise the streets. A taxi driver is available when the flag in the window on the passenger side is up and lit. At the time of writing, the meter starts at 200dr and adds 70dr per kilometre. The minimum fare is 500dr. There are various small surcharges (airport, port and station trips, and baggage), and all prices double between midnight and 5am. On major holidays, such as Easter, the driver gets a mandatory 'present' of a couple of hundred drachmae. A taxi between central Athens and the airport should cost 2,500–3,000dr; from the National Archaeological Museum to the Acropolis, about 1,000dr. Take proper yellow taxis with meters and official licence numbers only.

Sharing: Because fares are so low and demand so great, Athenians often share cabs. Usually, the cabbie leaves his flag lit, even if he has passengers, to indicate that he is willing to take more people. Hailing a cab this way is not for the faint-hearted; the usual procedure is to stand by the street, flag down any passing cab and, if they slow down and cock an ear, shout out your general destination. If the taxi is going that way, the driver will stop; if not, he won't. Check the meter when you board and pay from there, adding 200dr (the normal surcharge), plus any baggage charges. If the cabbie asks for the full fare, start writing down his licence number and ask for a receipt. That usually settles the issue on the spot.

Radio taxis charge 500dr to come from the moment you call, 1,000dr if you make an appointment. In many cases, especially for the airport, it is well worth it. In Athens, try Parthenon ✆ 532 3300, Enotita ✆ 645 9000, Ikaros ✆ 513 2316; in Piraeus, Piraeus I ✆ 418 2333. Numbers are listed in the English-language daily *Athens News*.

The traffic in Athens can be so snarled that there are now **motorcycle taxis**, ✆ 921 2000, that will zigzag you faster through the downtown traffic. The minimum fare is 500dr; 30min costs 3,000dr; 1 hour costs 6,000dr.

by car

Just don't. Besides the traffic jams, the one-way system is confusing and parking is almost impossible. If you need assistance, try ELPA (the Greek Automobile Club) at Mesogeion 395, ✆ 606 8800. You can call ✆ 104 for road assistance, wherever you are in Greece.

Athens ✆ (01–)   **Tourist Information**

The **tourist police** have a magic number: ✆ **171**. From 7am to 11pm daily, a voice in English will answer any question you may have. Between 11pm and 7am only, the emergency number is ✆ 924 2700. The Athens Tourist Police offices are out at Diumitrakoplou 77, in the Makrigiánni area, ✆ 925 3396, ✉ 924 3406, but, thanks to the magic number, you will probably never have to go there.

The **Greek National Tourist Organization** (EOT) is at 2 Amerikís St, between Stadíou and Panepistemíou, ✆ 331 0561/331 0565, ✉ 325 2895 (open Mon–Fri 9–7, Sat 9–2, closed Sun). They also have a booth in the East Air Terminal, ✆ 969 9500. EOT hands out a great free map with the city on one side, including bus routes, and Piraeus and Attica on the back. Ask for the free English *Now in Athens* magazine, with listings of museums, events, shops, etc. Another mine of information for Athens and Piraeus is the *Athens News*, in English, published every day except Monday and on sale at most central kiosks.

emergencies

first aid ✆ 166	**doctors on duty** ✆ 105
fire ✆ 199	**(2pm–7am only)**
police ✆ 100	**pharmacies on duty** ✆ 107

If you do not have a Greek speaker available when you make the call, try ✆ **171** and speak to the tourist police (*see* above).

left luggage

The East Air Terminal has a 24-hour facility. But if you are in mid-Athens with luggage, leave it at Bellair Travel, ✆ 323 9261, at 15 Níkis St (open Mon–Fri 9–6, Sat 9–2). Pacific Limited, 26 Níkis St, ✆ 324 1007, offers the same facility during business hours. In Piraeus, there is a left luggage facility in the metro station.

lost property

If you leave something on a bus, taxi or metro, call ✆ 642 1616.

The **Internet Café**, 5 Stadíou St, © 324 8105, *sofos1@ath.forthnet.gr*, charges 1,500dr an hour and is open Mon–Sat 10am–10pm, Sun 11am–7pm.

The megastore for books in central Athens is **Eleftheroudakis**, 17 Panepistimíou St, © 331 4180, with five floors of books in Greek and English. They also have a smaller branch right behind Sýntagma at 4 Níkis St, with a good selection of maps and tourist guides. **Compendium**, 28 Níkis St, is smaller, cozier, and has only English books, magazines and guides. It offers a good variety, plus an eclectic selection of used paperbacks to buy or swap.

Orientation: Athens in a Nutshell

Constitution Square, or **Plateía Sýntagma** (Συνταγμα), is the centre of the the city and the site of the Parliament Building, which backs onto the **National Gardens** and the **Záppeion Park**. These cool havens of shade allow an escape from the summer heat, with ducks to feed and a hundred benches useful for grabbing forty winks. Traffic is dense and noisy in Sýntagma, where you have trouble hearing yourself think at the outdoor tables, including those belonging to a great big McDonald's, predictably packed (mostly with Greeks). During the construction of the metro, a 3rd-century AD Roman bath and villa with lovely murals, an 11th-century BC grave and the tomb of a little dog were found under all the traffic jams; the archaeological finds are displayed in a smart underground concourse.

From Sýntagma Square it's a short walk up Filellínon St to Kidathinéon St, the main artery into the **Pláka** (Πλακα), Athens' old town below the Acropolis, where many houses have been converted into intimate tavernas or bars. This is a good place to look for mid-priced accommodation, especially now that cars have been banished from many streets. At the top of Pláka, tucked under the Acropolis rock, **Anafiótika** is a charming, uncommercialized enclave left by the builders of Otto's palaces, who came from the island of Anáfi and, homesick, re-created their island village here. Anafiótika is best reached from Tripódon and Epichármou Streets.

During the day, meander through Athens' flea-market district, west of **Monastiráki** metro station, where bulging shops sell everything from quality woollen goods and fake Caterpillar boots to furniture and second-hand fridges. Many streets hereabouts claim to be the 'genuine' flea-market, but most are tourist-trap alleys. They can be fun, though, and are certainly lively.

North of the Monastiráki metro station, Miaoúli St leads in two blocks to **Iróon Square**, the centre of **Psirrí**, a neighbourhood of winding little streets dating from Byron's time. He rented a room here. Recently, it has become one of the trendiest spots to eat and play in Athens.

A 10-minute walk east from Sýntagma, up Vas. Sophias St to the Benáki Museum and then left, will take you to **Kolonáki**, Athens' Knightsbridge in miniature, complete with fancypants shops, upmarket restaurants and plenty of well-heeled 'Kolonáki Greeks'—Athenian Sloane Rangers—to patronize them. Above the square rises **Lykavitós Hill**, illuminated like a fairytale tower at night (a long haul on foot, but there's a funicular every 10 minutes from the corner of Aristippoú and Ploutarchoúis). The summit offers the best panoramic views of Athens and Piraeus (*néfos* permitting), the chapel of St George, a restaurant/bar, a lovely outdoor theatre and a cannon fired on national holidays.

For something different, a 15-minute walk north of Sýntagma on Panepistimíou St/El. Venezélou will take you past the modern **University of Athens**, all dressed up in classical garb, and on to funky but soon-to-be-gentrified **Omónia Square**, the Athenian Times Square, open 24 hours a day and embracing a useful metro stop, as well as fast food, huge newsstands, pornmongers and screwballs. The **National Archaeology Museum** is further north, about a 10-minute walk along Patissíon St (at 28 Octovríou St), and behind it lies **Exárchia**, Athens' Latin Quarter, home of trendies, students and literati. *Terra incognita* for tourists, Plateía Exárchia comes alive after dark with traditional ouzeries and *boîtes*. For establishment Athens, Exárchia is synonymous with Anarchia, and home to druggies, disaffected youths and graffiti-sprayers. But it's tame by London or New York standards.

The area around the **Thissío**, at the base of the Acropolis, is giving Exárchia a run for its money for the young crowd, and may actually be surpassing it. The Thissío area, especially around Iraklídon Street, is packed with those who want to see and be seen, and do not mind spending a hefty amount of money for coffee or beer to be in the 'right' place.

The residential **Koukáki/Makrigiánni** area just south of the Acropolis is central and yet slightly off the tourist trail; the heart of this area is along Veíkou and Drákou Streets, where all the locals gather to gossip at the cafés and small eateries. This is the everyday Athens of the average citizen and can be reached on foot along Makrigiánni St. The nos.1, 5 and 9 trolley-bus routes pass through as well.

Across Vas. Konstantínos Avenue and the Záppeion Park, the landmark is the big white horseshoe of the **Olympic Stadium**, site of the 3rd-century BC original used during the Panathenaic festival, and rebuilt for the first modern Olympics in 1896. Behind this you'll find **Metz**, an old-fashioned neighbourhood popular with artists and media folk, with some fine old houses and authentic tavernas and *kafeneíons*. Bars are an old tradition here. Mr Metz was an enterprising German who ran a beer garden on the hill to cater to King Otto's Bavarian troops.

From Vas. Ólgas St, in front of the Záppeion Park, buses run frequently down to the coast and suburbs of **Glyfáda**, **Voúla** and **Vouliagménis**. Glyfáda, close to the airport, is a green and pleasant suburb that has grown into a busy resort and rival of fashionable Kolonáki. Smart city-dwellers shop at ritzy boutiques and haunt the marina. At the other end of the scale it's the hub of British package holidays, the so-called Apollo Coast. Here, and further down the coast at Voúla, are pay beaches run by EOT, usually jammed with Athenians. There are all kinds of facilities and the sea is cleaner at some than others—watch out for that sewage outfall. There's also good swimming beyond Voúla in the rocky coves at Vouliagménis, a smart place for a fish lunch and a haven for Greek yachties. It is possible (for a fee) to swim in the warm spa waters of Vouliagménis lake. En route, **Kavoúri** has excellent fish restaurants, ideal for a romantic dinner overlooking the sea. Beyond Vouliagménis, the road continues along the coast to **Várkiza**, another beach playground, and winds to stunning **Cape Soúnion** and its Temple of Poseidon (440 BC), famous for its magnificent position and sunsets, where there's always at least one tourist searching for the column where Byron carved his name.

Major Museums and Sites

The Acropolis

In summer, the museum and site are open 8am–7pm; in winter, the site is open Mon–Fri 8am–4.30pm, Sat and Sun 8.30–2.30, while the museum closes at 2.30pm every day ; adm exp.

Acropolis in Greek means 'top of the town'. Many Greek cities have similar naturally fortified citadels crowned with temples, but Athens has *the* Acropolis, the ultimate, standing proud above the city from a hundred different view points. First inhabited at the end of the Neolithic Age, it had a Cyclopean wall and was the site of the palace of Athens' Mycenaean king. It was later replaced by a temple of Poseidon and Athena, after those two divinities took part in a contest to decide who would be the patron of the city. Poseidon struck the spring of Klepsydra out of the rock of the Acropolis with his trident, while Athena invented the olive tree, which was judged the better trick. In later years the tyrant Pisístratos ordered a great gate to be constructed in the Mycenaean wall, but Delphi cursed it and the Athenians dismantled it. In 480 BC the temple's cult statue of Athena was hurriedly bundled off to Salamis, just before the Persians burnt and smashed the Acropolis. This allowed for renovations and the Acropolis as we see it today took shape.

The path to the Acropolis from the Agora follows the Panathenaic Way, laid out at the conse-cration of the Panathenaic Festival in 566 BC. The lower Acropolis entrance is the **Roman Beulé Gate**, named after the archaeologist who excavated it. The monumental stairways beyond are Roman too, and the two lions are Venetian. Themistocles reconstructed the Panathenaic ramp that leads to the **Propylaia**, the massive gateway built in Pentelic marble by Pericles' architect Mnesikles to compliment the Parthenon. Like the Parthenon, its ceiling was painted blue and accented with gilded stars. The ancient Greeks considered the Propylaia the architectural equal of the Parthenon itself, although it was never actually completed. On either side of the Propylaia's entrance are wings; the one to the north held a picture gallery (*pinakothéke*), while the smaller one to the south used a *trompe l'œil* technique to appear to have the same dimensions as the *pinakothéke*, although it was in fact truncated because the priests of the neighbouring Nike temple simply refused to have the wing in their precinct. The Propylaia had five doors, with massive wooden gates.

The Temple of Athena Nike

The Ionic Temple of Athena Nike was built in 478 BC of Pentelic marble on a stone-filled bastion of the Mycenaean wall by the architect Kallikrates. In 1687 the Turks destroyed the temple to build a tower, but it was rebuilt in 1835 and again in 1936, when the bastion beneath it threatened to crumble away. Cement copies replace the northern and western friezes taken to England by Lord Elgin.

From the temple of Athena Nike the whole of the Saronic Gulf could be seen in pre-*néfos* days, and it was here that King Aegeus watched for the return of his son Theseus from his Cretan adventure with the Minotaur. Theseus was to have signalled his victory with a white sail but forgot; at the sight of the black sail of death, Aegeus threw himself off the precipice in despair and, although he was miles from the water at the time, gave his name to the Aegean Sea.

The Parthenon

The Parthenon, the glory of the Acropolis and one of the most famous buildings in the world, is a Doric temple constructed between 447 and 432 BC by Iktinos and Kallikrates under the direction of Phidias, the greatest artist and sculptor of the Periclean age. Originally called the Great Temple, brightly painted and shimmering with gold, it took the name Parthenon (Chamber of the Virgins) a hundred years after its completion.

Constructed entirely of Pentelic marble, the Parthenon held Phidias' famous chryselephantine (ivory and gold) statue of Athena, which stood over 36ft high. The architects of the Parthenon wrote the book on mathematical perfection, subtlety, grace and *entasis*, the art of curving a form to create the visual illusion of perfection. Look closely and you'll see that there's not a straight line to be seen: the foundation is curved slightly to prevent an illusion of drooping caused by straight horizontals. The columns bend a few centimetres inward, and those on the corners are wider to complete the illusion of perfect form.

The outer colonnade consists of 46 columns, above them the remnants of the Doric frieze left behind by Lord Elgin: the east side portrayed the Battle of Giants and Gods, the south the Lapiths and Centaurs, on the west are the Greeks and the Amazons, and on the north the Battle of Troy. Little remains of the pediment sculptures of the gods. Above the interior colonnade, the masterful Ionic frieze designed by Phidias himself showed the quadrennial Panathenaic Procession, in which the cult statue of Athena in the Erechtheion was brought a golden crown and a new sacred garment, or *peplos*.

The Parthenon, used as a church and then a mosque, remained intact until 1687, when a Venetian bomb hit the Turks' powder stores and blew the roof off; an earthquake in 1894 was another serious blow.

Entrance to the interior has been forbidden to cut down on wear and tear. Preserving the building, as well as undoing the damage of previous restorations, has been the subject of intense study over the past two decades, when the alarming effects of the *néfos* on the marble could no longer be ignored. While discovering how to use hot, pressurized carbon dioxide to re-harden stone surfaces, Greek scientists have learned about ancient building techniques and, after all these years, are picking up the pieces to reconstruct as much of the temple as possible, stringing column drums on new non-rusting titanium rods.

The Erechtheion

The other great monument on the Acropolis is the Erechtheion, completed late, in 395 BC, a peculiar Ionic temple that owes its idiosyncrasies to the much older sanctuaries and sanctities it was built to encompass. The genius of its structure is that it appears harmonious and regular, although it is built on different levels and faces different directions.

Beneath the temple stood the Mycenaean House of Erechtheos, mentioned by Homer. The eastern *cella* was somehow divided up to serve Athena Polias and Poseidon Erechtheos. Within its confines stood the ancient primitive cult statue of Athena Polias, the biggest juju of them all, solemnly dressed in the sacred *peplos* and crown. Six tall Ionic columns define the north porch, where part of the floor and roof were cut away to reveal Poseidon's trident marks; it would have been sacrilegious to hide such divine work from the view of the gods. This porch was the tomb of Erechtheos, some say Kekrops, and the traditional home of the Acropolis guardian snake. The western court of the temple housed the sacred olive tree, and the southern porch is held up by the famous maidens, or caryatids, gracefully supporting the roof on their heads. Converted into a church in the 7th century, the Turks made it a harem and used the sacred place of the trident marks as a toilet. Lord Elgin nicked parts of this temple as well, including one of the six caryatids; the other girls, said to weep every night for their missing sister, have also come in from the *néfos*, this time to the Acropolis museum. The ones in place on the Erechtheion are casts.

The Acropolis Museum

The museum houses sculptures and reliefs from the Acropolis, arranged chronologically. There are lovely 6th-century BC statues of Kores (Maidens), offered as votives to Athena, still exhibiting traces of their original colour.

The Moschoforos (Calf-Bearer) of the same era is another gem. Bits and pieces of the Parthenon and statuary abound; note Athena's shield with the snakes. Anti-pollution filters have been installed to show the British parliament that Greece is ready to care for the Elgin marbles properly, if it should ever vote to give them back.

The Area around the Acropolis

Below the Acropolis entrance and slightly to the north towards the Agora, is the bald **Areópagos**, or hill of the war god Ares, once the seat of the High Council. It figured prominently in Aeschylus' play *The Eumenides*, where mercy defeated vengeance for the first time in history during the trial of the matricide Orestes. Although Pericles removed much of the original power of the High Council, under the control of the ex-*archons* it continued to advise on the Athenian constitution for hundreds of years. Beyond it, across Apostolou Pávlou St (now being pedestrianized), tucked in the side of Philopáppos hill, is the **Pnyx**, where the General Assembly of Athens met and heard the speeches of Pericles and Demosthenes. On Assembly days it was sometimes necessary to round up citizens in order to fill the minimum attendance quota of 5,000. For important debates, 18,000 could squeeze in here. Later the Assembly was transferred to the Theatre of Diónysos.

An attractive stone and marble lane leads by way of the lovely Byzantine church of **Ag. Dimítrios** up to the **Philopáppos Monument** (AD 114), built in honour of Caius Julius

Antiochos Philopáppos, a Syrian Prince and friend of Athens. The surrounding park is a good spot for a stroll, especially for romantic sunset views of the Acropolis and Piraeus (although avoid it at night, because it's very isolated). Nearby is the **Dora Stratou Theatre**, where Athens' folk dance troupe performs nightly.

The Theatre of Diónysos

Open 8.30–2.30 except Mon; adm; © 322 4625.

This theatre is probably the oldest playhouse in the world. However, the stone seats you see today never saw a first-night performance of any of the great plays they are constantly associated with. In fact, no stone theatre in Greece existed in the heyday of the great playwrights; they were all built in the 4th century BC or later. The likes of Aeschylus, Sophocles and Euripides had to make do with seats dug into the hillside or wooden bleachers, and wooden stages with canvas backdrops. The existing and much modified theatre was begun from 342 to 326 BC and reached its present form by the time of Nero (AD 54–68), when it seated 17,000. In this precinct, the Great Diónysia was held each year in the spring. This was a five-day *agon* (contest) held in honour of Diónysos, the god of wine and patron divinity of the theatre, in which playwrights presented plays to honour the god and to be judged by their peers.

A couple of streets over in Pláka is the **Monument of Lysikrátes**, a *choregos* (as the producers plays were known) in 334 BC. Every winner was allowed to put up a monument to his victory and, being typical Greeks, they all did. Lysikrátes' is one of the more elaborate. The Lysikrátes monument was later built into the wall of a Capuchin friary, which once hosted Lord Byron.

The Odeon of Herodes Atticus

Next to the Theatre of Diónysos, the Odeon was built in AD 161 by the Rockefeller of his day, Herodes Atticus (whose life reads like something out of the Arabian Nights—he inherited his extraordinary wealth from his father, who discovered treasure outside Rome). Now missing its original cedar-wood roof, the 6,000-seat Odeon hosts the annual mid-May and September Festival of Athens, where modern European and ancient Greek cultures meet in theatre, ballet and classical concerts performed by companies from all over the world.

The Heart of Ancient Athens: The Agora, Thissío and Stoa of Attalus

Open 8.30–3, closed Mon; adm; © 321 0815.

The Agora was, quite simply, the heart and heartbeat of Athens. It was not just a market, but a stage for public life, where elections, meetings, festivals and court proceedings took place. Athenian citizens spent as much time as possible there, and the conversations honed and polished in the atmosphere of the Agora changed the course of Western civilization.

The Agora started out as a large open space with stoas and buildings around its perimeter. After the Persians trashed it in 480 BC, it was rebuilt on a much grander scale. As time passed, it became more built up, but its classical buildings suffered desecration by angry Romans and firebug barbarians, and by Athenians in need of building stone.

The ruins you see today are a conglomeration of constructions from every era of ancient history. Only the foundations remain of the council house, or **Bouleuterion**, and the neighbouring Temple of the Mother of the Gods, the **Metroön**, built by the Athenians as reparation for the slaying of a priest from her cult. The annually elected *Prytanes* governed from the round **Tholos**, or Prytanéon. Since some had to be on call day and night, kitchens and sleeping quarters were included.

Near the Tholos is a **Horos**, one of the Agora's boundary stones. A path from here leads to the foundations of the prison where Socrates spent his last days and drank the fatal hemlock. Opposite the Metroön, only a wall remains of the **Sanctuary of the Eponymous Heroes of Athens**, which once housed the statues of the 10 heroes instituted by Kleisthenes to give their names to the 10 tribes of Athens (*see* p.49). The altar of Zeus Agoraios received the oaths of the new *archons*, a practice initiated by Solon.

The small 4th-century BC **Temple of Apollo** by the Metroön was dedicated to the grandfather of the Ionians, who believed themselves descended from Apollo's son Ion. Almost nothing remains of the **Stoa of Zeus Eleutherios**, one of the recorded haunts of Socrates. Some of it disappears into the railway tracks of the 'electrico', Athens' sometime subway, which is on the surface at this point.

Beyond the Stoa of Zeus, stands the **Altar of the Twelve Gods**, from which all distances in Attica were measured. This milestone of civic planning is partially destroyed by the *electrico*. A desecration, but when the tracks were laid, no-one knew where the Agora was; ruins lay everywhere. Beside the Altar of the Twelve Gods, right at the main entrance, is part of the sacred Panathenaic Way, the ceremonial path from the Kerameikós gate to the Acropolis to honour Athena Polias, the guardian of the city. The present path cuts past the Stoa of Attalos and continues up the hill along the original route. In Athens' heyday, it was a modest gravel path; the fancy stonework that appears further up is 2nd century AD Roman.

South of the Altar of the Twelve Gods stood a 5th-century BC Doric **Temple to Ares**. The **Three Giants** standing sentinel nearby were originally part of the **Odeon of Agrippa**, built in 15 BC; parts of the orchestra remain intact, but the massive roof collapsed in AD 190. Both the site and giants were reused in the façade of a 5th-century gymnasium.

Near the 2nd-century BC **Middle Stoa** are ruins of a Roman temple and the ancient shops and booths. On the other side of the Middle Stoa was the **South Stoa**, where the rooms used for symposia can still be made out. The doors of each room are slightly off-centre, so that a long couch could fit on one side of the inside wall. Small and intimate, these were the spots for a bachelor's bash, complete with wine, women and song. Beside the South Stoa, to the west, is the large, square, people's court, or **Heliaia**, established by Solon in the 6th century BC to hear political questions. It has been identified as one of the possible sites of the jury trials held by Athens. Since the jurors could number in the hundreds in the radical democracy, a big space was required for trials. It was used well into Roman times.

Between the South Stoa and **East Stoa**, (2nd-century BC) is the 11th-century **Church of the Holy Apostles** (Ag. Apóstoli), built on the site where St Paul addressed the Athenians; it was restored, along with its fine paintings, in 1952. Across the Panathenaic Way run the remains of **Valerian's Wall**, thrown up in 257 against the barbarians, its stone cannibalized from Agora buildings wrecked by the Romans. Between Valerian's Wall and the Stoa of Attalos are the higgledy-piggledy ruins of the **Library of Pantainos**, built by Flavius Pantainos in AD 100 and destroyed 167 years later. Beside it is the wonderfully renovated **Stoa of Attalos**, built in the 2nd century BC by one of Athens' benefactors, King Attalos II of

Pergamon, and reconstructed by another benefactor, John D. Rockefeller of Cleveland, Ohio. It houses the Agora Museum, containing artefacts found in the Agora in one large room (in the original building this would have been divided into many small rooms).

On the eastern edge of the Agora, the mid 5th-century BC **Theseum** is nothing less than the best-preserved Greek temple in existence. It was given this name by archaeologists who thought it was Theseus' grave. They were wrong. This Doric temple was, in fact, dedicated to Hephaistos, the god of metals and smiths. It may well have been designed by the architect of the temple at Sounion. It is constructed almost entirely of Pentelic marble and decorated with metopes depicting the lives of Heracles and Theseus. Converted into a church in the 5th century, it was the burial place for English Protestants until 1834, when the government declared it a national monument.

National Archaeology Museum

Patission and Tossítsa Sts. Open Mon 12.30–6.45, Tues–Fri 8–6.45, Sat and Sun 8.30–2.45; adm exp; © 821 7717.

This is the big one, and deserves much more space than permitted here. It contains some of the most spectacular and beautiful works of the ancient Greek world—the Minoan frescoes from Santoríni, gold from Mycenae (including the famous 'mask of Agamemnon'), statues, reliefs, tomb stelae, and ceramics and vases from every period. The Cycladic collection includes one of the first known musicians, the 4,000-year-old sculpture of the little harpist that has become the virtual symbol of the Cyclades. The star of the sculpture rooms is a virile bronze of Poseidon or Zeus (5th century BC) about to launch his trident or thunderbolt, found off Cape Artemission in 1928; around him are some outstanding archaic Kouros statues and the Stele of Hegeso, an Athenian beauty enveloped by the delicate folds of her robe, seated on a throne. Don't miss the Antikthera Mechanism, the world's first computer, made on Rhodes around 70 BC.

The museum has a shop on the lower level, with reproductions of exhibits by expert craftsmen, so accurate that each piece is issued with a certificate declaring it an authentic fake so you can take it out of the country.

Other Museums and Sites

Athens City Museum: 7 Paparigópoulou St, © 324 6164. *Open Mon, Wed, Fri and Sat 9–1.30; adm.* Located in a former residence of King Otto, this museum contains photos, memorabilia and excellent watercolours of Athens as it was soon after it became the capital of modern Greece.

Benáki Museum: Corner of Vas. Soffas and Koumbári Streets, © 361 1617. *Closed for renovations for several years now, and still counting, but the shop is open. Ring ahead.* Antónios Benáki spent 35 years amassing Byzantine and Islamic treasures in Europe and Asia, dating from the 6th to the 17th centuries. There are two icons painted by El Greco before he left his native Crete for Venice and Spain, and the section on folk art, dating from the Ottoman occupation, contains a superb collection of costumes and artefacts from the Ionian islands to Cyprus.

Byzantine Museum: 22 Vas. Soffas St, © 721 1027. *Open 8.30–3, closed Mon; adm.* A monumental collection of religious treasures ranging from the Early Byzantine period to the

19th century—not only icons but marble sculptures, mosaics, wood carvings, frescoes, manuscripts and ecclesiastical robes. There are three rooms on the ground floor arranged as chapels: one Early Christian, another Middle Byzantine and the third post-Byzantine.

Epigraphic Museum: 1 Tsoussítsa St (right by the Archaeological Museum). *Open Tues–Sat 8.30–2.45; Sun 8–2; Mon closed; free.* This one is for fanatics, a fascinating collection of inscriptions carved on stone and marble dating from the 6th century BC to 300 AD. At least you get an idea of how print-oriented the ancients were, something you don't see in the scoured, bare bones of the archaeological sites.

Goulandris Museum of Cycladic and Ancient Greek Art: 4 Neofýtou Doúka St (just off Vas. Sofías St), ✆ 722 8321. *Open Mon and Wed–Fri 10–4, Sat 10–3, closed Sun and Tues; adm.* The Goulandris collection of Cycladic figurines going back to 3000 BC, as well as ancient art from other parts of Greece, is second only to the National Museum, but it's better documented and intelligently displayed. Don't miss the Cycladic toastmaster, or the 5th-century BC cat carrying a kitten in her mouth.

Ilías Lalaonis Jewellery Museum: 4a Karyátidon St, Acropolis, ✆ 922 1044. *Open Mon 10.30–4.45, Tues–Sun 8.30–2.45; adm.* This showroom and workshop show the history of jewellery-making through the designs of the master jeweller.

Jewish Museum: 29 Níkis St, ✆ 322 5582. *Open Mon–Fri 9–2.30, Sun 10–2, closed Sat.* Most of Greece's Jewish population arrived in the 16th century, escaping from the Spanish Inquisition, and the majority was killed in the Second World War; documents and artefacts chronicle that period and back as early as the 3rd century BC.

Kanellópoulos Museum: Corner of Theorías and Panós Streets, in the upper Pláka, near the Agora, ✆ 321 2313. *Open 8:30–3, closed Mon; adm.* A highly eclectic private collection, in a neoclassical mansion, with lots of funeral vases, and Tanagra figurines from nearby Thebes.

Kerameikós and Museum: 148 Ermoú St, ✆ 346 3552. *Open 8.30–3, closed Mon; adm.* The ancient cemetery in the Kerameikós district was used for burials from the 12th century BC into Roman times, and is one of the most complex and fascinating (and quiet) sites in Athens. The most beautiful finds are from the rich private tombs built in the 4th century BC. Large stone vases mark the graves of the unmarried dead, while others are in the form of miniature temples and stelae; the best are in the National Museum. Excavations for the metro have revealed over a thousand more graves.

Museum of Popular Art: 17 Kyndathaíon St, Pláka, ✆ 322 9031. *Open 10–2, closed Mon; adm.* Exquisite Greek folk art, embroideries, wood-carvings, jewellery, paintings by naïve artists, and nearby, in a renovated mosque, a superb collection of ceramics.

National Gallery: 50 Vas. Konstantínou St, across from the Athens Hilton, ✆ 721 6560/723 5937. *Open 9–3, Sun and hols 10–2, closed Tues; adm.* The National Gallery concentrates on painting and sculpture by modern Greek artists. Works by the leading contemporary painter, Níkos Hadzikyriákos-Ghíkas, are permanently displayed on the ground floor, while the lower level is used for rotating exhibitions.

National Historical Museum: 13 Stadíou St, ✆ 323 7617. *Open 9–1.30, closed Mon; adm, free on Sun.* In the imposing neoclassical Old Parliament of Greece, guarded by a bronze equestrian Théodoros Kolokotrónis, are exhibits on Greek history, concentrating on the War of Independence. The highlight is the set of 25 small naïve paintings narrating Greek history from the fall of Constantinople to the War of Independence, commissioned by General Makrigiánnis, who described the events to the painter Zographos (another set of the paintings is in Windsor Castle library). Also see Byron's sword and helmet and his famous portrait dressed as a klepht, along with a sumptuous collection of folk costumes from every corner of Greece.

Numismatic Museum: 12 Panepistimíou St, ✆ 364 3774. *Open daily 8–2:30, closed Mon; adm, Sun free*. This terrific new museum is housed in Heinrich Schliemann's house, a neo-classical pile designed by Ernst Ziller that is worth a visit in itself. It houses 600,000 coins.

Popular Musical Instruments Museum: 1–3 Diogénous St, Pláka (near the Tower of the Winds), ✆ 325 0198. *Open Tues and Thurs–Sun 10–2, Wed 12–7, closed Mon; free*. A fascinating collection of old and new Greek instruments and interactive displays.

Roman Forum: Between the Agora and the Acropolis, at Pelopia and Eólou Streets, ✆ 324 5220. *Open 8.30–3, closed Mon; adm*. At the end of the Hellenistic age, the Romans built their own marketplace, or forum, feeling uncomfortable in the Greek Agora, especially after they had wasted it. The forum contains the celebrated 1st-century BC **Tower of the Winds**, or Clock of Andronikos Kyrrhestes, an all-marble tower, with a clock which was operated by an hydraulic mechanism, so the Athenians could know the time, day or night. Note the frieze of the eight winds that decorate its eight sides, although it has lost its ancient bronze Triton weathervane. The Turks made it into a mosque, hence the niche indicating the direction of Mecca. At its west end, the forum contains the **Gate of Athena Archegetis**, built with money sent over by Julius and Augustus Caesar. On one of its posts, still in place, are the market-pricing rules imposed by Hadrian. There is also a court and ruined stoa, and the Fethiye Camii, the Victory or **Corn Market Mosque**.

Temple of Olympian Zeus: Vas. Ólgas and Amalías Streets, ✆ 922 6330. *Open 8.30–3, closed Mon; adm*. Fifteen columns recall what Livy called 'the only temple on earth of a size adequate to the greatness of the god'. The foundations were laid by the tyrant Pisístratos, but work ground to a halt with the fall of his dynasty, only to be continued in 175 BC by a Roman architect, Cossutius. It was half-finished when Cossutius' patron, Antiochos IV of Syria, died, leaving Emperor Hadrian to complete it in AD 131. Nearby are the ruins of ancient houses and a bath and at the far end stands **Hadrian's Arch**, in Pentelic marble, erected by the Athenians to thank the emperor for his help. The complimentary inscription reads on the Acropolis side: 'This is Athens, the ancient city of Theseus', while the other side reads: 'This is the city of Hadrian, not of Theseus'. The Athenians come here to celebrate the Easter Resurrection.

War Museum of Greece: Vas. Soffas and Rizári Streets, ✆ 724 4464. *Open Tues–Fri 9–2, Sat and Sun 9.30–2, closed Mon; free on Sun*. Weapons and battle relics past and present.

Byzantine Churches and Monasteries

Ag. Theódori: An 11th-century church in Klafthmónos Square at the end of Dragatsaníou St, notable for its beautiful door; the bell tower and some decorations inside are more recent.

Kapnikaréa: A few blocks from Ag. Theódori, on Ermoú St, tiny Kapnikaréa (the chapel of the University of Athens) was built in the late 11th century in the shape of a Greek cross. Its central cupola is supported by four columns with Roman capitals.

Panagía Gorgoepíkoos (also called Ag. Elefthérios): 'Our Lady who Grants Requests Quickly' is in Mitropóleos Square. The loveliest church in Athens and known as the 'little cathedral', it was built in the 12th century almost entirely of ancient marbles: note the ancient calendar of state festivals and the signs of the zodiac. The adjacent 'big' **Cathedral**, or Metropolitan, was built in 1840–55 with the same collage technique, using bits and pieces from 72 destroyed churches. The Glucksberg kings of Greece were crowned here between 1863 and 1964, and it contains the tomb of the unofficial saint of the Greek revolution, the Patriarch of Constantinople Gregory V, hanged in 1821.

Ag. Ioánnis: A tiny church on Evripídou St and Diplári St, off Athenás St in Psirrí, with a Corinthian column sticking out of its roof which probably came from a temple to Asclepeius. People visited it to cure their fevers; the idea was to tie the fevers to the column with string or bits of wool. If you are lucky enough to find a custodian there, you can still see several dangling from the column behind the iconostasis.

Moní Pendéli (*bus from Mouseío to Paliá Pendéli*): Founded in 1578, in a lovely wooded setting on the mountain of Pentelic marble, this is one of the biggest monasteries in Greece, a popular weekend refuge from the *néfos*. Greek families come out for lunch under the gargantuan plane tree at the excellent **O Télis**, © 804 0484.

Dafní Monastery (*A16 bus from Plateía Koumandoúrou*): *Open 8:30–3pm, closed Mon; adm 500dr;* © 581 1558. The name Dafní derives from the Temple of Apollo Dafneíos (of the laurel), built on the Sacred Way from Athens to Eleusis to mark the spot where the nymph Daphni was spared the unwanted attentions of Apollo by being turned into a laurel tree. Dafní existed as a walled monastery by the 6th century and, when a new church was built in 1080, it was decorated with some of the best Byzantine mosaics in southern Greece. These mosaics are dominated by the figure of Christ Pantokrátor in the dome, his eyes spellbinding and tragic, 'as though He were in flight from an appaling doom' according to Patrick Leigh Fermor.

Athens (© 01–)   **Where to Stay**

Athens offers every imaginable hotel experience, with the possible exception of a dead quiet one. Naturally the expensive hotels have double glazing and heavy curtains, but if the more budget-minded choose carefully, relative quiet is possible. Hotels, especially those in the moderate to inexpensive range, are likely to drop their prices dramatically when the short summer high season is over. In July and August, booking is a good idea. If you can't find a room, try the Hotel Association's booking desk in Sýntagma Square, in the National Bank (during banking hours).

luxury

The beautiful **Grande Bretagne**, on Sýntagma Square, © 333 0000, @ 322 8034 (*lux*), was built in 1862 to house members of the Greek royal family who couldn't squeeze into the palace (the current Parliament building) up the square. It was used as a Nazi headquarters for a time, and by Winston Churchill, who had a lucky escape from a bomb planted in the hotel's sewer system while spending Christmas here in 1944. Totally modernized, with its vast marble lobby, elegant rooms and dining room, it offers grand style and service that the newer hotels may never achieve.

In the Pláka, three short blocks south of Filellínon St, the **Electra Palace**, at 18 Nikodímou, ✆ 377 0000, ✉ 324 1875 (*A*), has views of the Acropolis and a rooftop swimming pool in a garden setting. It even has a rare garage adjacent to the hotel. Facing the Temple of Olympian Zeus, the **Royal Olympic Hotel**, 28 Diákou St, ✆ 922 6411, ✉ 923 3317 (*lux*), has American-style rooms, with a number of family-sized suites, and a wonderful panorama from the rooftop bar or from the front-facing rooms. In Kolonáki, the **St George Lycabettus**, 2 Kleoménous (Plateía Dexamenis), ✆ 729 0711, ✉ 724 7610 (*lux*), has an intimate atmosphere and a pool, too. Its Grand Balcon dining room looks across to the Parthenon.

Just outside the centre towards the sea, the **Ledra Marriott**, at 113 Syngroú, ✆ 934 7711, ✉ 935 8603 (*lux*), features a Chinese-Japanese restaurant, and a hydrotherapy pool you can soak in with a view of the Acropolis. In the ritzy northern suburbs, you can't beat the gorgeous old **Pentelikon**, 66 Diligiánni St, in Kefalári-Kifissia, ✆ 808 0311, ✉ 801 0314 (*lux*), with a lovely garden and pool.

expensive

Right by Sýntagma Square, the **Astor**, 16 Karagiórgi Servías, ✆ 335 1000, ✉ 325 5115 (*A*), offers the usual amenities for its class and a rooftop garden restaurant. Close to Sýntagma near the Pláka, **Hermes**, 19 Apóllonos, ✆ 323 5514, ✉ 323 2073 (*C; exp in high season, mod in winter*), is comfortable, friendly and air-conditioned, with a small bar and roof garden with Acropolis views. Practically on top of lively, traffic-clogged Plateía Omónia, the large **Titania Hotel**, 52 Panepistimíou St, ✆ 330 0111, ✉ 330 0700 (*B*), has pleasant rooms and a very fashionable rooftop terrace, which is not only planted with old olive trees, but also affords gorgeous views over the Acropolis and Lykavittós. It has parking. In Koukáki/Makrigiánni, immediately south of the Acropolis, the **Parthenon**, 6 Makrí St, ✆ 923 4594, ✉ 923 5797 (*A*), has a great location and a pretty outdoor breakfast area. In the same neighbourhood is the quiet, well run and newly renovated **Hotel Philippos**, 3 Mitséon, ✆ 922 3611, ✉ 922 3615 (*B*). In swanky Kolonáki, the **Athenian Inn**, 22 Cháritos St, ✆ 723 8097, ✉ 724 2268 (*C*), was the favourite of Lawrence Durrell.

moderate

In the Pláka, **Adam's**, 6 Cherefóntos, ✆ 322 5381, ✉ 323 8553 (*C*), is low key, in a quiet central location off Kidathinéon St, with large rooms; the rooms without baths are good value. Nearby, also off Kidathinéon St, the quiet **Acropolis House**, 6–8 Kodrou St, ✆ 322 3244, ✉ 324 4143 (*C*), has modernized rooms in a traditional style, with antique furnishings, frescoes and a family welcome. It offers a few rooms in the moderate range. **Pension Adonis**, 3 Kódrou St (just off Kidathinéon St), ✆ 324 9737, ✉ 323 1602 (*C*), is a gem, clean and well run by the former manager of the Annapolis Hilton. All rooms have balconies, and there's a lovely breakfast roof garden and bar with views. Right at the back of the National Archaeological Museum, the **Museum Hotel**, 16 Bouboulínas St, ✆ 360 5611, ✉ 380 0507 (*C*), offers 58 rooms.

In the Sýntagma-Pláka area, the plain-Jane **Aphrodite**, 21 Apóllonos, ✆ 323 4357, ✉ 322 5244 (*C*), has basic rooms, air-conditioning and free parking in the garage. In Makrigiánni, just south of the Acropolis, the modern **Hera**, 9 Falírou at Veíkou,

© 923 6682/924 0672, © 924 7334 (*C*), has small gardens on the ground floor and the roof. Also in Makrigiánni, the **Art Gallery**, at 5 Erechthiou St and Veíkou St, © 923 8376, © 923 3025 (*E*), is a pleasant, quiet, well run old-style hotel. It's at the lower end of this category, but each room has its own bathroom, and the Pláka is a 15-minute walk away.

inexpensive

In the Pláka, near Hadrian's arch, **Dióskouros House**, 6 Pitakou St, © 324 8165, © 321 0907 (*D*), is a delightful, clean hostelry with high-ceilinged rooms in an old neoclassical building in quite a quiet spot. Old-fashioned, yes, and the kind you are terrified will be replaced by an office building before you return. **Kouros**, 11 Kódrou St, © 322 7431 (*E*), is quite an attractive old house just behind the small church on Kidathinéon. The owner's prices may be up for discussion if he's not full.

Near the Lysikrátes Monument, **Phaedra**, 16 Cherefóndos St and Adrianoú St, © 323 8461 (*D*), offers an unreconstructed pre-war interior, communal facilities and a great location. Free hot showers are promised. The **Student Inn**, 16 Kidathinéon St, © 324 4808, is organized along youth hostel lines (there is a 1.30am curfew).

Right behind the large Metrópolis church is the simple and cheap **John's Place**, 5 Patróou St, © 322 9719 (*E*), with bathrooms down the hall. Not far from the Monastiráki subway, **Tembi**, 29 Eólou St, © 321 3175, © 325 4179 (*D*), is nothing special, but it is cheap and has pleasant management, and a good central location. A stone's throw from the Monastiráki subway, the **Pella Inn**, 104 Ermoú St, © 321 2229, © 325 0598 (*D*), is simple but welcoming.

In Exárchia, at the Strefi Hill Park, book early for **Dryádes**, 105 Emm Benáki St and Anexartissías St, © 330 2388, © 380 5193 (*D*). All rooms have baths and the top three have lovely views. Next door is the **Orion**, run by the same manager, with common facilities and a roof garden with a great view.

In Koukáki, off Veikou St and Makrigiánni, a good 15-minute walk from the Pláka but on the trolley line, is **Marble House**, 35 A. Zínni, © 923 4058 (*E*), a comfortable Greek-French-run pension on a quiet street. Most rooms have baths. In Pangráti, the **Student's Hostel** at 75 Damaréos St and Frinis St, © 751 9530, © 751 0616, is far from the centre, but there is a nearby trolley-bus. This offers shared accommodation at about 2,000dr per head, with the possibility of a shared kitchen. Student cards are not required.

The nearest campsites to Athens are **Camping Athens**, 198 Athinon Ave, © 581 4114, © 582 0353, 7km out on the main road to Corinth, right as you are leaving the city, and **Camping N. Kifissia**, © 807 9579, © 807 5579, in the northern suburb of Kiffissiá.

hotels near the airport

If you have an early or delayed flight, or just one day to spend in Athens, there are quite a few hotels by the airport. Note that they tend to be desperately noisy—some are practically on the runway—and pricey for what they offer. **Emmantina**, 33 Vas. Georgíou, Glyfáda, © 898 0683, © 894 8110 (*A; lux*), is one of the better ones, and has a pool on the roof. **John's**, 3 Pandóras-Lazaráki, © 894 6837, © 898 0210

(*B; exp*), offers the same, at cheaper prices. The **Blue Sky**, 26 Eleftherías, ✆ 894 7722, @ 894 3445 (*C; mod–inexp*), is as good as it gets price-wise.

Eating Out

In Athens, prices are generally a bit higher than elsewhere in this book, and can even hit London levels. Menus are posted in the window or at the door, so you know what you're getting into. Know, too, that a late-night coffee, brandy or sweet in a café can cost as much as a whole meal. Note that prices below are per person.

Pláka

The Pláka, the traditional tourist ghetto, can still be the most fun, and it caters to the non-Greek urge to dine before 10pm. Inexpensive and moderate restaurants are clustered around Kidathinéon St and Adrianoú St, where tinkling glasses, music, chatter and laughter richochet through the narrow streets. Touts, however, can be real pests. A supercilious camel look or totally blank stare tends to discourage them.

You can still eat very well in a lovely setting at the **Byzántino**, 18 Kidathinéon St, ✆ 322 7368. Regulars still hate its tourist-baiting renovation, but come anyway because it serves big portions under the trees; the fish soup and lamb fricassée are excellent (*3,000–3,500dr*). The **Bacchus**, 10 Thrasýllou, ✆ 322 0385, is great for evenings. Up from the Lysikrátes Monument, right against the Acropolis, it has a lovely cloistered outdoor dining area under the Parthenon; try the savoury pies (*around 4,000dr*).

For a cut above taverna fare, book a table at **Daphne's**, 4 Lysikrátos St (by the monument), ✆ 322 7971. This was the 'typical Greek' taverna Hillary Clinton was taken to. Hardly. It's an elegant neoclassical mansion, where you can eat in a dining room decorated with Pompeiian frescoes and in a beautiful garden courtyard (heated in winter). It serves traditional Greek and international cuisine (*9,000–10,000dr*). **Eden**, Athens' oldest vegetarian restaurant,12 Lissíou St and Mnisikléous, ✆ 324 8858, offers vegetarian quiches and soya moussakas (*around 2,500dr*). *Closed Tues.*

Sýntagma

Sýntagma is fast-food heaven, with all the foreign and Greek chains represented. The best of the lot is **Loxandras**, 2 Ermoú St, ✆ 331 2211. The chicken is great, they even offer low-cal pittas and it is very inexpensive. You might even luck out and get a seat at one of its eight or so tables upstairs. For a real change of pace, try the **Furin Kazan**, 2 Apóllonos St, ✆ 322 9170. It offers delicious Japanese fast food at a reasonable price (*2,500–3,000dr*).

For an outdoor snack or lunch, head for **To Fagádiko**, ✆ 325 1350, in the large umbrella- and flag-studded open-air stoa that stretches from Boukourestíou St to Amerikís St, parallel to Stadíou St (right behind Wendy's). A surprising oasis of quiet in the middle of a civil service office complex, it serves inexpensive food from noon to 6pm Monday to Friday, and offers the government drones a discreet way to slip out of their offices, eat, grab a cigar, have a shave at the barbers, all without really leaving the premises. The Athens' Festival Box office is hidden away here, too.

Kolonáki and the Hilton Area

Close to Kolonáki Square, the legendary **Gerofinikas**, 10 Pindárou, ✆ 362 2719, still has the ancient palm tree that gave it its name, growing right out of the middle of the restaurant; the food is famous and the whole meal an experience (*7,000–8,000dr*). *Closed Sun.* **La Pasteria**, 17 Tsakálof St near Kolonáki Square, ✆ 363 2032, offers great pasta dishes (*5,000–6,000dr for the works*). In fact, Tsakálof St is lined with eateries catering to every pocket, most with outdoor tables. Two blocks above the US embassy, **Vlassis**, 8 Pasteúr St, ✆ 642 5337, is a superb family-run taverna serving true Greek cuisine, one of the rare breed with excellent wines and desserts (*around 5,000 dr*). *Closed Sun.* Behind the Hilton, **Othello's**, 45 Mikalakopoúlou St, ✆ 729 1481, serves authentic Cypriot cuisine, and has piano music (*around 4,000–5,000dr*).

Psirrí

Psirrí sprouts restaurants and *ouzeries* almost as fast as the city can do up the area, which so far attracts more Greeks than foreigners. Go after 9pm, or after 1pm on Sunday, when almost all the many restaurant-bars have some kind of live music. In terms of price, they vary a little, but not much: count on paying *4,000–6,000dr*. Right in Iróon Square, the epicentre of Psirrí, **To Rodakió**, ✆ 321 3922, offers bouzouki and guitar music. **Taki 13**, 13 Táki St, ✆ 325 4707, was the first, and still stands out as the most fun. It has a superb atmosphere, and although the food is simple, it's a great party bar, featuring live music (as we write, jazz/blues Tuesday and Wednesday, Greek at weekends) and sing-songs till 1.30am. On the outer edge of Psirrí, right behind the vegetable market, the **Klimatariá**, 2 Platei̱a Theátrou, ✆ 321 6629, is run-down and seedy, but has a loyal clientele for its guitar music and taverna fare.

There is one outstanding restaurant in Psirrí, **Frourarcheío** (The Guardhouse), 6 Platei̱a Psirrí, ✆ 321 5156. It is beautifully decorated with elegant restraint (*10,000–11,000dr*).

Monastiráki

Monastiráki is more famous for snacks than dining. If you have a hankering for an excellent and inexpensive *souvláki* and gyros, get yourself to **Thanássis**, 69 Mitropóleos St, ✆ 324 4705, or even better to **Sávas**, ✆ 324 5048, at No.86.

Hankering for the old Greece? **Peristéria**, off Mitropóleos St at 5 Patróou St behind the Metropolitan Church, ✆ 323 4535, is as plain as they come and still has the steam table of prepared dishes, at which you can point. *Open 9am–1am.*

Thissío and the Acropolis Area

Thissío's watering holes are up from the metro station, opposite the ancient Agora. Its main intersection is Irakleídon and Apostólou Pávlou St—the place for snacks and coffee with the trendies. The best and priciest joint is probably the **Stavlos**, 10 Irakleídon, ✆ 346 7206, housed in the old Royal Stables. It is an art gallery, bar and restaurant, with the old stable yard beautifully decorated to look like an old square in the Pláka (*5,000–6 000dr*). The blue-trimmed **Filístron**, two blocks up at 23 Apostólou Pávlou St, ☎ 346 7554, offers drinks, snacks and a wonderful terrace upstairs overlooking the Agora and the Stoa of Attalos.

Around Omónia Square

Omónia Square is a great place to try Greek street food. Just one block east of Omónia, in Themistokléous St, **Aráchova** (No.8), ☎ 384 1812, offers fast pittas and sandwiches, beer and so on, at cheap prices in an upmarket setting. They promise homemade bread too. The **Athinaikón**, 2 Themistokléous St, ☎ 363 8485, is a golden oldie and a great place to fill up on tasty *mezédes* (snacks) and swordfish or lamb kebabs while watching the passing crowds. *Closed Sun.* On the same street, at No.18, **Andréas and Sons**, ☎ 382 1522, offers tasty seafood at marble-topped tables in a cosy setting at reasonable prices. It is in a quiet, narrow street with some outside tables. *Open 11am–11.30pm, closed Sun.*

Central Meat Market

If you're near the Central Market, don't miss out on **Díporto**, ☎ 321 1463, an Athenian institution (so much so that there is no sign); it's down some cement stairs and has remained exactly the same for at least 50 years. It serves simple but delicious dishes and salads with barrelled retsina (eight barrels by the wall) on paper-covered tables set on a bare cement floor. Try whatever soup is on offer (the chickpea soup is delicious) and consider sharing portions—they are huge. *Patsás* (tripe soup), the traditional Greek hangover cure, as well as other Hellenic soul food is dished up for trendy drunkards and hungry butchers at the **Monastíri**, ☎ 324 0773, a glassed-in restaurant ensconced inside the main Athens meat market since 1924. The food is great, on display for you to point at, but the setting is not for the faint-hearted. Entering from the Evripídou St entrance closest to Eólou St is the easiest way to avoid too many dead bodies en route to eating them. These two inexpensive restaurants are open only in the morning and for lunch well into the afternoon hours. They close Sundays.

Exárchia

If in Exárchia around lunchtime, consider the clutch of inexpensive places around Plateía Exárchia, or Methónis St, higher up and close to Stréfi Hill. At Methónis 66, the **Ama Lachi**, ☎ 384 5978, housed in an old school, is cheap, good and very pleasant. *Open 1pm–2am, closed Sun.* For an evening out, try **Kostayiánnis**, 37 Zaími St, ☎ 821 2496, behind the National Archaeology Museum (off Stournári St), which has a succulent display of food in the glass cabinets near the entrance preparing you for a memorable culinary evening. To enjoy the after-theatre ambience, don't get there too early. Apart from the superb seafood, the many meat and vegetable dishes prepared each day are unbeatable— try the roast pork in wine and herb sauce or the rabbit *stifádo*, accompanied by barrelled retsina. Prices here are very reasonable—3,500–4,000dr for a full meal. *Open evenings only, closed Sun.* For a night out with music, book a table at **To Stéki tou Xanthis**, ☎ 882 0780, at Irinis Athinéas 5, on the northeast side of Stréfi Hill. Xánthis, owner and disciple of Theodorákis, leads the public in old Greek songs in a historic house. The food is good and plentiful (*around 4,500–5,000dr*). *Open evenings only, closed Sun.*

Koukáki and Makrigiánni

Lots of little eateries line Makrigiánni St. The **27**, at 27 Makrigiánni St, ✆ 923 8124, is about as imaginative as its name, but it is handy, open all day every day, and serves everything from pizza, to breakfast, to fixed-price meals in a rather Germanic atmosphere. At 16 Drakou St, join the locals at **Psitopoleío**, a modest hole in the wall that is worth finding: try the delicious grilled chicken with mustard sauce (*sáltsa moustárda*). *Around 2,000dr.* It is close to the **Vini**, 10 Drakou St, ✆ 922 6225, one of Athens' few pubs dedicated to serving a large variety of imported and local beer as well as snacks (*3,500dr* for a beer and snack). And just in case you think that this area lacks class, look for the **Diávlos**, 9 Drakou St, ✆ 923 9588, Koukáki's vegetarian restaurant, where *futofágoi* can swill carrot juice and mop up soya delicacies in a truly lovely renovated neoclassical house (*2,000–3,0000dr*). In the late evening it is transformed into a music restaurant with Iannis Glezos, a wonderful Greek composer, at the piano. Prices rise accordingly. Higher up in this area, opposite the Acropolis, the family-run **Strofí**, 125 Roberto Galli, ✆ 721 4130, is close to the Odeon, with a rooftop terrace and Acropolis views from its second-floor windows. It is famous for its *mezédes* (*3,500dr and up*). *Open every evening except Sunday.*

Entertainment and Nightlife

The summer is filled with festivals attracting international stars from around the world. These events are advertised in the *Athens News* and in *Welcome to Athens*. At other times, classical music fans should try to take in a performance at the **Mégaron**, on Vas. Sophías and Kokkáli Streets, ✆ 728 2333, Athens' brand new, acoustically wonderful concert hall. Maria Callas got her start at the **Greek National Opera House**, 59–61 Academías St, ✆ 361 2461, which is shared with the National Ballet. From May to September there are nightly folk dance performances at the **Dora Stratou Theatre** on Philapáppos Hill, ✆ 921 4650. *Rembétika*, the Greek blues, is having a serious revival in Athens; the real thing may be heard live at **Stoa Athanaton**, 19 Sophokléous St, ✆ 321 4362 (*closed Sun*), or at the **Perivóli T'Ouranoú**, 19 Lysikrátous St, Pláka, ✆ 323 5517 (*closed Sun and Mon*).

Irakleídon St in Thissío has popular rock bars, such as **Stávlos** and **Berlin**. The **Camel Club**, 268 Vouliaménis St, ✆ 971 6165, has mainstream rock, progressive house and techno on offer on two stages. For jazz, try the **Half Note**, 17 Trivonianoú St, ✆ 923 3460, which alternates between Greek and foreign artists.

The clubbing scene in Athens is as varied as it is volatile. The current hot spots for house are **The Crystal**, the former '+ Soda', 161 Ermoú St, ✆ 345 6187, one of the most popular clubs in Athens offering performance dancing during the week and dancing for all after that; and **HQ**, formerly 'King Size', 3 Amerikís St, ✆ 323 2500, which is for fashion victims and has a chill-out area. These two places have bouncers who delight in turning away the uncool. In the two hottest summer months, the cool head out to the temporary bars and clubs in Glyfáda and by the airport, set up by the big city clubs. These are as ephemeral as snowballs in a heat wave; the venues change and are often not announced until late June. Ask at your hotel or anyone under 30 in a Thissío bar for the current favourites.

Gay Athens gathers in Makrigiánni, at **Lamda**,15 Lebéssi St, ✆ 922 4202, and at **Koukles**, at Zan Moreas and Syngroú (no phone), for its famous Drag Show.

In the summer, **outdoor cinemas** are a treat and all the films are in their original language. Two nice ones are in Kolonáki: **Dexamení**, in Dexamenis Square halfway up Lykavittós St, ✆ 360 2363, and **Athináia**, 50 Cháritos St, ✆ 721 5717. The best is the **Cíne Paris**, in the Pláka on Kidathinéon St. If the picture is a bore, you can always gaze at the back of the Acropolis.

Crete

History	75
Chaniá	80
Nomós Chaniá	87
The Gorge of Samariá	90
Réthymnon	95
Nomós Réthymnon	98
Herákleon	103
Knossós	110
Nomós Herákleon	118
Nomós Lassíthi	130
Ag. Nikólaos	134

How Crete is Divided

Lofty mountain ranges neatly divide the island into four sections. These have become modern Crete's political divisions and are used for reference in this book. West of the White Mountains is the nomós (province) of Chaniá; between the White Mountains and Psilorítis (Mount Ida) is the nomós of Réthymnon; between Psilorítis and the Lassíthi Mountains lies the nomós of Herákleon; and east of the Lassíthi Mountains is the nomós of Lassíthi, of which Ag. Nikólaos is the capital. The description in the text covers Crete from west to east.

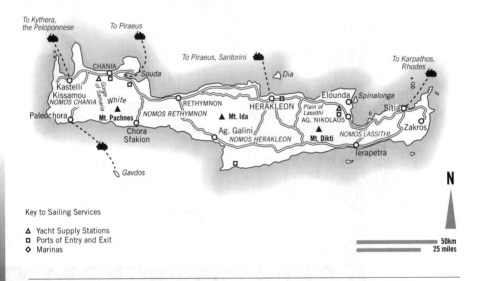

Key to Sailing Services

▲ Yacht Supply Stations
□ Ports of Entry and Exit
◇ Marinas

N

50km
25 miles

Column of the Levant,
My Crete, beautiful island,
Your soil is made of gold,
Your each stone a diamond.

traditional Cretan *mantináda*

Crete, on the map an odd, horned, wasp-waisted creature that seems to scoot along the 35th parallel, is Greece's largest island (roughly 260km by 50km), and in a hundred ways its most extraordinary. Endowed by a generous Nature with every earthly delight, Crete nurtured the very first civilization on European soil, the Minoan, which (at least according to its discoverer, Arthur Evans) was so advanced, graceful, peaceful and inventive that Europe has yet to see the like. Birthplace of Zeus, the father of the gods, Crete gave Greece its most ancient myths, and in its remote mountain villages customs survive that have long been abandoned elsewhere.

Despite Crete's violent past, today you're far less likely to be prematurely punctured by a shotgun than suffocated by the worst excesses of mass tourism. The lovely beaches along the north coast have been raped by toadstool strips of jerry-built hotels, shops, restaurants and discos, tourist compounds often run by Athenians or foreigners, where bars advertise daily video showings of *The Beverley Hillbillies*, the latest football scores, baked beans and permanent happy hours. Crete's hot climate makes it a major package holiday destination from early spring until the end of October. Each year it becomes more difficult to visit even fairly remote corners such as the Minoan palace of Zákros or the Diktean Cave without a dozen coachloads of tourists and rubber-tonsilled guides on your back. If you have mytho-poetic fantasies of tripping through the labyrinth of Knossós on your own, book your flight for December or January; after the Acropolis, it receives more visitors than any site in Greece.

As on Corfu, as on Rhodes, Crete's crushing popularity is a tribute to its extraordinary charms. Four mountain ranges lend the island a dramatic grandeur entirely disproportionate to its size; the White Mountains in the west are vast enough to hold the Gorge of Samariá, the longest in Europe. Some 1500 kinds of wild flowers, including a few hundred species unique to Crete, brighten the landscape in the spring with all the intensity of 1950s Technicolor. No island can approach Crete's agricultural importance or diversity: vineyards, olive and citrus groves cover the coastal plains and hillside terraces; cereals, potatoes, pears, apples, walnuts and chestnuts come from the well-watered mountain plains, especially up around Lassíthi; and acres of plastic greenhouses blanket the south coast—only 320km from Egypt—providing no advantage to the scenery but bushels of winter vegetables and fruit for the rest of Greece, including bananas and avocados. Cretan art and architecture afford an equally rich feast: the fabled Minoan sites and artefacts in Herákleon's superb archaeology museum; Byzantine churches and monasteries adorned with frescoes and icons by the Cretan School; the Venetian and Turkish quarters of Chaniá and Réthymnon; small mountain villages that do credit to the native Greek sense of design.

Of all the islands, Crete has the sharpest sense of a separate identity and the most ferocious love of liberty, manifest in its own culture, dialect, music and dances, and in the works of its most famous sons, El Greco, Elefthérios Venizélos, Níkos Kazantzákis and Míkis Theodorákis. This culture is even more predominantly patriarchal than that of other islands: in the mountain villages, older women still wrap themselves in drab scarves and rarely join in *kafeneíon* society, while their men cut a dash in their baggy breeches, high boots and black-fringed headbands, and pour disdain on 'the long-trousered men' who have exploited the coast. On feast days, people still sing *mantinádes* (improvised couplets) or *rizítika* ('songs from the roots') with themes of Cretan patriotism. And such patriotism is far from dead. In the face of a creeping homogenized and pasteurized Europe (not at all like the first Europe who came to Crete's shores—*see* below), many young Cretans are taking an active role in preserving their traditions, even moving back up to their ancestral villages, where EU subsidies assure them a decent living from grandfather's olives. Paradoxes are rife, but, after all, the island can take some credit for making paradox something of an art form, when the Cretan philosopher Epimenides declared: 'All Cretans are liars.'

Mythology

 As Cronos (the Roman Saturn), the ruler of the world, had been warned that he would be usurped by his own child, he swallowed every baby his wife Rhea, daughter of the Earth, presented to him. After this had happened five times, Rhea determined on a different fate for her sixth child, Zeus. When he was born she smuggled him to Crete and gave Cronos a stone to swallow instead. Mother Earth hid the baby in the Diktean Cave and set young Cretan warriors called Kouretes to guard him; they were ordered to shout and dance and beat their shields to drown out the baby's cries. And, as prophesied, Zeus grew up and dethroned his father by castrating him with a sickle.

When a Phoenician princess, Europa, caught Zeus' fancy, the god disguised himself as a beautiful bull and carried Europa off to Crete, where she bore him three sons: Minos, Rhadamanthys and Sarpedon, and gave her name to an entire continent. When Minos became the King of Crete at Knossós, he was asked to prove that his claim to the throne had divine sanction. Minos remembered the form his father had taken and asked Poseidon to send him a bull from the sea to sacrifice to the gods. However, the bull was so magnificent that Minos didn't kill it, but sent it to service his herds.

The kingdom of Minos prospered, ruling the seas and exacting tributes from across the Mediterranean. But Poseidon, weary of waiting for the promised sacrifice, caused Minos' wife Pasiphaë to fall in love with the bull. The unfortunate Pasiphaë confided her problem to the inventor Daedalus, who constructed a hollow wooden cow covered with hide for her to enter and mate with the bull. This union resulted in the Minotaur, born with the head of a bull and the body of a man. Minos hid the monster in another invention of Daedalus, the Labyrinth, an impossible maze of corridors under his palace, and fed it with the blood of his enemies. Among these were seven maidens and seven youths from Athens, sent to Crete every nine years, the tribute extorted by Minos when his son was slain in an Athenian game.

Two tributes had been paid when Theseus, the handsome son of Aegeus, King of Athens, demanded to be sent as one of the victims. Minos' daughter Ariadne fell in love with him as he stepped off the ship. She asked Daedalus to help her save his life, and the inventor gave her a ball of thread. Unwinding the thread as he went, Theseus made his way into the labyrinth, slew the Minotaur with his bare hands, retraced his way out with the ball of thread and escaped, taking Ariadne and the other Athenians with him.

Minos was furious when he discovered the part Daedalus had played in the business and threw the inventor and his young son Icarus into the Labyrinth. Although they managed to find their way out, escape from Crete was impossible, as Minos controlled the seas. But Daedalus, never at a loss, decided that what they couldn't accomplish by sea they would do by air. He fashioned wings of feathers and wax for himself and Icarus, and they flew towards Asia Minor. All went well until an exhilarated Icarus disobeyed his father's command not to fly too close to the sun. The wax in his wings melted, and he plunged and drowned off the island that took his name, Ikaría.

Minos heard of Daedalus' escape and pursued him all over the Mediterranean, hoping to trap the wily inventor by offering a great reward to whoever could pass a thread through a nautilus shell. Finally, in Sicily, Minos met a king who took the shell away and brought it back threaded—Daedalus was indeed there, and had performed the task by tying the thread to an ant. At once Minos demanded that Daedalus be turned over to him. The king hedged, and instead invited Minos to stay at his palace. While Minos was in his bath, Daedalus put a pipe through the ceiling and poured boiling water through it, scalding him to death. Zeus then sent Minos down to Hades to judge the dead, a task he shared with his brother Rhadamanthys and his enemy Aeacus.

History

The first Cretans were Neolithic sailors who arrived on the island around 8000 BC, and probably came from Asia Minor. They built small houses in Knossós and other future Minoan sites, with small rooms clustered around a central open area, presaging the floor-plans of the famous palaces. They worshipped fertility goddesses in the depths of caves, especially in caves on top of mountains—the future peak sanctuaries of the **Minoans**. As the first civilization on European soil, Minoan Crete exerts a special fascination. We knew of it first from Homer:

> One of the great islands of the world in midsea, in the winedark sea, is Krete: spacious and rich and populous, with ninety cities and a mingling of tongues. Akhaians there are found, along with Kretan hillmen of the old stock, and Kydonians, Dorians in three blood-lines, Pelasgians—and one among their ninety towns is Knossós. Here lived King Minos whom great Zeus received every ninth year in private council.

(translated by Robert Fitzgerald)

Archaeologically, we know the Minoans only since 1900, when Arthur Evans began excavating Knossós, searching for hieroglyphic seals and finding instead a whole new Copper and Bronze Age civilization that he called 'Minoan'. Since then, discoveries in Crete have continued apace, including some remarkable finds that have radically altered Evans' vision of the Minoans as a non-violent society of artsy flower children. Their accomplishments may also go back further in time than Evans thought; the latest dating techniques add another few centuries to the timescale, i.e. Santoríni is now believed to have erupted around 1750 BC.

Trade with Egypt, the Cyclades and the Middle East at the end of the Neolithic era introduced bronze to Crete and brought about the changes that distinguish the first Minoan period, the **Pre-Palatial** (2600–1900 BC), according to Níkos Pláton's widely accepted revision of Evans' chronology. Characteristic of the Pre-Palatial era are the first monumental *tholos* tombs (as at Archánes), the building of sanctuaries at high points, and the beginning of a ruling priestly (or priestessly) class, who dwelt in large palaces (or temples) with red-plastered walls. The Minoan taste for refinement shines through at the end of the period, in exquisite work in gold, semi-precious stones and sealstones, some bearing the first signs of writing in ideograms.

Pláton's **Old Palace period** (Evans' Middle Minoan; 1900–1700 BC) saw a hitherto unheard of concentration of wealth in Crete. Power, too, seems to have been concentrated in a few areas: in the 'palaces' of Knossós, Mália, Phaistós and Zákros. These were kitted out with the first-known plumbing and lavishly decorated with frescoes and stylized sacred 'horns of consecration'. Bulls played an important role in religion, which was dominated by the goddess, pictured in Minoan imagery in three aspects: as the mistress of the wild animals and earth; as the snake goddess, mistress of the underworld; and as the dove goddess, mistress of the sky.

Towns and palaces were unfortified, suggesting political unity on the island and giving substance to the myth of Minos' thalassocracy, or sea reign: Crete's powerful fleet precluded the need for walls. Their ships, laden with olive oil, honey, wine, precious balsams and art, traded extensively with Cyprus, Egypt and the Greek islands; Minoan colonies have been found at Kéa, Mílos and Kýthera. The palaces/temples all had important stores, acting either as warehouses or distribution points for the surrounding territory. There was a system of writing in ideograms, as on the Phaistós disc in the Herákleon museum. Roads paved with flagstones linked settlements on the island, and the first large irrigation projects were begun. Art reached new heights, in gold and in ceramics, especially decorated Kamáres-ware. Then in 1700 BC a huge earthquake ripped across the Eastern Mediterranean and devastated the buildings.

Forced to start afresh, the Minoans rebuilt better than ever in the **New Palace period** (1700–1450 BC). The palace complexes were rebuilt in the same style: a warren of rooms illuminated by light wells, overlooking a central and western court, where religious ceremonies and the famous bull-leaping may have occurred. To build the new palaces with more 'give' in case of earthquakes, wooden beams and columns (the distinctive reversed cedar trunks, thin at the bottom and wide at the top) were combined with stone. Workshops and vast store-rooms were clustered around the palaces, their contents recorded on clay tablets in a writing system known as Linear A. Fancy villas were built outside the palaces, most famously at Ag. Triáda, and scattered throughout the countryside were centralized farms, with kilns, wine presses and looms. Densely populated towns have been excavated at Gourniá, Móchlos, Palaíkastro, Zákros and Pseíra island. Burials became more elaborate, more monumental, more various; many were in painted clay sarcophagi, or *larnaxes*. Impressive port facilities were built, especially along the north and east coasts, and new trade centres were established on Santoríni, Rhodes, Skópelos, and on the mainlands of Greece and Asia Minor. Shields, daggers, swords and helmets have been found, although land defences were still non-existent.

The Herákleon museum is jammed full of testimonials to the extraordinary, exuberant art of the period. The Minoans delighted in natural forms and designs, especially floral and marine motifs. They portrayed themselves with wasp waists and long black curls, the men clad in codpieces and loincloths, the women with eyes blackened with kohl and lips painted red, clad in their famous bodices that exposed the breast, flounced skirts decorated with complex patterns, and exotic hats. All move with a natural, sensuous grace, completely unlike the stiffly stylized hieratical figures in Egyptian and Near Eastern art. The strong feminine quality of the art suggests that Minoan society was matriarchal, and that women were the equals of men, participating in the same sports, hunts and ceremonies. Vases and rhytons (libation vessels) made of basalt, marble and porphyry are unsurpassed in beauty and technique. Culturally Minoan influence spread north to mainland Greece, recently invaded by northerners known as Achaeans or Mycenaeans; the Minoans communicated with them in what seems to have been the lingua franca of the day, in the script Linear B—proto-ancient Greek.

But some time around 1450 BC disaster struck again. A tremendous volcanic eruption from Santoríni, and subsequent tidal waves and earthquakes, left Crete in ruins; in some places along the north coast a 20cm layer of tefra (volcanic ash) has been found—*under* structures belonging to the Late Minoan or **Post-Palace period** (1450–1100 BC). The old theory that Mycenaeans from the mainland invaded Crete, taking advantage of its disarray, has lost favour before the idea that their infiltration was much more gradual, and that for a long period the Mycenaeans co-existed peacefully side by side with the Minoans. Of the great palaces, Knossós alone was rebuilt, only to burn once and for all in *c.* 1380 BC; in other places, such as Ag. Triáda, typical Mycenaean palaces, or *megarons*, have been found. Linear B became the dominant script, and the natural, graceful decorative motifs of the New Palace period become ever more conventional and stylized. Clay figurines of the goddess lose not only their sex appeal but any pretensions to realism; they resemble bells with upraised arms, primitive faces and bee-sting breasts. The island maintained its great fleet (if often for piratical uses), and was able to contribute 90 ships to the Trojan War.

After the Minoans: The Doric Period

By 1100 BC, Minoan-Mycenaean civilization had ground to a halt; trade disintegrated as the Dorians, armed with the latest technology—iron weapons—invaded Greece, and then Crete. Their coming brought confusion and a cultural dark age (the **Proto-Geometric period**, 1100–900 BC). The last Minoans took to the hills, especially south of Sitía, surviving in memory as the Eteocretans, or true Cretans. Their art grew weird as they declined; in Praisós they left mysterious inscriptions in the Greek alphabet, still waiting to be translated. Other Cretans were treated according to the amount of resistance they had offered the Dorians; those who fought back the most were divided among the conquerors as slaves.

By the **Geometric period** (900–650 BC) Crete was politically divided, like the Greek mainland, into autonomous city-states: a hundred, according to ancient writers. The Minoan goddess was adopted into the patriarchal Greek pantheon—Atana became Athena, Britomartis became Artemis, her son and consort Welchanos became Zeus, father of the gods. Art from the period shows Eastern influences; works in bronze are especially fine. Towards the end of the period the first bronze statuettes by Daedalos (not to be confused with the inventor of myth) and his school appear, with their characteristic wide eyes, thick hair and parted legs.

The style reached its peak in the **Archaic period** (650–550 BC), when Doric Crete was one of the art centres of Greece. It declined, not only because of the Dorians' innate austerity, but in the face of expanding Ionian commercial and cultural influence in the Mediterranean that created Greece's **Classical Age**. Crete sat it out. By the 2nd century BC its coasts were little more than pirates' bases. When these pirates sufficiently niggled Rome by kidnapping the families of nobles at Ostia, right under Rome's nose, the Senate sent Quintus Metellus Creticus to subdue the anarchic island once and for all (69–67 BC).

Roman and Byzantine Crete

With the Romans, the centre of power on the island moved south to Górtyn, on the fertile Mesará plain, especially when it was made the capital of the Roman province of Crete and Cyrene (Libya) in West Africa. With peace, the population on Crete soared to some 300,000. Christianity came to the island early when St Paul appointed one of his Greek disciples, Titus, to found the first church at Górtyn in AD 58. Richly decorated basilicas were constructed across the island, most importantly at Knossós, Chersónisos, Górtyn, Lissós, Sýia, Itanos and Kainoúrios.

In 823, Saracen Arabs conquered Crete, plunging much of it into misery and decimating Górtyn. One lasting feature of their stay was the building of the first castle at Herákleon, called Kandak ('deep moat'), or Candia, a name which grew to encompass all of Crete in the Middle Ages (and eventually became synonymous with the sweet honey and nuts it exported, hence 'candy'). In 961 the future Byzantine emperor Nikephóros Phokás reconquered Crete and sent the fabulous treasure of the Arabs back to Constantinople. The victorious Greek soldiers were among the first new colonists given tracts of land; Emperor Aléxis Comnénus later sent his own son and other young Byzantine aristocrats, establishing a ruling class that would dominate Crete for centuries.

Venetian and Ottoman Crete

With the conquest of Constantinople in the Fourth Crusade in 1204 and the division of the empire's spoils among its conquerors, Crete was awarded to Boniface of Montferrat. He soon sold the island to the Venetians, who, after a brief tussle with arch-rival Genoa, occupied Crete from 1210 to 1669. The first two centuries of rule by the Most Serene Republic were neither serene nor republican; the Venetians high-handedly imposed the feudal system and their model of government, appointing a doge, or Duca, in Herákleon. Laws attempted to replace the Orthodox hierarchy with a Catholic one. Uprisings lasting several years occurred, often led by the *árchons*, or old Byzantine nobles. Usually they won important concessions from the Venetians, until, by the 15th century, the Orthodox and Catholics (some 10,000) lived in reasonable harmony. Happiness was for the few, however—the vast majority of Cretans, in addition to working long hours for their lords, were compelled to build the immense city walls, even though they were not allowed to live inside them.

Relations with Venice were cemented with the fall of Constantinople in 1453, when the Venetians were keen to keep the Cretans on their side. In Greece's age-old tradition of absorbing the invader, many Venetians became Hellenized, spoke Greek better than Italian and converted to Orthodoxy. As a refuge for scholars and painters from Constantinople and mainland Greece, Crete became the key point of contact between the East and the Italian Renaissance in the 15th and 16th centuries and in art produced, most famously, Doménico Theotokópoulos, who moved to Venice and Spain and became known as El Greco. Cretan-Venetian schools and academies, architecture, theatre, literature, song and romantic epic poetry blossomed, culminating in the dialect epic poem *Erotókritos* by Vicénzo Kornáros.

Although they had raided Crete periodically after the fall of Constantinople, the Ottomans finally caught the island by surprise. In 1645, Sultan Ibrahim declared war on the Knights of Malta and sent a fleet of 1,440 ships after them. They stopped in Kýthera for coffee and sugar, and the Venetian commander there sent word to his counterpart in Chaniá to allow the fleet safe passage; on 12 June, as the sultan's ships began to sail past, they turned their guns on the city. Chaniá fell but Herákleon resisted until 1669, after a 21-year siege.

Under the Ottoman Empire, Crete descended into a new spiritual and economic dark age. Turkish reprisals for Crete's long resistance were horrific, in human and material terms. The most fertile lands were given to Turkish colonists and, although the Orthodox religion was tolerated, many Cretans became crypto-Christians, publicly converted to Islam to avoid the punishing head and property taxes that turned them into serfs. Those who could emigrated to the Venetian-held Ionian islands; those who couldn't rose up against the Turks more than 400 times, in a crescendo of revolts throughout the 19th century.

In 1898, Greece declared war on Turkey and asked the Great Powers for aid. Britain did little, in spite of searing accounts of atrocities sent home by Arthur Evans, until the Turks made the fatal mistake of killing the British consul and 14 British soldiers in Herákleon. As British, French, Russian and Italian troops subdued sections of the island, Prince George was appointed High Commissioner of an independent Crete. Prince George's high-handed ways and imposition of a foreign administration led in 1905 to the Revolution of Therisso, led by Eleuthérios Venizélos of Chaniá. In 1909 Venizélos was appointed Prime Minister of Greece, a position that enabled him to secure Crete's union with Greece after the Balkan War of 1913.

The Battle of Crete

But Crete was to suffer one last invasion. As the Germans overran Greece, the government in Athens took refuge on Crete (23 April 1943), the last bit of Greek territory, defended by 30,000 British, New Zealand and Australian troops hastily transferred from the mainland. Crete's own battalions were trapped near the Albanian frontier; the only Greek soldiers on the island were cadets and untrained recruits. But then again, no-one suspected what Goering and General Student, his second-in-command of the Luftwaffe, had in store. After a week of bomb raids, Nazi paratroopers launched the world's first successful invasion by air on Crete (20 May 1941). The Allied and Greek forces, along with hundreds of poorly armed men, women and children, put up a such a stubborn resistance that the Germans were forced to expend the cream of their forces to subdue the island over the next 10 days—at the cost of 170 aircraft, 4,000 specially trained paratroopers, and their 7th airborne division. As Churchill wrote, 'In Crete Goering won a Pyrrhic victory, because with the forces he wasted there he could easily have conquered Cyprus, Syria, Iraq or even Persia...'

In spite of brutal German reprisals, resistance to the occupation, aided by British agents in the mountains and based in Egypt, was legendary, especially the daring abduction of German commander General Kreipe by Major Patrick Leigh Fermor and Captain Billy Moss in 1943. As a massive manhunt combed the island, the British and Cretan Resistance spirited Kreipe over the mountains and away to Egypt, earning a final, grudging compliment from the General: 'I am beginning to wonder who is occupying the island—us or the English.'

Food and Wine: The Old/New Cretan Diet

Back in 1947, researchers for the Rockefeller Foundation noted with astonishment how healthy elderly Cretans were compared to their American counterparts. In spite of the privations of the war and their 'primitive' way of life, people in their 90s were still running up mountains and working in the fields. In 1956 a 15-year study began in Japan, Finland, Yugoslavia, the USA, Holland, Italy, Corfu and Crete comparing diet, lifestyle and the incidence of cardiovascular disease and cancer. If health were a race, Crete not only won but lapped the competition several times; the difference in death rates, even compared with fellow Greek island Corfu, was striking. And this in spite of the fact that Cretans consume as much fat as the Finns, who did the worst in coronary disease; in fact, the only Cretan who died of coronary failure during the study was a butcher.

Olive oil (the main source of fat), lots of legumes, greens and fresh vegetables, and very little meat proved to be the secret and the basis of the Cretan diet that nutritionists, and now the Cretans, are beginning to promote. The island grows almost everything it needs: nuts, olives and every kind of fruit from apples to bananas and citrus; the farms along the south coast provide many of Greece's winter vegetables and market counters heave with herbs. Cretan honey and cheeses have had a high reputation since antiquity: the best is *myzíthra*, a white soft cheese similar to fresh ricotta, often served on rusks with tomatoes, as a starter (*dákos*); another is *stáka*, a rich white cheese, often baked in a cheese pie or served fried as a hot creamy dip. When Cretans do eat meat, they do delicious things to it, as in lamb *kriotópita* (baked in pastry with cheese), or kid stewed in fruit juice; and they eat more snails (*saligária*) than most Greeks.

No milk, but wine in moderation is definitely part of the diet. Crete's best wines are *Kritikós Topikós Oénos*, the Greek equivalent of a *vin de pays*: look for the fresh white wine of Péza, made from a unique variety of grape called *vilana*, and the spicy red wines of Archánes, made of *kotsífali* and tannin-rich *mandelári* grapes, the latter one of Greece's most ancient varieties. *Rakí* (more commonly *tsikoudiá*), an *eau-de-vie* distilled in a hundred mountain stills, is Crete's firewater, its moonshine, its pure hot-blooded soul, its cure-all; for a change try it hot, with a spoonful of honey.

Getting to Crete

Herákleon, and to a lesser extent Chaniá, are linked by direct charter flights to London Gatwick, Manchester, Glasgow, Newcastle, Dublin and Belfast. From Athens to Herákleon, Olympic runs five to six flights daily, Cronus and Aegean have four; from Athens to Chaniá, Olympic runs four flights daily, Cronus and Aegean have two; between Herákleon and Thessaloníki, Olympic has three flights a week, as does Aegean; between Chaniá and Thessaloníki, Olympic has two flights a week. From Rhodes to Herákleon, Olympic has four flights a week and Aegean has three; from Santoríni, Olympic has two flights a week. Crete's third airport, at Sitía, has a weekly flight from Athens. Olympic offices and agents are listed under individual towns.

When to Go

The ideal time to visit Crete is towards the end of April, when you'll avoid the worst crowds and rain; the Libyan Sea is usually warm enough for bathing, the flowers are glorious and the higher mountains are still capped with snow. Note that the Gorge of Samariá doesn't open until 1 May, when its torrent recedes sufficiently for safe passage. October is another good month, with many perfect days and a lingering warm sea.

Chaniá (ΞANIA)

Unless you have only a few days and want to concentrate on the high shrines of Minoan culture around Herákleon, consider easing yourself gently into this complex island by starting with Chaniá, Crete's second city (pop. 60,000) and easily the most elegant of the island's four provincial capitals. With the ghostly forms of the snow-capped White Mountains hovering over its rooflines and palm trees, Chaniá is a seductive town and an exceedingly old one, its streets lined with Venetian, Turkish and neoclassical monuments. Unfortunately, many others were lost in bombing raids during the Battle of Crete; fortunately, perhaps, the war-scarred ruins stood neglected for so many decades that they've now been incorporated into unique garden settings for bars and restaurants. The lovely inner and outer Venetian harbours become magnets in the evening, where unwinding over a drink can easily become addictive.

The ancient historian Diodoros Sikelus wrote that Chaniá was founded by Minos and that it was one of the three great cities of Crete. Buildings in the Kastélli quarter go back to 2200 BC, and archaeologists are pretty sure that the Minoan palace and town KY-DO-NI-JA, referred to on a Linear B tablet found at Knossós, lie hidden under the modern town. Kydonia was so important that for a time its name referred to all of Crete. In modern Greek, *kydónia* means quince, a fruit loved by the Minoans: the word (like 'hyacinth', 'labyrinth' and 'sandal') may have come from the ancient Minoan language.

Quince Town survived the rest of Cretan history to get a mention in Homer, to know glory days in the Hellenistic and Roman periods, then to decline so far between the 10th and 13th centuries that it was better known as 'Rubbish City'. Revived under the Venetians, who called it La Canea, it was so splendid by the 1500s that it was renamed the 'Venice of the East'. Crete's capital from 1850 to 1971, Chaniá was long the island's window on the outside world, with consulates and embassies, and it prospered as the fief of statesman Elefthérios Venizélos.

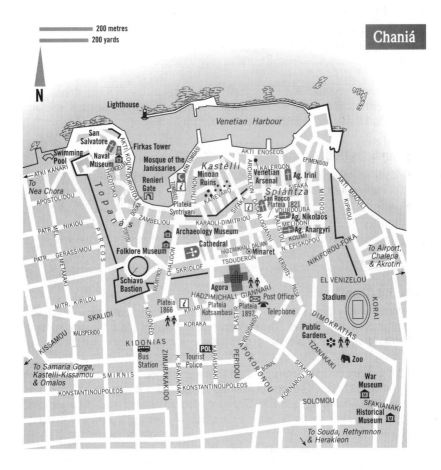

Chaniá **airport** is out on the Akrotíri peninsula, ℗ 63 264; a taxi to the centre costs about 2,000dr. The Olympic Airways office is at 88 Stratigoú Tzanakáki, ℗ 58 005; Aegean is at the airport, ℗ 63 366, and Cronus is at 12 El Venizélou, ℗ 51 100. **KTEL buses** travel from the station at Kidonías hourly to Herákleon and Réthymnon, at least hourly along the Stalos/Ag. Marina/Platanías/Gerani route and almost as often to Kolimbari; the other larger villages of the *nomós* are serviced at least daily: for transport to the Gorge of Samária, *see* p.90. For information call ℗ 93 306. **Car rental** can be organised at one of the many agencies lining Chalídon Street.

EOT: 40 Kriári St, ℗ 92 943, ✉ 92 624, open Mon–Fri 8.30am–2pm.

Tourist police: 23 Iraklion St, ℗ 53 333.

Internet: the new e-café on Theotokopoúlou has quiet cubicles where you can hook up (open to 2am); noisier services are provided on the harbour at Sante, Aktí Koundouriótou.

Telephone: Hermes, on the corner of Kondiláki, has a handy phone-now-pay-later system and accepts incoming calls (open 9am–11.30pm).

Festivals

Chaniá commemorates the anniversary of the Battle of Crete during the Chaniá Festival, which runs from the **middle to the end of May. 24 June** is St John's Day. On **15 August** Chaniá hosts the Pan Cretan Festival.

Excursions from Chaniá

1 If you're feeling active and ready for an early start, voyage down to the stunning Gorge of Samariá for a beautiful day's walk.

2 Visit the barren Akrotíri Peninsula, home to Moní Gouvernétou Monastery, the revered Bear Cave and the grotto of St John the Hermit; bring your swimming costume and cool off in the sea nearby. From here, continue on to the ancient ruins of Aptera before heading back to Chaniá.

Into Old Chaniá

The vortex of daily life in Chaniá is its cruciform covered market, or **Agora** (1911), standing at the entrance to the old town. The back stairs of the market and a left turn will take you to **Odós Skrídlof**, a narrow lane jam-packed for as long as anyone remembers with shops selling leather sandals, bags and boots, long a traditional craft of the city.

Skrídlof gives on to Odós Chalídon, Chaniá's jewellery-shop-lined funnel to the sea. Midway down, at No.21, in the 14th-century Gothic church of San Francesco, is Chaniá's excellent **Archaeology Museum** (*open 8.30–3, closed Mon; adm, free Sun*). Note especially the clay seal (*c.* 1450 BC) that shows the commanding figure of a Minoan holding a staff, standing over the sea as it breaks against the gates of a city where the roofs are crowned with horns of con-secration. Other exhibits include mosaic floors based on the legend of Dionysos from a

3rd-century AD house, the beautiful gold necklaces of Sossima, who perished in childbirth around the 3rd century BC, and cases of Linear A and the more common Linear B tablets, proved on a hunch by Michael Ventris in 1952 to be an ancient form of Greek. Disappointingly, the tablets are mostly inventories: 'Five jars of honey, 300 pigs, 120 cows for As-as-wa' is a typical entry.

Across the street, the sad-looking building with baby bubble domes is a Turkish bath. This is next to a large square holding the **Trimartyr Cathedral**, which should be more interesting than it is. In the 1850s a soap factory belonging to Mustafa Nily Pasha stood here; as a gesture of reconciliation he donated it to the Christians, along with enough money to build a church.

Around the Venetian Harbour

Chalídon Street flows into the crescent of the **outer port**, lined with handsome Venetian buildings. The neighbourhood on the west side of the port, **Topanás**, has been classified a landmark, although the interiors have nearly all been converted into bars, pensions and restaurants. The **Fírkas Tower** at the far west end of the port saw the official raising of the Greek flag over Crete in November 1913 in the presence of King Constantine and Prime Minister Venizélos. Long used as a prison, the tower now contains a summer theatre and the **Naval Museum** (*open 10–2, closed Mon; adm*). Crete, naturally, is the main focus; there are photos, models of Venetian galleys and fortifications, and mock-ups of key Greek naval victories throughout the ages, all described in nationalistic, hysterical English translations. The first floor has an evocative collection of photos and memorabilia from the Battle of Crete.

Behind the tower, simple little **San Salvatore** belonged to a Franciscan monastery and, like most of Chaniá's churches, was used by the Turks as a mosque. Near here begins **Theotokopoúlou**, the most picturesque street in the city, lined with Venetian houses remodelled by the Turks. On Theofánou Street (off Zambéliou) the **Renieri Gate** bears a Venetian coat-of-arms dated 1608. Further south stood the old Jewish ghetto, the Ovraiki; for more information on the dilapidated synagogue on Kondiláki Street, talk to the owner of Synagogi bar next door. At the top of Kondiláki, along Portoú Lane, you can see the last bastion of the **Venetian walls**. In 1538, just after Barbarossa devastated Réthymnon, the Venetians hired their fortifications wizard Michele Sammichele to surround Chaniá with walls and a moat more than 147ft wide and 28ft deep. They didn't exactly measure up to the job in 1645, when the Ottomans captured Chaniá in two months.

The **east end** of the outer port has Chaniá's two most photographed landmarks: a graceful Venetian **lighthouse** in golden stone, restored by the Egyptians, and the **Mosque of the Janissaries** (1645), crowned with its distinctive ostrich- and chicken-egg domes. Here the Christian-born slave troops of the Ottoman Empire worshipped, although little did it improve their character; not only did they terrorize the Greeks, but in 1690 they murdered the Pasha of Chaniá and fed his body to the dogs. In 1812, even the Sublime Porte had had enough and sent Hadji Osman Pasha, 'the Throttler', into Crete to hang the lot of them, an act that so impressed the Greeks that rumours flew around that 'the Throttler' must be a crypto-Christian.

Behind the mosque lies the **Kastélli** quarter, spread across a low hill above the inner harbour. This was the acropolis of ancient Kydonia, and **excavations** along Kaneváro Street revealed a complex of Middle Minoan buildings, most with two storeys, flagstoned floors and grand entrances onto narrow streets. The presence of nearly 100 Linear B tablets suggests the proximity of a palace; a large deposit of Linear A tablets was unearthed on nearby Katre Street. Kastélli took the brunt of the Luftwaffe bombs, but you can still pick out the odd Venetian architectural detail, especially along Kaneváro and Lithínon Streets. On the top of Ag. Markoú you can see the ruins of the Venetian cathedral, S. Maria degli Miracoli. Below, overlooking the inner harbour, rise seven of the original 17 vaulted shipyards of the **Venetian Arsenal** (1600).

Just east of Kastélli is **Splántza**, or the Turkish quarter. Some interesting churches are concentrated here, such as the underground **Ag. Iríni** from the 15th century, in Roúgia Square (Odós Kallinikou Sarpani). South in Vourdouba Street, near an enormous plane tree, the early 14th-century **Ag. Nikólaos** was a Dominican church, converted by the Turks into an imperial mosque to shelter a magical healing sword which the Imam would hold up while leading the Friday prayers. Note the *tugra*, or Sultan's stylized thumbprint, on the entrance and the minaret (and campanile); if it's open, pop in to see the coffered ceiling and the sword. The little **Mosque of Ahmet Aga** still stands in Hadzimichali Daliáni Street, while to the east 16th-century **Ag. Anargyri**, in Koumi Street, was long the only church in Chaniá allowed to hold Orthodox services during the Venetian and Turkish occupations.

Chaniá's Newer Quarters and Beaches

From the covered market, Odós Tzanakáki leads southeast to the shady **Public Gardens**, with a small zoo (your chance to see a *kri-kri*) and outdoor cinema, often showing films in English. On the corner of Tzanakáki and Sfakianáki, the **War Museum** (*open Tues–Sat 9–1*) chronicles the islanders' remarkable battle history, with photos and weapons, while a villa just south houses the **Historical Archives of Crete** (*open weekdays only 9–1*), 20 Sfakianáki, containing Greece's second largest archive, dating from the Venetian occupation to the liberation of Crete in 1944. Most of it will be incomprehensible if you don't read Greek. In Platía Venizélos stands the house (and statue) of Venizélos, the government palace built for Prince George (now the court-house), and a Russian Orthodox church donated by the mother of a former governor. Further east, by the sea, is the fancy **Chalepa** quarter, dotted with 19th-century neoclassical mansions and ex-consulates from Crete's years of autonomy.

The town beach, **Néa Chorá**, is a 15-minute walk west from the harbour, beyond the Fírkas tower. Although sandy, shallow and safe for children, it's not very attractive. The beaches improve as you go west; city buses from Plateía 1866 go as far as lovely sandy **Oasis beach** and **Kalamáki**. The strip is well developed, with good swimming and windsurfing, cafés and tavernas. There are other, less crowded beaches along the way, but prepare for a long walk.

Shopping

Chaniá certainly has no lack of shops. Among those selling handmade necklaces, bracelets and earrings based on traditional Greek designs are **Antoniou**, 22 Kondiláki; classy **Metamorphosis**, 50 Theokotópolou; **Eolos**, 7 Chalídon Street (with beautiful creations in lapis lazuli); and **Imeros**, 6 Zambéliou. Leather rules on Odós Skridlóf, and there are several traditional knifemakers along Sífaka, among them **Apostolos Pachtikos** at No.14, who also deals in mountain-goat horns and battered Nazi helmets. **Top Hanas**, 3 Angélou in the Old Town, is a red lair of traditional Cretan weavings and blankets. For books or newspapers in English, the big international shop in Plateía Sindrivani has the biggest choice; for books new or old, tapes and CDs, try **Apogio**, 80 Hatzimicháli Giannári. If it's handmade dolls and puppets you see, explore **Bizzarro**, 19 Zambéliou.

Chaniá's hotels have more character than any others in Crete, although be aware that some of the most picturesque places installed around the Venetian port can be noisy.

luxury

The fanciest hotels in Chaniá are out east in the Chalepa quarter, among them the former German consulate, **Villa Andromeda**, 150 El. Venizélou, ✆ 28 300, @ 28 303 (*B*), now divided into eight air-conditioned suites; a lush garden, Turkish bath and swimming pool are some of the amenities. In the Old Town, **Casa Delfino**, 9 Theofanous, ✆ 87 400, @ 96 500, *casadel@cha.forthnet.gr* (*B*), is a classy conversion of a 17th-century town house; suites feature data ports for fax/modem link-up as well as Jacuzzis.

expensive

The **Halepa**, 164 El. Venizélou, ✆ 28 440, @ 28 439 (*B*), housed Andromeda's British counterparts and, renovated in 1990, now offers 49 fully air-conditioned rooms in a quiet palm garden. Stylish **Hotel Doma** is nearby at No.124, ✆ 51 772, @ 41 578 (*B*), in a neoclassical mansion. The more modest **Contessa**, 15 Theofánous, ✆ 98 566, @ 98 565 (*A*), has the intimate air of an old-fashioned guesthouse, furnished in traditional style; book well in advance. A similar warning prevails for **El Greco**, 49 Theotokopoúlou, ✆ 90 432, @ 91 829, *hotel@elgreco.gr* (*B*), offering modern rooms in an old building on Chaniá's prettiest street. **Nostos**, Zambelíou 46, ✆ 94 743, @ 94 740 (*B*), is a smaller refurbished Venetian house on a quiet, flowery lane; many rooms have views.

moderate

Thereza, 8 Angélou, ✆/@ 92 798, offers charming rooms and studios oozing with character, and a tempting roof terrace in another restored Venetian house. For those seeking divine inspiration, **Palazzo**, 54 Theotokopoulou, ✆ 93 227, @ 93 229 (*A*), is the place, with each room named after a god. By the beach, **Faliro**, 36 Dodeckanissou, ✆/@ 41 904 (*C*), is only 300m from the centre and offers good-value doubles, breakfast, a roof garden and off-season discounts.

inexpensive

Chaniá's vast selection of pensions and inexpensive rooms are mostly located within a few blocks of the Venetian or inner harbour. The pick of the bunch are: **Stella**, 10 Angélou, ✆ 73 756, whose airy, traditional rooms (cheaper at the back) share a fridge, and perch above the eponymous boutique selling psychedelic hand-blown glass; **Meltemi**, 2 Angélou, ✆ 92 802, above the mellow Meltemi café, with space to swing several cats in the bigger rooms, some of which have lovely views across the port to the White Mountains, shared by **Maria's** next door, ✆ 51 052; and **Konaki**, 43 Kondiláki, ✆ 70 859, with eight rooms in a quirky house being tastefully renovated— the two ground-floor ones have private bathrooms and open on to the banana palm garden. **Kydonia**, 20 Chalídon, ✆ 74 650, has well-designed doubles, triples and quads in a quiet courtyard next to the archaeological museum. **Monastiri**, set in the ruined cloister of a Venetian church at 18 Ag. Markoú, ✆ 54 776 (*E*), has some rooms with views. There are two campsites near the beaches, though you'll need a bus to reach them: **Camping Ag. Marína**, ✆ 68 596, 8km west of the town and open throughout the season (buses from the bus station), and the more basic **Camping Chaniá**, ✆ 31 138, at Ag. Apóstoli, 5km west of town (city bus from Platéia 1866).

Chaniá ✆ (0821–)   Eating Out

It's hard not to find a restaurant in Chaniá—the harbour is one great crescent of tavernas and pizzerias. **Dino's**, overlooking the inner harbour on Aktí Enóseos and Sarpidóna, ✆ 41 865, is a long-time reliable favourite (*5,000dr*); **Aeriko**, a bit further away on Aktí Miaoúli, ✆ 59 307 is also good and considerably cheaper, with some seafood on the menu and chicken on a spit. **Tholos**, 36 Ag. Déka, ✆ 46 725, serves excellent food in the picturesque ruins of a Venetian town house (*5,000dr*). **Monastiri**, behind the Mosque of the Janissaries, serves fresh fish, traditional Cretan dishes and barrelled wine in the same price range and is well frequented by ex-prime ministers and the like. Other places serving Cretan specialities include **Ela**, 47 Kondiláki, ✆ 74 128, and **Konaki**, just opposite. **Apovrado**, Isódon Street, ✆ 58 151, serves a number of Chaniot specialities, including the local wine and country sausages. In the courtyard of a Venetian building dating from 1290, **Mirovolos**, 19 Zambelíou, features ample well-prepared dishes and Cretan dancing, not to mention the live Greek music. If you're after veggie fare, try **Ekstra**, 8 Zambelíou, ✆ 75 725, run by German ladies, an unpressurised place for the sole female traveller. Grab a taxi to Néa Chóra for excellent seafood at excellent prices at **Akrogiali**, ✆ 73 110. In the evening Chaniots like to head 7km east, up to Korakiés on the Akrotíri peninsula, to **Nikterida**, ✆ 64 215, one of the best tavernas in Crete, open since 1938, with music and dancing on Saturday nights; book in advance (*closed Sun*).

Entertainment and Nightlife

Chaniá is delightful after dark, just for strolling and watching the passing pageant. In the inner harbour, have a look at Chaniot post-modern design at **Trilogy**, 16a Radamánthous, by the northeast bastion. The inner courtyard of **Ideon Andron**, 26 Chalídon, is a mellow place playing classical or jazz records, while **Synagogi** is an atmospheric bar adjacent to the old synagogue. Around Salpidonos and the outer harbour, **Four Seasons** and **Street** are popular, while **Dhyo Lux** is a café to be seen in. For a more distinctly Cretan experience, try **Tsikoudadiko**, 31 Zambelioú, for *tsikoudi* and *mezédes*. **Fortetza**, by the lighthouse, has its own shuttle boat.

Chaniá loves its music. The hole-in-the-wall **Kriti**, at 22 Kallergón, is something of a local institution, where from 9pm on you can hear Cretan music for the price of a drink. **Plateia**, in the old harbour, frequently offers blues and other live music; similar plus jazz happens at **Fedra**, 7 Isóderon, ✆ 40 789. Chaniots decorate the cafés in Koum Kapi area, along Akti Miaouli and wend their way to **Owl** and **Nimfes** in Akrotíri. Alternatively, in Agia, 7km southwest of Chaniá, you can bop happily at **Vareladiko** or **Chaniá by Night**, a giant venue along the road to Herákleon which sometimes hosts big-name Greek performers. Clubbers head out to Plataniás' **Privilege**, **Splendid** and **O Mylos** discos, and the newish **Diogenis**, ✆ 60 360, with fountains and lovely views.

Plataniás also has a summer **cinema**.

Nomós Chaniá

Crete's westernmost province, *nomós* Chaniá, is the land of the White Mountains, which hit the sky at 2,451m at Mount Pachnés and are sliced down the middle by one of Crete's five-star attractions, the Gorge of Samariá, the classic day-walk that emerges by the Libyan Sea.

The Coast West of Chaniá

Not a single hotel along this sandy stretch of coast and fertile plain existed when a rain of white parachutes fell on 20 May 1941. 'Out of the sky the winged devils of Hitler were falling everywhere,' wrote George Psychoundákis in *The Cretan Runner*. Few signs of the battle remain, although 2km west of Chaniá stands the monument of the diving eagle, known locally as the **Kakó Poulí**, or 'Bad Bird', the German memorial to the 2nd Parachute Regiment.

Getting Around

By bus: at least hourly from Chaniá bus station to all the resorts as far as the Maleme Beach hotel; roughly every hour they continue to Kastélli-Kíssamou. There are also early-morning connections from the resorts to the Gorge of Samariá.

Festivals

Ag. Marína **17 July**. Kolimbári **15 August** and **29 August**—pilgrimage to the chapel of St John the Hermit. Tavronítis **14 September**.

Chaniá to Cape Spáda

Just beyond the reach of Chaniá's city bus lines, the beach strip of **Káto Stálos** merges with that of **Ag. Marína**, an old town with a smattering of Venetian and Turkish houses and a vast tourist sprawl. It looks out over the islet of **Ag. Theódori**, a refuge for the wild Cretan ibex, the *kri-kri*. The vast gaping mouth of its cave originally belonged to a sea monster which was bearing down on Ag. Marína with an appetite as big as all Crete when Zeus spotted the threat to his home island and petrified the monster with a thunderbolt. Just west, **Plataniás** has two faces: an old village above and a resort annexe by the sandy beach and cane forest, planted to protect the orange groves from the wind. The Battle of Crete began further west at **Máleme**; there's a large and extraordinarily moving German war cemetery as a grim reminder, simply set amongst olive groves near the Maleme Beach hotel.

At the foot of rugged Cape Spáda, just before the road to Kastélli splits into old and new, **Kolimbári** (ΚΟΛΥΜΒΑΡΙ) has a beach of large smooth pebbles and, a short walk north, the most important monastery in western Crete. **Moní Goniás**, or Odigítrias (*open Sun–Fri 8–12.30 and 4–8, Sat 4–8*), was founded in 1618 by monks and hermits, who decided to club together and build a monastery fortress high over a sandy cove (or *goniás*, in Greek). The patriotic monks were often besieged by the Turks; a cannon ball fired in 1866 is still embedded in the seaward wall. The church contains a fine gilt iconostasis carved with dragons, a venerable *Last Judgement* painted on wood and a beautifully drawn St Nicholas, although the juju seems to be concentrated in an icon of the Virgin, covered with votive *tamata*, jewellery and a digital watch.

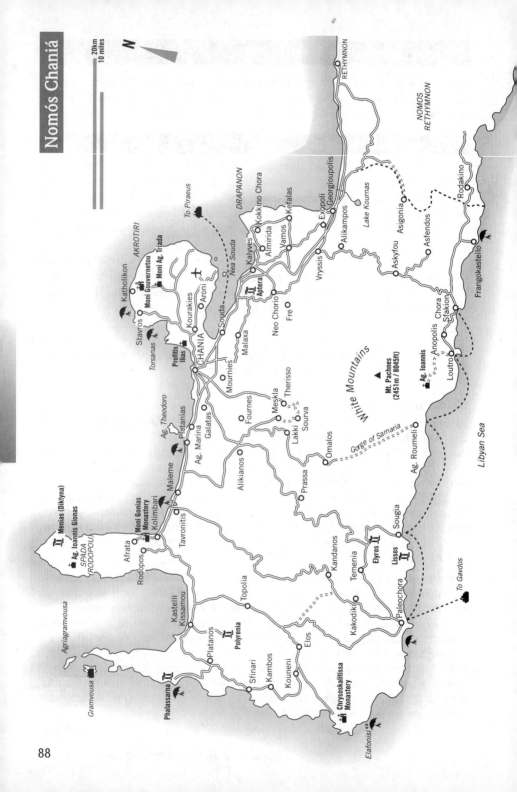

Nomós Chaniá

Beyond Moní Gonías, the road veers dizzyingly up and up the coast of Cape Spáda to **Afráta**, the last village accessible by car; from here you can follow the unpaved, treeless track north on foot or with a four-wheel-drive to **Diktyna**, in ancient times the most holy shrine in western Crete. Its little port, **Meniás**, is rocky, but the sea is transparent and caves offer shade. Diktyna's unexcavated shrine to Artemis dates back to the Minoans and had a popular following up to the end of the Roman Empire; enough remains to make it worth the scramble.

✆ (0821–)   *Where to Stay and Eating Out*

Ag. Marína ✉ 73100

German-run **Marina Sands**, ✆ 68 691, ✆ 68 694, *marinsands@hol.gr* (*exp*), is well laid out, with flowers surrounding the low-lying white buildings and a pool; rooms come with kitchen. **Santa Marina**, on the beach ✆ 68 460, ✆ 68 571 (*B; exp*), is somewhat bland but set in a garden with a pool, and often comes up with a room when the season is in full swing. Near the beach and at the Plataniás end of town, **Alexia Beach**, ✆ 68 110 (*C; inexp*), is small and attractive, with a pool and fridges in every room. **Angelika**, ✆ 68 642, has rooms with kitchen; **Villa Thodorou**, ✆ 60 665, ✆ 68 342, has rooms with fridges and balconies facing the sea; **Villa Margarita**, ✆ 68 581, has neither (*all inexp*). East in Káto Stalós, away from the noise of the main road, **Alector's Rooms**, ✆ 68 755, is immaculately run by Cretan-Californian Helen Zachariou (*mod–inexp*); take the lane up from the **Stavrodromi Restaurant**, ✆ 68 104, where the fried squid is delicious.

Plataniás ✉ 73014

Geraniotis Beach, ✆ 68 681, ✆ 68 683 (*B; exp*), is one of the more attractive of Plataniás' many hotels, set in lush green lawns on the edge of tourist town. **Kronos Apartments**, ✆ 68 630, ✆ 68574 (*C; exp*), is a well-kept, moderate-size complex of 53 units, with a pool near the sea. *Both open April–Oct.* In 1961 a 15th-century water mill on the west end of Plataniás was converted into the **Taverna Mylos**, ✆ 68 578, a lovely place under the tall trees (*5,000dr*). Up in Áno Plataniás, **Haroupia**, ✆ 68 603, not only enjoys lovely sunset views from its creeper-covered terrace but has delicious Cretan food.

Máleme ✉ 73014

The luxurious **Louis Creta Princess**, ✆ 62 221, ✆ 62 406, *maleme-beach@ cha.forthnet.gr* (*A; lux*), is shaped like a giant trident to give each of its 414 rooms a sea view. *Open April–Oct.* All the trimmings and more are also available at the more recent **Creta Paradise Beach**, in nearby Geráni, ✆ 61 315, ✆ 61 134, *cretpar@sail. vacation.forthnet.gr* (*A; lux*), which welcomes children. **Maleme Mare**, ✆ 62 121, ✆ 94 644 (*C; exp*), has more modest but uninspiring apartments by the beach with pool. Nearby, the tables of the **Maleme Taverna** are set on the grass by the beach.

Two Roads South of Chaniá: Venizélos and Citrus Villages

South of Chaniá, the 18km **Thérisson Gorge** is famous in Cretan history for the 1905 Revolution of Therisso, led by Venizélos in response to the reactionary policies of Prince George. Near the entrance to the gorge, you can stop off in large, sleepy **Mourniés**, birthplace of Venizélos, Greek prime minister most of the time between 1910 and 1932. Before he was born, his mother dreamed that he would liberate Crete and named him Elefthérios ('Freedom').

The best oranges in Crete grow in the Keríti valley south of Chaniá, on an estimated million trees. During the Battle of Crete, however, the lovely valley was known as Prison Valley after the big calaboose near **Alikianós**, just off the main Chaniá–Omalós road. A memorial honours the Cretans who kept on fighting here, cut off and unaware that the Allies elsewhere were in retreat; their ignorance enabled the majority of British and ANZAC troops to be safely evacuated from the Libyan coast. During the Occupation, prisoners were executed near the crossroads. The wedding massacre of Kantanoléo's Cretans took place at Alikianós' ruined Venetian tower; next to the tower, the little church of Ag. Geórgios (1243) has exceptional frescoes, painted in 1430 by Pávlos Provatás.

The Gorge of Samariá (ΦΑΡΑΓΓΙ ΣΑΜΑΡΙΑΣ)

The single most spectacular stretch of Crete is squeezed into the 18km Gorge of Samariá, the longest in Europe and the last refuge of much of the island's unique fauna and flora, especially rare chasm-loving plants known as *chasmopphytes*. Once a rather adventurous excursion, the walk is now offered by every tour operator; the gorge has been spruced up as a National Park and, in short, forget any private communion with Mother Nature. The walk takes most people between five and eight hours going down from Omalós south to Ag. Roúmeli on the Libyan Sea, and twice as long if they're Arnold Schwarzenegger or just plain crazy and walk up.

Not a few people return from Samariá having only seen their own feet and the back of the person in front. Staying in Ag. Roúmeli may be the answer; it will allow you more leisure to enjoy the beauty of the gorge and the rare flowers and herbs that infuse Samariá. Although the gorge is a refuge of the *kri-kri*, no-one ever sees them any more; the few that survived the 1993 epidemic of killer ticks, or *korpromantakes*, are shy of the hordes. Birds of prey (rare Griffon vultures, very rare Lammergeiers, buzzards and eagles) are bolder, and often circle high overhead.

Getting Around

Buses leave Chaniá for Omalós at 6.15, 7.30 and 8.30am and at 1.30pm; from Kastélli-Kíssamou at 6 and 7; and Réthymnon at 7. Others leave early from Plataniás, Ag. Marína, Tavronítis, Chandrís and Kolimbári. Organized **tour buses** leave almost as early (you can, however, get a slight jump on the crowds or at least more sleep by staying overnight at Omalós). Once through the gorge to Ag. Roúmeli, **boats** run all afternoon to Chóra Sfakíon, Soúgia and Paleochóra, where you can pick up a late-afternoon bus back to the north coast (5.30 and 7pm for Réthymnon). Consider paying the bit extra for a tour bus, especially in the summer, to make sure you have a seat on the return journey.

Practicalities

The gorge is open from 1 May to 31 Oct from 6am to 4pm, during which time the water is low enough to ensure safe fording of the streams and the staff of the National Forest Service patrols the area. Although last admission to the gorge is at 3pm, almost everyone starts much earlier, to avoid the midday heat and to make the *excursion a single day's round-trip outing. It is **absolutely essential** to wear good walking shoes and socks; a hat and a bite to eat are only slightly less vital, and binoculars a decided bonus for flower and bird observations. Dressing appropriately is difficult: it's usually chilly at Omalós and sizzling at Ag. Rouméli. Remove rings in case your hands swell. The fresh streams along the gorge provide good drinking water at regular intervals. Mules and a helicopter landing pad are on hand for emergency exits; tickets (1,200dr) are date-stamped and must be turned in at the lower gate, to make sure no-one is lost. If you haven't the energy to make the whole trek, you can at least sample Samariá by descending a mile or so into the gorge down the big wooden stair (the rub is you have to walk back up again). A less strenuous (and less rewarding) alternative, proposed by tourist agencies as 'the lazy way', is walking an hour or so up from Ag. Rouméli to the Sideróportes. For gorge information and walking conditions call © (0821) 67 179.*

Walking Down the Gorge

Just getting there is part of the fun. If you're on one of the early buses, dawn usually breaks in time for you to look over the most vertiginous section of the road as it climbs 1,200m to the pass before descending to the Omalós Plateau, 25 sq km and itself no shorty at 1,080m. In winter, snows from the fairy circle of White Mountain peaks flood this uncanny plateau so often that the one village, **Omalós** (OMAΛOΣ), is uninhabitable. The gorge **Tourist Pavilion** is a few kilometres south of Omalós. Some of the most spectacular views are from the pavilion, hanging over the edge of the chasm, overlooking the sheer limestone face of mighty 2,083m Mount Gýnglios, a favourite resort of Zeus when Olympos got on his nerves. If you come prepared and have some mountain experience under your belt, you can go up from here rather than down: a 90-minute trail from the pavilion leads up to the Greek Mountain Club's **Kallergi Shelter**, © (0821) 24 647 (book in high season), which sleeps 50.

Just after dawn, the first people of the day begin to trickle down the **Xylóskalo**, a zigzag stone path with a wooden railing and lookouts along the way. The name Samariá derives from Ossa Maria, a chapel (1379) and abandoned village halfway down the gorge, now used as the guardians' station and picnic ground. There are several other abandoned chapels along the way, traditional stone *mitáto* huts (used by shepherds for cheese-making) and, near the end, the famous **Sideróportes** ('iron gates'), the oft-photographed section of the gorge where the sheer walls rise almost 1,000ft on either side of a passage only 9ft wide.

At the southern end of the gorge stands old **Ag. Rouméli** (AΓ. POYMEΛI), abandoned after a torrent swept through in 1954. Recently, some of the empty houses have been recycled as stalls selling Greece's most expensive cold drinks. When tourists began to appear in the 1960s, a **new Ag. Rouméli** obligingly rose out of the cement mixer like a phoenix (toadstool is more apt), another blistering 2km away, on the coast—which makes it as enticing as a desert oasis to the weary and foot sore. This new Ag. Rouméli is built over ancient Tarra, where Apollo hid from the wrath of Zeus after slaying Python at Delphi. Here he fell so in love with a nymph that he forgot to make the sun rise and got into an even bigger jam with his dad. A sanctuary of Tarranean Apollo marked the spot, and on top of its foundations the Venetians built a church, **Panagías**. From Ag. Rouméli, caiques sail to Paleochóra, Chóra Sfakíon (p.000) and Soúgia. But if you linger and your feet don't hurt, the beach to aim for is **Ag. Pávlos**, a 90-minute walk away, with fresh springs and a lyrical 10th-century stone church.

Omalós ✉ 73005, ✆ (0821–)

> **Neos Omalos**, ✆ 67 590, 🖶 67 190 (*C; inexp*), is recently built, with centrally heated rooms, bar and restaurant. *Open year-round.* **To Exari**, ✆ 67 180, 🖶 67 124 (*C; inexp*), is a bit larger and almost as nice. **Drakoulaki**, ✆ 67 269, has simple and inexpensive rooms.

Ag. Roúmeli ✉ 73011, ✆ (0825–)

> Ag. Roúmeli has plenty of rooms, but prices are over the odds. There are several restaurant-pensions, such as **Aghia Roúmeli**, ✆ 91 241 (*C; inexp*). *Open Mar–Oct.* For something cheaper, try **Tara** taverna and rooms, ✆ 91 231, or **Lefka Ori**, ✆ 91 219.

East of Chaniá: Akrotíri (ΑΚΡΩΤΗΡΙ)

Akrotíri, the most bulbous and busiest of the three headlands that thrust out of Crete's northwest coast, wraps around to shelter the island's safest port, Soúda, from northerly winds. Its strategic position has assured it plenty of history, and now that Crete is safe from imminent invasion, the steep access road (Eleftheríou Venizélou) from Chaniá's Chalepa quarter is often chock-a-block with locals heading out to Akrotíri's beaches, nightclubs and seaside villas. Outside these suburban tentacles, Akrotíri is a moody place, dusty and junky with military zones towards the airport, lonely and wild around its famous monasteries.

First stop should be little **Profítis Ilías** church (4.5km from Chaniá), Crete's chief **memorial to Venizélos**, its favourite homegrown statesman. Elefthérios Venizélos (1864–1936) and his son Sophoklís (1896–1964) both asked to be buried here to enjoy superb posthumous views over Chaniá, but they had patriotic reasons as well: in the rebellion of 1897, Profítis Ilías was briefly the Revolutionary Military Camp of Akrotíri, located just within the Great Powers' 6km exclusion zone around Chaniá. To rout out the Greeks, the British, French, Italian and Russian navies bombarded it. In response, the Cretans raised the Greek flag. The admirals were so impressed by their courage as they stood there, holding up the flag with their bare hands even after it was shot off its pole, that they stopped bombing and applauded. Afterwards a Russian destroyed the monastery, but the Prophet Elijah (Ilías) got his revenge when the Russian ship was blown up the next day. News of the bombardment—that the Great Powers were bombing brave Christian Greeks—caused a stir in Europe and led the Allies to offer Crete its autonomy.

Akrotíri's first sandy seaside playgrounds are **Kalathás** (ΚΑΛΑΘΑΣ) and its nearby, quieter beach of **Torsanás**, rimmed with villas. **Stavrós** (ΣΤΑΥΡΟΣ), further north, is the end of the trail for buses from Chaniá and owes its growing popularity for longer stays to a lovely circular bay with shallow water; it was used for the beach scenes in the film *Zorba the Greek.* Above Stavrós sprawls the petrified body of one of Zeus' lovers, immortalised in stone by Hera, lying head-first in the deep blue sea. East of Stavrós, roads across the headland converge on the immaculate olive groves and tree-lined avenue that announce **Moní Ag. Triáda**, or Tzagaróliou (*open officially 6–2 and 5–7; adm*). The cruciform church has an austere, colonnaded Venetian façade, and in the narthex an inscription in Greek and Latin tells how Ag. Triáda was refounded in 1634 by Jeremiah Zangarola, a Venetian who became an Orthodox monk. Tangerine trees scent the courtyard and a museum contains a 17th-century *Last Judgement* among later icons and manuscripts.

A second and even older monastery, fortified **Moní Gouvernétou** (*open 8–12.30 and 4.30–7.30; adm*), stands on a remote plateau, 5km above Ag. Triáda along a narrow road that just squeezes through the wild rocky terrain. Gouvernétou played a major role in reconciling the Cretans and Venetians at the end of the 16th century; the grotesque sandstone heads on the portal, blasted by the sun and wind, are curious Venetian fancies far from home. Gouvernétou supplanted two older holy places—a shadeless but easy path from the car park leads in 10 minutes to the ruins of a hermitage by the cave named **Arkoudiótissa** ('Bear') after its striking bear-shaped stalagmite, worshipped since pre-Minoan times in the cult of Artemis, the Mistress of the Wild Animals. The stone bear leans over a cistern of water, filled by dripping stalactites; the low ceiling is blackened with millennia of candle-smoke. A walled-off corner in the cave contains a small 16th-century chapel dedicated to Panagía Arkoudiótissa, 'Our Lady of the Bear', who shares the same feast day as Artemis once did: 2 February (Candlemas).

From here the path continues down, a rough and steep 20 minutes or so, past hermits' huts and a sea rock shaped like a boat (a pirate ship petrified by the Panagía). The path ends with 150 steps carved in the rock, which leave you by the dark, complex **cave of St John the Hermit** (or Stranger), who sailed from Egypt to Crete on his mantle, founded a score of monasteries and retired here, becoming so stooped from his poor diet of roots and vegetables that a hunter shot him, mistaking him for an animal (7 October 1042—the anniversary still brings crowds of pilgrims here). In this wild ravine, St John founded the **Katholikón**, a church and buildings gouged into the living rock of the precipice, straddled by a stone bridge. Anchorites lived here until pirates in the 17th century made it too hot. A path descends to a rocky but delightful swimming nook, especially enjoyable when you contemplate the killer walk back.

Stavrós ✉ 73100, ✆ (0821–)   **Where to Stay and Eating Out**

Rea, back from the sea, ✆ 39 001, ✉ 39 541 (*B; exp*), is an air-conditioned complex offering everything from basketball and tennis to babysitting. *Open April–Oct.* Low-key **Zorba's Studio Flats**, by the beach, ✆ 52 525, ✉ 42 616 (*mod*), are also good for a family holiday, with a pool, tennis, garden, seaside taverna and a playground; the adjacent **Blue Beach** villa and apartments complex ✆ 39 404, ✉ 39 406, *vepe@cha.forthnet.gr* (*mod*), is even a tad nicer and oh so blue, with a pool, restaurant, bar and sea sports (*open April–Oct*). **Kavos Beach**, ✆ 68 623 (*inexp*), a bit further on, has some of the nicest rooms to rent. Between Zorba's and Blue Beach stands **Taverna Thanasis**, with a varied food and wine selection set against sea views.

Soúda and Ancient Aptera

Chaniá trickles scrubbily all along the road to **Soúda** (ΣΟΥΔΑ), the main port for western Crete, tucked into the magnificent sheltered bay (you can also drive down there from Akrotíri, through a military zone). Soúda will never win a beauty contest, in spite of its setting; its most prominent features include a Greek naval base behind yellow walls and a recently abandoned NATO base. The Venetians fortified the bay's islet, **Néa Soúda**, and when they and the Greeks who took refuge there finally surrendered to the Turks in 1715, it was only by way of a treaty, in spite of frequent attacks and a gruesome pyramid of 5,000 Christian heads piled around the walls by the Turks. Signs in Soúda point the way to the immaculate lawns of the seaside **Commonwealth War Cemetery**, where 1,497 English and ANZAC troops who perished in the Battle of Crete are buried, the majority of them too young to vote or lying anonymous under tombstones inscribed 'A soldier of the 1939–1945 War known unto God'. Two kilometres west of Soúda towards Chaniá, a road forks south for the 16th-century **Moní Chryssopigí** (*open 8–noon and 4–6*); the church and museum house an exceptional collection of icons from the 15th century on, and a superb cross decorated with gold filigree and precious stones.

The Turks had an excellent, if rather frustrating, view of the defiant islet of Néa Soúda from their fortress of **Idzeddin**, just east of Soúda on the promontory of Cape Kalámi. Now Chaniá's prison, Idzeddin was built of stone from the ancient **Aptera**, which was high on a plateau 8.5km east of Soúda, above **Megála Choráphia**. Aptera (*open 8.30–3, closed Mon*) was founded in the 11th century BC and remained one of the chief cities in western Crete until shattered by an earthquake in AD 700. Its mighty 4km walls have been compared to the great polygonal defences of Mycenaean Tiryns, and you can pick your way through the weeds to see classical temple foundations, a theatre and the skeleton of a Roman basilica. The Monastery of St John sits atop two magnificent, crumbling Roman cisterns the size of cathedrals. The city's name (*aptera*, or 'featherless') came from a singing contest held between the Muses and the Sirens. The Sirens were sore losers, and tore out their feathers and plunged into the sea, where they turned into the islets far below in Soúda Bay. Aptera also houses Maria Orfanoudaki's intriguing Laboratory of Peace, from where she paints and promotes peace and humanity.

Around Cape Drápanon

East of Aptera, the highway (and most of the buses) dives inland to avoid rugged Cape Drápanon, missing much lovely scenery: vineyards, olive groves and cypresses draped on rolling hills, and rocky fringes of maquis by the sea. A pair of resort towns dot the somewhat exposed north coast of Drápanon: **Kalýves**, with a long beach under the Apokoróna fortress, built by the Genoese when they tried to pinch Crete from the Venetians, and **Almirída**, smaller and more attractive, with a curved sandy beach, tiny harbour, and good windsurfing. From here, it's 4km to **Gavalochóri**, well worth a stop for its **Folklore Museum** (*open 10–1; adm*), where exhibits of old village life inspired a women's agrotourism co-operative to renew the local silk industry, in hibernation since the departure of the Turks. East of Almirída, the road begins to swing in from the rocky coast and continues up to picturesque **Pláka** and straggly **Kókkino Chóra**, the latter used for most of the village scenes in *Zorba the Greek*.

The best thing to do is circle around the cape, through **Drápanos** and **Kefalás**, sleepy villages reeking of past grandeur, with old stone villas, towers and gateways. The largest village, **Vámos** (ΒΑΜΟΣ), seems quite urban in comparison, its main street dark from the shade of trees, a Godsend on an August day. If you're headed towards Georgioúpolis from here, put off lunch until you reach **Exópoli**, where the tavernas enjoy a breathtaking view down to the sea.

✉ *73003,* ✆ *(0825–)*　　　　　　　　　　　　*Where to Stay and Eating Out*

Near Aptera

　　Megála Choráfia's blue and white **Taverna Aptera**, just under the archaeological site, is a good bet, but for more shade try **To Fangari**, in the centre of Stílos.

Kalýves/Almirída

　　In Kalýves, the seaside **Kalives Beach**, ✆ 31 285, 🖷 31 134 (*B; exp*), is the pick of the hotels; the travel agencies have lists of rooms and studios. Almirída has two rather stylish hotels, the **Almyrida**, 500m from the sea, ☎ 31 995 (*B; exp–mod*), with a pool, and the new **Dimitra Hotel**, ☎ 31 956 (*exp*), set back 100m from the water. There is a reasonable choice of tavernas, including **Dimitri's**, with good fresh fish.

Réthymnon (ΡΕΘΥΜΝΟ)

Delightful Réthymnon, Crete's third city (pop. 23,500), is the only one that 'weds the wave-washed sand', but for centuries the price it paid for its beach was the lack of a proper harbour. The Venetians dug a cute round one, but it keeps silting up. Not having a harbour may have proved a blessing, inhibiting the economy enough to spare Réthymnon much of what passes for progress. Like Chaniá, its Venetian and Turkish architecture has earned it landmark status, but Réthymnon escaped the attentions of the Luftwaffe. The fortress peering over its shoulder and its minarets lend the skyline an exotic touch; covered wooden balconies left over from the Turkish occupation project overhead, darkening the lanes. Its relative isolation attracted scholars who fled Constantinople, giving Réthymnon the reputation of the brain of Crete, confirmed by the recent construction of the University of Crete's faculties of the arts here.

Réthymnon ☎ (0831–)   ***Getting There and Around***

The new **bus** station is by the sea at the west end of town, between Igoum Gaviil and the Periferiaki, ☎ 22 785; those labelled 'El Greco/Skaleta' depart every 45min or so for the 10km stretch of hotels along the beaches east of town. **Olympic Airways** is at 5 Koumoundoúrou, ☎ 22 257.

Réthymnon ☎ (0831–)   ***Tourist Information***

EOT: along the town beach at E. Venizélou, ☎ 29 148 (*open Mon–Fri 8–2.30*).
Tourist police: next door, ☎ 28 156. Look for the free English-language *Creta-summer* paper, published monthly and full of things to do in and around town.
Ellotia Tours, at 161 Arkadiou, ☎ 24 533, ✉ 51 062, *elotia@ret.forthnet.gr*, are a particularly helpful and friendly agency, able to organize tickets, excursions, accommodation and car/bike rental.

Festivals

On **Wednesdays** Réthymnon hosts a big weekly market and fair off Odós Kanzantzáki. Look out for **Carnival** and **Midsummer's Day**, when there are bonfires. The Cretan **Wine Festival** and Handicrafts Exhibition is during the **last 10 days of July**, in the Public Gardens; there's also the Renaissance Festival for 20 days **in August and September**, with performances in the Venetian fortress: call ☎ 50 800, ✉ 29 879 for a list of events. The explosion at Moní Arkádi is commemorated **7–9 November**.

The Old Town

Although Réthymnon has been inhabited since Minoan times (the name, *Rithymna*, is pre-Greek), the oldest monuments in town are Venetian, beginning with the **Guóra Gate**, just below the Square of the Four Martyrs. Built in 1566 by the Venetian governor, the gate is the sole survivor of the city walls erected after the sackings by Barbarossa in 1538, and by Uluch Ali in 1562 and 1571. Before entering the gate, note the 17th-century Porta Grande or **Valide**

Sultana mosque, dedicated to the Sultan's mother; the Sultana's cemetery was converted after 1923 into the **Municipal Garden**. Its cool, melancholy paths seem haunted by discreet slippered ghosts—except during the wine festival, when it overflows with imbibers reviving ancient Dionysian rites.

From the Guóra Gate, Ethnikís Antistásis leads past **San Francesco**, the friary where Crete's contribution to the papacy, Alexander V, began his career; when elected pontiff, he paid for its elaborate Corinthian portal. The building now belongs to the University of Crete. Further down the street is the quaint lion-headed **Rimondi Fountain**, built in 1629 by another Venetian governor at the junction of several streets, now packed with bars.

The fountain has been the heart of town since Venetian times, and all the finest buildings were close by. The **Nerandzes Mosque** on Manoúli Vernárdou retains a monumental portal from its days as the Venetian church of Santa Maria. On its conversion into a mosque in 1657, it was capped with three domes; today the city uses it as a concert hall. Its graceful rocket of a minaret was added in 1890. The handsome Venetian **Loggia** (1550s), nearby on Arkadíou, was a club where the nobility and landowners would meet and gamble; it now does duty as an exhibition hall and museum replica shop. Just northeast of here is Réthymnon's bijou **Venetian harbour**, lined with seafood restaurants and patrolled by black and white swans.

The Fortezza and Archaeology Museum

In ancient times, when Cretans were bitten by rabid dogs they would resort to the temple of Artemis Roccaéa on Réthymnon's acropolis, and take a cure of dog's liver or seahorse innards. All traces of this interesting cult were obliterated in the late 16th century, when the Venetians decided that Réthymnon had been sacked once too often and forced the local peasants to build the **Fortezza** over the temple (*open daily 9–4; adm*). It is one of the best-preserved Venetian castles in Greece, and one of the largest, with room for the entire population of Réthymnon and its environs; yet in 1645, after a bitter two-month siege, the defending garrison was forced to surrender it to the Turks. The church, converted into a mosque—an austere cube with a dome—is fairly well preserved, but the rest has been left in dishevelled abandon.

Near the entrance to the Fortezza, the **Archaeology Museum** is in the former Turkish prison houses (*open 8.30–3, closed Mon; adm*), beautifully rearranged and air-conditioned. The most dazzling pieces hail from the Late Minoan cemetery at Arméni: a boar-tooth helmet, bronze double axes, lovely delicate vases, fragile remains of a loop-decorated basket from 1200 BC, and *larnaxes* (sarcophogi), including one painted with a wild goat and bull chase and a hunter holding a dog on a leash. A coin collection covers most of the ancient cities of Crete. Nearby, at 28 Mesolongíou, the **Historical and Folk Art Museum** (*open 9–1, closed Sun; adm*) offers a delicious collection of costumes, photos, farm tools and pottery from ancient times to 40 years ago. Nearby, on Chimáras, the **Municipal Centre of Contemporary Art** (*open 10–2 and 5–8, closed Mon*) features often excellent exhibitions of Greek art from the last 200 years.

Réthymnon ✆ (0831–)   ***Sports and Activities***

If you'd love to cycle down Mt Ida or the White Mountains but not up, contact **Hellas Bike Travel**, 118 Machis Kritis, ✆ 53 328 or (094) 525 056. **The Happy Walker**, 56 Tombázi St, ✆/◉ 52 920, offers organized treks in the most scenic areas of western Crete. **Portobello**, in Arkadio and Petáki, is the local scuba diving centre, and offers lessons, while **Atlantis** diving centre, ✆ 71 002, operates from the

Grecotel. The cornball **Pirate Ship** and its sister **Popeye** make daily excursions from the Venetian harbour to Maráthi (a fishing village in eastern Akrotíri) and to Balí, © 51 643; nearby there's a place that hires out mini motorboats.

Réthymnon © (0831–)   *Shopping*

Réthymnon's narrow tourist bazaar, **Odós Soúliou**, is crammed with desirable arty stuff and crafts to take home. Gold and jewellery shops line Arkadíou; for ceramics or handmade jewellery, try the little shops such as **Talisman** or **The Olive Tree** along Theodóros Arabatzóglou. For English-language papers, as well as a vast selection of guides and literature about Crete, try **International Press**, 81 El. Venizélou.

Réthymnon ✉ 74100, © (0831–)   *Where to Stay*
luxury

The **Grecotel Creta Palace**, 4km east, © 55 181, @ 54 085 (*lux*), is the most lavish, with an indoor heated pool and two outdoor ones, tennis courts and lots of sports, especially for children, who even have their own campground. *Open Mar–Nov.* Grecotel also owns the plush **Rithymna Beach** in Ádele (7km), © 29 491, @ 71 668 (*L*), on a lovely beach and with similar facilities; book early.

expensive

In town, **Mythos Suites Hotel**, 12 Plateía Karaóli, © 53 917, @ 51 036 (*B*), has 10 desirable suites sleeping 2–5 people and furnished in a traditional style, in a 16th-century manor house; all are air-conditioned and there's a pool in the central patio. **Palazzo Rimondi**, 19 Xanthoudidou, © 51 289, @ 51 013 (*A*), is similar, containing 25 suites in a renovated mansion, built around a courtyard with a small pool. **Fortezza** is just under the castle walls at 16 Melissínou, © 55 551, @ 54 073 (*B*), and is a much more modest affair; all rooms have balconies, and there's a garden courtyard and pool.

moderate

Ideon, Plateía Plastíra, © 28 667, @ 28 670 (*B*), enjoys a fine spot overlooking the dock and has a small pool; reserve a room. **Leon**, 2 Váfe, © 26 197 (*C*), is a central charmer, done up in traditional Cretan style. *Open all year.* **Brascos**, at Ch. Daskaláki and Th. Moátsou, © 23 721, @ 23 725 (*B*), is slick and clean. *Open all year.*

inexpensive

For peace and quiet, **Zorbas Beach** at the east end of the beach, © 28 540, @ 51 044 (*C*), is reasonably priced; rooms come with private shower and WC. **Zania**, Pávlou Vlasátou (a block from the sea), © 28 169, has a handful of pleasant rooms in a traditional house. **Ralia Rooms**, at Salamnós and Athan. Niákou, © 50 163, are more atmospheric than most, with lots of wood. **Katerina**, next door, © 28 834, has three attractive studios in another traditional house, up a somewhat vertiginous spiral staircase. Friendly **Ellotia Tours**, 161 Arkadiou, © 51 062, runs the pine-clad **Sea Front** rooms next door; the room at the top benefits from a terrace. The **youth hostel**, 41 Tombázi, © 22 848, is friendly, clean and central; breakfast and cooking facilities are available. **Elizabeth** campsite, a few kilometres east of Réthymnon, © 28 694, is recommended (*C class*).

With its tiny fish restaurants, the Venetian harbour is the obvious place to dine in the evening, but expect to pay at least 5,000dr for the privilege. Scan the menus—some places offer lobster lunches for two for 8,000dr. Other popular places are along the Periferiakós, the road under the fortress. Restaurants along the beach and El. Venizelou tend to be mediocre, except for **Samaria**, ✆ 24 681, which, despite plastic pictures and '*ordeure*' on the menu, has the tastiest Greek cooking, with good *giovétsi* and lamb *kléftiko* (*around 4,000dr*). Near the fountain, Plateía Petiháki has another row of touristy tavernas: **Agrimio** serves all the old favourites and pizza. Traditional **Kyria Maria**, 2 minutes away in a small alley, is well worth a meal, while **Alana**, with its pretty courtyard in Salamínos Street (just the other side of the fountain), is a nice enough place to bring your parents, serves a good fish-based menu for 7,000dr for two and even has Internet access.

Set up on different levels in a garden, **Avli**, 22 Xanthoudo, ✆ 24 356, is one of the prettiest places to eat but can get busy with groups. Just the opposite, **Antonias Zoumas**, across from the bus station, doesn't look like much but on Sunday afternoons it's packed with locals jawing through a 4-hour lunch. Just under the Fortezza on Chimáras, **Taverna Castelvecchio**, ✆ 55 163, has a good Cretan atmosphere and plenty of fish dishes, including sole in champagne; rooms are also available.

Entertainment and Nightlife

T. N. Gounaki on Koronaíou St (near the church of the Mikrí Panagías) is a simple but fun place summed up by its own sign: 'Every day folk Cretan music with Gounakis Sons and their father gratis/free/for nothing and Cretan meal/dish/food/dinner thank you'. The slicker **Odysseus Club**, by the port at Ioul. Peticháki, specializes in bouzouki and Cretan music, again mostly for tourists. Upstairs from 220 Arkadíou, **Dimman Music Bar** attracts a young crowd. **Baja**, on Salaminos, is a popular hangout, with a Greek and international music mix; serious groovers head for **Fortezza** disco near the water.

Nomós Réthymnon

Crete's smallest province, the *nomós* of Réthymnon, is also the most mountainous, wedged in between the White Mountains to the west and Zeus' Mount Ida, or Psilorítis (2,452m), to the east. Over the past 10 years its north coast, fringed by a 12km sandy beach on either side of Réthymnon, has become a popular base for exploring Crete; the Minoan sites to the east and beaches to the west are all within reasonable striking distance.

Close to Réthymnon: Arkádi and the Prasanó Gorge

Four buses a day go to **Moní Arkádi** (*open daily 6am–8pm; adm*), Crete's holy shrine of freedom. Founded in the 11th century on the lonesome flanks of Psilorítis, the monastery was mostly rebuilt in the 17th century, although the lovely sun-ripened façade of the church, Crete's finest essay in Venetian Mannerism, dates from 1587. During this time Arkádi was a repository for ancient Greek manuscripts, spirited out of Constantinople, and the monks performed important work in copying the texts and disseminating them in Europe. Arkádi resembles a small fort, which is one reason why Koronéos, as the head of the Revolutionary

Committee of 1866, chose it for a base and a store for his powder magazine. When the Turks demanded that the abbot hand over the rebels, he refused; in response, a Turkish expeditionary force marched on Arkádi and, in terror, people from the surrounding villages took refuge inside the monastery walls. On 7 November 1866 the Turks attacked, and after a 2-day siege they breached the walls. Rather than surrender, Abbot Gabriel set fire to the powder magazines, blowing up 829 Turks and Greeks. Another 35 who had hidden in the Refectory were summarily massacred by the furious Turks. The suicidal explosion caused a furore in Europe, as Swinburne and Victor Hugo took up the cause of Cretan independence. The Gunpowder Room, where the blast left a gaping hole in the roof, may still be seen, and there's the **Historical Museum** (*adm*), containing the holey, holy banner and portraits of the heroes of 1866, the vestments of Abbot Gabriel, monkish embroideries and icons. An old windmill was made into an ossuary, displaying a stack of skulls with holes blasted through them.

Just east of Réthymnon is one of Crete's prettiest gorges, the **Prasanó**, formed by the Plataniás river, which courteously dries up between mid-June and mid-October so you can walk down the gorge (allow 4 to 5 hours, wear sturdy shoes and bring water). Take the early Amári bus as far as the first bend in the road after Prassés, where the track begins; walk past the sheepfold and bear to the left. Lined with plane trees, dates, olives, cypresses and rhododendrons, the gorge has three sets of narrow 'gates' where the walls climb up to 480ft. The track ends near **Misiriá**, where you can swim and catch a bus back the last 5km to Réthymnon.

Amári: The Western Slopes of Mount Ida

Wedged under Mount Ida, the ancient province of Amári is well known not only for its fighting spirit and resistance in the last war, but also for its lush charms, cherry orchards, olive groves and frescoed Byzantine churches. These valleys that time forgot are prime walking and touring territory. If you have to choose one route, the **east valley** is lovelier, a proper Cretan Brigadoon. From Ag. Fotiní, turn left for **Thrónos**, the heir of ancient Sybrito, a city destroyed by the Saracens in 824. The setting, especially Sybrito's acropolis, is superb, and in the centre of Thrónos, the mosaic carpet of a large basilica overflows from under the simple little church of the Panagía, containing exceptional frescoes (late 13th and early 15th centuries). Just south, medieval **Moní Asómati** has a pretty Venetian church and a fountain.

Back on the main route, the University of Crete is excavating a Minoan Proto-Palatial villa, a 5min walk from **Monastiráki**. After Chaniá and Réthymnon, Monastiráki is the most important site yet discovered in western Crete (and still off limits to visitors): it had abundant workshops and storage rooms, where the *pithoi* still contained grape pips. The villa burned in 1700 BC, the same time as Knossós. **Amári**, one-time capital of the province, is one of the loveliest villages in Crete, surrounded by enchanting views, especially from the Venetian tower. **Ag. Ánna**, isolated outside the village, has the oldest dated frescoes in Crete (1225).

Réthymnon to Herákleon: The Coastal Route

Between Réthymnon and Herákleon you can choose between the coast-skirting highway, with a few small resorts squeezed underneath; or the old roads winding over the northern slopes of Mount Ida. The highway passes Réthymnon's beach sprawl, and then, before the mountains block access to the sea, arrives at **Pánormos** (ΠΑΝΟΡΜΟΣ), a pretty place with a ruined 5th-century basilica and small beach at the mouth of the Milópotamos river, guarded by a Genoese

Nomós Réthymnon

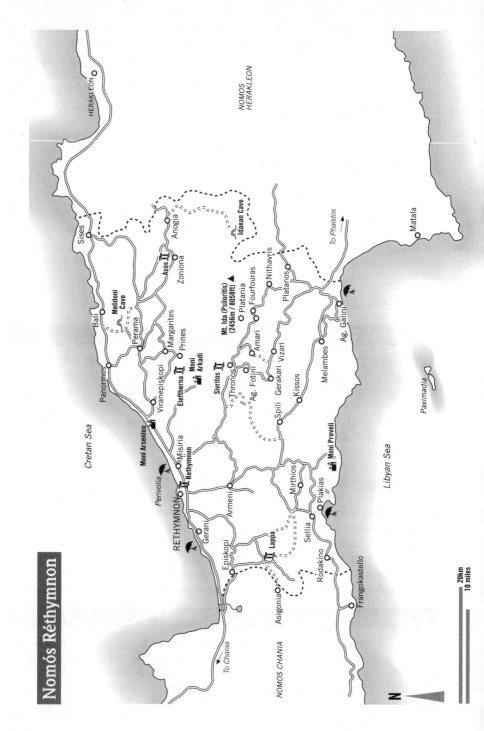

HERAKLEON

NOMOS
HERAKLEON

Sises

Bali

Melidoni
Cave

Panormos

Viranepiskopi

Perama

Prines

Margarites

Moni
Arkadi

Eleftherna II

Axos II

Anogia

Zoniona

Idaean Cave

Mt. Ida (Psiloritis)
(2456m / 8058ft) ▲

Platania

Fourfouras

Nithavris

Platanos

Sivritos II

Thronos

Ag. Fotini

Amari

Vizari

Gerakari

Spili

Kissos

Melambes

Ag. Galini

To Phaistos

Matala

Paximadia

Libyan Sea

Cretan Sea

Moni Arseniou

Misiria

Rethymnon

RETHYMNON

Perivolia

Gerani

Episkopi

Lappa II

Armeni

Mirthios

Moni Preveli

Plakias

Sellia

Rodakino

Asigonia

Frangokastello

To Chania

NOMOS CHANIA

N

20km
10 miles

fortress of 1206. Pánormos made its fortune in the last century as a specialist port for carob beans—once an essential ingredient in the manufacture of film.

Further east, **Balí** (ΜΠΑΛΙ), in part thanks to the exotic cachet of its name, has been transformed from a quiet steep-stepped fishing village overlooking a trio of lovely sandy coves to a jam-packed resort. On the hill over town, the lovely 17th-century **Monastery of Balí** is being restored; the Renaissance façade of the church and fountain are especially worth a look.

The **Old Road** between Pérama and Herákleon is pure rural Crete, where charcoal-burning is alive and well. Continuing east, **Fódele** (ΦΟΔΕΛΕ) lies between the Old and New Roads through solid orange groves. According to tradition, this sleepy village with its pretty Byzantine church of the Panagía (1383) was the birthplace in 1541 of Doménikos Theotokópoulos (El Greco), a tradition apparently confirmed by a plaque erected in his honour by the University of Toledo in 1934. Recently a '**House of El Greco**' has been set up, with a display about the master and his paintings. Although El Greco never returned to Crete after he sailed off in 1567 to make his career in Venice (where he studied with Titian and Tintoretto), Rome and Spain, he always signed his paintings with Greek letters, often followed by KRES, or CRETAN. East of Fódele, the highway continues to the junction for the attractive, upmarket resort of **Ag. Pelagía** (ΑΓ. ΠΕΛΑΓΙΑ), strewn like chunks of coconut over the headland and protected sandy beach that marks the outer gate of the Bay of Herákleon.

Réthymnon to Herákleon: Ancient Cities along the Inland Route

A choice of roads skirts the northern flanks of Psilorítis, and to see everything there is to see will involve backtracking. From Réthymnon, follow the coast as far as Stavroménos, where you can pick up the road for **Viranepiskopí**, with a 10th-century basilica near a sanctuary of Artemis, and a 16th-century Venetian church. Higher up, 7km south, colourful **Margarítes** is home to a thriving pottery industry (they even make huge *pithoi*) and two frescoed churches, 14th-century **Ag. Demétrius** and 12th-century **Ag. Ioánnis**, with a stone iconostasis.

Another 4km south, **Eléftherna** (ΕΛΕΥΘΕΡΝΑ) is just below the ancient city of the same name, founded by the Dorians in the 8th century BC. The setting, above two tributaries of the Milopótamos river, is spectacular; mighty walls and a formidable tower, rebuilt in Hellenistic times, kept out most foes. Historian Dio Cassius wrote that the Romans under Metellus Creticus were only able to capture Eleutherna after the tower was soaked in vinegar (!). Near here is a section of the aqueduct carved into the stone, which leads to two massive Roman cisterns capable of holding 10,000 cubic metres of water. At the bottom of the glade there's a well-preserved bridge, with Mycenaean-style corbelled stone arches.

Even higher and more precipitous, **Axós**, 30km east along the mountain road, was founded around 1100 BC by Minoans seeking refuge from the Dorians. Axós was the only town on Crete to have a king of its own into the 7th century BC, and it continued to thrive well into the Byzantine period, when it counted 46 churches; today 11 survive, of which Ag. Iríni, with frescoes, is the most important. The scattered remains of ancient Axós reveal a huge town. The acropolis is scattered on terraces below its 8th-century BC walls; arrange to go with Antonia Koutantou, ✆ (0834) 61 311, who runs one of the shops and has the key to the churches.

On the road to the east of Axós, a splendid panorama of all the hill towns of the Milopótamo opens up. Just below the first one, **Zonianá**, the **cave of Sendóni** contains one of Crete's most striking collections of stalactites, cave draperies and petrified waves.

Anógia and the Idean Cave

The next village east is **Anógia** (ΑΝΩΓΕΙΑ), to which the inhabitants of Axós moved in the Middle Ages. A stalwart resistance centre, it was burned by both the Turks and the Germans, the latter in reprisal for hiding the kidnapped General Kriepe, when all the men in the village were rounded up and shot. Today rebuilt in an upper, modern town and lower, more traditional-looking town, Anógia is not without charm, and lives off its weavings; brace yourself for a mugging by little old ladies (including a few surviving widows of the martyrs).

Just east of Anógia begins the paved, 26km road south to the **Idaean Cave** (ΙΔΑΙΟ ΑΝΤΡΟ), 1,540m. Back in Archaic times, the Idean Cave took over the Diktean Cave's thunder, so to speak, in claiming to be the birthplace of Zeus. Ancient even to the ancients, the Idaean cult preserved remnants of Minoan religion into classical times, presided over by Idaean Dactyls, or 'finger men'. According to his 5th-century BC biographer, Pythagoras was initiated by the Dactyls into the Orphic mysteries of midnight Zagreus (i.e. Zeus fused with the mystic role of Dionysos), a cult that was believed to be the origin of his mystical theories on numbers and vegetarianism. Since 1982 Ioánnis and Éfi Sakellarákis' excavations have produced roomfuls of votive offerings from 3000 BC to the 5th century AD; at the time of writing the cave is off limits. A ski resort has opened nearby, and there's a marked track from the cave to the summit of **Psilorítis**, Crete's highest peak (2,456m), about 7 hours' round trip if you're experienced and equipped. The Greek Mountaineering Federation operates a pair of shelters: at Prinos (1,100m, © (081) 227 609, sleeps 45), and at Toubotos Prinos (1,500m, © (0831) 23 666, sleeps 28).

From Anógia, the road continues east to **Goniés**, a village set in an amphitheatre at the entrance to the Malevízi, which produced Malmsey, a favourite sweet wine in medieval Venice and England, famous for filling the butt in which the Duke of Clarence drowned, allegedly a dastardly deed of his brother Richard III. Near here, at **Sklavokámbos**, a Minoan villa went up in flames so intense that its limestone walls were baked as if in a kiln; its ruins are right next to the road.

The Minoan Villas of Týlisos

Much more remains to be seen further east at **Týlisos** (ΤΥΛΙΣΟΣ), surrounded by mountains and swathed in olives and vineyards, where three large Minoan villas (*open daily, 8.30–3; adm*) were unearthed between 1902 and 1913. Built in the prosperous New Palace period and destroyed *c.* 1450 BC, the villas stood two or even three storeys high and contained small apartments and extensive storage facilities; palatial elements such as light-wells, lustral basins, colonnaded courts and cult shrines are produced here in miniature.

The Minoan love of twisting little corridors is further complicated here by the fact that the Dorians founded a town re-using many of the walls. Rectangular Villa B, nearest the entrance, is the oldest and least preserved; Villas A and C are extremely well built of finely dressed stone: door jambs, stairs, pillars and the drainage system survive. The presence of these elaborate villas in Týlisos and Sklavokámbos suggests that the Minoan nobility liked to take a few weeks off in the country, but the fact that they stand along the Knossós–Idean Cave road may be the true key to their purpose.

Hustling, bustling Herákleon is Crete's capital and Greece's fourth city, with a population of 120,000—the kind of place that most people go on holiday to escape. But Herákleon boasts two unmissable attractions: a museum containing the world's greatest collection of Minoan art, and the grand palace of Knossós in its suburbs.

Herákleon has gone through several name changes. It began modestly as Katsamba, the smaller of Knossós' two ports, and took on its current name in the classical period. In the 800s the Saracens saw the potential of the site and built their chief town here, naming it Kandak ('the moats') after the trench they dug around its walls. By the time it was reconquered by Nikephóros Phokás, Kandak was the leading slave market in the Mediterranean. The Venetians made Kandak into Candia, or Candy, and kept it as the capital of Crete; the mighty walls they built around it so impressed the Cretans that they called it Megálo Kástro, the 'Big Castle'. The Turks kept it their seat of government until 1850, when they transferred it to Chaniá. When Crete became autonomous, the classical name, Herákleon, was revived and it took back its capital role in 1971.

Excursions from Herákleon

1 Speed to picturesque Réthymnon along the fast sea road; after a leisurely look at the town, drive back to Herákleon along the scenic inland route, passing through colourful villages and past the ruins of Eléftherna and Axós and the striking Minoan villas of Týlisos. If time permits, stop off for a walk in the luscious Prasanó Gorge just east of Réthymnon, or make the detour to the venerated Moní Arkádi Monastery.

2 Head south through Veneráto, housing the pretty Palianí convent, towards lovely Zarós, for a delicious trout lunch; then slump on the beach at Mátala or head straight to stunningly situated Phaistós and nearby Ag Triáda. Stop off at the scattered ruins of Gortis on the way back if you've time.

3 Continue south from Knossós to historic Archánes; nearby is the necropolis of Phourni with its spectacular *tholos* tombs. A couple of kilometres further on are the scenically situated villas of Vathýpetro, from which you can meander home.

4 Drive east to quaint, cosmopolitan Ag Nikólaos via the panoramic Lassíthi Plateau; stop off at the birthplace of Zeus, the haunting Diktean Cave. Another short detour leads to the substantial Doric ruins of Lato.

© *(081–)* **Getting There and Around**

By air: Herákleon airport, 4km east, © 245 644, is linked to the city by public bus (no.1), beginning at Pórta Chaníon and passing through the centre of town. A taxi costs 2,000dr. For Olympic information, call © 223 400 or 229 191. Aegean is at the airport, © 330 475, and Cronus is at 10 1821 Street, © 286 394.

By bus: Herákleon has a number of bus stations. Buses for Knossós and destinations east (including the Lassíthi Plateau) depart from the port station outside the walls, just east of the Venetian port, © 245 017. The station for points west—Réthymnon and Chaniá—is across the street, © 221 765. From west of the Pórta Chaníon, buses head

southwest to Ag. Galíni, Górtyn, Phaistós, Mátala, Týlisos,
Anógia and Milapótamos, ✆ 255
965. From Plateía Kíprou buses
go to Áno Viános, Mýrtos and
Thrapsanó. Buses for Archánes
depart from Plateía Venizélou.

By car: there are no end of car
rental agencies liberally scattered
along 25 Ávgoustou and Doukos
Bofor; rates are reasonable, but be
prepared to haggle. Alfa Rent a Car,
✆ 243 885, ✉ 244 966, next to Hotel Kris, run
by the welcoming and helpful Seliniotakis
brothers, is recommended (especially their endless
supply of coffee and philosophical debate).

✆ *(081–)*   ***Tourist Information***

EOT: 1 Xanthoudídou St, across from the archaeology
museum, ✆ 228 225, ✉ 226 020 (*open Mon–Fri 8–2.30*).
Tourist police: 10 Dikeosínis St, ✆ 283 190. **British Vice
Consulate**: 16 Papalandroú St, ✆ 224 012.

Hospitals: Panelisteimiako, ✆ 269 111; Venizélou, ✆ 237 502. **First
Aid Centre**: ✆ 22 222.

Left Luggage: In the east and southwest bus stations (open until 8pm), and at
48 Odós 25 Ávgoustou, ✆ 281 750 (*open 7am–11pm*).

Internet: Istos Cybercafé, ✆ 222 120, is near the Archaeological Museum, at 2
Malikouti; further west, Netc@fé, ✆ 229 569, is at 4 1821 Street.

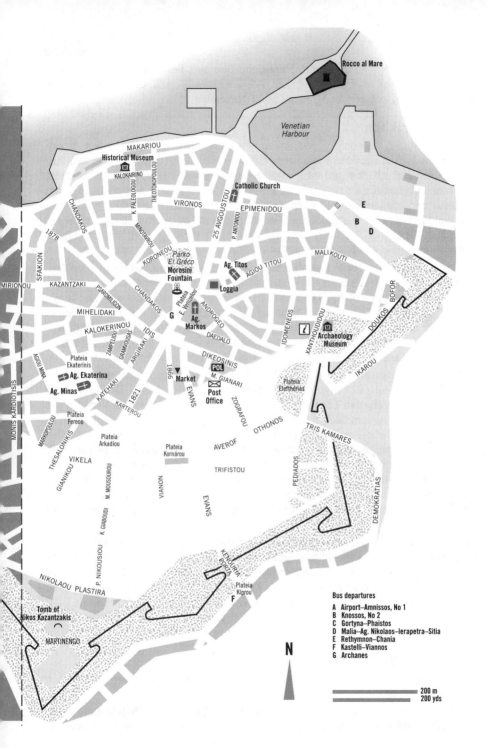

Rocco al Mare

Venetian Harbour

MAKARIOU

Historical Museum
Ⓜ KALOKAIRINO

CHANDAKOS

1878

SFAKION

MIRIONOU

KAZANTZAKI

MIHELIDAKI

KALOKERINOU

PSAROMILIGON

IDIS

ZAMPELIOU

GRAMBOUSSA

ARGIRAKI

K. PALEOLOGOU

THEOTOKOPOULOU

MINOTAVROU

KORONEOU

CHANDAKOS

VIRONOS

25 AVGOUSTOU

P. ANTONIOU

Catholic Church

EPIMENIDOU

E

B

D

Parko El Gréco
Morosini Fountain

Ag. Titos

AGIOU TITOU

MALIKOUTI

Plateia E. Venizelou

Loggia

ANDROGEO

G

Ag. Markos

DAEDALO

DIKEOSINIS

Plateia Ekaterinis

Ag. Ekaterina

Ag. Minas

KATEHAKI

1821

KARTEROU

1866

Market

M. GIANARI

Post Office

ZOGRAFOU

OTHONOS

IDOMENEOS

XANTHOUDIDOU

ⓘ

Ⓜ **Archaeology Museum**

DOUKOS

BOFOR

IKAROU

Plateia Eleuthérias

TRIS KAMARES

MONIS KARDIOTISIS

MARKOPOULOU

THESALONIKIS

GIANIKOU

VIKELA

P. NIKOUSIOU

K. GIABOUDI

M. MOUSOUROU

Plateia Fereou

Plateia Arkadíou

Plateia Kornárou

VIANON

AVEROF

TRIFISTOU

EVANS

PEDIADOS

DEMOKRATIAS

NIKOLAOU PLASTIRA

KENOURIA PORTA

Plateia Kiprou

F

Tomb of Nikos Kazantzakis

MARTINENGO

N

Bus departures

A Airport–Amnissos, No 1
B Knossos, No 2
C Gortyna–Phaistos
D Malia–Ag. Nikolaos–Ierapetra–Sitia
E Rethymnon–Chania
F Kastelli–Viannos
G Archanes

200 m
200 yds

Herákleon flower festival **2–6 June**. **Herákleon Summer Festival** brings in big-league theatre, ballet, opera and traditional music, ✆ 242 977, ✉ 227 180. Grape festival **11–19 September**. Huge *panegýri* for Ag. Minás on **11 November**.

Venetian Herákleon

When Crete won its autonomy in 1898, Arthur Evans, already a local hero for his news reports in Britain on Turkish atrocities, was instrumental in persuading the Cretans to safeguard their Venetian heritage, and it's a good thing he did because otherwise Herákleon would be a mess. The **Venetian Harbour**, a couple of hundred yards west of the modern ferry docks, still offers the best introduction to the city. Out on the harbour mole, the restored 16th-century fortress **Rocco al Mare** (or Koules) is guarded by a lion of St Mark and enjoys splendid views of the city (*open Tues–Sat 8.30–3, Sun 10–3; adm*). The **Arsenali**, or shipyards, recall Venetian seamanship and superior facilities at sea that supplied Herákleon during the great 21-year siege.

The main street up from the Venetian Harbour, **Odós 25 Avgoustou**, has always been lined with the sort of businesses it supports today: shipping agents, car rental outlets and banks. Halfway up, the church of **Ag. Títos** owes its cubic form to the Turks, who used it as a mosque and rebuilt it after several earthquakes. The chapel to the left of the narthex houses the island's most precious relic, the head of St Titus, a favourite disciple of St Paul, who converted the island to Christianity. When forced to give up Crete, the Venetians made off with Titus' skull and only returned it when the Pope Paul IV forced them to, in 1966.

It takes a bit of imagination to reconstruct, but the Venetians designed what is now **Plateía Venizélou**, at the top of 25 Avgoustou, as a miniature Piazza San Marco. Herákleon's City Hall occupies the **Venetian Loggia** (1628), built as a meeting place for the Venetian and Cretan nobility. It was completely reconstructed after taking a direct hit in the Battle of Crete. **San Marco** (Ag. Márkos), the first Venetian church on Crete (1239), was twice rebuilt after earthquakes, stripped of its lofty campanile and converted into a mosque by the Turks; it's now used as an exhibition centre. Water dribbles from the mouths of the lions of the **Morosini Fountain**, commissioned in 1626 by governor Francesco Morosini, who brought water in from Mount Júktas to replace the old wells and cisterns. Although the fountain is minus its figure of Neptune, the sea nymphs, mermen, dolphins and bulls are some of the finest Venetian work left on Crete.

South of Plateía Venizélou, the city's busy **outdoor market** runs along Odós 1866, a permanent display of Crete's extraordinary fecundity. Several stalls sell dried Cretan wedding cakes—golden wreaths decorated with scrolls and rosettes. Similar forays into the Baroque await at the south end of the market in Plateía Kornárou, in the carvings adorning the **Bembo Fountain** (1588), which was put together by the Venetians from ancient fragments; the Turks added the charming kiosk-fountain, or **Koúbes**, now converted into a café, and the Cretans added the sculptures of Erotókritos and Arethoúsa, the heroes of their national epic poem.

The Archaeology Museum

✆ 226 092. Open 8–7, Mon noon–7; adm exp, free Sun. If you get overwhelmed (or hungry) you can go out and return with your date-stamped ticket.

A few blocks east of Plateía Venizélou, on the north side of hemicyclical **Plateía Eleftherías**, is the **Archaeology Museum**, an ungainly coffer that holds the finest art of the Minoan civilization. Thanks to Cretan archaeologist Joseph Hadzidákis, a law was passed in the early days of Crete's autonomy which stated that every important antiquity found on the island belongs to the museum. The result is dazzling, delightful and entirely too much to digest in one visit. The collection is arranged in chronological order. In **Room I**, containing Neolithic (from 5000 BC) and Pre-Palatial periods (2600–2000 BC), the craftsmanship that would characterize Minoan civilization proper is already apparent in the delicate golden leaf pendants, the polished stone ritual vessels, the bold, irregularly fired red and black Vasilikí pottery and carved sealstones. Early Cycladic idols and Egyptian seals from the tombs of Mesara point to a precocious trade network. **Rooms II** and **III** are devoted to the Old Palace period (2000–1700 BC), when the Minoans made their first polychromatic Kamares-ware vases, marrying form and decoration with stylized motifs from the natural world. The virtuosity of Minoan potters 3500 years ago can be measured by their 'eggshell-ware' cups. One case displays the Knossós Town Mosaic: faïence plaques of miniature Minoan houses. The mysterious clay **Phaistós Disc** (c. 1700 BC) is the world's first example of moveable type: 45 different symbols, believed to be phonetic ideograms, are stamped on both sides in a spiral.

Items from the Minoans' Golden Age, the New Palace period (1700–1450 BC), are divided geographically in **Rooms IV–IX**. Potters turned to even freer, more naturalistic designs. Stone carving became ever more rarefied as the Minoans used porphyrys and semi-precious stones, cutting and polishing them to bring out their swirling grains. **Room IV** contains many of their masterpieces: a naturalistic bull's head rhyton carved in black steatite found in the Little Palace at Knossós, the leopard axe from Mália, and bare-breasted snake goddess statuettes from Knossós; the draughtsboard in ivory, rock crystal and blue glass paste; and the ivory bull leaper, the first known statue of a freely moving human figure, the muscles and tendons exquisitely carved. **Room V** contains finds from Knossós that just pre-date its destruction in 1450 BC. Note the model of a Minoan palace c. 1600 BC. Artefacts from cemeteries fill **Room VI**, where miniature sculptures offer hints about funerary practices, banquets and dances; an ivory *pyxis* shows a band of men hunting a bull. Goldwork reached its height in this period; see the Isopata ring, showing four ladies ecstatically dancing. The Mycenaeans are made to answer for the weapons—the boar-tusk helmets and 'gold-nailed swords' as described by Homer.

Items found in central Crete are displayed in **Room VII**. The show-stoppers here are the gold jewellery, particularly the exquisite pendant of two bees depositing a drop of honey in a comb from Mália, and the three steatite vessels from Ag. Triáda, decorated in low reliefs. The Harvesters' Vase shows a band of men with winnowing rods. On the 'Cup of the Chieftain', a young warrior reports to a long-haired chieftain. A rhyton has four zones of athletic scenes: boxing, wrestling and bull sports. The contents of **Room VIII** come from Zákros, the only large palace that escaped the ancient plunderers. The stone vases are superb, most notably a rock crystal amphora (it was in over 300 pieces when found) and a rhyton showing a scene of a Minoan peak sanctuary, with goats springing all around and birds presumably appearing as an epiphany of the goddess. **Room IX** has items from ordinary Minoan houses. The seal engravers achieved an astounding technique; suspicions that they had to use lenses to execute such tiny detail was confirmed when one made of rock crystal was found in Knossós.

After the Golden Age, the Post-Palace period artefacts in **Room X** (1450–1100 BC) show a coarsening and heavier Mycenaean influences. Figures lose their *joie de vivre*; the goddess are stiff, their flouncy skirts reduced to smooth bells, their arms invariably lifted, supplicating the fickle heavens. One goddess wears an opium poppy hat; Minoan use of opium and alcohol may possibly explain their apparent lack of aggression typical of other 'cradles of civilization'.

The Dorian invasion brought the artistic decline apparent in **Room XI** (1100–900 BC); the quality of the work is poor all round, whether made by pockets of unconquered Minoans or by the invaders. The pieces in **Room XII** show an improvement in the Mature Geometric and Orientalizing periods (900–650 BC). Familiar gods make an appearance: Zeus holding an eagle and thunderbolts on a pot lid, Hermes with sheep and goats on a bronze plaque. Orientalizing pottery shows the Eastern influences that dominated Greek civilization in the 8th–7th centuries. Griffons, sphinxes and lions are favourite motifs; one vase shows a pair of lovers, naturally presumed to be Theseus and Ariadne. At the foot of the stairs, **Room XIII** contains Minoan *larnaxes*, or terracotta sarcophagi. Minoans were laid out in a foetal position, so they are quite small. In the Old Palace days they were made of wood; the changeover to clay suggests the Minoans were over-exploiting their forests.

The Frescoes and Ag. Triáda Sarcophagus

Yet another art the Minoans excelled at was fresco, displayed upstairs in **Rooms XIV–XVI**. Almost as fascinating as the paintings themselves is the work that went into their reconstruction (sometimes based on only a fraction of the original) by the Swiss father-and-son team hired by Evans. Cretan artists followed Egyptian conventions in colour: women are white, men are red, monkeys are blue, a revelation that led to the re-restoration of *The Saffron Gatherers*, one of the oldest frescoes, originally restored as a boy and now reconstructed as a monkey picking crocuses after a similar subject was found on Santoríni.The first room contains the larger frescoes from the palace of Knossós, such as the nearly completely intact *Cup-Bearer* from the *Procession* fresco, which originally may have had 350 figures altogether. Here, too, are *The Dolphins*, *The Prince of the Lilies*, *The Shields*, and also the charming *Partridges* found in the 'Caravanserai', near Knossós. The 'miniature frescoes' in the other two rooms include the celebrated *Parisienne*, as she was dubbed by her discoverers in 1903, with her eye-paint, lipstick and 'sacral knot' jauntily tied at the back. Take a good look at the most famous fresco of them all, *The Bull Leapers* (or Toreador), which doubled as a calendar (*see* pp.111–12).

Occupying pride of place in the centre of the upper floor, the Ag. Triáda sarcophagus is the only one in stone ever found on Crete, but what really sets it apart is its elaborately painted layer of plaster. The subject is a Minoan ritual: a bull is sacrificed while a woman makes an offering on an altar next to a sacred tree with a bird in its branches, the epiphany of the goddess. On the other long side, two women bear buckets, perhaps of bull's blood, accompanied by a man in female dress, playing a lyre. On the right, three men are bearing animals and a model boat, which they offer to either a dead man, wrapped up like a mummy, or an idol (*xoanan*), as worshiped at Archánes. Near the sarcophagus is a wooden model of Knossós, and the entrance to the Giamalakis collection (**Room XVII**), containing unique items from all periods.

Downstairs, products of ancient Crete's last breath of artistic inspiration, the bold, severe and powerfully moulded 'Daedalic style' from the Archaic period (700–650 BC), are contained in **Rooms XVIII** and **XIX**. There is a striking frieze of warriors from a temple at Rizenia (modern Priniás) and lavish bronze shields and cymbals from the Idaean Cave. The bronze figures of Apollo, Artemis and Leto from Dreros are key works: the goddesses are reduced to anthropomorphic pillars, their arms glued to their sides, their hats, jewellery and flounced skirts as plain as a nun's habit. They could be a salt-and-pepper set. Yet the real anticlimax is reserved for **Room XX**, the classical Greek and Graeco-Roman periods (5th century BC–4th century AD), when Crete was reduced to an insignificant backwater.

Other Museums in Herákleon

The new **Battle of Crete and Resistance Museum** (𝄐 346 554; *open 9–1*) is just behind the archaeology museum, on the corner of Doukós Bófor and Hatjidáki Streets, with a collection of weapons, photos and uniforms. Across town, at 7 Kalokairinoú, the fascinating **Historical Museum of Crete** (𝄐 283 219; *open Mon–Fri 9–5, Sat 9–2, closed Sun and hols; adm exp*) picks up where the archaeology museum leaves off, with artefacts from Early Christian times. The basement contains delightful 18th-century Turkish frescoes of imaginary towns, pretty bits salvaged from Venetian churches, and a pleasing Venetian wall fountain made of tiny jutting ships' prows. On the ground floor are portraits of Cretan revolutionaries and their 'Freedom or Death' flag, and 14th-century murals in a chapel setting, from Kardoulianó Pediádos. Next door, in a little room all to itself, hangs the *Imaginary View of Mount Sinai and the Monastery of St Catherine* (*c.* 1576) by Doménikos Theotokópoulos (El Greco), his only known painting on Crete. It is also one of his few landscapes—in 16th-century Italy and Spain, where he spent the rest of his life, landscapes weren't very marketable. The first floor has photographs of Cretan *kapetános*, each more bristling than the last, a striking contrast with the reconstructed libraries of Níkos Kazantzákis and Emmanuél Tsouderós, once prime minister of Greece. Other rooms contain a sumptuous array of traditional arts, in particular intricate red embroideries and weavings, one of the most noteworthy artistic achievements by Ottoman Cretans.

The Cathedral and Byzantine Museum

West of Plateía Venizélou, and just south of Kalokairinoú, the overblown cathedral dedicated to Herákleon's patron **Ag. Miná** (1895) dwarfs its convivial predecessor. The interior is illuminated by an insanely over-decorated chandelier, the domes and vaults frescoed with stern and sad saints and a ferocious Pantocrator. Old Ag. Miná has a beautiful iconostasis and fine icons; that of Ag. Minas on his white horse has long been the protector of Herákleon (martyrologies claim that Minas was a 3rd-century Egyptian soldier, but you can't help wondering if his name might have had something to do with the devotion to him in this ancient port of Knossós).

Around the back, the sun-bleached **Ag. Ekateína** (1555) was in its day an important school linked to the Monastery of St Catherine in the Sinai. One subject taught here was icon-painting (El Greco studied here before leaving for Venice) and today the church, appropriately, holds a **Museum of Byzantine Icons** (𝄐 288 825; *open Mon–Sat 8.30–1.30, also Tues, Thurs and Fri 5–7; adm*). The pride of the museum is six icons by Mikális Damaskinós, the 16th-century contemporary of El Greco who also went to Venice but returned to Crete; the use of a gold background and Greek letters are the only Byzantine elements in his *Adoration of the Magi*; in his *Last Supper*, Damaskinós placed a Byzantine Jesus in a setting copied from an Italian engraving—a bizarre effect heightened by the fact that Christ seems to be holding a hamburger.

The Venetian Walls and the Tomb of Kazantzákis

Michele Sammicheli, the greatest military architect of the 16th century, designed Candia's walls so well that it took the Turks from 1648 to 1667 to breach them. From the beginning, the Venetians tried to rally Europe to the cause of defending Candia as the last Christian outpost in the East, but only received occasional, ineffectual aid from the French. Stalemate characterized the first 18 years of the siege; the sultan found it so frustrating that he banned the mention of Candia in his presence. In 1667 both sides, keen to end the stalemate, sent in their most brilliant generals, the Venetian Francesco Morosini (uncle of the Morosini who blew the top off the Parthenon) and the Turk Köprülü. The arrival of the latter outside the walls of Herákleon with 40,000 troops finally nudged the Europeans and the Holy Roman Emperor to action, but their fresh troops and supplies were too little, too late. Seeing that his men could only hold out a few more days, Morosini negotiated the city's surrender, and with 20 days of safe conduct sailed away with most of the Christian inhabitants (many ended up on the Ionian Islands) and the city's archives—an outcome that had cost the lives of 30,000 Christians and 137,000 Turks.

Brilliantly restored, Sammicheli's massive walls are nearly as vexing to get on top of today as they were for the besieging Turks—4km long, in places 13.5m thick, punctuated with 12 fort-like bastions. Tunnels been punched through the old gates, although the **Pórta Chaniá** (Chaniá Gate) at the end of Kalokairinoú preserves much of its original appearance. From Plastirá Street, a side street leads up to the Martinengo Bastion and the simple **tomb of Níkos Kazantzákis**, who died in 1957 and chose his own epitaph: 'I believe in nothing, I hope for nothing, I am free.' In the distance you can see the profile of Zeus in Mount Júktas (*see* p.118).

Knossós (ΚΝΩΣΟΣ)

Every 10 minutes a city bus (no.2) departs from Herákleon's main bus station for Knossós, with a stop in Plateía Venizélou. The site, © 231 940, is open daily except for important holidays, 8–7; adm exp. To avoid the crowds, arrive as the gate opens, or come late in the day.

The weird dream image has come down through the ages: Knossós, the House of the Double Axe, the Labyrinth of Minos. The bull dances, mysteries and archetypes evoke a mythopœic resonance that few places can equal. Thanks to Arthur Evans' imaginative reconstructions, rising up against the hill-girded plain, Knossós is now the most visited place in Greece after the Acropolis, with a million admissions a year. Evans' reconstructions are now themselves historical monuments, and the work you'll see on the site is reconstructions of reconstructions.

History

The first Neolithic houses on the hill next to the river Kairatos date from the 7th millennium BC, or earlier; few Neolithic sites in Europe lie so deeply embedded in the earth. In the 3rd millennium, a Minoan Pre-Palace settlement was built over the houses, and c. 1950 BC the first palace on Crete was erected on top. It collapsed in the earthquake of 1700 BC. A new, even grander palace, the Labyrinth, was built on its ruins. 'Labyrinth' derives from *labrys*, or 'Double Axe', a potent symbol that suggests the killing of both the victim and slayer; you'll see them etched in the pillars and walls throughout Knossós. In 1450 BC (give or take a century or two) Knossós was again destroyed, this time by fire but, unlike the other Minoan palaces, it was repaired once more, probably by Mycenaeans, and survived until at least 1380 BC. After a final destruction, the site of the Labyrinth was never built on again; it was considered cursed. Evans noted that the guardians he hired to watch the site heard ghosts moaning in the night.

In the Geometric era, a community near Knossós adopted the venerable name. By the 3rd century BC this new Knossós became Crete's second city after Górtyn and survived until the early Byzantine period. Meanwhile, the ruined palace was slowly buried, but not forgotten; unlike Troy and Mycenae, the site was always known. Cretans would go there to gather *galopetres*—'milkstones'—sealstones, which mothers prized as amulets to increase their milk.

The Labyrinth lay undisturbed until Schliemann's excavations of Troy and Mycenae electrified the world. In 1878, a merchant from Herákleon, appropriately named Mínos Kalokairinós, dug the first trenches into the palace of his namesake, at once finding walls, enormous *pithoi* and the first Linear B tablet. Schliemann heard the news, and in 1887 he negotiated the purchase of the Knossós site. However, the Turkish owners were impossible to deal with and the flamboyant, self-made German archaeologist gave up in despair; in 1890 he died.

The field thus cleared, Evans, then curator of the Ashmolean Museum in Oxford, arrived in Crete in 1894. A student of early forms of writing, he was fascinated by the sealstones and Linear B tablet shown him by Mínos Kalokairinós. With dogged persistence, he spent the next five years purchasing the property with the help of Cretan archaeologist Joseph Hadzadákis, while sending home reports of Turkish oppression. The purchase of Knossós coincided happily with Cretan independence, and in March 1900 Evans received permission to begin excavations in concert with the British School at Athens. Of the workmen hired, Evans insisted that half be Greek and half Turk as a symbol of co-operation for the newly independent Crete. Within the first three weeks the throne room had been excavated, along with fresco fragments and the first Linear A tablets, apparently belonging to a civilization that predated the Mycenaeans, which Evans labelled 'Minoan' for ever after.

In 1908, Evans used his considerable inheritance to embark on a project he had dreamed of from the beginning, to 'reconstitute' part of Minos' palace. Scholars dispute the wisdom and accuracy of these reconstructions, sniffing at them as if they were an archaeological Disneyland; they disagree perhaps even more on the purposes Evans assigned to the rooms of the palace, along with his interpretation of the Minoans as peaceful, flower-loving sophisticates. Evans' queen's bathroom, for instance, is another man's basin where dead bodies were pickled before mummification. No single conjecture seems to cover all the physical evidence, all the myths; the true meaning and use of Knossós may only lie in an epiphany of the imagination. The Cretans of 4,000 years ago saw a different world through different eyes.

The Bull in the Calendar

> *...there too is Knossos, a mighty city, where Minos was king for nine years, a familiar of mighty Zeus.*

Homer, The Odyssey, book XIX

 The so-called 'Toreador Fresco', found in the palace at Knossós, has become one of the most compelling icons of the lost world of ancient Crete. The slender, sensual, bare-breasted maidens who seem to be controlling the action are painted in white, the moon's colour, as in all Cretan frescoes, while the athlete vaulting through the bull's horns appears, like all males, in red, the colour of the sun. Mythology and archaeology begin to agree, and the roots of the story of Theseus, Ariadne and the Minotaur seem tantalizingly close at hand.

When you see this fresco in Herákleon's Archaeology Museum, take time to look at the decorative border—four striped bands and a row of multicoloured lunettes. Neither Arthur Evans nor any archaeologist since noticed anything unusual about it. A professor of English in Maine named Charles F. Herberger (*The Thread of Ariadne*, Philosophical Library, New York, 1972) was the first to discover that this border is in fact a complex

ritual calendar, the key to the myth of Theseus in the Labyrinth and to much else. The pairs of stripes on the tracks, alternately dark and light, for day and night, count on average 29 through each cycle of the five-coloured lunettes, representing the phases of the moon—this is the number of days in a lunar month. By counting all the stripes on the four tracks, Herberger found that each track gives roughly the number of days in a year; the whole, when doubled, totals exactly the number of days in an eight-year cycle of 99 lunar months, a period in which the solar and lunar years coincide—the marriage of the sun and moon.

To decipher the calendar, you can't simply count in circuits around the border; there are regular diagonal jumps to a new row, giving the course of the eight-year cycle the form of a rectangle with an 'x' in it. The box with the 'x' is intriguing, a motif in the art of the Cretans and other ancient peoples as far afield as the Urartians of eastern Anatolia. A Cretan seal shows a bull apparently diving into a crossed rectangle of this sort, while a human figure vaults through his horns. Similar in form is the most common and most enigmatic of all Cretan symbols, the double axe, or *labrys*. The form is echoed further in a number of Cretan signet-rings that show the x-shaped cross between the horns of a bull, or between what appear to be a pair of crescent moons.

The home of the *labrys*, the axe that cuts two ways, is the labyrinth. Arthur Evans believed the enormous, rambling palace of Knossós itself to be the labyrinth, a pile so confusing that even a Greek hero would have needed Ariadne's golden thread to find his way through it. In the childhood of archaeology, men could read myths so literally as to think there was a tangible labyrinth, and perhaps even a Minotaur. Now, it seems more likely that the labyrinth was the calendar itself, the twisting path that a Minos, a generic name for Cretan priest-kings, representing the sun, followed in his eight-year reign before his inevitable rendezvous with the great goddess. This meeting may originally have meant his death (in a bull mask perhaps) and replacement by another Theseus. Later it would have been simply a ceremony of remarriage to the priestess that stood in the transcendent goddess' place, celebrated by the bull-vaulting ritual. It has been claimed that the occasion was also accompanied by popular dancing, following the shape of the labyrinth, where the dancers proceeded in a line holding a cord— Ariadne's thread. Homer said 'nine years', and other sources give nine years as the period between each time that the Athenians had to send their captives to Crete to be devoured by the Minotaur—it's a common ancient confusion, really meaning 'until the ninth', in the way the French still call the interval of a week *huit jours*. Whatever this climax of the Cretan cycle was, it occurred with astronomical precision according to the calendar, and followed a rich, many-layered symbolism difficult for us scoffing moderns ever to comprehend.

That the Cretans had such a complex calendar should be no surprise—for a people that managed modern plumbing and three-storey apartment blocks, and still found time to rule the seas of the eastern Mediterranean. The real attraction lies not simply in the intricacies of the calendar (the Mesopotamians and many other peoples had equally interesting calendars), but more particularly in the scene in the middle, where the diagonals cross and where the ancient science translates into celebration, into dance. Cretan art speaks to everyone, with a colour, beauty and immediacy never before seen in art, and all too lacking in our own time. No other art of antiquity displays such an irresistible grace and joy, qualities which must have come from a profound appreciation of the beauties and rhythms of nature—the rhythms captured and framed in the ancient calendar.

The Site

Evans' reconstructions result from guesses as good as anyone else's and do succeed in his goal of making Knossós come alive for visitors, evoking the grandeur of a 1,500-room Minoan palace of *c.* 1700 BC that none of the unreconstructed sites can match; a visit here first will make Phaistós and Mália easier to understand. Tours go through so frequently that it's easy to overhear the explanations as you follow the maze.

Unlike most of their contemporaries in the Near East, the Minoans oriented their palaces to the west, not the east, and the modern entrance is still by way of the **West Court**. The three large pits were grain silos, originally protected by domes. A porch on the right from the West Court leads to the **Corridor of the Procession**, named after the fresco in the Herákleon museum, and the **Propylon**, or south entrance, with reproductions of original frescoes. A staircase from the Propylon leads to an upper floor, which Evans, inspired by Venetian palaces, called the '**Piano Nobile**'. Of all his reconstructions, this is considered the most fanciful. The **Tripartite Shrine**, with its three columns, is a typical feature of Minoan palaces, and may have been used to worship the Goddess in her three aspects of mistress of heaven, earth and the underworld.

A narrow staircase descends to the **Central Court**, measuring 190 by 95ft. Originally this was closed in by tall buildings, which may have provided safe seats to view the bull leaping (but how did they lead bulls in through the Labyrinth? How could they squeeze in all the action? It seems more likely that the Central Court would have been Homer's 'Ariadne's dancing floor'). The sacral horns that decorate the cornices and altars are the most universal Minoan symbol, and may have had multiple levels of meaning; in one Minoan picture, there's a bull with a double axe between its horns. Knossós was littered with sacral horns of all sizes (one pair, in fragments, was originally about 1m high). From the Central Court, enter the lower levels of the West Wing, site of the tiny **Throne Room**, where Evans uncovered a scallop-edged stone throne in the same place as it stood 3,800 years ago. Wear and tear has made it necessary to block off the room, so that you can no longer sit where Minos supposedly sat (although if you're a judge of the Court of International Justice in The Hague you may sit on a reproduction). On either side are gypsum benches and frescoes of griffons, the heraldic escorts of the goddess. The **Lustral Basin** in the Throne Room, like others throughout Knossós, may have held water used in rituals, or reflected light from light wells, or perhaps both. Evans found evidence here of what appeared to be a last-ditch effort to placate the gods as disaster swept through Knossós.

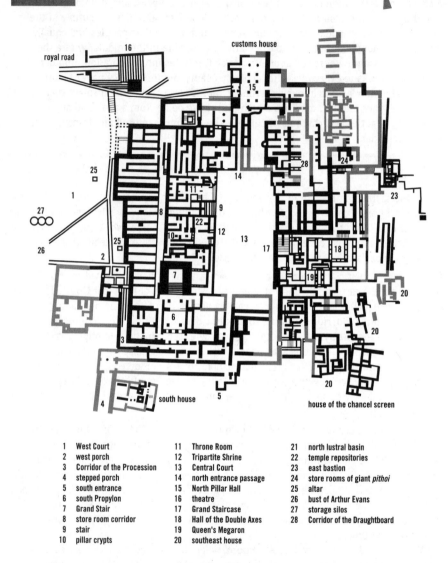

N

royal road

16

customs house

15

25

1

27

OOO

26

25

2

8

11

22

10

7

6

3

4

south house

5

14

9

12

13

17

28

24

23

18

19

20

20

20

house of the chancel screen

1	West Court	11	Throne Room	21	north lustral basin
2	west porch	12	Tripartite Shrine	22	temple repositories
3	Corridor of the Procession	13	Central Court	23	east bastion
4	stepped porch	14	north entrance passage	24	store rooms of giant *pithoi*
5	south entrance	15	North Pillar Hall	25	altar
6	south Propylon	16	theatre	26	bust of Arthur Evans
7	Grand Stair	17	Grand Staircase	27	storage silos
8	store room corridor	18	Hall of the Double Axes	28	Corridor of the Draughtboard
9	stair	19	Queen's Megaron		
10	pillar crypts	20	southeast house		

The stair south of the antechamber of the Throne Room ascends to an upper floor, used in part for storage, as in the **Room of the Tall *Pithos*** and the **Temple Repositories**, where the famous Snake Goddess statuette was found. The pillars thicken near the top, unique to Minoan architecture and distinctly similar to the trunk of the 'horizontal' cypress native to the Gorge of Samariá. Returning to the Central Court, note the high relief fresco copy of the '**Prince of the Lilies**' to the south, at the end of the Corridor of the Procession.

Evans, who grew up taking monarchies for granted, had no doubt that the more elaborate **East Wing** of the palace contained the 'Royal Apartments'. Here the **Grand Staircase** and **Central Light Well** are a dazzling architectural *tour de force*; almost five flights of broad gypsum steps are preserved. However, when you actually descend into the two lower floors (which were found intact) it is hard to imagine that anyone would choose to to be buried so deep, with little light and air; the near proximity of the 'Royal Workshops' would have made them noisy as well. The rooms did have something that modern royals couldn't live without: plumbing. The excellent water and sewer system is visible under the floor in the **Queen's Megaron** and its bathroom, complete with a flush toilet—an amenity that Versailles could scarcely manage. The King's Megaron, also known as the **Hall of the Double Axes**, due to the many carvings on the walls, opens on to the **Hall of the Royal Guard**, decorated with a copy of the fresco of cowhide figure-of-eight shields.

North of the royal apartments, the **Corridor of the Draughtboard** is where the game-board in the Herákleon Museum was found; here you can see the clay pipes from the Mount Júktas aqueduct. The **Magazines of Giant** *Pithoi* bring to mind the strange old myth of Minos' young son Glaukos. While wandering in the Labyrinth, the boy climbed up into a large *pithos* of honey to steal a taste, but fell in and drowned. The anxious father eventually located his body thanks to his prophet Polyidos. In grief, Minos locked Polyidos in a room with Glaukos' body and ordered him to bring the boy back to life. As Polyidos despaired, a snake came out of a hole in the wall. He killed it, and then watched in amazement as another snake appeared with a herb in its mouth, which it rubbed against its friend and brought it back to life. Polyidos tried the same on Glaukos and revived the boy, but Minos, rather than reward Polyidos, ordered him to teach Glaukos the art of prophecy. Polyidos had to obey, but as he sailed away from Crete, he told the boy to spit in his mouth, so that he forgot everything he had learned.

As you leave through the north, there's a relief copy of the bull fresco, and near this the so-called **Customs House**, supported by eight pillars, which may have been used for processing imports and exports. Below is the oldest paved road in Europe, the **Royal Road**, lined with various buildings and ending abruptly at the modern road; originally it continued to the Little Palace and beyond. The road ends at the so-called **Theatre** (it looks more like a large stairway), where 500 people could sit to view religious processions or dances, as pictured in the frescoes.

Around Knossós

Other Minoan buildings have been excavated outside the palace. Nearest to the palace are the reconstructed three-storey **South House**, complete with a bathroom and latrine, the **Southeast House**, and the **House of the Chancel Screen**, both believed to have been the residences of VIPs—the latter has a dais for a throne or altar. Other constructions require special permission to visit, such as the **Royal Villa**, with its throne and beautifully preserved Pillar Crypt. The **Little Palace**, just across the modern road, had three pillar crypts and was used after the Minoans as a shrine; the magnificent bull's head rhyton was found here.

To the south, a sign on the main road points the way to the **Caravanserai**, as Evans named it, believing weary travellers would pause here to wash the dust from their feet in the stone trough. The walls have a copy of the lovely partridge fresco. Further south are four pillars from the Minoan aqueduct that carried water over a stream, and south of that the unique **Royal Temple Tomb**, where the natural rock ceiling was painted blue and a stair leads up to a temple on top. One especially controversial find was Peter Warren's 1980 unearthing of the

House of the Sacrificed Children, named after a large cache of children's bones bearing the marks of knives, as if they had been carved up for supper. The Minoans, just having been found guilty of human sacrifice at Archánes (*see* pp.119–121), now had cannibalism to answer for. But it may be that that the children had already died and their bones were being stripped of any last flesh before re-burial—a custom that survived in parts of Greece into the 19th century.

Beaches around Herákleon

Herákleon is surrounded by sand, and you have a choice of backdrops for your beach idyll: a power plant, cement works and hotels at **Ammoudára** (ΑΜΜΟΥΔΑΡΑ), just west, frequently linked by bus no.6 from Hotel Astoria in Plateía Eleuthería; and to the east, the airport—from the same Hotel Astoria, bus no.7 crawls through the suburbs to the not exceptionally attractive city beach of **Kraterós** (7km) and beyond to **Amnisós** (ΑΜΝΙΣΟΣ), the first of the string of resorts east of Herákleon. It overlooks the islet of Día, a sanctuary for Crete's endangered ibexes, or *kri-kri,* who somehow have learned to cope with charter flights.

Amnisós has been a busy place since Neolithic times. A port of Knossós, it was from here that Idomeneus and his 90 ships sailed for Troy; here the ship of Odysseus, in the story he told Penelope, was long prevented from sailing by the north wind. The Minoans must have often encountered the same problem, and would get around it by loading and unloading at a south-facing port on Día islet. Minoan Amnisós had two harbours, on either side of a hard-scrabble hill, now topped by the ruins of a Venetian village. The east end is the fenced-off villa of 1600 BC that yielded the lovely *Fresco of the Lilies* in the Herákleon museum; on the northwest side is an Archaic sanctuary of Zeus Thenatas. In the 1930s, while excavating Amnisós' Minoan 'Harbour Master's Office', Spyridon Marinátos discovered a layer of pumice, the physical evidence he needed to support his theory that Minoan civilization had been devastated in its prime by ash flung from Santoríni's explosion.

One kilometre from Amnisós, up the road to Elia, is the **Cave of Eileithyia,** goddess of fertility and childbirth, daughter of Zeus and Hera and mother of Eros (ask at the Archaeological Service in the Archaeological Museum in Herákleon if you wish to visit). Few divinities enjoyed Eileithyia's staying power; her cave, which was also mentioned by Homer, attracted women from the Neolithic era to the 5th century AD. Stalagmites resembling a mother and her children were the main focus; pregnant women would rub their bellies against a third one, resembling a pregnant belly complete with a navel.

Herákleon ☏ (081–)   *Shopping*

The market along Odós 1866 is a good bet for edible and drinkable souvenirs and spices, as well as typical tourist claptrap. For Cretan wines, the **Kava Cellar,** 3 Daedálou, ☏ 243 506, is a touristy mine of bottles and information. Pedestrian-only Daedálou and its surroundings have most of the city's boutiques. **Cretaphone,** 6–10 Odós 1821, has a wide choice of Cretan music, as does **Aerákis,** Daedálou, which has honey and herbs too. For books in English, **Planet International** has a wide choice, at the corner of Kydonias and Chándakos; also try **Lexis,** on Platéia Kornárou, or **Astrakianakis,** on Platéia El. Venizélou.

Book in the summer. If you haven't, try the **Hotel Managers' Union**, Idomeneos and Malikoúti, ✆ 223 967, or the **Room Renters' Union**, 1 Gamaláki, ✆ 224 260.

luxury

Atlantis, near the archaeology museum at 2 Ighías, ✆ 229 103, ✉ 226 265, *atlantis@atl.grecotel.gr* (*A*), offers luxurious air-conditioned rooms (some with disabled access), a pool, satellite TV, roof garden, gym, hammam and a garage. Nearby, **Astoria Capsis Hotel**, Platía Eleftherias, ✆ 343 080, ✉ 229 078, *astoria@her.forthnet.gr* (*A*), is similarly priced and smart. West in Ammoudára, **Candia Maris**, ✆ 314 632, ✉ 250 669 (*L*), is the pricey business; there is even a thalassotherapy centre. **Agapi Beach**, ✆ 311 084, ✉ 258 731 (*A*), offers all the fancy beach accessories you could desire.

expensive

The **Galaxy**, just outside the walls to the southeast at 67 Demokratías, ✆ 238 812, ✉ 211 211 (*A*), offers contemporary serenity and full air-conditioning; ask for a room overlooking the pool. **Lato Hotel**, 15 Epimenídou, ✆ 228 103, ✉ 240 350, *lato@her.forthnet.gr*, has well-kitted-out, modern rooms with lovely sea views from the balconies. Then there are the resort hotels on the beaches: east in Amnisós, the **Minoa Palace**, ✆ 380 404, ✉ 380 422 (*A*), is a big, fancy beachside complex with a pool, floodlit tennis court, and activities and sports for all ages. The huge **Dophin Bay** in Ammoudára, ✆ 821 276, 821 312 (*A*), has similar facilities.

moderate

Many of these are conveniently located near the port and bus stations; among the best are: **Ilaira**, 1 Ariádnis, ✆ 227 103 (*C*), with traditionally decorated rooms with balcony, and a cafeteria roof terrace; and friendly **Kris**, 2 Doúkos Bófor, ✆ 223 221 (*C*), with its cheerful blue-and-red colour scheme and well-positioned rooms with fridge/sink. Plain and modern **Daedalos**, 15 Daedálou, ✆ 244 812, ✉ 224 391 (*C*), is convenient for the archaeological museum and centre, on a pedestrian-only street.

inexpensive

Lena, 10 Lahana, ✆ 223 280, ✉ 242 826 (*E*), has clean, simple rooms on a quiet street west of 25 Ávgoustou. **Rea**, 1 Kalimeráki, ✆ 223 638, ✉ 242 189 (*D*), is a good, quiet choice near the sea. **Atlas**, 6 Kandanoléontos, ✆ 288 989 (*E*), offers a touch of streamlined Art Deco on a noisy pedestrian-only street near the centre, although the rooms don't all live up to the promise of the exterior. *Open Apr–Oct.* The real **youth hostel** at 5 Víronos, ✆ 286 281, is well run and convenient, with usually a dorm bed to spare. The closest campsites are A-class **Creta**, at Chani Kokini, near Gournes, ✆ 41 400, and the smaller C-class **Chersónissos**, ✆ 22 902, both east of town.

Herákleon ✆ *(081–)* **Eating Out**

The fashionable set has created a car-free haven for themselves in the narrow streets between Daedálou and Ag. Títou; buildings have been restored and charming little restaurants and bars appeared on cue to fill them up; this is the young and hip place to be seen. One, **Loukoulous** on Koráli is an elegant Italian restaurant (*around 6,000dr; less for pizza*), and **Giovanni**, just opposite, offers a choice of fixed-price menus for two: fish, Greek or vegetarian. If you've a hankering for seafood, **Ippokampos** on the Sófokli Venizélou waterfront has the best, to go with its exquisite *mezés* (*6,000dr*).

The restaurants around the Morosini fountain tend to be rip-offs, but the tavernas jammed along the narrow Fotíou ('Dirty') Lane, between the market and Evans Street, all offer the Greek essentials and grills at moderate prices (*3,000–4,000dr*); **Ionia** on Evans claims to be the oldest taverna in town. **Kyriakos**, on Leof. Demokratías, is open all day and offers a wide choice. For a big night out, **La Tavola** in the Galaxy hotel (*see* above) prepares gourmet cuisine, but count on up to 9,000dr a head. Modest **Ta Psaria**, at the foot of 25 Avgoustou and with a view over the Rocco and the port, has the day's catch enticingly hooked up by your table. Other favourites outside the centre are the fish tavernas of Néa Alikarnassós just east; **Toumbrouk**, an excellent taverna in Katerós, east of Amnisós; **Chryssomenos** in Ag. Iríni, just after Knossós; or the typical tavernas of Rodiá, between Ammoudára and Ag. Pelagía.

Herákleon ⓒ (081–)   ***Entertainment and Nightlife***

When the Herákleoniots want to spend a night on the town, they often leave it in summer, when the clubs move out; the nightspots of Chersónisos and Ammoudára are especially popular (among the clubs, **Granazi** and **Edem** often have live music). In town, Doúkos Beaufort (aka Bófor) Street, above the main bus station, has a whole strip of trendy clubs, including a striptease joint and the **Kastro**, where you can hear Cretan music played nightly after 10pm by the island's best lýra maestros. There's live *rembétika* music at **I Palia Aigli**, at the end of Theríssou, ⓒ 252 600, or at the elegant **Café Veneto**, on Epimenídou, with an alluring roof terrace overlooking the port. There is a clutch of bars on Idomeneos Street (try **Blue Iguana** or **Xitzaz**). After that, if you're still full of beans, try **DNA** or **Fougaro**, both on Ikarou, in town. For quiet backgammon and drinks, head for the **Ideion Andron**.

Nomós Herákleon

This cradle between the Psilorítis range and the Diktean Mountain was the core of Minoan Crete: not only Knossós, but Mália, Phaistós, Archánes and Ag. Triáda, along with countless smaller sites are here. Besides the finest Cretan art and culture, the province also contains much of the worst—the hedonistic beach resorts along the lovely north coast, thrown up in the first flush of mass tourism in the 1960s, about which you often hear people say that what the Venetians, Turks and Germans couldn't conquer, money has undone without a fight.

South of Knossós: Archánes

One of the ancient proofs of Epimenides' paradox 'All Cretans are liars' was the fact that immortal Zeus was born on Crete, but buried here as well; the profile of his bearded face is easily discerned in Mount Júktas as you head south of Knossós. The road follows a main Minoan thoroughfare, and has seen some modern history as well: at the T-junction turn-off for

Archánes, Cretan Resistance fighters, led by Major Patrick Leigh Fermor and Captain W. Stanley Moss, kidnapped General Kreipe on 26 April 1944. His car was abandoned on Pánormos beach with a note saying that it was the work of English commandos and that any civilian reprisals would be against international law (*see* Captain Moss's *Ill Met by Moonlight*). But the Germans were (rightly) convinced that the General was still on Crete and launched a massive search for him.

Well-watered **Archánes** (ΑΡΧΑΝΕΣ) has often been called on to supply the north; the Minoan aqueduct to Knossós began here, as did the Venetian, ending in Morosini's fountain in Herákleon. Besides water, Archánes produces wine (Archánes and Armanti) and table grapes called *rozáki*. In the centre, the church of the **Panagía** has an exceptional collection of 16th–19th-century icons amassed by the parish priest (*open mornings*). Just south of town, the lovely church of the **Asómatos** is decorated with frescoes dated 1315: *The Battle of Jericho*, *The Sacrifice of Abraham* and the *Punishment of the Damned* are especially good.

From the 15th century on, visitors would come up to Archánes, intrigued by the story of Zeus' tomb, but the first hint that there was something more than stories here had to wait until the early 1900s, when an alabaster ladle inscribed with Linear A was found on the edge of town. In 1922 Evans surmised the existence of a 'summer palace' in Archánes. Then, in 1964, Ioánnis and Éfi Sakellarákis began excavating what was to become, after Zákros, the biggest Minoan discovery since the war. The **palace**, unfortunately for the archaeologists, is in the dead centre of town, on a site inhabited continuously since 2000 BC (the largest visible section lies between Mákri Sokáki and Ierolóchiton streets). Dating from the New Palace period (*c.* 1700–1450 BC), the walls are very thick, to support one or more storeys; only in Knossós and Phaistós were similar coloured marbles, gypsum and other luxury materials used. It had elaborate frescoes, a drainage system and a large cistern built over a spring. A 'theatrical area', with raised walkways forming the usual triangle, a small exedra, horns of consecration and an archive of Linear A tablets were also found.

In Minoan times, a paved road from the palace led to the **necropolis of Phourní** (*open daily 8.30–3, but it doesn't hurt to ring ahead, © (081) 751 907*), set atop a rocky ridge 1.5km to the southwest (a very steep walk up from the road; by car you can take the rural road up from Káto Archánes). This 5-acre site has proved to be one of the most important prehistoric cemeteries in the whole Aegean, in use for 1,250 years (2500–1250 BC). Most spectacular of all are the three *tholos* tombs, especially Tholos A, which was used as a hiding place in the Second World War. Debris filled the bottom floor, while below, tucked in a side chamber behind a false wall, lay a priestess or royal lady from the 14th century BC, buried in a gold-trimmed garment and surrounded by her grave offerings: gold and ivory jewellery, a footstool decorated with ivory and the remains of a sacrificed horse and bull, carved into ritualistic bits. The bottom layer of the collective burials in Tholos C goes back to 2500 BC and yielded marble Cycladic figurines and jewellery in the same style as the Treasure of Priam that Schliemann found at Troy. The Mycenaean grave enclosure with seven shaft tombs and three *stelae* is unique on Crete. Its libation pit, or *bothros*, was so saturated with offerings to the dead from thousands of years ago that when the Sakellarákis team found it they were overwhelmed by 'the unbearable stench'.

Five kilometres southwest of Archánes, above the town dump, on the windswept promontory of **Anemospiliá**, the Sakellarákises discovered an isolated **tripartite shrine** in 1979 (*same hours*). Often depicted in Minoan art, this was the first and, so far, the only one ever found. In

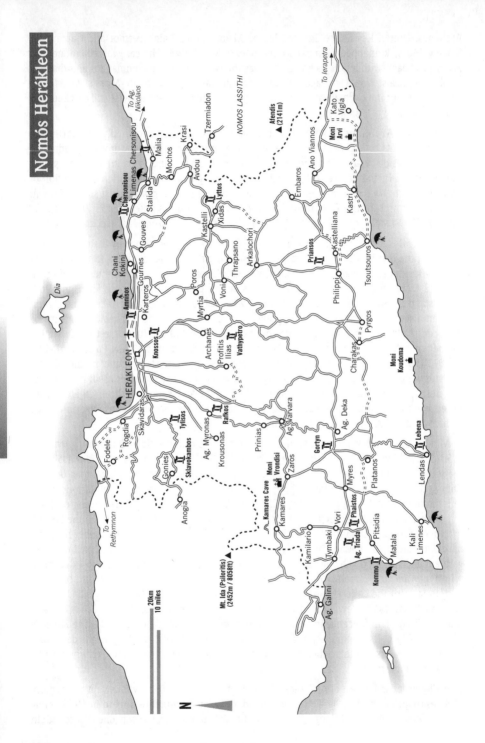

Dia

To Ag.
Nikolaos

NOMOS LASSITHI

To Ierapetra

Limenas Chersonisou
Chersonisou
Malia
Mochos
Krasi
Tzermiadon
Stalida
Avdou
Gouves
Kastelli
Lyttos
Xidas
Kato
Vigla
Afendis
(2141m)
Moni
Arvi
Ano Viannos
Embaros
Kastri
Chani
Kokini
Gournes
Poros
Voni
Thrapsano
Arkalochori
Kastelliana
Prianos
Philippi
Tsoutsouros
Amnisos
Karteros
Myrtia
HERAKLEON
Knossos
Archanes
Profitis
Ilias
Vathypetro
Pyrgos
Charakas
Moni
Koudoma
Skavidaras
Tylisos
Rafkos
Prinias
Ag. Varvara
Ag. Deka
Gortyn
Lebena
Rogdia
Fodele
Ag. Myronas
Krousonas
Zaros
Platanos
Lendas
Gonies
Skavokambos
Myres
To
Rethymnon
Anogia
Kamares Cave
Moni
Vrondisi
Kamares
Kamilario
Tymbaki
Vori
Phaistos
Pitsidia
Kali
Limenes
Ag. Triada
Matala
Mt. Ida (Psiloritis)
(2452m / 8058ft)
Kommo
Ag. Galini

20km
10 miles

N

the middle room was a pair of clay feet from a *xoanon,* or idol made from wood and other perishable materials worshipped in Greece since Neolithic times; Pausanius wrote that the Greeks believed they were first made by Daedalos on Crete. The eastern room was apparently used for bloodless sacrifices. The western room, however, produced one of the most startling finds in nearly a century of Minoan archaeology: it contained bodies of people caught in the sanctuary as the massive earthquake struck *c.* 1700 BC. The skeleton of a 17-year-old boy was found bound on an altar, next to a dagger; examination by the University of Manchester showed that the blood had been drained from his upper body, and that he had probably had his throat cut. The other skeletons belonged to a man wearing an iron ring and a woman who carried sickle cell anaemia: people of fine breeding, according to Manchester's palaeo-doctors. By a fourth skeleton, a precious Kamáres-ware vase was found; it may have been full of the boy's blood, perhaps an offering to appease their god, possibly Poseidon, the Earth-shaker.

The Anemospiliá findings came as a shock. The Minons evoked by Evans seemed too sophisticated for such barbarities, despite hints of human sacrifice in Cretan myth—there's the tribute of Athenian youths to the Minotaur, and an account tells how Epimenides went to Athens to deliver the city from a curse, which he did through human sacrifices. But such extreme acts were probably only resorted to in extraordinary situations, where the sacrifice of one is made in the hope of saving many, in this case from violent earth tremors. Even then, the practice was so disagreeable that it was not done in public, but hidden behind the doors of the shrine. A small, new archaeological museum (*same hours except Tues*) has an interesting collection of local finds.

Two kilometres south of Archánes, vines surround the villa complex of **Vathýpetro** (*same hours*), spectacularly set on a spur facing Mount Júktas. In plan it resembles a baby Knossós: it has a small west court and larger central court, a tripartite shrine, and a three-columned portico with a courtyard, closed off by a fancy, recessed structure of a type found nowhere else, supported by symmetrical square plinths. First built *c.* 1580 BC, the villa was shattered by an earthquake *c.* 1550. It seems to have been rebuilt as a craft centre; loom weights and potters' wheels were found, along with the oldest wine press in Greece: 3,500 years old. To this day, the vintners in the area repeat a ritual that may well be as old as Vathýpetro itself: every 6 August the first fruits of the harvest are ritually offered to the deity on the summit of **Mount Júktas.** A good road just before Vathýpetro leads up to the church where it all happens, the Christian replacement for the Minoan peak sanctuary of **Psilí Korfí** just to the north. This has yielded large quantities of votive gifts and bronze double axes. A young Poseidon was one of the gods worshipped here; the mountain was an important navigational landmark.

The broad road south of Vathýpetro continues to **Ag. Vasílios** and **Moní Spiliótissa,** a convent with a frescoed church built into a dim cave, hidden in a lush grove of plane trees; the spring water bubbling out of its foundations was known for its curative properties and was piped into Herákleon by the pashas. It's a pretty walk of a few hundred yards to the simple church of Ag. Ioánnis, with frescoes dated 1291, 'in the reign of Andronicus Palaeologue'. Just south, a white road to the west allows you to circle back behind Mount Júktas by way of **Kanlí Kastélli,** or the Bloody Fortress, built by Niképhoros Phókas in 961.

Myrtiá and Níkos Kazantzákis

Alternatively, and just as scenically, you could turn back east from Ag. Vasílios to Herákleon by way of Crete's most prestigious wine region, Pezá, and the village of **Myrtiá** (MYPTIA), set high on a ridge over a majestic sweeping landscape. If you're coming from Herákleon, the turn-off is just before the road to Archánes. Myrtiá has the **Kazantzákis Museum** (℗ 741 689, *open daily 9–1 and Mon, Wed, Sat and Sun 4–8, closed Thurs; adm*), in the house where Kazantzákis' father was born: photos, documents, dioramas and memorabilia evoke the life and travels of Crete's greatest novelist, the father of *Zorba the Greek*, who was inspired by a Macedonian miner and skirt-chaser named George Zorbas, with whom Kazantzákis operated a lignite mine in the Mani. Kazantzákis was 74 when he was nominated one last time for the Nobel Prize (the Church lobbied against him, and he lost by one vote to Albert Camus) and he died shortly after, in October 1957, from hepatitis contracted from a vaccination needle.

| ℗ (081–) | *Where to Stay and Eating Out* |

In Archánes, **Orestes Rent Rooms**, ℗ 751 619, are simple and just out of the centre; in the main square, **Myriofyto** offers light lunches under the trees. There are two other tavernas here, and another up at Myrtiá.

Southwest of Herákleon

The main road southwest of Herákleon to Górtyn, Phaistós and Mátala passes through dense vineyards. **Veneráto** offers the principal reason to stop, with a 2km detour to the serene convent of **Palianí**, home to 50 nuns. Besides early Christian capitals and 13th-century frescoes, Palianí has the venerable Holy Myrtle; the nuns claim there's an icon of the Virgin in the heart of the tree and use a pair of ancient capitals for the consecration of bread offerings every 23 September. To the south, the large, straggling village of **Ag. Varvára** stands amid cherry orchards at approximately the geographical centre of the big island, and in June shop fronts are festooned with garlands of delicious cherries; a chapel dedicated to the Prophet Elijah sits atop a large rock known as the '*omphalos*', or navel, of Crete. The weather here can be dramatic: at Mégali Vríssi, to the east, Crete's first 'Aeolian park' harnesses the cross-island winds with V-39 Vesta windmills, the biggest and strongest in Greece.

A lovely road west of Ag. Varvára skirts the groves and orchards on the southern flanks of Psilorítis. Nearly all the villages here began as Minoan farming communities, among them **Zarós** (ΖΑΡΟΣ), a famous local beauty spot and source of bottled mineral water. The Romans built an aqueduct from here to Górtyn so they wouldn't have to drink anything else. The **gorge of Zarós** is a good place to bring a picnic: the walk begins at the monastery of **Ag. Nikólaos**. Another monastery to the west, **Moní Vrondísi**, was burned by the Turks in 1821, but it still has a pretty gate and a charming 15th-century Venetian fountain, next to a massive plane tree. The tree's core, blasted hollow by a lightning bolt, houses the kitchen of the monastery's café. The 14th-century frescoes in the church are only a shadow of the treasures Vrondísi once had—in 1800, having had a premonition of its sacking, the abbot sent its finest works, by Michael Damáskinos, to Ag. Kateríni in Herákleon, where they remain. **Moní Valsamonérou**, 5km west, is reached by path from **Vorízia**, another village rebuilt after being obliterated by the Nazis (the guardian lives here, although he's usually at the church on weekday mornings). Once an important monastery, Valsamonérou is now reduced to an enchanting assymetrical church dedicated to Ag. Fanoúrios, in charge of heaven's lost and found; the exceptional 14th-century frescoes are by Konstantínos Ríkos.

The road continues to **Kamáres** (with tavernas and rooms), the base for the 3–4-hour walk up Mount Ida to the **Kamáres cave** (1,525m), an important Minoan cave sanctuary. Its gaping mouth, 66ft high and 130ft wide, is visible from Phaistós; pilgrims brought their offerings in the colourful pottery first discovered here—hence Kamares ware (*see* p.107).

Zarós ✉ *70002, ✆ (0892–)* **Where to Stay and Eating Out**

Idi Hotel, ✆ 31 301, 🍴 31 511 (*C; mod*), is one of the nicest mountain hotels on the island, with a verdant garden surrounding pools; its lovely views of the valley are shared by **Taverna Votomos**, ✆ 31 302, where fresh salmon and trout, served with delicious rice, hold pride of place on the menu (*4,500dr*).

The Mesará Plain and Górtyn (ΓΟΡΤΥΣ)

Górtyn is open daily 8–6; adm; ✆ (0892) 31 144. If you're arriving by bus, get off at the Górtyn entrance and make your way back towards the village of Ag. Déka.

Tucked under the southern flanks of Mount Ida, the long Mesará Plain is the breadbasket of Crete and one of its most densely populated areas since the days of the first Minoans. After the Dorian invasion, **Górtyn** (or Gortys) gradually supplanted Phaistós and later Knossós as the ruling city of Crete. Hannibal's brief sojourn here in 189 BC after his defeat by Rome may have given the inhabitants some insight into the Big Noise from Italy, because they helped the Romans capture Crete. In reward, Rome made Górtyn the capital not only of Crete but of their province of Cyrenaica, which included much of North Africa. In AD 828 the Saracens wiped it off the map.

In its prime, Górtyn counted 300,000 souls. Its ruins are enticingly scattered through a mile of olive groves—only the basilica and Odeon are fenced in. The apse is all that survives of the 6th-century **Basilica of Ag. Títos**, once one of the most important in Greece but now a roosting place for local birds. Titus, originally buried here, was one of Paul's favourite disciples and first bishop of Górtyn. Nearby, built into the walls of the elegant **Roman Odeon** (reconstructed by Trajan in AD 100), is Górtyn's prize, the **Law Code of Górtyn**, now covered by a shelter.

Human Rights, Dorian-style

The first block of engraved limestone, accidentally discovered in a mill stream in 1857, was purchased by the Louvre. It attracted a good deal of attention. At the time no-one had ever seen such an ancient Greek inscription, and it wasn't until 1878 that this first bit, dealing with adoption, was translated, using the writing on ancient coins as a study guide. No-one suspected that there was any more until one summer's day in 1884, when Halbherr, the Italian archaeologist, noticed a submerged building—the Odeon—while cooling his feet in the same mill stream, which was low because of a drought. The rest of the inscription, covering over 600 lines on 12 blocks, was found soon after in a farmer's field; only the tops of blocks X and XII and a piece of block IX are missing.

The code, written in *boustrophedon*, 'as the ox ploughs'—from left to right, then right to left—is in the Doric dialect of *c*. 500 BC. It is the longest such inscription to survive, and due to it the civil laws of Crete before the classical era are better known in their specific detail than Roman law. The code was made for public display, and significantly, in spite of the ancient Greek class system, which had a different set of rules for citizens, serfs (the native Minoans) and slaves, the Górtyn Code allows women property rights they've lacked in more recent laws (the Code Napoléon, for one); slaves had recourse against cruel masters, and there was a presumption of innocence until guilt is proven long before this became the core of Anglo-American law.

Just up and behind the Law Code is the rare and famous Cretan evergreen **Plane Tree of Górtyn**, by the Lethaios river. The story goes that it has kept its leaves for modesty's sake ever since Zeus in his bull costume brought the Phoenician princess Europa into its shade and had his evil way with her, resulting in the birth of Minos, Rhadamanthys and Sarpedon.

The rest of Górtyn is outside the enclosed area. If it's not too hot, consider climbing the **Acropolis**. Currently being excavated by the Italians, it has the remains of an 8th-century BC temple and sacrificial altar, Roman walls and a well-preserved defensive building, perhaps built at the expense of the **Theatre**, chewed away in the hillside below. A few minutes' walk down to **Mitrópolis** reveals an Early Byzantine church with a mosaic floor, cut in two by the modern road. Signs point to paths in the olive groves; the ground littered with broken tiles and the half-hearted fences make the ruins especially evocative, almost as if you were intruding into a 19th-century engraving. There's a small **Temple of Isis and Serapis**, the Egyptian gods popular in the late Empire, and the elaborate **Temple of Pythian Apollo**, the most important in Górtyn and often rebuilt since Archaic times; the inscription is another segment of Górtyn's law code, written in an even older dialect. Most imposing of all is the 2nd-century AD **Praetorium**, seat of the Roman governor; the building continued in use as a monastery until Venetian times. Part of the complex includes the **Nymphaeum**, where the waters from the Zarós aqueduct flowed into the city. Further south are the ruins of the gate, amphitheatre, stadium and cemetery, while the main path leads to the village **Ag. Déka**, named after 10 Christians martyred in *c.* AD 250. The block on which they were beheaded is kept in the church, and their tombs in the new chapel are the subject of much Cretan devotion.

Phaistós (ΦΑΙΣΤΟΣ)

Open daily 8–7; adm exp, free Sun; Ⓒ (0892) 42 315. Try to arrive early or late afternoon to avoid the crowds. A pavilion on the site has a café and food, and rooms, Ⓒ (0892) 42 360.

Superbly overlooking the Mesará plain and Psilorítis, Phaistós was one of the oldest cities in Crete, the fief of Minos' brother Rhadamanthys and the birthplace of the sage Epimenides. The first palace was constructed in the Old Palace period, around 2000 BC, and destroyed in an earthquake in 1700 BC; the second palace was built over the first and destroyed in turn in *c.* 1450 BC. Like Knossós but on a smaller scale, it was built of luxurious alabaster and gypsum, with a similar elaborate drainage system. Phaistós' workshops produced exquisite art, and yet, unlike at Knossós, no frescoes were found. Below the palace, 50,000 people lived and worked, and Minoan villages dependent on the palace were scattered across the Mesará. Into Hellenistic times Phaistós remained an independent little city-state, warring with Górtyn, until the latter crushed it once and for all in the 3rd century BC. Excavations by the Italians, led by the flamboyant Federico Halbherr, began in 1900, just after Evans began digging at Knossós.

Archaeological purists dismayed by Evans' reconstructions at Knossós will breathe a sigh of relief at Phaistós, where only your imagination will reconstruct the three-storey palace from the low, complicated walls and foundations; the fact that much of the second palace was built over the first means that, unless you have an especially good imagination, or opt for a guided tour, you may leave feeling singularly unenlightened. Visits begin in the northwest, in the paved **Upper Court** with its raised **Processional Way**. This continues down the steps into the **West Court**, originally part of the Old Palace—the only section the architects of the New Palace re-used after the earthquake, when the lines of the building were otherwise completely reorientated; the lower façade of the Old Palace survives just before the Grand Stairway. The West Court has the eight straight tiers known as the **Theatre**, where people may have watched dances and other performances, and two circular stone-lined granaries or silos, originally protected by domed roofs.

The **Grand Stairway** was carved with special care, partly from stone and partly from the living rock; note how the steps are slightly convex, to let rainwater run off quickly. At the top, the **Great Propylon**, the main entrance to the West Wing, stands just before a light-well with three columns. Another stair descends to the **Antechamber of the Store Rooms**, where Halbherr found a huge cache of sealstones, while beyond are the **Store Rooms**; one, covered with a roof, still contains its giant *pithoi*, along with a stone stool for standing on to scoop out

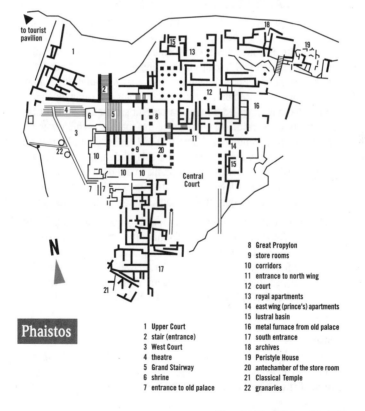

N

Phaistos

1 Upper Court
2 stair (entrance)
3 West Court
4 theatre
5 Grand Stairway
6 shrine
7 entrance to old palace

8 Great Propylon
9 store rooms
10 corridors
11 entrance to north wing
12 court
13 royal apartments
14 east wing (prince's) apartments
15 lustral basin
16 metal furnace from old palace
17 south entrance
18 archives
19 Peristyle House
20 antechamber of the store room
21 Classical Temple
22 granaries

the contents, and a built-in vessel in the floor to collect wine or oil run-offs. An important corridor separated the storage areas from the main **Shrine**, lined with stone benches.

From the Antechamber of the Store Rooms opens the **Central Court**, its long sides originally sheltered by porticoes; buildings on all sides would have hidden the tremendous views it enjoys today. A stepped block in the northwest corner may have been the platform used by bull dancers as a springboard for 'diving leaps'. To the southwest is a series of rooms fenced off and mingled with bits of the Old Palace and the foundations of a classical-era temple. Landslides have swept away much of the **East Wing**, but the small chamber just to the north, a bathroom and a a gypsum-paved lustral basin with steps earned it the name of 'Prince's Apartment'. A horseshoe-shaped **Forge**, built in the Old Palace era for smelting metals, is at the end of the corridor to the north, the earliest one yet discovered in Greece.

North of the Central Court, a grand entrance with niches in the walls and another corridor leads to yet more '**royal apartments**', paved with delicate alabaster and gypsum and now fenced off to prevent wear and tear; you can barely make out the **Queen's Megaron**, furnished with alabaster benches. An open peristyle court tops the **King's Megaron**, which once must have offered a royal view to the Kamáres cave sanctuary (that dark patch between the twin summits). The famous Phaistós Disc was found to the east of here, with a cache of pottery from 1700 BC, in the 'archives', a series of mud-brick rooms from the Old Palace.

The 'Summer Villa' of Ag. Triáda (ΑΓ. ΤΡΙΑΔΑ)

Just 3km west of Phaistós, a paved road runs to the car park just above the smaller Minoan palace of Ag. Triáda (✆ (0892) 91 360, *open daily 8.30–3; adm*), named after a diminutive Venetian church on the site. No-one knows why such a lavish little estate was built so close to Phaistós. Guesses are that a wealthy Minoan simply fell in love with the splendid setting, or it may have been a summer palace; Phaistós can turn into a frying pan in the summer and Ag. Triáda usually has a sea breeze. In Minoan times, the sea apparently came much further in and the ramp under the villa may have led down to a port. It's certainly an old site; Neolithic *tholos* tombs and dwellings were discovered under the 'palace', which was built around 1600 BC. It burned in the great island-wide destruction of 1450 BC. The Minoans rebuilt it and the Mycenaeans added a *megaron* over the top and a village, dominated by an area that curiously resembles a Hellenistic agora, with a row of shops in a *stoa*. The site, excavated by the Italians off and on since 1902, has yielded some of the Minoans' finest art, including frescoes, the Harvesters' Vase and the sarcophagus of Ag. Triáda, all now in the Herákleon museum.

The intimate scale and surroundings—and lack of tour groups—make Ag. Tríada the most charming of the major Minoan sites. The villa had two main wings, one orientated north–south, the other east–west. The north–south wing, overlooking the sea, was the most elaborate, with flagstone floors, and gypsum and alabaster walls and benches. One room had frescoes (the stalking cat), another had built-in closets. *Pithoi* still stand intact in the store rooms. At the entrance, **Ag. Geórgios Galatás** (1302) has good frescoes (the guardian has the key).

North of Phaistos

This corner offers more than the fossils of long-lost civilizations. Just to the north of Phaistós, the old village of **Vóri** (ΒΩΡΟΙ), on the road to Ag. Galíni, hopes to waylay you with its superb **Museum of Cretan Ethnology** (✆ (0892) 91 394, *open 10–6 in season and otherwise*

10–2; adm). It's the best place on the island to learn about traditional country life in Crete—a civilization not yet lost, if in danger of extinction—and has excellent detailed descriptions in English.

Southeast of Herákleon: Villages under the Diktean Mountains

Some attractive Cretan villages in the western foothills of Mount Díkti are linked by a good road south of Chersónisos. **Karouzaná** is a designated 'traditional village' for coach parties; but, hidden away south just before Kastélli, signs for 'Paradise Tavern' point the way to **Ag. Pandeleímonos**, under huge plane trees by a spring, built over a temple to Asklepeios (the taverna owners will summon the caretakers). Originally erected in AD 450, the church is said to have had 101 doors, but after being ravaged by the Saracens it was rebuilt on a more modest scale *c.* 1100. The bell is made out of a German shell and, inside, the nave is supported by marble columns from ancient Lyttos, including one made of nothing but Corinthian capitals.

Kastélli is the largest village of the Pediáda region, named after its long-gone Venetian castle. A short detour west to **Sklaverochóri** has its reward in the 15th-century church **Eisódia tis Theotókou**, decorated with excellent frescoes, the forerunners of the Cretan school: a fairytale scene with St George and the princess, allegories of the river gods in the Baptism and, on the north wall, a Catholic intruder—St Francis holding a rosary. Four kilometres east of Kastélli, ancient **Lyttos** (modern Xidás) was a fierce rival of Knossós after the Doric invasion and remained sufficiently wealthy to mint its own coins until 220 BC, when Knossós, allied with Górtyn, demolished it. As the Minoans hog the funds on Crete, Lyttos is just beginning to be investigated, but you can see Hellenistic walls, a theatre and remains of other buildings, including a frescoed church built on the early Christian basilica of Ag. Geórgios.

Families of potters in **Thrapsanó** (8km west) have made bowls and large *pithoi* for centuries. The technique for making the great jars, on wheels set in the ground, is the same as in Minoan times. **Arkalochóri**, just south, is the scene every Saturday of a large produce and animal fair. In 1932, Marinátos and Pláton excavated the village's sacred cave and brought forth some exceptionally meaty Minoan ritual weapons: gold axes, the longest prehistoric Greek bronze sword ever found and bronze axes, one engraved with Linear A, the other with symbols similar to those on the Phaistós Disc—which put paid to notions that the disc was a forgery.

The road rises at Panagía for **Embaros**: when Aeneas was wounded in the Trojan war, Aphrodite rushed over to Mount Ida to gather dittany to heal him; *Origanum ditamnus,* as it's officially known, is Crete's miracle herb, tea tonic and aphrodisiac. Cretans have often risked their lives to pluck it from the cliffs. In Embaros dittany is now safely cultivated.

The Coast: East of Herákleon to Chersónisos and Mália

East of Herákleon and Amnisós (*see* p.116), Europa, once raped on the island by Cretan Zeus in the form of a bull, gets her revenge on Crete. Even more depressing than the god-awfulness of the architecture of this region are the rusting rods curling out of the flat roofs, promising more layers of the same, and the skeletons of future monstrosities, usually crumbling away in a field of litter and weeds—some would-be Cesare Ritz's grubby field of dreams.

Even if a cup of REAL ENGLIHS (*sic*) TEA isn't yours, you may find a reason or two to put on the brakes, beginning at Vathianó Kambó to see **Nírou Cháni**, by the hotel Demetra, a well-preserved Minoan villa known as the House of the High Priest, where a trove of 40 tripods and double axes was found. It has two paved courts with stone benches, perhaps used in ceremonies (© (0897) 76 110, *open 8.30–3, closed Mon*). In **Goúves** (just inland), signs point the way to Skotinó, and beyond the village to the enormous **cave of Skotinó**; the path begins by a white chapel. The cave has a 180ft-high ballroom lit by sun pouring through the cave mouth, with a stalagmite mass in the centre. A huge amount of Minoan cult activity took place in the low-ceilinged chambers at the back, around formations like the 'head of Zeus' and natural altars.

Further east, past the turn-off at Lagada for the Lassíthi Plateau (*see* pp.130–3), **Chersónisos** (ΧΕΡΣΟΝΗΣΟΣ), or more properly Liménas Chersonísou, is a popular synthetic tourist ghetto from end to end, complete with a Cretan museum village (the **Lychnostachis Museum**, with a multilingual guided tour; *open 9.30–2, closed Mon; adm exp*) at one end for when the charms of the Hard Rock Café begin to pale. In more innocent times, Chersónisos was the port of ancient Lyttos and had a famous temple to Britomartis Artemis. Little remains of these ancient glories: a reconstructed Roman fountain by the beach, a Roman aqueduct (inland at Xerokámares, on the road to Lassíthi) and, on the west side of town, overlooking the harbour, the ruins of a 5th-century basilica, once the seat of one of Crete's first bishoprics.

Mália (ΜΑΛΙΑ)

East of Chersónisos, in the centre of a wide sandy bay, Mália has taken over as the busiest, most party-driven tentacle of the holiday sprawl east of Herákleon: at night, the bars lining the beach road thump and grind away. There is an older, wiser village of Mália inland, and, oldest of all, the **Minoan Palace of Mália** (© (0897) 31 597, *open 8.30–3, closed Mon; adm, free on Sun*), near a quiet stretch of beach 3km further east (any bus to Ag. Nikólaos will drop you nearby). Traditionally the fief of Minos' brother Sarpedon, Mália controlled the fertile coastal plain under the Lassíthi mountains. Its history follows the same pattern as Knossós: inhabited from the Neolithic era, the first palace was built on the site in 1900 BC. When it was devastated by the earthquake 200 years later, another palace was built over the first, then ruined in the mysterious catastrophe traditionally dated 1450 BC. Compared to Knossós and Phaistós, Mália is 'provincial': it's built from local stone rather than alabaster, marble and gypsum, and it had no frescoes. On the other hand, the lack of later constructions makes it easy to understand. Excavations were begun in 1915 by Cretan archaeologist Joseph Hadzidákis and continued by the French.

The entrance to the palace is by way of the **West Court**, crossed by the usual raised flagstones of the Processional Way. Eight grain 'silos', originally covered with beehive domes, are at the south end of this (similar ones have been found in Egypt). The **Central Court**, re-used from the Old Palace, had galleries at the north and east ends; in the middle are the supports of a hollow altar, or sacrificial pit. A Grand Stairway led up into the important **West Wing**, which may have had some kind of ritual role: the raised **Loggia**, where religious ceremonies may have been performed, is near a mysterious round stone stuck in the ground. The **Treasury**, behind it, yielded a sword with a rock crystal pommel and a stone axe shaped like a pouncing panther. The **Pillar Crypt** has a variety of potent symbols (double axes, stars and tridents) carved in its square pillars. The four broad steps here may have been used as a theatre, while in the southwest corner is the unique limestone *kernos*, a round wheel of an altar with a deeper hollow in the centre and 34 smaller hollows around the circumference. Its similarity to the *kernos* used in classical times is striking, and it may have been the Minoans who originated the rite of *panspermia*, or offering of the first fruits to the deity.

A long portico of square stone pillars and round wooden columns ran along the east side of the Central Court. Mália had no lack of store rooms, and the narrow ones that take up most of the East Wing (now protected by a roof) are equipped with drainage channels from the first palace. North of the centre, the **Pillar Hall** is the largest room in the palace; the chamber directly above it, reached by the surviving stair, may have been for banquets. Behind it is another pillar room, and the **oblique room**, its different orientation suggesting some kind of astronomical or lunar observation. A suite of so-called **royal apartments**, with a stepped, sunken lustral basin, are in the northwest corner. A number of Linear A tablets were found in the **Archive Room**, with the base of a single pillar. A paved road leads north to the so-called **Hypostyle Crypt**, under a barrel-vaulted shelter; no-one has the foggiest idea what went on here.

If Mália seems somewhat poor next to Knossós and Phaistós, the Minoan estates found in the outskirts were sumptuous, especially the one to the northeast of the palace, where the only fresco at Mália has been found. In the cemetery by the sea, the **Chrysolakkos tomb** may have been the family vault of Mália's rulers; although the 'gold pit' was looted for centuries, the French found the magnificent Mália twin bee pendant inside. Stylistic similarities suggest that the Aegina Treasure in the British Museum was pillaged from here in antiquity.

© *(0897–)*   ***Where to Stay and Eating Out***
Chersónisos (Liménas Chersonísou) ✉ 70014

Don't expect to find any cheap rooms here, or even a hotel in season, although the tourist office on Giaboúdaki Street will do its best to help. Aegean-style **Creta Maris**, © 22 115, @ 22 130 (*L; lux*), is the most luxurious, with lots of sports, six bars, free kindergarten, open-air cinema and the works; Aldemar runs the **Knossos Royal Village**, © 23 375, @ 23 150, *marketing@aldemar.gr* (*L; lux*), newer and glossier, with outdoor and indoor pools, water slide and floodlit tennis courts, and the lesser **Cretan Village**, © 23 750, @ 22 300, same email (*A; lux*). **Silva Maris**, another pseudo Cretan village, © 22 850, @ 21 404 (*A; lux*), has an attractive pool, water sports and frequent buses to Herákleon. *Open Apr–Oct.* In quieter Stalída, just east of Chersónisos, **Katrin Hotel**, © 32 137, @ 32 136 (*B; mod*), is the pick of this category, with three pools. There's also **Caravan Camping**, with shade, © 22 025. **Artemis**, © 32 131, by the beach in Stalída, serves Greek and Cretan specialities; in Chersónisos try **Kavouri**, at Archéou Théatro, with better than usual Greek foods. After dinner, everyone gathers in the bars and clubs around El. Venizélou.

Mália ✉ 70007

Towards the Minoan palace, **Grecotel Mália Park**, © 31 461, @ 31 460 (*A; lux*), has plush, air-conditioned bungalows, watersports and a mountain-bike centre. **Ikaros Village**, © 31 267, @ 31 341 (*A; exp*), is a large hotel complex, designed as one of those traditional Cretan villages; pool, tennis and sea sports are among the offerings. *Open Apr–Oct.* **Alexander Beach**, © 32 134, @ 31 038 (*B; exp–mod*), is a recently built complex a stone's throw from the beach, with a heated pool as well as tennis and other sports.

In Mália proper, **Ermioni**, © 31 093 (*E; inexp*), is a blessing for budget travellers, while just along the main road is **Ibiscus**, © 31 313, ✆ 32 042 (*inexp*), with a pool.

The best place to eat is in the old village, south of the main road, where tavernas serve barrelled wine and good food at fair prices: try **Yannis** and **Kalimera**, or any of the others around the main square, all far from the cacophony along the beach road.

Nomós Lassíthi (ΛΑΣΙΘΙ)

The name of Crete's easternmost province comes from the Greek mispronunciation of the Venetian La Sitía, one of its chief towns. Lassíthi doesn't have the towering peaks that characterize the rest of Crete (although Mt Díkti, on its western fringes, isn't exactly a peewee at 2,142m), but it manages to be the most varied county on the island, framed at its western end by a plateau hanging in the clouds, planted with apple orchards and wheat, while its east coast ends at Vaï with a luxuriant, palm-lined tropical beach. Ag. Nikólaos, set in the magnificent Gulf of Mirabélo, is the most cosmopolitan of Crete's four capitals, with most of the island's luxury hotels in its environs. But traditional Crete, as always, awaits only a few miles inland.

Lassíthi was densely populated in Minoan times: if the unplundered palace of Zákros is the most spectacular find, town sites such as Gourniá, Paleokástro, Vasilikí, Fournoú Korifí and Móchlos have proved important in providing clues about day-to-day Minoan life.

Lassíthians tend to be gentler than other Cretans and claim to be the best lovers on the island; other Cretans grant them only superior potatoes and pigs.

The Plateau of Lassíthi and the Birthplace of Zeus

A parade of tour buses make the ascent to the spectacular Plateau of Lassíthi, one of the high points of Crete, both in altitude and atmosphere; you may want to spend a night or two there after the tour groups have gone, to get a feel for the place. For it is unique: a green carpet hemmed in on all sides by the Díktean Mountains, snowcapped into April and irrigated in summer by windmills designed by Venetian engineers in 1564; the hundreds that still turn make a splendid sight. The uncanny cave where Zeus was born is the chief attraction, while Karphí, a Minoan last refuge, is just as weird, harder to get to, and unvisited.

Getting There and Around

One or two daily **buses** from Herákleon, Mália and Ag. Nikólaos wind their way up to the plateau, taking in most of the villages and ending up at the Diktean Cave.

Festivals

23 April: Ag. Geórgios; **15 August**: Mochós; **29–31 August**: Psychró.

The Lassíthi Plateau: Approaches from the West

With your own transport you have a choice of scenic routes. The main one from Chersónisos passes a series of old villages; just above one of these, **Potamiés**, the lovely cruciform church

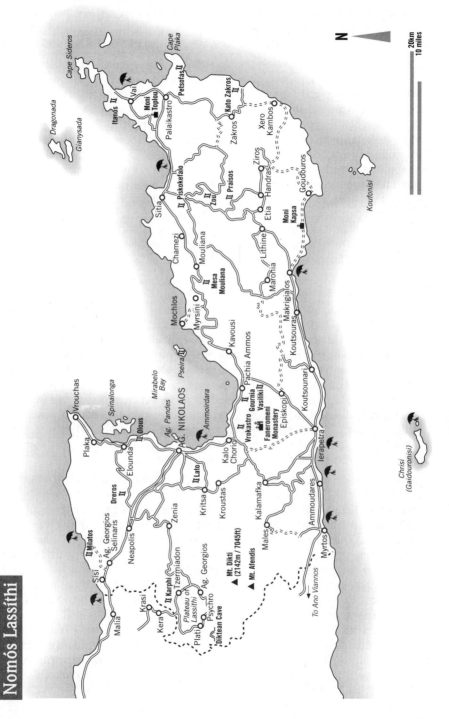

Nomós Lassíthi

Cape Sideros
Dragonada
Gianysada
Cape Plaka
Vai
Itanós II
Moni Toplou
Palaikastro
Petsofas II
Kato Zakros II
Zakros
Xero Kambos
Ziros
Piskokefalo II
Sitia
Zou II
Praisos II
Handras
Etia
Goúdouros
Koufonisi
Chamezi
Mouliana
Mesa Mouliana
Lithine
Moni Kapsa
Myrsini
Mochlos
Maronia
Makrigialos
Kavousi
Koutsouras
Pseira II
Koutsounari
Pachia Ammos
Ammoirdara
Vrouchas
Spinalonga
Mirabelo Bay
Ag. Pandes
AG. NIKOLAOS
Gournia
Vasiliki II
Episkopi
Ierapetra
Plaka
Olous II
Prokastro II
Faneromeni Monastery
Elounda
Kalo Chorio
Dreros II
Lato II
Kritsa
Kroustas
Kalamafka
Ammoudares
Chrisi (Gaidouronisi)
Sisi
Milatos II
Ag. Georgios Selinaris
Zenia
Neapolis
Males
Myrtos
Krasi
Karphi II
Tzermiadon
Ag. Georgios
Mt. Dikti (2142m / 7045ft)
Mt. Afendis
To Ano Viannos
Malia
Kera
Plateau of Lassithi
Psychro
Plati
Dikteon Cave

N
20km
10 miles

at abandoned Moní Gouverniótissa has excellent 14th-century frescoes, including a powerful Pantocrator who stares holes into sinners (key at the *kafeneíon*). Frescoes from the same period decorate Ag. Antónios at **Avdoú**, a pretty village dotted with small Byzantine churches.

On the road east of Chersónisos at Stalída, the ascent is far more abrupt. After 8.5km of bird's eye views over the sea, **Mochós** comes as a pleasant antidote to the coastal cacophony. There are a few places to eat and some rooms, mostly occupied by Swedish tourists, who know Mochós through their assassinated prime minister Olof Palme; his simple summer residence, Villa Palme, is now a local shrine. South of Mochós, **Krási** is famous for its curative spring. Perhaps the best advertisement for the waters is the village plane tree, which has thrived on them for the past 2,000 years or so. In the 19th century, a café with three tables did business inside the hollow trunk. Very near Krási, in **Kerá**, the **Convent of Kardiótissa** was founded in the 1100s and contains a miraculous icon that was twice carried off by the Turks to Constantinople but made its way home on its own; the third time the Turks chained it to a column, but it flew back to Crete with the column and chain attached. The column is still in the courtyard, while the chain, hanging on the iconostasis, is said to relieve pain if wrapped around the body. During restoration work on the church, beautiful 14th-century frescoes were discovered, with a fine portrait of the lady donor.

The Villages of the Plateau

Beyond the stone windmills—still used for grinding wheat—the road finally reaches the pass at the Seli Ampelou Taverna and Grill, then descends into the Lassíthi plateau. Down below, the round emerald plain presents at its best a kind of epiphany; Werner Herzog used it as such, hypnotically, in his film *Signs of Life*. A fertile chequerboard divided by drainage ditches, in a bowl of barren mountains, the plateau was farmed by the Minoans, and later by the Dorians of Lyttos, but in 1293 it was such a nest of resistance that the Venetians forced everyone out, demolished the villages, set up a guard around the passes and persecuted anyone who came near. Only in 1543 were Greek refugees from the Turkish-occupied Peloponnese permitted to resettle the plateau. To re-establish the orchards, the Venetians built 10,000 white-sailed irrigation windmills. In the 1970s they were still a remarkable sight, but, sadly, since then most have become derelict in favour of the more reliable petrol pump.

Eighteen villages dot the circumference of the plateau, to preserve the best land for farming and to keep their toes dry; the plain becomes boggy from melted snow. The largest village, **Tzermiádon** (TZEPMIAΔO; pop. 1,500), is near a sacred cave and peak sanctuary. The cave, **Trápeza**, was used from 5000 BC; long before the first temples, Cretans left ivory votive offerings in the mysterious penumbra behind its narrow opening; the Middle Minoans used it for burials (bring a light, or take a local guide). An hour's walk up a strenuous path (a dirt road goes part way, marked 'Tinios Stavros'), **Karphí** (KAPΦI), the 'nail', is a fairly accurate description of the mountain, a weird place that holds the loftiest of all Minoan peak sanctuaries (1,158m). Excavated by the affable one-eyed giant John Pendlebury between 1937 and 1939—his last project before he was killed, fighting alongside the locals in the Battle of Crete—Karphí had been the refuge of some 3,000 Minoans, or Eteocretans ('True Cretans'), during the Dorian invasion in 1100 BC. For a century they tried to keep the fires of their civilization burning, before the harsh winters apparently got to them. In this mighty setting, Pendlebury found 150 small houses, a temple, a chieftain's house with a porch and hearthroom, a tower and barracks, and a shrine that contained five of the very last Minoan clay idols of the goddess (*c.* 1050 BC, now in the Herákleon museum), weird, distorted and a metre tall, with a cylinder skirt, detachable feet and long neck, like Alice when she was mistaken for a serpent.

Clockwise from Tzermiádon, **Ag. Konstantínos** has the most souvenir shops on the plateau, while just above it the 13th-century **Moní Kroustallénia** enjoys a lovely panoramic spot. In **Ag. Geórgios**, the next village, a 200-year-old farmhouse contains a **Folk Museum** (*open June–Aug 10–4*), complete with everything a Cretan family needed to get by, including a wine-press that doubled as a bed; it also has a fascinating collection of photos of Níkos Kazantzákis.

Psychró and the Diktean Cave

Psychró (ΨΥΧΡΟ), at the southwest end of the plateau, is the base for visiting the **Diktean Cave**, the birthplace of Zeus (*open 8–5; adm*). From the car park (*300dr*) it's a 1km ascent up a rocky, stepped path; sure-footed donkeys are available, while local guides at the entrance hire lanterns in case you haven't brought your own, although it's wise to set a price from the start. Rubber-soled shoes are important; the descent is slippery and dangerous (tour leaders often fail to warn their elderly clients, creating massive single-file jams).

If you get there before or after the groups, the cave is a haunting, other-worldly place well worthy of myth. Only rediscovered in the 1880s, it contained cult items from Middle Minoan up to Archaic times; its role as the birthplace and hiding place of Zeus from his cannibal father Cronos was confirmed by the discovery in Paleókastro of the *Hymn of the Kouretes* (the young men who banged their shields to drown out the baby's cries). Down in the cave's damp, shadowy bowels the guides point out formations that, if you squint just so, resemble the baby god, his cradle, his mantle and the place where the nanny goat Amaltheia nursed him; to help conceal the birth, Rhea, his mother, spurted her own breast milk into the heavens, creating the Milky Way. A strong tradition has it that Minos came up here to receive the Law of Zeus every nine years, and that Epimenides the Sage lived in the cave as a hermit, having strange visions.

✉ *72052,* ☎ *(0844–)*   ***Where to Stay and Eating Out***

Tzermiádon/Ag. Geórgios

In Tzermiádon, **Kourites**, ☎ 22 194 (*B; inexp*), is the smartest place to stay on the plateau. **Lassithi**, owned by the same family, ☎ 22 194 (*E; inexp*), is just as small and has a restaurant. *Both open all year.* In Ag. Geórgios, try **Rhea**, ☎ 31 209 (*E; inexp*).

Psychró

In Psychró, there are quite a few rooms to supplement **Hotel Zeus**, ☎/🖷 31 284 (*D; inexp*), and the **Dikteon Andron**, ☎ 31 504 (*E; inexp*). There are several traditional tavernas on the main street to sup at.

Between Mália and Ag. Nikólaos

After Mália, the New Road cuts inland, avoiding the rugged Cape Ag. Ioánnis. This is good news for the last two resorts, Sísi and Milátos, which are free of the grind of heavy traffic that bedevils the coast to the west. Laid-back **Sísi** (ΣΙΣΙ) is like a chunk of southern California, with its modern pastel architecture, sandy beaches and cute little port—a turquoise crique under the cliffs, lined with a palm garden and a cascade of tavernas, bars and pubs.

Just east, **Paralía Milátou** (ΠΑΡΑΛΙΑ ΜΙΛΑΤΟΥ) is just the opposite: low-key, a bit dumpy, its pebble beach graced with a few fish tavernas. Yet ancient Milátos was one of the most important cities of Homeric Crete. Myth has it that Minos, Rhadamanthys and Sarpedon once competed for a beautiful boy. When the boy chose Sarpedon, his brothers were such poor sports that Sarpedon moved to Asia Minor, taking with him not only the boy but the inhabitants of Milátos, where they founded the great city of Miletus. Up on its hill, the dusty old village still wears a forsaken air. It has a more recent reason to look forlorn. In 1823, during the War of Independence, the large stalactite **Cave of Milátos** (on the edge of a wild, rocky ravine, 6km from the beach then a 10-minute walk from the narrow parking area) served as a refuge for two weeks for 3,600 people. The Turks besieged them, and after two battles the refugees surrendered. Although the Turkish leader promised them safe conduct, he massacred all the men and children and enslaved the women. Under the bulbous rock at the entrance, the cave has a low, smoke-blackened ceiling supported by slender stalactites. One large chamber has a chapel, or *heroön*, containing a glass reliquary full of bones.

Neápolis (ΝΕΑΠΟΛΙΣ) and Ancient Dreros

Immersed in greenery and almond groves, **Neápolis** is the largest town on the Herákleon–Ag. Nikólaos road. In its former incarnation as Karés, it saw the birth of Pétros Fílagros in 1340. Raised by Catholics, he became a professor of theology and was elected Pope Alexander V in 1409, one of several popes-for-a-year during the Great Schism. Karés predeceased him, however, when the Venetians destroyed it in 1347 after a revolt. The rebuilt village grew into the 'new town', Neápolis, the provincial capital before Ag. Nikólaos. It has a leafy central square and a small **museum** (*open 10–1 and 6–9, closed Mon; adm*) housing traditional crafts and a few finds from **Dreros**, a lonely, wild place a few miles north up a narrow winding road (cross under the New Road and follow signs for Kouroúnes; from the tiny parking area, a rough path leads up to a saddle between two peaks). Excavated in the early 1900s, there's an Archaic agora and, under a protective shelter, a 7th-century BC Geometric temple to Apollo Delphinios; the latter yielded the oldest hammered bronze statues ever found in Greece (now in the Herákleon museum) and Eteocretan inscriptions—Minoan words in Greek letters.

Ag. Nikólaos (ΑΓ. ΝΙΚΟΛΑΟΣ)

When Ag. Nikólaos was selected capital of *nomós* Lassíthi in 1905, only 95 people lived in the village, built as an amphitheatre overlooking a round lake and the breathtaking Mirabélo Bay. It didn't have a proper port; ships had to call at Pachiá Ámmos to the east. A new port in 1965 attracted the first yachties, and what has happened since is not exactly hard to guess: the resident population of Agnik, as the Brits call it, has multiplied by 100. A few years back it was the first place on Crete to cross over the courtesy threshold when signs were erected, pleading: 'Please respect our local mores and customs. Do not disrupt the town's tranquillity and keep the environment clean. Thank you. The Mayor.' They must have worked—the rowdies now concentrate at Mália, leaving Agnik older, wiser and noticeably nicer.

The Olympic Airways office is at 20 Plastíra, ☎ 22 033. The **bus station** (☎ 22 234) is near the rocky beach of Ámmos at the end of Sof. Venizélou. Beaches within easy bus range are Eloúnda and Kaló Chorió (on the road to Sitía).

Tourist office: Between the lake and the sea, 20 Aktí S. Koundoúrou, ☎ 82 384 (*open 8.30am–9.30pm daily in season*).
Tourist police and **lost property**: 34 Kontogiáni, ☎ 26 900.

Festivals

New Year. Easter festivities include the burning of an effigy of Judas on a platform in the middle of the harbour. **29 May**: Ag. Triáda; **27 June–3 July**: nautical week, with fireworks on the last day; **6 December**: Ag. Nikólaos.

Around Town

Ag. Nikólaos stands on the ruins of Lato Pros Kamara, the port of ancient Lato, and the town still concentrates much of its mercenary soul around the port, overlooking the islet of **Ag. Pándes**. The chapel of the same name on the islet draws pilgrims on 20 June, but at other times you need to go with a cruise party to visit the *kri-kri* goats, the only inhabitants, who will probably play hide-and-seek anyway. The other vortex is circular **Lake Voulisméni**, the 'bottomless' (although it has been measured at 210ft). It was often stagnant until 1867, when the local pasha connected it to the sea. From the cliffs there's a fine view of the fish that call it home, some over 2ft long and fattened by bread from the restaurants, only to appear later on their menus. Behind the tourist office, there's a small but choice **Ethnographic Museum** (*open 10–3, closed Sat; adm*), with icons, embroideries, instruments and stamps from independent Crete. Aktí S. Koundoúrou follows the waterfront past rocky places where you can swim. There is a beach at the end and the little stone church that gave the town its name, **Ag. Nikólaos**, with rare 9th-century Geometric frescoes from the Iconoclastic period (key at the Minos Palace Hotel).

The **Archaeology Museum**, up the hill at 68 K. Paleológou (*open 8.30–3, closed Mon; adm*), displays artefacts discovered in eastern Crete; among the highlights are a Neolithic phallus-shaped idol from Zákros, the peculiar Early Minoan pinhead chicken-like 'Goddess of Myrtos', lovely gold jewellery from Móchlos, a stone vase in the form of a triton shell, engraved with two demons making a libation (from Mália), a Daedalic bust from the 7th century BC that looks like Christopher Columbus and a unique lamp from Olous with 70 nozzles. In the last room, a 1st-century AD skull still has a fine set of teeth, a gold burial wreath embedded in the bone of its brow, a silver coin from Polyrenia (to pay Charon, the ferryman of the Underworld), and a plate of knucklebones, perhaps used for divination.

Many tourists are surprised to discover that Agnik was asleep when God was handing out beaches: there's little sand at shingly **Kitroplateía**, sheltered and safe for children, named after the cypress wood once exported from here. The pocket-sized sand beach of **Ammoúdi** is at the end of Aktí S. Koundoúrou, while at the other end of town, near the bus station,

Ámmos is a clean, but not terribly atmospheric, piece of sand. To the south, on the other side of the stadium, is the crowded but clean **municipal beach** (*entrance fee*); from here, a walking path leads past little, sandy **Gargardóros** beach and beyond that to **Almyrós**, the best.

Shopping

Don't confuse the three streets named after the Koundoúrou family. Mixed in with the shops flogging embarrassing T-shirts, Ag. Nikólaos has some excellent boutiques, such as **Maria Patsaki**, at 2 K. Sfakianáki, with embroideries, clothes and antiques, and **Syllogi**, on Aktí S. Koundoúrou, with old paintings, antiques, silver and other fine crafts. **Sofia**, 33 R. Koundoúrou, has a good selection of Cretan crafts, jewellery and weavings. **Kerazoza**, 42 R. Koundoúrou, has puppets, toys and postcards from the 1950s. **Anna Karteri**, 5 R. Koundoúrou, has a wide range of titles in English.

Ag. Nikólaos ✉ *72100,* ✆ *(0841–)*   **Where to Stay**

luxury

Ag. Nikólaos' reputation as a posy tourist hotspot owes much to the posh hotels in the area, such as the **St Nicholas Bay**, spread over a narrow peninsula 2km from Ag. Nikólaos, ✆ 25 041, ✉ 24 556, *stnicolas@otenet.gr* (*L*), a 130-bungalow complex which includes a private sandy beach, four outdoor and one indoor pool (not to mention the private pools accompanying some suites), a health club and an art gallery. *Open Mar–Nov.* **Minos Beach**, on the secluded, garden-covered promontory of Ammoúdi, ✆ 22 345, ✉ 22 548 (*L*), has 132 sumptuous bungalows, good restaurant, bars, private beach and diving school; although built practically in the Minoan era by Agnik standards (1962), it was renovated in 1990 and is still one of the best.

expensive

Ormos, near the sea, ✆ 24 094, ✉ 25 394 (*B*), is family orientated, with air-conditioning, pool and playground; rates plummet off-season. **Coral Hotel**, on the waterfront along Aktí Kondoúrou, ✆ 28 363, ✉ 28 754 (*B*), is a smart town option, with pool and terrace, while **Melas**, along the road at No.26, ✆ 28 734, has stylish apartments for 2–5 people (winter ✆ (01) 647 0133).

moderate

Panorama, also on Aktí Koundoúrou, ✆ 28 890, ✉ 27 268 (*C*), offers just that over the harbour, and all rooms come with bath.

inexpensive

Rea, on the corner of Marathonos and Milatou, ✆ 28 321, ✉ 28 324 (*B*), is a good-value hotel with character and excellent sea views. **Doxa** is another good, year-round bet, at 7 Idomeneos, ✆ 24 214, ✉ 24 614 (*C*). The **Green House**, 15 Modátsou, ✆ 22 025, is a cheapie with little rooms leading out to a small courtyard, filled to overflowing with greenery, and patrolled by a small army of cats. Other pleasant, clean guesthouses to try are the central **Perla**, ✆ 23 379 (*E*), and **Adonis**, ✆ 22 931 (*E*). The tourist office lists over 1,000 other rooms to rent if you get stuck.

Pelagos, on Str. Kóraka (just in from Aktí Koundoúrou), is a trendy (if pricey) seafood restaurant, with a long list of tasty *mezédes* to start with (*6,000dr*). When the Greeks want to dine on the lake, they make for **Pefko**, with delicious, reasonably priced taverna food.

Although it has no view at all, **Itanos,** next to the cathedral on Str. Kíprou, ✆ 25 340, has some of the finest traditional cooking in eastern Crete (the lamb and spinach in egg-lemon sauce is excellent), good barrelled wine and a terrace. Halfway up to the archaeology museum, on K. Paleológou, **Aouas** is small, inexpensive and good, serving Cretan dishes in a green shady courtyard far from the madding crowd.

Near Kitroplateía beach, **Trata,** on Akti Pangalou, has a roof garden where you can lap up fish soup or chicken *kleftíko* (with cream, cheese and ham), as well as a long list of casserole dishes. Of the tavernas along Kitroplateía, **Ofou to Io** at the far end offers boiled kid, *tigania* pork with white sauce, roast lamb stuffed with garlic and various cheeses.

Down at Ammoúdi Beach the **Dolphin** has good food served by jovial twin waiters (*3,000dr*); **Grigoris,** at Stavrós, 200m after the bridge to Almyrós, is exceptionally friendly and cheap, or head out of town altogether for **Synantysi,** a popular taverna along the Old Road to Herákleon. **Kaklis,** ✆ 26 645, 4km towards Elounda, is a favourite for Cretan food and, frequently, live Cretan music.

Entertainment and Nightlife

After-dark action is not hard to find, concentrated around the lake and port. For background music, there's the perennially popular roof terrace at **Alexandros,** on K. Paleológou; if you want more pulsating sounds, head for the dancing disco bars: **Lipstick,** overlooking the main port, or try one of the string along 25 Martíon. On Almyrós beach, **Erodios** bar, ✆ 23 733, has live Greek music on Friday and Saturday nights.

Eloúnda, Olous and Spinalónga

Tantalizing views across the Gulf of Mirabélo and its islands unfold along the 12km from Ag. Nikólaos north to Eloúnda; below, the rocky coastline is interspersed with tiny coves, draped with Crete's most glamorous hotels. **Eloúnda** (ΕΛΟΥΝΤΑ) attracts a high percentage of Brits, many of whom never seem to drift too far from the bars in the central square overlooking the sea.

On the south edge of Eloúnda, a bridge crosses an artificial channel dug by the French in 1897 to separate the promontory of Spinalónga from mainland Crete. Along this channel, under the windmills, lies the sunken harbour of **Olous,** the port of ancient Dreros (*see* p.134) and goal of the 'sunken city' excursions from Ag. Nikólaos. The moon goddess Britomartis, inventor of the fishing net, was worshiped here, represented by a wooden cult statue (a *xoanon*) with a fishtail, made by Daedalos; one story has her turning into a fish to wriggle away from the embrace of Minos. Fish also figure in the mosaic floor of an Early Byzantine basilica near the Canal Bar.

The tiny island of **Spinalónga** (ΣΠΙΝΑΛΟΓΚΑ; not to be confused with the promontory) is a half-hour caique trip from Eloúnda, or an hour by excursion boat from Ag. Nikólaos. Venetian engineers detached it from the promontory in 1579 when they dug a channel to defend their fortress, built over the ancient fort of Olous. It held out against the Turks, like the islet forts of Nea Soúda and Gramvoúsa, until 1715, when the Venetians surrendered them by treaty. When the Turks were evacuated in 1904, Spinalónga became a leper colony—the last in Europe—surviving until 1957. Today the poignant little streets, houses and lepers' church are abandoned and forlorn. **Pláka**, opposite the islet, was the supply centre for the lepers and now has a tiny laid-back colony of its own, dedicated to relaxation by a little pebble beach.

Eloúnda ✉ *72053,* ☏ *(0841–)*　　　　**Where to Stay and Eating Out**

Decadent **Elounda Mare**, ☏ 41 102, 🖅 41 307, *elmare@agn.forthnet.gr* (*L; lux*), is a member of the prestigious Relais & Chateaux complex, renovated in 2000, with 47 hotel rooms and 46 bungalows with private pools on the seafront, not to mention all the restaurants and watersports. **Eloúnda Beach**, ☏ 41 412, 🖅 41 373, *elohotel@ elounda-beach.gr* (*L; lux*), incorporates traditional Cretan architecture and has a sandy beach as well as its own cinema, deep-sea-diving expeditions, fitness centre and heated pool; Royal Suites boast pools, private butler, pianist and gym with trainer. **Elounda Blue Bay**, ☏ 41 924, 🖅 41 816 (*B; exp*), is a rather more modest complex offering a pool, playground and tennis. Near the causeway **Akti Olous**, ☏ 41 270. 🖅 41 425 (*C; exp*), is a popular place, with a pool and roof garden. **Korfos Beach**, ☏ 41 591, 🖅 41 034 (*C; inexp*), is within spitting distance of the strand, with watersports on offer.

Eloúnda is well endowed with restaurants, especially around the port area. **Vritomartis**, out on its little islet, serves well-prepared seafood and lobster. Nearby **Kalidon** has tables out on a small pontoon and a good selection of vegetarian dishes and *mezédes*. **Marilena**, ☏ 41 322, has a vine-covered rear garden and Cypriot dishes on the menu. On the Pláka road, **Taverna Despina** has a good name for fish.

Above Ag. Nikólaos: Kéra Panagía and Kritsá

From Ag. Nikólaos, it's only a short hop up to Kritsá and, 1km before the village, **Kéra Panagía** (*open 8.30–3; adm*), set back from a road in an olive grove. It looks like no other church on the island: the three naves, coated with centuries of whitewash, trailing long triangular buttresses and crowned by the simplest of bell towers and a drum dome. Within, the entire surface is alive with the colours of Crete's most celebrated fresco cycle, one that well illustrates the evolution of Byzantine art before it ceased with the Turks. The central aisle, dedicated to the Virgin, dates from the 12th to mid-13th centuries: on the northwest pillar look for *St Francis*, with his Catholic tonsure. It's rare that a Western saint earns a place among the Orthodox, but Francis, introduced by the Venetians, made a considerable impression among the common people. The two side aisles were later additions, painted in the more naturalistic style emanating from Constantinople in the early 14th century. The south aisle is devoted to St Anne (whose picture fills the apse), and many of the scenes are based on apocryphal gospels. The north aisle belongs to Christ Pantocrator, while a *Last Judgement* covers most of the nearby vaults. Among the saints here, don't miss the donors with their small daughter, rare portraits of medieval Cretans.

In 1956, director Jules Dassin chose the lovely white village of **Kritsá** (ΚΡΙΤΣΑ) as the location for his film *He Who Must Die* starring Melina Mercouri, and ever since its role has been as something of a film set—a traditional Cretan village swamped by Agnik tourists, who are in turn swamped by villagers selling them tablecloths, rugs and lace, some rather more handmade than others. Kritsá is famous for throwing real roll-out-the-barrel Cretan weddings, and in August weddings are re-enacted with food, drink and dancing for fee-paying 'guests'.

Ancient Lato

A scenic 3km walk (the path begins near the crossroads) or drive north of Kritsá leads up to the extensive remains of Dorian **Lato** or, more properly, Lato Etera (*open 8.30–2.30, closed Mon*), its ruins curling down the saddle between the hills, with bird's-eye views over the sea. Named after the Minoan goddess Leto (Lato in Dorian Greek), the city was founded in the 7th century BC; it flourished through the classical era and gave birth to Nearchus, Alexander the Great's admiral and explorer, before it was abandoned in favour of its port, Lato Kamara (Ag. Nikólaos). Lato displays some unusual Minoan influences on Dorian design: the double gateway, the street of 80 steps lined with small houses and workshops, and the architecture of its agora, with its columnless sanctuary and cistern in the centre. The wide steps that continue up to a peristyle court and *Prytaneion*, where the sacred fire burned day and night, date from the 7th century BC and may have been inspired by Minoan 'theatres'; spectators could sit and watch events in the agora below. Monumental towers stood on either side of a narrower stair leading up to the altar. On the second hill stands a beautiful, column-less temple (probably dedicated to Leto), an isolated altar and a primitive theatre seating a few hundred people.

East of Ag. Nikólaos: The Gulf of Mirabélo

The coastline that lends Ag. Nikólaos its panache owes its name to the Genoese fortress of Mirabélo, 'Beautiful View', demolished by the Turks. Where precipices aren't crowding the sea the land is immensely fertile, and has been populated for the past 5,000 years; fortunately archaeological zoning has kept more recent Agnikish development down. Frequent buses run the 12km out to the sandy beach of **Kaló Chório**; the road east continues past the up-and-coming resort of **Ístro** to the turn-off for the 12th-century **Moní Faneroménis**, possessing a stupendous view over the Mirabélo gulf. The monastery is built like a fortress into the cliff, sheltering a frescoed cave church with a miraculous icon of the Virgin found by a shepherd.

Minoans along the Riviera: Gourniá, Vasiliki and Mochlos

East of Ístro, the road passes directly below the striking hillside site of Gourniá (℗ (0842) 94 604; *open 8.30–3, closed Mon; adm*), excavated between 1901 and 1904 by American Harriet Boyd, the first woman to lead a major dig. Gourniá reached its peak in the Late Minoan period, around 1550 BC, and was never rebuilt after a fire in c. 1225 BC. Stone-paved lanes meander past workshops, store rooms and houses. At the highest point, a small 'palace' with store rooms surrounds a rectangular court; there's a mini theatrical area and Shrine of the Snake Goddess, with a shelf for long, tube-like snake vases.

From Gourniá, it's a short drive down to **Pachiá Ámmos**, a woebegone resort village along a sandy beach that corners most of the garbage in the Cretan sea; the much-talked-about plans for doing something about it are yet to be enacted. It stands at the beginning of the Ierápetra road (*see* p.146) bisecting the isthmus of Crete, a mere 12km of land separating the Aegean from the Libyan sea. The isthmus is undergoing a close survey; as Gourniá wasn't a palace, archaeologists suspect one must be somewhere nearby, especially as this was one of the first places settled by the Minoans. By 2600 BC, in the Pre-Palace era, they had built a settlement at **Vasilikí**, 5km south of Pachiá Ámmos. Discovered in 1906, it yielded the first known specimens of what has since been known as 'Vasilikí ware', the Minoans' first distinctive pottery style, boldly mottled in red and black, an effect produced by uneven firing. Excavations here have recently been taken up again in search of clues to the Minoans' origin, as Vasilikí is one of the few sites from the period that was abandoned (2000 BC) and never rebuilt.

Pachiá Ámmos is also the crossroads for Sitía, some 47km east down the Cretan riviera, on a corniche road that slithers along the jagged, precipitous coast of the Gulf of Mirabélo, with the bright lights of Ag. Nikólaos twinkling far below. Stop at **Plátanos**, with a wonderful belvedere over the gulf and a pair of tavernas to linger over the sunset. Beyond, signs point the way down to **Móchlos** (ΜΟΧΛΟΣ), a charming fishing village with a pebbly beach, set between barren cliffs and a small islet barely a stone's throw from the shore. This islet was originally attached to the mainland, giving Minoan Móchlos the advantage of two harbours. Abandoned after the disaster of 1470 BC, Móchlos specialized in pots with lid handles shaped like reclining dogs. Recently, seven intact chamber tombs were discovered cut into the cliffs. One building is called 'the House of the Theran Refugees' for its architectural similarities to the top-floor timbered houses at Akrotíri, on Santoríni; pot shards from Akrotíri littered the floor *on top of* a 20cm layer of volcanic ash. Life went on after the Big Bang.

Yet another Minoan settlement existed from 3000 BC on **Pseíra**, 2km offshore, where the inhabitants used the pumice that floated ashore from Santoríni to build up the floor of their shrine. The town was excavated in 1907 by American Richard Seager and, judging by the rich finds, it was a prosperous little port town in its day, although now it's completely barren. Pseíra's House of the Pillar Partitions, with a bathroom equipped with a sunken tub, plughole and drains, is the most elegant in eastern Crete. Other ruins belong to a Roman lighthouse.

Móchlos ✉ *72057,* ✆ *(0834–)*　　　　　**Where to Stay and Eating Out**

Aldiana, ✆/☞ 94 491 (*B; mod*), precludes the need to go anywhere else, with a restaurant, sports, pool and nightclub. **Sofia**, ✆ 94 554, ☞ 94 238 (*D; inexp*), is pleasant and small. **Mochlos**, ✆ 94 205 (*E; inexp*), is similarly priced and 20 yards from the beach. *Open all year.* **Sta Limenaria**, at the far end of the beach, has good food, including vegetarian meals, and more rooms; nearly all the seaside tavernas specialize in fresh fish.

Sitía (ΣΗΤΕΙΑ)

As an antidote to Ag. Nikólaos, sunny Sitía has kept its Greek soul and natural courtesy, perhaps because it has a livelihood of its own, based on sultanas and wine. It is more pleasant than stunningly beautiful, set in an amphitheatre and endowed with a long, sandy beach that flies the blue flag of environmental righteousness. Its Byzantine, Genoese and Venetian walls fell to earthquakes and the bombardments of Barbarossa, leaving only a restored Venetian fortress as a souvenir to close off the western end of the port.

Sitía ✆ (0843–)　　　　　　　　　　　　　　　　　**Getting There and Around**

Sitía's little **airport is** 1km out of town; a taxi costs around 1,000dr. The Olympic office is by the Tourist Information Office, ✆ 22 270; for airport information, ✆ 24 666. The **bus station** is at the south end of the waterfront, ✆ 22 272, and has 5–6 buses daily to Ag. Nikólaos, Herákleon, Palaíkastro, Vaï and Ierápetra, and 2–3 to Káto Zákro.

Sitía ✆ (0843–)　　　　　　　　　　　　　　　　　　　**Tourist Information**

Municipal Tourist Office: ✆ 28 300, on the marina.

Tourist police: ✆ 24 200.

Festivals

24 June: large local festival, Piskokéfalo; **summer** Kornaria cultural festival; **mid-August:** a 3-day wine and sultana festival, Sitía.

Around the Town

Sitía, filled with the bustle of a provincial town, the pranks of its pet pelicans and general schmoozing along the waterfront, is a paradise for lazy visitors. But *la dolce vita* is nothing new here; under the fortress you can see the ruins of a Roman fish tank, where denizens of the deep were kept alive and fresh for the table. The **Archaeology Museum**, incongruously set among the garages at the top of Ítanos Street (✆ (0843) 23 917, *open 8.30–3, closed Mon; adm*), has a small collection Minoan *larnaxes*, a wine press and a cache of Linear A tablets from Zákros, and offerings from the 7th century in the Daedalic style. Some of the newest finds are some from Pétras, just south of Sitía, where a large structure from the New Palace period is currently being explored: it may well be the Se-to-i-ja of the Minoan tablets.

If the town beach at Sitía is too crowded, try the sandy cove of **Ag. Fotía,** 5km to the east. In 1971 a large Pre-Palatial Minoan cemetery of 250 chamber tombs was discovered near the sea here (fenced in, off a path at the east end of the village). The hill above is the site of a large Old Temple building that was mysteriously but peacefully destroyed just after its construction and replaced with a round fortlike building—perhaps part of a coastal warning system.

Crete's Popular Epic: The Erotókritos

On Crete, Sitía is best known for Vincénzo Kornáros, the 17th-century Creto-Venetian author of the *Erotókritos*, the island's national epic. A 10,000-line romance, written in the Cretan dialect, the *Erotókritos* is still memorized and sung today to the *lýra* and *laúto*; some shepherds can rattle off thousands of verses off the top of their heads. The story, inspired by Ariosto's *Orlando Furioso*, is set in Byzantine times and tells of the love and trials of Erotókritos, son of a poor commoner, and Aretousa, daughter of King Heracles of Athens. Eventually, Erotókritos in disguise (a magic potion has turned him black) saves Athens singlehandedly from the Vlachs. The king then gives in at last and lets the couple marry, and the hero accedes to the throne of Athens. Interspersed with all the action, Kornáros included enough philosophy to make the *Erotókritos* a rich source for *mantinade* singers or others in search of the *mot juste* for any occasion. One favourite:

> *Clouds and mists in*
> *Time disperse;*
> *Great blessings in time*
> *Become a curse.*

Sitía ✉ *72300,* ✆ *(0843–)*   **Where to Stay**

Plushest and biggest here, **Sitia Beach**, ✆ 28 821, @ 28 826 (*A; exp*), has two pools, tennis, sea sports, a 'musculation centre', archery and disco. **Itanos**, 4 Karamanli, ✆ 22 146, @ 22 915 (*C; inexp*), is a stylish hotel near the park with roof garden and special rooms for the disabled. **Alice**, 34 Papanastassíou, ✆ 28 450 (*C; inexp*), is good value, modern and offers Cretan evenings once a week. Little **Archontikon**, 16 Kondiláki, ✆ 28 172 (*D; inexp*), is clean, quiet and friendly, with a terrace, on the west edge of town. **Stars**, 37 M. Kalyváki, ✆ 22 917 (*D; inexp*), offers some peace and quiet; ditto for **Nora**, 31 Rouseláki, ✆ 23 017 (*D, inexp*). The **youth hostel**, 4 Theríssou St, ✆ 22 693, is just east of town, pleasant and friendly, with kitchen use and camping in the garden.

Sitía ✆ *(0843–)*   **Eating Out**

Sitía is a civilized place, where *mézedes* automatically come with your drink. **Zorba's** has a wonderful location on the waterfront, and delicious seafood and grills (*5,000dr*); **Mixos Taverna Ouzeri**, two streets in from the port, serves lamb baked or on the spit with barrelled wine (*4,000dr*). Just up Kazantzaki from the water, the **Balcony** offers a Greco-Italo-Mexican array of dishes (*6,000dr*). For a good meal with a good view, **Neromilos**, 4km east, is the local favourite, located in a former water mill. There's a stylish clutch of bars near the pelicans' house; for more of a sweat, head for the **Summer** disco, where you can cool off in the pool afterwards, or the huge **Planitarion** disco, 1km out past the ferry port.

Inland from Sitía: the Last True Cretans and a Venetian Villa

Along the main road south, 2km past whitewashed **Maronía**, the road forks for Néa Praisós, just below ancient **Praisós**, the last stronghold of the Eteocretans—the 'true Cretans', or Minoans—who took refuge here during the Dorian invasion and survived into the 3rd century BC, co-existing with the Dorians, running their shrine of Diktean Zeus at Palaíkastro and keeping other cults alive on their three acropoli. When Praisós began to compete too openly with Dorian Ierapytna (Ierápetra) in 146 BC, it was decimated. Ironically, this last Minoan town was one of the very first to be discovered, in 1884 by Federico Halbherr, who was mystified by the unfathomable inscriptions in Greek letters, now generally held to be in the native Minoan language of Linear A. The scenery is lovely, the ruins pretty sparce.

The slightly more substantial remains of another vanished civilization may be seen further south in **Etiá**, a village noted for its pretty setting. In the Middle Ages, Etiá was the fief of the Di Mezzo family, who in the 15th century built themselves a fortified villa, the most beautiful on Crete—three storeys high, with vaulted ceilings and intricate decorations. Destruction of it began when a band of Turkish administrators were besieged here by angry locals in 1828, and a fire and earthquake finished the job. Now partially restored by the Greek Archaeological Service, the entrance, ground floor and fountain house offer a hint of the villa's former grandeur.

East of Sitía: the Monastery of Toploú

This, one of Crete's wealthiest monasteries, is formally called Panagía Akroterianí, but Toploú ('cannoned' in Turkish) more aptly evokes this fortress of the faith, isolated on a plateau 3.5km from the Sitía–Palaíkastro road. It started off with a chapel dating from Nikephóros Phokás' liberation of Crete (961), while the monastery itself (*open 9–1 and 2–6*) was founded in the 15th century by the Kornáros family and rebuilt after the earthquake of 1612. Square 30ft walls defend Toploú; the gate is directly under a hole named the *foniás* ('killer'), through which the besieged monks used to pour rocks and boiling oil on their attackers. Much of Toploú's building stone came from ancient Itanos: note the inscription from the 2nd century BC embedded in the façade, recording the arbitration of Magnesia in a dispute between Itanos and Ierapytna. The campanile bears the date 1558, while the courtyard is a miniature floral oasis.

Toploú has a venerable history as a place of refuge, revolution and resistance, and more than once the monks have paid dearly for their activities. At the beginning of the War of Independence in 1821, the Turks hanged 12 monks over the gate as a warning to other rebels, although it only made the Cretans mad as hell and by the end of the war Toploú was theirs again. During the Second World War, the abbot was shot by the Germans for operating a radio transmitter for the Resistance. Next to the icons, artefacts from Toploú's battles are on display in the museum (*adm*); the finest icon is one of the masterpieces of Cretan art: the *Great is the Lord* by Ioánnis Kornáros (1770), has 61 lively, intricate scenes illustrating an Orthodox prayer.

Palaíkastro, Vaï and Itanos

All roads on the east coast converge at **Palaíkastro** (ΠΑΛΑΙΚΑΣΤΡΟ), an increasingly popular place to stop over, with a fine beach a kilometre below. The first edition of Palaíkastro was down here, en route to Chiona beach, at **Roussolakos**, a Late Minoan settlement with streets, houses and workshops similar to Gourniá. In summer, excavations continue apace. Later, the inhabitants moved up the hill to **Kastrí**, where in the ruins of a 4th-century BC temple to Diktean Zeus—the same one controlled by the Eteocretans of Praisós—the *Hymn of the Kouretes* (*see* p.74) was found engraved on a stone; in fact the words are much older than the temple. Two kilometres north, **Koureménos Beach** is a favourite for windsurfing.

Palaíkastro is the last bus stop before **Vaï** (ΒΑΪ), the island's most stunningly beautiful beach. Its silver sands are lined with Europe's only wild palm trees, a species unique to Crete called *Phoenix theophrastii*. A banana plantation completes the Caribbean ambience; bunches are on sale around Vaï's bus-gorged car park. The only way to avoid sharing this tropical paradise with thousands of body-bakers is to get there at the crack of dawn, come out of season or star in the next Bounty ad filmed on the beach. An overpriced taverna overlooks the sands—and if you wonder why people hop about in the water, it's because the fish sometimes bite.

Small beaches around Vaï act as crowd overflow tanks and free campsites. The three best have a few palms of their own and lie along the path north of Vaï, 1.5km up Cape Sideros near ancient **Itanos**. Inhabited from Early Minoan times, Itanos minted the first coins on Crete.

After the razing of Praisós, the city was a fierce rival of Ierápetra for control of Palaíkastro's temple of Diktean Zeus, leading to the Arbitration of the Magnesians of 132 BC—a decision in Itanos' favour, as we know from the inscription embedded in the Toploú's wall. The Ptolemies of Egypt used Itanos as a naval station, but pirates forced its abandonment in the 8th century; best preserved of the remains are a basilica and fine cut Hellenistic wall.

The Minoan Palace of Zákros

© (0843) 93 323. Open 8–7 in season, otherwise 8–2.30, closed Mon; adm.

From Palaíkastro, the road south cuts through a porphyry-coloured country of olives and sleepy hamlets to **Zákros** (ΖΑΚΡΟΣ). A rich Minoan villa of the New Palace era, with wall paintings, sewers, wine presses and cellars, was found near the head of a dramatic gorge, the 'Valley of Death', named not for tourists with broken necks but after the Minoan tombs from 2600 BC cut into the cliffs. On feet clad in reasonable shoes it's a not terribly difficult 8km walk down to Káto Zákros. The new road is plied by two or three buses a day from Sitía.

For decades farmers kept digging up seals by the sea at Káto Zákros, and it was there that English archaeologist David Hogarth, who excavated the villa at upper Zákros in 1901, next planted his spade, uncovering 12 houses before a torrential downpour forced him to abandon the site—literally a few feet from the prize. This, the **Palace of Zákros**, the fourth largest on Crete, waited patiently underground until 1961, when Greek archaeologist Níkos Pláton began digging where Hogarth left off. Built over an older site in the New Palace period (*c.* 1700 BC), the town that surrounded the palace was probably the Minoans' chief port for Egypt, the base of the 'Keftiu' (as the Egyptians called them, and as the Minoans may well have called themselves); the importance of trade for Zákros is highlighted by the fact that the valley could never have supplied such a large settlement with enough food.

The palace collapsed in the general catastrophe of 1450 BC, followed by fire, and was never rebuilt, never plundered; Pláton found large quantities of unworked ivory, which may have been a local speciality. The discovery of cult items suggests that disaster overwhelmed the residents. Thanks to the slow subsidence of the east coast of Crete (or rise in Mediterranean sea-levels according to others), the once important harbour of Zákros is now under the sea.

The entrance to the palace is by way of the original harbour road, leading into the northeast court; the covered area is a foundry predating the palace. A corridor leads into the long **Central Court**, which preserves the base of an altar. As usual, there are sanctuaries and ritual chambers in the West Wing, entered by way of a monolithic portal near the altar base. **Store Rooms** of giant *pithoi* are to the northwest, while the large **Hall of Ceremonies** extends to the west, with a paved light-well in front and two windows; traces of frescoes were found here. A quantity of wine vessels found in the large room to the south led the archaeologists to dub it the **Banquet Hall**. Behind this are a **Shrine** and **Lustral Basin**, probably used for purification, and the **Shrine Treasury**, where Pláton found the precious rock-crystal libation vase now in Herákleon's archaeology museum and other stone vases. Boxes of Linear A tablets came out of the shrine's **Archive**; unfortunately the wet dissolved the bulk of them into a clay mass. **Workshops** closed in the southern end of the Central Court. In the southeast corner, a **Well** with worn steps was used for sacrificial offerings. At the bottom, Pláton found a bowl of perfectly preserved Minoan olives; they tasted pretty good, too, according to Pláton and his team.The East Wing of the palace is tentatively identified as the **Royal Apartments**. The so-

Zákros

1	Central Court	19	cistern room
2	Banquet Hall	20	spring
3	Hall of Ceremonies	21	well
4	lustral basin	22	lustral basin
5	shrine	23	altar base
6	archive room of the shrine	24	dye house
7	shrine treasury	25	store rooms
8–15	store rooms	26	entrance
16	kitchen-dining room	27	main road to harbour
17	Queen's apartment	28	courtyard
18	King's apartment	29	workshops

called **Cistern Room** behind the apartments is even more of an enigma: was this plaster-walled basin, with a balustrade and steps leading down to the paved floor, a swimming pool, a fish pond, or used to float a sacred ship as in Egypt? Nearby, steps lead down to a '**well-fashioned spring**', as Pláton called it after Homer's description, which may have been a shrine connected to the spring that fed the cistern. At the north end is a large **Kitchen**—the only one ever found in a palace.

As a protected archaeological zone, the little fishing hamlet of **Káto Zákro** seems utterly idyllic, with no new buildings or big hotels. The pebbly beach is fine for a swim or a snorkel, but if it is remote soft white sands you have a yen for, make your way 10km south down the tortuous coastal road to **Xerókambos** (signposted off the new road), where the Liviko View Restaurant will feed you.

✉ *72300,* ☎ *(0843–)*   ***Where to Stay and Eating Out***

Palaíkastro

Marina Village, 500m from the sea, ☎ 61 284, ✉ 61 285 (*C; exp*), is a little resort complex with its own restaurant, pool and tennis courts. **Hellas**, near the central square, ☎ 61 240 (*C; inexp*), is good value. *Open all year.* **Thalia**, ☎ 61 448, ✉ 61 558 (*D; inexp*), is on a side street, smothered in bougainvillea. *Open all year.*

Zákros

In the upper village, **Zákros**, ✆/✉ 93 379 (*C; inexp*), is small and a bit frayed at the edges. *Open all year.* In summer there are a few rooms to let along the road to Káto Zákros, and about 50 beds scattered in the various rent-rooms near the sea that are in great demand and preferable, among them **George**, ✆ 93 201 (*inexp*), with clean, tastefully furnished rooms and a terrace, and seaside **Athena**, ✆ 93 458 (*inexp*), at the end of the beach road. Three tavernas hug the shore; **Maria's**, serving fresh fish under the tamarisks, is the best.

Ierápetra (ΙΕΡΑΠΕΤΡΑ)

By rights, **Ierápetra**, as the southernmost town in Europe—a mere 370km from Africa—and main market centre for Crete's banana, pineapple and winter veg crops, should be a fascinating place instead of an irritatingly dull dodoburg with a grey sand beach. It's still a popular day-trip destination from the north coast of Crete, though, with frequent bus connections from Sitía and Ag. Nikólaos.

Dominating Ierápetra's seafront is the 13th-century Venetian **Kastélli**, rebuilt by Sammicheli; it stands on the south mole of the ancient harbour, once Roman Crete's chief port for Africa, now bobbing with fishing and pleasure craft. Near here, the domed church of **Aféndi Christós** was first built in the 1300s and has a fine carved wooden iconostasis. Behind, in a warren of narrow streets, is a house where Napoleon supposedly spent the night of 26 June 1798, before sailing off to campaign in Egypt. The most beautiful things in Ierápetra are a Late Minoan *larnax* painted with scenes of animals and a hunt, and a charming Roman Demeter, both residents of the **Archaeology Museum**, Plateía Dimarchéiou (*supposedly open Tues–Sat 9–3; adm*).

All in all, the best thing to do in Ierápetra is leave—take Thethelatákis' caique or one of several other excursions out to the golden sands of **Nisos Chrisí** (or Gaidouronísi, or 'Donkey Island'), an uninhabited islet where one of Crete's last natural cedar forests survives intact. The sea deposits seashells by the million on Chrisí's shores; in season tavernas by the beach ward off any chance of starvation. In summer you can also find excursion boats to **Koufonísi**, a remote island to the east, where the seashells were mostly of the murex variety, used to dye cloth royal purple. This resource made it a prize, and Ierápetra and Itanos fought over it endlessly; a theatre and settlement have been excavated, and the water is crystal-clear for snorkelling.

Corfu   148

Kefaloniá   173

Kos   188

  Psérimos   199

Lefkáda   200

  Meganísi   210

Direct from the UK

Lésbos   210

Náxos   228

Rhodes   236

  Sými   265

Sámos   271

Skiáthos   286

Thássos   293

Zákynthos   299

The islands in this chapter are all package-tour destinations from the UK, as well as being served by flights from Athens. While this does mean that they contain some of the biggest and busiest resorts on the Greek islands, they are by no means completely spoilt by the effects of mass tourism, and it is still possible to find havens of peace, beauty and tranquillity on each of them.

Corfu/Kérkyra (KEPKYPA)

Corfu is a luxuriant Garden of Eden cast up in the northwest corner of Greece, a sweet mockery of the grim, grey mountains of Albania, so close and so unenticing. The Venetian city-capital of the island is one of the loveliest towns in Greece; the beaches that have managed to escape the infectious claw of package tourism are still gorgeous; the gentler mountain slopes, sprinkled with pastel villas and farms, could be in Tuscany.

Corfu's reputation as a distant paradise began with Homer, who called it Scheria, the happy isle of the Phaeacians, beloved of the gods, where the shipwrecked Odysseus was found washed up on a golden beach by the lovely Nausicaa. Shakespeare had it in mind when creating the magical isle of *The Tempest*, even if Prospero offered a different sort of hospitality to his shipwrecked guests. Edward Lear and Gerald and Lawrence Durrell evoked its charms so delightfully that it found a special niche in the English heart—with staggering consequences. During Corfu's first British occupation, it learned to play cricket; during the second (nearly a million British tourists come a year, and there are 7,000 British and Irish female permanent residents), the island has learned the consequences of run-amok mass tourism speculation—of letting its beauty be cheaply bought and sold. Corfiots have been stunned by the Calibanish behaviour of British lager louts, then stung by the negative reports of their island in the British press. It hardly seemed fair.

The rotten publicity spurred a serious 'culture versus crud' debate on Corfu, and not a moment too soon (in fact way too late for the 10km of coastline either side of Corfu town, where a depressing jerry-built sprawl litters the road and pebble beaches). A new sewage system has sorted out most of the sea pollution complaints. Stricter zoning and licensing laws are being enforced and a spit and polish of Corfu town has begun to set the tone for a classier, more genteel Corfu. An Autumn Chamber Music Festival has been added to its successful annual Spring Chamber Music Festival (three quarters of the musicians in the Greek National Orchestra are from Corfu), and the Art Café and the Old and New Fortresses now host innovative art exhibitions, subsidised by the municipality. Count Spíros Flambouriári, member of an old Corfiot family ennobled by the Venetians, has begun an island 'National Trust' to restore its lovely but mouldering country estates, beautifully photographed in his book *Corfu: The Garden Isle*.

These estates of the gentry are scattered in the gorgeous hinterland (especially to the north of Corfu town), where villages are free of monster concrete hotels, enclaves of expensive villas, and tourist compounds. In some of Corfu's more distant nooks and crannies are lovely beaches that somehow slipped past the cement mixer. Come in the early spring, when the almonds blossom, or around Palm Sunday or the first part of November (coinciding with the colourful celebrations of Ag. Spyrídon), and seek out the old cobbled donkey paths that once provided the main link between villages—you'll be rewarded with a poignant vision of the old Corfu, strewn with wild flowers (including 43 kinds of orchids), scented with the blossoms of lemons

Corfu/Kérkyra

and kumquats, and silvery with billowing forests of ancient olives interspersed with towers of straight black cypresses. The olive trees still outnumber tourists by three and a half million.

History

In ancient times Corfu was Corcyra, named after a mistress of the sea god Poseidon. According to ancient tradition, she bore him a son called Phaeax, who became the founder of the gentle and noble Phaeacian race. Archaeological evidence suggests that the Phaeacians were cultur-ally quite distinct from the Mycenaeans, and had much in common not with any people in Greece but with cultures in Apulia, in southern Italy. In 734 BC the Corinthians sent a trading colony to the island and founded a city at Paliaopolis (the modern suburbs of Anemómylos and Análypsis). A temple there housed the sickle that Zeus used to castrate his father Cronos, whose testicles fell to form the two hills around the Old Fortress (*corypho* in Greek means 'peaks', hence 'Corfu'). A prophecy current in classical Greece foretold that Apollo would one day fetch the sickle to do the same to his father Zeus.

Although Corcyra thrived to become the richest of the Ionian islands, it was cursed with violent political rivalries between its democrats and the oligarchs. According to Thucydides, the Corcyrans fought the first sea battle in Greek history, against Corinth in 664 BC. In 435 BC, after the same two city-states quarrelled over a colony in Albania in the Battle of Sybota (the dispute that set off the Peloponnesian War), internal strife left Corcyra so weakened that it was captured by Syracuse, and then by King Pyrrhus of Epirus, and in 229 BC by the Illyrians. In the first century BC, Corcyra was loyal to Mark Antony—he left his wife Octavia here before sailing off with Cleopatra—and as a reprisal after his defeat Octavian's army under Agrippa destroyed every civic monument on the island. Yet whatever the turmoil, ancient Corcyra never lost its lofty reputation for fertility and beauty; Emperor Nero paid it a special visit in AD 67 to dance and sing at the temple of Zeus in modern Kassiópi.

The remnants of the population that survived the ravages of the Goths in AD 550 decided to rebuild their town on the more easily defended site of the Old Fortress and two hills of Cape Sidáro, where they would be better protected. This failed to thwart the Normans in 1081, but in 1148, when their raids menaced the Byzantine Empire itself, Emperor Emmanuel Comnenus sent a special force and fleet to dislodge them. When the siege of the Byzantines made no progress, Emmanuel came to lead the attack in person. By craftily seeding subversion among the Normans themselves, he succeeded in winning back the island.

Venetian Corfu

In 1204, when Venice came to claim Corfu as part of its spoils in the Fourth Crusade, the inhabitants put up a stiff resistance. Although the Venetians succeeded in taking the island's forts, the islanders aligned themselves with the Despotat of Epirus, an Orthodox state. Fifty years later, however, the King of Naples and brother of St Louis of France, Charles I of Anjou, snatched Corfu and the rest of Achaia when his son married the princess of Villehardouin. Angevin rule, already infamous for provoking the Sicilian Vespers, was equally intolerant and hated on Corfu. After 120 years, the Corfiots swallowed their pride and in 1386 asked Venice to put them under the protection of the Republic.

In 1537 a serious threat, not only to Corfu but to all of Europe, landed at Igoumenítsa in the form of Suleiman the Magnificent. Suleiman, the greatest of the Turkish sultans, already had most of the rest of Greece in his pocket and was determined to take Corfu as a base for attacking Italy and western Europe. Thanks to a peace treaty with Venice, Suleiman was able to plot his attack in the utmost secrecy. When the Corfiots discovered only a few days in advance what was in store for them, they tore down their houses for stone to repair the fortress and to leave nothing behind for the Turks. The terrible Barbarossa was the first to arrive and begin the siege of the city, during which he suffered massive losses. Thousands of Corfiots who had been pitilessly abandoned outside the fortress were caught in the Venetian and Turkish crossfire, and fell prey to Barbarossa's fits of rage at his continual setbacks. Those who managed to survive were carted off to the slave markets of Constantinople when Suleiman, discouraged by his losses and bad weather, ordered the lifting of the siege.

Only 21 years later Venice, under pressure from the Corfiots, expanded the island's fortifications to include the town. Many houses remained unprotected, however, and when the Turks reappeared in 1571 under Ouloudj Ali, these and the rest of the villages, trees and vineyards of Corfu were decimated. This time the Turks took no prisoners and massacred whoever they caught. A final blow was struck two years later by another pirate admiral, Sinan Pasha: of the entire Corfiot population, only a tenth remained on the island after 1573.

In 1576, Venice finally began to build walls to protect all the surviving islanders. The New Fortress and other fortifications designed by the expert Sammicheli were considered superb, state-of-the art works in their day—the equal of Sammicheli's bastions around Herákleon. The Venetians also undertook measures to restore Corfu's economy, most notably by offering a bounty of 42 *tsekínia* for every olive tree planted (today there are an estimated 4.5 million trees, producing 3 per cent of the world supply of oil). To ingratiate themselves with local power brokers, they allowed wealthy Corfiots to purchase titles, creating a class society unique on the Greek islands. Sammicheli's walls were given the ultimate test in 1716, when Turks staged furious attacks for one terrible month before being repulsed by the stratagems of a German mercenary soldier, Field Marshal Schulenberg, and a tempest sent by Corfu's guardian, St Spyrídon.

After the fall of Venice to Napoleon, the French occupied Corfu and immediately improved the education system and set up the first public library (1797), but they lost the island two years later in a fierce battle against the Russo-Turkish fleet. When Napoleon finally got it back, he personally designed new fortifications for the town; he loved Corfu, 'more interesting to us than all of Italy put together'. Napoleon's walls were so formidable that the British, when allotted the Ionian islands after Waterloo, did not care to argue the point when the French commander Donzelot refused to give them up. The French government finally had to order Donzelot home, and in 1815, with the signing of the Treaty of Vienna, Corfu and the other Ionians became a British Protectorate, with the blessing of Count John Capodístria. Capodístria, soon to be the first president of Greece, was a native of Corfu and, like many of the island's noblemen and scholars, had been in the employ of the tsars after 1799.

British and Greek Corfu

While Capodístria had requested 'military protection', the British, based in Corfu, took it upon themselves to run all the affairs of the Ionian State, which they 'legalized' by a constitution imposed under the first Lord High Commissioner, Sir Thomas Maitland, whose brutal and unbelievably rude behaviour earned him the nickname 'King Tom'. One of his first acts was to demolish part of the Venetian walls to build new, stronger ones in their place, calling upon the Ionian government to cough up more than a million gold sovereigns to pay for the improvements. Maitland made himself even more disliked by forcing neutrality on the islands as the Greek War of Independence broke out, disarming the population and imprisoning, and even executing, members of the secret patriotic Society of Friends. The constitution ensured that the peasantry lived in near-feudal conditions, and denied Corfu's educated and middle classes any political role; the Ionians weren't even given favourable trade status with Britain. It was, as one British High Commissioner put it, 'a sort of middle state between a colony and a perfectly independent country, without possessing the advantage of either.' Other public works were more positive and long-lasting—the building of new roads and schools and a university (the 'Ionian Academy', founded by Hellenophile Lord Guilford), and the establishment of a permanent water supply to Corfu town. The locals took up cricket, and Edward Lear spent months on the island, painting pretty watercolours and writing in his journal.

In 1858, with the political situation growing increasingly uncomfortable, Gladstone was sent down as a special investigator to propose a solution to the crisis, but, constrained by the international situation (British distrust of King Otho and Greece's support of Russia, Britain's enemy in the Crimean War), he only proposed a reconstruction of the government. The 1862 overthrow of Otho gave Britain a chance to cede the islands gracefully to Greece, on condition that Greece found an acceptable king. This was Prince William of Denmark, crowned George I, King of the Hellenes; on 21 May 1864 the Ionians were presented as the new king's 'dowry'. There was one ungracious condition to the deal: that the British ensure the islands' neutrality by destroying the fortresses of Corfu—not only the walls they themselves had just made the Corfiots build, but also the historic Venetian buildings. A wave of protest from all corners of the Greek world failed to move the British, and the bulk of the fortifications were blown sky high.

In 1923, Mussolini gave the world a preview of his intentions when he bombarded and occupied Corfu after the assassination on Greek territory of an Italian delegate to the Greek-Albanian border council; the Italians left only when Greece paid a large indemnity. An even worse bombardment occurred in 1943, when the Germans blasted the city and its Italian garrison for 10 days; a year later, the British and Americans bombed the Germans. At the end of the war, a quarter of the old city was destroyed, including 14 of the loveliest churches.

✆ (0661–)   *Getting There and Around*

By air: frequent charter flights from London, Manchester, Glasgow and other UK airports; also regular flights from many European cities; three flights a day from Athens, two in the winter with either Aegean Airlines or Olympic. The Olympic Airways office in Corfu town is at 20 Kapodistríou, ✆ 38 694/5/6; Aegean is at the airport, ✆ 27 100. There is no special bus service linking Corfu's airport to the town but there is a regular bus stop on the main road, several hundred metres away, or a taxi for 1,000dr. For general **airport information**, call ✆ 30 180 or 37 398.

By sea: there's a year-round ferry service to Paxí. Ferry links from Corfu town to the small islands of Eríkousa, Othoní and Mathráki are only twice a week (for details call ✆ 36 355), but **excursion boats** go there from Sidári and Ag. Stéfanos. **Caiques** go regularly from the Old Port to Vído, home to many Serbian graves, and take tourists from Dassiá along the coast to Kassiópi and Benítses. **Port authority**: ✆ 32 655.

By bus: the bus depot in Platéia Theotóki–San Rócco Square, ✆ 31 595, has blue KTEL buses to villages just beyond Corfu town (Kanóni, Pótamos, Konokali, Goúvia, Dassiá, Pérama, Ag. Ioánnis, Benítses, Pélekas, Kastelláni, Kouramádes, Áfra, Achilleíon and Gastoúri). From the depot in Avramíou Street, ✆ 39 985 or 30 627, green buses run to the more distant villages (Ipsos, Pírgi, Glyfáda, Barbáti, Kassiópi, Paliokastrítsa, Sidári, Ag. Stéfanos [west coast], Róda, Kávos, Messóghi, Ag. Górdis, and both resorts named Ag. Geórgios).

By foot: the ubiquitous Mrs Paipeti has also written a book on hidden trails across the island; you can purchase it at Likoudis bookstore, next to the National Bank.

By bicycle: the Dutch Bicycle company, Ag. Ioánnis Tríklino, ✆/✉ 52 407, rents out mountain bikes for exploring the hidden corners of Corfu. The Corfu Mountainbike Shop in Dassiá, ✆ 93 344, ✉ 46 100, also rents out bikes galore and organizes tours.

By car: although lately much improved, Corfu's roads are not always well signposted, and there seem to be more than the usual number of Greek island hazards: dangerous curves and farm vehicles, careless tourists on motorbikes or sudden deteriorations in the surface. Road maps often confuse donkey tracks with unpaved roads. Try International Rent A Car if you want wheels, ✆ 33 411 or 37 710, ✉ 46 350, centrally located at 20a Kapodistríou Street and run by a friendly Greek-Irish couple with 35 years' rental and travel agency experience. They will deliver your car free to anywhere on the island and transport you from the airport into town. Petrol stations are generally open Mon–Fri 7am–7pm, Sat 7am–3pm, but opening hours can be flexible. Make sure you get a decent map; best at the time of writing is *The Precise All New Road Atlas of Corfu*, hand drawn by S. Jaskulowski.

Tours: travel agents in Corfu offer one-day Classical tours to the mainland: to Epirus to visit the Oracle of the Dead (consulted by Odysseus after crossing the perilous River Styx), and the ancient cities of Kassopea and Nicopolis, founded by Augustus after the defeat of Mark Antony and Cleopatra in 31 BC. A second tour takes in Dodóni, with its ancient theatre, and Ioannína, the modern capital of Epirus, with its island of Ali Pasha and museum. Excursions to Albania to visit the ancient Roman city of Saranda have recently been resumed.

✆ *(0661–)*   ***Tourist Information***

EOT: 7 Rizospaston Voulefton, ✆ 37 520, ✉ 30 298 (open weekdays 8–2).

Tourist police: Samartzi Street, near San Rocco Square, ✆ 30 265.

OTE telephones: Mántzarou and Kapodistríou Streets, and in the New Port.

Post office: Alexándras Avenue, ✆ 39 265 (open 8–8).

Internet: Café Online, 28 Kapodistríou Street, ✆ 46 226 (open 9am–1am), and the slightly cheaper Centraal, ✆ 72 255.

Doctor: Dr J.P. Yannopapas speaks excellent English, 1 Mántzarou, ✆ 49 350/587.

✆ *(0661–)*   ***Consulates***

Denmark	50 Stratigou, ✆ 35 698.
France	22 Polila, ✆ 26 312/30 067.
Germany	57 Guilford Street, ✆ 31 453.
Great Britain	1 Penecratus, ✆ 30 055/37 995.
Ireland	20a Kapodistríou Street, ✆ 32 469/39 910.
Netherlands	2 Idroménou Street, ✆ 39 900.
Norway	9 Donzelótou Street, ✆ 39 667.

Festivals

Procession of Ag. Spyrídon in Corfu town on **Palm Sunday, Easter Saturday, 11 August** and **first Sunday in November**. **Holy Saturday** is celebrated in Corfu town with a bang—the sound of everyone tossing out their chipped and cracked crockery. **First Friday after Easter**, Paliokastrítsa; **21 May**, Union with Greece; **5–8 July**, in Lefkimi; **10 July**, Ag. Prokópios in Kávos; **14 August**, the Procession of Lights in Mandoúki; **15 August**, Panagías in Kassiópi. The Corfu Festival in **September** brings concerts, ballet, opera and theatre to the island.

Excursions on Corfu

1 North—Shorter Circuit: Drive up to charming Agní bay for lunch, then follow the beautiful wooded coastline until the road off to the traditional village of Old Perithía; consider walking up to Mount Pantokrátor's summit for superlative views. Drive on to Láfki and down towards Strinílas, through beautiful countryside, past olive wood shops. Continue down past Pírgi to Corfu town.

2 North—Longer Circuit: Head up to Agní for lunch again and continue along the wooded coast and around the north of the island to Róda; turn inland here and meander through traditional villages and hills of wild flowers and cypresses down towards Troumbetas and Makrades. You'll pass the stunningly situated Angelókastro before reaching charming Lákones, perched on the hillside; stop off for a drink at one of the panoramic cafés and then wind down to Paleokastrítsa. There's a good road from here back to Corfu town.

3 South—Inland and Beach: Branch inland at Kinopiástes down towards alluring little Ag. Déka and Strongilí; make for Korissíon lagoon, a twitcher's delight in spring and autumn, with unspoilt beaches sandwiched between it and the sea. Then head up to traditional Ag. Mattheos, epicentre for many rural walks, and follow the delightful road on to Vouniatades, Sinarádes and Pélekas before heading east to Corfu town.

Corfu Town

Corfu town, or Kérkyra (pop. 40,000), the largest town in the Ionian islands, was laid out by the Venetians in the 14th century when the medieval town, crowded on to the peninsula of Cape Sidáro (where the Old Fortress now stands), had no room to expand. They began with the quarter known as Campiello (from *campo*, Venetian for 'square'), where three- or four-storey houses loom over the narrow streets, as they do back in the lagoon capital. By the time the new walls were added in the 16th century, the Venetians built at a more leisurely pace in the more open style of the Renaissance, laying out an exquisite series of central streets and small squares. Some of the finest Venetian houses, their arches decorated with masks and half-moon windows over the door, can be seen along the upper Esplanade, and everywhere you look there are gentle shades of Savoy red and pinks peeling off gracious Venetian façades. The British knocked down most of the old Venetian walls to allow the pent-up town to expand again, and then constructed a set of elegant Georgian public buildings.

Besides Campiello, the old city is divided into a number of small quarters such as Garítsa, the 19th-century residential district to the south. The Old Port, on the east side of the New Fortress, is now used by only one ferry—the excursion boat to Paxí; all the other ferries and excursion boats come in and out of town through its back door at Mandoúki or New Port, west of the New Fortress.

The New Fortress

The New Fortress, or Néo Froúrio, is the mass of walls that dominates the view if you arrive by sea, built after 1576 by the Venetians following the Ottomans' third attack on Corfu. It bore the brunt of the Turkish siege of 1716, and although most of the walls were dynamited by the British, enough masonry survived for the installation of a Greek naval base. Over the gates are carved Lions of St Mark and inscriptions in various states of erosion. Now open to the public (*daily 9–8.30; adm; entrance from Solomós Street*), there are excellent views of Corfu town from the top of its bastions, and two underground tunnels to explore. **Corfu's Market** is in the Fortress moat along G. Markorá Street; if you're self-catering or planning a picnic, try to come early to get the pick of the fresh fish and produce. Quite a bit further west, beyond the hospital on Polichroni Konstantá Street, the **Monastery of Platýteras** contains two beautiful icons given to the island by Catherine the Great in honour of Count Capodístria, who is buried here; also note the silver and gilt columns by the altar, a typical Russian feature.

To the east of the New Fortress in Spiliá, near New Fortress Square, stands the 1749 Catholic **church of Ténedos**, named after an icon brought to Corfu by the Venetians from the now Turkish island of Ténedos. You can reach the centre of town from the Old Port through the 16th-century Spiliá Gate, incorporated into a later structure, or take the narrow steps up into the medieval Campiello Quarter (*see* below); the **Jewish Quarter**, equally old and picturesque, lies south of Plateía Solomoú. Although the Greek synagogue and a school remain in the heart of the quarter, in Velissáriou Street (the Italian synagogue was bombed and burned in 1943), only 170 out of the 1,800 members of the congregation sent to Auschwitz survived to return to Corfu after the war.

The Esplanade (Spianáda) and the Listón

A series of long parallel streets—the main residential district of the Venetians—all lead to the town's centre, the great green space called the Spianáda, or Esplanade, one of the largest public squares in Europe. Originally a field left open for defensive purposes, it began to take its present form as a garden and promenade when Napoleon ordered the building of the arcaded **Listón** on the west edge of the Esplanade, in imitation of one of his proudest Paris creations, the rue de Rivoli. At the time, it was the only place in all of Greece reserved exclusively for the aristocracy (or those on the list, hence the name). Then, as now, the Listón was a solid row of elegant cafés; at night the monuments and trees are floodlit for dramatic effect.

The northern end of the Esplanade is filled by the Georgian **Palace of St Michael and St George**, with its two grand gates. Designed by Sir George Whitmore, the palace was built as the residence of Sir Thomas Maitland, first High Commissioner of the Ionian state—note the symbols of the seven islands on its Maltese marble façade. In 1864 it became the summer residence of the King of Greece, then fell into disuse until it was renovated in 1953 to house a magnificent **Museum of Asiatic Art** (*open 8.30–3, closed Mon; adm*), one of the largest and most important privately formed collections in the world, and the only one of its kind in Greece. A gift to Corfu from Greek diplomat Gregórios Mános, with further contributions from Michélis Chadjivasilíou and others, the museum contains 10,000 works (masks, ceramics, armour and weapons, and much more) from all the countries of the Far East, dating back to 1000 BC. At the **Art Café**, in a corner of the palace, you can linger over coffee and drinks and enjoy one of the permanent or temporary local art exhibitions. Adjacent to the palace is

Map labels:

OLD PORT

NEW PORT

XENOFONDOS STRATIGOU

NEW VENETIAN FORTRESS

To Mandouki

Ktel long distance (Green) Bus Terminal

AVRAMIOU

AVRAMI HILL

G. MARKORA

I. THEOTOKI

Plateia G. Theotoki (Sanrocco)

Hospital

POLICHRONI KONSTANDA

City (Blue) Bus Terminal

DIMOULITSA

MITROPOLITI METHODIOU

ZAFIROPOULOU

Post Office

KOLOKOTRONI

British Cemetery

MARASLI

Prison

KIPROU

To Kanoni

GARITSA

EHTO Tourist Police

POL

Plateia Solomou

the *loggia* of the **Reading Society** (*open daily 9–1*), founded in 1836 by a group of young Corfiot idealists freshly returned from their studies in France; the library has a fine collection of books on the Ionian islands. Just in front of the palace is another British legacy—the **cricket ground**, where little boys play football until their older white-clad brothers chase them off the field. In the summer, matches pit the six local teams (which aren't at all bad) against visitors from Britain, the Greek mainland and Europe.

Numerous monuments embellish the Esplanade. In the centre of the Upper Plateía is the **memorial to Sir Thomas Maitland**, another work by Sir George Whitmore, designed in the form of an Ionian rotunda, where local brass bands serenade the summertime crowds; you can often hear them practising in the evening in the old quarters. There is a marble **statue of Marshal Schulenberg**, the crafty and heroic soldier of fortune from Saxony who outwitted the Turkish High Admiral in the Great Siege to spoil the last major attempt of the Ottoman Empire to expand in the west. The **Guilford Memorial** is

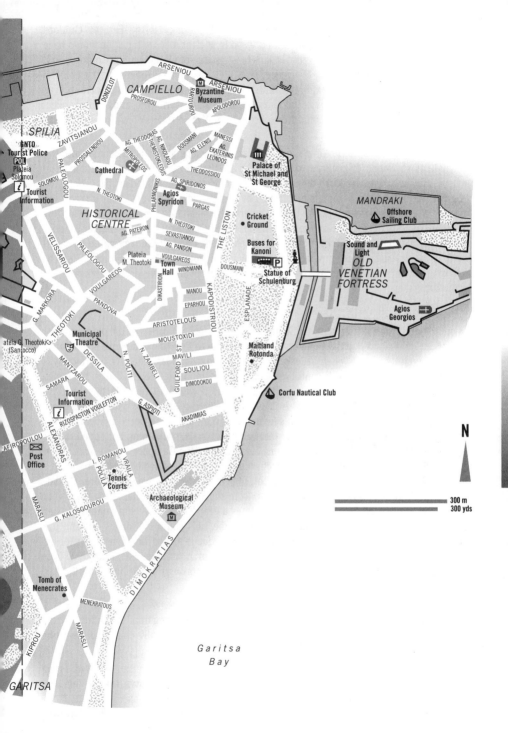

to Corfu's favourite Englishman, the Hellenophile Frederick North, Earl of Guilford (1769–1828). The seated statue portrays him dressed in ancient robes, a touch he would have appreciated. On the southern end of the Esplanade is a statue of his ambiguous Corfiot friend, Count Capodístria, first president of Greece, who was assassinated for his murky political machinations. Nearby, on Moustoxídi, one of the streets traversing Guilford, is a **Serbian War Museum** (*open 9–noon*). This is not at all what immediately springs to mind, but a collection of photographs and memorabilia from the Balkan War of 1915–17 which covers also Corfu's role in aiding the refugees.

The **Old Fortress** (*open 8.30–3, closed Mon; adm*) on Cape Sidáro is separated from the Esplanade by the moat, or *contra fosse*, dug over a 100-year period by the Venetians. The medieval town of Corfu was located on the two little hills of the cape; scholars have identified the site with the Heraion acropolis mentioned by Thucydides. The walls, built up over the centuries, were badly damaged by the British; others have fallen into decay. Part of the fortress is still used by the Greek army, but you can wander about and explore the Venetian tunnels, battlements, drawbridge, well, cannons dating back to 1684 and **St George's**, the bleached church of the British garrison, now an Orthodox place of worship. The Old Fortress Café has an alluring vista out to sea from its privileged position; best of all, however, is the view of the city from the hills.

Ag. Spyrídon

The church of Corfu's patron saint Ag. Spyrídon—the original Spíros—is in the old town, not far from the Ionian and Popular Bank of Greece. It's easy to find: the campanile soars above town like the mast of a ship, often bedecked with flags and Christmas lights. Ag. Spyrídon was the Bishop of Cyprus in the 4th century; when Constantinople fell to the Turks, his bones were smuggled in a sack of straw to Corfu. The church was built in 1596 to house the precious relics, no longer in straw but in a silver Renaissance reliquary which, with great pomp, is carted though town on the saint's feast days. According to the Corfiots, Spyrídon 'the Miracle-Worker' has brought them safely through many trials, frightening both cholera and the Turks away from his beloved worshippers. He even gave the Catholics a good scare when they considered placing an altar in his church; the night before its dedication, he blew up a powder magazine in the Old Fortress with a bolt of lightning to show his displeasure. He did, however, peacefully accept a large silver lamp from the Venetians in thanks for his divine intervention against the Turks in 1716. Four times a year (Orthodox Palm Sunday, Easter Saturday, 11 August and the first Sunday in November) his coffin is brought out and the faithful gather from all over Corfu and the mainland and queue to kiss the lid in thanks for his saving the island from plague, famine and Turks. In the church, amid mediocre Italianate frescoes blackened by the smoke of ages, the gold shimmers through in the flickering light of votive candles.

The nearby Ionian Bank houses a **Museum of Paper Money** (*open 9–1, closed Sun*), with a collection of banknotes from around the world and Greek notes dating from the nation's birth; upstairs, you can learn how they're printed. Across the square, the 1689 church of the **Holy Virgin Faneroméni** contains some fine icons of the Ionian School.

The square gives on to the main street, Nikifórou Theotóki, one of the prettiest in town. From there, head up E. Voulgáreos Street to the elegant square with Corfu's **Town Hall**, a Venetian confection begun in 1691 that later did duty as the municipal opera house; grotesque faces grimace all around the building and a bas-relief shows a triumphant Doge. The **Catholic**

Cathedral of St James on the square was seriously damaged by the German bombing in 1943. Only the bell tower survived intact; the rest has been reconstructed.

Campiello

There are a number of buildings worth seeking out in the Campiello Quarter between the Old Port and the Esplanade, beginning with the 1577 **Orthodox Cathedral**, its 18th-century façade rather unfortunately located next to the rudest T-shirt shop in town. The cathedral is dedicated to Ag. Theodóra Augústa, Empress of Byzantium (829–842), who was canonized for her role in restoring icon worship in the Orthodox Church following the Iconoclasm. Her relics were brought to Corfu along with those of Ag. Spyrídon and lie in a silver casket in the chapel to the right of the altar; if the priest in charge likes the look of you, you can kiss her and take home titbits of her slipper; donations more than welcome. The gold-grounded icons are lovely, reminscent of 13th-century Italian art.

The **Byzantine Museum of Corfu** (*open 8.45–3, Sun and holidays 9.30–2, closed Mon; adm*) is near here, up the steps from Arseníou Street. The collection is housed in the beautifully restored 15th-century Antivouniótissa, typical of the Ionian style of church with its single aisle, timber roof and exonarthex, or indoor porch, that runs around three sides of the building. Among the eminent Corfiots buried under the flagstones is Capodístria's sister, who was a nun here. The church has one of the elaborately decorated ceilings or *ourania* ('heaven') that the Ionians were so fond of, a stone iconostasis from a later date and very Italianate 17th-century Old Testament murals on the walls. Icons from all over the island have been brought here; note especially the mid-16th-century *SS. Sergius, Bacchus and Justine* by Michael Damaskinós, the 17th-century *St Cyril of Alexandria* by Emmanuel Tzanes, the 17th-century four-handed *Ag. Panteléimon* and icons by the 18th-century painter Geórgios Chrysolorás. On the same street is the **Solomós Museum** (*open weekdays 9–1; adm*), with a collection of old photographs and memorabilia associated with the great Zákynthos poet Diónysos Solomós, who lived here in his later years (*see* p.303).

On a narrow stairway off Philharmonikí Street, **Ag. Nikólaos** had the distinction of once serving as the parish church of the King of Serbia. After the defeat of the Serbian army by the Austro-Hungarians in 1916, the king, his government and some 150,000 Serbs took refuge on Corfu. A third of them died shortly thereafter from the flu and are buried on **Vído island**. Boats from the Old Port regularly make the trip to Vído; the Venetians fortified it after the Turks built a gun battery on it to attack the Old Fortress in 1537. The walls were demolished by the British. Today the island is a quiet refuge with footpaths, a little beach and a memorial to the Serbs.

South of Corfu Town: Garítsa and the Archaeology Museum

South of the Old Fortress, Garítsa Bay is believed to have been the harbour of King Alcinous of the Phaeacians; it became a fashionable residential district in the 19th century, just in time for the neoclassical building craze. On Kolokotróni Street, the beautiful, peaceful **British Cemetery** is famous as a natural botanic garden, where rare species of wild flowers bloom; the graves, many with intriguing headstones, date from the beginning of the British protectorate.

The star attraction in Garítsa is the **Archaeology Museum** (*open 8.30–3, closed Mon; adm*), with an excellent collection of finds from the island and nearby mainland, flanked by outsized amphorae worthy of Pirandello. Opened in 1967, the musuem has already been extended but is still too small to display the more recent discoveries. Among the new exhibits are bronze statuettes from Archaic to Roman times, a horde of silver staters (coins) from the 6th century BC, an iron helmet with silver overlay from the 4th century BC, and Cycladic sculptures, discovered in 1992 by a customs officer as the smugglers attempted to spirit them abroad from Igoumenítsa. Upstairs are grave-offerings, Archaic statues of the *kore* and *kouros*, and two statues of Aphrodite, the favourite goddess of the lusty Corinthians; here, too, are the snarling, stylized 'Lion of Menecrates', found on the tomb of the same name (*see* below), and the relief of a Dionysiac Symposium (*c.* 500 BC), showing the god Dionysos with a youth, lying on a couch; their eyes are focused intently on something that is probably lost forever. A lion sleeps under the couch; a dog comes striding up.

One room is given over to the striking wall-sized Gorgon Pediment (585 BC) discovered near the temple of Artemis in Kanóni; the oldest preserved stone pediment, and one of the largest (56ft wide), it shows how advanced the Corinthians were in the early days of monumental sculpture. The grinning Gorgon Medusa is powerfully drawn, running with one knee on the ground, flanked by her two diminutive children, Pegasus the winged horse and Chrysaor; according to myth they were born from her blood when she was slain by Perseus, although here she looks very alive indeed. Two large leopards on either side suggest that this is actually Artemis herself in her form of 'the Lady of the Wild Animals', a fearsome goddess who demanded an annual holocaust of the creatures she protected, burned alive on the altar; in the far corners of the pediment, much smaller scenes show the Clash of the Titans.

The circular, 7th-century BC **Menecrates tomb** was discovered in the 19th century in an excellent state of preservation. Its lower sections are still intact in the garden of a building at the junction of Marasslí and Kíprou Streets, three blocks south of the museum.

Southern Suburbs along the Kanóni Peninsula

City bus no.3 from Corfu town passes through all the garden suburbs draped over the little **Kanóni peninsula** that dangles south of Garítsa Bay. Ancient Corcyra originally occupied much of this peninsula and had two harbours: what is now the Chalikiopóulos lagoon to the west and the ring-shaped 'harbour of King Alcinous' (now filled in) in the northeastern corner of the peninsula, at Anemómylos. Above it, right on top of the centre of ancient Corcyra, Sir Frederick Adam, the second High Commissioner of the Ionian State, built the little Regency villa of **Mon Repos** for his Corfiot wife. The Greek royal family later adopted it as a summer villa; Queen Elizabeth II's consort, Philip, Duke of Edinburgh, was born here in 1921. In 1994 the Greek government allowed the Municipality of Corfu to repossess the estate from ex-King Constantine and the beautiful wooded park is to be developed as an archaeological park. So far a Roman villa and bath have been discovered on the periphery, at Kasfíki, opposite the ruined 5th-century basilica of **Ag. Kérkyra** at Paleópolis (by the crossroads, opposite the gate of Mon Repos). Little Mon Repos beach—Corfu town's beach—is just below if you need a dip. A few lanes back, don't miss the 11th-century church of **Ag. Iássonos and Sosipater**, the only Byzantine-style church on the whole island; inside are lovely icons and iconostasis and the tombs of the church's namesakes, two martyrs instructed by St Paul, who brought Christianity to Corfu in AD 70. Near the Venetian church, along the wall of Mon Repos, a path leads to the bucolic spring of **Kardáki**, which flows year-round from the mouth of a stone lion; the Venetians used it to supply their ships. The cold water is good, but an inscription above warns: 'Every stranger who wets his lips here to his home will not return.' Below the spring are the ruins of a 6th-century BC Doric temple. From here it's an easy walk to the lush and lovely residential area of Análypsos.

Further south, a minor road leads to the Doric **Temple of Artemis** (585 BC), source of the magnificent Gorgon Pediment in the Archaeology Museum. The large altar and the retaining wall of the Hellenistic stoa survive; some of its stones were cannibalized in the 5th century to build the adjacent convent of **Ag. Teodóri**. At the southern tip of the lovely little peninsula, **Kanóni** is named for the old cannon once situated on the bluff, where two cafés now overlook the pretty bay, the harbour of ancient Corcyra. Two islets protected it: that of the oft-photographed convent **Panagía Vlacharína**, connected to the shore by a causeway, and **Pondikonísi**, the Isle of the Mouse, with its 13th-century chapel, Ag. Pnévmatos. Pondikonísi was the Phaeacian ship that brought Odysseus home to Ithaca, but on its way back to Corfu the angry Poseidon smote 'with his open palm, and made the ship a rock, fast rooted in the bed of the deep sea', according to the *Odyssey*. An airport runway built on a landfill site now crosses the west end of the shallow lagoon, and a collection of big new hotels has toadstooled nearby, in spite of the noise of planes day and night, which can interrupt a good night's sleep.

Pérama, Gastoúri and the Achilleíon

Past the Kanóni peninsula and linked to it by a pedestrian causeway over the lagoon, **Pérama** claims to be the site of King Alcinous' wonderful garden and is where the Durrell family first lived when they arrived (for more details on the brothers Durrell, pick up a copy of Hilary Whitton Paipeti's *In the Footsteps of Lawrence Durrell and Gerald Durrell in Corfu*). The pretty village of **Gastoúri** is the dreamy setting for a neoclassical neo-Pompeiian villa called the **Achilleíon** (*open for tours daily in summer, 8–3.30; adm*), with lovely views in all directions. The villa itself is more of a nightmare, sufficiently kitsch to be used as a location for the James Bond film *For Your Eyes Only*. Built in 1890 by the Empress Elisabeth ('Sissi') of Austria after the tragic death of her only son Rudolphe, the villa was named for Sissi's passion for the hero of Homer's *Iliad*; Sissi fancied herself as the immortal sea goddess Thetis, with Rudolphe as her son Achilles, idealized by a large marble statue she had made of the *Dying Achilles* for the garden. Ten years after Sissi was assassinated in 1898 by an Italian anarchist, Kaiser Wilhelm II purchased the Achilleíon and made it his summer residence from 1908 to 1914, and, true to character, had the *Dying Achilles* replaced with a huge bronze *Victorious Achilles*, with the inscription 'To the Greatest of the Greeks from the Greatest of the Germans.' Among the bevy of more delicate statues, note the Grace standing next to Apollo, sculpted by Canova using Napoleon's sister Pauline Borghese as his model. The small museum contains, among its collection of imperial mementoes, one of the Kaiser's swivelling saddles, from which he dictated plans for the First World War, and photos of him swanning around on his huge yacht, the *Hohenzollern*, which he used to anchor off the 'Kaiser's Bridge' just south of Pérama. Amid this fetid mix of bad art and power, note, over the gate of Troy in Franz Matsch's stomach-churning painting of the *Triumph of Achilles*, a little swastika.

Shopping

Xenoglosso, 45 Ger. Markóra, near San Rocco Square, has a good selection of books in English. Autolycus Gallery, now closed, sells some of its fine collection of antique prints, maps, postcards and watercolours at Mrs Paipeti's antiques shop next to the Cavalieri Corfu Hotel. There are a number of high-fashion shops, the most famous of which must be Panton on Panton Street, the main outlet of Corfu designer Lisa Palavicini, whose clothes have been featured in Vogue and are sold in outlets in Athens, London and Jordan. Shops with a predominantly touristy clientèle hardly ever seem to close, but non-tourist shops are closed every evening except Tuesday, Thursday and Friday.

Corfu Town ✉ 49100, ☎ (0661–) Where to Stay

luxury

Just south of the centre, the enormous **Corfu Palace**, Dimokratías Ave, ☎ 39 485, @ 31 749, *cfupalace@hol.gr* (*L*), has two swimming pools and all the trimmings, from baby sitting to 24-hour room service. Most rooms have sea views but can cost as much as 65,000dr in high season. There's also a cache of luxurious high-rise palaces in Kanóni: the **Corfu Holiday Palace** (*née* Hilton), ☎ 36 540, @ 36 551 (*L*), is a hotel and bungalow complex with casino, bowling alley and golf course; rooms have either sea or lake views. *Both open all year.*

expensive

For old-style elegance, no hotel on Corfu can compete with the **Cavalieri Corfu**, located on the end of the Esplanade at 4 Kapodistríou, ☎ 39 336, @ 39 283 (*A*), in a renovated French mansion; it's comfortable, air-conditioned and has a magnificent roof garden, open for drinks to non-guests and overlooking the town in all directions. The salmon-coloured **Bella Venezia**, just back from the Esplanade at 4 Napoleon Zambeli, ☎ 44 290, @ 20 708 (*B*), is a renovated old mansion in a relatively quiet, yet central, part of town, with a pretty garden terrace in which to linger over the sumptuous buffet breakfasts. *Open all year.* On the waterfront in the Old Port, **Konstantinoupolis**, ☎ 48 716/7, @ 48 718 (*C*), is a good choice, originally established as a hotel in 1878 and very well refurbished in 1997. *Open all year.* In an old building overlooking the Old Port and the New Fort, there's the **Astron Hotel** at 15 Donzelótou, ☎ 39 505, @ 33 708 (*B*); the rooms mostly have balconies but are a bit basic for the price despite good bathrooms. *Open all year.*

moderate

The **Arcadion**, at 44 Kapsdistríou, ☎ 37 671 (*C*), is very central and comfortable (but closed for renovation at the time of writing). The **Royal**, in Kanóni, ☎ 35 345, @ 38 786 (*C*), enjoys a commanding position and could be a class higher with its three swimming pools on descending levels, and roof garden with views over Mouse Island and the airport.

inexpensive

Hermes, 4 Ger. Markóra, ☎ 39 268, @ 31 747 (*C*), is a moderate-sized hotel away from the tourist crowds but next to the early-morning food market, on the inland side of the New Fortress. **Europa**, 10 Gitsiáli, at the New Port, ☎ 39 304 (*D*), is one of the better modern choices. For something even less dear, try the list of rooms to rent from the **EOT**, 7 Rizospaston Voulefton, ☎ 37 520. Most of these are in the old quarters and cost 5,000dr upwards for a bed in season. The **Accommodation Center**, on the corner of Donzelótou and Zavits in the Old Port, may also be able to help. The youth hostel, and nearest campsite, are 8km north in Kontókali (*see* below).

Corfu shows its Venetian heritage in the kitchen as well as in its architecture. Look for *sofríto*, a veal stew flavoured with garlic, vinegar and parsley; *bourdétto*, a fish stew, liberally peppered; and *pastitsátha*, a pasta and veal dish. The island's own sweet is *sikomaeda*, or fig pie. Bear in mind when choosing your taverna that they generally specialize in meat or fish, but not both. Eating out on the genteel Listón, with front-row seats on the crowds, can be expensive unless you stick to pizza. One street back at 66 Kapodistríou, **Rex**, ✆ 39 649, has a good varied menu—try the *sofríto* and other Corfiot dishes, and pay 3,500dr for a meal. **Yoryias Taverna** on Guilford Street is a popular traditional taverna. Just opposite, **Porta Remounda** has a well-earned reputation for fish. On the seafront below the Palace of St Michael and St George, **Faleraki**, ✆ 30 392, is tucked away in a historic spot where the steam passengers used to disembark; now an ouzerie/restaurant, it has mesmerizing views of the sea, old walls and the off-shore yacht club, but average fare. In Kremastí Square, the characterful **Venetian Well**, ✆ 44 761, has a good-value varied and international menu with a wide choice of costly Greek wines (*4,000dr*). **Del Sole** offers Italian food in the centre for 4,000dr. The **Averof**, at Alipíou and Prossalendíou, is a long-established favourite of tourists and locals alike, and **L. Gigisdakis**, at 28 Solomoú, is as authentic an old Greek taverna as you could hope for, with old pots bubbling away in the kitchen and ready oven dishes; try their pickled octopus (*achtapóthi xytháto*); meals around 2,500dr. By the New Port, in Xen. Stratigoú St, the smart **Orestes** has dining inside and in a pleasant little garden opposite; seafood specialities from 4,000dr. For something much cheaper, **Becchios** in Mandoúki, opposite the ferries to Igoumenítsa, does splendid charcoal-grilled meats; and in the suburb of Potamós try **Nicholas** for outstanding traditional fare. The elegant **Xenichtes**, on the road to Paleokastrítsa, ✆ 24 911, has served excellent Greek food with a sprinkling of dishes from other countries for 20 years; fresh salmon is delivered every morning on the Oslo–Corfu flight (*4,000dr*).

In Garítsa, near the Church of Ag. Iássonos and Sosipater, **Yannis** is one of the few remaining tavernas where you are still invited to go into the kitchen, lift lids off pots and choose your food. Futher out in Kanóni, **Restaurant Nausicaa**, 11 Nausicá, ✆ 44 354, serves delicious Greek, French and Eastern dishes under the garden trellis (fairly dear, but they take credit cards). Its close neighbour, **Taverna Pelargos**, looks a bit corny from the outside but serves a vast array of well-prepared Greek dishes: the *stifádo* and *sofríto* are superb. In Kinopiástes, 3km from Gastoúri, **Taverna Tripa** ('Hole in the Wall'), run by the Anyfantís family since 1947, is something of a Corfu national monument, completely cluttered inside with bottles, knick-knacks, a hurdy gurdy and photos (mostly of the late Spiros Anyfantís with celebrity diners), while up on the ceiling strings of salamis, sausages, peppers and garlic are linked by cobwebs. Greek nights here are renowned, with up to 10 courses served; although it's not cheap, the food and service are excellent and the costumed waiters put on a folk-dancing show to boot. Nearby, on the Achilleion road (about 7km from town), are two tavernas with live music and good, reasonably priced food: the **Barbathomas**, with meat specialities, and **Pontis**, with a big selection of *mezédes*, spit-roasted lamb, charcoal grills and local dishes.

Pick up a copy of the monthly *The Corfiot* for local news and a calendar of events; published primarily for ex-pat residents, it makes interesting reading. Other media are even better served: Corfu has three cable TV stations and 17 radio stations, and a flip through the FM dial may even dig up an English-speaking DJ. Apart from the disco ghetto, north of town, and, a bit less brash, in the Kanóni area, most of Corfu's nightlife revolves around the Listón, with a smattering of bars playing late-night music; **Magnet Bar** is a good choice to be drawn to. For more of a bop, **Karnayio** has dancing until the wee hours and two of the most popular bar/clubs are **Coca** and **Bora Bora**. There are a number of *bouzoúki* joints, most of which can be avoided without fear of missing anything wonderful; the best live Greek music, with dancers and the works, is at the **Loutrovio** restaurant in Kefalomandoukó, on the hill overlooking 'disco strip'. **The Gallery**, on Ag. Spyrídon Street, is a favourite watering hole of Greeks and ex-pats, and **Remezzo** is fun for late-night ice-cream. The café/bar perched up in the Old Fort is also a scenic spot, with music and an alluring view (*open 9am–2am*).

There are two cinemas that show undubbed English-language films: the **Pallas** and the **Orfeus**.

North of Corfu Town

The roads along the east coast of Corfu are fast moving and hotel developers have followed them every inch of the way. To the immediate north of Corfu town begins a 10km stretch of beach, hotel, self-catering, campsite and restaurant sprawl, most intensely at Kontókali, Goúvia, Dássia, Ipsos and Pírgi; yet if they all missed the boat in architecture and design, there's visual redemption in the dishevelled beauty of the surrounding green hills and olive groves. Eight kilometres from Corfu town, the coast road veers sharply right through **Gouviá** (ΓΟΥΒΙΑ), overlooking a lagoon once used by the Venetians as a harbour; in return, the impressive remains of the Venetian **arsenal** overlook Gouviá's popular marina. The pebble beach offers watersports and reasonable swimming. A bit further along the dual-carriageway, emerald **Cape Komméno** extends out, but looks better from a distance and has poor beaches to boot. A few kilometres further north on the still excruciatingly built-up main road, **Dassiá** (ΔΑΣΙΑ) has a long, narrow sand and shingle beach fringed by olive groves, a favourite for sports from waterskiing to paragliding; keep on heading north to avoid the seemingly endless pub/bar sprawl. Excursion boats run as far as Kassiópi (north) and Benítses (south).

A few years ago, if a good night's sleep was a priority, it was best to avoid **Ípsos** (ΥΨΟΣ) and **Pírgi** (ΠΥΡΓΙ), former fishing villages at either end of Corfu's 'Golden Mile' north of Dassiá. Although the plethora of bars and discos no longer reverberate till dawn, you still might want to head for the scenic hinterland or continue up the coast if you want to escape the carousels of inflatable crocodiles and 'I ♥ Corfu' postcards which line the long scimitar of shingle beach, leaving barely enough room for a good wiggle. From Ípsos, head inland to **Ano Korakiána**, with its olive wood workshop and delightful exhibition of folk sculpture at the **Museum of Aristedes Metalinós**, © (0663) 22 317 (*open 8.30–2.30, closed Mon*). The road leading up into the Troumpetta range via Sokraki is an awesome series of hairpins and about as green and gorgeous as it gets. From Pírgi, noodle up though Spartílas to Strinílas for lunch and excellent local wine in the beautifully shaded main square; or browse through olive wood shops, like family-run 'Pantokratora', with its workshop at the entrance to the village.

Kontókali ✉ 49100

Corfu's **youth hostel** is here (take bus no.7 from San Rocco Square), © 91 202; an IYHA card is required. The nearest **campsite** to Corfu town (© 91 202) is here as well, although those in Dassiá are fancier. The **New Locanda** flirts with the cuisines of the world, including many vegetarian dishes. **Gerekos**, in the village, and **Roula's**, on the promontory past the Corkyra Beach Hotel, are both excellent for fish.

Gouviá ✉ 49100

The **Grecotel Corfu Imperial**, © 91 481, ✆ 91 881 (*L; lux*), occupies a private peninsula overlooking Koméno Bay and has no fewer than five bars, a disco, tennis, pool and watersports. **Debonos**, © 91 755, ✆ 90 009 (*A; exp*), has a garden with a pool. *Open Mar–Oct.* **Louvre**, © 91 506, ✆ 91 979 (*C; mod*), has a cheaper pool, but don't expect any masterpieces. **Bella Mama**, on the edge of the strip, is Greek owned and run in spite of its name, and serves a delicious *sofríto*, lamb *kléftiko*, and other meats and chicken, with a house wine to quaff. **Tartufo**, up the hill, is owned by the same family and is similar, but set in a quieter area (*both from 3,000–5,000dr*). **La Bonita** is a good Italian and **O'Kapetanios** is best for fish. Bars aren't exactly tranquil here, but **Whistles**, next door, is reasonable for a tipple.

Dassiá ✉ 49100

Corfu Chandris and **Dassia Chandris**, © 97 100, ✆ 93 458, *www.chandris.gr* (*A; lux*), form a huge double resort on the beach; their bungalows and villas in the environs also have use of the pools, tennis, playground, restaurants and a free shuttle service into Corfu town. The Corfu is currently the most recently renovated; ask for a sea view since the so-called mountain view faces right on to the hideous main road. *Open Apr–Oct.* Rather more modest but perfectly pleasant is the family-run **Scheria Beach**, © 93 233, ✆ 93 289 (*C; mod*); try to get a sea-facing balcony. For campers, **Kormari**, © 93 587, and **Karda Beach**, © 93 595, both offer ample facilities, including pool.

Ípsos ✉ 49083

Costas Beach, © 93 205 (*D; mod*), is one possibility on the seafront. Although no longer allowed to boom all night, there are still plenty of young bars in Ípsos; **Hector's Club** and **B52** are especially popular.

The Northeast Corner: Barbáti to Ag. Spirídon

Continuing north, **Barbáti** (ΜΠΑΡΜΠΑΤΗ) has a long stretch of pebbles and every conceivable facility to go with it, but from here on there is a gentle and welcome gear-change; as the coastal road wiggles its way up from the sea, the resorts below become smaller and cosier. No longer spread over vast stretches of coastline with wall-to-wall shops and tavernas, the traditional village charm of these smaller resorts is allowed to peek through. The first, **Nissáki**, is a fishing hamlet which trickles along the main road; below, roads and goat tracks lead to a number of quiet coves, although its tiny eponymous beach has two good tavernas and a good arts and crafts shop (The Loom) so tends to get pretty full. Even if you don't venture off the main road here, it is worth pausing at Nissáki's fine olive wood shop, opposite the Hotel Ilios. Just on from Nissáki, you can drive down to **Kamináki**: a pebbly bay bordered by villas (*many bookable through CV Travel, see p.31*), with the clearest of water, perfect for snorkelling. There are some watersports here, boat hire and two beach tavernas. Still heading north is the picturesque and unspoilt bay of **Agní**, with crystal-clear waters and three outstandingly good tavernas, all with sunbeds on the beach for collapsing after lunch. The next little resort off the main road is built around the popular pebble beach of **Kalámi** (ΚΑΛΑΜΙ), one of the biggest self-catering compounds on Corfu, where you can stay overlooking the bay in Lawrence Durrell's famous White House (*see* below). **Kouloúra**, a kilometre or so from the rugged Albanian coast, is a lovely seaside hamlet on a narrow horseshoe bay with a shingle beach, which has not yet succumbed to the developers; the brothers Durrell spent their youth here. Kouloúra was also favoured by Venetians: note the 16th-century **Koúartanou Gennatá**, part villa and part fortified tower, and two 17th-century mansions, **Vassilá** and **Prosalenti**. The next beach north is **Kerásia**, a pretty strand of white pebbles with shade and a taverna, most easily reached by doubling back 2km from beautiful, pricey South Kensington-on-Sea, known locally as **Ag. Stéfanos** and hiding the exclusive villas of the Rothschild set.

Kassiópi (ΚΑΣΣΙΟΠΗ), an important Hellenistic town founded by Pyrrhus of Epirus (the famous generalissimo of pseudo-victories), is now the largest and busiest resort on the northeast coast. It flourished under the Romans, who surrounded it with great walls; its famous shrine of Zeus Cassius was visited by Cicero and Emperor Nero, and Tiberius had a villa here. The Byzantine fortress was the first place in Greece to fall to Robert Guiscard's Normans, who invaded from their fief in Calabria after first pillaging Rome. As every subsequent marauder from the north passed by Kassiópi to reach Corfu town, the town bore the brunt of their attacks. When after a long struggle the Venetians finally took the fortress, they rendered it useless to avenge themselves. Without any defences the Kassiopiots suffered terribly at the hands of the Turks and the town lost all of its former importance.

The ruined fortress still stands above the village, guarding only wild flowers and sheep. Although still a fishing village with a pretty waterfront, Kassiópi has discovered the profits to be made from the tourist trade and the main shopping street is positively groaning with touristy trinkets; however, on the road skirting town 'Barbara's' is worth a peek if you're after locally designed and painted ceramics. Four small, well-equipped beaches can be reached by footpath from the headland, and when you're tired of windsurfing or basting yourself on the beach, you can explore the rocky coastline on foot. Two of Corfu's most tastefully developed beaches, **Avláki** and **Koyévinas**, are a quick drive, or 20–30-minute walk, south of Kassiópi; both beautiful white pebble bays, Koyévinas sports a taverna, while Avláki has two, along with boats, pedalos and windsurfers for hire.

Continuing west beyond the grey sand beach of **Kalamáki** (also with a taverna), a sign for Loútses and Perithía announces the way up the brooding slopes of 900m **Mount Pantokrátor**, Corfu's highest point. You can take a car as far as **Old Perithía**, one of Corfu's erstwhile secrets: a charming cobblestoned village of stone houses, abandoned by all but three farming families, one of whom now runs the Capricorn Grill, an understated taverna in the hub of the old village. Lost in a mountain hollow, Old Perithía's once lush garden terraces are slowly disintegrating since everyone left for the coast to seek their fortune. The path from here to the summit of Pantokrátor takes about an hour, but rewards you with a wondrous display of flora even into the hot summer months, and views of emerald Corfu spread at your feet and white-capped Albanian peaks on the mainland, a vista enjoyed every day by the single monk and his somewhat less orthodox pylon in the mountaintop monastery. The rutted road from Old Perithía by way of Láfki takes in some of Corfu's most enchanting countryside.

Back down on the coast road, **Ag. Spyrídonos** may be the answer if you've been seeking a small sandy beach, a simple taverna or two and a handful of rooms to rent, although Corfiots converge on it on Sundays.

Ⓣ (0663–)   *Where to Stay and Eating Out*

Nissáki/Kalámi/Ag. Stéfanos/Agní ✉ 49100

The **Sol Elite Nissaki Beach Hotel**, Ⓣ 91 232, ⌨ 22 079, *nissaki@otenet.gr* (*A; lux*), is the only big hotel on this stretch of coast; despite being a mammoth eyesore, it offers great views, a pool, gym, shops, restaurants and good facilities for kids.

This is the perfect area for a glimpse of the old Corfu and to rent from an exquisite selection of villas, ranging in size and plushness, including the upstairs (downstairs is a good taverna) of Lawrence Durrell's White House in Kalámi; book through CV Travel in London, Ⓣ (020) 7581 0851 (*see* p.31); in Corfu, Ⓣ 40 644 or 39 900. Up on the coast road through Nissáki, **Vitamins** is a smart and friendly taverna with excellent food and a lovely terrace. **Mitsos** on Nissáki beach is always busy for lunch, with good reason. One evening a week, three local musicians play good old-fashioned Greek music at next-door **Nikos**, and the **Olive Press** celebrates with the occasional and relatively tasteful Greek Night. For a bit of unparalleled romance on a moonlit evening, take a water-taxi from Kalámi to any one of the three excellent tavernas in Agní: **Nikolas**, Ⓣ 91 243, offers wondrous fare for around 4,000dr; **Agní** attracts the glitterati; and **Toulas** is next door. Agní is also reachable by road, for a long, lazy lunch.

Kassiópi ✉ 49100

Kassiópi bulges with Italians in August and, unless you are pre-booked (*see* the specialist companies on pp.10–12), forget it. Even at other times, the hotel situation is pretty meagre. **Manessis Apartments**, Ⓣ 32 664, ⌨ 36 935, *diana@otenet.gr* (*mod*), are a delightful exception right on the port, in a building overflowing with vines and bougainvillea, run by friendly Irish Diana. It's worth asking at **Villas Elli**, Ⓣ 81 483, and **Angela**, Ⓣ 81 036 (*both mod–inexp*), to see if they have a free apartment. If not, try **Cosmic Tourist Centre**, Ⓣ 81 624; **Kassiopi Travel Service**, Ⓣ 81 388; or **The Travel Corner**, Ⓣ 81 220, ⌨ 81 108. **Kassiopi Star** and **The Three Brothers** on the waterfront serve Greek and Corfiot specialities (*4,000dr*). Next door, **Porto** is more fishy, while **Psilos** is a traditional no-frills taverna. For a lighter meal, newly opened **Marina** bar has a range of snacks and salads. At Imerólia, the nearest beach, the **Imerolia Beach Taverna** has good food, and dancing every other night. In the opposite direction, **Cavo Barbaro** is a good choice on Avláki beach. If you're going to groove, try **Satyros** disco, at the port, or **Axis Club**.

Ag. Spyrídon ✉ 49100

Tucked away in the olive groves, 100m from the sea, **St Spíridon Bay**, Ⓣ 98 294, ⌨ 98 295 (*B; mod*), is a quiet, unpretentious bungalow complex with pool, only open in season. **Olive** bar opposite is a mellow place to eat, with good fresh fish and the beach only 100m away; ask here if you're looking for a room.

The North Coast

Almirós, at the quiet east end of Corfu's longest beach, is a warm shallow lagoon with trees and migratory birds. The rest of the coast has been clobbered with the magic wand of package tourism, from **Acharávi** (AXAPABH), where the beach is framed by pretty scenery, to **Róda** (POΔA), where egg and chips seems to be everyone's special of the day, but at least there's enough sand to escape the worst of the crowds by walking a bit in either direction. **Astrakéri** and next-door **Agnos**, at the west end, have a downbeat feel but might have free rooms.

Inland from Acharávi, **Ag. Pauteléimonos**, has a huge ruined tower mansion called **Polylas**, complete with prisons used during the Venetian occupation; another Venetian manor lies further up in **Episkepsís**. Inland from Róda, **Plátanos** is in the heart of Corfu's kumquat country. Introduced from the Far East half a century ago, kumquats look like baby oranges but are too sour for many tastes; the annual harvest of 35 tonnes produced by 70 farmers is distilled into kumquat liqueur (using both blossoms and fruit) and preserved as kumquat jams and conserves. Inland from Astrakerí, **Karoussádes** is a pretty agricultural village with the 16th-century Theotóki mansion as its landmark.

Sidári (ΣIΔAPI) has rolled over and surrendered itself wholesale to package tourism and mosquitoes. If you're passing through, the **Canal d'Amour** is a peculiar rock formation said to be two lovers—swim between them and you are guaranteed eternal love, which is more than promised by the local disco. If you have your own transport, less crowded beaches await west of Sidári below the village of **Perouládes**; the wind-sculpted tawny cliffs are high enough to cast the sandy beach in shade in the early afternoon.

✆ (0663–) ***Where to Stay and Eating Out***

Róda/Agnos/Astrakéri ✉ 49081

In season nearly every room in Róda is block-booked, but give the friendly Greek-Canadian-run **Roda Inn** a try, ✆ 63 358 or in the UK ✆ (01332) 776353 (*C; inexp*); they'll organize a boat trip on one of George's Dreamer Cruises for you too. Just along the street is **Aphrodite**, ✆ 63 147, ✆ 63 125 (*C; inexp*), but it tends to be packaged in high season. If you like the outdoors, **Roda Camping**, ✆ 93 120, may oblige. Once the only taverna in town, **Kind Hearted Place** (at the eastern end of the waterfront), has been offering a good, if limited, Greek menu since the early 60s; a small back terrace overlooks the water.

Over in Agnos, the **Angela Beach Hotel**, ✆ 31 291, ✆ 31 279 (*mod*), is an uninspiring package development, but does offer a pool by the gently shelving sands and is two minutes from a couple of good-value fish tavernas. Further west along the strand at Astrakéri, yet another **Three Brothers** taverna offers traditional fare and ambience on the beach.

Platonas ✉ 49080

Platonas, ✆/✆ 94 396 (*D; mod*), is a pleasant place to escape the crowds on the coast, and there's a taverna, too.

Islands near Corfu: Othoní, Eríkousa and Mathráki

Northwest of Sidári, three sleepy islets, Othoní (the largest), Eríkousa and Mathráki, comprise the westernmost territory of Greece. Transport to them is not always reliable: there are organized excursions and caiques from Sidári (caiques run most of the year, depending on demand and weather), ferries from Corfu town, or a summer excursion from Ag. Stéfanos. The population is disproportionately feminine, the wives of husbands who fish, or work in the USA. Olives and aromatic table grapes are produced locally, and fresh fish is nearly always available; each island has rooms to rent, but food supplies can be scarce.

Of the three, **Othoní** is the largest and driest (a lack of water is one of the problems), but has the friendliest atmosphere and the most to offer if you like to ramble. There are a handful of shingle beaches and donkey trails up to the pretty, nearly abandoned villages and a well-preserved medieval fort on a pine-covered hill. Most of the excursions make for **Eríkousa**, which has the best sandy beach and a pair of villages set in the cypresses and olives. **Mathráki**, the smallest island, also has a sandy beach—a nesting place for loggerhead turtles (*see* p.304)—and very limited facilities.

© *(0663–)*   *Where to Stay and Eating Out*

Othoní/Eríkousa/Mathráki ✉ 49081

> Book early for the **Locanda dei Sogni**, on Othoní, © 71 640, which offers pretty rooms and good Italian food, or eat at the **Rainbow** taverna. Ditto for **Hotel Erikousa**, © 71 555 (*C; mod*), the only hotel on Eríkousa, directly on the beach.

Western Beaches: North to South

The whole northwest corner of Corfu is covered with forests. The main roads have been re-surfaced, but once off the beaten track be warned that the roads can bottom out the best shock-absorbers. The main coastal road from Sidári cuts off the corner of the northwest en route to **Ag. Stéfanos** (not to be confused with the Ag. Stéfanos on the east coast), a large and uninspiring bay with brown sand and windsurfing; **Aríllas** just south has a wide, sandy, steep bay with an attractive backdrop of green hills. The village of **Afiónas** is on a headland with magnificent views in either direction, its sandy beach steadily developing. Best of all is **Ag. Geórgios** (Pagói), a long, magnificent stretch of beach under steep cliffs; as yet it is not over-developed, but already offers watersports (especially windsurfing), tavernas and discos; during the day it fills up with trippers from Paleokastrítsa.

One of Corfu's celebrated beauty spots and the major resort in west Corfu, **Paleokastrítsa** (ΠΑΛΑΙΟΚΑΣΤΡΙΤΣΑ) spreads out from a small horseshoe bay, flanked by sandy and pebbly coves, olive and almond groves, mountains and forests. Paleokastrítsa is chock-a-block in the summer with holiday-makers; in the early spring, however, you can believe its claim to have been the fabled home of King Alcinous and Princess Nausicaa. The sea is said to be colder here than anywhere else in Corfu. On a promontory above town, **Zoodóchos Pigí** (or Paleokastrítsa) monastery was built in 1228 on the site of a Byzantine fortress, and tarted up by an abbot with rococo tastes in the 1700s. Tour groups queue up to buy a candle (the price of admission) as a monk hands out black skirts and shawls to the underclad. Inside, a one-room museum contains some very old icons and an olive press; outside, there's a peach of a view of the sapphire sea below. The most spectacular view of the magnificent coastline is on the steep climb (or drive) out of Paleokastrítsa through cypress and pine woods north towards the charming traditional village of **Lákones** and its celebrated Bella Vista Café, affording nothing less than 'the Most Beautiful View in Europe'. Lákones itself is the hub of some of the loveliest walks on Corfu, especially to Kríni and the formidable **Angelókastro** (you can also walk from Paleokastrítsa). Built in the 13th century by the Byzantine despot of Epirus, Michael Angelos, Angelókastro is mostly ruined, but makes an impressive sight clinging to the wild red rocks over a 1,000ft precipice. Angelókastro played a major role during the various raids on the island, sheltering the surrounding villagers (as well as the Venetian governor, who lived there). However, the Corfiots were rarely content to stay behind the walls of Angelókastro, and often spilled out to attack their attackers. If you have a car, the mountain roads from Lákones north to Róda through the little villages of **Chorepískopi**, **Valanión** (3km on a by-road) and **Nímfes** offer a bucolic journey through the Corfu of yesteryear, and in spring and early summer the air is laden with the aromatic perfumes of the wild herbs and flowers; little old ladies line the road tempting you with oregano, honey, almonds and olive oil for sale.

South of Paleokastrítsa stretches the fertile, startlingly flat **Rópa Valley**, where Homer's description of the island rings true: 'Pear follows pear, apple after apple grows, fig after fig, and grape yields grape again.' Along with orchards, Rópa has the **Corfu Golf Club**, 18 holes designed by Harradine and Pencross Bent, rated one of the 100 top courses in the world; club hire available (✆ (0661) 94 220). Westwards on the coast, **Ermónes**, with its pebble beaches and hotels, is another candidate for Odysseus' landing point; Nausicaa and her servants would have been washing the palace laundry in a little cascade, near the present-day Snackbar Nausicaa. **Pélekas**, a 17th-century village up on a mountain ridge, was Kaiser Wilhelm II's favourite spot to watch the sunset; busloads of people arrive every evening in the summer to do the same, from a tower known as **Kaiser's Throne**. Pélekas was one of Corfu's nudie beaches until a road built from Gialiskári brought in crowds of trippers; now completely unadorned walk down the steep track leads to lovely **Mirtiótissa** beach (the other half of the beach, by the monastery, is not nudist). After sunset the village throbs to the sound of disco music. **Glyfáda**, one of the island's best beaches, is a long gentle swathe of golden sand. It fills up during the day with hotel residents and day-trippers, but early evening is perfect for a swim here, with steep cliffs dropping straight down into the blue bay.

Where to Stay and Eating Out

Ag. Geórgios/Afiónas ✉ 49080, ✆ (0663–)

Golden Sands, ✆ 51 225, ✉ 51 140 (*B; mod*), is reasonably priced, given its pool and tennis courts, and appropriately by the beach. St George, ✆ 96 213 (*D; inexp*), is convenient for the beach. *Open Apr–Oct.* Vrachos is the best place for freshwater crayfish and lobster. Nearby Afiónas is a good place to rent rooms away from the brouhaha. At **Dionysos**, delicious *mezédes* complement the spectacular views over Ag. Geórgios bay, while **The Three Brothers** is a bar-restaurant with a splendid terrace from which to watch the sunset. A bit further north, on the road to Kavádes from Aríllas, **Mon Amour** is one of the best tavernas on Corfu, specializing in lamb-on-the-spit and other meaty delicacies.

Paleokastrítsa ✉ 49083, ✆ (0663–)

Prices have come down here, but so have standards; most apartments are pre-booked and the choice of hotels isn't rivetting. The **Akrotiri Beach**, ✆ 41 275, ✉ 41 277 (*A; exp*), 5 minutes uphill from the beach, enjoys some of the best views, and there's a seawater pool for those who don't want to commute to the real thing. **Odysseus Hotel**, also above the beach, ✆ 41 209, ✉ 41 342 (*C; mod*), is a smart complex, while **Hotel Apollón**, ✆ 41 124, ✉ 41 211 (*C; mod*), is a more modest affair, with balconies facing the sea. Ask at **Astacos** restaurant, ✆ 41 068, for its quiet, good-value rooms (*inexp*); the **Diving Centre**, just past Astacos, also has rooms. **Paleokastritsa Camping**, ✆ 41 204, is probably the nicest campsite on Corfu. There's a number of seafood restaurants. **Chez George** commands the prime location and the highest prices; residents and long-term visitors prefer the **Astacos**. Alternatively, if you can stomach the name, try **Smurf's**, along the beach.

Ermónes ✉ 49100, ✆ (0661–)

Ermones Beach, ✆ 94 241, ✉ 94 248 (*A; exp*), is a huge bungalow complex, with every facility. The much more intimate **Athena Hermones Golf**, ✆ 94 236, ✉ 94 605 (*C; mod*), is near the course.

Pélekas/Glyfáda ✉ 49100, ✆ (0661–)

The **Louis Grand Hotel Glyfada**, ✆ 94 140, ✉ 94 146 (*A; lux–exp*), and its many watersport activities dominate the beach. The **Glyfada Beach**, ✆/✉ 94 257 (*B; mod*), is an alternative. Perched on top of Pélekas by the Kaiser's Throne, the **Levant Hotel**, ✆ 94 230, ✉ 94 115 (*A; exp*), has superb views and a pool away from it all.

Southern Corfu

The southern half of the island has attracted the worst excesses of tourism. For years **Benítses** (ΜΠΕΝΙΤΣΕΣ) was the numero uno offender, a British package resort bubbling with hormones and devouring a little Greek fishing village (with its permission, of course) inhabited since ancient times. More recently, tour operators have pulled out and Benítses is an altogether gentler place again, but the damage is already done. The patches of beach it offers will always be too close to the coastal highway and the rowdies seem to have chased the resort's former enthusiasts away for good. But if you look hard enough, you can still find a few remnants of Benítses' more aesthetic past. The arches and mosaics just behind the harbour belonged to a Roman bathhouse. And you can walk through the old, residential quarter of the village, past the local cemetery through delightful rural scenery towards **Stavrós**, where the Benítses Waterworks were built by Sir Frederick Adam, British High Commissioner from 1824 to 1832. Originally, the waterworks supplied Corfu town; now Benítses somehow manages to use it all, even though few people there would be caught dead drinking from it. Benítses also currently houses the itinerant **Corfu Shell Museum**, ✆ 72 227 (*open daily 10–8; adm*), with its thousands of beautiful sea treasures. Further south, the nearly continuous resort sprawls past the beaches of **Moraítika** (ΜΟΡΑΙΤΙΚΑ) and **Messónghi** (ΜΕΣΣΟΓΓΗ), a cut above Benítses. If you're down here for the scenery, skip the coast altogether and take the inland route, beginning at Kinopiástes (near Gastoúri), passing by way of Ag. Déka (one of Corfu's prettiest villages), Makráta, Kornáta and Strongilí.

The more inaccessible west coast is also worthwhile: **Ag. Górdis** (ΑΓ. ΓΟΡΔΗΣ) is one of Corfu's more attractive village-resorts with a lovely, sheltered 2-mile-long beach of soft golden sand and minimal waves, although it is increasingly dominated by package-holiday operators. Inland, **Sinarádes** is a large and pretty village surrounded by vineyards and home to a fine folk museum (*open 9.30–2.30, closed Mon; adm*); accommodation can be arranged through Karoukas Travel (*see* below). The road south to Ag. Mattheos is a delightful meander through olive groves and cypresses; stop at Golden View café to admire the view. **Ag. Mattheos**, planted on its own mountain, is a serene place to daydream under the plane tree and write up your diary, disturbed only by the occasional roar of hired scooters and jeeps as they zip through the village on a quest for true peace and quiet. The village remains delightfully Greek—full of traditional houses with wonky wooden verandas overflowing with geraniums and bougainvillea, and reverberating with birdsong—and the locals are more concerned about their olive crop than threatened decreases in tourist numbers. There are 24 churches in or near the village, and by asking around you can find your way down the steep slopes to the really peaceful beaches of **Tría Avlákia**, **Paramónas** and **Skithi**, with a few rooms and the odd inexpensive taverna. An octagonal Byzantine castle at **Gardíki**, south of Ag. Mattheos, was another work by the despot of Epirus, Michael Angelos II. This is one of the most unspoilt areas of Corfu, and is a good starting point for some excellent walks. A minor road by Gardíki leads in 4km to one of Corfu's few lakes, the lagoony **Límni Korissíon**, which is separated from the sea by a long stretch of huge, wild dunes; in spring and autumn it fills with migratory birds. Take your mosquito defences, however; they grow as big as pterodactyls here and have appetites to match. **Lagoúdia**, two islets off the southwest coast, are home to a tribe of donkeys; some of their ancestors were eaten by a boatload of Napoleon's troops who were wrecked there for three days.

The scenery from here down to Corfu's tail is flat and agricultural, but the beaches are sandy and clean. South of Lake Korissíon a busy family resort has grown up around (another) **Ag. Geórgios**. **Linía**, the northern extension of Ag. Geórgios beach, is more tranquil and backed by dunes; the beach of **Marathiás** is the southern extension of the same strand, with a few tavernas. In the centre of a large fertile plain, **Lefkími**, the largest town in the south, is dusty and uninviting; the nearest beaches, **Mólos** and **Alykés**, 2km away on the east coast, are flat and grey, set amid salt pans.

Kávos (ΚΑΒΟΣ) is a one-time fishing village turned all-day-and-night package holiday rave party where things have got so out of hand that locals now refuse to work there. At the southernmost tip of Corfu, the quieter beaches of **Asprókavos** and **Arkoudílas** (near a ruined monastery, reached by a path from Sparterá) have white sand and tavernas; the pretty beach below **Dragotiná** is a long walk from the village but never crowded.

© (0661–)   ***Where to Stay and Eating Out***

Ag. Górdis ✉ 49084

> **Yaliskari Palace**, © 54 401, ✆ 52 234 (*A; exp*), a vast fancy complex with a pool, tennis courts and sea sports, is 3km from the beach; **Ag. Gordis**, © 53 320, ✆ 52 234 (*A; exp*), is similarly large, ultra modern, and endowed with facilities, but right on the sand. **Dandidis Pension-Restaurant**, © 53 232, ✆ 523 183 (*mod*), offers plain doubles with fridge and balcony on the beach. **Pink Paradise**, © 53 103 (*E; inexp*), is a resort complex run by Americans for backpackers. Alternatively, **Karoukas Travel**, © 53 909, ✆ 53 887, *karoukas@otenet.gr*, on the main street, can fix you up with a room or apartment. Restaurants and café/bars abound on and around the beach; try **Michali's Place** or **Alex in the Garden**.

Benítses ✉ 49084

> A few kilometres past Benítses stands the classy **Marbella**, © 71 183, ✆ 71 189, *marbella@otenet.gr* (*A; lux*), one of the most luxurious establishments along the

coastal strip; recently refurbished in grand style it exudes tranquil opulence. The À la Carte restaurant is reasonably priced. **San Stefano**, ✆ 36 036, 🖷 72 272 (*A; exp*), is spread across terraces, overlooking the sea; it has the largest swimming pool on the island, sea sports and other facilities. **Le Mirage** (*C; inexp*) offers more modest rooms, quietly situated around a swimming pool off the main pub strip. Alternatively, **All Tourist Services**, ✆ 72 223, on the main road, can find you a private room. Benítses is not known for its cuisine, but the **Marabou** bravely presents some tasty local dishes (*3,000dr*). **Stefanos Pizzeria** whips up delicious authentic pies, while **Paxinos**, ✆ 72 339, in the old village, serves some more traditional fare. After eating your fill, you can try your voice at laser karaoke and proceed to **Disco Valentino** to dance the night away.

Moraítika/Messónghi ✉ 49080

Calimera Miramare Beach, Moraítika, ✆ 75 224, 🖷 75 305 (*L; lux*), is a superior complex set in 200-year-old olive groves and citrus orchards, with pool, tennis, theatre and disco. **Messonghi Beach Hotel and Bungalows**, ✆ 76 684 (*B; exp*), is a giant, self-contained family fun complex. **Koryfo Apartments**, in Moraítika ✆ 75 511, in Athens (01) 981 8889, 🖷 982 2445 (*exp*), are pretty flats, 400m from the sea. **Apollo Palace**, in Messónghi, ✆ 75 433, 🖷 75 602, *apollopl@mail.hol.gr* (*A; exp*), is one of the grander places here, in a relatively tasteful way, offering all facilities and half-board. **Margarita Beach Hotel**, in Moraítika, ✆/🖷 75 267 (*C; mod*), offers more modest seaside doubles with balcony. **Roulis**, Messónghi, ✆ 55 353 (*C; mod*), small and near the sea, with some sea sports. It's fairly easy to find a room to rent (ask at **Moraítika Tourist Center**, ✆ 77 008, confusingly on the road into Messónghi). When it comes to eating, **Islands** restaurant, on the main road in Moraítika, is an option, or else head up to **Bella Vista** taverna in the old village for a calmer evening.

Ag. Mattheos ✉ 49084

Nearby Paramónas beach houses the **Paramonas**, ✆ 75 686, 🖷 76 596 (*B; mod*). There's a row of cafés with small terraces on the main road; the **Mouria** grill house is worth a try.

Kefaloniá (ΚΕΦΑΛΟΝΙΑ)

'The half-forgotten island of Cephallonia rises improvidently and inadvisedly from the Ionian Sea,' writes Dr Iannis in Louis de Bernières' *Captain Corelli's Mandolin*, perhaps the best book to be set on a Greek island in years—although it is not at all popular with islanders due to its one-sided portrayal of the events of the Second World War. Kefaloniá's Jabberwocky silhouette contains 781 square kilometres of ruggedly beautiful mountains, making it the largest of the Ionian islands by far, although it supports a mere 30,000 people (and even many of these live in Athens in the winter). Kefalonians have always been famous for wandering (one, Constantine Yerákis, made a fortune in the British East India Company and became Regent of Siam), and it's not uncommon to meet someone whose entire family lives in Canada, Australia or the United States. Only in the last few years has tourism begun to slow the diaspora and keep more people put. Most Kefalonians are friendly, good-humoured and clever, but have the reputation of being hard-headed, cunning, eccentric, tight with their money and the worst blasphemers in Greece, swearing at their patron Ag. Gerásimos one minute and swearing by him the next. Other Greeks say the Kefalonians have drunk a toast with the devil himself.

Although the earthquake in 1953 shattered all but a fraction of Kefaloniá's traditional architecture and all the quaintness and charm that goes with it, the big, sprawling island has lost none of its striking natural beauty. It has fine beaches (one of which, Mýrtos, is perhaps the most dramatic in all of Greece), two of the country's loveliest caves, lofty fir forests, splendid views and Robóla wine. Because Kefaloniá is so large, it is easy to escape the summertime crowds, although be aware that even on the main roads driving distances and times can be exhausting.

History

Fossil and tool finds in Fiskárdo, Sámi and Skála go back to at least 50,000 BC and perhaps earlier, making Fiskárdo man (and woman, one supposes) among the earliest known inhabitants in Greece. Later inhabitants appear to have been culturally related to the Pelasgians in western Sicily and Epirus; their skulls, all banged about, suggest that Kefalonians have always been a feisty lot. The Achaeans introduced Mycenaean culture from the Peloponnese in the 14th century BC; Krani, near Argostóli, was their most important colony. Although the name Kefaloniá does not occur in Homer, scholars believe that the 'glittering Samos' of the *Odyssey* actually refers to Kefaloniá's town of Sámi. Others believe Homer doesn't mention Kefaloniá because, as part of the kingdom of Odysseus, he simply calls it Ithaca. The recent discovery of a major Mycenaean tomb near Póros has given the argument new weight as archaeologists scramble to locate the big jackpot—the Palace of Odysseus.

Historically, the first sure references to Kefaloniá are in Herodotus and Thucydides, who describes its four autonomous city-states—Sami, Pali, Krani and Pronnoi—allies of Corinth who spent much of their history fighting for their independence from Athens. In Byzantine times it prospered, in spite of many attacks by the pirates from Spain and Sicily, and in the 9th century was made the capital of its own *theme*. In 1085, Normans based in southern Italy unsuccessfully besieged the Byzantine forts of the island; their duke, Robert Guiscard, died of fever in the village that has taken his name—Fiskárdo (*see* below). If the Kefalonians breathed a sigh of relief then, it was too soon; for the next 800 years the island, like its sisters, was to become the plaything of the Normans, of Venice and of the Vatican (but mostly the Venetians), as well as a motley assortment of dukes and counts in need of a tax income; the most colourful of its masters was the pirate Count Matteo Orsini, who founded a murderous, dowry-snatching dynasty at the end of the 13th century. In 1483 the Turks captured the island, but lost it again in 1504 when Venice and Spain under the Gran Capitan, Gonzalo Fernández de Córdoba, besieged and took the fort of Ag. Geórgios and slaughtered the Turkish garrison.

After this the fortress was repaired and the nearby town became the Venetian capital. A huge earthquake caused heavy damage to Ag. Geórgios in 1636, and in the 18th century it was abandoned and Argostóli became the new capital. In 1823, Lord Byron spent three months on Kefaloniá (along with a retinue including his faithful Venetian gondolier, Tita) working as an agent of the Greek Committee in London before going to die a pathetic death from fever in Missolóngi. During the British occupation of the Ionian islands, the Kefalonians demanded union with Greece and revolted; 21 nationalist leaders were hanged in 1849.

Ioánnis Metaxás, prime minister-dictator of Greece from 1936 to 1941, came from Kefaloniá, and for all his faults has gone down in history for laconically (and, apparently, apocryphally) saying 'No' to Mussolini's ultimatum at the beginning of the Second World War—celebrated

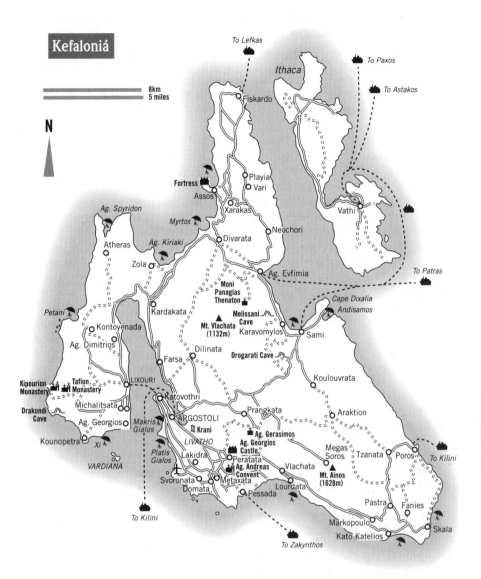

Kefaloniá

8km
5 miles

N

To Lefkas

To Paxos

To Astakos

Ithaca

Fiskardo

Fortress

Playia
Vari

Assos

Xarakas

Vathi

Ag. Spyridon

Myrtos

Neochori

Atheras

Ag. Kiriaki

Divarata

Zola

Ag. Evfimia

To Patras

Moni
Panagias
Thenaton

Cape Dixalia

Andisamos

Petani

Kardakata

Melissani
Cave

Mt. Vlachata
(1132m)

Karavomylos

Sami

Kontogenada

Ag. Dimitrios

Dilinata

Farsa

Drogarati Cave

Kipourion
Monastery

Tafion
Monastery

LIXOURI

Koulouvrata

Drakondi
Cave

Michalitsata

Katovothri

Prangkata

Araktion

Ag. Georgios

Makris
Gialos

ARGOSTOLI

II Krani

Kounopetra

Xi

LIVATHO

Ag. Gerasimos

Megas
Soros

Tzanata

Poros

To Kilini

Platis
Gialos

Lakidra

Ag. Georgios
Castle

Peratata

VARDIANA

Ag. Andreas
Convent

Vlachata

Mt. Ainos
(1628m)

Svoronata

Metaxata

Lourdata

Domata

Pessada

Pastra

Fanies

To Kilini

Markopoulo

Kato Katelios

Skala

To Zakynthos

nationally on 28 October as *Ochi* ('No') Day. In 1943, after the surrender of Italy, the occupying Italian Acqui Division joined the Greeks and for seven days fought the invading Germans. Five thousand Italians, or perhaps twice that many, died in the subsequent mass executions ordered, it is said, by Hitler himself; their bodies were all burned to hide the evidence; the Greeks call them the Kefaloniá martyrs.

A decade later nature itself struck Kefaloniá a blow which made all the previous earthquakes on the island seem like cocktail shakers. For five days in August 1953, 113 tremors reduced the island's 350 towns and villages to dust; the first, deadliest quake had the estimated force of

60 atom bombs. As the dust slowly cleared, money for reconstruction poured in from Europe and the tens of thousands of Kefalonians who live abroad.

Getting There and Around

By air: daily flights from Athens (1–2 a day in summer); frequent charters from British cities. The Olympic Airways office is in Argostóli, at 1 R. Vergotí, ✆ (0671) 28 808/881; the **airport** is 9km south of Argostóli, ✆ (0671) 41 511, and reachable by pricey taxi.

By sea: Kefaloniá has six ports. Sámi (✆ (0674) 22 031) has daily boats to Váthi and Píso Aetós (Ithaca), Vasilikí (Lefkáda) and Fiskárdo. In summer there are daily excursions from Fiskárdo (✆ (0674) 51 212) to Frikés (Ithaca) and Nídri and Vasilikí in Lefkáda. The ferry betwen Argostóli and Lixoúri goes every half-hour in season and otherwise hourly, costing 310dr for a foot passenger. In Lixoúri, sail boats can be rented with or without skipper (but only with the appropriate licence) by the day or by the week, ✆ 91 541. **Port authority**: ✆ (0671) 22 224.

By road: bus services to the main centres of the island are fairly good if not frequent: four or five buses head daily from Argostóli for Lassi and Sámi; there are two to Fiskárdo, Ag. Evfimia and Skála; and three buses connect Lixoúri to Xi beach. Next to the KTEL station near the bridge on the waterfront in Argostóli there's a local KTEL tourist office to help you plan excursions—some go as far as Olympia in the Peloponnese. For information, call ✆ (0671) 22 276 or 22 281. To really see the island, however, you need your own transport, readily available in the towns (although particularly pricey in Fiskárdo): try to avoid any mileage restrictions. Many **taxi** drivers specialize in trips around the island, and **caiques** go to the more popular beaches.

Tourist Information

EOT, Argostóli, on the waterfront, ✆ (0671) 22 248, ✆ 24 466 (*open weekdays 8–2*), is a very helpful office where you can pick up freebies like *Kefaloniá Tourist News*, *Trails of Cephallonia* and info on the Kefalonian Marine Turtle Project. **Tourist police**: Argostóli, ✆ (0671) 22 815. Also very helpful are **Filoxenos Travel**, 2 Vergoti, ✆ (0671) 23 055, and in Fiskárdo, **Fiskardo Travel**, near the post office, ✆/✆ (0674) 41 315, and **Nautilus Travel**, on the waterfront, ✆/✆ (0674) 41 500.

Festivals

21 May, Festival of the Radicals (celebrating union with Greece) in Argostóli; **21 May**, Ag. Konstantínos near Argostóli; carnival celebrations on the **last Sunday and Monday before Lent**; **Easter** festival in Lixoúri; **23 April**, Ag. Geórgios; **23 June**, Ag. Ioánnis in Argostóli; **15 August**, Panagías in Markópoulo; **16 August** and **20 October**, Ag. Gerásimos; **first Saturday after 15 August**, Robóla festival of wine in Fragáta.

Argostóli (ΑΡΓΟΣΤΟΛΙ)

Argostóli (pop. 10,000), magnificently set on a thumb of the great bay in the west, is a big, busy Greek town. It started life as a smugglers' hamlet under the Venetians and gradually, as the threat of piracy diminished, grew up around vast warehouses full of raisins, where ships from all over Europe would dock to fill their holds; the port of Argostóli is especially deep and safe, and to this day is used for winter berthing of yachts and larger ships. As Ag. Geórgios, the Venetian capital, declined, the inhabitants petitioned Venice to make Argostóli capital and in 1759 their wish was granted, to the eternal disgust of archrival Lixoúri. After the earthquake of 1953, the Kefalonians abroad lavished money to rebuild the town in a style worthy of a provincial capital. As a result, Argostóli has more public buildings than most island capitals, grouped neatly around the large, central and palmy **Plateía Vallianóu**. Pre-earthquake Argostóli was famous for its bell towers, two of which have been rebuilt—there's something vaguely German Expressionist about the one by the Catholic church near the square.

Argostóli itself has two museums: the **Koryalenios Historical and Folklore Museum** (© 28 835, *open 9–2, closed Sun; adm*), below the library on Ilía Zervoú Street, is one of the best of its kind and gives great insight into the island's history and the devastation of the earthquake. It contains the Venetian records of the island, including its Libro d'Oro listing the local nobility, photos of old Kefaloniá icons and of pre-1953 Argostóli, a traditional bedroom, memorabilia recalling Kefaloniá's early love affair with opera and theatre, and a carved ebony desk that belonged to Ferdinand Lesseps, the mastermind behind the Suez Canal. The library itself is the ground floor of an elegant mansion rebuilt since the quake. The **Archaeology Museum** (© 28 300, *open 8.30–3, closed Mon; adm*), on G. Vergóti, contains ex-votos to the god Pan from the cave of Melissáni, a room of Mycenaean finds (bronze swords, vases with spirals, and gold and ivory jewellery), coins from the four ancient cities of Kefaloniá and a startlingly modern bronze bust of a man from the early 3rd century AD. The island's first theatre, the **Kéfalos**, has been reconstructed above the museum. Five kilometres north of town, at Davgata, is the low-key **Museum of Natural History of Cephalonia and Ithaca** (© 84 400, *open Mon–Sat 9–1 and 6–8, Sun 9–1 only*), with educational exhibits and a library.

The one structure to survive the earthquake in one piece was the 800m **Drapanós Bridge**, built by the British in 1813 over the shallowest part of the bay, punctuated with a commemorative obelisk. Cross it to join the road to Sámi; a few minutes on by car, the picturesque church of **Ag. Barbára** peers from the rockface over a little bridge. About 1km further, at Razáta, a dirt road leads up to ancient **Krani** (Paleókastro), where the huge stone blocks of the 7th-century BC Cyclopean walls snake through the trees. There are some fragments of a Doric temple to Demeter and a rectangular hollow carved out of the top of the hill called the Drakospilia, or Dragon's Lair, although it was probably really just a Roman tomb.

The Lassí Peninsula

One thing to do in Argostóli is to shoot the loop by foot, bike or car—there's no bus—around the little Lassí peninsula, just north of the city. There are a number of sandy beaches and a clutch of bars, tavernas and discos around the **Katovothri**, or swallow holes, where the sea is sucked into two large tunnels deep under the ground. Where the sea water actually went was a big mystery until 1963, when Austrian geologists poured 140 kilos of green dye into the water. Fifteen days later the dye appeared in the lake of the Melissáni cave and at Karavómylos, near Sámi, on the other side of the island. Sea mills to harness the rushing water for electricity were destroyed by the earthquake (which also greatly diminished the suction). One has been reconstructed, for decoration more than anything else; the mill is now used as a lobster nursery. At the tip of the Lassí peninsula is the lovely **lighthouse of Ag. Theódori**, a Doric rotunda built by one of Kefaloniá's great benefactors, British High Commissioner Charles Napier, and reconstructed to its original plans after the 1875 earthquake. A 20-minute walk inland is a memorial to the Italian troops who hid nearby but were found and slaughtered by the Germans.

The coastal strip south of Argostóli with its huge beaches, **Platís Gialós** and **Makris Gialós**, was once a place of great natural beauty—a sandy paradise for the town dwellers. Now the locals steer clear and leave it for the razzle-dazzle of package tourism, but since Kefaloniá is hardly lacking in beautiful places to swim, don't feel deprived if you give it a miss.

Excursions from Argostóli

1 Take the ferry over to rival Lixoúri and head for Xi beach, then visit Kipouríon monastery, perched on the cliffs, and Drákondi Spílio cave nearby. Stop off at Petáni beach as you drive back around the headland.

2 Drive up to marvel at the caves near Sámi, then head to Paradise taverna near Ag. Evfimía for lunch and on to Mýrtos beach for a siesta. From there drive south back to Argostóli.

3 Drive up through traditional villages and past superb sea vistas to quaint Fiskárdo. After a fishy lunch, make for Ássos beach and see the sun set from the Venetian castle before heading home.

Argostóli ✉ *28100,* ✆ *(0671–)*　　　　　　　　　　　**Where to Stay**

Two of the island's swankiest hotels are bang in the middle of the coastal strip decribed above. **Mediterranée**, on the beach at Makris Gialós, ✆ 28 760, ✆ 24 758 (*A; exp*), caters for the fat wallets of a youngish crowd in an international bland fashion; it has all mod cons and a variety of land and sea sports. **White Rocks**, at Platís Gialós beach, 3km from Argostóli, ✆ 28 332, ✆ 28 755 (*A; exp*), appeals to a slightly older clientèle and is just as pricey and well equipped. In town, **Hotel Ionian Plaza**, in central Plateía Valliánou, ✆ 25 581, ✆ 25 585 (*C; mod*), is a stylish hotel, each room with a balcony. **Cefalonia Star**, at 50 Metaxá St, ✆/✆ 23 180 (*C; mod*), is at the quieter end of the waterfront in a clean modern block. *Open all year.* For a little less, cosy, family-run **Irilena**, ✆ 23 118 (*C; mod*), is a pleasant choice on the Lassí peninsula, near a little beach. *Open May–Oct.* You can get basic, cheap rooms at **Hara**, 87 Leof. Vergotí, ✆ 22 427 (*D; inexp*). *Open all year.* **Argostoli Beach Camping** is 2km north, by the lighthouse, ✆ 23 487.

Argostóli ✆ *(0671–)*　　　　　　　　　　　　　　　　**Eating Out**

O Mezes, in Lauranga St, and **Sto Psito**, two streets up from the Folklore Museum, are both set in a pretty gardens and excel in traditional grills, *mezédes* and Kefalonian specialities like *sheftália* (minced meatballs on a spit, with pitta bread) for 4,000–5,500dr. If you prefer a more musical setting, head for **Captain's Table**, ✆ 23 896. In the main square, **Kefalos** serves a large menu of Greek favourites on pretty pink tablecloths; **El Greco** (on Vergoti) and **Caliva** (also in the main square) are good choices too. **Taverna Diana**, on the waterfront near the fruit market, does good moussaka and *kreatópita* (Kefalonian meat pie: beef and pork with rice in filo pastry). If you have a hankering for charcoal-grilled chicken with a lemon marinade or lamb *kléftiko*, washed down with a house wine, get a table at **Psitaria Elliniko**, near Hotel Olga, © 23 529. Locals enjoy **Patsouras**, on the waterfront near the EOT, and **Phaedra**, on the Lassí peninsula; those in the know go for good, robust lunches at **Tzivras**, on a side street by the fruit market (*2,500dr*).

Lixoúri and the Palikí Peninsula

Ferries trundle across the bay from Argostóli to the bulging Palikí peninsula and **Lixoúri** (ΛΗΧΟΥΡΙ), Kefaloniá's second city, all new houses on wide streets and in itself not terribly interesting, even if it's the home of the Pale Philharmonic. Lixoúri is known for its sense of humour and in its central square near the waterfront the town has put up a dapper **statue of Andréas Laskarátos**, holding his top hat. Born into the island aristocracy, Laskarátos (1811–1901) was a poet and satirist who directed most of his broadsides at the Orthodox Church; he heckled the clergy so much that they finally excommunicated him—in Greek, *aforismós*, meaning that the body will not decompose after death. When Laskarátos found out he hurried home, collected his innumerable children's decomposing shoes and returned to the priest, asking him to please excommunicate the footwear, too. You can get a glimmer of what pre-earthquake Lixoúri was like at the west end of town at the **Iakovátos Mansion**, a rare survival and now a library and icon museum (*open Mon–Fri 8–1.30, Sat 9.30–12.30*); one of the works is attributed to Mikális Damaskinós. Fresco fragments and an iconostasis salvaged from the earthquake have been installed in the town's newer churches. North of Lixoúri, the unexcavated ancient city of Pali (or Pale) stood on the hill of Paliókastro.

The Palikí peninsula is well endowed with beaches. Closest is **Ag. Spyrídon**, just north of town and safe for children, while 4km south are **Michalitsáta** and **Lépeda**, both sandy, the latter near the abandoned cave-monastery (now church) of Ag. Paraskeví. In the same area, **Soulári**'s church of Ag. Marína has fine icons and a handsome Venetian doorway; the next village, **Mantzavináta**, has good frescoes in its church of Ag. Sofía. From here a road leads south to the lovely beach of **Ag. Geórgios** (or **Miá Lákko**), a long stretch of golden-red sand, which merges to the west with the Palikí's preferred beach, simply known as **Xi**, a long crescent of pinkish sand, with sun beds and a taverna.

Just south of it is the famous **Kounópetra**, a huge monolith a few inches from the shore that rocked to and fro, pulsating at the rate of 20 times a minute. The earthquake of 1953 fouled up the magic by stabilizing the sea bed beneath and likewise destroyed the houses on pretty, deserted **Vardianá islet** off the coast.

A by-road to the west of Lixoúri passes the abandoned monastery of **Tafíon**, en route to a second monastery, **Kipouríon**, rebuilt as it was before the earthquake in the 1960s and perched on the west cliffs, with spectacular sunset views and guest rooms where you can spend the night. The peninsula is shot full of caves: the most interesting, **Drákondi Spílio**, 40m deep, can be reached from the monastery with a guide.

The sparsely populated northern part of the Palikí has a scattering of pretty villages such as **Damoulináta**, **Delaportáta** and **Kaminaráta** (the latter has a small folk museum in the old olive press at its centre and is famous for its folk dances), and more beaches: the large, lovely white sands of **Petáni** are rarely over-crowded and are known as Paralía Xouras ('Old Geezer beach'), after the old man who used to run the seaside taverna. Even more remote—accessible by a minor road—is **Ag. Spyrídon**, a stretch of sand tucked into the northernmost tip of the Palikí peninsula.

Cefalonia Palace Hotel, next to Xi beach, ℰ 93 112, winter bookings ℰ 92 555, 🖂 92 638, *cphotel@compulink.gr* (*A; lux*), is a new hotel offering half-board accommodation with pools; all rooms have a sea view and balcony. *Open May–Oct.* Although used by tour operators, the **Summery** in Lixoúri, ℰ 91 771, 🖂 91 062, *summery@otenet.gr* (*C; mod*), is a tranquil place to stay and has a pool; taxi transfers from the airport are provided. *Open all year.* **Pension Bella Vista**, ℰ 91 911 (*A; inexp*), is small, modern and comfortable; all rooms have bath, simple kitchen and sea view. **Akrogiali** has good fish in season and **Zorbas** has a nice terrace garden; neither costs an arm and a leg. The main square in Lixoúri provides ample cafés for gentle navel gazing.

Southeast of Argostóli: The Livathó and Mount Aínos

Most of Kefaloniá's rural population is concentrated in the fertile region of valleys, gardens and green rolling hills called the Livathó, southeast of Argostóli. After Platís Gialós beach, emerging free from the tourist tinsel is **Miniés**, home to a ruined Doric temple from the 6th century BC and some of Greece's finest white wine.

Kefaloniá in a Glass

Kefaloniá is one of the most important islands for wines, especially Robóla, a grape variety introduced by the Venetians in the 13th century that ferments into distinctive lemony dry white wines. Lately it's been better than ever: the Robóla from Gentilini, a small vineyard in Miniés owned and operated by Nichólas Cosmetátos, has been something of a revalation in the country, demonstrating just how good Greek wines can be when made with the latest techniques and *savoir faire*, even when starting from scratch. In 1978, Cosmetátos purchased an estate in these limestone hills, planted his first vines, built a small but ultra-modern winery, and carved a cellar out of the cliffs to attain the perfect storage temperature. Each year his vintages improve: pale gold Gentili Animus, 100 per cent Robóla, is a crisp, delicious wine well worth looking out for; Gentili Fume is a Robóla aged in oak casks, with an oaky fragrance. Gentili also does a fine Muscat fortified dessert wine (Amando) and a lovely apéritif wine (half Muscat, half Robóla) called Dulcis, which goes perfectly with fresh fruit. Another label to look for, Calligas, was founded in the early 1960s, and produces lovely Robólas and other dry whites and reds, and occasionally the very rare Thiniatikó—a velvety port-like wine. In fish tavernas, the common house wine is Tsoussi, made from a white grape unique to Kefaloniá. You may also see Mavrodáphni Kefallinías, another sweet wine.

The coastal road south of Miniés continues to **Svoronáta**, where the red sands of **Avithos beach** (with a *cantina* and taverna) look out to the tiny islet of **Días**. This is named after a tiny islet off the coast of Crete, and like that one had an altar to Zeus: sacrifices were coordinated by smoke signals with those on Mount Aínos. **Domáta**, the next village east, boasts Kefaloniá's oldest olive tree (able to squeeze 20 people in the hollow of its ancient trunk) and the beautiful church of the **Panagía**, with a pretty reconstructed Baroque façade and a giant 19th-century carved and gilded iconostasis that cost 12,000 gold sovereigns—all melted down to form it.

Nearby **Kourkomeláta** was rebuilt by the wealthy Kefalonian shipowner Vergotís; everything is as bright, new and pastel-coloured as a suburban southern Californian town. The neo-classical cultural centre and surrounding vineyards add to the effect. If you wish to wine-taste, turn off at the sign that reads 'visit the familiar farm—free wine tasting' and sample the produce on this attractive farm. At **Metaxáta**, where printing was introduced to Greece, Byron rented a house for four months in 1823, finished his satirical rejection of romanticism, *Don Juan*, and dithered over what to do as the representative of the London Committee while each Greek faction fighting for independence jostled for the poet's attention—and more particularly his money. Just northwest, **Lakídra**, rebuilt by French donations after the earthquake, is the most important village of the Livathó and believed by some archaeologists to be the site of Odysseus' palace; in the suburb of Kallithéa, near the plain little church of **Ag. Nikólaos ton Aliprantídon**, four Mycenaean tombs yielded a good deal of pottery dating from 1250 to 1150 BC. Byron used to come here and sit on a rock, inspired by the views, and a line from the poem he wrote is inscribed on a plaque: ΑΝ ΕΙΜΑΙ ΠΟΙΗΤΗΣ ΤΟ ΟΦΕΙΛΩ ΕΙΣ ΤΟΝ ΑΕΡΑ ΤΗΣ ΕΛΛΑΔΟΣ ('If I am a poet, I owe it to the air of Greece').

Inland: Ag. Andréas, Ag. Geórgios and Ag. Gerasímos

North of Metaxáta is the Byzantine convent of **Ag. Andréas**, originally known as Panagía Milapídia (the Apple Virgin) after an icon discovered on an apple tree trunk. Perhaps the one and only good deed done by the quake of 1953 was to shake loose the whitewash on the walls, revealing frescoes that date back to the 13th century (in the chancel) and the 17th and 18th centuries (along the nave). The church is now called the **Ag. Andreas Monastery Museum** (*open Mon–Fri 9–1.30 and 5–8, Sat 9–1.30, closed Sun; adm*), and houses icons, fresco fragments and saintly relics orphaned by the eathquake, among them the Veneto-Byzantine icon of *Panagía Akáthistos*, painted in 1700 by Stéfanos Tsankárolos from Crete. After the earthquake, a new Basilica of Panagía Milapídia was built next door to house its bizarre prize possession: the sole of St Andrew's right foot, donated in the 17th century by Princess Roxanne of Epiros.

Above the church looms the tree-filled **Castle of Ag. Geórgios** (*open Jun–Oct Tues–Sat 8.30–3, Sun 9–3, closed Mon*), spread over a 320m hill and commanding a wonderful view of the surrounding plains and mountains. Founded by the Byzantine emperors, the citadel was completely rebuilt by the Venetians and Greeks under Nikólaos Tsimarás after the fierce seige of 1500 dislodged the Turkish occupants. The centre of life and religion on Kefaloniá until 1757, Ag. Geórgios once had a population of 14,000 people living in or just outside the polygonal walls. Storerooms, prisons, Venetian coats-of-arms, a ruined Catholic church and a bridge built by the French during their occupation crumble away within the battlements; of the 15 churches, the **Evangelístria**, with Byzantine icons, still stands in the present-day little village.

To the east lies the green **plain of Omalós** and the **monastery of Ag. Gerásimos**, where the bones of Kefaloniá's patron saint rest in a silver reliquary in a small church built over his little grotto hermitage. If half of the male population of Corfu are named Spíros after St Spyrídon, 50 per cent of Kefalonian men are named Gerásimos. The saint's speciality is intervening in mental disturbances and exorcising demons, especially if the patient keeps an all-night vigil at his church on 20 October, his feast day, but pilgrims from all over Greece pour in year round; a small hostel allows 20 to stay overnight. The monastery is dwarfed by an enormous plane tree and its tall, pseudo-rococo freestanding belfry. Opposite is a local winery, **Si.Ro.Ke**, sometimes open for tastings.

From the Argostóli–Sámi road a branch winds up to the summit of Mount Aínos, **Mégas Sóros** (1,628m), the highest point of the majestic Aínos range, the loftiest in the Ionian islands, and covered with snow from December to March. The road goes as far the tourist pavilion, 1,300m up, and from there you can easily hike the rest of the way, an impressive stroll among the tall, scented trees, seemingly on top of the world. On a clear day, the Peloponnese, Zákynthos, Ithaca, Lefkáda, the Gulf of Pátras and Corfu are spread out below as if on a great blue platter. At one time the entire range was blanketed with its unique, indigenous species of black fir— *Abies cefalonica*—with a distinctive bushy appearance and upward-pointing branches; the forests were so dense that Strabo and other ancient writers called the island Melaina ('the Dark'). From ancient times, timber was the main source of Kefaloniá's prosperity; recent studies at Knossós show that the Minoans imported Kefaloniá's firs for the pillars of the labyrinth. Venetian shipbuilders over-harvested the trees, but two disastrous fires, in 1590 and 1797, share the blame for destroying nine-tenths of the forest; the second fire burned for three months. In 1962 what had survived of the forest was made into Mount Aínos National Park. A handful of wild horses, the last survivors of an ancient breed which live in the park, are near extinction. Hesiod mentioned the 8th-century BC temple of **Aenesian Zeus**, the foundations of which are just below Mégas Sóros; you can see the bones from the great animal sacrifices that took place there.

The South Coast: Beaches and the Virgin's Little Snakes

The south coast of Kefaloniá is bursting with good sandy beaches shielded from the north winds by Mégas Sóros. There are good beaches just down from **Spartiá**, under sheer white cliffs, and at **Trapezáki**, 1.5km from the tiny harbour of **Pessáda** (ΠΕΣΑΔΑ)—Kefaloniá's chief link to Zákynthos (with a summer *cantina* but no telephone for the unwary foot passenger to ring for a cab, so be first off the boat and grab one that's waiting). East, below **Karavádos**, is another pretty little sand beach with a taverna perched above and plane trees and reeds spread behind.

The beach at **Lourdáta** (ΛΟΥΡΔΑΤΑ) is the longest and most crowded. Lourdáta's name is said to derive from the English lords who spent time here in the 19th century, perhaps attracted by the village's warm microclimate. Its main square, with a spring and an enormous plane tree, is the beginning of Kefaloniá's first nature trail, blazed with funds from the WWF. It takes about 2½ hours to walk and passes through a representative sample of the island's flora—orange and olive groves, macchia shrubs and scrubby phyrgana, pine woods and kermes oaks, and masses of wild flowers in the spring. The path goes by the ruined **Monastery of Síssia**, founded in 1218 by St Francis of Assisi (hence its name) on his return from the Crusades in Egypt, and converted to Orthodoxy in the 16th century; a new monastery was built just above after 1953.

Káto Kateliós is a small resort, a pretty place with springs, greenery and a beach that curves along Moúnda Bay. Just east, Potomákia beach, below Ratzaklí, is a favourite nocturnal nesting place of loggerhead turtles (*see* p.304) from June to mid-August; stay off the beaches at night during this period, as the nesting mothers are easily scared off and may just dump their eggs at sea.

Just inland, Kefaloniá's most unusual religious event takes place in the village of **Markópoulo**, set over the sea on a natural balcony. During the first 15 days of August, small harmless snakes 'inoffensive to the Virgin Mary', with little crosses on their heads, suddenly appear in the village streets. Formerly they slithered into the church (rebuilt in exactly the same place after the earthquake) and mysteriously disappeared near the silver icon of the Panagía Fidón ('Virgin of the Snakes'). Nowadays, to keep them from being run over, the villagers collect them in glass jars and bring them to the church, where they are released after the service and immediately disappear as they did in the past. Although sceptics believe that the church is simply along the route of the little snakes' natural migratory trail, the faithful point out that the snakes fail to appear when the island is in distress—as during the German occupation and in 1953, the year of the earthquake.

Skála (ΣΚΑΛΑ), with its long beach and low dunes, is the biggest resort in this corner, with plenty of watersports, sunbeds, bars—the works—but still relatively low key. The Romans liked the area; a Roman villa was excavated near Skála, with 2nd-century AD mosaic floors, one portraying Envy being devoured by wild beasts and two men making sacrifices to the gods. Two kilometres north of Skála, a 7th-century BC temple of Apollo has also been discovered, though most of its porous stone was cannibalized to build the nearby chapel of Ag. Geórgios.

Pronnoi, one of the four ancient cities of Kefaloniá, was located inland, above the village of **Pástra**, although only a necropolis and some walls of the acropolis have survived. In 1992, in the nearby hamlet of **Tzanáta**, Danish and Greek archaeologists uncovered a huge 12th-century BC domed tomb 7m under a vineyard, said to be the most important ever discovered in western Greece. The bones, gold jewellery and seals discovered inside are now being studied at the University of Pátras, but the discovery (the Kefalonians immediately declared it the tomb of Odysseus) has added new fuel to the 'where was Ithaca really?' debate.

From Tzanáta the road descends through the wild and narrow 'Póros Gap', carved, according to myth, by Heracles, who ploughed his impatient way through the mountains. **Póros** (ΠΟΡΟΣ), with direct ferry links to Kilíni, was originally the port of Pronnoi. In the 1820s, British High Commissioner Napier settled Maltese farmers here to create a model farming community called New Malta. It never got off the ground; now the village, with its clear turquoise waters, abundant fresh fish and beach, shows the tell-tale signs of resortdom and is none the better for it.

© *(0671–)*   *Where to Stay and Eating Out*

Pessáda ✉ 28083

> **Sunrise Inn**, 1.5km from the port, © 69 586, @ 69 621 (*B; lux*), is comfortable and air-conditioned, set in the trees, with a pool and children's activities. In nearby Spartiá, **Poseidon**, © 86 475, book in Athens @ (01) 895 9899, @ 69 649 (*mod–exp*), has apartments with sea-view balconies, a tennis court, pool and a large garden. **Karavados Beach Hotel**, near Ag. Thomas beach, © 69 400, @ 69 689 (*B; exp*), offers two pools, tennis and a mini-bus service to Argostóli.

Lourdáta ✉ 28083

> **Lara**, © 31 157, @ 31 156 (*C; mod–exp*), is a pleasant moderate-sized hotel with a pool and playground, set in greenery a few minutes from the sea. *Open May–Oct.* **Pension Thalassíno Trifilli**, ©/@ 31 113 (*inexp–mod*), has just opened; its rooms

are bedecked with flowers and it is run by members of Archipelagos, the local environmental group, who can inform you about any new nature trails and activities on the island. Rooms to let abound (and are being constructed at a rate of knots): try **Lucky House** or **Ionian Sun** on the beach. Two of the best tavernas in the village, **To Thalassíno Trifilli** (by the pension of the same name) and **Klimatis** are also run by Archipelagos. If it's on offer, try the *prentza* cheese made in nearby Simotáta.

Skála ✉ 28082

Tara Beach hotel, ✆ 83 341, 🖷 83 344 (*C; mod–exp*), has rooms and bungalows by the beach. *Open May–Oct.* **Aliki,** ✆ 83 427, 🖷 83 426 (*B; mod*), overlooks the sea, has a large garden and is good value. **Ostria's House,** 600m from Ratzaklí, ✆ 83 383, book in Athens ✆ (01) 202 4555 (*mod*), is a small and attractive pension. Skála has a reasonable supply of restaurants, after which **The Loft** will concoct a cocktail or two for you. Up the coast at Póros, the first taverna on the waterfront is particularly agreeable and known for good home-cooking.

North Kefaloniá: Caverns and Castles

Sámi, the port for ships to Pátras, Corfu and Italy, has beaches and a campsite and makes a half-hearted attempt at being a resort in its own right. Although the bay, with mountainous Ithaca as a frontdrop, is not unattractive, the town and its beach are of little interest, although at the time of writing Sami is under seige for the shooting of the film version of *Captain Corelli's Mandolin*, for which a wonderful mock-Venetian waterfront façade has been constructed; it must be the first time for almost 60 years that Italian Second World War artillery has been seen thundering through the streets. Kefalonians wait anxiously to see what the impact will be on the island's tourism in years to come. Four kilometres east is one of the most exquisite pebble beaches, **Andisámos**, set in a bay of exceptional beauty with lushly forested hills spilling down to the postcard-clear water; and because facilities don't stretch beyond a simple *cantina*, the crowds stay away.

On the two hills behind Sámi are the town's **ancient walls**, where the citizens put up a heroic four-month resistance to the Romans in 187 BC before their inevitable defeat and equally inevitable sale into slavery. Sámi is also close to Kefaloniá's magnificent grottoes. The **Drogaráti cave** (*adm*), near the hamlet of Chaliotáta, is a lugubrious den of orange and yellow stalactites and stalagmites; one of its great chambers has such fine acoustics that Maria Callas came here to sing, and concerts are occasionally held in the summer (ask for details at EOT in Argostóli). The other, the more magical steep-sided **Melissáni** ('purple cave'; *adm exp*), is a half-hour walk from Sámi; small boats wait to paddle you across its mysterious salt water lake (supplied by the swallow holes near Argostóli; *see* p176), immersing you in a vast shimmering play of blue and violet colours caught by the sun filtering through a hole in the roof of the chasm, 100ft overhead. According to the school of thought that Homer's 'Ithaca' consisted of both Itháki and Kefaloniá, this was the Cave of the Nymphs, where the Phaeacians deposited Odysseus. *Both caves open sunrise–sunset in summer, but are closed after October.* There are other, undeveloped caves for spelunkers only in the vicinity of Sámi, many with lakes and dangerous, precipitous drops; the best of them is **Angláki cave**, near Pouláta.

At the base of Kefaloniá's northernmost peninsula, pretty **Ag. Evfimía** (ΑΓ. ΕΥΦΗΜΙΑ) is the port for Ithaca and Astakós, and a far cosier resort base than Sámi. There's good swimming off a scattering of white pebbly beaches along the Sámi road. A mosaic uncovered in Archeotíton Street is believed to have been the floor of the early Byzantine church of Ag. Evfimía, and the pretty village of **Drakopouláta**, a few kilometres above the port, was spared by the earthquake. Further west, scattered across the slopes of Mount Ag. Dinatí, are more of Kefaloniá's most traditional villages—and goats with silver-plated teeth, caused by the high mica content in the soil.

Ⓒ (0674–)   *Where to Stay and Eating Out*

Sámi ✉ 28080

Pericles, Ⓒ 22 780, ✆ 22 787 (*B; exp*), is a largeish unexceptional complex on the edge of town, with two round pools, tennis and a nightclub. **Melissani**, Ⓒ 22 464, in Athens Ⓒ (01) 417 5830 (*D; mod*), set back from the waterfront in greenery, is a small and friendly hotel. *Open May–Oct.* **Kastro**, Ⓒ 22 656, ✆ 23 004 (*C; mod*), has sea-view balconies and is convenient for ferries (temporarily closed for the filming of *Captain Corelli's Mandolin*; due to reopen in 2001). **Karavomilos Beach Camping**, 1km from town, Ⓒ 22 480, is well equipped. The taverna selection is unexciting, though Delfini, Adonis and Port Sámi are pretty reliable. Look out for local specialities such as octopus pie and meat cooked in a ceramic *stámna*, and expect to pay around 3,500dr.

Ag. Evfimía ✉ 28081

Smartest is family-run **Hotel Gonatas**, Ⓒ 61 500, ✆ 61 464 (*B; exp*), with a pool and sea views, at Paradise Beach, a 5-minute amble from the little port. **Hotel Boulevard Pyllaros**, Ⓒ 61 800, ✆ 61 801 (*exp*), on the waterfront, has rooms and suites full of dark repro furniture, as well as boat hire and tennis. Floral **Hotel Logaras**, Ⓒ/✆ 61 202 (*C; mod*), has apartments but may be package-booked; if so, try institutional **Moustakis**, Ⓒ 61 060, ✆ 61 030 (*C; mod*), down the street. *Open Apr–Sept.* Paradise Beach is also blessed with **Paradise** (also known as Dendrinos, after its owner) taverna, which has earned itself a big reputation for Greek and international dishes; stick to the Greek. **Finikas** has pizza and traditional food on the waterfront. If you're peckish or self-catering, visit the bakery nearby, which uses a traditional oven.

Up the Northwest Coast: To Mýrtos, Ássos and Fiskárdo

The journey from Argostóli north to Fiskárdo is magnificently scenic—perhaps a good reason to take the bus, so you don't have to keep your eyes on the road, although there are some very tempting stops along the way. The first good beach, white pebbly **Ag. Kiriakí**, with several bars and tavernas, rims the crotch of land linking the Palikí peninsula to the rest of Kefaloniá, a few kilometres below the village of **Zóla**. An unpaved road links Zóla to **Angónas** (it's also on the main Argostóli road), where local folk artist Razos has decorated the village square with paintings. Eight kilometres to the north and 2km below **Divaráta** (though the signpost indicates 4km) curves the U-shaped bay of **Mýrtos**, where sheer white cliffs carpeted with green maquis frame a stunning crescent of tiny white pebbles and patches of sand against a deep sea so blue it hurts. There are sunbeds, but if you want to make a day of it bring provisions (and a hat—there's no shade in the afternoon) or settle for a pricey sandwich at the beach café.

The road winds along a corniche to another famous, stunning view, over **Ássos** (ΑΣΟΣ), where the Venetian citadel and colourful little fishing hamlet tucked under the arm of the isthmus look like toys. The village was rebuilt by the French after the earthquake and, though its sleepy charm may get a bit frazzled by day-trippers, Ássos becomes a friendly little Greek village in the evening; there are umpteen rooms to rent and a couple of tavernas. The **Venetian fortress**—a favourite sunset destination, by foot or, much more easily, by car— dates from 1585, when the Turks occupied Lefkáda and began raiding this coast; it was the seat of the Venetian proveditor until 1797. His house survives in ruins, along with the church of San Marco and a rural prison, used until 1815. The venerable olive tree in principal Plateía Paris is said to have shaded the open-air sermons of St Cosmás the Aetolian, an 18th-century missionary; at one point, the story goes, his words were being drowned out by the buzzing cicadas. Cosmás told the insects to hush, and they obligingly did.

East of the main road, an unpaved road rises up through the inland villages of the peninsula. One, **Varí**, has by its cemetery a late Byzantine church called Panagía Kougianá, with rare and curious frescoes painted by a folk artist who decorated the left wall with scenes from hell, and the right one with scenes of paradise until the villagers applied a coat of whitewash. The church is usually locked; ask in the village for the key.

Continuing up to Cape Ather, the northernmost tip of Kefaloniá, the road passes the white rocky beach of **Chalikéri**, where people come to soak in the exceptionally briny water and leave pleasantly pickled. In **Ántipata Erissóu**, the unusual Russian church of 1934 was built by a Kefalonian who made a fortune in the Soviet Union; opposite, by the pine tree, there are good *mezédes*.

Fiskárdo (ΦΙΣΚΑΡΔΟ) is by a landslide the prettiest and trendiest village on the island, its 18th-century houses gathered in a brightly coloured apron around a yacht-filled port. A fluke in its innermost geological depths spared it from the 1953 earthquake, and it's a poignant reminder of the architecture Kefaloniá once had, now turned to dust. Some of the old houses have been fixed up for guests (*see* below); others are decorated with folk paintings of mermaids and ships. Four carved stone sarcophagi and the ruins of a Roman bath are fenced off by the Panormos Hotel. The newly opened **Nautical and Environmental Museum**, at the top of the village (*open 10–2 and 5–9*), displays objects trawled up from the depths (including the Bristol Beaufighter, a plane shot down in 1943), as well as marine life and current projects. The museum hosts slide shows and presentations (*Weds, around 9pm*) on its history and environmental issues. You can work as a volunteer for a few months with Fiskárdo's Nautical & Environmental Club, which runs the museum, and be trained to dive for underwater research into the bargain (© 41 181, 📧 41 182, *fnec@compulink.gr* for further details).

Genius and Extrovert

The name Fiskárdo is derived from Robert Guiscard, the *terror mundi* of his day, whose very name once made popes, emperors and kings tremble in their boots. Born in 1017, the sixth of 13 sons of a minor Norman nobleman named Tancred de Hauteville, Robert began his career as a mercenary adventurer working for (and against) the Byzantines and Lombards in Italy. By a mix of adroit military leadership, an eye for the main chance and cunning (his nickname *Guiscard* means 'crafty'), he made himself Duke of Apulia, master of southern Italy. Other Hauteville brothers came to join him; the most successful was the youngest, Roger, who married a cousin of William the Conqueror, defeated the Arabs of Sicily and founded an extraordinary dynasty of Norman-Sicilian kings.

Having just sacked Rome after defeating Emperor Henry IV's attempt to dethrone Pope Gregory VII (Hildebrand), Robert Guiscard and his Normans stopped off here on their way to do the same to Constantinople, on the excuse that Byzantine Emperor Michael VII had locked his empress—Guiscard's daughter—up in a convent. In 1085 the Normans had just scored a major victory at Corfu over the Venetians, Byzantium's allies, when a typhoid epidemic at last laid low the 68-year-old warrior; Giuscard was brought ashore here and died in the arms of his Lombard warrior wife, Sichelgaita. His body was preserved in salt and sent back to Italy to be buried with his brothers; the coffin was washed overboard in a storm, but later recovered off Otranto and the messy remains of Guiscard were buried at Venosa. As John Julius Norwich wrote in *The Normans of the South*: 'He was that rarest of combinations, a genius and an extrovert...a gigantic blond buccaneer who not only carved out for himself the most extraordinary career of the Middle Ages but who also, quite shamelessly, enjoyed it.' Such was the power of his name that the old pirate was granted a posthumous and completely false reputation as a virtuous Crusader; two centuries after his death Dante installed him in *Paradiso*.

Ássos

✉ 28084, ✆ (0674–)   ***Where to Stay and Eating Out***

There are more than 200 beds in private rooms, but they fill up fast in the summer. Try **Linardos Apartments**, ✆ 51 563 or winter in Athens ✆ (01) 652 2594; **Cavos**, ✆ 51 564; **Papa Spiratos Apartments**, ✆ 51 360; or **Kanakis Apartments**, ✆ 51 631, with its own tiny pool. There's a handful of tavernas, of which **Kokolis** is the most established.

Fiskárdo

In bijou Fiskárdo, where everybody likes to stay, four typical houses have been renovated by EOT; for reservations, write to Paradosiakós Ikismós Fiskárdou, Kefaloniá, or call ✆ 41 398. There are two pensions which are renovated and done out in traditional style: the **Filoxenia**, ✆/✆ 41 319 (*A; exp–mod*), and the **Dendrinos**, just out of town, ✆ 41 326. Self-contained apartments include **Stella**, ✆ 41 211, ✆ 41 262 (*B; exp–mod*), and **Kaminakia**, ✆ 41 218 (*C; mod*), while **Nitsa**, ✆ 41 143 (*A; inexp*), has cheaper rooms and a studio. The Greek Islands Club (see p.32) has tasteful waterfront apartments and houses here and in nearby villages. Cheap rooms are also available; ask at Fiskárdo Travel. **Tassia**, ✆ 41 205, is a fine fish restaurant in the harbour, serving up ample portions of the day's catch to landlubbers and yachters who like to drop in (*4,500dr*); nearby **Nefelis** is similar. **Lagoundera**, ✆ 41 275, is a good, friendly grill house set in a square just back from the water; try the fresh anchovies when they are in season. **Nikolas**, ✆ 41 307, perched above the harbour, has a fine location and food (as well as rooms—*A; mod*), with nightly Greek dancing to boot. **Solenti's Bar** is an enticing winter haunt set in the old school, with open fires and mandolin music. Five kilometres away in Máganos, **Ionio** is an excellent traditional café and taverna.

Kos (ΚΩΣ)

Dolphin-shaped Kos, with its wealth of fascinating antiquities, flowers and orchards, sandy beaches and comfortable climate, is Rhodes' major Dodecanese rival in the tourist industry. In other words, don't come here looking for anything very Greek—the *kafeneíon* and *ouzerie* serving octopus sizzling from the grill have long been replaced with fast-food joints and tourist-trap cafés. The streets are packed with T-shirt and tatty gift shops; where garlanded donkeys once carried their patrons home from the fields, swarms of rent-a-bikes rev. In high season English, German and Swedish tourists fill the island's myriad big, self-contained resort hotels and countless discos. Even the architecture isn't particularly Greek, partly owing to an earthquake in 1933: the Italian occupation contributed some attractive buildings, and the pair of minarets rising from the mosques add an aura of elegance and *cosmopolitana* to the capital. Inland, Kos in summer looks uncannily like a mini California: sweeping golden hills, with a few vineyards, groves and orchards, grazing cattle and sheep, and pale cliffs, but otherwise empty, contrasting with the rashes of building—pseudo-Spanish villas seem to be the rage—crowding the countless sandy coves that ruffle the coasts.

History

Evidence in Áspri Pétra cave suggests people have been living on Kos since 3500 BC. A Minoan colony flourished on the site of the modern city; the Mycenaeans who superseded them traded extensively throughout the Mediterranean. The island went through a number of name changes, including Meropis, after its mythical king; Karis, for its shrimp shape; and Nymphaeon, for its numerous nymphs. Kos, which finally won out, is either from a princess named Koon or a crab, an early symbol. In the 11th century, the Dorians invaded and made Astypálaia their capital, and in 700 BC they joined the Dorian Hexapolis: a political, religious and economic union that included the three cities of Rhodes, and Cnidos and Halicarnassus on the Asia Minor coast.

Poised between East and West (Asian Turkey is, after all, just over the channel), Kos flourished with the trade of precious goods—and revolutionary ideas. Halicarnassus was the birthplace of Herodotus, the 'father of history', the first to attempt to distinguish legend from fact, and in the 5th century BC Kos produced an innovating papa of its own, Hippocrates, father of medicine. Believing that diseases were not punishments sent from the gods but had natural causes, Hippocrates was the first to suggest that healers should learn as much as possible about each patient and their symptoms before making a diagnosis. His school on Kos, where he taught a wholesome medicine based on waters, special diets, herbal remedies and relaxation, was renowned throughout the ancient world, and he set the standard of medical ethics incorporated in the Hippocratic oath taken by doctors to this day. When Hippocrates died, the Asklepeion (dedicated to Asklepios, the healing god) was founded, and people from all over the Mediterranean came to be cured in its hospital-sanctuary.

In 411 BC, during the Peloponnesian War, the Spartans played a nasty trick on the island; pretending to be friends, they entered the capital Astypálaia and sacked it. In 366 BC the survivors refounded the old Minoan/Mycenaean city of Kos, conveniently near the by now flourishing Asklepeion. The next few centuries were good ones; besides physicians, Kos produced a school of bucolic poetry, led by Theocritus, a native of Sicily (319–250 BC) and the most charming of all ancient Greek poets. His *Harvest Time in Kos*, in which he evokes a walk across the island to drink wine by Demeter's altar, and meeting a poetic goatherd on the way,

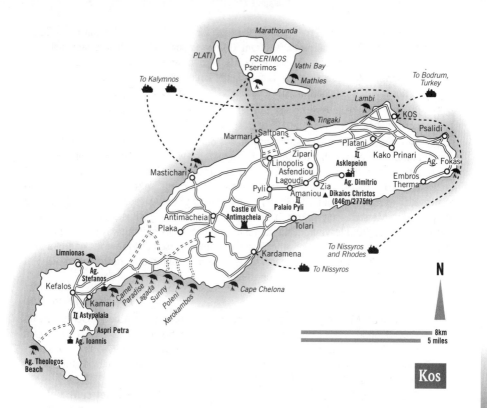

Kos

is one of his masterpieces and gave English the word 'idyllic'. Apelles, the greatest painter during the lifetime of Alexander, was a native of Kos, as was Philetas, inventor of the Alexandrine and teacher of another native, Ptolemy II Philadelphos, who went on to become king of Egypt; many subsequent Ptolemies were sent over to Kos for their education. The Romans were later to prize Kos for its translucent purple silks, wines and perfumes and gave it a special autonomy because of the Asklepeion. St Paul called in and began the island's conversion to Christianity; so far 21 early basilicas have been discovered.

Kos' wealth and strategic position made it a prize for invading Persians, Saracens, pirates and Crusaders. The gods themselves, it seems, were jealous, and earthquakes in AD 142, 469 and 554 levelled most of the island's buildings. In 1315 the Knights of St John took control, and in 1391 began fortifications using the ancient city as a quarry, incorporating even marble statues from the Asklepeion in their walls. In 1457 and 1477 the Turks besieged Kos without success, but they gained the fortress in 1523 by treaty after the fall of Rhodes. After almost 400 years, the Italians toppled the Turks, then introduced a fascist regime in the 1920s. The Germans took over in 1943; when the 'thousand-year Reich' fell two years later, Kos was left in the custody of the British. It was united with the rest of Greece in 1948.

© (0242–)   *Getting There and Around*

By air: there are charters direct from London and other European cities, and four flights a day from Athens. Olympic's office is at 22 Leof. Vass. Pávlou, © 28 331. For one-way tickets home, try Plotin, in town, ℂ 22 871, ✉ 25 154. The airport is 26km from town. Olympic airport buses from Kos town depart 2 hours before each flight and transport arriving Olympic passengers into town and Mastichári, or there are infrequent public buses (the stop is outside the airport gate—ask for Taverna Panorama) to Kos town, Mastichári, Kardámena and Kéfalos. **Airport:** ℂ 51 229.

By sea: daily **excursions** sail to Psérimos from Kos town, as well as Mastichári, Kardaména, Bodrum (Turkey), Níssyros, Platí and Léros.

By road: flat Kos town and the small roads out west are especially suited to **bicycles** and there are a number of shops that hire them, as well as an abundance of **car rental** agencies on the waterfront. The city **bus** runs every 15 minutes at peak times and regularly otherwise from the centre of the waterfront (7 Akti Koundouriotou, ℂ 26 276) to Ag. Fokas and Lampi; roughly every hour to the Asklepeion; and eight times a day to Messaria (buy tickets in the office before boarding). Buses to other points on Kos, ℂ 22 292, leave from the terminal behind the Olympic Airways office, but they get packed so arrive early; otherwise you'll find yourself at the wrong end of a long queue waiting for a taxi. In theory, at least, you can summon a **radio cab**, ℂ 23 333 or 27 777, but keep a close eye on the meter.

ℂ *(0242–)*   *Tourist Information*

The helpful **Municipal Tourist Office** is in the ornate old Albergo Gelsomino on Vass. Georgíou just before the hydrofoil berth, ℂ 26 585 or 28 724, ✉ 21 111 (*open Mon–Fri 8am–8.30pm, Sat–Sun 8am–3pm*). The **tourist police**, ℂ 26 666, shares the yellow edifice with the clocktower opposite the main harbour with the regular **police**, ℂ 22 222, and EOT (closed at present).

Post office: 14 Venizélou, by the OTE telephone office. **Internet café**: Café del Mare, 4a Alexandrou, offers pricey access in pleasant surroundings. **British consulate**: in Aeolos Travel, 8 An. Laoumtzi St, ℂ 26 203.

Festivals

25 March, Evangelismós in Asfendíou; **23 April**, Ag. Geórgios in Pylí; **24 June**, Ag. Ioánnis, bonfires everywhere; **29 June**, Ag. Apóstoli in Antimácheia; **29 August**, Ag. Ioánnis in Kéfalos. In **August** the *Hippocratia* features art exhibitions, concerts, theatre and films. **8 September**, Panagías in Kardaména. **21 November**, Isódia tis Panagías in Ziá; **6 December**, Ag. Nikólaos in Kos town.

Kos Town

Bustling Kos, capital city and main port, is roughly in the region of the dolphin's eye. As you sail into the harbour it looks magical, especially at twilight, the port still guarded by a medieval castle, the silhouettes of mountains behind and lush garden setting, the multitude of flowers and stately palm trees and the fragrant evening scent of jasmine; opposite, the coast of Turkey fills the horizon. At close quarters, the town doesn't quite live up to the promise. Most of it postdates the 1933 earthquake, although this means it has more Art Deco buildings than the average Greek island town. Another side-effect of the quake: when the rubble was cleared away, several ancient sites were revealed, leaving a serene Greek and Roman oasis of antiquities peppered amongst throbbing holiday bedlam. Declared 'European City of 1995' for its self-improvements, Kos has a new water treatment system guaranteeing pristine beaches, the monuments are being restored and new pedestrian areas and a one-way traffic system have been established, to cut down on some of the cacophony. But the tourist fleshpots have not lost any of their uninhibited garishness: there's no lack of fast food, touts, T-shirt shops, and even a hard sell from the excursion boats all lit up along the front.

One block up from the harbour, the city's main square **Plateía Eleftherías** has been freed of cars, leaving it eerie and empty, like a Pirandello character in search of a play. Here you'll find the 18th-century **Defterdar Mosque** (*still used by the 50 or so Moslem families on the island, but not open to the public*), and two Italian Art Deco buildings. One, laid out like a Roman house, holds the **Archaeology Museum** (© (0242) 28 326, *open Tues–Sun, 8.30–3; adm*). Fittingly, the prize exhibit is a 4th-century BC statue of Hippocrates with a noble, compassionate expression. Other items include an intriguing fragment of an archaic Symposium; a 2nd-century AD seated Hermes, with a little pet ram and red thumb; a statuette of a pugilist with enormous boxing gloves; and another of Hygeia, the goddess of health, feeding an egg to a snake. There are also fine mosaics, of a fish and of the god Asklepios with his snake, stepping from a boat and welcomed by Hippocrates.

Plateía Eleftherías also has the city's **market**, with fruit, vegetables and seashell kitsch—walk through it to Ag. Paraskévi square, with its shady cafés, and don't miss the superb bougainvillea arching over the back of the market. Buying and selling is old hat here; Plateía Eleftherías also has the entrance into the ancient **Agora**, by way of the **Pórta tou Foroú**, draped with another massive bougainvillea. This was where the Knights of St John built their town and auberges, just as in Rhodes (*see* pp.240–1). When these collapsed in the earthquake, they revealed not only the market, with the re-erected columns of its *stoa*, but the harbour quarter of the ancient city, a temple of Aphrodite Pandemos, and a 5th-century Christian basilica. Whilst wandering round, you'll probably stumble across trails of dried cat food scattered by the Kos Animal Protection League.

On the northern end of the Agora, Plateía Platánou is almost entirely filled by **Hippocrates' plane tree**, its trunk 52ft in diameter, its huge boughs now supported by an intricate metal scaffolding instead of the marble columns that once kept the venerable tree from disaster. At an estimated 700 years old it may well be the most senior plane in Europe. Hippocrates may well have taught under its great-grandmother, for he believed, as do modern Greeks, that of all the trees the shade of the plane is the most salubrious. The Turks loved the old plane just as much, and built a fountain under it with a sarcophagus for a basin, and overlooking it constructed the lovely **Mosque of the Loggia** (1786). On 1 September the citizens of Kos pluck a leaf from the tree to include in their harvest wreaths as a symbol of abundance.

The Tree of Life

One of the great meeting centres of Greek life is the mighty plane tree, or *plátanos*, for centuries the focal point of village life, where politics and philosophy have been argued since time immemorial. Since Hippocrates, the Greeks have believed that plane-tree shade is wholesome and beneficial (unlike the enervating shadow cast by the fig). In Greek the expression *cheréte mou ton plátano* loosely translates as 'go tell it to the marines', presumably because the tree has heard all that nonsense before.
The *plátanos* represents the village's identity; the tree is a source of life, for it only grows near abundant fresh water, its deep roots a symbol of stability, continuity and

protection—a huge majestic umbrella, as even the rain cannot penetrate its sturdy leaves. Sit under its spreading branches and sip a coffee as the morning unfolds before you; the temptation to linger there for the day is irresistible.

The Castle of the Knights

A stone bridge off Plateía Platánou takes you over the former moat (now the Finilon, or palm grove) to the entrance of the **Castle of the Knights of St John** (© (0242) 28 326; *open Tues–Sun 8.30–3; adm*). Combined with their fortress across the strait in Bodrum, this was the premier outer defence of Rhodes. After an earthquake in 1495, Grand Master Pierre d'Aubusson rebuilt the walls and added the outer enceinte, and the tower overlooking the harbour bears his name and coat-of-arms. Since d'Aubusson mostly used stones from the Agora, the masonry is a curious patchwork quilt of ancient inscriptions and reliefs of the knights' coats-of-arms. Some have been removed to the castle's **antiquarium**, to join other stacks of defunct columns and marble that nobody seems to know what to do with. The castle's dishevelled weeds and wild-flowers and the stillness of the noonday sun attracted director Werner Herzog, who set his first black and white film, *Signs of Life* (1966), partly within its walls, although the elaborate cock-roach traps and hypnotized chickens that played a major role are no longer in evidence.

Roman Kos

From Plateía Eleftherías, Vas. Pávlou leads to Kos' other main archaeological sites. In the quarter called the Seraglio (don't expect any harem girls), Minoan and Mycenaean houses were discovered, as well as later structures. Opposite the Olympic Airways office stands a ramped Hellenistic **Altar of Dionysos**, and across Grigoríou Street, the ruins of the **Central Baths** (site of the Vourina spring, praised by Theocritus) and the **Casa Romana** (© (0242) 23 234; *open Tues–Sun 8.30–3; adm*), both victims of the earthquake of AD 554, and excavated and reconstructed in grim concrete shell by the Italians in 1940. The house, begun in the Hellenistic era, has well-preserved mosaics—one owner at least was fond of panthers—and offers a fair idea of the spacious elegance to which the wealthy could aspire; even on the hottest days it remains cool inside. To the west along Grigoríou Street, by the Catholic church, the **Roman Odeon**, or concert hall, has its rows of white marble seats, partially restored by the Italians; the statue of Hippocrates was discovered under its arches. Besides this the city had three other theatres and a music school. Strabo wrote of it: 'The city of the Koans is not large, but one lives better here than in others, and it appears beautiful to all who pass it by in their ships'.

Some of this good living is evident in the **Western Excavations** just opposite. On one side of the main path rise the great Hellenistic walls built around the **acropolis** (now studded with a minaret); on the other side you can pick out the marble-paved *Cardo* and *Decumanus*, the main arteries of Roman Kos, lined with ruined houses. Although the Italians took many of the best mosaics off to Rhodes, some good bits remain (often under a protective layer of sand), especially the **House of Europa**, on the *Decumanus*. Just north of this, lining the *Cardo*, are an elegant 3rd-century BC **nymphaeum**, or fountain house, which supplied running water to the nearby **public toilets** with marble seats. The gymnasium has a **xystos**, a running track covered by a marble colonnade, used in the winter months—a rare ancient luxury that even Kos' most luxurious beach hotels lack. The Romans also had a heated pool, near the brick **baths** (the *thermae* still survive). Part of this was transformed into a Christian basilica in the

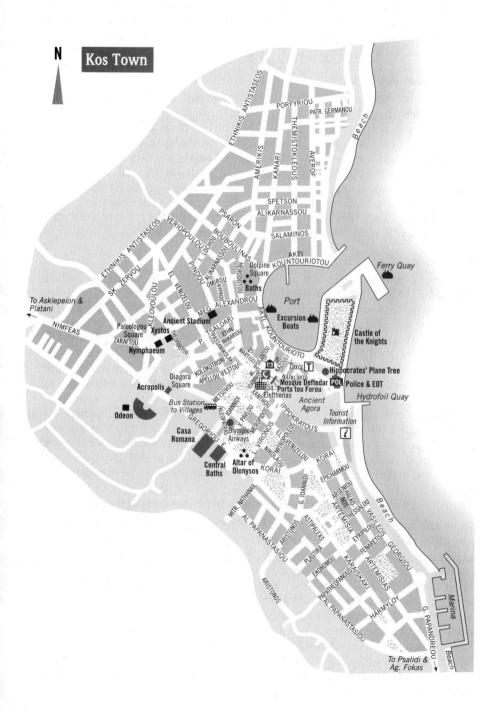

5th century; the lintel has been rebuilt and the baptistry has a well-preserved font. At the north end, an unidentified 3rd-century BC building contains mosaics of battling bulls, bears and boars. The **Stadium** is a block north, along Tsaldári St; only a few of the seats have been excavated and work continues, but on the far side near the church is a well-preserved *aphesis*, or starting gate.

Beaches near Kos Town

Since the advent of the water treatment plant these have won blue flags for cleanliness, but that's about the nicest thing you can say about them. The sandy and pebbly town beaches are packed with rows of sunbeds and umbrellas edge-to-edge; in places along Vas. Georgíou the smell of gallons of sun lotion is overpowering. The city bus will take you in a few minutes to better, less crowded beaches to the north of town at **Lampí** (ΛAMΠI), now occupied by package tourists rather than the military; the closest strands to the south are at **Psalídi** (ΨAΛIΔI), 3km away, and **Ag. Fokás** (8km), both sporting fancy hotel complexes. For something more remote, get your own transport to continue to **Embrós Thermá** (13km), where volcanic black sands and thermal springs make the bathing a few degrees warmer; a new spa is currently planned to replace the old hot pit where the water oozes out.

The Asklepeion and Platáni

City bus or a short bike climb will take you up to the island's most important site, the **Asklepeion** (AΣKΛEΠEION) (✆ (0242) 28 763; *open Tues–Sun 8.30–3; adm*), 4km west of the city. The German archaeologist Herzog, following Strabo's description, discovered it in 1902, and it was partially restored by the Italians during their tenure. This was one of the ancient world's most important shrines to the healing god Asklepios, served by the Asklepiada, a secret order of priests (Hippocrates was one) who sensibly found that good water and air and relaxing in beautiful surroundings did much to remedy the ills of body and soul. The cult symbol was the snake, the ancestor of the same one on the modern medical symbol, twining itself around the caduesis. Snakes, sacred intermediaries between the living and the dead (they used to always be found in holes in cemeteries, eating mice fattened on grave offerings), were believed to have a knack for seeking out healing herbs and transmitting dreams, which were part of the therapy—the Asklepiada made good use of hallucinogens and the power of sugges-tion in their cures. The sanctuary on Kos was built after the death of Hippocrates, who left a whole school of disciples behind him, but most of the buildings visible today date from the Hellenistic age, when the earthquake-damaged Asklepeion was last reconstructed. Many of the structures were cannibalized by the Knights, who found it too convenient a quarry.

Set on a hillside, the Asklepeion is built in a series of terraces sliced by a grand stair. On the lowest level are Roman baths, built in the 3rd century AD. The next level, once surrounded by a huge portico, has the main entrance and another large bath; here was the medical school, and the museum of anatomy and pathology, with descriptions of cures and votive offerings from grateful patients. Near the stair are the remains of a temple dedicated by the Kos-born physician G. Stertinius Xenophon, who served as the Emperor Claudius' personal doctor and murdered his patient by sticking a poisoned feather down his throat, before retiring on Kos as a hero (so much for the Hippocratic oath!). On this level, too, was the sacred spring of the god Pan, used in the cures. On the next terrace is the altar of Asklepios, and Ionic temples dedi-cated to Apollo and Asklepios (a few of the columns have been reconstructed by the Italians); on the top stood a Doric temple of Asklepios from the 2nd century BC, the grandest and most sacred of all, and enjoying a view that in itself might shake away the blues. In August, for the

Hippocratia, the teenagers of Kos get off their motorbikes for a day to don ancient chitons and wreaths to re-enact the old rituals and recite the Hippocratic oath.

Just up the road, the modern **International Hippocrates Foundation** is dedicated to medical research. In 1996, several Nobel Prize winners and other leading lights attended the first 'International Medical Olympiad' here, and no no no, they didn't hold brain surgery races but gave out awards and held conferences. Similar Olympiads may be held in the future, although nothing has been organized to date. Here the five rings of the Olympic symbol are used to sum up Hippocratic philosophy: 'Life is short. Science is long. Opportunity is elusive. Experiment is dangerous. Judgement is difficult.'

On the way back to Kos town, downhill all the way along the cool cypress-lined avenue, stop for refreshments in **Plátani**, Kos' main Turkish settlement, although tension since the Cyprus troubles has decreased the population by two-thirds. They're busy and a bit touristy, like everything on Kos, but the Turkish food is excellent and relatively cheap; if you want a more peaceful setting, try the taverna on the way down the hill. A little out of Plátani, on the road back to the harbour, the **Jewish Cemetery** stands in a pine grove near the Muslim graveyard. The inscriptions on its headstones end abruptly after 1940. Without any parishoners, the pretty synagogue back in Kos town (4 Alexándrou Diákou, by the ancient Agora) has been converted into the civic cultural centre.

Kos Town ✆ *(0242–)*   *Sports*

Learn to **dive** from certified instructors at the Kos Diving Centre, 5 Koritsas Square, ✆ 20 269 or 22 782; if you already know how, go out with the Dolphin Divers, ✆ (094) 548 149, whose *Happy Puppy* boat is moored every evening with the excursion craft. The proximity of Turkey and other islands makes for lovely **sailing**: contact Sunsail, 3 Artemisias, ✆ 27 547, or Kavos Moorings, 7 Themistokleous, ✆ 27 115, ✆ 27 116. Or go **riding** in Mármari (*see* below).

Kos Town ✉ *85300,* ✆ *(0242–)*   *Where to Stay*

In days of yore, visitors in need of a cure would stay in the Asklepeion and sacrifice a chicken to the gods. These days, beds can be so scarce in high season that you still might need that chicken. Book, or if you get offered a room as you get off the ferry, take it. If you want to stay in the centre *and* get a good night's sleep, buy earplugs. Package companies block book everything in the moderate range, so splurge or slum.

luxury

These are all A class and out in Psalídi. **Hippocrates Palace Hotel**, ✆ 24 401, ✆ 24 410, has the Olympic Health Centre spa, indoor and outdoor pools and tennis. *Open Apr–Oct*. The newer **Kipriotis Village**, ✆ 27 640, ✆ 23 590, is huge and packed with amenities: two pools, one Olympic-sized; hammam; tennis; Jacuzzi; gym; etc. It also has rooms for the disabled; open same months. **Dimitra Beach**, ✆ 28 581, is another beachside complex; nearby, there's the neo-Venetian, air-conditioned **Platanista**, ✆ 27 551, ✆ 25 029, with tennis and pool.

expensive

Ramira Beach, ✆ 22 891, ✆ 28 489 (*A*), is slightly more affordable and still well endowed with facilities.

Afendoulis, 1 Evripílou, © 25 321, ✉ 25 797 (*C*), is a friendly and comfortable pension with a fragrant terrace in a quiet road near the sea, run by Ippokrátis and brother Aléxis Zíkas of the **Pension Alexis**, 9 Irodótou, © 28 798, ✉ 25 797 (*E*), the Mecca for backpackers and full of character. Alex is amazingly helpful and the large veranda at the Pension Alexis positively reeks of jasmine of an evening from the overgrown creeper. Alternatively, **Manos Hotel**, 19 Artemisias, © 28 931, ✉ 23 212 (*C*), has reasonable rooms with balcony. **Kos Camping**, © 23 910, 3km from the port, is a well-run site with a wide range of facilities from laundry to bike hire. A minibus meets the ferries.

Kos Town © (0242–)   *Eating Out*

Eating out in town is like playing Russian roulette if you want real food. Avoid the harbour-front, where waiters aggressively *kamáki* or 'harpoon' punters in. One of the lovelier places to dine is the **Anatolia Hamam,** 3 Diagora Square overlooking the Western Excavations, © 28 323, in the sumptuously restored Turkish bath with a garden terrace; the food has an appropriate Anatolian touch, but beware the pricey wine. **Taverna Petrino,** © 27 251, nearby, is also classy, set in a pleasant terrace courtyard, and serving huge salads. The **Kástro**, near the ancient Agora on 15 Hippocratous, © 23 692, has pricey French food in an alluring setting. Atmospheric creeper-draped **Platanos**, © 28 991, offers expensive international and traditional dishes, cakes and live music at enticing tables adorning the square around Hippocrates' beloved tree. For a real neighborhood taverna with good food, big portions, and low prices, seek out **Antonis**, at Koutarys St, behind Hotel Anna, or for even better food go out to **Taverna Ambavri**, a ten-minute walk south of the Casa Romana. **Nick the Fisherman**, on the corner of Averof and Alikarnassou, offers his catch at good prices, accompanied by bouzouki when he's in the mood. *Ouzeries* are reappearing: **Kohili**, 9 Alikarnassou St, has the finest *mezédes* but they don't come cheap.

Outside town in bi-ethnic Platáni, a handful of tavernas serve Turkish food. The best of the bunch is the **Arap**, offering excellent aubergine with yoghurt, borek, grilled shish kebab and chicken. On the way to Psalídi near the Ramira Beach Hotel, **Mavromatis** is a tranquil place with traditional food; ditto **Nestoras** near the campsite.

Entertainment and Nightlife

Kos is one big party at night. The ancient Agora is alive with the thumping sound of house music from 'Disco Alley' on pedestrian Navklírou Street, where every establishment is a bar pumping out conflicting beats. Discos go in and out of fashion season by season, but **Kalua** and **Heaven**, both at Lámpi, have a watery backyard and garden and remain popular. **Aesolos** café-bar on the waterfront nearby plays mellow music at night and serves excellent Baileys frappés. For Greek music and *rembetika*, there's **Happy Club**, 1 Navarinou. **Jazz Opera**, 5 Arseniou, is a great place playing jazz, funk, reggae and the blues. Alternatively, for some amusement, try your feet at Greek dancing classes, advertised in many restaurants. If you want to catch a film, **Orpheus** has an indoor screen in Plateía Eleftherías and an outdoor screen along Vas. Georgiou

St, ✆ 25 713. For anyone homesick for football, rugby, cricket, or just about any other sport, **Taurus Bar**, 9 Mandilara St, keeps up with all the scores and events and shows many matches live.

Around Kos

The northeast of Kos is flat and very fertile, with fields of watermelons and tomatoes. Beyond Lampí and the reach of the town bus, **Tingáki** (ΤΙΓΚΑΚΙ) is a smart little resort overlooking the island of Psérimos and still has a village feel, especially when the day-trippers have gone. Boat beach (so nicknamed by locals because of the beached whale of a vessel there), before Tingáki, is quiet and has a taverna. In March and April, the nearby salt pans, Alikes, are a favourite port of call for flamingoes and numerous migratory birds, while the sandy coast and estuary are a loggerhead turtle nesting area. At the far end of the wet lands, **Marmári** (MAPMAPI) is increasingly given over to packages, but offers a generous sandy beach and a chance to explore local byways on horseback at the **Marmari Riding Centre**, ✆ (0242) 41 783. Just inland, two ruined Byzantine basilicas (Ag. Pávlos and Ag. Ioánnis) lie on the outskirts of **Zipári**; above, Kos' spinal ridge has a bumpy, curiously two-dimensional profile.

But these are real mountains, not a child's drawing. From Zipári the road ascends to **Asfendíou**, a cluster of five peaceful hamlets set in the woods, with whitewashed houses and flower-filled gardens, many now being turned into holiday homes. The highest of the five hamlets, **Ziá** is a pretty place, of fresh springs, fruit and walnut groves—the bucolic Pryioton described by Theocritus—now converted wholesale into a 'traditional village' for package tours, receiving busloads every evening for the absolutely spectacular sunsets and a Disneylandish Greek Night out in the schlocky tavernas; but there are others, too, such as the excellent Olympiada, minus dancing 'oopa oopa' waiters. Kos' ancient sculptors came up here to quarry marble from Kos' highest peak, **Díkaios Christós**, 'Justice of Christ' (846m), the summit of which can be reached without too much difficulty in about three hours from Ziá, and well worth it for the god-like views of Dodecanese and Turkish geography.

From the Asfendíou a road runs across country to **Lagoúdi** and continues from there to **Amaníou**, where there's a turn-off to **Palaío Pýli**, once a Byzantine capital of Kos, now a ghost town on a crag surrounded by concentric walls camouflaged in the rocks. Within its walls is the church of Panagía Ypapandí, built in the 11th century by the Blessed Christódoulos before he made a trade for land on Pátmos; it and two others, Ag. Antonio and Ag. Nikólaos, have 14th-century frescoes. Another side lane, just west of Amaníou, leads to the **Charmyleion**, an ancient tholos tomb-hero shrine with twelve little vaults, re-used as a church crypt. The modern, grotty village of **Pýli** below is a major agriculture centre, although the upper part of town has a great place to stop for lunch, in the taverna by a handsome spring-fed fountain (or *pygí*) built in 1592. On 23 April, for the feast of St George, Pýli holds a horse race, with an Easter egg as prize, cracked on the forehead of the winning horse—a custom going back to remotest antiquity. Further west, in a wild setting and enjoying more great sunset views, the **Castle of Antimácheia** was built by the Knights as a prison for bad knights in the mid-14th century. Within its great, battlemented triangular walls are two churches (one with a fresco of St Christopher carrying baby Jesus), a few surviving cisterns and, over the gateway, the arms of Pierre d'Aubusson. The sprawling village of **Antimácheia**, near the airport, had the island's last operational windmill as its landmark, which doubled as a wheat grinder (although it has ground to a halt at present). Opposite is a traditional house (*open*

8–4.30); the typical boxed-in beds were often even higher than this so olives and wine could be stored underneath. Even better, head up to **Pláka**, on a paved road from the airport: a green oasis and favourite picnic ground, with wild peacocks and yet more sunsets.

There are more beaches on either coast: to the south, the sand stretches between **Tolíri** and much hotter **Kardámena** (ΚΑΡΔΑΜΑΙΝΑ), once a charming fishing village famous for its ceramics and now a heaving resort. Commercialized to Costa Brava proportions, it's very much the Brit and Scandinavian family package destination, complete with pubs, chips and smorgasbord. But there is also golden sand, boats to Níssyros, and watersports and entertainment for all ages. On the north coast, **Mastichári** (ΜΑΣΤΙΧΑΡΙ) is quieter, and has frequent boats for Kálymnos and Psérimos, and, a 20-minute walk beyond the Kanari Beach Hotel, the ruins of a 5th-century **basilica of Ag. Ioánnis** with a fine mosaic floor.

There are more mosaics (again, under a layer of sand), Ionian columns and remains of an atrium and baptistries with the extensive ruins of the lovely twin 5th-century basilicas of **Ag. Stéfanos**, near the beach at **Kamári**, towards the dolphin's tail. In the bay you can contemplate the islet of **Kastri**, a natural volcanic bulwark, often surrounded by the butterfly wings of windsurfers skimming over the blue sheet, with a Club Med complex as a foreground. A long fringe of sand runs under the cliffs to the east with a few access roads; the steepest descent is to pretty **Camel Beach**, by picturesque rocks, and the easiest to **Paradise Beach** (or 'Bubble Beach' after the bubbles that rise to the surface through the clear waters at one end of the bay); it's perfect for children, although they'll have to fight their way through the forest of sunbeds and umbrellas to get to the water. Further along the headland to the left, the beaches **Lagáda** (or Banana; generally considered the most beautiful with its dunes), **Sunny**, attractive **Poléni** (or Magic) and **Xerokambos** are much quieter although still offering their share of sunbeds, parasols and little cantinas.

The road twists up to **Kéfalos** (ΚΕΦΑΛΟΣ) to the west, high up on the headland of the dolphin's tail. This is where the bus terminates and, when the hotels are bursting full elsewhere, you just may find a room here. Another Knights' castle stands looking over Kamári and isn't particularly impressive, although it inspired many travellers' tales in the Middle Ages, all involving a dragon; Mandeville in his *Travels* claims the serpent was none other than Hippocrates' daughter, enchanted by Artemis and awaiting a knight brave enough to kiss her to transform her back into a maiden. South, just off the road, there's a Byzantine chapel of the Panagía built out of a temple that once belonged to the ancient capital of Kos, **Astypálaia** (signposted Palatia), the birthplace of Hippocrates. A few bits of the ancient city remain, including a theatre. Isthmioton, another ancient city on the peninsula, was important enough in the past to send its own delegation to Délos, but not a trace of it remains. A paved road descends to **Ag. Theológos** beach, offering some of the island's most secluded swimming (but often big waves) and a nice taverna. Neolithic remains from 3500 BC were found in the **Áspri Pétra cave** just south, reached by a (unmarked) path. The road passes through dramatic scenery, past sheer cliffs and a telecommunications tower, then ends at the charming **Monastery Ag. Ioánnis Thimianós**, 6km from Kéfalos.

Kos ✆ (0242–)   ***Where to Stay and Eating Out***

Tingáki/Marmári ✉ 85300

In Tingáki, **Park Lane**, 150m back from the beach, ✆ 69 170 (*B; mod;* book through Aeolos Travel in Kos town ✆ 26 203), is a package-dominated family hotel, with pool, playground and friendly staff. **Meni Beach**, ✆ 69 181, @ 69 217 (*C; inexp*), is close to the sea and has a pool; or venture out of town to **Paxinos**, ✆ 69 306 (*C; inexp*). **Alikes Taverna**, on the edge of town, should satisfy your appetite. In Marmári, the **Caravia Beach**, ✆ 41 291, @ 41 215 (*A; exp*), is a super club hotel set in beautiful grounds a little out of town with a vast range of facilities. *Open Apr–Oct*. Between Marmári and Mastichári, **Tam Tam Beach Taverna**, by Troulos beach, is a lovely place. In Marmári, **Dimitris** and **Apostolis** are decent eateries.

Mastichári ✉ 85301

Mastichari Bay, ✆ 59 300, @ 59 307 (*A; exp*), is good for families, with lots of activities, nice pool and beach, playground, floodlit tennis, open-air theatre and satellite TV. **Mastichari Beach**, ✆ 59 252 (*C; inexp*), is plain, clean and near the harbour with sea views, and the **Arant**, ✆ 51 167 (*C; inexp*), is also reasonable. Just back from the road and very close to the beach, **Evagelia Argoula** has cheap, clean and cheerful studios, ✆ 59 047 (*inexp*). The first taverna in town, **Kalikardia**, is still good, as is the long-established **Taverna Makis**, just off the waterside.

Kardámena ✉ 85302

Kardámena has scores of hotels, but unless you go on a package you may only find rooms on the edges of the season. **Porto Bello Beach**, ✆ 91 217, @ 91 168, *portobello@kos.forthnet.gr* (*A; exp*), has a luxurious setting with views of Níssyros, an enormous pool and private beach, not to mention its original flooring. **Restaurant Andreas** refuses to pander to tourists and has a good ethnic range of dishes; **Christopoulos Taverna**, by the beach, is also recommended. Kardámena lives it up with happy hours and has something for night owls of all ages, seasoned with a pint of good old-fashioned seaside Brit vulgarity.

Kéfalos ✉ 85301

Panorama, perched above packageville overlooking Kastri island, ✆/@ 71 524 (*inexp*), has quiet studios that live up to its name and a garden; breakfast included. Down in town, **Paradise Pension**, ✆ 71 068 (*inexp*), has cheap rooms with fridge, kettle, balcony and a café below. In the hill village **Esmeralda** does quails and liver as well as more usual Greek fare; **Kastro** has OK food and a good view of the bay; **Stamatia** by the sea has a wide selection of fish, including 'dogs' teeth' for adventurous diners. If you have wheels, **Milos Taverna**, above the tiny fishing port of Limnionas, serves up a fishy feast.

Psérimos (ΨΕΡΙΜΟΣ)

Psérimos, wedged between Kos and Kálymnos, has a beautiful sandy beach, which its 70 residents have come to regard as a curse, as day in and day out during high season it becomes invisible under rows of day-trippers like well-oiled sardines. Even in September, excursion boats from Kos town, Mastichári and Kálymnos queue up to dock, the tavernas are thronged and the islanders short-tempered. It becomes even more crowded on 15 August, when hundreds of pilgrims attend the *panegýri* at its monastery Grafiótissa. If you are staying any length of time (when the day boats have gone the people become quite friendly), you'll probably want to take to the interior by day, or hunt up one of the smaller pebbly strands on the east coast; the main beach can be murder. Some boats now head instead to the adjacent islet of **Platí**, with another sandy beach, and make a day of it by stopping for lunch in Kálymnos.

Psérimos ℗ (0243–)

Where to Stay and Eating Out

The seaside **Tripolitis**, ℗ 23 196, is pleasant, located over Mr Saroukos' taverna; the **Pension Niki-Ross** is also worth a try (Ross is Australian Greek). The **monastery** has simple accommodation for up to 10 people. There are a few rooms to be had in the village; try **Katerina Xiloura**, ℗ 23 497, or **Glynatsis** on ℗ 23 596. If the rooms are full, you can sleep out on one of the island's more distant beaches, a kilometre from the village. Most of the tavernas on the main beach are packed, and the service in them surly at lunchtime. The unnamed one with the garden area does excellent and reasonably priced fresh *kalamári*.

Lefkáda (ΛΕΦΚΑΔΑ)

The island of Lefkás (more popularly known in Greece by its genitive form Lefkáda) was named for the whiteness (*leukos*) of its cliffs. It barely qualifies as an island; in ancient times Corinthian colonists dug what is now the 20m (66ft) wide Lefkáda ship canal, separating the peninsula from the mainland. This is kept dredged by the Greek government and is easily crossed by a swing bridge; beyond the canal a series of causeways surrounds a large, shallow lagoon, where herons and pelicans figure among the migratory visitors. As on Kefaloniá, Ithaca and Zákynthos, a series of earthquakes—most recently in 1953—destroyed nearly all of the island's buildings.

Lefkáda is not a love-at-first-sight island; the approach from land is unpromising, and first impressions may be disappointing. This changes once you make your way down the coast, where the island's long sandy beaches make a rich blend with the natural beauty and traditionalism of the interior. Lefkáda is especially well known for the laces and embroideries produced by its women, some of whom still keep a loom in the back room of their house; it is just as famous for its perfect windsurfing at Vassilikí and sailing through the enchanted isles off Nidrí. Dolphins seem to like it as well: there are more varieties seen off the coasts of Lefkáda than anywhere else, including the rare *Delphinus delphis*.

History

Although inhabited at least as far back as the late Paleolithic era (8000 BC), Lefkáda first enters the scene of recorded history as part of ancient Akarnania, site of the city Nerikus, located at modern Kallithéa. Nerikus is recorded as being huge, but over the years farms and houses have almost completely overtaken all the remains. In 640 BC, the Corinthians used a ruse to snatch the island from the Akarnanians, and founded the city of Lefkáda where it is today, dug the channel separating Lefkáda from the mainland, and built the first fort at the northern tip, which throughout history would be the key to the island. During the Peloponnesian War, Lefkáda, as a loyal ally of Corinth, sided with Sparta and was devastated twice, by the Corcyraeans and the Athenians.

The biggest blow to ancient Lefkáda came with the war between Macedonia and Rome in the mid-3rd century BC, when the island was punished for Akarnania's siding with Macedonia. Another dark moment was the Battle of Aktium, where Augustus outmanoeuvred and defeated the fleets of Mark Antony and Cleopatra and won the Roman Empire as his prize. To celebrate his victory, Augustus founded a new city, Nikopolis (near modern Aktion) which drained away Lefkáda's wealth and population.

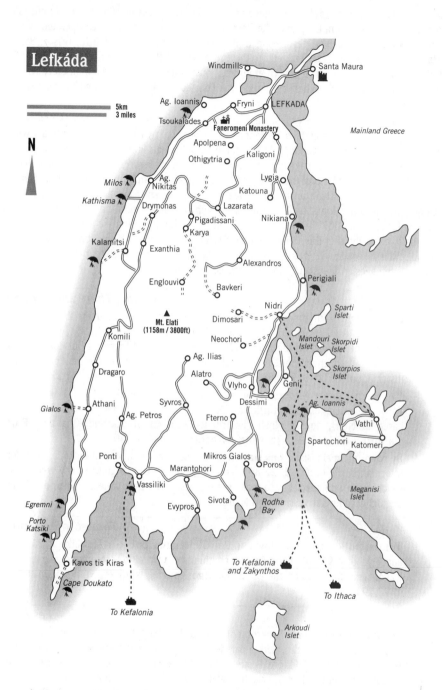

Lefkáda

5km
3 miles

N

Although Lefkáda was granted to Venice after the Fourth Crusade, it took the Venetians a century to wrench it from the grip of the Despot of Epirus. The inhabitants, exasperated by the fights and pirates, received permission from Venice to built the original fortress of Santa Maura, a name that soon came to refer to the entire island. When Constantinople fell in 1453, Helene Palaeológos, mother of the last emperor, Constantínos XI, founded a monastery within the walls of Santa Maura. When the Turks took Lefkáda in 1479, they turned the monastery into a mosque.

In 1500 the combined forces of Spain and Venice under the Gran Capitan Gonzales de Cordoba captured Lefkáda and Santa Maura, but the very next year Venice made a treaty with Turkey and returned the island. In 1684, Venetian nobleman Francesco Morosini, angry at losing his own fortress at Herákleon, Crete, was determined to win Lefkáda back for Venice, which he did with the help of the Bishop of Kefaloniá, leading an army of priests and monks. Venice held on to the island until its own fall in 1796, but never managed to influence it as strongly as the other Ionians. With the fall of Venice, the French and then the Russians grabbed Lefkáda; in 1807 the tyrant Ali Pasha of Epirus tried to purchase it from Russia, but was held back by the Russian-appointed Secretary of State, Count John Capodístria. Capodístria is said to have later sworn to support the cause of an independent Greece with the rebellious refugees on the island, among them Kolokotrónis.

Getting There and Around

By air: flights four times a week from Athens and regular charters from England (Monarch, Air Ferries, and Air Caledonian among them), to Aktion, the nearest airport, 26km away on the mainland; from May–mid-Oct there are bus connections to Lefkáda from the airport. Another charter, Britannia, flies to Préveza. For Olympic information, ✆ (0645) 22 881; for Aktion/Préveza airport, ✆ (0682) 22 355.

By sea: in summer, **excursion boats** from Nidrí and Vassilikí to Sámi, Fiskárdo and Póros (Kefaloniá) and Kióni (Ithaca). Daily boat from Nidrí to Meganísi. The *Ikaros*, based in Nidrí, does a plush day trip to Meganísi, Ithaca and Kefaloniá. **Port authority**: ✆ (0645) 22 176; **Nidrí harbour**: ✆ (0645) 92 509.

By road: the main island **bus station** is located at the north end of Lefkáda town; for information call ✆ (0645) 22 364. Routes to Nidrí, Vassilikí and touristy west coast beaches are well plied, but to really see the island you need at least a **moped**; there are plenty to hire at Vassilikí and Nidrí.

✆ (0645–)   Tourist Information

Tourist police in Lefkáda town, ✆ 26 450; **regular police** in Vassilikí, ✆ 31 218, and Vlychó, ✆ 95 207. For help with anything from travel to accommodation, the first travel agent to set up on the island, **George Kourtis**, is still on Nidrí's main street, ✆ 92 494, ✉ 92 297.

Festivals

50 days after Easter, Faneroméni Monastery; **26 July**, Ag. Paraskeví near Ag. Pétros, carnival festivities, with a parade; in **August**, the Arts and Letters Festival and large International Folklore Festival, in Lefkáda town; throughout the **first two weeks of August**, Karyá, which is well known for its handmade lace and woven carpets, puts on a stream of festivities including a clarinet festival on the **11th** (in the same vein, nearby Englouvi has a clarinet and lentil festival on 6 and 7 August) and 'Riganada', the re-creation of a traditional wedding, where everyone wears their finest old costumes); **11 November**, Ag. Minás in Lefkáda town.

Lefkáda Town

Approaching Lefkáda over the floating bridge, the first thing you'll see as you cross the causeway over the lagoon is the massive **Fortress of Santa Maura**, dipping its feet in the sea near Akarnania (as the region is still known) on the mainland. Most of what stands dates from the Venetian and Turkish reconstructions. Although the buildings in the walls were blown to smithereens in an accidental powder explosion in 1888, the fortress continued to serve as a military camp, and, for 10 years after the 1922 Asia Minor Disaster, as a refugee camp.

Santa Maura has survived the periodic earthquakes that rattle Lefkáda better than the capital, **Lefkáda town**, which collapsed like a house of cards in the earthquake in 1948, and was hit hard again in 1971. The rebuilt town is like no other in Greece: narrow lanes lined with brightly painted houses, stone on the ground floor, topped by a fragile wooden or more often corrugated metal upper storey as an antiseismic measure. Another unusual feature of the town is its iron bell towers, rearing up like oil derricks. For all this, it is a bustling market town with more genuine Greek atmosphere than anything you'll find in the resorts.

Bosketo Park, the large shady square near the end of the causeway, displays busts of Lefkáda's three great contributors to letters: Valaorítis, Sikelianós (for more on both, *see* below), and Lafcadio Hearn (1850–1904), whose British father and Kytheran mother named him after his birthplace. He went on to become a journalist in the States, and in 1890 went to Japan, where he became an expert on Japanese language and culture, teaching the Japanese about Western literature and vice versa; every now and then Japanese tourists make the pilgrimage to the island to honour the man they know as Yakomo Kuizumi.

Lefkáda's churches, constructed mostly in the 18th century under the Venetians, are square, domeless and solidly built of stone, and have largely survived the tremors; fine examples of the Ionian school of painting are in **Ag. Minás** (1707), and the three icons in **Ag. Dimítrios** (1688), although the chances of finding either open are not good. Another church, the **Pantokrátor**, has a pretty façade, last reworked in 1890, with an original curved roofline. **Ag. Spyrídon** (17th century) has a fine carved wooden screen.

There are four small museums in Lefkáda town. Near Ag. Spyrídon, the **Orpheus Folklore Museum** (*follow the little signs; closed for renovation at the time of writing*) has four rooms displaying the beautiful embroideries and weavings made on the island, dating back to the last century; there are also old maps, including a precious original map of Lefkáda made by the Venetian mapmaker Coronelli in 1687. The **Archaeology Museum** (*open weekdays 10–1; adm*) has recently moved to a new building on the northwestern edge of the seafront and houses mostly the finds from cave sanctuaries and the 30 12th-century BC tombs discovered by Dörpfeld in Nidrí; the **Icon** (or **Post-Byzantine**) **Museum** (*open 10.30–12.30; adm*), with works of the Ionian school, is housed in the municipal library (*© (0645) 22 502*); and, appropriately for the town that established the first municipal brass band in Greece (1850), the **Lefkáda Phonograph Museum**, beyond the square at 12–14 Kalkáni Street (*open 10–1.30 and 6.30–11 in season*), founded by a local collector. The only museum of its kind in Greece, it contains old gramophones sent over by relatives from the United States, records of Cantades and popular Greek songs of the 1920s, and one of the first discs recorded by a Greek company, 'Orpheon' of Constantinople, founded in 1914. A cemetery dating from 600 BC was discovered a few years ago on the outskirts of town, and is in a permanent state of excavation, and still not open to the public.

Just Outside Town

The closest place to town for a swim is the **Gýra**, the long, sandy if often windy lido that closes off the west side of the lagoon, with a few tavernas. On the other side of the windmills, a second beach, good for surfing, **Ag. Ioánnis Antzoúsis**, is tucked under a chapel, supposedly named for the Angevin Knights who founded it during the Crusades. In the opposite direction, by the cemetery, stop at the Café Pallas for a refreshing glass of almond milk, or *soumáda*, and watch the old men in the olive grove opposite play *t'ambáli*, Lefkáda's version of boules, played with egg-shaped balls on a concave ground, which as far as anyone knows is played nowhere else in the world. Two kilometres south, set among the ruins of a monastery, the stone church of the **Panagía Odhigýtria** (1450) is the oldest on the island and the only one to have withstood all the earthquakes.

Just above town is the 17th-century **Faneroméni Monastery**, rebuilt in the 19th century after a fire. It is a serene place in the pine woods, with bird's-eye views over the town, lagoon and the walls of Santa Maura. On the islet with the ruined chapel of **Ag. Nikólaos** was a cottage where Angelos Sikelianós and his wife Eva would spend their summers.

Sikelianós and the Delphic Idea

Angelos Sikelianós, born on Lefkáda in 1884 and as romantically handsome as a poet should be, was a good friend of Valaorítis. Although he duly followed his parents' wishes by going off to law school in Athens, he left after a couple of years to join a theatre company with two of his sisters, Helen and Penelope. Penelope married the brother of Isadora Duncan, and through him Sikelianós met his own American spouse, Eva. All shared an interest in reviving the mythic passion and power of ancient Greece, in active artistic expression rather than in the dusty, pedantic spirit of the time. Sikelianós did his part by writing startling lyrical poetry, infused with the spirit of Dionysian mysticism in a longing to join the world of the gods to the world of men.

In the 1920s, Sikelianós and Eva came up with the idea of reviving the 'Delphic Idea' of learning and the arts, in the same spirit as the revival of the Olympics. Their goal was to create an International Delphic Centre and University, and stage a Delphic Festival of drama, dance, music, sports and crafts; this actually took place in 1927 and 1930, funded in part by a mortgage on the Sikelianós house and Eva's inheritance. But the Depression closed in, and the following years were bitter; Eva went back to America, and although they divorced she continued to support the 'Delphic Idea' and send Sikelianós money. Sikelianós remarried and sat out the war years in a small flat in Athens, in declining health; his finest moment came when he gave the funeral oration of his fellow poet Palamas, and declared 'In this coffin lies Greece' and boldly led the singing of the banned Greek national anthem, even though he was surrounded by German soldiers. The dark years of the war and Greek Civil War added a tragic power to his poetry, but his progressive ideas barred him from membership of the Athens Academy, and, as they will tell you in Lefkáda, from winning the Nobel Prize, although he was twice nominated. In 1951 he died when he mistook a bottle of Lysol for his medicine.

Lefkáda ✉ 31100, ✆ (0645–) Where to Stay

Most rooms at the **Nirikos Hotel**, ✆ 24 132, ✉ 23 756 (*C; exp*), face the water, and there's a nice café-bar downstairs. The newly renovated **Pension Pirofani**, ✆ 25 844 (*mod*), has spacious, air-conditioned rooms with balconies looking on to the pedestrianized main street. **Byzantio Hotel**, ✆ 21 315 (*E; inexp*), is a basic but well-kept and friendly pension at the waterfront end of the same street.

Lefkáda ✆ (0645–) Eating Out

Restaurants are numerous and reasonably priced on Lefkáda and portions seem to be larger than elsewhere in Greece. If they are on offer, try the increasingly rare local wines *vartsámi, kerópati* or *yomatári*. In the quaint, central Plateía Antistási there are plenty of colourful cafés and tavernas, good for people-watching; **Café Boschetto** on the seafront is also a pleasant place to vegetate. In Dimaríou Verrioti, near the Folklore Museum, **Taverna O Regantos** is blue and white and cute, with solid fare for around 3,000dr. On the edge of town, towards Ag. Nikítas, **Adriatika**, in a pleasant garden setting, is pricier but has some good Greek specialities and excellent service (*4,000dr*).

The East Coast

The east coast of Lefkáda is as lovely, green and bedecked with beaches as the choice coasts of Corfu, and not surprisingly most of Lefkáda's tourist facilities have sprung up here. Just a few kilometres south of Lefkáda town, at Kaligóni on a hill near the shore, are the scant ruins of **ancient Nerikus**, the pre-Corinthian city, where Dörpfeld (*see* below) found Cyclopean walls, traces of roads, arches, a watertank, and a pre-Roman theatre, as well as some early Byzantine ruins, which can be seen after some scrambling through the olives. Further along is the once cute fishing village of **Lygiá**, now a sprawling commercial resort with narrow beaches; **Nikiána**, spread out more attractively, has good striking views of the mainland.

Further south is **Perigiáli**, with a fine beach and some new hotels, and, two kilometres further on, **Nidrí** (ΝΥΔΡΙ), Lefkáda's busiest resort town and something of a package-ville. Nidrí looks out over lovely Vlýcho Bay, closed in like a lake by the Géni peninsula, its still waters dotted with the privately owned wooded islets of **Mandourí, Sparti, Skorpídi** and **Skórpios**. The last still belongs to what remains of the Onassis family—Aristotle's little granddaughter. From the sea you can spy Aristotle's tomb, and excursion boats now have permission to land on the beaches if no one is in residence. You may notice a little red caique taking over a small army of workers who maintain the island; Onassis stipulated in his will that they must be from Nidrí. His obsession with privacy and payoffs in the right places kept tourist facilities at Nidrí at a bare minimum during his lifetime, but the locals have since made up for lost time. By Lefkáda standards Nidrí is cosmopolitan, commercial and smack on the main road; the tavernas are mostly lined up along the seafront, all of which can get very very busy and noisy in the summer. Much of the old beach was sacrificed for the building of a quay, so most people head up to Perigiáli for a swim.

Sit at a café in Nidrí at twilight—there's one so near the shore you can sit with your feet in the sea—and, to the sound of croaking frogs, watch Mandourí, 'the poet's island' as the locals call it, float above the horizon on a magic carpet of mist. The mansion on Mandourí belongs to the family of the poet Aristotélis Valaorítis (1824–79). Like many intellectuals from the Ionian islands, Valaorítis studied abroad, and when he returned it was first to serve as a member of the Ionian Parliament, and later the Greek Parliament, where he was renowned as a public speaker. Highly romantic like his friend Sikelianós and as patriotic as any in his day, he was one of the first to write verse in the demotic language of the people.

Excursions from Nidrí

1 Head up the verdant east coast to quaint Lefkáda town, to see the museums, then climb up the picturesque inland hills to traditional Karyá, home of lace-making and embroidery. After a drink in the shady *plateía*, wind down the stunning small roads to Ag. Nikítas, in time for lunch and a beach siesta on any of the beautiful western beaches, lapped by sky-blue water. Return via Faneroméni Monastery for an evening view.

2 Head south along the left-hand fork of the road to Vassilikí for a surf and then inland through the panoramic, fragrant scenery to Komíli. Then head down the peninsula, stopping off at any of the stunning beaches en route to the sheer white cliffs of Cape Doukáto. On the way back, take the left-hand fork from Vassilikí, towards Sývros, and climb up to lofty Ag. Ilías for magnificent views.

3 One of the nicest, and shortest, excursions from Nidrí is the 45-minute walk by way of the hamlet of Rachí to the waterfall, at the end of the Dimosári gorge. In the spring it gushes forth with enthusiasm; in the summer it is little more than a high-altitude squirt, but it's wonderfully cool and refreshing, and there's a pool for a swim.

Vlyhó, the next village south of Nidrí, is a quiet charmer, famous for its traditional boat-builders. Sandy **Dessími** beach, with a campsite, lies within walking distance, as does the **Géni peninsula**, covered with ancient, writhing olive groves. Wilhelm Dörpfeld, Schliemann's assistant in the excavation of Troy, found a number of Bronze Age tombs behind Nidrí and instantly became a local hero when he announced that they proved his theory that Lefkáda was the Ithaca of Homer. He died in 1940 and is buried near the house in which he lived, by the Géni's white church of Ag. Kyriakí. Further south, **Póros** is near the very pretty white pebble beach of **Mikrós Gialós**, set under the olive trees. **Sívota**, the next town south, has an exceptionally safe anchorage that draws yacht flotillas; many use it for winter berthing. The nearest swimming is at **Kastrí**, to the west.

Lefkáda ✉ *31100,* ✆ *(0645–)*   ***Where to Stay and Eating Out***

Nikiána

The hotel-apartment complex **Red Tower**, ✆ 92 951, 📠 92 852 (*C; exp*), sits high up like a castle with wonderful views over the water. **Porto Galini**, ✆ 92 431, 📠 92 672 (*B; exp*), provides luxurious furnished apartments among the cypresses and olives, and watersports down on the beach. For a bit less, try the **Pension Ionian**, ✆ 71 720 (*C; exp*), a stone's throw from the sea. **Aliki**, ✆ 71 602, 📠 72 071 (*C; exp–mod*), is a top-notch small hotel in a superb location; pool and air-conditioned rooms overlook the sea and its own small beach. *Open all year.*

The **Hotel Konaki**, at Lygiá, ✆ 71 397, ✉ 71 125 (*C; exp–mod*), has a garden setting, overlooking a large pool. There are also rooms to let in abundance. Just north of Lygiá, **Kariotes Beach Camping**, ✆ 71 103, ironically has a pool but no beach in sight. If you are in Nikiána, its fish tavernas should more than satisfy your appetite.

Nidrí

Ta Nisakia, 1km from Nidrí, ✆ 92 777, book in Athens ✉ (01) 764 5440 (*A; exp*), are studio apartments with commanding views, 200m above the sea.

Two kilometres north in Perigiáli, **Scorpios**, ✆ 92 452, ✉ 92 652 (C; *exp*), is an upmarket apartment complex with pool; **Armeno Beach**, ✆ 92 018, ✉ 92 341 (C; *exp*), has modern air-conditioned rooms right on the beach, with watersports available. The **Nidrí Akti** pension, ✆ 92 400 (*B; mod*), has good views and is open all year. **Bella Vista**, ✆ 92 650 (*mod*), is set in a garden 500m from Nidrí and two minutes from the beach; studios have pretty views of Vlýho Bay. **Hotel Gorgona**, ✆ 92 268, ✉ 95 634 (*E; mod*), is set back from the razzmatazz in its own quiet garden. Direct Greece (*see* p.31) has apartments and a hotel here, and George Kourtis can fix you up with a room (visit his agency on the main road or call ✆ 92 494). There is camping at Simi Bay, near Vlýho at the end of the peninsula. There are plenty of restaurants in Nidrí: **Kavos** has consistently good food for 4,000dr, and **Il Saporre** is worth a try. Just out of town, Haradiatika village is popular with locals for its good-quality meat and *mezé;* and the **Olive Tree** and **Paliokatouna** towards Neochóri are also well liked.

Póros/Sívota

Okeanis at Mikrós Gialós, ✆ 95 399 (*mod*), is a relatively quiet place on the beach, with comfortable rooms. *Open May–Sept.* You can stay in the lap of luxury at **Poros Beach Camping**, ✆ 23 203, with 50 sites, some bungalows (*mod*), a bar, restaurant and pool. Sívota has rooms to rent, but is better known for its excellent fish tavernas, where you can pick a lobster from the sea cage.

Inland Villages: Lace and Lentils

At least once while on Lefkáda venture inland, where traditional farming villages occupy the fertile uplands framed in mountains, and it's not unusual to encounter an older woman still dressed in her traditional costume of brown and black, with a headscarf tied at the back, sitting with distaff in hand, at her loom, or over her embroidery. Although many villages are facing the usual rural exodus of their young people for the bright lights and easier money to be made on the coast, **Karyá** is one large village to aim for, the centre of the island's lace and embroidery cottage industry, where the ethnographic **Museum Maria Koutsochéro** (*open 9am–8pm in high season; adm*) is dedicated to the most famous embroiderer of them all, a woman from Karyá whose works were in international demand around 1900. Most of the women sell their goods direct, although don't come looking for bargains: look for signs reading KENTHMATA. Another well-known traditional lace and embroidery town is **Englouví**, the highest village on Lefkáda (730m), tucked in a green mountain valley; it is even prouder of its lentils, which win prizes at Greek lentil competitions. In the interior there are several notable churches with frescoes, among them the Red Church (Kókkini Eklisía) and Monastery of Ag. Geórgios (from around 1620) near **Aléxandros**, a nearly abandoned village crumbling to bits, and the 15th-century church of Ag. Geórgios at **Odhigytría** (near Apólpaina), its design incorporating Byzantine and Western influences. **Drymónas** to the west is a pretty village of stone houses and old tile roofs.

Lefkáda ☎ (0645–)	**Where to Stay and Eating Out**

Karyá ✉ 31080

The **Karyá Village**, ☎ 41 030 (*B; mod*), has pleasant rooms if you want to get away from the beach crowds (phone ahead out of season). There are also some rooms available, and tavernas and traditional lazy *kafeneíons* under the plane trees. In the event of homesickness, be sure to have some Tetleys and one of Brenda's toasties in the main square. After working for years as a guide on the island, she can find an answer to most questions (and probably find you a room).

Down the West Coast

The much less developed west coast of Lefkáda is rocky and rugged, and the sea is often rough—perfect for people who complain that the Mediterranean is a big warm bathtub. For under the cliffs and mountains are some of the widest and most stunning stretches of sand in the Ionian, that are only just beginning to be exploited. The road from Lefkáda town avoids the shore as far as the farming village of **Tsoukaládes**, from where a 2km road leads down to narrow pebbly **Kalímini** beach and the most turquoise water imaginable (take provisions and swimming shoes). The route down to the coast from Karyá is a superb approach offering stunning views down to the sea; from Karyá head back towards Lefkáda, turning right at the T-junction; then take the first left to Ag. Nikítas and enjoy. The long sandy beach of **Pefkóulia** begins under the mountains and stretches around the coast to **Ag. Nikítas** (ΑΓ. ΝΙΚΗΤΑΣ). With only a cluster of hotels at the top, the nucleus of the village, with its pretty tile roofs and old tavernas, is off limits to developers; the narrow streets are overhung with flowers and vines. Beware that parking is a major headache, especially on summer weekends. With nothing between here and Italy, the sea is a crystal-clear pale blue and clean, but cold. Don't let your windsurfer run away with you, though—the odd shark fin has been spotted off the coast. Just south of here, 2km off the main road, **Káthisma** is another good, wavy place to swim, with a taverna and cantinas on the wide beach of golden sand, dotted with places to dive and little caves to explore. An unpaved road leads to yet another beautiful sandy beach below the village of **Kalamítsi**, set among giant rocks, with rooms and tavernas that make it a good quiet base.

The Original Lovers' Leap, Vassilikí and Windsurfing

To reach Lefkáda's southwest peninsula, a secondary road from Kalamítsi crosses to the pretty leafy village of **Chortáta** and **Komíli**, where the road forks. Buses continue down the coastal road only as far as **Atháni**, a tiny village famous for its honey that struggles to meet the demands of tourists heading further south to the superb beaches along the peninsula. The first, long and undeveloped **Gialós**, can be easily reached by a path from Atháni; the next, glorious golden **Egrémni**, requires a labour of love to reach from land—a long unpaved road followed by 200 steep steps. Sandy **Pórto Katsíki** ('goat port') further south is magnificently set under pinkish white cliffs, reached by another long walkway-stair from the road (*500dr for parking*) and is a popular excursion boat destination; there's a taverna too.

At the end of the road are the famous 190ft sheer white cliffs of **Cape Doukáto** or **Kávo tis Kyrás** (Lady's Cape), where Sappho, rejected by Phaon, hurled herself into the sea below; one old tradition says that she was only imitating the goddess Aphrodite, who took the plunge in despair over the death of her lover Adonis. Later, Romans rejected by their sweethearts would make the leap—with the precaution of strapping on feathers or even live birds and employing rescue parties to pull them out of the sea below. Young Greeks still soar off the edge, but now use hang-gliders instead of feathers. Before becoming a cure-all for unrequited love, the leap was made by unwilling sacrifices to stormy Poseidon—prisoners or criminal scapegoats. When human sacrifices dropped out of fashion, priests serving at the temple of Apollo Lefkáda 'of the Dolphins' (of which only the scantiest ruins remain) would make the jump safely as part of their cult, called *katapontismós* ('sea plunging'), rather like the divers at Acapulco, one imagines; no doubt the leaps were accompanied by animal sacrifices—read barbecues—for a pleasant ancient Greek outing. The white cliffs are a famous landmark for sailors and now are topped by a light-house. Byron, sailing past in 1812 during his first visit to Greece, was strangely moved, and put down the experience in *Childe Harold* (canto II):

> But when he saw the evening star above
> Leucadia's far-projecting rock of woe
> And hail'd the last resort of fruitless love,
> He felt, or deem'd he felt, no common glow
> And as the stately vessel glided slow
> Beneath the shadow of that ancient mount,
> He watch'd the billow's melancholy flow,
> And, sunk albeit in thought as he was wont,
> More placid seem'd his eye, and smooth his pallid front.

The left-hand fork in the road at Komíli passes through inspiring scenery, divinely perfumed by the wild flowers in late spring (no wonder the honey is so good!), by way of the pretty farming village of **Ag. Pétros** on the way to **Vassilikí** (ΒΑΣΙΛΙΚΗ), one of the very best places in Europe to windsurf and Lefkáda's second biggest resort after Nidrí, although not half so compromised by package tourism. A shady, charming village, Vassilikí has a little tree-rimmed port with pleasant cafés and shops that specialize in all types of boards for sale or hire. The long beach running north of town isn't the best for swimming, full as it is with surfers whizzing around the bay, their brightly coloured sails like butterflies skimming the water. On most days a gentle breeze blows up by mid-morning, perfect to teach beginners the fundamentals, and by mid-afternoon it's blowing strong for the experts; by evening, the wind, like a real gent, takes a bow and exits, allowing a pleasant dinner by the water's edge before the discos open; the nightlife is almost as exhilarating as the wind. For a swim, walk along the sand to Pondi or catch a caique from Vassilikí round the white cliffs of Cape Doukáto for the beach of Pórto Katsíki (*see* above) or the pretty white beach of **Agiofýlli**, accessible only by sea.

Lefkáda's highest peak, Eláti (1,158m) cuts off the inland villages of the south, which can only be reached from Vassilikí or the Póros–Sívota road in the southeast. The road rises from the plain of Vassilikí, covered with olives and fields of flowers (flower seeds for gardeners are an important local product), to **Sývros**, one of the larger villages in the interior, with places to eat and Lefkáda's largest cave, **Karoucha**. From here the road tackles the increasingly bare slopes of Eláti to lofty little **Ag. Ilías**, with magnificent views.

Ag. Nikítas ✉ 31080

Odyssey, ℗ 97 351, ⊛ 97 421, *filippas@otenet.gr* (*C; exp*), is one of the island's nicest hotels, with a roof garden and pool. **Ag. Nikítas**, ℗ 97 460, ⊛ 97 462 (*C; exp*), is a tastefully decorated, tranquil hotel at the top of the village. Alternatively, **Ostria Pension**, ℗ 97 483, ⊛ 97 300 (*A; mod*), is in a pretty blue and white house over-looking the bay, or seek a private room with bath overlooking the sea for 6–10,000dr depending on season. **Sapfo** on the beach and **Poseidon** on the main street both offer good fare, while **Captain's Corner** is the place to alcoholically survey the bays.

Vassilikí ✉ 31082

Smartest here is **Ponti Beach**, ℗ 31 572, ⊛ 31 576 (*B; exp*), above the bay, air-conditioned and with a pool and fabulous views. **Christina Polete**, ℗ 31 440 (*mod*), has newly converted rooms and two small apartments in a beautiful house, one field back from the sea, or try **Billy's House**, ℗ 31 418 (*mod*), with nice rooms, private baths and kitchen, 70m from the beach. **Katina's Place**, ℗ 31 262 (*mod–inexp*), is a simple, clean and tremendously hospitable pension with great views over the village and port. In Pondi, the brand-new **Surf Hotel**, ℗ 31 740, ⊛ 31 706 (*C; inexp*), has balconied rooms by the beach. **Vassilikí Beach** campsite is well located halfway along the bay, ℗ 31 308, ⊛ 31 458. **Miramare** and **Mythos** are among the better tavernas and, depending on how raucous you're feeling, there's a terrific choice in the way of nightlife. **Zeus** is the crazy late-night bar for young windsurfers, while **After Eight** attracts a slightly gentler crowd, with a pool table and playing 60s–80s music.

Meganísi (ΜΕΓΑΝΗΣΙ)

Spectacular rocky and wild Meganísi, an hour and a half by daily ferry or excursion boat from Nidrí, lies off the southeast coast of Lefkáda. Believed to be the island of Taphos mentioned in the *Odyssey*, it was the main base of the semi-mythical Teleboans, sailors and pirates who at one point were powerful enough to take on the King of Mycenae. The population of 1,800 is still employed in traditional occupations—seafaring for the men, embroidery and lacemaking for the women. Ferries call at **Váthi**, a pretty port with lots of good fish tavernas, rooms to rent and a campsite, packed to the gills for the *panegýri* of Ag. Konstantínos on 21 May. A road leads up to the cheerful flowery hamlet of **Katoméri**, where a track heads down to the beach of Polistafíon in narrow Athéni Bay, and there's even the small, nice, moderately priced **Hotel Meganísi**, ℗ (0645) 51 639 (*B; mod*). The paved road continues around to **Spartochóri**, with a couple of good tavernas, and back to Váthi. Excursion boats from Nidrí usually call at the yawning 90m-deep **Papanikólaos' Grotto**, said to be the second largest in Greece and named for the daring Greek resistance submariner who used to hide here and dart out to attack Italian ships, and at the sandy beach of **Ag. Ioánnis**, with a summer cantina.

Lésbos/Mytilíni (ΛΕΣΒΟΣ/ΜΥΤΙΛΗΝΗ)

Officially Lésbos, but more often called Mytilíni after its principal city, Sappho's island (pop. 116,000) is the third largest in Greece, and one of the more elusive, many-sided in more ways than merely geographical. Traditional rural life remains strong in the quiet villages, 15 of which have been declared traditional settlements: its undulating hills support an astonishing 11–13 million olive trees, which glisten silver in the sunlight, while the higher peaks are swathed in deep chestnut and pine forests. Its size (it's nearly 100km from Mytilíni town to Sígri) makes transport difficult unless you have a car or scooter. Although much of the countryside is quite lovely, little stands out in particular—an attractive artists' colony, a handful of charming villages with houses made of dark basalt with Levantine wooden galleries, a few excellent beaches where tourists congregate. But it has a bewitching magic. The people are friendly, easygoing, lyrical and fond of a drink, like Greek Celts, prepared to burst into song and dance when the mood takes them; Lésbos has been a cradle of some of Greece's greatest poets, from Sappho, Alcaeus and Longus (the 3rd-century BC author of the romance *Daphnis and Chloe*) to Nobel Laureate Odysséas Elýtis, whose parents belong to one of the island's most important industrial families. On the other hand, it also produced the Barbarossa brothers, red-bearded Greeks turned pirates for the Sultan, and the worst terrors the Aegean has ever known. Although becoming more developed, with charters in summer, the island is still very much a place where people go about their business untainted by the great wave of international tourism that has swept over the other islands. Visitors are made welcome but Lésbos—known as the Red Island for its politics—still retains its own strong identity.

Mythology

 Even in myth Lésbos is connected with music and poetry. The mytho-historical musician Arion, accredited with the invention of the dithyramb, was a son of the island. His talents brought him great wealth—and headaches. After a musical contest in Italy, where he had won all the prizes, the crew of the ship returning him to Lésbos decided to throw him overboard and keep his rich prizes for themselves. Arion was allowed to sing one last tune, after which he dived into the sea. But his swan song had charmed the dolphins, and they saved his life, carrying him safely to shore. The ship's crew were later executed for their treachery. Another myth deals with the great poet Orpheus, who was torn to pieces by orgiastic maenads and followers of Dionysos and thrown into a river of Thrace. His beautiful head floated to Lésbos, where the inhabitants carried it to a cave. There Orpheus' head sang and prophesied so well that people stopped patronizing the Delphic oracle. This loss of business angered Apollo, the god of Delphi, who made a special trip to Lésbos to order the head to shut up.

History

Like many of the islands that hug the coast of Asia Minor, Lésbos both enjoyed the benefits and suffered the penalties of its east–west location as early as the Trojan War. Homer describes the island as an ally of Troy, and it suffered raids by both Odysseus and Achilles. In the 10th century BC Aeolians from Thessaly, led by Penthilos, son of Orestes, colonized the island and the coast of Asia Minor. The Aeolians lacked the vital intellectual curiosity of the Ionians, but by the 6th century BC they made Lésbos a cultural centre, especially under the rule of Pittachos, one of the Seven Sages of ancient Greece. He went far in healing the ancient rivalry between Lésbos' two principal cities, Mytilíni and Míthymna, and promoted trade with Egypt. Míthymna, having lost the fight for island dominance, avenged itself on Mytilíni when the latter decided to leave the Delian league and join Sparta in the Peloponnesian War, in 428 BC.

Míthymna tattle-taled to Athens, and according to Thucydides an order was sent for a general massacre in Mytilíni. However, soon after the ship with the order sailed, the Athenians reconsidered (for once) and sent a second ship countermanding the massacre. It arrived in the nick of time, and the citizens were spared.

In the 4th century BC, Lésbos continued to change hands frequently, its most memorable ruler being Hermeias, who governed both the island and the Troad, or region around Troy, on the mainland. Hermeias was a eunuch and a student at Plato's Academy, and he attempted to rule his principality on the precepts of the *Republic* and the ideal city-state; Aristotle helped him found a branch of the Academy in ancient Assos (just opposite Lésbos, in Asia Minor) and while there married Hermeias' niece. Later the island was occupied by Mithridates of Pontus, who was in turn ousted by the Romans in a battle believed to be Julius Caesar's first.

Like Chíos, Lésbos was given by the Byzantine Emperor Michael Palaeológos to the Genoese for their help in restoring the Byzantine Empire (1261). In 1462 Mohammed the Conqueror captured the island, despite the heroic resistance led by Lady Oretta d'Oria, and the island remained in Turkish hands until 1912.

Getting There and Around

By air: numerous charters from various European cities; at least three daily flights from Athens with Olympic and Aegean; daily to/from Thessaloníki, three times a week to/from Límnos and twice a week to/from Chíos (all with Olympic). The Olympic office is at 44 Kavétsou, ✆ (0251) 28 660; Aegean is only at the airport, ✆ (0251) 61 120; the airport is 8km from Mytilíni town, ✆ (0251) 61 234 or 61 212, and reachable by taxi (*around 2,000dr from town*).

By sea: in the summer, there is a daily boat to the pleasant little resort of Ayvalik, Turkey (with a possibility of a three-day trip that includes Bergama—ancient Pergamon). **Excursion boats** run from Mólyvos to Skála Sikaminiás and beaches, or you can hire a caique from Evangelos Pairaktaris, ✆ (0251) 31 766; from Sígri, caiques visit nearby Nisiópi islet. **Port authority:** ✆ (0251) 28 827.

By road: buses from Mytilíni town depart from two stations: distant villages are served by the station at the south end of the harbour, on the edge of the public gardens, ✆ (0251) 28 138/873 (3–4 buses a day to the tourist spots on the west of the island in season); buses to the suburbs and closer villages depart from the station in the centre of the harbour, ✆ (0251) 46 436, every hour or so. **Taxis:** Mytilíni, ✆ (0251) 23 500 or 25 900; Mólyvos taxi rank is on the road in from Petra, ✆ (0253) 71 480; in Petra, ✆ (0253) 42 022. Renting a **car** helps cover Lésbos' considerable distances. Koundouriotou St has a number of rental agencies: Holiday Car Rental, by the city bus station, ✆ (0251) 43 311, and Just, ✆ (0251) 43 080, are reliable.

Tourist Information

EOT, ✆ (0251) 42 511 or 42 513 (*open weekdays 8–2.30 and 6–8.30*), is up the street from the **tourist police,** ✆ (0251) 22 776, near the ferry at Mytilíni. There is also an information desk at the airport, and a very helpful **Municipal Tourist Information Office** on the main street in Mólyvos, ✆ (0253) 71 347/71 069, ✉ 72 277, *mithimna@aigaio.gr* (*open weekdays 7.30–4*). For Eressos information, call ✆ (0253) 53 557 (*open Mon–Fri 10–noon and 7–9, Sat 10–noon*); for Plomári, ✆ (0252) 32 535; in Sígri, Jan Adonakis, ✆ (0253) 54 295, is an informal mine of

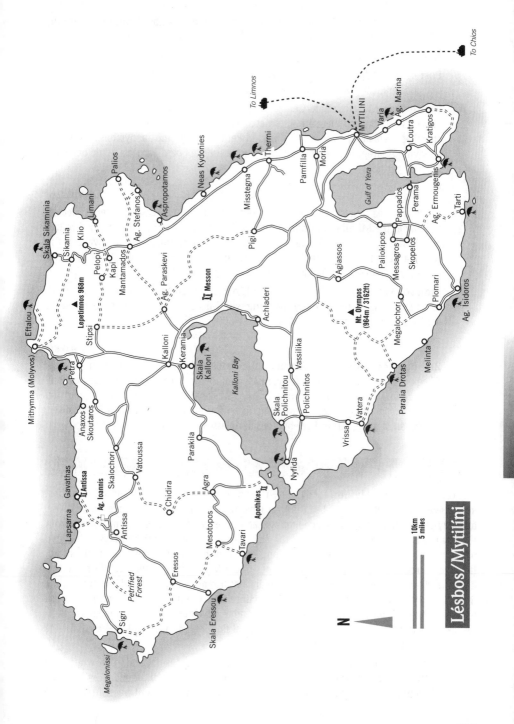

Lésbos/Mytilíni

10km
5 miles

N

information. For more help with accommodation, try the **Hoteliers' Union**, ℰ (0251) 41 787, 🌐 40 008.

ATMs: Apart from in the capital, there are holes in the wall in Mólyvos and Kalloni.

Post office: in Mytilíni, up Vournazon, near the summer cinema. There are smaller branches in most towns and tourist villages.

Internet: in Mólyvos, Café Centraal, by the harbour (*open 10–3am*), has various offers; during the day there are 'Internet Specials' (with breakfast, for example), while after 10pm emails are free with a drink. In Pétra, seek out the anonymous shop on an anonymous street nestling next to the wonderful clapboard barber's, which charges 1,300dr per hour.

Activities

There are yoga courses with an international clientèle run by Gisa and Detlev Siebert-Bartling at the **Milelia Seminar House**, ℰ/🌐 (0251) 72 030, where trained British and Australian bodyworkers also do therapies. More spiritual feeding awaits at the **Karuna Meditiation Retreat Centre**, 3km outside of town, ℰ (0251) 71 486, run by Geórgios (Greek) and Yosoda (Nepalese) Kassipides.

Molyvos Watersports, ℰ (0253) 71 861, offers parasailing, water skiing, and windsurfing lessons. There's **donkey trekking** with Michaelis, day and evening treks with barbeque supper on the beach, ℰ (0253) 71 309.

Festivals

2nd day of Easter and **15 August**, in Agiássos; **8 May**, Ag. Theológos in Ántissa; 'Week of Prose and Drama' in **May**, in Mytilíni town; **3rd Sunday after Easter**, bull sacrifice in Mandamádos; **26 July**, in Ag. Paraskeví; **15 August**, in Pétra, and Ag. Magdalinís in Skópelos; **26 August**, Ag. Ermoláou in Paliókipos; **end of September**, in Plomári, and big carnival celebrations in Agiássos.

Mytilíni

The capital of Lésbos, **Mytilíni** (MΥΤΙΛΗΝΗ) is a large town of magnificent old mansions, impressive public buildings and beautiful gardens. At the same time it manages to be dusty, higgledy-piggledy, ungentrified, cacophonous, and, outside of its cavernous dark waterfront ticket agencies and the odd hotel, not the slightest bit bothered with tourism. It has two harbours, one to the south, protected by a long jetty, and the abandoned harbour to the north. In ancient times a canal known as the 'Euripos of the Mytilineans' flowed between the two harbours, a fact dramatically proved when an ancient trireme was found under a street in the middle of town, having been stranded in the accumulation of sand and sediment. For the last few years, half of the city's streets have been dug up as a biological waste treatment system is installed; every time the works hit an archaeological find it all grinds to a halt—a gift for the archaeologists and a curse for anyone in a car.

The former islet—once the ancient acropolis—became a peninsula, and is crowned by a sprawling **Byzantine-Genoese castle**, or *kástro* (*open 8–2.30; adm*), founded by Justinian in the 6th century, who is said to have blinded every prisoner he sent here. In 1373 the

Genoese enlarged and repaired it with any available material, including columns from the 600 BC Temple of Apollo hastily crammed in between the stones like a collage. Inside are numerous buildings left by the various occupants of the fortress, one bearing the coat-of-arms of the Paleológos family; there's also a well-preserved Roman cistern and a Turkish *medrese*, or Koranic school, prisons, and a *tekes*, the cell of an Islamic holy man. In July and August, some of the most popular performers in Greece put on concerts in the *kástro*; once, the heart-throb bouzouki singer Dalaras had his trousers ripped off by ardent female fans. There are some picnic tables in the pine groves below and a town pay beach run by EOT at **Tsamákia**.

In the south harbour, arrivals by sea are greeted by a large statue of Freedom. Standing on a traffic island amid the bustle of the waterfront, a prettily restored old white house, formerly belonging to the harbourmaster, now holds the **Museum of Traditional Arts and Crafts** (*open 8–2.30; adm*), with a collection of lace, weapons, ceramics, tools, engraved copper pans and costumes. Back from the pier on 8 November Street, the **Archaeology Museum** (*open 8.30–3, closed Mon; adm*) is housed in an old aristocratic mansion and the new museum building, and prides itself on reliefs found in a Roman house depicting scenes from the comedies of Menander, a statue of the Lion of Yéra, Greek mosaics found at Chórafa, Roman mosaics from Ag. Therapón and Páno Skála, and prehistoric finds from Thérma. The cathedral **Ag. Athanásios** (16th–17th century) has a finely carved wooden iconostasis. The lofty dome that dominates the skyline belongs to **Ag. Therápon**, dedicated to a penniless but saintly doctor. Built over a temple of Apollo, or perhaps even the School of Sappho, in the 5th century it became a Christian basilica; the present church dates from 1850. In front of the church the priest runs an interesting **Byzantine Museum** (© (0251) 28 916; *phone to check when open; adm*) stocked with icons from the 13th to 18th centuries, including one by Theóphilos (*see* below). The **Municipal Theatre** (1968) sits right on the Municipal Gardens, a delightful green and shady oasis with a scattering of cafés where everyone goes to escape the hurly-burly.

North of the *kástro*, the abandoned Old North Port or **Páno Skála** is a neighbourhood in the first stages of reinventing itself. The waterfront can be haunting in its desolation; a ruined mosque, the **Yení Tzamí**, and its truncated minaret stand forlorn in the centre, with trees growing out of the walls; carpenters and metalworkers work in the grimy shops; kids on bikes hurtle around the warren of lanes. Now small antiques shops are moving in, worth a look if you fancy the unusual or bizarre. By the pine forest to the west, at the end of Theátrou Eschílou Street, the Hellenistic **Theatre** was one of the largest of ancient Greece (with a capacity of 15,000, now seating as many small shrubs and closed for renovation until at least 2001); Pompey admired it so much that he used its plans to build his theatre in Rome in 55 BC. Just south are the remains of a Roman aqueduct, and near the cemetery of **Ag. Kyriakí** are some of the walls of ancient Mytilíni.

If Páno Skála is funky, the quarters south of the centre (Sourada and Kióski) are dotted with grand and very un-Greek Victorian or Bavarian neoclassical mansions built by Mytilíni's olive oil and ouzo barons. Known as '*archontika*', loosely meaning 'aristocratic', they have, for the most part, been beautifully restored with government help and some are now upmarket hotels.

South of Mytilíni Town

Buses from the waterfront municipal station will take you hourly to **Variá** (BAPEIA), the home town of Theóphilos Hadzimichális (1873–1934), a former door guard at the Greek consulate at Smyrna who earned his ouzo in exchange for the liveliest, most passionate and truest paintings modern Greece has produced, sometimes on walls of shops, tins or rags—whatever he could find. The old school house, set in an ancient olive grove a few minutes' walk from the main road, is now a charmingly rustic **Theóphilos Museum** (© (0251) 41 644; *open 9–2.30 and 6–8, closed Mon; adm*), founded by Tériade (*see* below) in 1964. Its

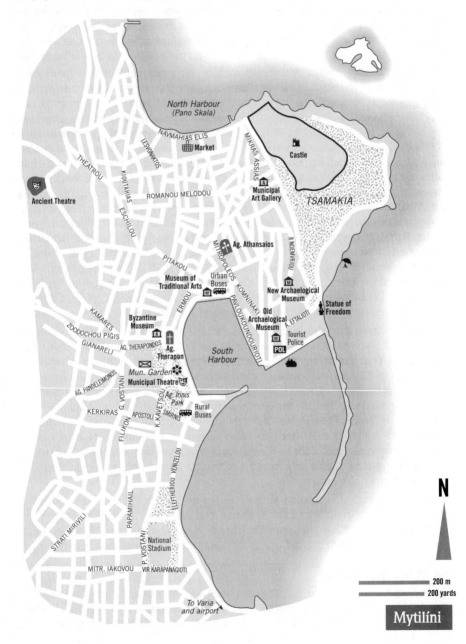

Mytilíni

80 paintings are 'like the trembling of the dew', as Seferis wrote of them, and evoke far more than any photograph ever could; note the way Theóphilos painted frames around his paintings, since he couldn't afford to buy them, and, because he aimed for total lucidity, carefully wrote long descriptions around each scene so there's no mistaking what's going on, whether it is a scene from mythology, the lives of the saints, a postcard, the Greek War of Independence, current events (Vesuvius' eruption) or a local festival; smokestacks belch smoke over Lésbos, aeroplanes fly over it, steam boats call at its ports. Don't miss the 19th-century studio photos, of Greeks posing in the same splendid costumes that Theóphilos loved to paint; he himself, dumpy and middle-aged, liked to dress up as Alexander the Great (note the portrait by Tsarouchis), followed by his 'Macedonians' or street urchins in carnival gear. Not surprisingly most of his contemporaries thought he was a lunatic.

A stone's throw away, a modern building houses the **Tériade Museum and Library** (*©* (0251) 23 372; *open Tues–Sun 9–2 and 5–8; adm*), founded in 1979 by Stratís Eleftheriádes, better known by his adopted French name Tériade. Born in Mytilíni in 1897, Eleftheriádes went to study law in Paris at age 18, where he was drawn to the lively, pioneering artistic world of the time. Although he loved to paint, his real interest soon moved on to art theory and criticism, and in 1937 he launched his own art publishing house, *VERVE*, printing both art books and a respected quarterly review of the same name that lasted until 1971. Long fascinated by medieval illuminated manuscripts, Tériade produced a series of 'Grands Livres' with text and lithographs by the greatest artists of the day—Picasso, Miró, Léger, Chagall, Roualt, Giacometti, Henri Laurens, and Juan Gris—handprinted on handmade paper in limited editions, many of which are on display here, along with minor paintings by the same names (although a burglary put a dent in the collection). On the ground floor there's a room with more paintings by Theóphilos. Tériade 'discovered' him in 1930, but not in time to save the artist from dying unknown and penniless.

Neápolis just south of Variá has a beach and ruined 5th-century basilica, but the main attraction south of Mytilíni is a lovely pair of beaches at the extreme south tip of the peninsula at **Ag. Ermougénis**, on either side of the eponymous chapel, and with an excellent taverna on the hill. From Skála Loutrón, a ferry crosses the Gulf of Géras, completely encompassed with dense olive groves, for Pérama; at nearby **Loutrá Géras** you indulge in a relaxing warm soak in the gentlest of Lésbos' five spas, in pools segregated by sex (*open daily 8–8; nominal adm*).

Mytilíni ✉ *81100, © (0251–)*   **Where to Stay**

Tourism and Travel Agency, © 21 329, near the bus station is able to arrange rooms in 16 island villages; the **Sappho Rented Rooms Association**, © 43 375, has 22 owners on the books offering accommodation in town. Both are cooperatives.

Mytilíni Town

Blue Sea, © 23 994, @ 29 656 (*B; exp*), has smart, clean rooms with balconies overlooking the ferries (not without noise). For a more tranquil time, one of Mytilíni's neoclassical mansions, a 10-minute walk south of the harbour, is now run as an atmospheric guesthouse, **Villa 1900**, 28 Vostáni, © 23 448, @ 28 034 (*A; mod*). *Open Apr–Oct.* Back on the waterfront, the **Sappho Hotel**, © 28 415 (*C; mod*), has lively views from a modern block. There is a fair selection of rooms to rent: **Salina's Garden Rooms**, © 42 073, are recommended and the garden is lovely. The

Cuckoo's Nest, ✆ 23 901, is crowded with family knick-knacks (*both inexpensive, with shared bathrooms*).

Around Mytilíni Town

Out in Variá, near the beach and Theóphilos Museum and en route to the airport, **Loriet**, ✆ 43 111, ✉ 41 629, *loriet@hotmail.com* (*A; exp*), has 10 suites charmingly situated in a converted stone mansion, with pool and wheelchair access. **Zaira**, at Loutrá, ✆ 91 188, ✉ 44 270 (*C; exp*), is in a converted old stone olive press, complete with chimney, air-con and minibars to boot. **Silver Bay Hotel and Bungalows**, just over 5km west of the capital at Alifanta, ✆ 42 410, ✉ 42 860 (*B; exp*), is a soulless complex but offers pool, golf, tennis and sea views. For a more modest but delightful stay, head north to Thermi, where **Hotel Votsala**, ✆ 71 231, ✉ 71 179, *votsala@ otenet.gr* (*B; mod*), has a relaxing garden by the water where you can contemplate the Turkish coast, and the friendly owner will ferry you to and from Mytilíni. Variá also has cheaper rooms on offer: try **Filoxenia**, ✆ 61 110, or **Akrotiri**, ✆ 26 452 (*both inexp*).

Mytilíni ✆ (0251–)   ***Eating Out***

Mytilíni is fairly well supplied with restaurants and tavernas, where you can savour the island's famous fresh sardines and giant prawns; local specialities include *kakávia* (fish soup), *astakós magiátikos* (lobster with vegetables), *skoumbri foúrnou* (baked mackerel) and *kotópoulo me karýdia* (stuffed chicken and chicken with walnut sauce). A row of small fish tavernas lines the south end of the south harbour; try **To Fanari**, ✆ 46 417, with a wide selection of wines to go with your fish, where the owner will regale you with historical details about Mytilíni. **Apolafsi**, ✆ 27 178, is a good bet for *mezédes*, grilled meat and fresh fish. The harbour area, Variá and Neapolis are all popular bar venues where young Greeks aren't in the least inhibited about dancing a *zembékiko* when the mood strikes.

North of Mytilíni

There are two roads to the north coast and its resorts. The longer, east-coast road passes **Mória**, where more arches of Mytilíni's Roman aqueduct remain intact, and **Thérmi**, a spa with hot iron-rich springs recommended by Galen (good for diseases of the joints and skin, gynaecological ailments and rheumatoid arthritis, ✆/✉ (0251) 71 277 for information), and the 12th-century Byzantine church of **Panagía Trouiloutí**. Thérmi was inhabited before 3000 BC; its five successive levels of civilization were excavated by Winifred Lamb between 1923 and 1933. Ancient Thérmi had connections with Troy, and during the Trojan War the Achaeans burnt it to the ground; the dates match the traditional dates of the Trojan War (1250 BC). A large Turkish tower stands near the baths, and there are rooms, restaurants and a beach nearby.

Leaving the coast, the road north rises to **Mantamádos** (ΜΑΝΤΑΜΑΔΟΣ), a large village of grey stone houses, best known for its yoghurt and 18th-century church **Taxiárchis Michael**, with a miraculous black icon of Archangel Michael that is said to smell of wildflowers. One story has it that pirates killed all the monks except one, who collected the blood-soaked earth and moulded it into an icon; another says St Michael made it himself. As on Évia, parishioners press a coin to the icon; if it sticks, the wish they make will be granted. Mantamádos, like Ag. Paraskeví, ritually sacrifices a bull on the third Sunday after Easter, a feast that draws pilgrims from across the island. Further north, **Kápi**, one of several villages circling the 968m Mount Lepétimnos, is the start of one of the new marked hiking trails on Lésbos that takes in some ravishing, luxuriant ravines and gorges. Further north lies the fetching village of **Sikaminiá** and, at the end of the road, the little fishing port of **Skála Sikaminiás**, in many ways the quintessence of a Greek island fishing village, renowned on Lésbos for its mild winters and housing good tavernas. The novelist Stratís Myrivílis was born in Sikaminiá, and next to the Restaurant Sikaminia in Skála you can see the ancient mulberry tree (*'sikaminiás'* means mulberries) where the author used to sleep in a tree bed. His novel *The Mermaid Madonna* was inspired by the chapel of the **Panagía**, about which he once had a dream, although don't come looking for the icon that gave the book its name—Myrivílis invented it. Another novel, *The Schoolmistress with the Golden Eyes*, was based on a woman from Mólyvos who collaborated with the Germans, went mad and burnt her house down. Although you can swim at Skála Sikaminiás, the nearest good beach, a strand of rose-tinted volcanic sand (with tavernas and showers) is at **Tsónia** to the southeast, but you have to go by way of Klió to get there on wheels. There's a footpath through the olive groves from Skála.

The Inland Route

The buses from Mytilíni to Mólyvos take the shorter, inland road (still, it takes an hour and 45 minutes). Keep your eyes peeled for a tree known as **Ag. Therapís Tzatzaliáris** (St Therapis of the Rags), where the superstitious hang bits of clothing belonging to ill relatives, hoping for a cure. The road passes near **Keramiá**, a village beloved by the Greeks for its fresh springs and centuries-old trees; further along, it skirts the wide Gulf of Kalloní, where a lovely, intensely cultivated plain is dotted with Lombardy poplars. A signposted road leads to the Ionic **Temple of Mesi**, built in the 4th or 3rd century BC and dedicated to Aphrodite; the foundations and column drums remain. **Kalloní** (ΚΑΛΛΟΝΗ), the large village here, replaces the ancient city of Arisbe; its acropolis was located where the medieval **Kástro** stands today. Arisbe flourished until a few local swains abducted some girls from Míthymna. The girls' kinsfolk perhaps overreacted, destroying Arisbe and enslaving all its people. **Skála Kalloní** is a quiet family resort, its sandy beach ideal for small children. Famous for its sardines (eaten raw as a *mezéde*) and anchovies, it's also a mecca for birdwatchers, with many kinds of waders and visiting storks nesting on the chimney-pots.

West of Kalloní, the 16th-century monastery **Ag. Ignatios Limónos** was used as a secret Greek school under the Turks. Men only are allowed in to see the frescoes in the central church, but women don't have to feel too hard done by. There are over 40 other chapels dotted around the grounds and plenty more places that are worth a peek: St Ignatius' own room, monks' cells, and the petrified wood, folk art and ecclesiastical artefacts in the excellent little museum. From Kalloní a road leads east up to the village of **Ag. Paraskeví**, where, in a rite that seems to recall the Roman rites of Mithras, a bull is bedecked with flowers and ribbons, paraded through the village, sacrificed and eaten in the three-day feast in late May of Ag. Charálambos, in conjunction with horse races. Apart from having an unusually old-time feel (and an extraordinary number of men playing chess and backgammon, spilling out on to the street from the *kafeneíons*), the village is best known for making olive oil. Old presses adorn the surrounding countryside and some have been attractively converted into centres for conferences and local fun and festivals. Further north, the green Ligona ravine below **Stýpsi**, on the slopes of Mount Lepétimnos, has the remains of 20 water mills and is a favourite venue for organized 'Greek Nights'.

Míthymna/Mólyvos and the North Coast Resorts

Up at the northernmost tip of the island is **Míthymna** (MHΘΥMNA), although the locals still call it **Mólyvos** (MOΛΥBOΣ), its Venetian name. By whatever name, it is the most popular and prettiest town on Lésbos, Mytilíni's arch rival for centuries, although it has now dropped to third town on the island in terms of population. Míthymna was the birthplace of the poets Arion and Longus and the site of the tomb of the Achaean hero Palamedes, buried here by Achilles and Ajax. Achilles besieged Míthymna, but with little success until the daughter of the king fell in love with him and opened the city gates, a kindness Achilles rewarded by having her slain for betraying her father.

Mólyvos is a symphony of dark-grey stone houses with red-tiled roofs, windows with brightly coloured shutters and gardens full of flowers, stacked above the lovely harbour and beach. For years a haunt of artists and the artsy, Mólyvos has lost little of its charm despite package tourism. The steep cobbled lanes of the village centre, known as the **Agorá**, are canopied with vines and wisteria and lined with boutiques, while the taverna terraces are perched high on stilts with wonderful views across to Turkey. Climbing through the Agorá, you'll pass a small **Archaeology Museum** (*open 8.30–3, closed Mon*) on the way up to the striking **Genoese Castle** (*same times*). In 1373, Francesco Gattilusi repaired this old Byzantine fortress on top of the hill, but it fell to Mohammed the Conqueror in 1462. However, he didn't get it without a fight. Onetta d'Oria, wife of the Genoese governor, repulsed an earlier Turkish onslaught when she put on her husband's armour and led the people into battle. Note the Turkish inscription in marble over the gate. The fine, long pebble town beach lined with feathery tamarisks has loungers and watersports and gradually becomes shingly sand at the far end, popular with nudists.

East of Mólyvos, **Eftaloú** has a tree-fringed beach, also popular with nudists, an excellent taverna and a bathhouse with very hot thermal springs. A local bus now runs on a regular basis between Eftaloú and Náxos, stopping at Mólyvos, Pétra and the beaches in between. Pick up a timetable at the Mólyvos tourist office or at Petra Tours.

Pétra and Náxos

Pétra means rock, and in particular a sheer rocky spike, carved with 114 steps and crowned by the church of **Panagía Glykofiloússa**, 'Virgin of the Sweet Kiss' (1747). The icon of the same name originally belonged to a captain, but it insisted on staying atop this pinnacle, sneaking away every night even after the captain nailed it to his mast. He finally gave up and let the icon go, and the next thing you know the Panagía was bullying the mayor of Pétra to build her a church. When he at last gave in and the church was built, a special ceremony was held for its dedication. A boy bringing up a tray of raki for the workers slipped and fell over the precipice. But the Panagía wasn't far, and she caught the boy in a puff of air and brought him back to the top of the cliff—not spilling a single drop of the raki, either. No wonder, in spite of the heat, flocks of pilgrims tackle the climb up on August 15, when they're rewarded with the traditional dish of *keskesi*, made of meat, grain, onions and spices.

Below, the pretty village has winding lanes, Levantine-style wooden balconies, a fine sweep of beach rapidly being developed, and the **Women's Agricultural Cooperative**, which in 1985 launched its own taverna, where men have been spotted doing the washing-up.

A Minor Revolution

For centuries Greek country women have been virtual slaves to the land, bent double under piles of fodder like beasts of burden, tending the flocks, toiling with the olive harvests and grape-picking. Among the most hard-working and least liberated in Europe, and additionally burdened by the dowry tradition (*see* pp.288–9), many found that life changed in 1985 when the Greek Council for Equality launched Women's Agricultural Cooperatives to enable tourists to visit rural areas and stay with local families. Women at last were given the chance to grab some economic independence, and discover their own abilities; after centuries of being marginalized through sexual oppression, they suddenly found themselves on training seminars, sorting out the administrative and financial nuts and bolts of their village collectives. Of course they had juggled families, housekeeping and farmwork for years, and were a strong yet unrecognized force. At last they were not just doing, but seen to be doing, taking control of their lives. As well as providing women with opportunities, the scheme is a move towards Green tourism, offering hospitality in traditional houses and refurbished village settlements in a bid to halt the march of the concrete mixer across the land. The Council also seeks to preserve old customs, handicrafts and local cuisine, believing that Greece will lose out unless its women play an active part in public life. Each cooperative has different specialities; besides the taverna and rooms to rent, the women of Pétra sell their traditional sweets and fruits in syrup (*glykó*), weavings, crochet and pottery.

Other beaches lie within easy striking distance of Pétra: **Avláki**, 1km west, a small sandy beach with two tavernas and some sea grass, and **Náxos**, 3km away, a fine sandy bay nearly a kilometre long with fabulous views of Mólyvos, although unfortunately a burgeoning, ugly resort in its own right. From Náxos a lovely coastal path skirts the dark volcanic shore to the west leading to **Mikrí Tsichránta** and **Megáli Tsichránta**, tiny hamlets, the latter set on a charming little bay. This is oak country, and the larger buildings are oak warehouses; in the next village on the path, **Kaló Limáni**, the warehouses have been converted into homes.

© *(0253–)*   ***Where to Stay and Eating Out***

Skála Kalloní ✉ 81107

Pasiphae, *©* 23 212, *✉* 23 154 (*B; exp*), is a comfortable hotel with a saltwater pool, one of several large, family-orientated complexes on the gulf, or there's the decent 10-apartment **Arisvi**, *©* 22 456 (*inexp*). The fish tavernas are cheap and specialize in *avthrini*, rather like fresh sardines.

Mólyvos/Eftaloú ✉ 81108

There are plenty of hotels and pensions here, although they can be pricey and packaged. Choose between four areas: just outside town; down to the beach, where there are some very attractive converted stone houses (but beware the package tour); on the harbour; and in the old town climbing up to the *kástro*, which is blissfully car-free but requires hoicking up the luggage. The latter houses pensions and rooms rather than fancy hotels.

Of the pricier options out of town, **Sun Rise Hotel** is a bungalow complex 2km from Mólyvos, ✆ 71 713/779, ✉ 71 791 (*B; exp*), with a pool, tennis, playground and minibus service to whisk you to the coast. **Delfinia** is just outside, ✆ 71 373, ✉ 71 524 (*B; exp*), with a pool, tennis, beach sports and lazy terrace. *Open all year.* By the beach, **Molyvos I**, ✆ 71 496, ✉ 71 640 (*B; exp*), has cool terracotta-floored rooms in a converted traditional building with a spacious terrace overlooking the beach. Two minutes' walk inland, **Amfitriti**, ✆ 71 741, ✉ 71 744 (*B; exp*), is mainly taken up by tour operators, but has a pool set in verdant grass surrounded by apricot trees. The **Sea Horse**, ✆ 71 630, ✉ 71 374 (*C; exp–mod*), has sewn up the harbour accommodation, with a variety of airy rooms; the bathrooms are alluring and front-facing rooms have good views of the day's catch. The cafeteria below has shady seating by the water's edge, while the owner runs boat trips from his travel agency next door.

More modest options by the beach include the **Olive Press**, ✆ 71 205, ✉ 71 647 (*B; mod*), a lovely conversion of an olive press, with tennis court, charming café and dining terrace, and the attractive **Adonis**, ✆ 71 866, ✉ 71 636 (*C; mod*), set amongst trees nearby. Cheaper places include the good-value, quiet **Posidon** near the beach, ✆ 71 981, ✉ 71 570 (*inexp*), where some rooms have picture-postcard castle views, and up in the old town, **Pension** (endearingly spelt 'Passion' on their cards) **Mema**, ✆ 71 284 (*inexp*), with clean, marble-floored rooms and balconies set amongst trees and flowers; head to the top floor for good views. If the Mema is full, almost as good is the **Malli**, ✆ 71 010 (*inexp*), a little further up the hill, equipped with a veranda offering spectacular views. Further along the cobbled path to the castle are **Studios Voula**, ✆ 71 305 (*inexp*); as well as the simple studios, there's a brand-new, detached 'villa' with two double bedrooms, a spacious living area, cool stone floors and pine ceilings.

The harbour is by far the most atmospheric, but inevitably touristy, place to eat fish: **To Xtapodi** is authentic, good for fish and not overpriced, even though it appears on most of the island's postcards. **The Captain's Table** has a varied menu and is a bit more expensive; **Faros** at the end is very good as well, serving tasty seafood specialities. The **Mermaid**, on the way down, is famous for its fish and lobster 'with Lesbian sauces'. Up in the Agorá, where prices are inching up while portions and quality are shrinking, **To Pithari** (or **O Gatos**) is good, with its balconies high on stilts and great views, while the traditional **Salguimi Kafeneíon** offers welcome respite from the tourist trash. **Ramona Taverna** is a lovely, untouristy lunch spot, but for the ultimate view **To Panorama** beside the castle is worth the strenuous hike up in time for a sundown drink or meal. Outside Mólyvos near the Eftaloú road, **T'Alonia Taverna** is excellent and cheap and very popular with the locals; besides traditional Greek dishes it also cooks up breakfast. In Vafiós (the village just above Mólyvos), **Vafios** and **Ilias** are traditional meat tavernas with wide menus, good local pies and wine from the barrel. In Eftaloú, **Hotel Molyvos II**, ✆ 71 497, ✉ 71 694 (*B; exp*), boasts a children's playground, tennis, volleyball, pool and poolside bar, not to mention minibus service from sister hotel **Molyvos I** in town; **Panselinos**, ✆ 71 905, ✉ 71 904 (*B; exp*), is by the sea with the works, including wheelchair access. The **Eftalou Taverna**, ✆ 71 049, is one of the best on Lésbos and the home of delicious stuffed courgette flowers and other delicacies, served in a shady garden, neither expensive nor touristy.

Pétra ✉ 81109

Clara, at Avláki (1.5km from Pétra, with a shuttle bus), ✆ 41 532, 🖃 41 535 (*B; exp*), offers a hotel and bungalows around a seawater pool; all rooms have balconies and sea views. Moderately priced choices include **Michaelia**, on the beach, ✆ 41 730, 🖃 22 067 (*C; mod*), with sea views and sea sports, but mainly tour operated, and **Theofilos**, ✆ 41 080, 🖃 41 493 (*C; mod*), larger with a pool. Next to Michaelia, **Studios Niki**, ✆ 41 601 (*inexp*), has plain, clean and quiet accommodation set in a garden of flowers and birds. **The Women's Agrotourist Cooperative**, ✆ 41 238, 🖃 41 309, is open all year, and now rents more than a hundred rooms to visitors; at 6,000dr, they are immaculately clean, tastefully decorated and good value. Their taverna has some of the most scrumptious food on Lésbos, especially the delicious *mezédes*—try the fresh *dolmades* and mouthwatering aubergine jam and reserve one of the dinky little balconies over the *plateía* if you can. You are welcome to join in family life, fishing and working in the fields if you want. That's the theory anyway! **Niko's** is recommended for seafood (*4,000dr*). For details of the open-air cinema, check outside Vrissa Travel in season.

Entertainment and Nightlife

Besides Mólyvos' more traditional summer entertainments—an open-air cinema opposite the taxi rank, a summer theatre festival with spectacular evening productions of ancient Greek drama and modern works, and music and dancing in the castle—there's the amazing alfresco **Gatelousi** (ΓΑΤΕΛΟΥΣΙ) nightclub between Mólyvos and Pétra (walkable from the latter), resembling a cruise liner with its deck projecting from the rock face. It has a restaurant and a shuttle bus service that runs from 10pm to 5am. **Gatelousi** in Mólyvos, on the other hand, offers live Greek music. Mólyvos also has a wide range of bars, but nothing too raucous. **Pirates** plays the music of polite seduction, while if you prefer coffee and cake try **To Panorama** (the Agorá branch). **Conga** is an open-air bar and club where you can sit by the waves, while **Bazaar**, nearer the harbour, has an atmospheric little terrace. **The Other Place**, another dancing bar in the harbour, is happily sound-proofed in a very atmospheric old house, with Greek nights and traditional dancing on Thursdays. The **Bouzouki Taverna** down a track on the road to Eftaloú is in romantic gardens with good Greek musicians and singers and the chance to dance. It serves expensive drinks, but that's how you pay for the entertainment, and it's well worth a go, as much for the excellent local dancers as the tourists; and there's always the **Mólyvos beachside disco**. In Pétra, the shorefront **Machine Dancing Bar**, in the former olive factory, oozes atmosphere with all the press machinery in view and the top two floors engagingly derelict. The **Magenta bar**, bizarrely blue and yellow, pumps out a club sandwich of sounds until the early hours.

Western Lésbos and the Petrified Forest

The northwest quarter of Lésbos is dramatic, volcanic and noticeably less humid than Mólyvos and Pétra. Despite its barren appearance, it is brimming with unusual wild herbs and birdlife: rose-coloured starlings, bee eaters, hoopoes and pairs of golden orioles. Until modern times it was the home of wild horses—some believe they may be the last link with the horse-breeding culture of the Troad in the late Bronze Age, mentioned in the *Iliad*. The modern village of **Ántissa** (ΑΝΤΙΣΣΑ) has inherited the name of **ancient Antissa**, up on the north coast: to get there, follow the road as far **Gavathás**, with a so-so beach and nice family-run hotel and taverna (Hotel Restaurant Paradise, ✆ 56 376; *mod*), and then walk east on a 1km path skirting the coast. Founded in the Bronze Age, Ántissa was violently joined to Lésbos in an earthquake. It was a musical place; after he was torn to shreds by the Maenads, the most important bits of Orpheus—his prophetic head and lyre—washed up here, perhaps inspiring Terpander, the 'father of Greek music' born in Ántissa *c.* 710 BC and credited with the invention of choric poetry, the seven-string lyre and the foundation of Sparta's first music school. The Romans destroyed the town to punish the inhabitants for their support of the Macedonians, and all the meagre remains lie below **Ivriókastro**, 'Castle of the Hebrew' but really a Genoese fort facing the sea. The wonderful quiet beaches with views over to Mólyvos are the main reason for making the trek, and if you're lucky you'll hear the nightingales who are said to have learned to sing so sweetly from Orpheus. A path follows the coast east towards Náxos and Ag. Pétra (*see* above).

West of modern Ántissa, the handsome monastery **Ag. Ioánnis Theológos Ipsiloú** is stunningly set on the promontory of a dead volcano. Founded in the 9th century and rebuilt in the 12th, it shares its pinnacle with military buildings and has a museum containing a collection of antique religious paraphernalia. In the courtyard you can examine bits of petrified wood—more than most people usually find in the forest near Sígri. The petrification began, apparently, when the monastery's volcano erupted two million years ago, and was further abetted by the quakes that have rocked this coast over the aeons.

Continuing west to the farthest end of Lésbos (a two-hour drive from Mytilíni), **Sígri** (ΣΙΓΡΙ) is a delight (though it can be windy), a bustling fishing village and carefully growing resortlet, complete with 18th-century Turkish castle and a gently shelving, sheltered sandy beach. For the sake of variety, within an hour's walk either side of Sígri there are plenty of other coves and beaches, including **Fanerómeni**, which has contrastingly deep water.

Between **Sígri** and Eressós is Lésbos' **petrified forest** (ΑΠΟΛΙΘΩΜΕΝΟ ΔΑΣΟΣ)— sequoias fossilized after being buried in volcanic ash; the colourful remains of the trunks have slowly become visible as the ash erodes. Others are on the offshore islets of Nisiópi (which also has a sandy beach to which caiques venture) and Sarakína. Some of the best specimens on Lésbos—a pair of fallen trunks that survived souvenir-hunters—are near Sígri itself, but entail a long walk in the sun (following the path to the south marked with yellow rectangles, past the beaches and the valley of the Tsichlíondas river). Sígri's newly opened **Natural History Museum** (*open daily 8–8; adm*) occupies an august setting by the windmill and focuses on the petrified forest, with well-displayed examples and talks. For more information on Sígri, its intriguing water cistern, the forests and local walks, pick up a copy of Roy Lawrence's *Where the Road Ends: Sígri* from Jan Adonakis.

The path ends up at the attractive village of **Eressós** (ΕΡΕΣΟΣ), overlooking a lush emerald plain tucked amid the rough volcanic tumult. Eressós is a low-key, ramshackle place with a shady main square of cafés, tavernas and old men. It inherited the name from ancient Eressos, some fragments of which still stand just east of **Skála Eressoú**, 4km away, reached down an avenue of whitewashed trees. Skála is endowed with a long, steeply shelving sand beach, lined with tamarisks and serviced by a lively if modern seaside village, a favourite of Greek families and gay women. In the attractive square is a bust of famous Eressian Theoprastus (372–287 BC), botanist and author of the *Characters*, a set of essays and moral studies on the picturesque people of his day. The inland road from Sígri to Eressós is an epic, primeval drive scented by sea daffodils, with scarred rock faces, ancient contoured stone walls and an amazing sense of space and purity.

The Tenth Muse

The most famous and influential Eressian of them all was Sappho, born in the late 7th century BC; Eressós proudly minted coins bearing her portrait. Little else is known for certain of Sappho's life, besides that she was married to a Kerklyas of Andros and perhaps had a daughter, and ran a marriage school for young ladies, to whom she dedicated many of her poems. Like her fellow islander and contempory Alcaeus, she wrote what is known as melic poetry, personal and choral lyrics with complex rhythms (sometimes known as Sapphic stanzas) intended to be sung at private parties before a select company. One of her songs dedicated to a young girl is the first, and rarely surpassed, description of passion: 'Equal to the gods seems that man who sits opposite you, close to you, listening to your sweet words and lovely laugh, which has passionately excited the heart in my breast. For whenever I look at you, even for a moment, no voice comes to me, but my tongue is frozen, and at once a delicate fire flickers under my skin. I no longer see anything with my eyes, and my ears are full of strange sounds. Sweat pours down me, and trembling seizes me. I am paler than the grass, and seem to be only a little short of death...' Her influence was so powerful that Plato called her the 'Tenth Muse'. A strong but probably apocryphal tradition has it that she threw herself from the white cliffs of Lefkáda (*see* p209) in despair over an unrequited love—for a man. Her poems that have survived have only done so by accident; considered morally offensive in 1073, they were the subject of book burnings in Rome and Constantinople.

Where to Stay and Eating Out

Sígri / Skála Eressoú ✉ 81105, ✆ (0253–)

One of the best ways to stay in Sígri and Skala Eressoú is in an apartment booked through **Direct Greece** (*see* p.31). Various other studios for rent pop up in Sígri in season, and 1km outside sits the well-designed **Hotel Vision**, ✆ 54 226, ✉ 54 450 (*C; mod*); all rooms have sea view and benefit from the pool, but there's no beach. Sígri has quite a spread of tavernas, of which classy **Remezzo** has the pick of the positions and the largest lobster tank. The taverna that everyone knows as **The Blue Wave**, down by the fishing boats with octopus tentacles gripped by clothes pegs on a line, has excellent, good-value fish, although the owner's bolshy style is not to everyone's taste. **The Golden Key** has unbeatable *yigantes* and other home-baked dishes, while the *kafeneíon* **To Kendro** is great for *souvlaki, tavli* and watching the world go by. Afterwards, head for **Notia** bar, which never ceases to musically please with the very individual CD collection of the owner; it's an extremely atmospheric little red-walled place. The bar above The Blue Wave is also friendly and good for boat watching.

Between Eressoú and Skála Eressoú sprawls the **Aeolian Village**, ✆ 53 585, ✉ 53 795 (*A; exp*), a pastel complex with large pools and a supervised children's club for a few hours' respite. In Skála, **Sappho the Eressian**, ✆ 53 495 (*C; mod*), is an orange, lesbian-only haven on the seafront, with comfy chairs down by the strand. **Hotel Galini**, ✆ 53 138, ✉ 53 137 (*B; inexp*), has good-value air-con rooms set back from the beach amongst trees and flowers, while **Pansion Eresos**, © 53 560 (*inexp*), has clean, plain rooms and a subterranean reception area. Friendly **Sappho Travel** on the main street, © 52 140, 📧 52 000, *sappho@otenet.gr*, will organize your accommodation for you and has a helpful Web site of accommodation all over Lésbos (*www.lesvos.co.uk*). For fresh fish, head for **Soulatso** on the waterfront, where translucent octopus are hung up in the sun with only the big blue sea beyond. Whitewashed **Cine Sapho** hosts very pleasant, open-air films, while **Naos Club** offers you the 'spirit of the music' from midnight.

Southern Lésbos

Southern Lésbos, between the inland seas of Kallóni and Géras, is dominated by **Mount Olympos** (967m). At the last count, there were 19 mountains in the Mediterranean named Olympos. Almost all were peaks sacred to the local sky god, who, in this most syncretic corner of the world, became associated with Zeus; hence, the local sky god's mountain would take the name of Zeus' home. In the shadow of Olympos, reached down a delightful road flanked by olive groves and natural springs, lies the lovely village of **Agiássos** (ΑΓΙΑΣΣΟΣ), a coach tour stop treating tourists accordingly, but still one of the most interesting on Lésbos, with its red-tile-roofed houses, medieval castle, and addictive, creeper-shaded market streets where locals gather for coffee at the traditional *kafeneío* with the peppermint-blue tables and fine copper kettle; carry on up to the bakery on your left for excellent walnut baklava and cheese pies. Founded in the 1100s by the Archbishop of Mytilíni, Valérios Konstantínos, the **Church of the Panagía** houses an icon of the Virgin, said to have been made by St Luke from mastic and wax and rescued from the iconoclasts. The present church building was constructed in 1812 after a fire destroyed the older structure, and it has one of the most beautiful 19th-century interiors of any Greek church, all grey and gilt, lit by hundreds of suspended lamps and chandeliers. Various of the icons are very fine, with perspective redolent of the 15th-century Italian Renaissance in some on the iconostasis. There is a small Byzantine Museum to the right of the church in the courtyard (*open 8–8; adm*), with a motley collection. One of the priests was a master at the *sandoúri*, or hammer dulcimer, and some of the shops sell his recordings, as well as the island's ceramics. Agiássos is famous for its pre-Lent Carnival and special vases. From the Kípos Panagías taverna (up the steps from the bus stop and dominated by a majestic old plane tree, like the 'Tree that Sat Down') there's a splendid view of the village and its orchards that produce excellent black plums and walnuts. Park your car at the foot of the village, rather than grinding to a halt in the serpentine streets of the old town. A lovely marked path leads from Agiássos to Plomári on the coast, passing by way of the ruins of **Palaiókastro**, of uncertain date, and the pleasant village and fountains of **Melaglochóri**.

Chestnut and pine groves cover much of the region, one of Lésbos' prettiest, and the road west to **Polichnítos** (ΠΟΛΙΧΝΙΤΟΣ) is especially lovely. Polichnítos isn't much itself, although it houses the quirkiest display of taxidermy, with stuffed storks to accompany the real ones nesting on the chimneys, reconstructed amphorae and a life-sized, garish doll in a ground-floor workshop at the entrance to the village. There is also a recently built **Municipal Folklore and Historical Museum**, © (0252) 42 992, not to mention the thermal spa, **Gera Yera**, oozing out the hottest waters in Europe (91°C), good for arthritis and gynaecological disorders (© (0252) 41 229; *open 7–11am and 4–7pm in season; adm*). Erika, who runs it with partner Lefteris, recommends a dip even in mid-summer, reminding you to 'fight heat with heat'—it is very refreshing. Near the harbour of **Skála Polichnítou**, there's a beach with noticeably warmer water than off the exposed coastal strips, and many tavernas. Another pretty beach near the mouth of Kallonís Bay, **Nyfída** flies the blue flag of EU righteousness, although it can be windy. South of Polichnítos, **Vríssa** was the home town of Briseis, the captive princess who caused the rift between Achilles and Agamemnon at Troy. Only a wall remains of the ancient Trojan town destroyed in 1180 BC, and a Genoese tower stands to the west of Vríssa; the modern town can only claim a *kafeneíon*. Ruins of a 1st-century BC Doric temple of Dionysos Vrysageni 'Born of the Springs' stand on Cape Ag. Fókas. Ag. Fókas marks the start of Lésbos' longest beach, **Vaterá** (BATEPA), 9km of sand, dotted with seasports facilities, pensions, tavernas and fragrant sea daffodils. For a lovely excursion, walk up the path marked with yellow circles, beginning at the river Voúrkos, to **Áno Stavrós** and **Ampelikó**, a charming village in a ravine under Mount Olympos, with Roman ruins, a castle, pretty church and cafés. Two years ago, the discovery of an extraordinary variety of animal and plant fossils in the area was announced, including the fossilized shell of a tortoise the size of an old VW beetle. Investigations are under way by the universities of Athens and Utrecht, and finds are displayed in the temporary museum at Vríssa (© (0252) 61 711). Back along the coast to the east, **Plomári** (ΠΛΟΜΑΡΙ) is Lésbos' second city and port (pop 10,000), with attractive houses decorated with traditional *sachnissinía* (wooden galleries). The centre is as funky as Mytilíni town and it reeks of Greece's favourite aperitif—Kéfi, Veto, Tikelli and Barbayiánni ouzos are all distilled here, and increasingly much of it is drunk by tourists (especially Scandinavian) in situ as Plomári discovers resort life in a big way under the palm trees. Plomári has a beach but **Ag. Isídoros** just east has an even better one of pebble and sand. The inland roads are quite attractive and woodsy; from the main road, an unpaved one descends to the very pretty sandy cove at **Tárti**, with a good taverna or two. At Pérama, a dingy oil port (olive oil, that is), you'll find a ferry across the Gulf of Géras, 'the Bay of Olives', to Skála Loutrá, near Mytilíni town.

© *(0252–)*   **Where to Stay and Eating Out**

Polichnítos/Skála Polichnítou ✉ 81300

At **Gera Yera** spa, there are tranquil rooms, © 41 229 (*inexp*). To eat, **Polikentro Taverna**, at the entrance to the village, is the best. At Skála, Erika and Lefteris run **Soft Tourism**, © 42 678 (*inexp*), usually hosting courses for small groups, but happy to help individuals if they can. A handful of tavernas line the harbour and strand serving some of the freshest fish on the island, sold directly from the dock; the *mezédes* are delicious and there are customers who seem to be there 24 hours a day nursing *karafákis* of ouzo; a good bet is **Tzitzifies**, with the blue and red tablecloths. Down at Nyfída, **Taverna Tsitsanos** and **Iotis** are excellent.

Vaterá ✉ 81300

Hotel Vatera Beach, © 61 212, 🖷 61 164, *hovatera@otenet.gr* (*C; mod*), run in a relaxed fashion by the inimitable Barbara and George in a tranquil floral setting, lets you unwind to your heart's content; the beach-side restaurant offers half-board and vegetarian options to boot. *Open May–mid-Oct.* The **Dionysos Club**, one of two discos in Vaterá, has a very good campsite with a swimming pool. On the west end, by Ag. Fokás, are two superb fish tavernas, with gorgeous views; **Chakadakis** is also good. **Mylos** is a soporific café-bar decked out in reggae colours on the beach.

Plomári ✉ 81200

Almost everything here is block-booked by Vikings, but you may find a room in the old centre—try traditionally housed **Lida I** or **II**, ✆ 32 507 (*B; inexp*)—or out of season at **Okeanis**, ✆ 32 469 (*C; inexp*), 100m from the sea. The **Rented Rooms Union**, ✆ 31 666, should be able to help. In Ag. Isídoro, try **Ammodis Akti**, ✆ 32 825 (*C; inexp*). *Open Apr–Oct.*

Náxos (ΝΑΞΟΣ)

Náxos, 448sq km in area, is the largest of the Cyclades and the most mountainous, its highest point, Mount Zas, crowning the archipelago at 1,004m. The second most populated island, with 17,000 year-round residents, it can also claim to be the most fertile: the only one that could get by without importing food, its valleys a refreshing green even in the height of the sun-browned Cycladic summer. Sacred to Dionysos, Náxos makes excellent wine, and Kítron, a fragrant liqueur distilled from citron leaves (an ungainly cousin of the lemon), although seed potatoes are the main export. The entire west coast is almost one uninterrupted beach of silvery sands. Náxos was Byron's favourite island, perhaps because it comes in romantic proportions: rugged mountains and lush valleys, sprinkled with the ruins of the ancient Greeks, the gilded Byzantines, and his beloved Venetians. There are plenty of tourists, including heavy German and Scandinavian contingents, but they stay by the beaches, leaving the rest of the big island to wanderers and poets.

History

Náxos was one of the major centres of the Neolithic Cycladic civilization. Around 3000 BC, as now, the main settlements were near Chóra, on the hill of the Kástro, and at Grótta, where the sea-eroded remains of the Cycladic town can still be seen in the clear water. Tradition has it that the island was later colonized by a party from Karia, led by a son of Apollo named Náxos. Although these Naxians were Ionians, their most troublesome enemy was Miletus in Ionia proper, where some Naxian refugees, eager to take back the island for themselves, helped foment trouble. According to Plutarch, many battles were fought between the two rivals at the fort called Delion, of which a few vestiges remain near Náxos town. One story has come down as follows: once when Miletus attacked Náxos, the beautiful island heroine Polykrite arrived at Delion too late and found the fortress gate closed against her. One of the Miletan leaders found her, fell in love with her and proved it by telling her of all the movements of his armies. His information enabled the Naxians to make a sudden attack on the Miletians, but in the confusion of the battle Polykrite's lover was also killed, and the girl died of sorrow the next day.

Náxos was one of the first islands to work in marble. In the Archaic period Naxian sculptors produced the lions of Délos and *kouros* statues of incredible size. Big was beautiful on Náxos; in 523 BC the tyrant Lugdamis declared he would make Náxos' buildings the highest and most glorious in Greece, although only the massive lintel from the Temple of Apollo survives to tell the tale of his ambition. Náxos next makes the history books in 1207 when the Venetian Marco Sanudo captured the island's chief Byzantine castle, T'Apaliroú, and declared himself Duke of Náxos, ruler over all the adventurers who had grabbed up islands after the conquest of Constantinople in 1204. In 1210, when Venice refused to grant Sanudo the status he desired, he hitched his wagon to the Roman Emperor and took the official title Duke of the Archipelago, the Byzantine name for the 'chief sea', or Aegean; under Sanudo and his successors, the word gained its current meaning. Even after the Turkish conquest in 1564, the Dukes of Náxos remained in nominal control of the Cyclades, although answerable to the sultan.

Mythology

After slaying the Minotaur, the Athenian Theseus and Ariadne, the Cretan princess who loved him, stopped to rest at Náxos on their way to Athens. Yet the next morning, while Ariadne slept, Theseus set sail and abandoned her. This, even in the eyes of the Athenians, was dishonourable, especially as Theseus had promised to marry Ariadne in return for the assistance she had rendered him in negotiating the Labyrinth. Various explanations for Theseus' ungallant behaviour have sprung up over the centuries. Did he simply forget her, did he find a new mistress, or did the god Dionysos, who later found Ariadne and married her, somehow warn Theseus off? Everyone agrees that it was the jilted bride's curse on Theseus that made him forget to change his black sails to white to signal his safe homecoming, causing his father to commit suicide in despair. Ariadne lived happily ever after with Dionysos, who taught the Naxians how to make their excellent wine and set Ariadne's crown, the Corona Borealis, amongst the stars; the Celts called it Ariansrod, where their heroes went after death. The story inspired later artists as well, including Richard Strauss, who wrote the opera *Ariadne auf Náxos*.

© (0285–)   ***Getting There and Around***

By air: one or two flights a day from Athens with Olympic; charters from London and Manchester. **Airport**: © 23 292; take a taxi. **Zas Travel**, next to Náxos Tourist Information Centre, © 23 330, @ 23 419, *zas-travel@nax.forthnet.gr*, handles Olympic Airways.

By sea: excursion boats to Délos, Mýkonos and Santoríni. **Port authority**: © 22 300.

By road: frequent **bus** services from Náxos town, © 22 291, at least every hour down to Ag. Ánna Beach; six times a day to Filoti and Chalki; five times to Apiranthos; four times to Apollonía, Koronos, Pirgaki, Kastraki and Tripodes; 2–3 times to Komiaki and Melanes, © 22 291. **Taxi** rank near bus station. Many **car rental** agencies are represented; Auto Tour offers full insurance at competitive rates, © 25 480, @ 25 968.

© (0285–)   ***Tourist Information***

The privately run **Náxos Tourist Information Centre**, © 24 358, @ 25 200, right by the quay, organizes accommodation and manages various establishments. It also has luggage-storage and laundry facilities, organizes excursions and sells Christian Veke's helpful *Walking Tours in Náxos*. Also look for the Harms Verlag map of Náxos, available in shops, with all the paths, the best ones marked in red.

Internet: it's not cheap, but access is available in Néa Chora, at Vaporia Play Room, © 23 469, until 5am, and the nearby Rental Center.

Festivals

Some of the many celebrations are: **23 April**, Ag. Geórgios in Kinídaros; **1 July**, Ag. Anargýroi in Sangrí; **14 July**, the biggest of all for Ag. Nikódimos, patron saint of

Náxos, with a procession of the icon and folk festival; **17 July**, in Kóronos; the **first week of August** usually sees the Dionýsia festival in Náxos town, with folk dancing in local costume and free food and wine in the central square; **15 August**, Panagía in Filotí; **23 August**, in Trípodes; **29 August**, Ag. Ioánnis in Apóllon and Apíranthos.

Excursions from Náxos Town

1 Head down to the beautiful swathes of sand south of town, especially the remote beaches around Cape Kouroúpia. Circle back via Sangrí, to visit the reconstructed Temple of Demeter; for more of a walk, head for the Byzantine castle of T'Apaliróu.

2 Drive inland through the fertile plateau to Chálki, bursting with Byzantine and Venetian towers, castles and churches with fine frescoes; be sure to taste the local Kitron. Head on to panoramic Filóti and the remarkable preserved Hellenistic Tower of Chimárou; from there, lovely, marble-coated Apíranthos is within reach. Drive back via Kinídaros and Mélanes (*see* 3).

3 Drive east towards Mélanes, turning off at Flerio to marvel at the giant *kouros* asleep amongst the cypresses. Continuing on to Kinídaros, you'll be tempted by the enchanting walk laced with waterfalls, after which head up to Apóllonas' 33ft *kouros*. From here follow the northern coastal road back to town via idyllic Ormós Ábram beach.

Náxos Town

Náxos, the island's port and capital, is a hustling bustling place that has sprawled all along the waterfront, leaving the old districts on the hill above intact. As you pull into port, the island's Π-shaped trademark, the massive doorway to nowhere, is the **Portára** of Lugdamis' unfinished **Temple of Apollo** (522 BC), standing out like an ancient version of the enigmatic monolith in *2001: A Space Odyssey*. Set on the islet of **Palátia**, linked by an ancient causeway to the port, it comes in handy as a dramatic frame for sunset photos. The ancient **harbour mole** was rebuilt by Duke Marco Sanudo; in front of the port, a little chapel sits on its own islet. Statues of two famous sons of Náxos greet you: Michaeli Damiralis (d. 1917), who translated Shakespeare into Greek, and the slightly disappointed-looking Pétros Protopapadákis, who planned the Corinth canal but had the misfortune of serving as Minister of Economics during the 1920–22 catastrophe in Asia Minor; he was executed with five other ministers as scapegoats by the subsequent regime.

Near the main waterfront, by the Agrarian Bank, the 11th-century church of **Panagía Pantanássa** was once part of a Byzantine monastery and famous for its very early icon of the Virgin. Lanes here lead up into old Náxos, a fine Cycladic town, although some people find its twisting streets almost claustrophobic and bewildering, which is just as the natives intended them to be, to confuse invading marauders. The town was divided into three neighbourhoods: **Boúrgos** where the Greeks lived; **Evraiki**, the Jewish quarter; and up above, **Kástro**, where the Venetian Catholic nobility lived. In Boúrgos, the Orthodox cathedral, the **Metropolis of Zoodóchos Pigí**, was created in the 18th century out of an old temple and older churches; its iconostasis is by Dimítrios Valvis of the Cretan school. Archaeologists would gladly knock it down for a slam-bang dig if only the bishop would let

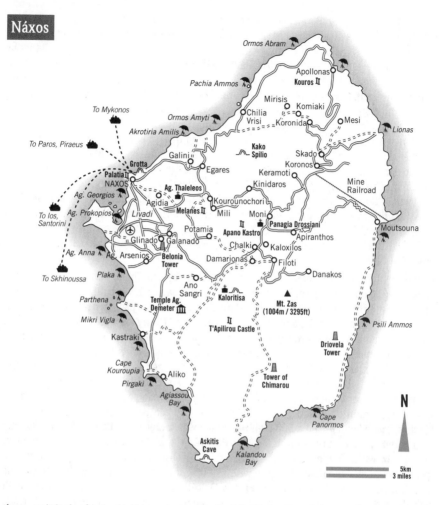

Ormos Abram

Apollonas
Kouros II

Pachia Ammos

To Mykonos

Mirisis

Komiaki

Chilia
Vrisi

Ormos Amyti

Koronida

Mesi

Akrotiria Amilis

Lionas

To Paros, Piraeus

**Kako
Spilio**

Skado

Galini

Grotta

Egares

Keramoti

Koronos

Palatia
NAXOS

Kinidaros

Mine
Railroad

Ag. Georgios

Ag. Thaleleos

Agidia

Kourounochori

To Ios,
Santorini

Ag. Prokopios

Melanes II

Mili

Moni

Livadi

Potamia

Apano Kastro

Panagia Drossiani

Moutsouna

Glinado

Galanado

Chalki

Apiranthos

Ag. Anna

Ag. Arsenios

Kaloxilos

**Belonia
Tower**

Damarionas

Filoti

Plaka

Danakos

Ano
Sangri

Kaloritisa

Parthena

**Temple Ag.
Demeter**

Mt. Zas
(1004m / 3295ft)

Mikri Vigla

T'Apilirou Castle

Psili Ammos

Kastraki

**Driovela
Tower**

Cape
Kouroupia

Aliko

**Tower of
Chimarou**

Pirgaki

Agiassou
Bay

Cape
Panormos

N

**Askitis
Cave**

Kalandou
Bay

5km
3 miles

them; as it is they've had to be content with the Mitropolis Site Museum under the adjacent square (*open Tues–Sun 8–2*), displaying Mycenaean remains of the city. The cathedral looks down over **Grótta**, the coast named for its numerous caves (naturally re-dubbed Grotty by Brits); if it's not windy you can see remains of the Cycladic town and a road under the water; one hollow in the rock is the 'Bath of Ariadne'. Ancient **Fort Delion**, scene of starcrossed love, stood just to the east.

The Evraiki district is just above, but any traces of its former inhabitants have been obliterated. On top, the high-walled **Kástro** preserves one of its seven original towers, still guarding one of only three entrances into the district—a higgledy-piggledy jumble of stunning houses, flowers and dark alleys. Some 19 Venetian houses still bear their coats-of-arms—something you'll almost never see in Venice proper, where displays of pride were severely frowned upon. Most of the Kástro's residents claim Venetian descent, and many of their grandparents' tombstones in the 13th-century **Catholic Cathedral** boast grand titles. The cathedral, clad from head to toe in pale grey marble, was founded by Marco Sanudo, whose own palace, or what remains of it, can be seen directly across the square. During the Turkish occupation Kástro had a reputation for its School of Commerce, run by Catholic friars, attended for two years by Níkos Kazantzákis. This is now the **Archaeology Museum**, at least until a new one is built (*open Tues–Sun 8–2.30; adm*), with artefacts from the 5th millenium BC to 5th century AD, including a superb collection of Cycladic figurines in all sizes, a Cycladic pig about to be sick in a sack from 2800 BC, Mycenaean pottery (note the *hydria* painted with fishermen) and a Roman mosaic of Europa. The **Venetian Museum** (Domus Della-Rocca-Barozzi) preserves a traditional Kástro house (*open 10–3 and 6–10; adm*) and is the venue for atmospheric summer concerts. **Antico Veneziano** antique shop is also housed in an 800-year-old mansion with lovingly restored 2,000-year-old Ionian columns original to the house in the erstwhile servants' quarters (now the shop); it also has fascinating photos of Náxos and Santoríni through the 20th century and a room exhibiting works by international artists. A beautifully carved portico by the Kástro entrance leads to a choice terrace containing tables, chairs and a drinks machine.

South of Náxos Town

Further south, numerous hotels and a whole new suburb, Néa Chóra, have sprung up around popular **Ag. Geórgios** beach. Much of the rest of holiday Náxos is built up along the sand-strewn coast further south. The road then skirts the fertile **Livádi** plain, where Náxos grows its famous spuds; here, near the airport at Iria, a **temple of Dionysos** was discovered in 1986. The road continues to **Ag. Prokópio**s, with nice, coarse non-sticky sand, and then **Ag. Ánna**, the most popular beach, well sheltered from the notorious *meltémi*, and **Pláka** just south, considered by many the best in Náxos, with a variety of watersports, and an alternative camp-site popular with the counter culture. From Ag. Ánna, boats and bifurcating dirt roads hidden in the bamboo continue south to the beaches; by asphalt road you have to divert inland, by way of **Ag. Arsénios** (if you get off the bus here, you can take a lovely path down to the beaches, past windmills and a 30ft-high Hellenistic watch tower, the **Paleó Pírgos**). The vast white sandy beaches to the south begin at **Parthéna**, excellent for surfing and swimming, followed by **Mikrí Vígla**, where the sea is brilliantly clear; **Sahára** is well equipped for sea sports, and merges into **Kastráki**, again with sparkling sea and white sands, ideal for letting the kids run wild. Above the road stands **Pírgos Oskéllou**, a ruined Mycenaean fortress, built over the remains of a Cycladic acropolis. If the above beaches are too busy for your taste, there's a more remote strip of sand beyond Kastráki on either side of **Cape Kouroúpia**.

Inland Villages, the Southerly Route: Venetian Towers and Olive Groves

A few kilometres east of Náxos town the main inland road forks, the southerly right-hand branch heading first to **Galanádo**, site of the restored Venetian **Belonia Tower**, bearing the lion of St Mark, and the Venetian church of **St John**, with a Catholic chapel on the left and an Orthodox one on the right: a typical arrangement on Náxos. It is also seen in the island's first cathedral, the recently restored 8th-century **Ag. Mámas**, dedicated to the patron saint of thieves, located a short walk from the road, towards **Sangrí** (ΣΑΝΥΚΡΙ). Actually three small villages picturesquely spread out over the plateau, Sangrí gets its name from the Hellenized version of Sainte Croix, the French for the 16th-century tower monastery Tímiou Stavroú or True Cross. There are many Byzantine frescoed chapels (usually locked) and medieval towers in the vicinity and, a pretty mile's walk south of Áno Sangrí, a 6th-century BC **Temple of**

Demeter. A church on the site used much of the stone, but archaeologists have taken revenge on the Christians and dismantled the church and scoured surrounding farms for other bits to fit the temple back together like a giant jigsaw. A much more strenuous walk southeast of Áno Sangrí will take you up to the ruins of **T'Apalioú**, the Byzantine castle high on its rock that defied Marco Sanudo and his mercenaries for two months.

Inland Villages: The Tragéa and Slopes of Mount Zas

From Sangrí the road rises up to the beautiful Tragéa plateau, planted with fruit trees and lilacs, flanked on either side by Náxos' highest mountains. Olives are the main product of the numerous small villages in the valley, including **Chálki**, where both the Byzantines and Venetians built tower houses: the Byzantine **Frankópoulo**, in the centre, and up a steep, difficult path the 13th-century Venetian **Apáno Kástro**, used by Marco Sanudo as a summer hideaway. He was not, however, the first to enjoy the splendid panorama from the summit; the fortress sits on Cyclopean foundations, and Geometric era and Mycenaean tombs have been discovered just to the southeast; rare for Greece, there's even a menhir. In Chálki itself there are two fine churches with frescoes: 12th-century **Panagía Protóthronis** (ask in the village for the priest if it's closed) and 9th-century **Ag. Diasorítis**, and a paved road leads up to a shady glade sheltering the most striking church on Náxos, **Panagía Drossianí**, built in the 5th century and crowned with ancient corbelled domes of field stones. Open most mornings (offering expected), it contains excellent frescoes of the Pantokrator, Virgin, and two saints. Chálki is also in the heart of Kítron territory; if you wish to understand the production process (the thought of the free tipple at the end does wonders for your concentration), try the well-established **Vallindras Náxos Citron distillery.**

The main road continues on to **Filóti** (ΦΙΛΟΤΙ), on the slopes of Mount Zas, the largest village in the Tragéa, where contented ewes and nannies produce the island's best cheese; it also offers splendid views and the chance to eavesdrop on everyday village life. Monuments include the Venetian towerhouse of the De Lasti family, the churches **Koímisis tis Theotókou**, with a fine carved marble iconostasis, and **Panagía Filótissa**, with a marble steeple. There are many scenic paths, one leading up the slopes of **Mount Zas**, passing by way of an ancient inscription ΟΡΟΣ ΔΙΟΣ ΜΗΛΩΣΙΟΥ ('Mount Zeus, Herd-Protector'). There's a sacred cave near the summit, where one story says baby Zeus of Crete (*see* p.74) was briefly deposited for a while; be careful and bring a light if you want to explore—the only inhabitants now are bats. A 3-hour path (or unpaved road) from Filóti follows the west flanks of the mountain south to the isolated and hence excellently preserved Hellenistic **Tower of Chimárou**, built by Ptolemy of Egypt of white marble blocks, lost in the wildest part of Náxos.

From Filóti the road skirts the slopes of Mt Zas on its way to **Apíranthos** (ΑΠΕΙΡΑΝΘΟΣ), where the Venetian families Crispi and Sommaripa built towers. Many contemporary families, however, are Cretan, descended from migrants who came during the Turkish occupation to work in Greece's only emery mines. It's the most picturesque village on Náxos, with narrow winding paths paved with marble; Byron loved it so much that he declared that he wanted to die in Apíranthos (there are a few rooms to rent if you feel the same way). The churches, to saints Georgios, Sofia and Ilias, are built on ancient temples to Ares, Athena and Helios respectively. A few women still weave on looms and farmers sell their produce. Don't miss the ancient barber shop. In August, though, the atmosphere changes with cocktail bars and revelry. Visit the small **Cycladic museum**, devoted to mostly Neolithic finds (*open 9–3; adm*), and a **geological and folklore museum** (*same hours*) in the school. A road from here descends to the port of **Moutsoúna**, where emery (used in ancient time to polish Cycladic statues) is brought down from the mountains near Kóronos by a rope funicular (more successful than the disastrous one used in *Zorba the Greek*) and loaded on to ships. Moutsoúna has a fine beach; from here a dirt road follows the east coast south to the remote beach of **Psilí Ámmos**.

The Northerly Route: Mélanes to Apóllonas and Down the West Coast

The left branch of the main road from Náxos town leads to **Mélanes** and the ancient marble quarries in the heart of Náxos; at Flerio, signposted off the road (it's a 700m walk), lies a 7th-century BC 20ft-high *kouros* in a cypress grove. *Kouros* means 'young man', and in the Archaic period such statues—highly stylized, stiff figures, their arms hugging their sides, one foot stepping forward—were inspired by Egyptian art; the young men they portray are believed to have been Zeus' ancient guardians (the Cretan Curetes) or perhaps the Ionian god Apollo. This one was abandoned because of a broken leg; a second one, 300m south, is in poorer shape. At **Kourounochóri** near Mélanes stand ruins of a Venetian castle; **Ag. Thaléleos** in the same area has a monastery with a fine 13th-century church. Náxos' marble is almost as fine as Páros' (although Naxians will insist it is the best), and is still quarried to the east at **Kinídaros**. One of the most beautiful walks on Náxos begins here; the path descends past the chapel of the woodland goddess Ag. Artemis, and follows the lush Xerotakari river valley down to Egarés. The Xerotakari is the only river in the Cyclades to flow even in August; it has little waterfalls and provides a pleasant home for turtles and eels, as well as drinking water for Náxos town.

A paved road links **Kóronos** to **Liónas** beach, while the main road north turns into a winding, hairpin serpent leading to pretty **Komiakí**, highest of the island's villages, with stunning views over terraced vineyards. The road leads back down to **Apóllonas** (ΑΠΟΛΛΩΝΑΣ), a dreary little town with a (very) public sandy beach, several tavernas heavily patronized by tour buses, and some mid-range pensions. Ancient marble quarries are carved out of the slopes of the mountain, and steps lead up to a colossal, 33ft-long *kouros*, abandoned in the 7th century BC because of flaws in the marble. Because Apóllonas was sacred to Apollo (an inscription is still visible on the marble wall) the statue is believed to represent the god; even more intriguingly, the long-vanished temple that stood here is part of a perfect equilateral triangle formed by the temples of Apollo on Délos and Páros. Apóllonas is as far as the bus goes; by car you can chance the road along the north coast back to Náxos town, passing the isolated beaches of idyllic **Ormós Ábram** with a taverna and rooms and a curious giant marble head abandoned on a rock, and **Pachiá Ámmos** near the **Monastery of Faneroméni** dating from 1606. There are lovely beaches in this northwest coast, although when the *meltémi* roars you'll want to give them a miss.

Náxos ✉ 84300, © (0285–)   *Where to Stay and Eating Out*

If you don't have accommodation, dodge the touts and head for the booking desk by the quay or for Náxos Tourist Information Centre, by Créperie Bikini, which will find you a room. Many rooms are in Néa Chóra, unlovely but handy for the beach; if you stay there, make sure you can find your way 'home' through its anonymous streets.

Náxos Town

Staying up in car-free Chóra is delightful; you can hear the waves washing on the waterfront from right up by the Kástro at night. If you want to spoil yourself, stay in the plush **Château Zevgoli**, ✆ 22 993, ✉ 25 200, *chateau-zevgoli@forthnet.gr* (*C; exp*), in an old mansion, small and exclusive with roof garden, antique décor and a four-poster for honeymooners. It's run by the manager of the Náxos Tourist Information Centre; enquire there. **Hotel Grotta**, just north of Chóra, ✆ 22 101, ✉ 22 000, *grotta@náxos-island.com* (*C; exp*), is another blue and white creation with wonderful sea views; the owner will collect you from the quay. Opposite are **Iliada Studios**, ✆ 23 303, ✉ 24 687, *iliada@naxos-island.com* (*mod*), also overlooking the sea. Brand-new **Apollonia**, ✆ 24 358 (*mod*), is closer to Chóra (ask at the Náxos Tourist Information Centre), while **Hotel Anixis**, ✆ 22 932, ✉ 22 112 (*D; mod*), is very moderate, up by the Kástro, overlooking the sea from its verandas and terraces.

Of the small hotels in Boúrgos, just outside Kástro's walls, **Panorama**, ✆/✉ 24 404 (*C; inexp*), on Amphitris Street is pleasant, with a marvellous sea view, as is adjacent **Bourgos**, ✆/✉ 25 979 (*inexp*), especially the airy studio off the roof terrace. **Despina Panteou's rooms**, ✆ 22 356 (*inexp*), are also nice, with balcony and roof-terrace views out to sea.

Just south, in Néa Chóra and Ag. Geórgios, there's a wide selection of blander places: **Nissaki Beach Hotel**, ✆ 25 710, ✉ 23 876 (*C; exp*), has rooms circling a pool by the beach, with restaurant-bar. **Barbouni**, ✆ 22 535, ✉ 23 137 (*C; mod*), is a welcoming, family-run operation, but on a noisy road. **St George Beach**, ✆ 23 162 (*E; mod*), is by the strand. In Néa Chóra, quiet, family-run **Irene Pension**, ✆ 23 169, *irenepension@hotmail.com* (*inexp*), offers better-value air-conditioned studios. **Camping Náxos**, ✆ 23 501, is by the beach.

If you want to splash out for dinner, there are two fine but touristy places up in Bradóuna Square, just under the Kástro's walls: **Oniro**, ✆ 23 846, has candlelit tables in a courtyard, and a roof garden with a dream view over town; try the *arni bouti yemistó*, lamb stuffed with garlic and bacon; a few steps away the **Kastro**, ✆ 22 005, has delicious rabbit *stifádo* and *exochikó*, filo pastry parcels. **Manolis**, in a quiet courtyard on Old Market Street, which used to be the heart of Chóra, has good-value traditional food: ask for the specials and try the homemade *rakí* (good in itself and even better in '*rakimelo*', warmed with honey to cure the worst of writers' hacking coughs). **Koutouki** is another hearty Kástro option. **Apolafsis** by the waterfront serves fine Greek food with live Greek music, and **Karnaiyo** is a decent fishery. A 10-minute stroll brings you to **Gallini**, ✆ 25 206, a proper Greek fish tavern with friendly service. **Kavouri** is an old favourite on Ag. Geórgios beach, serving good fish soup and other dishes with Naxian wine for over 40 years. You can taste the local Kítron liqueur (regular, mint or banana flavour) in the **Probonas** shop on the waterfront; Náxos wine is good as well, but best drunk from a barrel in situ; it's famous for not travelling well. For a traditional café, try to find **To Roupel** in Chóra (erratic nocturnal opening).

Beaches South of Chóra: Ag. Prokópios, Ag. Ánna, Pláka, Mikri Vigla,and Kastráki

At Ag. Prokópios the **Kavouras Village**, ✆ 25 580, ✉ 23 705 (*B; exp*), offers flower-bedecked studios and villas and a pool; here too is **Camping Apollon**, ✆ 24 117, with minibus service. At Ag. Ánna, the **Iria Beach Apartments**, ✆ 42 600, ✉ 42 603 (*C; mod*), are right by the beach, with a range of facilities including car hire (upstairs studios have attractive balconies); **Ag. Anna**, ✆ 42 576, ✉ 42 704 (*C; inexp*), is also right by the sea, with verandas and fruits of the orchard to feast on. Alternatively, try the **Studios Anemos**, above the bakery, ☎ 41 919 (*mod–inexp*). Immaculate, German-run **Camping Maragas**, ☎ 24 552, is nearby. For dinner, try **Paradise Taverna** for tasty Greek dishes, a terrace shaded by a vast pine tree and an infectious atmosphere, or **Gorgonas** for fishier dishes. At **Pláka**, **Villa Medusa** (book in Athens, ☎ (01) 894 6469, 🖥 412 0422, *A; exp*) is a favourite of sophisticated wind surfers; rooms are furnished with antiques from around the world, mini bars and satellite TV. **Aronis Taverna**, on the Ag. Ánna–Pláka beach road, ☎ 42 019, 🖥 42 021 (*mod*), has clean studios by the sea and a hippy eatery; the road is lined with similar studios. At Mikrí Vígla, the newish **Mikri Vigla**, ☎ 75 241, 🖥 75 240 (*B; exp*), is a low-rise mini-resort in Cycladic style, on the beach with a pool and surfing centre; **Mikri Vigla restaurant**, ☎ 75 214, at one end of the beach, and **Kostas' taverna** are good gastronomic bets. At Kastráki, **Summerland Complex**, ☎ 75 461, 🖥 75 399, *summerland@ath.forthnet.gr* (*exp*), has a relaxed collection of apartments around two pools and bars, with gym, Jacuzzi and mini-market on site, good for entertaining kids. Plainer studios are available at **Yiannis**, near the beach, ☎ 75 413 (*mod*).

Apollónas

Flora's Apartments, ☎ 67 070 (*mod*), are pleasant, built around a garden. **Adonis**, ☎ 67 060 (*C; mod*), is comfortable, but if you want to get away from it all head for Órmos Ábram and **Pension Efthimios**, ☎ 63 244 (*inexp*), which also has a taverna.

Entertainment and Nightlife

Náxos has a buzzing nightlife with masses of bars; smartish **Veggera**, near the OTE, is popular, while adjacent **Med Bar**'s terrace overlooks the water. Should you wish to grace the main waterfront, **Cocos Café** is a relaxed place to sit, or make a date at **Rendezvous**. In Chóra, **Lakridi Jazz Bar**, Old Market Street, is the mellowest of places of an evening. Alternatively, you can dance the night away, watching the sun rise through the giant window at the **Ocean Club** right on the sea, or at **Cream**, 'a club that is always on top', or the thumping **Super Island**, in Grotta. In Ag. Ánna, **Enosis**, ☎ 24 644, is a popular club in an old warehouse playing Greek music.

Rhodes/Ródos (ΡΟΔΟΣ)

Rhodes, 'more beautiful than the sun' according to the ancient Greeks, is the largest and most fertile of the Dodecanese, ringed by sandy beaches, bedecked with flowers, blessed with some 300 days of sun a year, dotted with handsome towns and villages full of monuments evoking a long, colourful history—in a nutshell, all that it takes to sit securely throned as the reigning queen of tourism in Greece. As a year-round resort for cold northerners and top international package destination (in increasingly swanky, fancy-pants packages) it's not quite fair to compare it with Greece's other islands. Rhodes is a holiday Babylon, Europe's answer to Florida, a glittering, sun-drenched chill pill in the sea where people shed their inhibitions with their woollens, if not always their black socks with their sandals. Germans, Brits and Scandinavians outnumber everyone (there's even a special post box for Sweden at the central Post Office) but Israelis, Czechs and even Turks are now adding some different accents to the Babelling brew.

When and if you get fed up with the hordes, head inland, or for the southern half of Rhodes, beyond Líndos and Péfkos, and watch the sun set to see if you can find any lingering hints of the island evoked from Lawrence Durrell's imagination in his *Reflections on a Marine Venus*, written just after the war: 'Ahead of us the night gathers, a different night, and Rhodes begins to fall into the unresponding sea from which only memory can rescue it. The clouds hang high over Anatolia. Other islands? Other futures? Not, I think, after one has lived with the Marine Venus. The wound she gives one must carry to the world's end.'

Mythology

In myth, Rhodes is the subject of a messy number of very ancient and very often contradictory traditions. According to one, the first inhabitants of Rhodes were the Children of the Sea, the nine dog-headed enchantresses called Telchines, who had flippers for hands. In spite of this apparent handicap, they made the sickle that Cronos used to castrate Uranus, carved the first statues of the gods, and founded Kámiros, Ialysós and Líndos before moving to Crete. There Rhea, the great mother goddess of the earth, made them the nurses of her son Poseidon, and they forged the sea god's trident.

Poseidon fell in love with the Telchines' sister, Alia, and had six sons and a daughter by her. The daughter, the nymph Rhodos, became the sole heiress of the island when Zeus decided to destroy the Telchines for meddling with the weather (they were fond of weaving magical mists), although their real crime was belonging to a pre-Olympian matriarchal religion. He flooded Rhodes, but the Telchines managed to escape in various forms, most notoriously as the hounds of Artemis, who tore Actaeon to bits.

The same cast of characters are on stage in another version, although this time the Telchines change sex and shed their dog heads and flippers. The sons of Pontos and Thalassa (the sea), they were artisans, magicians and ministers of Zeus, with the same sister, Alia, who was loved by Poseidon and gave birth to Rhodos and a number of sons. When these sons refused to let Aphrodite dock as she sailed between her favourite islands of Kýthera and Cyprus, the goddess of love put a curse of incestuous passion on them and they raped their mother Alia. In despair Alia flung herself into the sea and became 'Lefkothea' (the White Goddess). The wicked sons hid in the bowels of the earth and became demons as Poseidon in his wrath flooded Rhodes (the Telchines, tipped off by Artemis, escaped before the deluge).

The sun god Helios later fell in love with Rhodos, evaporated the stagnant waters with his hot rays and married the nymph. They had a daughter and seven sons, known as the Heliades. Athena gave them wisdom and taught them nautical and astrophysical lore. But the wisest of the Heliades, Tenagis, was killed in a jealous fit by four of the brothers, who then fled to Lésbos, Kos, Ikaría and Egypt. The two innocent brothers, Ohimos and Kerkafos, remained and founded the city of Achaia; Ohimos' daughter Kydippi, a priestess of Hera, married her uncle Kerkafos and had three sons, Líndos, Kámiros and Ialysós, who founded the three city-states that bear their names.

A later, tidier Olympian version of the story relates that while the gods were dividing up the world's real estate among themselves, Zeus realized that he had forgotten to set aside a portion for Helios. Dismayed, Zeus asked Helios what he could do to make up for his omission. The sun god replied that he knew of an island just emerging from the sea off the coast of Asia Minor which would suit him admirably. Helios married Rhodos and their seven sons, famous astronomers, ruled the island. One of the sons, or perhaps Tlepolemos (who led the ships of Rhodes to Troy), refounded the ancient Telchine towns.

Kámiros even has another possible founder: Althaemenes, son of the Cretan King Katreus and grandson of Minos. When an oracle predicted that Katreus would be slain by one of his offspring, Althaemenes tried to avoid destiny by going off to Rhodes, where he founded Kámiros and built an altar of Zeus, surrounding it with magical metal bulls that would bellow if the island were invaded. In later life Katreus sailed to Rhodes to visit his son, whom he missed dearly. He arrived at night, and what with the darkness and the bellowing of the metal bulls, Althaemenes failed to recognize his father and fellow Cretans and slew them. When he realized his error in the morning he piteously begged Mother Earth to swallow him up whole, which she did.

History

Inhabited since Paleolithic times, Rhodes was colonized by the Minoans, who built shrines to the moon at Filérimos, Líndos and Kámiros, and when the Achaeans took over in the 15th century BC, they founded the town of Achaia. Before settling on Rhodes for its name, the island was often known as Telchinia (*see* above), or Ophioussa, for its numerous vipers; even today villagers wear snake-repelling goatskin boots when working out in the fields. The Achaeans were supplanted in the 12th century BC by the Dorians, whose three cities—Líndos, Ialysós and Kámiros—dominated the island's affairs. According to Homer, they sent nine ships to Troy, led by Tlepolemos, son of Hercules, who met an unhappy end before the Trojan walls. Positioned along the main Mediterranean trade routes, Rhodes was important early on in both trade and naval power. Around 1000 BC, in response to the first Ionian confederacy, the island's three cities formed a Doric Hexapolis along with Kos, Cnidos and Halicarnassus, a prototype EU that united the six city-states politically, religiously and economically. For four centuries the Hexapolis prospered, establishing trade colonies from Naples to the Costa Brava.

The Founding of Rhodes City, and its Colossus

Rhodes sided with the Persians in both of their major campaigns against Greece, but upon their defeat quickly switched sides and joined the Delian confederacy. In 408 BC, in order to prevent rivalries and increase their wealth and strength, Líndos, Ialysós and Kámiros united to found one central capital, Rhodes, or Ródos, 'the Rose'. Hippodamos of Miletus, the geometrician, designed the new town on a grid plan similar to the one he provided for Piraeus, and the result was considered one of the most beautiful cities of ancient times. It was huge, its walls encompassing a much greater area than that enclosed by the existing medieval walls. Celebrated schools of philosophy, philology and oratory were founded, and the port had facilities far in advance of its time. Although Líndos, Kámiros and Ialysós continued to exist, they lost all their importance and most of their populations to the new capital.

One reason for Rhodes' prosperity was its unabashedly expedient foreign policy. During the Peloponnesian War, it adroitly sided with whichever power was on top, and later hitched its wagon to the rising star of Alexander the Great in 336 BC. Alexander in turn favoured Rhodes at the expense of hostile Athens, and enabled the island to dominate Mediterranean trade; like Athens in classical times, the Rhodian navy ruled the waves and policed the seas of the Hellenistic era, and founded colonies all over the known world; its trade and navigation laws were later adopted by the Romans and remain the basis of maritime trade today.

Egypt was one of Rhodes' most lucrative trading partners, and in the struggles between the Macedonian generals after Alexander's death, Rhodes allied itself with Ptolemy, who had taken Egypt as his spoils. When another of Alexander's generals, the powerful Antigonas, ordered Rhodes to join him against Ptolemy, the Rhodians refused. To change their minds, Antigonas sent his son Dimitrios Poliorketes (the Besieger) at the head of the 40,000-strong Syrian army and the Phoenician fleet to besiege the uppity islanders.

The ensuing year-long siege (305–304 BC) by one of the greatest generals of all time against the greatest city of the day has gone down in history, not only as a contest of strength and

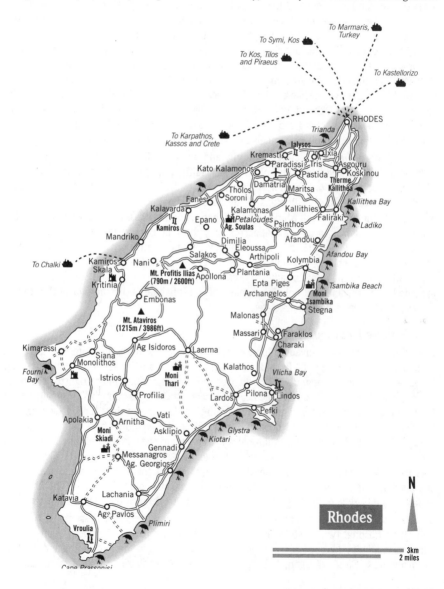

endurance, but as a battle of wits. Over and over again Dimitrios would invent some new ingenious machine, such as the 10-storey Helepolis siege tower, only to have it ingeniously foiled by the Rhodian defenders (who tripped up the Helepolis with a hidden, shallow ditch). After a year both sides grew weary of fighting and made a truce, Rhodes agreeing to assist Dimitrios' father Antigonas in wars except in battles against Ptolemy.

So Dimitrios departed, leaving his vast siege machinery behind. This the Rhodians either sold or melted down to construct a great bronze statue of Helios, their patron god of the sun. The famous sculptor from Líndos, Chares, was put in charge of the project, and in 290 BC, after 12 years of work and at a cost of 20,000 pounds of silver, Chares completed the Colossus, or didn't quite: he found he had made a miscalculation and committed suicide just before it was cast. Standing somewhere between 100 and 140ft tall (at her crown the Statue of Liberty is 111ft), the Colossus did not straddle the entrance of Rhodes harbour, as is popularly believed, but probably stood near the present Castle of the Knights, gleaming bright in the sun, one of the Seven Wonders of the Ancient World. But of all the Wonders the Colossus had the shortest lifespan; in 225 BC, an earthquake cracked its knees and brought it crashing to the ground. The Oracle at Delphi told the Rhodians to leave it there and it lay forlorn until AD 653 when the Saracens, who had captured Rhodes, sold it as scrap to a merchant from Edessa. According to legend, it took 900 camels to transport the bronze to the ships.

In 164 BC, when they had repaired their city and walls, the Rhodians signed a peace treaty with Rome. Alexandria was their only rival in wealth, and tiny Délos, with all its duty-free trade concessions, their only rival in Mediterranean trade. The famous School of Rhetoric on Rhodes attracted all the top Romans of the day—Pompey, Cicero, Cassius, Julius Caesar, Brutus, Cato the Younger and Mark Antony. When Caesar was assassinated, Rhodes as always backed the right horse, in this case Augustus, only this time the wrong horse, Cassius, was in the neighbourhood; he sacked the city, captured its fleet, and sent its treasures to Rome (43–42 BC). It was a blow from which Rhodes never recovered. She lost control of her colonies and islands, and other Roman allies muscled in on her booming trade. In 57 AD St Paul preached on the island and converted many of the inhabitants; by the end of the Roman empire, Rhodes was a sleepy backwater.

Two Hundred Years of Knights

Byzantium brought many invaders and adventurers to Rhodes: Arabs and Saracens (including in 804 a siege by Harun al Rachid, of *Arabian Nights* fame), Genoese, Venetians and Crusaders all passed through; in 1191 Richard the Lionheart and Philip Augustus of France came to recruit mercenaries. After the fall of Jerusalem in 1291, the Knights Hospitallers of St John, dedicated to protecting pilgrims and running hospitals in the Holy Land, took refuge on Cyprus, but by 1306 they had become interested in the wealthier and better-positioned Rhodes. They asked the Emperor Andronicus Palaeológos to cede them the island in return for their loyalty, but after 1204 the Byzantines had learned better than to trust the Franks. The Knights, under Grand Master Foulques de Villaret, then took the matter into their own hands and purchased the Dodecanese from their current occupants: Genoese pirates. The Rhodians weren't impressed, and the Knights had to spend their first three years subduing the natives.

By 1309, with the help of the pope, the Knights were secure in their possession and began to build their hospital (which still exists) and inns in Rhodes town. They built eight inns or auberges in all, one for each of the 'tongues', or nationalities, in the Order (England, France, Germany, Italy, Castile, Aragon, Auvergne and Provence). Each tongue had a bailiff, and the eight bailiffs elected the Grand Master, who lived in a palace. There were never more than 650 men in the Order and, although as always dedicated to the care of pilgrims, their focus shifted to their role as freebooting, front-line defenders of Christendom. Already wealthy, they were given a tremendous boost in 1312, when Pope Clement V and Philip the Fair of France dissolved the fabulously wealthy Knights Templars, confiscated their fortune and gave the Hospitallers a hefty share of the loot. With their new funds, the Knights of St John replaced the fortifications—and continued to replace them up until the 16th century, hiring the best Italian fortification engineers until they could claim one of the most splendid defences of the day.

Meanwhile, the knights had made themselves such a thorn in the side of Muslim shipping that they were besieged by the Sultan of Egypt in 1444 and by Mohammed II the Conqueror in 1480 with 70,000 men, both times without success, thanks to those tremendous walls. Then in 1522 Suleiman the Magnificent moved in with 200,000 troops; the Rhodians (there were 6,000 of them, plus 1,000 Italian mercenaries, and 650 knights) bitterly joked that the Colossus was now coming back at them, in the form of cannon balls. After a frustrating six-month siege, Suleiman was on the point of abandoning Rhodes when a German traitor informed him that, of the original Knights, only 180 survived, and they were on their last legs. The sultan redoubled his efforts and the Knights at last were forced to surrender. In honour of their courage, Suleiman permitted them to leave in safety, with their Christian retainers and possessions. They made their new headquarters in Malta—at the nominal rent of a falcon a year—and in 1565 they successfully withstood a tremendous all-out assault by the Ottoman fleet. After gradually losing sight of their reason for being on Malta, they caved in to Napoleon. In 1831 the Knights re-formed as a benevolent charity in Rome, from where they still fund hospitals and fight leprosy; the English Order, revived in the 19th century, established the St John Ambulance, as well as the St John Ophthalmic Hospital back where it all started, in Jerusalem.

Ottomans and Italians

The Greeks were forced to move outside the walls, which became the exclusive domain of the Turkish and Jewish population of the island. The new Ottoman rulers built a few buildings, but in general left things as they were, content to enjoy Rhodes. When the Rhodians attempted to revolt during the War of Independence, the Turks reacted with atrocities; their popularity dropped even more in the Great Gunpowder Explosion of 1856, when lightning struck a minaret and exploded a powder magazine, blowing much of the Old Town to bits and killing 800 people. The Italians took Rhodes after a siege in 1912, and cheekily claimed that the island was their inheritance from the Knights of St John, and Mussolini, fancying himself as a new Grand Master, had their palace reconstructed to swan around in. He never saw it: war intervened. After 1943 the Germans took over until May 1945; long enough to send most of the island's 2,000-strong Jewish community to the concentration camps. Rhodes, with the rest of the Dodecanese, officially joined Greece in 1948, whereupon the government declared it a free port, boosting its already great tourist potential.

© (0241–)   *Getting There and Around*

By air: Rhodes airport, the third busiest in Greece, *©* 83 400, has recently been enlarged. There are numerous UK, German and Scandinavian direct charters from April to mid-October and nearly a million charter tourists during the season. From Athens, there are at least five daily flights with Olympic, two with Aegean and one with Cronus; from Crete (Herákleon), Olympic and Aegean have three weekly flights;

from Thessaloniki, Olympic has two a week and Aegean has three; Olympic also has flights from Mýkonos (twice a week), Santoríni (five a week), Kárpathos (two a day), Kastellórizo (one a day) and Kássos (three a week). Olympic is at 9 Iérou Lóchou, Rhodes town, ✆ 24 571; Aegean is at the airport, ✆ 98 345; and Cronus as at No.5 25 Martiou, Rhodes town, ✆ 25 444. **Airport Flight Information Desk:** ✆ 83 214, 83 200 or 83 202. The bus to Parádissi passes near the airport every 30 minutes or so until 11pm; taxi fares to town are around 2,500dr. If your return flight is delayed— charters always seem to be—it's only a three-minute walk to the nearest bar and taverna (Anixis) in Parádissi, and the latter stays open until 2am.

By sea: daily **excursion boats** and *Sými I* and *Sými II* ferries from **Mandráki Harbour** to Líndos, Sými (also by hydrofoil) and beaches at Lárdos, Tsambíka, Faliráki, Kallithéa, Ladiko and Kolymbia. Daily caiques ply their way from Kámiros Skala on the west coast to Chálki; for Marmaris, Turkey, there are daily hydrofoils (currently 14,000dr return) and ferries. **Port authority:** ✆ 28 695 and 28 888.

By road: there is a frequent **bus service**. East-coast buses (✆ 24 129) are yellow and depart from Plateía Rimini in Rhodes town; they service Faliraki (18 times daily), Líndos and Kolymbia (8–10 times), Genadi and Psinthos (3–5 times). West-coast buses (✆ 27 706) are white and blue, departing from around the corner by the market; these travel to Kalithéa Thermi (16 times), Koskinou (10 times), Salakos (five times), and Kamiros, Monolithos and Embonas (once). **Taxis** are plentiful and reasonably priced. The central taxi rank is in Plateía Alexandrias, Rhodes town, ✆ 27 666. Radio taxis run round the clock and are a bit more expensive, ✆ 64 712, 66 790 or 64 734. It's worth hiring wheels to get off the beaten track, especially in the interior; nearly anything from four-wheel-drive beach buggies to motorbikes are available, although four wheels are better than two if you want to cover any distances; out of high season prices are negotiable. Note that petrol stations are closed Sunday, holidays and after 7pm.

The **Dodecanese Association of People with Special Needs**, ✆ 73 109, will, with 48-hour warning, provide free transport in special vans to any destination on Rhodes, between 7am and 3pm.

✆ *(0241–)*   ***Tourist Information***

The **EOT** office on the corner of Papágou and Makaríou Street, Rhodes town, ✆ 21 921, ✉ 26 955, *eot-rodos@otenet.gr*, has very helpful multilingual staff and a wide range of maps, leaflets and information (*open Mon–Fri 8–3*). The **Tourist police** have a 24-hour multilingual number, ✆ 27 423, for any information or complaints. **City of Rhodes Tourist Information Centre**, in Plateía Rimini, ✆ 35 945 (*open Mon–Sat 9–8, Sun 9–noon*) is mostly a money exchange. Hotels and both tourist offices have copies of the free and helpful English-language newspaper *Ródos News*. For **recorded info**, call ✆ 78 489.

American consulate: the Voice of America station at Afándou may help, ✆ 52 555. **British consulate:** Mr and Mrs Dimitriádis, 3 P. Mela, ✆ 27 247. **Irish consulate:** Mr Skevos Mougros, 111 Amerikís, ✆ 22 461.

Internet: in Rhodes Old Town, Mango café-bar, Plateía Dor: and . : os, obliges; otherwise, head for Rockstyle, 7 Dimokratías, near the stadium. (For Líndos, *see* that section.)

Post office: on Mandráki harbour, Rhodes town (*open Mon–Fri 7.30am–8pm*).

Telephones: in Rhodes town, head for the OTE, 91 Amerikis (*open daily 7am–11pm*).

© *(0241–)*   *Watersports*

Dive Med, © 33 654, and Waterhoppers, © 38 146, both operate from Mandráki harbour in Rhodes town, although the only permitted diving is at Kalithéa. Cape Prassonís is the place to windsurf: Procenter, © 91 045, *procenter.prasonisi@ eunet.at*, operates from April to October.

Festivals

Lenten carnival **just before Easter**; **14 June**, Profítis Amós in Faliráki; Scandinavian **midsummer** festivities in Rhodes town, organized by tour operators (yes, really); **28 June**, in Líndos; **first 10 days of July**, Musical Meetings in Rhodes; **29–30 July**, Ag. Soúlas in Soroní, with donkey races; **26 July**, Ag. Panteleímonos in Siána; in **August**, dance festivals in Kallithiés, Maritsa and Embónas; **14–22 August**, Tis Panagías in Kremastí; **26 August**, Ag. Fanoúrious in the Old Town; **5 September**, Ag. Trías near Rhodes Town; **7 September**, in Moní Tsambíkas (for fertility); **13 September**, Stávros in Apóllona and Kallithiés; **26 September**, Ag. Ioánnis Theológos in Artamíti; **18 October**, Ag. Lukás in Afándou; **7 November** in Archángelos.

Excursions on Rhodes

1 From Líndos: head west to Moní Thari, the oldest Rhodian monastery to survive, and on to the lovely traditional village of Ag. Isidoros; from here, you're close to the delightful stone village of Siana. Continue south to Monólithos, with its spectacularly positioned Knights' castle, and on to hilltop Moní Skiádi, which boasts a miraculous icon. If you like wind buffetting, head for the southern tip; otherwise cut east and back up to Líndos, stopping at any of the tempting beaches en route.

2 From Líndos or Rhodes town: travel to the remarkably preserved west-coast site of Kámiros; pause for lunch in little Arthípoli and then head for shady Sálakos, set in forests and surrounded by panoramic walks.

3 From Rhodes town: head out to Mount Filérimos, the acropolis-citadel at Ialysós, and then down to enchanting, perfumed Butterfly Valley, Petaloúdes; from there, trails lead up to two monasteries with inspirational views (and huge festivities on 30 July).

Rhodes Town

Spread across the northern tip of the island, Rhodes (ΡΟΔΟΣ) is the largest town, with a population of 50–60,000 (out of the 98,000 on the island), and capital of the Dodecanese. It celebrated its 2,400th anniversary in 1993. Rhodes divides neatly into Old and New Towns. Tourism reigns in both—prepare to be bombarded by English signs—although these days the New Town is increasingly filling up with designer boutiques aimed at the prosperous Rhodians and visiting upmarket Greeks who come to shop duty-free. The medieval city is so remarkably preserved it looks like a film set in places, and has often been used as such (for example, *Pascali's Island*).

Rhodes presents an opulent face to the sea, and sailing in is much the prettiest way to arrive and get your bearings. The massive walls of the Old Town, crowned by the Palace of the Grand Masters, rise out of a lush subtropical garden; graceful minarets and the arcaded waterfront market, bright with strings of lightbulbs at night, add an exotic touch. Monumental pseudo-Venetian public buildings trying to look serious decorate the shore to the left, while opposite three 14th-century **windmills** (down from the original 15) turn lazily behind a forest of masts. Yachts, smaller ferries and excursion boats dock at the smallest of three harbours, **Mandráki** (ΜΑΝΔΡΑΚΙ). The entrance is guarded by the lighthouse and fort of **Ag. Nikólaos**, built in the 1460s to bear the brunt of the Turkish attacks, and a **bronze stag and doe**, marking where the Colossus may have stood. Under the Knights, a chain crossed the port here, and every ship that entered had to pay a 2% tax of its cargo value towards the war effort. Larger ferries, any craft to Turkey, and cruise ships enter the **commercial harbour** (ΕΜΠΟΡΙΚΟΣ ΛΙΜΕΝΑΣ) nearer the Old Town walls.

These **walls** are a masterpiece of late medieval fortifications, and, although you'll often be tempted to climb up for a walk or view, access is by guided tour only (*Tues and Sat, meet in front of the Palace of the Grand Master at 2.30; adm exp*), although you can get a good, free squiz at them by walking round the bottom of the dry moat: the main entrance is off Plateía Alexandrías. Constructed over the old Byzantine walls under four of the most ambitious Grand Masters (d'Aubusson, d'Amboise, del Carretto and Villiers de l'Isle Adam), they stretch 4km and average 38ft thick. Curved the better to deflect missiles, the landward sides were safeguarded by the 100ft-wide dry moat. Each national group of Knights was assigned its own bastion and towers to defend, except the Italians, who were the best sailors and put in charge of the Knights' fleet.

Of the many gates that linked the walled Old Town with the village outside, the most magnificent is the Gate of Emery d'Amboise (**Píli Ambouaz**, in Greek) near the Palace of the Grand Masters, built in 1512 (entrance off Papágou Street). Under the Turks, all Greeks had to be outside the walls by sundown or forfeit their heads.

The Old Town (ΠΑΛΑΙΑ ΠΟΛΗ)

The town within these walls was fairly dilapidated when the Italians took charge. They restored much, but fortunately lost the war before they could get on with their plan to widen all the streets for cars and build a ring road. To keep any such future heretical notions at bay, UNESCO has declared the Old Town a World Heritage Site, and is providing funds for historical restoration and infrastructure, and burying electric and phone cables.

Entering the aforementioned Gate d'Amboise, passing the tablecloth sellers and quick-draw portrait artists, you'll find yourself in the inner sanctum or **Collachium**, where the Knights could retreat if the outer curtain wall were taken. By the gate, at the highest point, a castle within a castle, stands the **Palace of the Grand Masters** (*open Tues–Fri 8–7, Sat and Sun 8–3, Mon 12.30–7; adm exp*), built over a temple to Helios; some archaeologists believe that the Colossus actually stood here, overlooking the harbour. Construction of this citadel was completed in 1346, modelled after the Popes' palace in Avignon—not by accident: 14 of the 19 Grand Masters on Rhodes were French and French was the official spoken language of the Order. Underground rooms were used as storage and as a refuge for the civilian population in case of attack. The Turks used the whole as a prison, even after the Great Gunpowder Explosion of 1856, when the first floor caved in, and the Italians did the same until Mussolini ordered that it be reconstructed as one of his famous summer villas. The Italians covered the floors with lovely Roman mosaics from Kos, a hotch-potch of Renaissance furniture, and installed a lift and modern plumbing, but war broke out and ended before the Duce had enjoyed its 158 rooms (don't panic: only a tenth are open to the public). Note the huge marble coat-of-arms on one of the fireplaces: 'Restored by Vitt. Eman. III, King and Emperor 1939.' On the ground floor, two excellent permanent exhibitions have been set up: **The City of Rhodes from its Foundation to the Roman Period** and **Rhodes from the 4th Century to its Capture by the Turks**, with English translations and full of curious sidelines on lightweight Rhodian bricks (used for the dome of Ag. Sophia in Constantinople) and the Knights' production of sugar, an item worth its weight in gold in the Middle Ages. There's a collection of detached frescoes, coins, icons and the tombstone of the Grand Master Villier de l'Isle Adam, who defied Suleiman the Magnificent's advance for six months even though outmanned nearly 40 to one.

The main street descending from the palace into the heart of the Collachium is a favourite of film makers: quiet, evocative, cobblestoned **Odós Ippotón** (Knights' Street), beautifully restored by the Italians. It passes under the arcaded **Loggia** that originally linked the Palace to the Knights' 14th-century cathedral of St John, where the Grand Masters were buried; after being shattered in the Gunpowder Explosion, a Turkish school was built in the midst of the ruins. Ippotón has most of the Knights' inns, where they had meetings and meals. There were eight, each housing a 'tongue' and emblazoned with the arms of the Grand Master in charge when it was built: the **Inn of Provence** on the left and the two buildings of the **Inn of Spain** on the right, then the French chapel and elaborate **Inn of France** (1509), adorned with escutcheons and crocodile gargoyles; as there were always more French knights than any other 'tongue', their inn was the most spacious. Next door stands a townhouse, belonging to Villier de l'Isle Adam; opposite was the Knights' entrance to the hospital. The **Inn of Italy** (1519) stands at the foot of the street.

Two squares open up at the end of the street; just to right, on the corner of Plateía Moussion, stands the much restored **Inn of England** (1483), abandoned in 1534, when the Pope excommunicated Henry VIII. It was hard hit by an earthquake in 1851, then rebuilt by the British, bombed and rebuilt again in 1947. The British consul of Rhodes (*see* above for the address) has the key. Opposite stands the flamboyant Gothic hospital of the Knights, built between 1440 and 1481 and restored by the Italians in 1918, now home to the **Archaeology Museum,** still awaiting a much needed overhaul (*open 8–2.30, closed Mon; adm*). The long ward, where the Knights' surgeons (from the ranks of commoners) cared for patients in elaborate canopy beds, still has its heraldic devices. In the sculpture gallery the star attraction is Lawrence Durrell's beloved 3rd-century BC *Marine Venus* (marine because she was found in the sea) and the pretty kneeling *Aphrodite of Rhodes* (90 BC), combing out her hair after emerging from the sea; also note the bust of Helios from the 2nd century BC, complete with holes in the head to hold his metal sunrays. Ceramics, stelae, Mycenaean jewellery, and mosaics round off the collection. In the adjacent square, 11th-century **Panagía Kástrou**, used by the Knights as their cathedral of St Mary until they built their own, now contains a little **Byzantine Museum** (*open 8.30–3, closed Mon; adm*), with frescoes and icons from disused churches across the island and Chálki.

Through the arch, charming Plateía Argyrokástro has the loveliest inn, the 15th-century **Inn of Auvergne** (now a cultural centre), with a **fountain** made from a Byzantine baptismal font. Here, too, is the 14th-century **Palace of the Armeria**, constructed by Grand Master Roger de Pins as the Knights' first hospital on Rhodes. The **Museum of Decorative Arts** (*open 8.30–3, closed Mon; adm*) has folk arts and handicrafts from all over the Dodecanese, including costumes, embroideries and a reconstruction of a traditional room. Nearby, in Plateía Sýmis, is the **Municipal Art Gallery** (*open 8–2, closed Sun*), housing a significant collection of 20th-century Greek painting and engraving. Also in the square are the ruins of a 3rd-century BC **Temple of Aphrodite**, discovered by the Italians in 1922. Fragments of another temple of the same epoch, dedicated to **Dionysos**, are in a corner behind the Ionian and Popular Bank. The Italians reopened the two harbour gates that the Turks had blocked up, **Píli Eleftherías** to Mandráki ('Freedom Gate' named by the Italians, who regarded themselves as Rhodes' liberators) and **Píli Navarchio** (or Arsenal Gate) to the marina and Commerical Harbour.

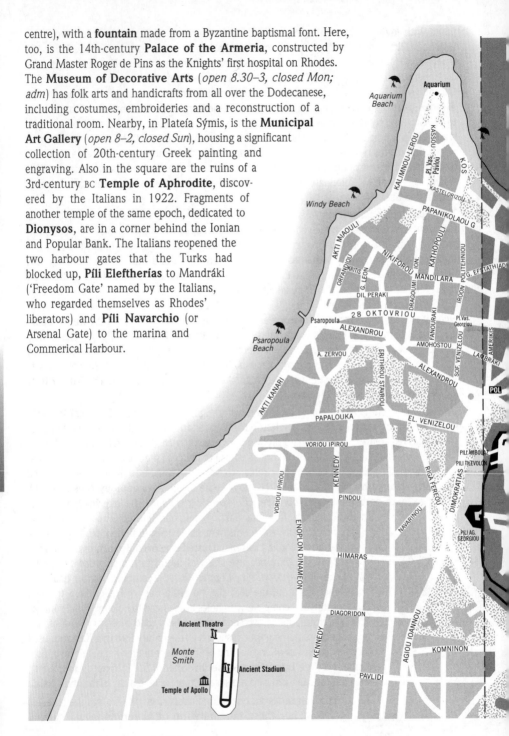

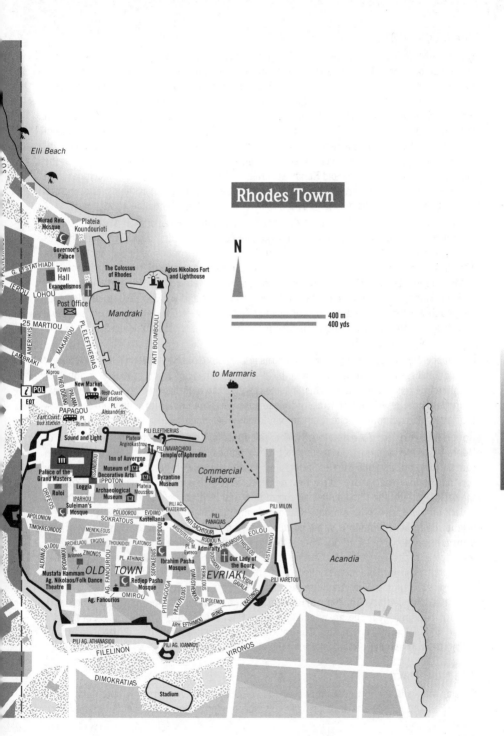

Rhodes Town

N

400 m
400 yds

Elli Beach

Murad Reis Mosque
Plateia Koundourioti
Governor's Palace
Town Hall
Evangelismos
Post Office
25 MARTIOU
G. FESTATHIADI
IEROU
LOHOU
LAMBRAKI
AMERIKIS
MAKARIOU
PL ELEFTHERIAS
THEO DORAKI
PI. Kiprou
New Market
West Coast bus station
PAPAGOU
East Coast bus station
PI. Rimini.
PI. Alexandrias
POL
EOT
PALAMA
The Colossus of Rhodes
Agios Nikolaos Fort and Lighthouse
Mandraki
AKTI BOUMBOULI

to Marmaris

PILI ELEFTHERIAS
Sound and Light
Plateia Argirokastrou
PILI NAVARCHIOU
Temple of Aphrodite
Inn of Auvergne
Museum of Decorative Arts
IPPOTON
Palace of the Grand Masters
Archaeological Museum
Byzantine Museum
Plateia Moussiou
Loggia
Roloi
IPARHOU
Suleiman's Mosque
OREOS
APOLONION
TIMOKREONDOS
POLIDOROU
EVDIMO
SOKRATOUS
Kastellania
PILI AG. EKATERINIS
PILI PANAGIAS
PILI MILON

Commercial Harbour

MENEKLEOUS
ARCHELAOU
ERGIOU
THOUKIDIDI
PLATONOS
RODIOU K.
AKTI SACHTOURI
ARISTOTELOUS
EOLOU
PINDAROU
THRESEOS
KISTHINIOU
ALEXANDRIDOU
IPPODAMOU
ZINONOS
Arionos
PL. ATHINAS
SOFOKLEOUS
EVRIPIDOU
Ibrahim Pasha Mosque
PI. M. Evreon
Admiralty
DIMOSTHENOUS
DOSIADOU
PERIKLEOUS
Our Lady of the Bourg
Mustafa Hammam
Ag. Nikolaos/Folk Dance Theatre
AG. FANOURIOU
Redjep Pasha Mosque
OMIROU
Ag. Fanourios
PITHAGORA
PRAXITELOUS
DIMOSTHENOUS
IRINIS
EVRIAKI
GAVALA
TIDIA
EKATONIS
TLIPOLEMOU
PILI KARETOU

Acandia

OLD TOWN

PILI AG. ATHANASIOU
FILELINON
PILI AG. IOANNOU
ARH. EFTHIMIOU
VIRONOS
DIMOKRATIAS
Stadium

The Medieval Town

South of the Collachium of the Knights is the former Turkish bazaar and shopping district, centred on bustling **Sokrátous Street**, to this day thick with tourist and duty-free luxury shops. Midway along, at No.17, the Turkish-owned *kafeneíon* has remained steadfastly unchanged for the past century: some say, ditto its coffee-drinking, backgammon-playing clientèle. At the top of Sokrátous Street stands the slender minaret of the lovely, faded red **Mosque of Suleiman** (*now closed*), built in 1523 by Suleiman the Magnificent to celebrate his conquest of Rhodes. The **Muselman Library** (*open Mon–Fri 7.30–2.30 and 6–9, Sat and Sun 8–noon*) opposite (1793) contains rare Persian and Arabian manuscripts and illuminated copies of the Koran. Two precious 700-year-old Korans stolen in 1990 and worth 100 million drachmas have now been recovered and are back on show. Behind Suleiman's mosque, the Byzantine clock tower, **To Roloi**, has splendid views over the town, if you're lucky enough to find it open.

South of Sokrátous Street, the Turkish Quarter dissolves into a zigzag of narrow streets, where charming Turkish balconies of latticed wood project beside crumbling stone arches and houses built directly over the street. On scruffy Plateía Arionos, off Archeláos Street, the **Mustafa Mosque** keeps company with the atmospheric **Mustafa Hammam**, or Turkish baths, built in 1558 and remodeled in 1765, when the relaxation rooms were added. Still heated by a ton of olive logs a day, it has mosaic floors and marble fountains and a lovely ceiling, divided into men's and women's labyrinthine sections (*open Tues–Fri 11–7, Sat 8–6; bring own soap and towel; adm*). Another old mosque, **Ibrahim Pasha** (1531), is off Sofokléous Street; executions took place in front of it.

On Hippocrátes Square, where Sokrátous turns into Aristotélous Street, stands the picturesque Gothic-Renaissance **Kastellania**, built by d'Amboise in 1507, perhaps as a tribunal or commercial exchange for the Knights. It stands at the head of Pithágora Street, the main street of **Evriakí**, the Jewish quarter; according to Josephus, the community dates from the 1st century AD; later chronicles cite them among Rhodes' defenders against the Turks.

Continuing east along Aristotélous Street, the **Plateía Evrión Martyrón** (the Square of Hebrew Martyrs) honours the memory of the Rhodians sent off to die in the concentration camps. Just south stands Rhodes' remaining synagogue, highly decorated and still in use; commemorative plaques pay homage to the deported Jewish population and a small display at the back illustrates the Rhodian Jewish community and its diaspora. The so-called **Admirality** is back on the square, with a bronze seahorse fountain; it was more likely the seat of Rhodes' bishop. From here, Pindárou Street continues to the impressive ruins of **Our Lady of the Bourg**, once the largest Catholic church on Rhodes, built by the Knights in thanksgiving for their defeat of the Turks in 1480 but never the same after it took a British bomb in the war. The Turkish and Jewish Quarters offer many other little cobbled lanes to explore, dotted with old frescoed churches converted into mosques and converted back again: it's worth trying to find little 13th-century **Ag. Fanourios** with its fine frescoes off Omirou, hidden behind a modern building, near the abandoned **Redjep Pasha Mosque** (1588), once completely coated with colourful Persian tiles. The gate at the end of Pithágora Street, **Píli Ag. Ioánnou**, or Red Door, is another demonstration of the walls' strength.

The New Town

Outside the walls, the row of seafront cafés look enticingly over Mandráki harbour, but they're overpriced and mainly aim at dragging in unsuspecting greenhorns. Just behind them, in the

Italian-built octagonal **New Market**, tomatoes and watermelons have been replaced by gýros and *souvláki* stands. Further along Mandráki is an austere ensemble of Mussolini-style public buildings built in the 1920s—post office, theatre and town hall. The Italians also left Rhodes some rather more lighthearted architecture: the **Governor's Palace**, a pseudo-Doge's Palace decorated with a garish red diaper pattern, and the cathedral **Evangelísmos**, a copy of St John's, the cathedral blown up in the Gunpowder accident. The fountain is a copy of Viterbo's Gothic Fontana Grande.

The Turks regarded Rhodes as an island paradise, and many Muslim notables in exile (including a Shah of Persia) chose to spend the rest of their lives here. Many lie buried in the cemetery north of the municipal theatre, next to the **Mosque of Murad Reis**, named after the admiral of the Egyptian sultan who was killed during the siege of Rhodes in 1522 and buried in a turban-shaped tomb, or *turbeh*. The mosque has a lovely minaret reconstructed by the last people you would guess—the Greek government. Stretching along the shore from here is Rhodes' busiest strand, shingly **Élli Beach**, sheltered from the prevailing southwest winds and packed chock-a-block with parasols and sunbeds; signs everywhere warn about illegal beach touts poisoning people with out-of-date food. There's a diving platform for high divers and a lifeguard, but people floating on airbeds should beware of being swept out to sea.

At the northernmost tip of the island is the **Aquarium** (*open daily in season 9–9, otherwise 9–4.30; adm*), built by the Italians in 1938 and the only one in Greece, with tanks of Mediterranean fish and sea turtles, a pair of which are over 100 years old, and a startling collection of stuffed denizens of the deep, their twisted grimaces the result not of any prolonged agony but of amateur taxidermy. Local farmers have contributed an eight-legged calf and four-legged chicken for more horror-show fun. On the headland, **Aquarium Beach** has deep water, but its breezes make it more popular for windsurfing and paragliding than sunsoaking; ditto **Windy Beach**, which stretches down to Aktí Miaoúli. A bit further south, **Psaropoúla** is a safe, sandy beach running from the Hotel Blue Sky to the Belvedere. Although often breezy, the biggest danger is crossing the busy road to get to it. South of Psaropoúla are numerous small coves with safe swimming unless the wind is strong. Women should beware another drawback: the area is nicknamed Flasher's Paradise.

Just Outside Rhodes Town

City bus no.5 heads south of the New Town to the ancient acropolis of Rhodes, **Monte Smith**, named after Admiral Sydney Smith who in 1802 kept track of Napoleon's Egyptian escapades from here; today most people come up for the romantic sunset. On the way (North Epírou Street) are the ruins of an **Asklepeion**, dedicated to the god of healing, and a **Cave of the Nymphs**. On the top of Monte Smith, the Italians have partly reconstructed a 2nd-century BC Doric **Temple of Pythian Apollo**, who was later associated with Rhodian Helios, and a 3rd-century BC **Stadium**, which sometimes hosts classical dramas in the summer. A few columns remain of temples of Zeus and Athena. The adjacent, reconstructed **Ancient Theatre** is the only square one found on the islands.

City bus no.3 will take you the 2km out to **Rodíni Park**, with its cypresses, pines, oleanders, maples, peacocks and **Deer Park** (the Delphic oracle told the ancient Rhodians to import deer to solve their snake problem, and they have been here ever since). Rodíni Park marks the spot where Aeschines established his celebrated School of Rhetoric in 330 BC, where the likes of Julius Caesar and Cicero learned how to speak—there's a rock-cut tomb from the 4th century BC, the so-called 'Tomb of Ptolemy', and the ruins of a Roman aqueduct. The Knights grew their medicinal herbs here, and now merry drinkers can join Rodíni's peacocks for the **Rhodes Wine Festival**, recently resurrected by the council during three weeks in late July–early August with music, dance and food. Special buses transport revellers to and from Mandráki harbour. During the evenings you can try Rhodes' own wines: Chevaliers de Rhodes; Ilios; the prize-winning premium red from CAIR, Archontiko; and the excellent Emery white, Villaré; as well as other Greek vintages.

Shopping

Rhodes' duty-free status has made for some odd sights; it may be the island of the sun, but nowhere on earth will you find more fur shops, or umbrella shops: a popular model opens up to reveal Michael Jackson's mug in alarming proportions. In the Old town Sokrátous is the main bazaar street, and Sakhellaridis, in Plateía Moussíou, is the place to look for Greek music. The New Town near Mandráki is full of designer shops and a Marks and Spencer for the homesick. For shoes, try Platéia Kýprou; for a reasonably priced tailor-made suit made from the finest British fabrics, try the Kakakios Brothers, 47 G. Labráki, who made them for the likes of Gregory Peck and Anthony Quinn. The biggest market in the Dodecanese takes place on Zefiros Street (by the cemetery) every Saturday morning; get there early if you want to find a bargain. Another, lesser one takes place on Wednesdays, at Vironas by the Stadium.

Rhodes Town ✉ *85100,* ✆ *(0241–)*　　　　　　**Where to Stay**

Rhodes has a plethora of accommodation in every class and price from one of the most expensive hotels ever to be built in Greece to humble village rooms. Most places are booked solid by package companies, some for winter breaks too, so if you're island-hopping in high season it's worth phoning ahead. On the Internet: *www.helios. gr/dis/rhodes* has more info on hotels, and sights, while *www.helios.gr/hotels/* offers on-line descriptions and bookings for a selection of luxury to C-class hotels across the island.

luxury

Most of the luxury hotels are in Ixiá and Triánda, although the mega-luxury, seven-star suites at the **Rodos Park**, next to the historic centre at 12 Riga Fereou, ✆ 24 612, 🖷 24 613 (*L*), in town overlooking the park are just as opulent, with private Jacuzzis, pool, health club, ballroom and every other amenity. The **Grand Hotel Rhodes** on Aktí Miaoúli, ✆ 26 284, 🖷 35 589 (*L*), has one of the island's casinos, a nightclub, tennis courts and what's reputed to be the largest swimming pool in the country.

expensive

The **Plaza Hotel Best Western** on Ieroú Lóchou, ✆ 22 501, 🖷 22 544, *plaza@otenet.gr* (*A*), has been done up and is centrally situated with a pool, baby-sitting and English buffet breakfast. **S. Nicolis**, 61 Ippodámou, ✆ 34 561, 🖷 32 034 (*E*), offers atmospheric accommodation in a lovely old house in the heart of the Old Town with excellent bed and breakfast, large garden and rooftop terrace with great views. The Greek-Danish proprietors also have new apartments to sleep four nearby and a cheaper pension; booking essential. **Marco Polo Mansion**, 42 Ag. Fanouríou, ✆/🖷 25 562 (*exp*), is a delightfully converted Turkish house, tastefully furnished and with hammam; the breakfasts are recommended. Recently renovated **Marie**, 7 Kos, ✆ 30 577, 🖷 22 751 (*C*), is near Élli beach, and offers a pool, sea sports, and satelite TV.

It was good enough for Michael Palin on his *Pole to Pole* jaunt so the **Cavo d'Oro**, © 36 980, is well worth a try. The delightful 13th-century house at 15 Kisthiníou, near the Commercial Harbour, has been beautifully restored by the owner and his German wife and he'll even meet you from the ferry. **Victoria**, 22 25th Mariou, © 24 626, ◉ 36 675 (*C*), is central, family-run, and the owner's son, a UK-trained doctor, has consulting rooms next door. Near the Old Town **Popi**, Stratigou Zisi and Maliaraki 21, © 23 479, ◉ 33 453, has studios in the old fashioned Greek style, each sleeping four. **Paris**, 88 Ag. Fanouríou, © 26 356 (*D*), has nice rooms and a quiet courtyard with shady orange and banana trees, and prices at the bottom of this range.

One of the best value is the **Ambassadeur**, 53 Othonos and Amalías, © 24 679 (*C*). Recommended is **Andreas**, 28D Omírou, © 34 156, ◉ 74 285, under friendly French-Greek management and with uplifting views of the Old Town from some of the rooms and the bar. In the heart of the Old Town, **Attiki**, Haritos and Theofiliskou, © 27 767 (*E*), is quietly tucked away in the corner, in a medieval building, a bit dishevelled but children welcome. *Open all year.* La Luna, © 25 856 (*E*), and its bar are in a perfectly quiet courtyard with hammam, next to a tiny church on Ierokleous just off Orfeos. *Open all year.* Some of the cheap backpackers' haunts have become a bit unsavoury, but **Spot**, Perikléous 21, © 34 737 (*E*), is very good value with light, airy rooms plus en suite bathrooms; **Maria's Rooms**, on Menekléous, © 22 169, are a comfortable choice around a quiet courtyard. Nearby the **Iliana**, 1 Gavála, © 30 251 (*E*), is in an old Jewish family house and has a small bar and terrace; no charge for childen under 10 and cheap for everyone else. **Minos Pension**, 5 Omírou, © 31 813, is also pristine and offers panoramic roof-garden views.

Rhodes Town © (0241–)   **Eating Out**

Rhodes has a cosmopolitan range of eating places from luxury hotel restaurants to dives selling tripe (*patsás*). The Rhodians are to the Greek islands what the Parisians are to France. They are fashionable, often fickle, and love new food trends. Rhodes has several good places serving a Greek version of *nouvelle cuisine*, some just out of town (*see* p.255). In the New Town with its strong Italian influence you can eat great authentic pizza, pasta and other Italian dishes as well as fast food and burgers (the local rivalry is Greece's Goody's vs. Ohio's Wendy's), or there's Danish, Swedish, Indian, Chinese, French, Mexican and even Yorkshire cuisine on the menu. And then there's Greek...

New Town

Probably the best place for *mezédes* is **Palia Istoria** ('Old Story'), © 32 421 (*exp*), on the corner of Mitrópoleos and Dendrínou south of the new stadium. This award-winning restaurant isn't cheap but you get what you pay for—an imaginative array of dishes from celery hearts in *avgolémono* sauce to scallops with mushrooms and arti-chokes, and a good choice of vegeterian dishes. Food is served out under the pergola in a private house atmosphere; the fruit salad has twenty kinds of fruit. Excellent Greek wine list; booking advisable; splurge for a taxi.

Ellinikon, 29 Alexandrou Diákou, ✆ 28 111, is another popular choice with the locals, serving a choice of Greek and international dishes and excellent desserts (*6,000dr*). The wacky **7.5 ΘΑΥΜΑ** ('Wonder') at Dilperáki 15, ✆ 39 805 (*mod–exp*), advertises 'food, drink and party hats since 292 BC' and turns out to be Swedish chefs, ancient Greek décor, Eastern-inspired dishes and seriously good food served in a secret garden. One of the best and most authentic tavernas for lunch is **Christos** out in the suburb of Zéfiros beyond the commercial harbour. A favourite with local families and taxis drivers—no problem finding it—food is excellent, good value and accompanied by an astonishing range of ouzos. Another genuine, friendly ouzerie is **Steno**, Ag. Anargíron (just south of Ag. Athanasiou gate). For a real taste of Denmark try **Dania** at Iroon Polytechniou 3, ✆ 20 540 (*mod*), near the Royal Bank of Scotland, with traditional herring dishes and a running smorgasbord on Sunday evenings. The New Market is full of holes in the wall offering good 'n' greasy *gýros* with outdoor tables.

Old Town

After an aperitif, plunge into the maze of backstreets, which are almost deserted after about 8pm—in some industrious shops you'll see tailors and cobblers still hard at work and you'll find a wide range of eating places, some still untouristy and authentic, others all the rage with trendy locals. **Alexis**, with tables around a Turkish fountain on Sokrátous Street, is one of the top fish restaurants, expensive but good. For cheap and cheerful Greek staples try **Ioánnis**, under the Sydney Hotel in Apéllou Street. **Nireas**, 22 Plateía Sofokléous, is ace for Greek home cooking (booking advisable, ✆ 21 703). **Araliki**, 45 Aristofánous, offers superb *mezédes* in a medieval setting. Home-style **Dodekanissos**, 45 Plateía Evrión Martyrón, ✆ 28 412, has moderate-priced seafood and an exceptionally good shrimp *saganáki*; another old but distinctly pricey favourite is **Dinoris**, 14 Plateía Moussíou, ✆ 35 530, tucked down a narrow alley by the museum, with a romantic garden patio and more lovely fish; **Fotis**, 8 Menekleóus St, ✆ 27 359, does excellent grilled fish—simple and delicious.

Cleo's on Ag. Fanouríou is one of the most elegant places to dine in the heart of the medieval city, serving upmarket Italian or French cuisine (to reserve, call ✆ 28 415). At the other end of the scale, join the working men for a bowl of *patsás* soup at **Meraklis**, 32 Aristotélous (*open 3am–7am*), or **Patsas Sotiris** in an alley off Sokrátous.

Rhodes Town ✆ *(0241–)*　　　　　　　　　　**Entertainment and Nightlife**

Rhodes has something for everyone, with around 600 bars in the town alone. There are discos with all the latest sounds, laser shows and swimming pools; Irish pubs; theme bars; super-cool cocktail bars or live-music tavernas in restored Old Town houses; bars full of gyrating girls and wet T-shirt nights; and even simple *ouzeries* where a game of backgammon is the high spot (notably at 76 Sokvátous Street). The island has all kinds of music from traditional folk sung to the *lýra*, funk, soul, house and rap to vintage Elvis. Traditional Greeks head for the late-night **bouzoúki club** at Élli Beach, while for more sophisticated Greek sounds, the **Grand Hotel** on Aktí Miaoúli has the **Moons Rock**, featuring top bouzouki singers and musicians, and a **casino**, ✆ 24 458 (no jeans or shorts), although it now has to compete with a new casino operated by Playboy International in the handsome Hotel des Roses, a 1930s landmark. For a romantically intimate garden evening among the jasmine, there's nearby **Christos**, 59 Dilperaki.

Orfanídou Street just in from Akti Miaouli is known as the street of bars—Irish **Flanagan's**, **Colorado** (with pub, club and bar), **Hard Rock Caffé** (*sic*) and **Down Under Bar** are currently popular—and **Diákou Street** to the south is also heaving with nightlife, British and Scandinavian tourists spilling out of the bars into the road in high season. Rockers should head for the ever popular **Sticky Fingers**, A. Zervou 6, south of Psaropoula, or to live out your fantasies in a totally themed and tropical environment, head for the **Blue Lagoon Pool Bar**, No.2 25 Martíou. In the Old Town, **O Mylos**, just off Sokrátous, is a pretty open garden music bar, or join the smart set in the clock-tower, **To Roloi**, up the ramp on Orféos and distinctly pricey, or follow the cognoscenti to the fabulous **Karpouzi**, in a lovely medieval building off Sokrátous in the Old Town with *rembetíka*, wine and *mezédes*. For an Antipodean atmosphere, head for **Café Besara**, 11 Sofokléous, never dull and featuring live music three times a week.

You can take in a film (subtitled, in the original language) at one of the open-air cinemas (indoors out of season): the **Metropol**, corner of Venetoken and Vironos Streets near the stadium, the nearby **Pallas** on Dimokratías, or at the **Muncipal Cinema**, by the town hall, with artier fare. The history of Rhodes unfolds at the **Son et Lumière** show in the Palace of the Grand Masters (*in English on Mon and Tues at 8.15pm, Wed, Fri and Sat at 9.15pm, Thurs 10.15pm*). Alternatively, watch real if coolly professional **traditional Greek folk dances** by the Nelly Dimoglóu Company in the Old Town Theatre, Androníkou (*May–Oct Mon, Wed and Fri 9.20pm–11pm; for information © 20 157 or 29 085; dance lessons also available*). Bop till you drop at **Le Palais** disco or **Privato**, 2 Iliadon, © 33 267.

Western Suburbs: Rhodes Town to Ancient Ialysós and Mt Filérimos

On the way out of town, look out for the little ethnic houses on the left at **Kritiká**, built by Turkish immigrants from Crete facing their homeland. **Triánda** (TPIANTA) or Tris, the modern name for Ialysós, has become the island's prime hotel area, and Ialysós Avenue, which runs via **Ixiá** into Rhodes town, is lined with apartments, hotels and luxury complexes out for the conference trade all the year round, as well as catering for rich summer clientèle. The beaches along here are a favourite of windsurfers (nearly every hotel has a pool for calmer swims), the sea is a lovely turquoise colour, and there are views across to Turkey. This coast was settled by Minoans in 1600 BC, and may have been damaged in the eruptions and subsequent tidal wave from Santoríni; more recently this golden mile has been devastated by neon-lit bars, fast-food places and eateries providing English breakfasts and *smorgasbord.*

Triánda village occupies the not completely excavated site of **ancient Ialysós**, the least important of the three Dorian cities. When the Phoenicians inhabited Ialysós, an oracle foretold that they would only leave when crows turned white and fish appeared inside the water jars. Iphicles, who beseiged the town, heard the prediction and with the help of a servant planted fish in the amphorae and daubed a few ravens with plaster. The Phoenicians duly fled (and whatever the ancient Greek for 'suckers' might have been, we can be sure Iphicles said it). Ialysós was the birthplace of the boxer Diagoras, praised by Pindar in the *Seventh Olympian Ode*, but with the foundation of the city of Rhodes it went into such a decline that when

Strabo visited in the 1st century AD he found a mere village, albeit with a rich, extensive cemetery that yielded the Mycenaean jewellery in the archaeology museum.

The main interest in Ialysós lies in the beautiful garden-like acropolis-citadel above Triánda, on **Mount Filérimos**, thought to be the initial nucelus of the 15th-century BC Achaean settlement of Achaia (*open 8–6, closed Mon; adm; wear modest dress to visit the monastery*). John Cantacuzene defended the Byzantine fortress on the site against the Genoese in 1248 and Suleiman the Magnificent made it his base during the final assault on the Knights in 1522. Built over the foundations of a Phoenician temple are the remains of the great 3rd-century BC **Temple of Athena Polias and Zeus Polieus**, in turn partly covered by Byzantine churches. A 4th-century **Doric fountain** with lionhead spouts has been reconstructed, but the main focal point is the monastery of **Our Lady of Filérimos**, converted by the Knights from a 5th-century basilica church and heavily restored by the Italians. Reached by a cypress-lined flight of steps, the monastery and its domed chapels wear the coat-of-arms of Grand Master d'Aubusson, under whom the church diplomatically had both Catholic and Orthodox altars. Beneath the ruins of a small Byzantine church with a cruciform font is the tiny underground chapel of **Ag. Geórgios**, with frescoes from the 1300s. The monks will be pleased to sell you a bottle of their own green liqueur called Sette, made from seven herbs.

For more wonderful views, there's an uphill path from the monastery lined with the Stations of the Cross. In 1934 the Italian governor erected an enormous Cross on the summit although seven years later the Italians themselves shot it down to prevent the Allies from using it as a target. In 1994 the Lions Club financed the current one, 52ft high, dominating an otherwise very secular coast.

Rhodes Town ✉ *85100,* ✆ *(0241–)*   **Where to Stay**

The Ixiá and Triánda strip is one long stretch of hotels, with the prime luxury compounds in Ixiá. At the top of the list is the vast **Grecotel Rhodos Imperial**, ✆ 75 000, ✉ 76 690 (*L; lux*), the most luxurious five-star hotel on the island and the most expensive hotel project in Greece so far, with a range of top restaurants, watersports centre, fitness club, children's mini club, and every delight from *syrtáki* dance lessons to Greek language courses, squash to cabaret.

The **Miramare Wonderland**, ✆ 96 251/4, ✉ 95 954 (*L; lux*), was built in 1998 for those 'seeking paradise on earth', with swish cottages slap on the beach, all facilities and even a train around the complex! Another rival, the **Rodos Palace**, ✆ 25 222, ✉ 25 350 (*L; lux*), is one of the most up-to-date hotels in the Med, with twin digital state-of-the-art communications systems and catering for the conference trade. The striking domed, heated Olympic-size indoor pool is partly built with Sými's former solar water still; you'll also find three outdoor pools, a sauna, gym, tennis courts and all the trimmings.

Rodos Bay, ✆ 23 661, ✉ 21 344 (*A; exp*), sprawls over a hillside, with a pool and bungalows by its private beach, while the rooftop restaurant has one of Rhodes' finest views. Scores of A- and B-class hotels and apartments, plus cheaper pensions, are available all along from here to the airport. **Galini Hotel Apartments** in Ialysós, ✆ 94 496, ✉ 91 251 (*B; mod*), has apartments for two to six people, pool, children's pool and playground. *Open May–Oct.*

Two of the island's gourmet citadels are here. **Ta Koupia**, ✆ 91 824, in Triánda by Ialysós (take a taxi), is simply the cat's pyjamas among Rhodian trendies and visiting movie stars. Wonderfully decorated with antique Greek furniture, the food matches the décor in quality—excellent *mezé* and upmarket Greek dishes with an Eastern touch. **La Rotisserie**, in the Rodos Palace, ✆ 25 222, is the place for French and Greek *nouvelle cuisine*, with an exquisite wine list, followed by dessert trolley and a cigar from the humidor; the Rhodians love the set-price lunch, which changes daily. **Trata** on Triánda beach is good and much kinder to the pocket. In Ialysós the **Sandy Beach Taverna** right on the beach is a favourite lunchtime haunt with a garden terrace; try its *kopanistí*, cheese puréed with cracked olives. In Ixiá, **Restaurant Tzaki** is known for its *mezédes* and also has bouzouki music.

Down the East Shore to Líndos

Like the windier west shore, the sandy but not so clean shore southeast of Rhodes town is lined with modern luxury hotels and holiday resorts, beginning with the safe Blue Flag beaches of **Réni Koskinoú**, popular with families. The inland village of **Koskinoú** is known for its houses with decorative cobblestoned floors and courtyards, the distinctive Rhodian pebble mosaics, or *choklákia*, a technique introduced by the 7th-century Byzantines. En route, industry has taken over **Asgouroú**, a Turkish village; the mosque was originally a church of St John.

Further along the coast the coves of **Kalithéa** are a popular spot for swimming and snorkelling. The waters of Kalithéa were personally recommended by Hippocrates, and now the old, disused thermal spa, in a magnificent kitsch Italianate-Moorish building from the 1920s, is being restored at great expense by EOT. There's a small lido and scuba diving on offer from Dive Med's boat, *The Phoenix*. Beyond here, holiday La-La Land begins in earnest with **Faliráki Bay North**, a massive development of upmarket hotel complexes along the sandy beach, complete with a shopping mall. Bad enough, if that's what you've come to a Greek island to escape from, but reserve judgement until you meet the original **Faliráki**, the vortex, with its sweeping golden sands, awarded a Blue Flag for excellence and featuring all kinds of watersports and wild nightlife. A playground for the 18–30s predominantly Brit crowd, fur and jewellery shops rub shoulders with fast-food places, bars featuring wet T-shirt contests and local supermarkets that call themselves Safeway, ASDA and Kwik Save, copying the logos from UK carrier bags. If the beach to the south is the nudist hang-out, the rest of Faliráki attracts families with diversions such as sailing catamarans, jumping off Godzilla's Meccano set at the **New World Bungy**, ✆ (0241) 76 178, the **Faliráki Snake House** with tropical fish and live reptiles (*open 11am–11pm; adm*) and **Aqua Adventure**, 'the longest waterslide in Greece!' located in the grounds of the Hotel Pelagos. Ironically, as Faliráki tries to become a sunny version of Blackpool, some exclusive hotel complexes in Cycladic village style are springing up in the area. Faliráki also has the island's only campsite. The town's backdrop is all the bleaker due to recent fires which scorched the scrub from here heading south.

Ladiko Bay just south is a small rocky cove also known as Anthony Queen Beach (*sic*) after the actor who bought land from the Greek government (or thought he did—he's never been able to get the title) while filming *The Guns of Navarone* at Líndos; some scenes were shot on the beach. Next door, the hidden village of **Afándou** is less frenetic and has the ultimate rarity in this part of the world—an 18-hole golf course by the sea, ✆ (0241) 51 256, as well as tennis courts. Once known for its carpet-weaving and apricots, Afándou now relies on tourism (complete with a little tourist choo choo train and a Chinese takeaway) thanks to its 7km pebble beach, deep crystal waters and excellent fish tavernas; a few people also work at the Voice of America radio station. By this point you may have noticed a plethora of roadside ceramic 'factories' with coach-sized parking lots, which are exactly what they seem to be.

Next comes **Kolýmbia**, a soulless, rapidly developing resort with many new large hotels. A scenic avenue of eucalyptus trees leads to **Vágia Point** with some great beaches south of the headland. Local farms are irrigated thanks to the nymph-haunted lake fed by the **Eptá Pigés**, the 'Seven Springs', 5km inland. A wooded beauty spot with scented pines, it's a tranquil place to escape the sun, with strutting peacocks, lush vegetation and a wonderful streamside taverna. You can walk through ankle-deep icy water along the low, narrow, tunnel dug by the Italians (claustrophobes have an alternative route, from the road) which opens out into the spring-fed lake. But beware: the Greeks tend to wade back up again, colliding with everyone.

The long sandy bay at **Tsambíka** is very popular (although bereft of accommodation), with its tiny white monastery perched high on the cliffs above. Rhodes' answer to fertility drugs, the monastery's icon of the Virgin Mary attracts childless women who make the barefoot pilgrimage and pledge to name their children after the icon. Their prayers are answered often enough; look out for the names Tsambíkos or Tsambíka, unique to Rhodes. The road leads on to **Stégna**, where charming fisherman's houses are being engulfed by tourist development. There's a shingle beach set in a pretty bay. The rugged coastal path, redolent of Cornwall, offers rewarding walks: from Tsambíka to Faraklós takes around 3 hours.

Next stop on the main road, **Archángelos** (pop. 3,500) is the largest village on Rhodes, with a North African feel, its little white houses spread under a chewed-up castle of the Knights, although much of the original charm has been lost to tourism now. Its churches, **Archángelos Gabriél** and **Archángelos Michaél**, are two of the prettiest on the island; another nearby, **Ag. Theodóroi**, has 14th-century frescoes, but be prepared to find all three shut. Fiercely patriotic, the villagers have even painted the graveyard blue and white. Archángelos is famous for its ceramics and has several potteries-cum-gift-shops—regular stops on island tours. Otherwise the village is still somewhat untouched by tourism and its major industries are agriculture and fruit farming. The villagers speak in their own dialect, and also have a reputation for their musicial abilities, carpet-making and special leather boots that keep snakes at bay in the fields. Local cobblers can make you a pair to order; they fit either foot but don't come cheap.

Once one of the strongest citadels on Rhodes, the ruined **Castle of Faraklós** is dramatically positioned on the promontory below **Malónas**, overlooking Charáki and **Vlícha Bay**. It was originally occupied by pirates, until the Knights gave them the boot, repaired the walls and used the fort as a prison. Even after the rest of the island fell to Suleiman, Faraklós held, only surrendering after a long, determined siege. The nearby fishing hamlet of **Charáki** has a pretty shaded esplanade running along a small crescent-shaped pebble beach, and makes a welcome stop after the coastal walk. There are good waterside fish tavernas, excellent swimming and postcard views of Líndos. In **Mássari**, just inland, one of the Knights' sugar refineries was discovered where olives and orange groves now reign.

Koskinoú ✉ 85100

Most tavernas are like the village itself, small and typically Greek. **O Yiannis**, once cheap and cheerful, has become the place to see and be seen. There'll be queues but it's worth the wait.

Faliráki ✉ 85100

Between Kalithéa and Faliráki, **Esperos Village**, ℗ 86 046, ✆ 85 741 (*L; lux*), set high in its own grounds with Disney-inspired castle gates, is so Cycladic it looks as if it escaped from Tinos; facilities on offer include conference centre, pools and tennis courts. At the other end of the scale there are droves of C-class hotels (any package operator can set you up) and **Faliráki Camping**, ℗ 85 516, now the island's only official campsite, which has every comfort. After dark, Faliráki is one big party. **Champers**, ℗ 85 939, is the eighth wonder of the world for young package ravers: karaoke and dancing on giant barrels are among the attractions; young sun-and-fun crowds also head for **Slammer's Pub**.

Afándou ✉ 85103

Lippia Golf Resort, ℗ 52 007, ✆ 52 367 (*A; exp–mod*), is an all-inclusive air-conditioned resort, with indoor and outdoor pools, tennis and proximity to the links; **Reni Sky**, ℗ 51 125, ✆ 52 413 (*B; inexp*), has a pool and good-value rooms. For exceptional fish, follow the jet-set to **Reni's**, ℗ 51 280 (*exp*), probably the best on the island.

Líndos

Dramatically situated on a promontory high over the sea, beautiful Líndos (ΛΙΝΔΟΣ) is Rhodes' second town, with a year-round population of 800. With its sugar-cube houses wrapped around the fortified acropolis, it looks more Cycladic than Rhodian. It has kept its integrity only because the whole town is classified as an archaeological site, unique in Greece; even painting the shutters a new colour requires permission, and no hotels are allowed to be built within sighting distance of the windows. Líndos was a magnet for artists and beautiful people back in the swinging sixties, when, they say, you could hear the clink of cocktail glasses as far away as Rhodes town. It still has a few showbiz Brits (Pink Floyd's Dave Gilmour), Italians, Germans and Saudi princes and diplomats—who have snapped up many of the lovely old captains' houses. Incredibly beautiful as Líndos is, there's little left of real village life apart from locals selling a few vegetables and produce in the early morning when most people are sleeping off the night before. In July and August the cobbled streets are heaving with day-trippers and you can literally be carried along by the crowds—around half a million visitors are siphoned through each year—although it quietens down at night. The locals have adjusted to the seasonal invasion and pander to the tourists' every need, from pornographic playing cards to English breakfasts. If you want to avoid the hordes visit in the off season; Greek Easter (confusingly, either before or after the Western variety) is wonderful in Líndos. But if you can't take the heat, be warned: Líndos is the frying pan of Rhodes and temperatures can be unbearable in August (several places rent out electric fans). The nightlife also sizzles.

Líndos was the most important of the three ancient cities of Rhodes, first inhabited around 2000 BC; the first temple on its magnificent, precipitous acropolis was erected in 1510 BC. The city grew rich from its many colonies, especially Parthenope (modern Naples). Ancient Líndos, four times the size of the present town, owed its precocious importance to its twin natural harbours, the only ones on Rhodes, and to the foresight of its benevolent 6th-century BC tyrant Cleoboulos, one of the Seven Sages of Greece, a man famous for his beauty, his belief in the intellectual equality of women, and his many maxims, one of which, 'Measure is in all the best' (moderation in all things), was engraved on the oracle at Delphi. The reservoir and rock tunnels dug by his father, King Evander, supplied water to Líndos until only a few years back. St Paul landed at St Paul's Bay, bringing Christianity to the Lindians; the Knights fortified Líndos, and during the Turkish occupation of Rhodes Lindian merchants handled most of the island's trade. To this day there's a rivalry between the people of Rhodes and Líndos, and the Lindians are still known for their business acumen.

✆ (0244–)   *Getting Around*

Besides daily **boats** from Rhodes town, Líndos has its own direct hydrofoil to Sými and to Marmaris, Turkey; book through Pefkos Rent-a-Car, ✆ 31 387. **Donkey taxis** to the Acropolis cost 1,500dr.; the possibility of buying a photo of the experience comes with the deal. If you're staying, little 3-wheeled vehicles will transport your luggage.

✆ (0244–)   *Tourist Information*

Municipal tourist office: Plateía Eleftherías, ✆ 31 900, ✉ 31 282 (*open daily 7.30am–10pm*).

Internet: there's an Internet café by the post office.

Telephone: try the phones at Lindos Suntours.

A Walk Around Town

The serpentine pebbled lanes and stairs of Líndos are lined with dramatic and unique houses, many of them elegant sea captains' mansions built between the 15th and 17th centuries. Usually constructed around courtyards with elaborate pebbled mosaics (*choklákia*), secluded behind high walls and imposing doorways, the houses have high ceilings to keep cool and unusual raised living rooms (*sala*), and beds are often on sleeping platforms. According to tradition, the number of cables carved around the doors or windows represented the number of ships owned by the resident captain. Many are now holiday homes or bars, which take full advantage of their flat roofs: great for sunbathing and admiring the views. Some houses still have collections of Lindian ware, delightful plates painted with highly stylized Oriental motifs first manufactured in Asia Minor; legend has it that the Knights of St John once captured a ship full of Persian potters and would not let them go until they taught their craft to the islanders. They used to be displayed in the fancy **Papakonstandís Mansion**, once the museum, now the Museum Bar. As some compensation, stop in at the Byzantine church of the **Assumption**, built on the site of a 10th-century church and restored by Grand Master d'Aubusson in 1489–90. It may take a few moments for your eyes to adjust to the dim light to see its frescoes of the Apostles, painted by the artist Gregory of Sými in 1779 and refurbished in 1927. One has a camel head. The back wall is covered with a scene of the *Last Judgement*, with St Michael weighing souls and a misogynist St Peter welcoming the Elect into heaven's gate.

The Acropolis of Líndos

Floating high over Líndos' housing is the **Temple of Lindian Athena** (*open in season Mon 12.30–6.40, Tues–Fri 8–6.40, Sat and Sun 8.30–2.40; rest of the year Tues–Sun 8.30–2.40; adm exp*), one of the most stunningly sited in Greece, accessible by foot or 'Lindian taxi'—hired donkey. The steep route up is lined with billowing blouses, embroidered tablecloths and other handicrafts put out for sale by local women, who sit by their wares, mugging passers-by. Líndos' reputation for embroidery dates back to the time of Alexander the Great. Some needlework is authentically hand-made but the vast majority is mass-produced, imported and overpriced.

Just before the Knights' stairway, note the prow of a trireme carved into the living rock. This once served as a podium for a statue of Agissándros, priest of Poseidon, sculpted by Pythokretes of Rhodes, whose dramatic, windblown *Victory of Samothrace* now graces the Louvre. The inscription says that the Lindians gave Agissándros a golden wreath, portrayed on the statue, as a reward for judging their athletics events. At the top of the stair are two vaulted rooms, and to the right a crumbling 13th-century church of **St John**. Continue straight on for the raised Dorian arcade, or **Stoa of Lindian Athena**, the patron goddess of the city. She was a chaste goddess; to enter beyond here, any woman who was menstruating or had recently made love had to take a purifying bath, heads had to be covered, and even men were obliged to have clean bare feet, or wear white shoes that were not made of horsehair. From here the 'stairway to Heaven' leads up to the mighty foundations of the **Propylaea** and, on the edge of the precipice, the **Temple of Athena** itself, of which only seven columns are standing. Both were built by Cleoboulos, rebuilt after a fire in 342 BC and reconstructed by the Italians; the reconstructions are now being restored in turn and a fair bit of scaffolding surrounds the site at the time of writing. In ancient times, the temple was celebrated for its primitive wooden statue of Athena, capped with gold, and its golden inscription of Pindar's Seventh Olympian Ode, now gone without a trace. On the northern slope of the Acropolis, the **Voukópion** is a small sanctuary in the recess of the rock which was used to sacrifice bullocks in honour of Athena, at a distance from her temple, which was presumably to be left uncontaminated by blood.

The views from the acropolis are stunning, especially over the azure round pool of the small harbour, **St Paul's Bay**, where St Paul landed in AD 58; the diminutive beach gets quite busy despite encroaching pollution. Below this, the **Grand Harbour** with the decent town beach and small but trendy **Pallas Beach** was the home port of ancient Líndos' navy, 500 ships strong. On the far end of this, the cylindrical **Tomb of Cleoboulos** intriguingly actually predates the king, and in the Middle Ages was converted into the church of Ag. Aililiános.

Villages and Beaches around Líndos

Péfki (ΠΕΥΚΟΙ), just south of Líndos, has a narrow sandy beach fringed by the pine trees which give it its name. Much quieter than Líndos, it's still a fast-developing resort with holiday apartments, mini-markets, cocktail bars, some good tavernas, fish and chips and a Chinese restaurant. Sprawling **Lárdos** (ΛΑΡΔΟΣ), inland west of Líndos, has a pretty valley village as its core, with a charming central square where you can watch the local world go by. Just to the southwest, in the valley of **Keskinto**, farmers in 1893 dug up half of a stone stele from *c.* 100 BC with references to the orbits of Mercury, Mars, Jupiter and Saturn, and believed to be the work of Attalus. Keskinto, on the same latitude as the Pillars of Hercules (*aka* Gibraltar), was the site of the observatory believed to have produced the famous Antikýthera Mechanism (*see* pp.350–1).

If you're under your own steam, head 12km inland to **Laerma**, turn 2km down the Profila road and travel another 2km on a rather dodgy road to **Moní Thari**, founded in the 9th century—the oldest surviving religious foundation on Rhodes, well hidden from pirates and now reoccupied by monks from Pátras. The monastery is said to have been founded by a princess held hostage by pirates, who had a dream from the Archangel Michael promising her that she would soon be free. The princess had a gold ring, and in turn promised St Mike to build as many monasteries as cubits that she flung her ring. She threw it so far she lost it, and ended up building only Thari. The church has some of the finest frescoes on Rhodes, dating back to the 12th century; in places they are four layers thick. Note the more unusual scenes: the *Storm on the Sea of Galilee* and the *Encounter with the Magdalene*.

South of Lárdos the beach on sweeping **Lárdos Bay** has sand dunes bordered by reeds and marshes. This area is being developed with upmarket village-style hotels, but you can still find very peaceful, even deserted beaches further along the coast: **Glystra** is a gem, with a perfect sheltered cove. **Kiotári** now has sophisticated hotel complexes isolated in the surrounding wilderness, while its beach stretches for miles, with a hilly backdrop, stylish international holidaymakers and laid-back seafront tavernas. A detour inland leads to the medieval hill village of **Asklipío** (ΑΣΚΛΗΠΙΕΙΟ) huddled beneath the remains of yet another crusader castle. The church of the recently restored **Monastery of Metamórfossi** dates from 1060, and has frescoes from the 15th century depicting stories from the Old Testament, arranged like comic-strips around the walls (*open daily 9–6*).

Further south, buses go as far as **Gennádi,** an agricultural town with a beach which looks like a vast pebble mosaic. Nearby **Ag. Georgios** has water sports and refreshments; inland, **Váti**, with its huge plane tree in the centre, is typical of the new Rhodes; only 35 people hold the fort during the week, while everyone else has a flat in the city and returns at weekends. A Bohemian, arty crowd of mostly German ex-pats have livened up the similar one-horse village of **Lachaniá**. Plimíri (ΠΛΗΜΥΡΙ) has a spanking-new marina, a fish farm and a popular fish restaurant as well as some wonderful deserted beaches along a California-like coast.

Líndos ✉ *85107,* ☎ *(0244–)*   **Where to Stay**

In Líndos, where it's illegal to build new hotels, nearly every house has been converted into a holiday villa, all but a few with the name of a British holiday company on the door: **Direct Greece** is one of the bigger operators (book from the UK; *see* p.31). Locally run **Pallas Travel,** ☎ 31 494, ◙ 31 595, can also arrange villas and rooms. If you prefer to turn up and take pot luck, you may well be offered a room on arrival; if not, **Nikolas,** ☎ 48 076 (*exp*), has pricey apartments sleeping 2–6. **Lindos Sun,** ☎ 31 453, ◙ 22 019 (*C; exp–mod*), offers tennis and pool from April to Oct. More modest are **Kyria Teresa**'s pretty garden rooms, ☎ 31 765 (*mod*), or try the staple pensions: **Electra,** ☎ 31 266 (*mod–inexp*), whose shady garden wins the day, or adjacent **Katholiki,** ☎ 31 445 (*inexp*), in a traditional house built in 1640 (shared bathroom).

Outside Líndos going north, several excellent hotels are beautifully positioned on Vlícha Bay, 3km from town. The big news here is the **Atrium Palace**, at Kálathos, ☎ 31 601, ◙ 31 600, atrium@otenet.gr (*L; lux*), with every conceivable amenity. The **Lindos Bay,** ☎ 31 501, ◙ 31 500 (*A; lux*), is on the beach with great views of Líndos, tennis, watersports, pool and wheelchair access. The **Steps of Lindos,** ☎ 31 062, ◙ 31 067 (*A; exp*), has luxury rooms and facilities, and offers a variety of watersports. **Lindos Mare,** ☎ 31 102, ◙ 31 131 (*A; exp*), also has a pool overlooking the sea.

There are plenty of village rooms and pensions south of Líndos—just look out for the signs. Further down the coast outside Lárdos the **Lydian Village**, © 47 361, ✆ 47 364 (*B; lux–exp*), is a stylish club-type complex, exquisitely designed, with white Aegean-style houses clustered around paved courtyards. Furnishings are luxurious but with an ethnic feel: pale blue wooden taverna chairs and old ceramics. There's every facility, and it's right on the beach, with hills behind.

Líndos © (0244–) Eating Out

International cuisine rules in town; prices are high and a traditional Greek coffee as scarce as gold dust. **Mavriko's** (established in 1933) just off the square is good, with an imaginative menu (*5,000dr*). On a more modest budget, **Dionysos Taverna**, in the centre, has all the usual Greek favourites in a rooftop setting, and the **Lindos Restaurant**, bang in the centre by the bank, serves good, reasonably priced tourist fare in a two-tiered roof garden; **Agostino's**, with another romantic roof garden, does tasty grills, village dishes and Embónas wine by the carafe. It's also open for breakfast and brunch. At Péfki, carnivores can head to the **Butcher's Grill**, run by family butchers from Lárdos, with excellent fresh meat and traditional village cooking, while **To Spitaki**, an old house in the village centre, offers Greek dishes with a cordon bleu touch in peaceful gardens. In the main square at Lárdos, **Anna's Garden Taverna** is as pleasant as it sounds. Alternatively, venturing north to Charáki is well worth the effort for the excellent **Argo**, © 51 410, or **Haraki Bay**, © 51 680, with an enormous *mezédes* selection.

Entertainment and Nightlife

Líndos has all types of bars that come into their own once the trippers have gone, many in converted sea captains' mansions: try the **Captain's House**, with the most elaborate doorway in Líndos, decorated with birds, chains and pomegranate flowers (the symbol of Rhodes), a charming, friendly and tranquil place for a tipple. The 400-year-old **Lindian House**, with painted ceiling and lovely windows, is a grand place and **Socrates** opposite is another attractive captain's house. **Jody's Flat**, encompassing a tree, with English papers and board games, is full of character. **Lindos By Night** is quite an institution, on three floors with lovely roof gardens just above the donkey station, laying out superb Acropolis views, but lost in thumping music in season. Three nightclubs also reverberate at night: **Namas** and **Akropolis**, halfway down to the beach, and **Amphitheatre** on the hillside. Lárdos has a good selection of music bars as well.

The Far South: Windsurfing and Weddings

Kataviá (KATTABIA), the southernmost village on Rhodes, has an end-of-the-line atmosphere, and, more importantly, a petrol station. In July and August it gets invaded by migrating windsurfers who adore the southernmost tip of Rhodes, **Cape Prassonísi**, 'the Green Island', reached by road from Kataviá. The desolate landscape may as well be the end of the world. The narrow sandy isthmus which links Prassoníssi with Rhodes partially disappeared after storms, although one side remains wild and wavy, the other perfectly calm; take a caique to reach the very tip. There are a couple of tavernas, rooms and unofficial camping. Near the isthmus, Danish archaeologists discovered ruins of a 7th–6th-century BC walled settlement at **Vroulia**, set on a panoramic shelf over the sea.

For more grand views over both coasts of Rhodes, take the high corniche road from Kataviá up to **Messanagrós**, an old-fashioned mountain village. Just west, if you get stuck, you can spend the night (ask on arrival) at **Moní Skiádi**, a hilltop monastery sheltering a miraculous icon of the Panagía and Child which was said to have flowed blood when a 15th-century heretic stabbed the Virgin's cheek. The wound, and stains, are still visible. The unpaved road continues down to the west coast, where there are spectacular views but a wind battered sea. Sheltered in a valley, **Apolakiá** (ΑΠΟΛΑΚΚΙΑ) is a modern, unexceptional town with a few tavernas and rooms to rent, but producing the best watermelons and marriage feasts on Rhodes.

Getting Hitched on Rhodes

As marriages or renewing-wedding-vows ceremonies become big business on Rhodes, it's interesting to note that, even 50 years ago, real Rhodian weddings were the stuff of folklore and lingering pagan rites. The ceremony began with gifts: the bridegroom presented his fiancée with a braided jacket, a veil embroidered with gold, a skirt and shoes, and the bride reciprocated with a shirt and a tobacco pouch she had embroidered herself. To show she was no longer available, the bride's long hair was cut in front in a fringe, while the rest was gathered in numerous small plaits. Her hands were anointed with cinnamon. When she was ready, the wedding musicians were brought in to pass their instruments over her head (a meaningful gesture repeated several times during the wedding day). The bridegroom was given much the same treatment.

After the wedding, the young couple were led to their new home—the bride's dowry (as it often is to this day, although unofficially). The new husband then dipped his finger in a pot of honey and made the sign of the cross on the door, while all the guests cried: 'Be as good and sweet as this honey!' He next stamped on a pomegranate placed on the threshhold, its bursting seeds a guarantee of future fertility, while the guests showered the couple with corn, cotton seeds and orange flower water. After the musicians had sung the praises of the bride and groom, the bride knelt before the father and mother of the groom and kissed their hands, then was led away by her female friends to eat at a neighbour's house to the wild crashing of cymbals and song. The dancing would begin at night and last for two days.

Up the West Coast: Monólithos, Embónas and Mount Atáviros

Monólithos is the most important village of the region, the monolith in question a fantastical 700ft rocky spur rising sheer above the sea, capped spectacularly by a **castle** built by the ubiquitous Grand Master d'Aubusson. A precarious stairway winds to the top and, within the castle walls, there's the little 15th-century chapel of **Ag. Geórgios** with some interesting frescoes. There are fabulous views, especially at sunset, across to the islands of Alimnia and Chálki; a couple of panoramic tavernas make the viewing easier. There are strong currents off Cape Monólithos, but 5km below the castle, down a tortuous road, the shady bay of **Foúrni** has a sandy beach and a seasonal cantina. There are early Christian cave dwellings round the headland.

The road continues through **Siána**, an attractive old stone village built on a hillside, offering a superb view of the coast and islets. Siána is famous for its superb wild honey and *suma*, a local firewater reminiscent of schnapps. You can sample both at roadside cafés in the village, where the oldest houses have roofs made of clay. The church of **Ag. Pantaléimon** has a beautiful interior and basil growing at the doorway.

Renowned for for its wine, olives, tobacco, dancing and festivals, the mountain village of **Embónas** (ΕΜΠΩΝΑΣ) has tried to preserve its traditional ways. The dances of the women are exceptionally graceful and the *panegýri* in August are among the best on the island, fuelled by the local vintages. Some of the older people still wear local costumes, but only those who don't mind being camera fodder for the Greek Nights and Folk Dance busloads from Rhodes town. Embónas is the centre of the Rhodes winemaking cooperative, **CAIR** (their sparkling white makes a superb Buck's Fizz), and **Emery Winery**, founded by the Triantafýllou family in the 1920s. Visitors are welcome in their handsome tasting room (*C* (0246) 41 208; *open Mon–Fri 9–3*). Their mighty red Cava (12.5°) is made from a local grape, *mandilari* (or *amoryiani*), but the wine that has really made them famous, white Villaré, owes its distinctness to indigenous grape *athiri* that refuses to grow well outside its own microclimate, at 700m altitude, on the slopes of the island's highest peak, **Mount Atáviros** (1215m); the summit is a tough 3hr climb from Embónas. Here Althaemenes (*see* p.238) built the temple of Zeus Atavros, although little remains to be seen. Besides eagle-eye views of the whole island, you can (they say) see Crete on a clear morning; poor Althaemenes used to come up here when he longed, like all Cretans, for his mother island.

While up on the roof of Rhodes, head around to **Ag. Isidóros**, like Embónas minus tourists, with vineyards and tavernas. Legend says Althaemenes founded the white hillside village below Embónas, **Kritiní**, which he named in honour of Crete.

Just below Kritiní lies **Kámiros Skála** (ΣΚΑΛΑ ΚΑΜΙΡΟΥ), a fishing harbour with two good tavernas that served as the port of ancient Kámiros, 16km north. These days it's where the local ferries depart for Chálki. The ferries link with the buses to and from Monólithos and Rhodes town, taking the children of Chálki to school and the islanders shopping. Towering high above Kámiros Skála, the **Kastéllo** (signposted Kástro Kritinías) was one of the Knights' most impressive ruins, set above lemon groves and pinewoods and affording spectacular views.

Ancient Kámiros

Althaemenes' most celebrated foundation, however, was **Kámiros** (ΚΑΜΙΡΟΣ) (*open Tues–Sun 8.30–5; adm*), one of Rhodes' three Dorian cities, built in terraces up the hillside. Destroyed by an earthquake in the 2nd century BC, the city was simply abandoned and forgotten, covered with the dust of centuries until no one remembered it was there. In the 19th century, local farmers discovered a few interesting graves, and in 1859 the improbably named British Consul and French archaeologist, Biliotti and Alzman respectively, began excavating. The city they eventually brought to light has been compared to Pompeii: well preserved, untouched by Byzantium, Christianity or the Knights. The cemetery, in particular, rendered many beautiful items now in the British Museum, and in archaeological terms the discovery was one of the richest ever in Greece. An excellent water and drainage system, supplied by a large reservoir, served around 400 families in the excavated Hellenistic-era houses.

A second dig in 1914 carried out by the Italians uncovered most of the ancient city: the baths, the Agora with its rostrum for public speeches, the Agora's Great Stoa with its Doric portico, Roman houses, two temples—one 6th-century BC dedicated to Athena of Kámiros and the other Doric from the 3rd century—and an altar dedicated to sunny Helios.

Down on the coast at modern Kámiros there are tavernas for pit-stops. **Fanés**, further north, has a long, narrow stony beach with a few tavernas.

Inland, on a high hill over the village of **Sálakos**, are the ruins of another medieval fort; Sálakos itself is beloved for its shade and fresh water from the Spring of the Nymphs. This region, with its cedar and pine forests and views of the sea, is one of the prettiest for walks. Further up, the road leads to **Mount Profítis Ilías** (790m) and its two derelict Swiss chalet hotels. The trees here belong to the Prophet Elijah, who according to legend strikes down any sinner who dares to cut one down. The chief settlements on its slopes are **Apóllona** with a museum of popular art and **Eleoússa** with a pretty Byzantine church. Nearby **Arthípoli**, with its good tavernas, is a favourite green oasis for lunch.

Back on the Northwest Coast

Theológos (or **Thólos**) announces the proximity of Rhodes town with hotels and a collection of roadside supermarkets and tavernas. Beyond is the straggling village of **Paradíssi** (ΠΑΡΑΔΕΙΣΙ) next door to the **airport**. Hardly heaven, it's still a useful place for an overnight stay after a night flight—plenty of 'rooms to let' signs—and there's a small beach, constantly zapped by roaring planes. The strip in neighbouring **Kremastí** (ΚΡΕΜΑΣΤΗ) bustles with foreign tourists and Greek soldiers from the island's main barracks. The village itself is famous for its wonder-working icon, **Panagías Kremastí**, occasioning one of the biggest *panegýri* in the Dodecanese, lasting from 15 to 23 August. During this there's a funfair, *souvláki* stands and all kinds of hawkers selling their wares. At the climax on the 23rd the villagers don traditional costumes and dance a very fast *sousta*.

Inland, a road between Theológos and Paradíssi leads to **Káto Kalamónas** and from there to one last enchanting spot, more so if you manage to get there before or after the tour buses: **Petaloúdes**, the **Valley of the Butterflies** (*open May–Sept daily 8.30–7; adm*). Sliced by a stream and laughing waterfalls, the narrow gorge is crowned by a roof of fairytale storax trees, whose vanilla-scented resin is used to make frankincense. From June to September rare Quadrina butterflies (actally moths, *Callimorpha quadripuntaria*, named for the Roman numeral IV on their black, brown, white and red wings) flock here, attracted by the resin. This is one of their two breeding grounds in the world, and in recent years their numbers have declined because of tourists clapping their hands to see their wings: every flight weakens them, so resist the urge.

You can follow the trail up the valley to the monastery of the **Panagía Kalópetra**, built in 1782 by Alexander Ypsilántis, grandfather of the two brothers who wanted to be kings at the start of the 1821 Greek War of Independence (and gave their name to the town in Michigan). It's a tranquil place well worth the uphill trek, with wonderful views and picnic tables in the grounds. From here another wooded trail leads to the **Monastery of Ag. Soúlas**, just off the road down to **Soroní**. Here they have a giant festival on 30 July with donkey races and folk dancing immortalized in *Reflections on a Marine Venus*.

✆ (0246–)   *Where to Stay and Eating Out*

In Monólithos, try the little **Thomas**, ✆ 61 291, ✉ 28 834 (*D; inexp*). *Open all year.* Kámiros Skála is popular for fresh fish, especially at weekends, with several tavernas overlooking the sea: **Loukas** at the harbourside is good and a jolly place to wait for the

Chálki ferry. By the sea on the old Kámiros road, the **Taverna New Kamiros** isn't much to look at but serves good seafood and meat dishes.

To escape from the sun-and-fun crowds, head for the hills and Sálakos, home of Rhodes' new natural spring water, where the **Nymfi** © 22 206 (*B; mod*), is a real oasis with four traditional rooms: the perfect island hideaway. *Open all year.* Favourites, especially for a cool, shady prolonged Sunday lunch, are near Arthípoli: **Psinthos** is one, **Pigi Fasouli** under the plane trees another, or **Artemida**, with charcoal grills and good house wines. **Taverna Oasis** at Eleoússa is another fine choice, lost in the trees.

Sými (ΣΥΜΗ)

Inevitably, there's a fusillade of clicking camera shutters and purring of camcorders when the ferries swing into Sými's main harbour, Gialós, one of the most breathtaking sights in Greece. Few other islands have Sými's crisp brightness and its amphitheatre of imposing neoclassical mansions, in soft ochre or traditional deep shades, stacked one on top of the other up the barren hillsides. There are few trees to block the sun, for unlike its neighbour Rhodes, Sými is an arid island, with insufficient water to support many visitors. Most who do come arrive on daily excursion boats from Rhodes, when pandemonium reigns in several languages as groups are herded along the waterfront or head for the small town beach at Nos. When the boats have sounded their sirens and the invaders departed Sými regains much of its serenity; at night when the lights come on it is pure romance. As its lovely houses are all bought up and immaculately restored, the island has become a very trendy place, with a major cultural festival and fancy restaurants. Sými is very popular with the sailing fraternity, who fill the harbour with yachts, flotillas and jet-set cruisers flying flags of all nations. Avoid August when the island is heaving, rooms are expensive and tempers frayed in the heat; because it's in a basin and the heat bounces off the rocks, Sými sizzles like a cat on a hot tin roof from July to September. On the other hand, it stays warm into October and is particularly lovely in spring.

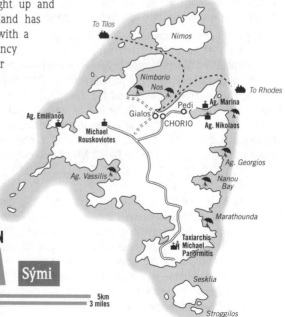

History

According to legend, Sými was a princess, daughter of King Ialysos on Rhodes, who was abducted by the sea god Glaukos, an eminent sponge-diver and sailor who also built the *Argo* for Jason. He brought her to the island and gave it her name. If such was the case, Princess Sými's descendants inherited Glaukos' shipbuilding skills: throughout history Sými was famous for its ships. Sými was also known as Metapontis, or Aigle, after a daughter of Apollo and mother of the Three Graces. In another myth, Prometheus modelled a man from clay here, angering Zeus so much that he turned the Titan into a monkey for the rest of his natural days on the island. Ever since, the word 'simian' has been connected with apes.

Pelasgian walls in Chorió attest to the prehistoric settlement of Sými. In the *Iliad* Homer tells how the island mustered three ships for the Achaeans at Troy, led by King Nireus. After Achilles, Nireus was the most beautiful of all the Greeks, but, as in Achilles' case, beauty proved to be no defence against the Trojans. In historical times Sými was part of the Dorian Hexapolis, but dominated by Rhodes. The Romans fortified the acropolis at Chorió; the Byzantines converted it into a fort, which was renovated by the first Grand Master of the Knights of Rhodes, Foulques de Villaret. From Sými's Kástro the Knights could signal to Rhodes, and they favoured swift Sýmiot skiffs or *skafés* for their raiding activities.

Thanks to the Knights, Sými prospered through shipbuilding and trade. When Suleiman the Magnificent came to the Dodecanese in 1522, the Sýmiots, known as the most daring divers in the Aegean, avoided being attacked by offering him the most beautiful sponges he had ever seen. In return for a relative degree of independence, Sými sent a yearly consignment of sponges to the sultan's harem. Like the Knights, the Turks made use of the swift Symiot ships, this time for relaying messages. In order to keep Sými thriving, the sultan made it a free port and allowed the inhabitants to dive freely for sponges in Turkish waters.

Little Sými thus became the third richest island of the Dodecanese, a position it held from the 17th to the 19th centuries. Large mansions were constructed befitting the islanders' new status; shipbuilders bought forests in Asia Minor; schools thrived. Even after certain privileges were withdrawn because of its participation in the 1821 revolution, Sými continued to flourish. The Italian occupation and the steamship, however, spelt the end of its luck: the Italians closed the lands of Asia Minor and the steamship killed the demand for wooden sailing vessels altogether; during the Italian tenure the population of Sými dropped from 23,000 to 600 by the outbreak of the Second World War. At its end the treaty giving the Dodecanese to Greece was signed on Sými on VE Day, 8 May 1945, later ratified on 7 March 1948.

© (0241–)   **Getting There and Around**

By boat: the island's own **ferries**, *Symi I* and *Symi II*, leave Mandráki Harbour, Rhodes, daily early evening and return to Rhodes in the early morning. There are at least three daily tourist boats from Rhodes, some calling at Panormítis Monastery, and a daily hydrofoil. Local **excursion boats** visit different beaches, and the islets of Sesklí and Nímos; lovely old caiques like the *Triton* circle the island, plying you with ouzo and retsína on the way. Water taxis go to Nimborió from Gialós and Ag. Nikólaos from Pédi Beach. There's a weekly excursion to Datcha (Turkey) run by Symi Tours, *©* 71 307. **Port authority**: *©* 71 205.

By road: the taxi rank and bus stop are on the east of the harbour, *©* 72 666; the island has four **taxis** and the Sými Bus, departing every hour from 8.30am to

10.30pm from Gialós to Pédi via Chorió. Various places rent **motorbikes and scooters** nearby at a cost.

Tourist Information

The **police** share the **post office** building near the Clock Tower, Gialós, ℗ (0241) 71 111. Pick up a copy of the free *Sými Visitor* for helpful tips on the island.
Internet: try Vapori Bar, near the start of the stairs to Chório.

Walks

Organised walks are popular here: ask at Symi Tours. Look out for Mr Noble's *Walking on Sými*, too.

Festivals

2 May, Ag. Athanásios; **5 May**, Ag. Iríni; **21 May**, Ag. Konstantínos; **4 June**, Análypsis; **24 June**, Ag. Ioánnis; **July–September**, Sými Festival, with big-name performers, especially music; **17 July**, Ag. Marína on the islet; **20 July**, Profítis Ilías; **6 August**, Nimborió and Panormítis; **15 August**, Panagías; **24 August**, Panagía on Nímos islet, and Panagía Alithiní; **8 November**, Taxiárchis at the monasteries of Panormítis and Roukouniótis.

Gialós and Chorió

Sými divides into down, up and over—Gialós around the harbour, Chorió, the older settlement high above, Kástro even higher, on the site of the ancient acropolis, and Pédi clustered round the bay over the hill. In **Gialós** (a derivation of its ancient name Aigialos), arrivals are greeted by the elaborate free-standing bell tower of Ag. Ioánnis, surrounded by *choklákia* pavements, and most of Sými's tourist facilities, tavernas and gift shops. Harbour stalls sell sponges and local herbs, filling the air with the pungent scent of oregano and spices. In honour of the island's shipbuilding tradition and the signing of the Treaty of the Dodecanese, a copy of the trireme from Líndos has been carved into the rock with the inscription: 'Today freedom spoke to me secretly; Cease, Twelve Islands, from being pensive. 8th May, 1945.' The treaty was signed in the nearby restaurant, Les Katerinettes. Behind the small recreation ground next to the bridge which links the two halves of the harbour, a neoclassical mansion houses the **Nautical Museum** (*open Mon–Sat 10–3; adm*), with models of Sými's sailing ships, sponge-diving equipment, old photos and a stuffed heron.

At the end of the harbour, behind the clock tower and bronze statue of a boy fishing, the road leads to shingly **Nos Beach** via **Charani Bay**, still a small hive of industry where wooden caiques are being built or repaired while chickens strut about and cats lurk under the beached prows. Heavily bombed during the Second World War, many of the houses here are now being renovated in traditional Sými style with elegant plasterwork in blues, greys, yellows and Venetian red. **Nos**, complete with waterside taverna and sun-loungers, is a small strand popular with families. But it's also the first place the day-trippers hit, so it soon gets packed. It's better to walk further along the coastal path to the flat rocks and small coves popular with nudists on the way to **Nimborió**, a pretty tree-shaded harbour with a good taverna, loungers and a pebbly shore. Sand has been imported further round the bay to make **Zeus Beach**, which also has a cantina.

Most of the neoclassical houses in Gialós date from the 19th century, while older architecture dominates the **Chorió**. The lower part can be reached by road from the port; the alternative is a slog up the 375 steps of the **Kalí Stráta**, a mansion-lined stairway which starts near the Kaloudoukas agency off Plateía Oekonómou, or Plateía tis Skálas, to reach the houses in the maze of narrow lanes in the high town. Worn smooth and slippery over the years, the steps can zap even the fittest in the heat of high summer, even though local grannies trip up and down like mountain goats. The stairway can be sinister after dark: a torch is a must. In the centre of lower Chorió near the derelict windmills, a **stone monument** was erected by the Spartans for their victory over the Athenians off the coast of Sými. On the headland overlooking Pédi Bay are the **Pillars of Sými**, dating from when the island was an important part of the Dorian Hexapolis.

Now mostly restored, the houses in Chorió are crammed together, often forming arches and vaults over the narrow lanes. They're built in the Aegean sugar-cube style, small and asymmetrical, but with neoclassical elements incorporated into their doorways and windows. Many have lovely interiors with carved woodwork and Turkish-style *moussándra*, beds on raised platforms or galleries. Among the most interesting buildings are the **19th-century pharmacy** with an apparent remedy for every malady in its many drawers and jars; the fortress-mansion **Chatziagápitos**; and the churches of **Ag. Panteleímon** and **Ag. Giórgios** with their pebble mosaics of evil mermaids sinking hapless ships. Follow the signs to the island's **museum** (© (0241) 71 114; *open Tues–Sun 10–2; adm*), which houses icons, coins, pottery, a reconstructed 19th-century Symiot room and bits and bobs going back to the 5th century AD. Up at the top, the **Kástro** is on the site of the ancient acropolis; its Byzantine and medieval walls top a temple of Athena; the coat-of-arms belongs to d'Aubusson, Grand Master supreme. Within the fortifications the church of **Megáli Panagía** has good frescoes and post-Byzantine icons. The orginal church was blown up by the Germans when they discovered an arms cache. As a memorial, one of the church bells is made from the nose-cone of a bomb.

Around Sými

From Chorió it's a half-hour walk downhill to **Pédi** (ΠΕΔΙ) along a shady avenue of eucalyptus trees. The most fertile area of the island, there are smallholdings along the way, herds of goats, a few donkeys and fig trees in the fields. A petite sandy beach and boatyard plus excellent taverna await to the left where the road forks, while to the right past the church you'll find rooms to let and a more developed beach with cafés and the Pedi Beach Hotel. Pédi is pretty, with typical fishermen's cottages edging the bay. From here you can follow the left-hand path up over the headland to **Ag. Marína** with a chapel-topped islet within swimming distance, site of a famous secret school before the War of Independence broke out. Water taxis from Pédi buzz to the 18th-century church of **Ag. Nikólaos** with its shingly tree-fringed beach and cantina. Otherwise follow the goat-track, marked with red paint, which begins to the far right of the bay, up and over the headland.

A road from Chorió now goes to the extreme southern tip of the island and Sými's main attraction, the vast 18th-century **Monastery of Taxiárchis Michael Panormítis** (*open daily 9–2 and 4–8*), set against a backdrop of cypresses and pine. In the summer, tourist boats from Rhodes descend on it for an hour at 11am, making for massive crowds. Archangel Michael of Panormítis Bay is Sými's patron, a favourite of all Greek sailors, and the monastery's the goal of pilgrimages throughout the summer—hence the seaside guest rooms, where the underwear of

Greek families flaps merrily by signs demanding modest dress. The monastery's landmark colourful neoclassical bell-tower was built in 1905; its *choklákia* courtyard is strewn with flags; the church, coated with frescoes blackened by smoke, has, on a remarkable wooden **iconostasis,** the stern, larger-than-life silver-plated icon of St Michael, painted by Ioánnis of the Peloponnese in 1724. Taxiárchis Michael is a busy archangel: at once heaven's generalissimo, slayer of the satanic dragon, weigher of souls (one of his nicknames on Sými is *Kailiótis* because of the pain he brings mortal hearts), and patron saint of the Greek Air Force, he can also be called upon to come through in storms and induce fertility. You can hardly miss the gold and silver ship ex-votos, and the wax babies left behind by the grateful faithful.

There are two small **museums** (*adm*), one filled with more rich gifts from sailors, model ships and prayers in bottles which miraculously found their way to Panormítis bearing money for the monastery, Chinese plates and ivories donated by Symiots living in Africa, stuffed crocodiles, a weasel and mongoose. The second contains household furnishings, and the radio for British commandoes operated by the abbot and two members of the Resistance, who were executed by the Germans in 1944. Outside, there's a small shop/*kafeneíon* with miserable service, a bakery selling white and 'brawn' bread, a decent taverna with wonderful sunset views (with a memorial to the abbot), a small sandy beach, and an army barracks. You can walk in the woods surrounding the monastery, or follow the forest trail to the pebbly beach at **Marathoúnda** with resident goats.

Seskú, the islet facing Panormítis, also belongs to the monastery. Its ancient name was Teutlousa, and Thucydides writes that it was here that the Athenians took refuge after their defeat by the Spartan navy during the Peloponnesian War. A few Pelasgian walls remain and there are regular barbecue trips from Gialos. Seskú has a long pebbly beach shaded with tamarisk trees, and crystal waters. There are a few ruins on the nearby islet **Stroggilós**, while boat trips also visit the islet of **Nímos**, a stone's throw from the Turkish coast.

Sými has 77 churches, many dedicated to Archangel Michael. One of the most interesting is **Michael Roukouniótis**, an hour's walk from Gialós. Built in the 18th century, it is a curious combination of Gothic and folk architecture, and holds its feast day beneath an old umbrella-shaped cypress. **Ag. Emiliános** is on an islet in the bay of the same name, connected to the shore by a causeway with a pleasant pebbly beach nearby. On the east coast, best reached by caique, **Ag. Giórgios** has a tree-shaded sandy beach and **Nánou Bay** has an excellent shingly one, fringed by trees—another favourite barbecue spot. There's a small chapel and masses of wild herbs to flavour the food. Other beaches include **Faneroméni** opposite Panormítis and the scenic bay of **Ag. Vassílis**, a two-hour-plus walk across the island.

Sými ✉ *85600,* ✆ *(0241–)* **Where to Stay and Eating Out**

Most of the island's accommodation is in Gialós but there are also rooms to let in Chorió and Pédi. Kalodoukas Holidays, ✆ 71 077, 🖳 71 491, at the foot of the Kalí Stráta, has character property to let, excursion programmes and a book exchange; Sými Tours, ✆ 71 307/689, 🖳 72 292, also has villas and rooms to rent, and it's worth glancing at *www.symi-island.com* while you're at it. Sými is very expensive in July and August and suffers from cockroaches then anyway. Cheaper rooms are often let on condition that you stay three nights or more to economize on sheet-washing. There's no campsite but unofficial camping is tolerated on remote beaches.

Gialós

The old municipal **Nereus**, ✆ 72 400, @ 72 404 (*C; exp*), has been sympathetically restored and wonderfully painted in traditional colours. A few doors along, the elegant **Aliki**, ✆/@ 71 665 (*A; lux–exp*), and **Dorian**, ✆ 71 181, @ 72 292 (*A; lux–exp*), up the steps just behind, are two of the most stylish places to stay: both old sea captains' mansions, lovingly restored with fine wood interiors; the Aliki has a roof garden, and air-conditioning in some rooms, the Dorian has nine self-catering studios. **Grace**, ✆ 71 415 (*B; exp*), is in another traditional house and has recently added smart studios; the **Opera House**, ✆ 71 856, @ 72 035 (*A; exp*), has lovely family suites with air-conditioning set back from the harbour in a garden.

For more modest but recommended rooms, try the **Albatros** in the marketplace, ✆ 71 707, @ 72 257 (*C; mod*), well decorated and with air-con. There are several small pensions and rooms to let in the quiet backwater beyond the town hall. For stunning views over the harbour, especially at night, **Les Katerinettes** takes some beating, ✆ 72 698; it's situated above the restaurant in an eccentric traditional house with pleasingly painted ceilings. You could also try the scenic **Katerina's Rooms**, ✆ 71 813, with kitchen facilities and tremendous vista. Other options are **Kokona**, ✆ 71 451, @ 72 620 (*mod*), with decent, en suite rooms, but no sea view; and the **Egli**, ✆ 71 392 (*inexp*), at the base of the stairway to Chório, with clean, no frills rooms usually only open in high season.

The eateries in Sými fall into two clear-cut categories: really good and genuine, and tourist traps along the harbour. Away from all this in the backstreets beyond the bank, **Meraklis** is one of the island's most authentic tavernas with excellent Greek home-cooking and reasonable prices. The **Neraida** has delicious untouristy food at budget prices behind Hotel Glafkos; **Hellenikon**, just back from the bridge, serves unusual *mezédes* and 140 kinds of Greek wine (*7,000dr*).

Over the bridge, **Taverna Yiannis** is another good place where you might hear impromptu Greek music. Out on the headland, restaurant **O Tholos** has an impressive menu in a romantic setting and great fresh grills. On the way out of town, **Dimítris** is a family-run *ouzerie* with scrumptious fish dishes.

Old favourite **Les Katerinettes** is back under original management: don't miss the octopus and *pikilía* or selection of *mezédes*. You can send an e-mail home, or read the quality UK newspapers and magazines over baked potatoes or home-made chocolate cake at the **Vapori Bar** near the square.

Chorió

Horio, ✆ 71 800, @ 71 802 (*B; exp–mod, inc breakfast*), has been built in the traditional style with smart air-conditioned rooms and stunning views, surrounded by fields plus goats and donkeys. In upper Chorió the **Metapontis**, ✆ 71 491 (*B; exp–mod*), is in a very old Sými house cleverly converted to keep many of the traditional wooden features like the *moussandra* sleeping gallery. **Taxiarchis**, ✆ 72 012, @ 72 013 (*C; mod*), is an elegant neoclassical development of family-run apartments with a small bar, breakfast terrace, and breathtaking panorama of Pédi (as well as the occasional package group).

Lower down the village **Fiona**, ✆ 72 088 (*mod*), is a comfortable and tasteful bed and breakfast; the owner plays the *sandouri*—Zorba's instrument. Affable Jean at her **Jean**

and Tonic bar, ✆ 71 819, ✉ 72 172 (*mod*), also has several well-situated traditional houses to rent. **Georgio's Taverna** is an institution at night, famous for exquisite Sými shrimps and the man himself on the accordion.

Pédi

There are a few rooms to let plus the **Pedi Beach**, ✆ 71 870, ✉ 71 982 (*B; exp–mod*), but this is usually booked solid by package operators. There are several eateries: **Taverna Tolis** on the beach next to the boat yard is best for food and atmosphere, or else try **Kamares**.

Nimborió

If you really want to get away from it all, **Taverna Metapontis**, ✆ 71 820, has rooms to let, besides being a pretty spot for lunch; their taxi boat *Panagióta* will take you back to Gialós.

Entertainment and Nightlife

Sými buzzes at night, the lights from the houses and the bars reflecting their colours in the harbour like stained glass. The island's old *ouzerie* **Paco's** is still an institution but has a rival in **Elpida**, the smart new *ouzerie* doing traditional *mezédes* across the water in Mouragio. Nightlife revolves around three bars off the square, popular with locals and tourists alike. **Mina's** and former rival **Vapori** next door have finally clubbed together now, jointly attracting yachties and up-market Brits. For less conspicuous rivalry and conflicting sounds head for laid-back **Meltemi Bar** and the excellent Τεμβελα Σκαλα ('Lazy Steps') along the harbour where locals sometimes play traditional Greek music if the mood takes them. The yachting crowd and sophisticated night owls head for the **Roof Garden**, which also does snacks, for mellow sounds and romantic views, not to mention the panoramic **Kalí Stráta**, just down the steps. There are a few bars in Chorió but friendly **Jean and Tonic** caters for locals as well as tourists and still reigns supreme for early outdoors happy hour and late nightcaps. You can bop at **The Club** dancing bar in Gialós, or go to real bouzouki nights with traditional music and dance at the **Alethini Taverna** on the road to Pédi. Futher along, the **Valanidia** also has bouzouki with top singing stars in high season.

Sámos (ΣΑΜΟΣ)

A ship goes away from Chíos/With two small rowing boats
She came to Sámos and moored there/And sat and reckoned
How much is a kiss worth/In the East, in the West?
A married woman's, four/A widow's, fourteen.
An unmarried girl's is cheaper/You take it with a joke.
But if it touches your heart/Oh, then, Christ and the Virgin, help!

traditional song from Chíos

Famous for its wine, women and ships, Sámos, the 'Isle of the Blest', has historically and economically always been one of the most important islands in Greece, and since the 1980s it has become one of the most touristy as well. Despite savage forest fires in July 2000, when a state of emergency was briefly declared, pine forests, olive groves and vineyards still cover most of its emerald hills, so fertile that Menander wrote in the 4th century BC *Kai tou pouliou to gala*, 'Here even the hens give milk'—an expression now used as the slogan of a supermarket chain in Athens! The countryside ranges from lovely, gentle and bucolic to the spectacular and dramatic; the coast is indented with numerous sandy coves, and two mighty mountains furnish imposing background scenery: central Mount Ámpelos (1,140m) and in the west, Mount Kérkis, a looming 1445m, both a continuation of the mainland chain that Sámos broke away from in a cataclysm millennia ago. Two famous couples, Zeus and Hera and Antony and Cleopatra, chose Sámos for romantic dallying, and to this day it seems to have the power of awakening romance in second or third honeymoons, mostly now in the form of northern European couples on self-catering packages (a far cry from Cleopatra's gilded barge, pet leopards, perfume baths and dance troupes, but there you go). On the other hand, it is one of the most expensive islands, and to arrive without a hotel reservation in the summer is tantamount to sleeping on the beach.

History

By 3000 BC Sámos was inhabited, first by the mysterious Pelasgians and later by the Carians from the mainland opposite. Its name comes from *sama*, Phoenician for high place (similar to Samothráki and Sámi in Kefaloniá; in myth the founder of the latter city was the first to colonize Sámos). The worship of the goddess Hera began early by the river Imbroussas; her first shrine, made of wood, was built by the Argonaut King Angaios in the 13th century BC. The Ionians made their appearance in the 11th century, and by the Archaic period wine-exporting Sámos was one of the most prosperous states in the Aegean.

In 670 BC, the island became a democracy, which unleashed its creative juices, especially in the invention of a long, swift warship known as the *sámaina*, in which Samians fearlessly sailed the open seas and frequently down to Egypt; in 650 BC a local captain named Kolaios became the first known man to sail through the Straits of Gibraltar (the Phoenicians most certainly did, but they never told anyone about it). Pythagoras, the most famous Samian of them all, lived during the rule of the tyrant Polykrates, who came to power in 550 BC and was probably the most powerful man in Greece at the time. He became the first to rule the Aegean since Crete's King Minos, thanks to his fleet, incredibly large for the day, consisting of 150 *samainae*, which he used to extract tolls and protection money; he was also the first, along with Corinth, to introduce triremes into his navy. Even more lastingly, Polykrates was the first tyrant to patronize the arts and poetry. He oversaw the three greatest public works of the day: the building of the great temple of Hera, the creation of the massive harbour mole, and the digging of the Efplinion tunnel through a mountain to bring water to his capital, modern Pythagório. Under their tyrant, the Samians swanned around in the finest clothes and jewels and knocked down their *palastra* or gym to build pleasure dens with names of the order of the 'Samian Flowers' and the 'Samian Hotbed'. Polykrates' great good fortune worried his friend and ally, King Amassis of Egypt, who warned he would attract the envy of the gods unless he brought at least a small disaster or deprivation upon himself. Polykrates considered, and threw his favourite ring into the sea, thinking it would placate Fate. Three days later a fisherman caught a fish with the ring in its stomach, and returned it to Polykrates. Amassis recognized this as an evil omen, and broke off their friendship to spare himself grief later on. To ward off doom Polykrates paid a thousand archers to surround him. But they couldn't save him from

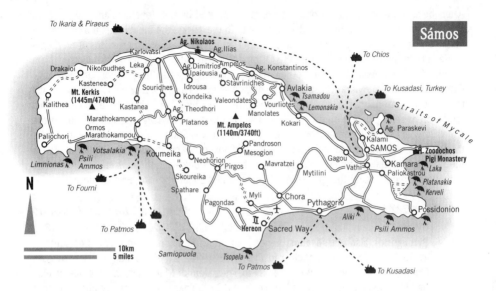

his own greed; lured by the promise of treasure by Cyrus' satrap Orsitis, he was crucified on a bluff overlooking his beloved Sámos.

A constant throughout ancient history is Sámos' lifelong feud with its chief Ionian rival on the mainland, Milétus. Whatever Milétus did, Sámos did the opposite, siding in turn with the Persians, the Spartans and the Athenians in the great disputes of the age. During their second invasion of Greece, the Persians occupied Sámos and kept their fleet at the island. During the battle of Plataea (479 BC) the Greeks attacked the Persian fleet at the Strait of Mykále, soundly defeating them—helped by the defection of the Samians in the Persian navy. The battle of Mykále was one of the most crucial in the war, and once and for all eliminated Persian threats from the sea. After the battle, Sámos allied herself with Athens, and under that city's influence became a democracy (again); when Milétus sided with Athens, Sámos as usual didn't and even defeated the Athenian fleet under Pericles in 441. The leader of the fleet was Melissus, who was also an important pre-Socratic philosopher. Melissus believed in the essential unity of creation, which was spatially and temporally infinite, and only appeared to move. In the next century Sámos produced the mathematician Aristarchus (310–230 BC), nowadays considered the best astronomer of his time. Although the other Greek astronomers all took it for granted that the Earth was the centre of the universe, and that the planets moved about it in perfect circles, Aristarchus, in an attempt to account for the retrograde motion of Mars and the fluctuations in the planets' brightness, boldly declared that the Earth was a mere planet among planets, and that all planets circled the sun. This was simply too much for his fellow mathematicians and astronomers to take on board, as it would be for many of their descendants, when Copernicus told them the same thing in the 16th century.

In 129 BC Rome incorporated Sámos into her Asia Province, and Augustus often visited the island in the winter, granting it many privileges, despite the fact that his enemies, Antony and Cleopatra, courted there for a short time; according to Plutarch, it was on Sámos that Antony became so infatuated that he threw away the world for a woman.

After the sacking of Constantinople, Sámos was captured by the Venetians and Genoese. In 1453, when the Genoese handed the island over to the Turks, the inhabitants took refuge en masse on Chíos, leaving their island all but deserted for 80 years. With promises of privileges and a certain amount of autonomy, the Ottomans repopulated the island with Greeks from mainland Greece, Asia Minor and other islands—names reflected in many of Sámos' village names (i.e. Mytilíni, Marathókambos, Pírgos). Over the centuries, however, the Ottomans' taxes became insupportable, and the Samians joined the revolution. They made good their old repuation at sea by defeating the Turks at a second battle of Mykále in 1824. Although the Great Powers excluded Sámos from Greece in 1830, it was granted semi-independence under the 'hegemony of the prince of Sámos', a Christian governor appointed by the sultan. In 1912, the Samian National Assembly took advantage of Turkey's defeats in the Balkan Wars to declare unity with Greece, under the leadership of Themostiklés Sophoúlis, later Prime Minister.

✆ *(0273–)*   **Getting There and Around**

By air: five daily flights from Athens with Olympic (✆ 27 237 in Sámos, ✆ 61 213 in Pythagório); also with Manos, Aegean, Cronus and Axon (Rhenia Tours has details, ✆ 88 800 in Sámos, branches in Pythagório, Kokkári, Votsalakia and Karlóvassi). Olympic and Manos fly twice weekly to Thessaloniki; Manos also hops twice weekly to Mýkonos and Santoríni. **Airport**: ✆ 61 219. There are too many charters from northern Europe, rising to 20 a day in July and August. The airport is 17km from Sámos and 4km west of Pythagório. The bus only runs between Sámos, Pythagório and the airport four times a day, so taking a taxi may be preferable.

By sea: from Órmos Marathókampos there are **hydrofoil excursions** to Foúrni, Pátmos and the islet Samiopoúla (*5,500dr inc. barbeque lunch*).

By road: From the station (a 10-minute walk from the dock at Sámos), **buses** run every hour or two (until 5pm) to Pythagório, Ag. Konstantínos, Karlóvassi, Kokkári, Tsamadoú; five to six times a day to Mytilíni and Chóra; four to Heréon; and once to Marathókampos, Votsalákia and Pírgos. **Car rental** is widely available; Speedy RentaCar, Pythagório, ✆ 61 502, 🖷 61 042, *auto1@otenet.gr*, is a reliable, family-run agency offering comprehensive insurance. **Taxi**: Sámos ✆ 28 404, Pythagório ✆ 61 450.

✆ *(0273–)*   **Tourist Information**

Pythagório has a particularly on-the-ball **Municipal Tourist Information Office**, on the main street, ✆ 61 389, 🖷 61 022 (*open 8am–10pm*), which can help with accommodation, day trips and boat excursions; Jocelyn, on the afternoon shift, is particularly helpful and can solve most problems. Meanwhile, in Sámos, the **EOT** hides away on Martíou Street, ✆ 28 530, and is open only from 9 to 2 on weekdays in season, leaving the job to the various travel agencies that line the waterfront (Rhenia Tours is one; *see* above). Also pick up a free copy of *Summer Days* for useful titbits and suggested walks. **Tourist police**: Sámos, ✆ 27 333; Pythagório, ✆ 61 333; Kokkári, ✆ 92 333; Karlóvassi, ✆ 31 444. **British Vice Consulate**: 15 Themístokli Sofúli St, Samos, ✆ 27 314.

Internet: Diavlos, beside Sámos police station, offers round-the-clock Internet access; in Pythagório, Nefeli bar on the waterfront obliges.

20 July, Profítis Ilías celebrated in many villages; 26 July, Ag. Paraskeví in Vathí; 27 July, Ag. Panteleímonos in Kokkári (one of the most popular); the Sámos Wine Festival takes place every year in August and dancing groups perform dances from various parts of Greece; 6 August, Celebration of the Revolution, Sámos, and of Metamorphosis, Pythagório; 29 August, Ag. Ioánnis in Pythagório; 8 September at Vrontiáni Monastery; 21 November, Panagía Spilianí by Pythagório.

Sámos/Vathí (ΒΑΘΥ)

Names on Sámos are a tad confusing. In ancient times the city of Sámos was what is now Pythagório. The present capital and main port of the island, set in a sweeping amphitheatre of green hills, inherited the name Sámos a few decades ago; when the autonomous 'Hegemony' moved here from Chóra in 1834 it was called Vathí, but this name is now only used on ferry schedules and to describe the upper, older town (Áno Vathí) at the 'deep end' of the city's magnificent harbour. If the immediate port area of Sámos town seems permeated with unfulfilled expectations (the abandoned hulk of the old Xenia Hotel on the waterfront doesn't help), the higgledy-piggledy, often arcaded lanes of Áno Vathí reek with atmosphere, linked with white and pastel houses covered with weathered tile roofs.

Most of the life down in Sámos town is concentrated in the pedestrianized backstreets and Plateía Pythagório near the middle of the overwhelmingly long waterfront. Here café dawdlers are shaded by palms and guarded by a stone lion, perhaps because Pythagorians believed that lions were the highest animals for a transmigrating soul to lodge in (the laurel was the pick of the plants). Four streets south and one block inland, the town's small public garden offers shelter from the afternoon sun, complete with a little café beside a trickling fountain. Diagonally opposite the garden, the fascinating finds from the island are displayed in the two buildings of the Archaeology Museum (*open 8–2.30, closed Mon; adm*). Top billing goes to the set of stylish and elegant Archaic statues in drapery folded as finely as pinstripes, a prelude to the majestic, finely sculpted, 7th-century BC *kouros* from the temple of Hera, at five metres one of the largest such statues ever found (they had to lower the floor to fit it in, and when the head was found, they had to raise the roof), with features as serene as a Buddha. There are geometric vases and prehistoric tools, and masses of ex-votos from the temple of Hera, dating back to little terracotta figurines from the 10th century BC; others were manufactured as far away as Cyprus, Egypt, Etruria and Andalucía. Many are quite costly, testifying to Hera's prestige: even bits of wooden furniture have been found, along with splendid bronzes and a magnificent array of bronze griffon heads (a Mesopotamian calendar beast introduced to the west through Sámos in the 8th century BC), most of them originally attached to bronze cauldrons.

The rather unpromising road north of the harbour leads to the so-so town beach, Gággou, near the fashionable suburb of Kalámi; the road continues, getting narrower and narrower, eventually ending in Ag. Paraskeví. Short excursions east of town offer views over the beautiful, narrow Strait of Mykále and the rugged coast of Turkey, where velvet-green slopes hem in the turquoise sea; the monastery Zoodóchos Pigí (1756), set on the cliffs over the fishing hamlet of Mourtiá, is a popular vantage point. Roads south of Sámos lead 10 to 14km to the beaches at Kervelí (pretty but stony), Possidónion (sheltered and shingly) and Psilí Ámmos (sandy, busy, and a bus ride from Sámos or a hop from Turkey). Very near to Psilí Ámmos, the lagoons around **Áliki** are now protected as a nature reserve; between November and July storks, flamingoes, ducks and herons are frequent visitors.

Sámos ✉ *83100,* ✆ *(0273–)*   ***Where to Stay and Eating Out***

Beware that nearly every hotel with any pretensions to comfort is mercilessly block-booked in season, and independent travellers may as well throw themselves on the

tender mercies of the travel offices lining the massive waterfront. Out of season, you'll find some bargains. Of the clutch of new, upmarket hotels at Kalámi, **Kirki Beach**, © 23 030 (*B; exp*), with a pool, is worth a stay. The stylish **Aeolis** is a waterfront option at Them. Sofouli 33, © 28 904, @ 28 063 (*B; exp*), with petite pool, Jacuzzi and bar perched on the roof terrace. **Hotel Galaxy**, © 22 665 (*C; mod*), is a few streets inland, with rooms facing on to a leafy pool area. Up in atmospheric Áno Vathí, **Christiana**, © 23 084 (*B; mod*), also has a pool. Back by the port, **Hotel Samos**, © 28 377, @ 23 771, *hotsamos@otenet.gr* (*C; inexp*), is an impersonal choice, but offers good value and sea views from the roof terrace (with pool and bar). The delightful **Pension Avli**, © 22 939 (*inexp*), is run by a sympathetic Athenian lawyer in the beautiful buildings of the former French convent, enclosing a shady courtyard; the simple rooms have wooden floors and furniture, deliciously at odds with the lurid red, moulded bathroom capsules. Off the road up to Áno Vathí, friendly family-run **Vathy**, © 28 124. @ 24 045(*C ; inexp*), sits with its teeny but welcome pool above the town and harbour. The quirky **Ionia Pension** three streets in from the sea at 5 Kalómiri, run by chatty Evagelía Zavitsánou, © 28 782 (*inexp*), is about as cheap as you get (shared bathrooms), while **Helen**, @ 28 215, @ 22 866 (*C; inexp*), has quiet, clean rooms with balcony. **St Nicholas**, on Mykáli beach (Psili Ammos) heading south, © 25 230, @ 28 522 (*B; exp*), has shuttle buses to both Sámos and Pythagório, along with two pools, plenty of watersports and tennis.

Beware the tacky bars and restaurants on the harbourfront. Instead, walk three minutes towards Kalámi to **La Calma**, a restaurant-bar where, for once, the noise of the waves drowns the roar of the mopeds. *Open eves only.* In the centre of town, five minutes up Lekati Street, past the bus station and post office, **Kotópoula** on Mykális and Vlamaris, © 28 415, is an excellent vine-covered taverna and favourite of the locals. **Petrino**, behind Samos Hotel, is also reasonable. In Áno Vathí, relax under a canopy of vine, sampling home-cooked Samian specialities such as fried chick pea balls, at **Agrabeli**. (Don't try to take a car further than the Hotel Christiana at the edge of the village: the streets are impossibly narrow.)

Entertainment and Nightlife

Many of the Sámos' waterfront bars stay open till the small hours, but their names and popularity change. Some of the more permanent include **Club Gallery**, **Escape** (open air and romantic, on the cliffs beyond the ferry) and **Cleary's Pub** (behind Plateía Pythagório). **Totem** (on the road to Pythagório) is a current favourite while, most summers, **Metropolis** sets up tent in the orchards near the bus station and attracts a younger crowd. For live Greek music try **Nisi** (the taverna at the end of the road at Ag. Paraskeví). *Friday and Saturday nights only.*

Pythagório (ΠΥΘΑΓΟΡΕΙΟ)

Pythagório on the southeast coast has for the past two decades been the island's most popular resort, although as it's climbed upmarket it's lost some of its old pith—not only is the 'Samian Hotbed' long gone, but so are some of the Greeks, who now commute to work in the resort from Chóra and the other inland villages. When it was the tyrant Polykrates' capital, its population reached 300,000; by the 20th century it was reduced to a little fishing village called Tigáni, or frying pan, not because of its sizzling heat but because of the shape of Polykrates' jetty. In 1955 the town was renamed to honour Sámos' most famous son, synonymous with the right-angled-triangle theorem that put his name on the lips of every schoolchild in the world. It was not only a brilliant theorem, but the first theorem: Pythagoras was the first to apply the same philosophical 'proofs' used by the earliest philosophers of Milétus to the subject of mathematics.

Pythagoras: Geometry, Beans and the Music of the Spheres

Pythagoras is a rather murky character who never wrote anything down himself, and is only known through the writing of his followers and enemies. Born on Sámos some time around 580 BC, he is known to have visited Egypt and Babylonia, either before or after his quarrel with Polykrates that sent him to Croton in southern Italy. In Croton he and his followers formed a brotherhood 'of the best' that governed the city for 20 years, before it revolted. This brotherhood was a secret society, similar to Freemasonry, that spread throughout the Greek world; brothers recognized each other by their symbol—the pentangle, or five-pointed star. But politics was hardly the main thrust of Pythagorean belief and philosophy, which was to have considerable influence, especially on Plato. On the religious level, Pythagoras believed the soul was immortal, and after death it transmigrated not only into new humans but into plants and animals, and that by purifying the soul one might improve it, and perhaps escape the need for re-incarnations. There were important prohibitions on eating meat (that chicken might be your grandmother, after all) and, more mysteriously, against eating fava beans. Over the centuries scholars have wondered: did Pythagoras somehow think that beans held human souls, expressed in unharmonious flatulence, or did he know about favism, a sometimes deadly reaction many Mediterranean people have to fava beans and their dust? Recently, however, it has been shown that Pythagoras has been the victim of a couple of millennia of misunderstanding: the ancient Greeks used letters for numbers, and what reads 'lay off fava beans' is actually another theorem of angles.

Pythagoras wasn't full of beans, but he was full of numbers. He was the first to apply *kosmos*, a Greek word meaning arrangement and ornamentation (hence our 'cosmetics') to the universe. The order of the cosmos, according to Pythagoras, was based on the connections of its various parts, which he called harmonia, and that harmonia was based on numbers. He discovered that music could be expressed mathematically by ratios and the tuning of the seven-string lyre, and he extended the harmonia he found there to 'the music of the spheres', the motions of the seven planets (the five visible ones, and the moon and sun)—and to the Golden Mean, proportions in beauty which were to give classical architecture and sculpture their perfect harmony. Although the belief that everything could be defined by number took the Pythagoreans down some wild and woolly paths, the key idea was that the study of the order of the Cosmos and its harmony would help to eliminate the disorder in our souls. No one agreed more than a latter-day Pythagorean, Johannes Kepler, who worked out the true elliptical orbits of the planets and later formulated the Third Law of Planetary Motion (1619): 'The square of the period of revolution is proportional to the cube of the mean distance from the sun.' Kepler noted that the varying speeds of the planets' revolutions corresponded with the ratios of the polyphonies used by Renaissance composers; in

1980, one of the mementoes of Earth that NASA scientists packed aboard *Voyager* for its journey out of our solar system was a computer-generated recording of Pythagoras' and Kepler's music of the spheres.

Excavations of the city itself, begun in 1985, occasionally turn Pythagório into a minefield of trenches. Pythagoras, however, didn't leave as much behind in his home town as Polykrates' chief engineer, Efplinos, designer of the 360m **ancient harbour mole**, which Herodotus declared was one of the three great wonders of ancient Greece; it now supports a new harbour wall, where white yachts swish in and out in place of sharp-bowed *samainae*. The **long walls** that surrounded ancient Pythagório were originally 6,500m from end to end and stretched all the way to Cape Foniás, bristling with towers and gates; partly destroyed by Lysander when the Spartans took Sámos during the Peloponnesian War, bits and pieces remain scattered along the edge of town. Lykúrgos Logothétis, a hero of the 1821 revolution, built the castle by the town— mostly at the expense of the Temple of Hera. Pythagório's sand and pebble **beach** begins at Logothétis' castle and extends off and on several kilometres to the west. The great victory at sea over the Turks in 1824 is commemorated by a plaque ('Christ Saved Samos the 6 August 1824') in the pretty white church of the **Metamórfosis**. There's a small **archaeological museum** in the Community Hall (*open 8.45–2, closed Mon*) which houses finds from the area.

Little remains of the **Roman Baths** (*open 8.30–2.45, closed Mon*) west of town, but a summer season of music and theatre takes place at the ancient **theatre** (ask for details at the Tourist Office). Don't miss the extraordinary **Efplinion Tunnel** (*open 8.45– 2.40, closed Mon; adm*) half a kilometre up the road. Polykrates wanted his aqueduct kept secret, to prevent an enemy cutting off the water. Under Efplinos two crews of slaves started digging through the solid rock on either side of Mount Kástri and, thanks to his amazingly precise calculations, met on the same level, only a few inches off total Channel Tunnel perfection. Nearly 1,000m long, the tunnel's earthenware pipes kept the baths full in Pythagório for 1000 years or so—until the 6th century AD, after which the tunnel was forgotten until it was accidentally rediscovered in the late 19th century. The lamps and tools of the workmen were found in the parallel maintenance tunnel. Recently the tunnel has been electrically lit, so it no longer seems quite as old and mysterious as it used to; visitors are allowed in the first 700m, but the middle of the tunnel has collapsed. Another road from the ancient theatre leads up to the cave where the sybil Phyto prophesied a one and true god. Along with her sister sybils, Phyto would provide an important link between antiquity and Christianity; appropriately the cave shelters a church, **Panagía Spilianí**, last rebuilt in 1836, near a tiny monastery in the cypresses.

The Temple of Hera and Heréon

From Pythagório, the marble-paved **Sacred Way** (now 90 per cent under the profane airport road and runway) led the faithful 8km west past an estimated 2,000 statues, tombs and elaborate monuments to the **Temple of Hera** (*open 8.30–2.45, closed Mon; adm*). The site was already sacred to 'cow-eyed' Hera back in the Bronze Age. She was the first of all the gods to have temples erected in her honour; two temples of mud, wood and bricks had already been built here by 718 BC, when an architect named Roikos built what is considered to have been the first of all true Greek temples (i.e. a stone building completely surrounded by a colonnaded peristyle). When this was destroyed by Cyrus' satrap Orsitis in his war on Sámos, Polykrates, who never did believe in half measures, decided to replace it in a big way.

Shortlisted as one of the Seven Wonders of the Ancient World, Polykrates' Great Temple was, after the temple of Artemis at Ephesus and the Temple of Zeus in Akragas (Agrigento), the third largest temple ever built by the Greeks (approximately 354 by 165ft or 108 by 52m); today only a single column of its original 133 remains intact as sole witness to its extraordinary size and height, even if looks like a wobbly stack of mouth-freshening mints.

Mythology

 Zeus had to use cunning to seduce an uninterested Hera (perhaps because he was her brother), and they spent a 300-year-long wedding night on Sámos 'concealed from their dear parents'. Bathing in the Imbrassos perpetually renewed Hera's virginity. She was pre-eminently the goddess of marriage, worshipped in three aspects: The Girl, The Fulfilled and The Separated, but never in an erotic fashion or as a mother (though often a wicked stepmother); she was always the Great Goddess, ambivalent about her relationship with her upstart consort. Although her temple was filled with great works of art, the holy of holies was a plank of wood crudely painted with the goddess's features, believed to have fallen from heaven, too sacred to be touched; the priests tied it with twigs of osier, the willow sacred to Hera, and carried it thus. Twice a year grand celebrations took place at the temple: the Heraia, in honour of her marriage, and the Tonea, recalling the attempt of the Argives to snatch the sacred wooden plank for their own Temple of Hera, only to be thwarted by the goddess, who refused to let their ship sail away until they returned it. By her altar were her symbols: two peacocks and an osier.

The temple was destroyed in the 3rd century AD by raiding Herulians; earthquakes in the 4th and 5th centuries and builders looking for ready-cut stone finished it off. Only the base of the massive **altar**, **a Mycenaean wall**, other small temples, a **tribute** sent by Cicero and the apse of a Christian basilica have survived. Some of the stone went into the **Sarakíni Castle**, built by a Patmian naval officer of the same name in 1560, appointed by the sultan to govern Sámos.

The nearby seaside village of **Heréon** (ΗΡΑΙΟ), a dusty backwater a decade ago, now has its portion of hotels, apartments and bars on a short stretch of beach that gets too crowded in the summer; jets pouncing on to the nearby airport add to the noise. To get away from it all, check out caiques running south to the remote sandy beach of **Tsopela**. If you have your own transport, inland villages offer some respite as well: **Chóra**, west of Pythagório, was made the capital of Sámos by the aforementioned Sarakíni and kept its status until 1855. It's still a lively little place with good tavernas. To the north the road passes through a steep valley to the rather sprawling village of **Mýtilíni**, where animal fossils dating back 15 million years—believed to have been washed into a deposit by the Meander River, before Sámos broke free from the mainland—have been gathered in Greece's only **Palaeontological Museum** in the Town Hall (*open weekdays 9–2 and sometimes in the afternoons; call ahead to check, © (0273) 52 055*). Sámos had a reputation for fierce monsters in mythology; one story has it that the island broke off from the mainland like glass when the monsters let loose a particular high-pitched shriek. The museum's prize exhibit, among the skulls and teeth of prehistoric hippopotomi and rhinoceres, is a 13-million-year-old fossilized horse brain.

Above Heréon, lemon groves surround **Mýli**, the source of the Imvrassos, where an important Mycenaean tomb was accidently found near the village school. From equally well-watered **Pagóndas** ('the land of springs'), the road circles around through Sámos' finest untamed, majestic south-coast scenery en route to **Spatharáioi** (7½km) and **Pírgos** (another 6km), a pretty mountain village in the now charred pines, founded by settlers from the city of the same name in the Peloponnese. Down in a ravine below Pírgos, **Koútsi** is the kind of place preferred by the ancient nymphs, a grove of venerable plane trees, clear waters and cool mountain air and something the nymphs didn't have—a good taverna, perfect on a hot, lazy afternoon. Unfortunately tour operators know about it too, so you may want to get there early or late for lunch.

From Pírgos you can circle around back towards Pythagório without retracing your steps (although sadly, the trees along this stretch in particular took a good scorching in the rampant fires in July 2000), going by way of **Koumaradáioi**, where a track leads up to the **Moní Megális Panagías**, founded in 1586; the walls of the monastery encompass one of the island's most beautiful churches, with good icons and frescoes inside (unfortunately closed to visitors). One of the monks who built it also founded **Timíou Stavroú Monastery** (1592) to the east, after a dream he had of a buried icon of the Holy Cross; the icon was duly found, and has been completely plated with silver and ex-votos in gratitude for its miraculous cures. On Holy Wednesday people gather here from all over Sámos to watch the Archbishop re-enact the washing of the Apostles' feet. North of the monastery, ceramics and pottery are made at **Mavratzeí**, which specializes in the goofy 'Pythagorean Cup'; the main road heads back to Chóra.

Sámos ✆ *(0273–)*   ***Where to Stay and Eating Out***

Pythagório ✉ 83103

If not in the trendy little town, the hotels of Pythagório are clustered out of most camera angles but in easy walking distance around the beach at Potokáki or just north of town. The big and luxurious **Doryssa Bay Hotel**, Potokáki, ✆ 61 360, ✆ 61 463 (*A; lux*), with rooms in an older hotel or spread through a perfect asymmetrical village of air-conditioned bungalows, has a pool, tennis courts, watersports and even a minigolf course for the small fry. Smaller **Glycoriza Beach**, ✆ 61 321 ✆ 61596 (*C; mod*), is another good out-of-town choice by the sea with pool. **Hera II**, ✆ 61 879, ✆ 61 190 (*C; med*), is a cool, pink establishment: elegant with panoramic town and sea views. **Kastelli**, ✆ 61 728, ✆ 61 863 (*C; exp*), a tad further out and 100m from the sea, with soaring views, breakfast and air-conditioning, is a good bet if you can beat the crowds. **Gallini**, ✆ 61 167, ✆ 61 168 (C; mod), is central and quiet, with a friendly owner; the rooms on top have verandas and more of those views. Pythagório is packed with small up-scale pensions and studios that are packed in summer; ask the tourist office for a list of available rooms, ✆ 61 389, ✆ 61 022. **Areli Studios**, ✆ 61 245, ✆ 62 320 (*inexp*), are some of the most pristine in the Aegean, with an olive grove and abundance of flowers between you and the road. **Afrodite**, ✆/✆ 61 540 (*inexp*), also offers studios and an airy apartment; port-facing rooms have extensive views. **Alexandra**, ✆ 61 429 (*D; inexp*), has simple, charming and cheap rooms with a lovely, shady garden on the lower level, replete with reclining chairs. **Hotel Stratos**, ✆ 61 157, ✆ 61 181, *vasiliades@aol.com* (*C; inexp*), has a non-smoking policy and rooms of varying prices and standards under the aegis of an affable Greek American.

The waterfront is one uninterrupted line of tavernas and cafés that charge well over the odds for what you get, so compare menus before you sit down. Alternatively, seek out **Maritsa**, Ⓒ 61 957, a street in from the harbour and with excellent octopus (but unimpressive service); **Platania**, under the plane trees in the main square, offers gargantuan portions and good *saganáki*. The last restaurant in the group of tavernas on the beach, at the far side of the children's playground, is also pretty reliable, or consider taking a taxi up to Chóra and trying **Andonis** or **Sintrofia**.

Entertainment and Nightlife

Ask at the Tourist Office about the summer music and theatre programme in the ancient theatre. **Notos** bar, Tarsanas beach, has a chilled-out concoction of world music throughout the day; of an evening, this turns to beautiful, live bouzouki courtesy of the talented Yannis (check times at the Tourist Office). To admire the finely inlaid bouzoukis he crafts and to talk shop, visit Pythagorios on Metamorfosis Sotiros Street; it also has a good selection of Samian handicrafts and soothing olive oil soap. **Riva** bar is a romantic spot to stargaze, and **Edem**, on the way into town from Sámos, has live Greek music.

The North Coast: Beaches and Vineyards

On the great bay just opposite Sámos town, **Malagári**, immersed in pines, is the headquarters of the Union of Sámos Wine Producing Cooperatives, where wines are aged in great oaken barrels in the handsome stone warehouses known as *tavérnes*. Ten kilometres west of Vathí, pretty **Kokkári** (KOKKAPI) was once a whitewashed fishing village that owes its funny name 'onion bulbs' to its old speciality, although now package tourism has replaced most of the onions. Still, the setting is lovely, the houses spread over two narrow headlands. In addition to its own busy beach, there are several nearby. **Lemonákia** is a 20-minute walk away and the more beautiful **Tsamadoú**, a partly nudist beach 2km from Kokkári (and a steep descent from the car), is a crescent of multi-coloured pebbles where you can rub elbows with your neighbouring sunworshippers. Further west, **Avlákia** has an altogether different, old-time atmosphere: a delightfully low-key resort with a sprinkling of accommodation on the beach and a second small pebble beach at **Tsaboú**. It is a good base for exploring the ravishing green hinterland, where cypresses and pines rise up like towers along the majestic slopes of Mount Ámpelos, 1153m; its name, from the 1st century BC, means 'Mount Vineyard'.

'Fill High the Bowl with Samian Wine...'

 The north-facing mountain villages of Vourliótes, Manolátes and Stavrinídes are the top wine-growing villages on Sámos, where one famous variety of grape, Moscháto Sámou, has reigned for the last 2,000 years or so. The old vines are thickly planted on small anti-erosion terraces called *pezoúles* from 150m to 800m above sea level and, like all quality dessert wines, have an extremely low yield. After years of neglect in the Middle Ages, Samian wine began its comeback under the Greek settlers brought over by the Ottomans in the late 16th century. By the 18th century it was imported in large quantities to Sweden and even France, and the Catholic Church gave Sámos a concession to provide wine for Mass, something it still does to a degree in Austria, Switzerland and Belgium. All Samian wine has been sold through the cooperative since 1933, after winegrowers, reduced to penury by profiteering international wine merchants, revolted against the system and demanded control of their own production. The most prized wine of Sámos is its light amber Grand Cru Vin Doux Naturel, with 15% alcohol, given its *appellation* in France in 1982 (the only Greek wine so honoured); also try a chilled bottle of fruity Nectar, aged in its wooden cask and splendid with strong cheeses, fruit salads or sorbets. Of the dry wines, the green-tinted Samena Dry White is made from grapes grown above 600m, and is popular as an aperitif.

From the handsome village of **Vourliótes**, it's a delightful, leafy 3km walk up to Sámos' oldest monastery, **Panagía Vrontiáni**, founded in 1560, with some of its original wall paintings, although access is limited now that the monks have been replaced by soldiers. Further east along the coast, a road leads up to lovely **Manolátes**, which overlooks an arcadian valley beloved by nightingales, one of the beauty spots of Sámos; at **Platanákia**, you can eat under the magnificent grove of plane trees and drink barrelled red wine, but beware the 'Greek Night' excursion busloads. The last place where the mountains cede to the coast is at anti-climactic **Ag. Konstantínos**, quieter and rawer than some other resorts, but lacking their traditional character.

Sámos ☎ (0273–)   ***Where to Stay and Eating Out***

Malagári ✉ 83100

> **Poseidon**, ☎ 23 201, 🖷 24 592 (*A; lexp*), is equipped with a pool, roof garden and other creature comforts.

Kokkári ✉ 83100

> Much of the accommodation here is packaged out in season. Five hundred metres above Kokkári is the air-conditioned **Arion**, ☎ 92 020, 🖷 92 006 (*A; exp*), built in traditional Samian style with shady lawns among the trees, as well as a pool, sauna, Jacuzzi and even ping pong; the hotel bus provides transport to Kokkári. *Open May–Oct.* **Olympia Village**, ☎ 92 420, 🖷 92 457 (*exp*), has principally packaged bungalows in a flowery complex; its sister, **Olympia Beach** (same numbers, *mod*) is appropriately by the strand, with aquatic views. **Pension Paradisos**, ☎ 92 162 (*mod*), has moderately priced studio apartments near the Arion. Kokkári also has some 250 rooms in private houses, but don't hold your breath. On the water's edge **Kima** has tasty, freshly prepared Greek dishes (*3,000dr*); for Italian, head for satisfying **Porto Picolo**. If you're dying for a disco, try **Cabana Club** in the centre.

Avlákia/Vourliótes/Manolátes ✉ 83100

> **Avlákia**, ☎ 94 230 (*C; inexp*), is a very pleasant old-fashioned hotel right on the beach, with **Oscar**, its restaurant, on the strand; there are several more traditional seaside tavernas along the strip. **Pension Markos**, up in Vourliótes, ☎ 93 291, and **Angela's Studio**, in Manolátes, ☎ 94 478 (*both inexp*), are great places for peace and quiet away from the sea. Angela has a shady, grassy garden from which to contemplate the hills.

> At the beginning of the 4km road up to Manolátes, **Palataki**, in a grove of plane trees, is open in season and is liked for its spit-roasted meats and wood-oven dishes. Halfway

up the village itself, look out for **Giorgides**, ✆ 94 239, a delightful taverna spilling out on both sides of the street. Follow signs all the way to the top of the village to **Loukas**, blissfully overlooking the hills and sea. Everything here is home-made from their own olive oil, cheese, wine and *suma* (a local schnapps) to the stuffed vine leaves and courgette flowers (picked daily at 6am before they close) and then baked in their traditional wood-burning oven. Manolátes also has some excellent little craft shops including ΙΒΥΚΟΣ, or simply, **The Shop**, ✆ 94 338, with handpainted ceramics and local modern art.

Ag. Konstantínos ✉ 83200

Apollonia Bay, ✆ 94 444, ✆ 94 090 (*C; mod*), is a smart apartment complex with pool, while the old **Atlantis**, ✆ 94 257 (*E; inexp*), is a good budget bet. There are no end of rooms and pensions down by the water, of which **Coral's apartments**, ✆ 94 390 (*inexp*), are a good example; try for a sea-facing room. Two kilometeres inland at Andóni, a hillside hamlet of old stone two-storey houses called **Aindónokastro**, ✆ 94 404, in Athens ✆ (01) 544 0182 (*B; mod*), has been beautifully converted into traditionally decorated apartments sleeping 2–4 people. *Open Apr–Oct.*

Karlóvassi and Western Sámos

Wallflower **Karlóvassi** (ΚΑΡΛΟΒΑΣΙ), Sámos' second city and port, was an industrial tanning centre before the Second World War and, although the hides and stink are long gone, the empty warehouses along the port present a dreary face to the world. After the first baleful introduction, however, the little city is pleasant enough, and neatly divided (in descending order of interest) into old, middle and new (Paléo, Meséo and Néo) Karlóvassi, punctuated here and there with the pale blue domes of absurdly large 19th-century churches. It is much sleepier and Greekier than Vathí or Pythagório, and most visitors stay in a small cluster of hotels in the picturesque old town of Limáni, with a far more appealing and intimate atmosphere than Néo Karlóvassi, although this is where you'll find the regional bus stop, banks, post office and other useful services, not to mention the timeless Paradise, an old-man's ouzerie with tables and chairs strewn under a shady tree. A city bus provides good transport to the nearest beach, **Potámi** (ΠΟΤΑΜΙ), 2km west, a fine sweep of beach with a few rooms and a fish taverna or two, watched over by a chapel that can charitably be described as an attempt at Orthodox moderne.

Western Sámos has been compared to western Crete: fewer sights, fewer tourists, but amply rewarding in the walking scenery and beach department. A track from Potámi leads back to the church of **Panagía tou Potamoú** (Our Lady of the River), Sámos' oldest church dating from the 10th century, and, if you carry on, to the lovely river canyon, a magical place of chilly rock pools and little waterfalls that you have to swim to cross; but don't expect to have it to yourself in the summer. There are superb sandy beaches further west: the lovely cove of **Mikró Seitáni** (1km beyond the end of Potámi) and **Megálo Seitáni** (4km) at the foot of a striking ravine, but you need your hiking shoes to reach them, as well as your own provisions. The track, one of the most stunning, continues another 8km along the towering west shore as far as **Drakáioi**, a farming village and time-capsule glimpse of traditional Greece at the end of the rough road from Marathókampos and a very rare bus line. South of Drakaíoi the road continues round, past **Kallithéa**, with rooms and food.

Buses run on Mondays from Karlóvassi to **Plátanos**, the island's second most important wine-growing area and down to the sea by way of **Koumeïka**, a little village with an overgrown marble fountain; the sand-pebble beach with shade and a quieter summer community is alternatively known as **Ormós Koumíikou** or **Bállos**. The more westerly road south of Karlovássi curls around the soaring mass of Sámos' highest peak, **Mount Kérkis**, 1,575m, a dormant volcano often crowned with a halo of cloud and mist like a remembrance of eruptions past. **Kastanéa**, surrounded by chestnut groves and laughing brooks, is a popular place to aim for on hot days, but remembered by locals as the location for 27 deaths at the hands of the occupying Italians. To the south, **Marathókampos** is an attractive village on tiny lanes spilling down the slopes, where the residents have restored some old abandoned houses for guests. Below is the beach, pleasantly low-key resort and regional port of **Órmos Márathokámpos** (ΟΡΜΟΣ ΜΑΡΑΘΟΚΑΜΠΟΣ), from where caiques sail several times a week to Samiopoúla, a tiny islet with a fine stretch of sand. Extending west of Ormos is the long white sandy beach and package resort of **Votsalákia**, now well and truly lined with tourist shops, restaurants and flashing lights. For a brief escape, follow the marked path through the olives to the **Convent of the Evangelístria**, and beyond to the summit of Mount Kérkis; fit walkers can storm the peak and return for a swim in five or six hours. Alternatively, and especially if you have small children in tow, keep heading west to the safe, exceedingly shallow seas at **Psilí Ámmos** (not to be confused with Psilí Ámmos in the east). Continuing on, there are still some unspoiled sandy coves, accessible only by foot or boat. If you have your own transport, to escape the madding crowds a bit more, drive on to the delightful cove of Limnionas, with excellent swimming and relaxation guaranteed.

Sámos ✆ (0273–)   **Where to Stay and Eating Out**

Karlóvassi ✉ 83200

In Limáni, the Samaina Group has the international-chain-style **Samaina Inn**, ✆ 30 401, ✉ 34 471 (*A; exp*), with smart, cool rooms, large pool area and crèche; their **Samaina Bay**, ✆ 30 812 (*B; exp*), is less flashy but still with pool. Towards Potámi beach, **Aspasia**, ✆ 32 363, ✉ 34 777 (*B; mod*), is the smartest place to sleep, with air-conditioned rooms, a pool, roof garden and minibus service. *Open Apr–Oct*. In Néo Karlóvassi, **Hotel Merope**, ✆ 32 650, ✉ 32 652 (*B; inexp*), is a favourite of many for its old-world service and amazingly good value, with period rooms and collectors' TVs, as well as pool. There are also cheap rooms in Limáni, on the pedestrian lane behind the port road. At dinnertime make your way to the seaside **Kyma**, for well-prepared *mezédes*. On the road east, halfway to Ag. Nikoláos, **Psarades**, ✆ 32 489, also has excellent fresh fish along with dreamy sunsets over the sea. Near Karlóvassi harbour, **Anema** pool-bar enticingly advertises 'many unexpectables, passion, rythym [sic]'.

Ormos Márathokámpos/Limnionas ✉ 83102

Anthemousa Studios, ✆ 37 073 (*inexp*), are up by the church in olive groves above the port, with tranquil views; the owner also has seafront studios and offers boat trips. **Kleopatra Studios**, ✆ 37 486 (*inexp*), are plain but decent; upstairs maisonettes have balconies and the kind owner has more flats right by the sea along the road. **Kerkis Bay**, ✆ 37 202, ✉ 37 372 (*B; inexp*), has seen better days but has a good restaurant. There are also some 15 rooms to rent up in pretty Plátanos. Ormos

Márathokámpos has a decent array of tavernas and the very friendly **Pizza Cave**. If you fancy a tipple, there's even the **Mucho Drinko** bar.

Lovely Limnionas offers the low-lying, whitewashed **Limnionas Bay Hotel**, ✆ 37 057 (*mod*), with pool, and **Limnionas Studios**, ✆ 31 294 (*inexp*), beautifully secluded at the corner of the cove, with views across it. Meanwhile, **Limnionas Taverna**, on the beach, is a small place with fish and traditional fare. Just past the turning down to Limnionas on the main road, **Sophia's Taverna** is recommended.

Skiáthos (ΣΚΙΑΘΟΣ)

Racy, cosmopolitan Skiáthos is not for the shy teetotaller or anyone looking for a slice of 'authentic' Greece. Although still an isolated peasant island community in the early 1970s, Skiáthos has been catapulted faster than any other island into the frantic world of tourism, with all the pros and cons that this inevitably entails, beginning with the predatory attitudes of the *nouveau riche* ex-fishermen and farmers. Corruption and violence (violence by Greek island standards, at any rate) have long been a factor in local life; those in the know speak darkly of generations of untreated syphilis. Nevertheless, Skiáthos is one of the most popular destinations in Greece: away from the main road, it is stunningly beautiful, and its magnificent beaches (by most counts there are 62) provide some of the best swimming in Greece. Add to this a host of lively bars and restaurants and you have the ingredients for a potent, heady cocktail that attracts the young and the young at heart from the four corners of the globe.

History

When the enormous Persian fleet of King Xerxes sailed to conquer Greece in 480 BC, it encountered a fierce storm in the waters off Skiáthos. So many of Xerxes' ships were damaged that he put in for repairs. During his stay Xerxes came up with the world's first-known navigational aid, to keep his fleet from wrecking on a reef called Myrmes (now called Lepheteris and to this day a dangerous menace to ships sailing between Skiáthos and the mainland). 'Thither the barbarians brought and set up a pillar of stone that the shoal might be clearly visible,' as Herodotus wrote; thanks to its guidance, Xerxes succeeded in slipping safely past the Athenian patrol ships towards his first sea battle at Artemisseon and eventual defeat at Salamis. Part of the pillar can still be seen today, in the courtyard of the Naval Cadet School in Piraeus.

The rest of Skiáthos' history follows that of the other Sporades. The Gizzi ruled the island in the name of Venice and built the fort on Boúrtzi islet by the present-day town, which was settled in 1790 by refugees from Límni on Évia. The Skiathot navy assisted the Russians in the campaign at Cêsme, when they defeated the Ottomans. The islanders revolted against the distant Turks in 1805, and sent so many ships to aid the cause of independence that Skiáthos itself was left unprotected and prey to marauders. It was one of the first places to be touched by the Orthodox reformist movement, Kollivádes, emanating from Mount Áthos (although Skiáthos means 'shadow of Áthos' in Greek, its name comes from a pre-Hellenic source).

✆ (0427–)   **Getting There and Around**

By air: two flights a day from Athens (except Weds: one flight), and numerous charters from European cities. Olympic Airways is at Papadiamánti, Skiáthos town, ✆ 22 040. **Airport information**: ✆ 22 049. The 4km to the airport can be taxied for around 2,000dr.

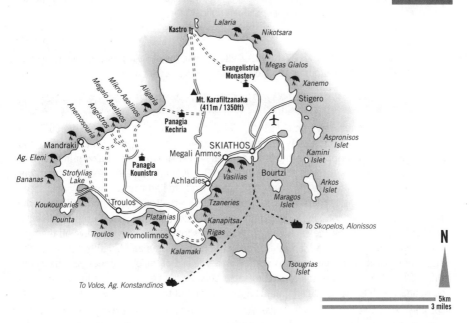

By sea: daily **excursion boats** go to Skópelos and Alónissos. The boats bobbing up and down in front of the cafés in the old harbour will take you to most beaches and you'll hear the owners calling out their destinations. Some offer round-island trips but be warned that on the north side there is a fairly uninteresting stretch of coast and the sea can be rough—many a daytripper returns green about the gills. You can also rent your own boat by the day or hour. **Port authority**: ✆ 22 017.

By road: **buses** to other parts of the island run at least hourly in season (until 11pm from Skiáthos town to Koukonariés, 1am vice versa) from the new harbour in Skiáthos town. Demand is so great in summer that your feet may not touch the floor throughout the journey. If you want to get about the island under your own steam, there are a number of places to **rent cars**, motorbikes and scooters along the harbour, but be careful on the roads—traffic is fast-moving. **Taxis**, ✆ 21 460, are a popular, if expensive, option; never be shy of sharing.

By mule: various agencies will take you around the island on muleback; more upmarket riding (of the **horse** variety) is available in Koukounariés, from Pinewood Riding Club.

By foot: a network of walking paths offers the opportunity to explore Skiáthos on two feet rather than four; look out for Rita and Dietrich Harkort's local guide.

✆ *(0427–)*   *Tourist Information*

Tourist police: Papadiamánti, ✆ 23 172 (*open 8am–9pm in season*).

Geof Baldry is a great source of information on Skiáthos; call © 49 473 or visit his illuminating Web site: *www.skiathosinfo.com.* He's also happy to organize special activity (e.g. painting, walking or sailing) holidays for you.

Festivals

26 July, Ag. Paraskeví; 27 July, Ag. Panteleímonos; 15 August, in Evangelismós; 27 August, Ag. Fanóurios; 21 November, Kounistra Monastery.

Skiáthos Town

The capital and only real town on the island, Skiáthos has a split personality. On the one hand it is a gentle spread of traditional whitewashed houses, overhung with bougainvillea and freshly washed sheets rippling in the breeze; on the other, it is a razzmatazz of in-your-face commercialism. A walk through the backstreets will help you escape some of the latter, but don't expect to encounter any donkeys; you're more likely to find yourself dodging high-speed trail bikes. The town has two harbours, separated by the pretty **Boúrtzi** promontory, where the medieval fortress now contains a restaurant and an outdoor theatre used during summer. If you simply can't summon the energy to join the queues for bus, boat or taxi, dive off the rock here and pretend you're in a Martini ad. For a sweeping panorama of Skiáthos town and the neighbouring island of Skópelos, take the steps up at the end of the old harbour past the water-front cafés, restaurant touts and souvenir shops. Cocktail hour seems to last forever here, as you sit and watch an extraordinary international selection of the human race go by.

Morning excursion boats wait to whisk you off in half an hour to **Tsougriás** islet, facing Skiáthos town. In the sixties the Beatles wanted to buy it. It's an ideal place to escape the droves of summer visitors, with its fine sand and excellent swimming. The simple snack bar usually provides freshly caught *marídes* (whitebait) to munch at a table under the trees, but you may have to share your food with the resident wasp population. Tsougriás has two other beaches, accessible only by foot, where you really can play Robinson Crusoe for the day.

If this flagrant hedonism pricks the conscience, you can get a shot of culture by locating the **house of Alexander Papadiamántis** (1851–1911), situated just off the main street (*open 9.30–1 and 5–8, closed Mon*).

Papadiamántis, the Master of Neo-Hellenic Prose

One of modern Greece's finest novelists, Papadiamántis wouldn't recognize his home town today. The Skiáthos he immortalized in his stories, with stark realism and serene, dispassionate prose, was a poor, tragic place, where most of the men were forced to emigrate or spend years at sea, and the women lived hard lives of servitude, often in total penury to accumulate a *príka*, or dowry, for each daughter; this was such a burden that, when a little girl died, other women would comfort the mother by saying: 'Happy woman, all you need to marry this one off is a sheet.' Papadiamántis' strongest story, *I Phonissa* (*The Murderess*), written in 1903, concerns an old woman who, reflecting on the conditions of her own life, sees the monstruous injustice of the system and quietly smothers her sickly newborn granddaughter, to spare her daughter the need to slave away for her dowry. Always the island's herbal doctor (the one herb she could never find was the herb of sterility), the woman believes that her destiny is to alleviate the suffering of others, and she drowns and smothers four other daughters of poor families before being pursued to her own death. As she drowns, the last thing she sees is the wretched vegetable garden that was her own dowry.

Skiáthos ✉ 37002, ✆ (0427–)   **Where to Stay**

For more information on hotels, contact the hoteliers' association, ✆ 22 187 or 21 019, 🖷 22 526, or the rented room owners' association, ✆ 22 990 (kiosk on the quay). Skiáthos has accommodation to suit everyone's taste and pocket, but in high season, when it seems the island will sink beneath the weight of its visitors—who outnumber the locals 11 to one—finding a bed without a reservation or package booking is the devil. If you come unstuck in your quest, try the brown tourist kiosk or any of the tourist offices on the waterfront.

Hotel Akti, ✆ 22 024 (*C; exp*), has watery harbour views, especially from the four-person top-floor suite. The **Alkyon**, on the new harbour front, ✆ 22 981 (*A; mod*), is the town's biggest hotel with an airy lobby and comfortable rooms overlooking pleasant gardens. Nearby, the **Meltemi**, ✆ 22 493 (*C; exp–mod*), has a loyal following and is generally booked solid, though their bar is a good vantage point for the antics of the flotilla crowd as they moor and unmoor with zealous gung-ho. *Open Apr–Oct.* Away from the harbourfront, but central and set in delightful little gardens are two sister hotels: **Pothos**, ✆ 22 694 (*D; exp*), and **Bourtzi**, ✆ 21 304 (*C; exp*); all rooms are en suite, with telephone, fridge and balcony. In terms of overall appeal, Pothos just has the edge, but both have great charm. **San Remo**, ✆ 22 078, 🖷 21 918 (*D; inexp*), is a colourful hotel whose terraced rooms give you dress circle seats to observe the harbour traffic and wave at the greenhorns on the incoming charter jets. For something quieter, in the Old Town, two traditional Skiathot houses have been converted to make the small **Hotel Orsa**, ✆ 22 300, 🖷 21 975 (*B; mod*); or head up to nearby Ag. Fanourios, where the **Messinis family**, ✆/🖷 22 134 (*mod*), have quiet rooms with panoramic views from the balconies, carefully tended by Stavros Messinis, a master craftsman. Central and cheaper, **Australia Hotel**, just off Papadiamántis Street, behind the post office, ✆ 22 488 (*E; inexp*), has simple en suite rooms. Surrounded by flowers and olives, and a 10-minute walk from the centre, the **Fanariotis** family has tranquil studios with terrace, accessed from the ring road (ask husband Miltos, who works in Jimmy's Bar on the waterfront; *mod–inexp*).

Skiáthos ✆ (0427–)   **Eating Out**

Eating out in Skiáthos is a hit-and-miss affair; often the most beautifully located tavernas serve the worst food. The tavernas on the steps at the western end of the old harbour tend to be over-priced and in high season just walking past is to run a gauntlet of pushy touts, while some of the places tucked away on backstreets may be harder to find but are well worth the effort. **Mesogia**, ✆ 21 440, is the oldest taverna on Skiáthos and has an excellent repertoire of Greek delicacies including outstanding fried courgette balls. For more good Greek fare and a pleasant atmosphere, try **Family**, up near the clock tower, overlooking the Boúrtzi. **Helliníkon** is another solid local favourite, set in a garden away from the ritzy port. For a more international flavour and a lovely view, the **Windmill**, in a converted guess-what behind the San Remo Hotel, is popular though pricey. **Casa Blanca/Primavera**, in a small square near the church behind the fish market end of the waterfront, serves excellent pasta and other Italian delights, or try **Cuba**, east of Papadiamánti in a leafy *plateía*. Overlooking the sea, **Agnantio**, ✆ 22 016, on the road to the Evangelístria monastery, is a delight with its chic navy and white interior, and its terrace with beautiful views over the Pounta promontory.

Entertainment and Nightlife

Having eaten, you'll be spoilt for choice when it comes to bars, but they're not cheap. The little **Admiral Benbow Inn** (Polytechníou St) provides a corner of old England and hippie music on Skiáthos, while, in the same street, the **Borzoi** is worth a try after midnight if you can afford the drinks. An oasis of tranquillity in the Skiáthos summer madhouse, **Adagio**, opposite Stavros taverna in Evangelístrias St, is a friendly and non-exclusive gay bar with pleasant décor and classical music to soothe the eye and ear; a favourite place for an after-dinner drink or coffee. **Kentavros** promises more of a funky jazz and blues atmosphere, near Papadiamántis' house. On a warm summer evening, the picturesque waterfront bars come into their own, one of the best being **Jimmy's**. For a blaring bop, the heaving hordes go to **Kavos**, **Remezzo**, and the ever popular seafront **BBC**. In high season, the only place to get a good dose of genuine live Greek music is at **Aselinos**, ✆ 49 394, the huge cattleshed of a taverna on Asélinos beach; *Friday and Saturday from 2am*. If you prefer celluloid, **Paradise** outdoor cinema offers undubbed films on the ring road.

Koukounariés and Other Beaches

Beaches, beaches and more beaches are the key to Skiáthos' success, and they rim the emerald isle like lace. Mobile sardine tins called buses follow the main road along the south coast, stopping within easy walking distance of the island's best strands, nearly all equipped with places to lunch and someone hiring out windsurf boards and other watersports gear. From town, the most convenient is **Megáli Ámmos**, although it's generally too crowded for comfort. Moving westward, **Achládies** (ΑΧΛΑΔΙΕΣ) beach, dominated by the large Esperides Hotel (with tennis court open to the public), is also densely populated for most of the summer season.

Beyond that, 5km from town, the **Kalamáki** peninsula juts out with a coating of holiday villas. Beaches here include **Kanapítsa** (ΚΑΝΑΠΙΤΣΑ), a popular cove for swimming and watersports, with a restaurant by the water, and nearby **Vromólimnos** ('dirty lake'), hard to pronounce and hard to find, but one of the finest places to swim on the island, with powder-puff-soft sand (but don't hold your breath for solitude); the bar at the right-hand end of the strand is worth a tipple or two. When the rest of Skiáthos is bulging at the seams, you can often find room to toss a frisbee around on the next beach, **Platánias**.

Convenient by bus or boat, **Troúlos** has plenty of tavernas waiting to welcome the round-the-island trippers; be sure to get there well before or after them to avoid the busy rush. The last stop, 12km from Skiáthos town, is the legendary **Koukounariés** (ΚΟΥΚΟΥΝΑΡΙΕΣ), with 'the Best Beach in Greece' pretensions: a superb sweeping crescent bay of soft sand that somehow escaped from the South Pacific, fringed with pine trees, although in August it seems that not only can you 'see a world in a grain of sand' as Blake wrote, but that each grain of sand has a world sitting on top of it. Tavernas, hotels and a campsite are hidden away from the sea behind trees and a rather uninspiring lake. Hyper-trendy **Krássa**, nowadays called **Banana** beach, is up the hill with the sea on your left when you get off the bus at Koukounariés. **Little Banana** (or Spartacus), next door, is where you can peel off everything in high season and lie cheek-to-cheek in a bunch. Next is the lovely **Ag. Eléni**, the last beach accessible by road, a somewhat quieter spot with a view across to the Pelion peninsula on the mainland and a welcome breeze; or take the dirt road just before reaching the beach, which leads after 1km or so to the way down to **Kryfos Ammoudia** beach, with its cool taverna.

In general, beaches on the north coast are subject to the *meltémi* winds. **Mandráki**, known as the hippy beach, is reached in 15 minutes by a lovely footpath from the lagoon behind Koukounariés, with two stretches of sand and a snack bar. Further east, **Asélinos** is a sandy beach in an arcadian setting with reed shelters rather than the usual eyesore parasols and a taverna that swings with live Greek music on Friday and Saturday nights; beware the undertow. Just off the road that leads to nearby **Mikro Asélinos** (tricky to find and not worth the bother), is the exquisitely painted, candlelit chapel of the 17th-century monastery **Panagía Kounistrá**, overlooking the north coast, where an icon of the Virgin was found dangling in a tree and refused to be rehoused, in the way these stubborn icons do. Past Kástro, the beach at **Laláría** (accessible only by sea) is a marvel of silvery pebbles, shimmering like a crescent moon beneath the cliff, with a natural arch closing off one end and nearby sea grottoes—**Skotiní**, 'the dark' (so bring a light if you want to see anything), **Galázia**, 'the blue', and **Chálkini**, 'the copper'.

Inland to Kástro

When charter-set life begins to pall, there are several escape hatches and a network of walking paths. A road (with the occasional bus) and a donkey path, beginning just before the turning to the airport road, lead 4km through some of the most beautiful and uninhabited scenery on Skiáthos, up to the island's last working monastery. **Evangelístria** (*open 8–noon and 4–8pm; proper attire required*) was founded in 1797 by monks forced to flee Mount Áthos for their support of the traditionalist Kollivádes movement. A lovely, peaceful place with a triple-domed church and garden courtyard, the monastery became a refuge for both monks and scholars, as well as for members of the revolutionary militia movement from the Olympus area, known as the *armatolés*. With the support of the Russians, the *armatolés* raised a small pirate fleet to harass the Turks. When Russia signed a peace treaty with Turkey in 1807, the Greek revolutionaries were abandoned, and many took refuge on Skiáthos; under Giánnis Stathás, they united in an irregular army, and over the monastery hoisted the blue and white flag of independent Greece that they had just invented. The Ottoman fleet soon put an end to their pretensions, but a statement had been made which inspired fighters in the War of Independence 14 years later. Only a rusting cannon and a few displays in the small museum, cared for by a sole monk and his helper, recall the monastery's belligerent past.

Continue on from Evangelístria or make the 2-hour walk from Ag. Konstantínos near Skiáthos town across the island (the path is well marked) to **Kástro**, a town founded on a difficult, windswept niche in the 14th century, when pirates were on the warpath, and inhabited until 1829, when everyone moved down to the sheltered comfort of Skiáthos town. Eight of the original 30 Byzantine churches more or less still stand (one, **Christós**, has good frescoes and a chandelier) among the houses and a Turkish hammam. The view from the top is quite lovely and there's a quiet beach below, used to smuggle out trapped Allied troops in the war. Skíathot writer Papadiamántis describes Kástro's churches in a short story, 'The Poor Saint': 'some of them stood on rocks or on reefs by the shore, in the sea, gilded in summer by the dazzling light, washed in the winter by the waves. The raging north wind whipped and shook them, resolutely ploughing that sea, sowing wreckage and debris on the shore, grinding the granite into sand, kneading the sand into rocks and stalactites, winnowing the foam into spokes of spray.' If the *meltémi* is blowing, you can see that he wasn't exaggerating.

A detour on the path could be made to the pretty 15th-century monastery **Panagía Kechriá**, containing some fine frescoes painted after 1745. A path from here continues down to the lovely, isolated Kechriá beach, where the local goatherd runs a delightful taverna.

Skiáthos ✉ 37002, ✆ *(0427–)*　　　　　　　　　**Where to Stay and Eating Out**

Kanapítsa/Achládies

The **Plaza**, ✆ 21 971, 🖷 22 109, *plaza@n-skiathos.gr* (*B; lux*), is scenically situated amongst pines and olive groves 100m from Kanapítsa beach; there's a pool, gym and the inevitable Greek nights. **Villa Diamanti** at Kanapítsa, ✆ 22 491, Athens ✆ (01) 590 3280 (*A; exp*), 50m from the sea, has stylish apartments in a garden setting, with a barbecue terrace. *Open May–Oct.* For something less pricey, try **Villa Anni**, ✆ 21 105 (*C; mod*), at Achládies. Alternatively, contact **Mare Nostrum Holidays** in town at 21 Papadiamánti, ✆ 21 463, who rent places in the vicinity. If you prefer to stay with the hordes on the beach at Megáli Ámmos, try **Angeliki**, ✆ 22 354 (*E; mod*), or smaller **Rea**, ✆ 21 013 (*C; inexp*), where the thriving flora on the terraces lends an exotic atmosphere.

Koukounariés/Ag. Paraskeví/Inland

The **Skiathos Palace**, Koukounariés Bay, ✆ 49 700, 🖷 49 666 (*L; lux*), overlooks the bay amid pines, with pool, tennis, massage and roof garden. *Open May–Oct.* The **Skiáthos Princess**, Ag. Paraskeví beach, ✆ 49 226 or 49 369, 🖷 49 666 (*L; lux*), is bright and airy and enjoys one of the best positions on one of the best beaches, with wheelchair access and a diving school. *Open May–Oct.* Near the Princess, **Atrium Hotel** (with monastic Mount Áthos-style foyer) **and Bungalows**, ✆ 49 376, 🖷 49 444 (*A; exp*), have excellent views, a 5-minute stroll from the beach. *Open Apr–Oct.* On the hillside overlooking Troúlos bay, **La Luna**, ✆ 49 262 (*A; exp–mod*), has well-equipped air-conditioned studios and maisonettes, a lovely pool and great views, 10 minutes' walk from the sea. **Korali**, on Troúlos Beach, ✆ 49 212, 🖷 49 551 (*C; exp*), is a friendly flat complex, with fully equipped kitchens and balconies with sea views and pool. *Open May–Oct.* **Boudourgianni's House**, ✆ 49 280 (*B; exp*), also has a pool. For true rural peace and quiet, seek out Geof and Lida Baldry's **Zorbathes**, ✆/🖷 49 473, *geof@skiathosinfo.com* (*exp–mod*), with two fully equipped stone, wood and terracotta houses sleeping 4–6 in a lush valley; book in advance.

Camping Koukounaries, ✆ 49 250, is the nicest campsite on the island (and the only official one), at the east end of the eponymous beach. **Camping Aselinos**, ✆ 49 394, is next best, in a farm setting near Megalo Asélinos beach.

Thássos (ΘΑΣΟΣ)

An island crowned with forests and lying in the sea like the backbone of an ass.

Archilochos

The northernmost Greek island, Thássos is also one of the fairest, almost perfectly round, well-watered, ringed with soft beaches and mantled with fragrant, intensely green pinewoods, plane trees, walnuts and chestnuts. Unlike the other Aegean islands, it is almost never afflicted by the huffing and puffing of the big bad *meltémi*, but has a moist climate, much subject to lingering mists; on hot summer days the intense scent of the pines by the calm sapphire sea can make even the most practical soul sink into a sensuous languor. For many years its relative inaccessibility kept it a secret holiday nook of northern Greeks, but it wasn't long before Germans and Austrians soon discovered how quickly they could reach Thássos by car, while the opening of Kavála airport to international charter flights has definitely changed the all-Greek character of the island, but not too outrageously. Thássos is a great island for camping, but is especially vulnerable to forest fires (terrible ones in 1985 and 1989—the latter set by an arsonist—devastated large swathes of woodland in the southeast), so take extra care. Where ever you sleep, come armed: the native mosquitoes are vivacious, vicious and voracious.

History

Herodotus wrote that the island was settled by the Phoenicians in 1500 BC, who under their leaders Cadmus and Thássos had been seeking Cadmus' sister Europa after her abduction by Zeus in the form of a bull. When Thássos gave up, he found an island to name after himself and established a colony to exploit its rich gold mines and timberlands. These first settlers had close relations with Páros, and in 710 BC, when attacked by Thracians, they called on Páros for aid. The likeable Parian poet, Archilochos, was sent to do battle with them, but found himself outmanoeuvred and ran away; his description of the incident is the first known self-deprecating poem: 'Some Thracian now is pleased with my shield/which I unwilling left on a bush in perfect condition on our side of the field/but I escaped death. To hell with the shield!/I shall get another, no worse.' The Parians who remained on Thássos in obedience to the Delphic Oracle that commanded them to found a city 'on the island of mists' had better luck, extracting some 900 talents of gold a year from the rich mines and the lands they annexed on the mainland.

In 490 BC Thássos was attacked by the Persians, who razed the walls. When Xerxes and his Persian army turned up again 10 years later, the defenceless islanders prevented another attack by holding a fabulous banquet in their honour, and with many slaps on the back sent the Persians off to defeat at Salamis. When Thássos later revolted against the Delian league, Athens sent Kimon to teach it a lesson, which he did—after a two-year siege. After that Thássos was ruled by Athens or Sparta, or whoever had the upper hand; Philip of Macedon seized its mainland gold mines.

In 197 BC the Romans defeated the Macedonians and Thássos gladly became part of Rome, enjoying many special privileges, which led to a new period of prosperity. Among the un-invited guests who troubled the island in later years, the Genoese stayed the longest, from the 1300s until the Turks chased them out in 1460. Russia took over from 1770 to 1774. In 1813 the sultan gave the island to Mohammed Ali, Governor of Egypt, who had been brought up in the village of Theológos and loved Thássos; he at once lowered the taxes and granted the island virtual autonomy. Benevolent Egyptian rule lasted until 1902, when the Turks returned briefly before union with Greece during the Balkan Wars, in 1912. In 1916 the Allies occupied it and, from 1941 to the end of the war, the Bulgarians. These days many of the mountain villages are being bought up wholesale by Germans as holiday homes.

Getting There and Around

By air: there are twice-daily flights from Athens to Kavála on the mainland with both Olympic Airways and Aegean. For Olympic information in Kavála, call © (0591) 830 711; Aegean are at the airport, © (0591) 53 333. Kavála airport is also open to international charter flights; for airport information, call © (0591) 53 273. From Kavála, Thássos is only a short ferry or hydrofoil ride away.

By sea: **ferry** from Kavála (port authority © (0591) 223 716) to Skála Prínos almost every hour and to Liménas once a day. There are **hydrofoils** from Kavála to Liménas (at least eight a day), Limenária, Liménas Potós and Kalliráchi. Daily boat **excursions** go from Liménas to Chryssí Ámmos, Glyfáda and Papalimáni beaches, and there are day trips to Philippi to see the royal tombs. **Port authority**: © (0593) 22 106.

By road: the **bus** service © (0593) 22 162 is good and regular; from Liménas quayside there are at least 10 services daily to Skála Prínos, Skála Potamiá, and Limenária, and six to Theológos and all around the island. Alternatively, take a **taxi** from in front of the bus station. **Car hire** is available at the agencies around the central *plateía* in Liménas; for motorbikes or **bicycles**, try Billy's Bikes, © (0593) 22 490, on Theogenous.

Tourist Police

In Liménas, on the waterfront, © (0593) 22 500.

Festivals

18 January, Ag. Athanásiou in Kástro; **first Tuesday after Easter**, all over the island; **28 April** in Ag. Geórgios; **end of July–beginning of August**, traditional weddings performed in Theológos; the Thássos festival runs from **10 July to 15 August**; **6 August**, Metamórphosis tou Sotírou in Sotíras; **15 August**, Panagía in Panagía; **27 August**, in Limenária with special dances; **26 October**, Ag. Dimítrios in Theológos; **6 December**, Ag. Nikólaos in Liménas.

Liménas (Thássos Town)

The bustling capital and port of the island is officially Thássos, but is better known as **Liménas** (ΛΙΜΕΝΑΣ) or sometimes just Limen (not to be confused with the island's second town, Limenária). Liménas is not exceptionally pretty, but it's lively enough, with nearly as many flags as the United Nations waving along the waterfront; massive plane trees shade the squares, and shops wait to sell you walnut sweets and honey. Abandoned between the Middle Ages and the mid-19th century, the town has only 2,300 inhabitants (many of whom came over from Asia Minor in 1922), who can hardly begin to fill the shoes of **ancient Thássos**; its ruins crop up everywhere and give the new town much of its character. The ancients used an amazing amount of marble—the island's highest peak, 1,070m Mount Ipsárion, is one huge white and greenish marble block. The marble is especially beautiful in the **Roman Agora** in the centre of town, near the little ancient harbour. Here are the foundations of porticoes and

To Kavala

To Keramoti,
Thassopoula

To Kavala,
Parama

Papalimani

Skala Rachoni

LIMENAS (THASSOS)

Glyfada

Makryammos

Ag. Georgios

Skala Prinos

Rachoni

Chrysi Ammoudia

Skala Sotiros

Mikro Kasavati

Panagia

Prinos

Skala
Kallirachis

Sotiros

Megalo Kasavati

Potamia

Skala Potamia

Maries

Mt. Ipsarion
(1070m /3531ft)

Paliochora

Kallirachis

Kastro

Klisma

Theologos

Kinira

N. Kinira

Skala
Marion

Kalivia
(Ag. Georgios)

Cape
Stavros

Pefkari

Tripeti

Limenaria

Leivadi Thimonia

Aliki

Potos

Astris

Archangelou

Psili Ammos

Panagia

Cape Sapuni

N

10km
5 miles

stoas, a massive altar, sanctuaries, and from the 7th century BC, predating the rest of the Agora by 500 years, the mysterious paved 'Passage of Theoria' leading to a Temple of Artemis.

The adjacent **museum** (*closed at the time of writing*) has a fine collection: among the bits in the courtyard, there's a dead ringer for the Maltese Falcon, while inside highlights include a magnificent 6th-century BC *Kriophoros*—a young man bearing a lamb on his shoulders—an ivory lion's head (550 BC), an enormous, unfinished *kouros*, a relief of two griffons devouring a doe (2nd century AD), a lovely head of Dionysos from the 3rd century BC, little turtle votive offerings and Aphrodite riding a dolphin. Several items relate to the island's ancient wine-making: a tablet from *c.* 420 BC with wine regulations, written in *boustrophedon*, 'as the ox plows'; an *oinira*, or wine weight measure; and an amphora stamped with the island's special wine seal. Also near the Agora is part of an ancient street, an **exedra**, a few tiers of the **Odeon** and the **Sanctuary of Hercules**, the oldest on Thássos—Hercules was the island's patron saint, in a cult first established by the Phoenicians.

A path from behind a stately Turkish customs building on the harbour follows the extensive marble **walls** and gates of the ancient city and acropolis. These were reconstructed after the first Persian invasion and the later Athenian siege, and were last repaired by the Genoese. Many of the gates still bear the bas-reliefs, including the two naval gates, the **Chariot Gate** (with Artemis) and the **Gate of Semel-Thyone** (with Hermes). Near these stood sanctuaries dedicated to Poseidon and Dionysos. From here the walls extend beyond the ancient moles of the commercial harbour and rise to the 5th-century BC **Greek Theatre** on the lower slopes of the acropolis, magnificent not so much for its state of preservation as for the marvellous view it affords of pinewoods and sea. At the time of writing it's still the subject of an extensive EU-financed dig by French and Belgian archaeologists. A colourful character named Gianni runs the little bar nearby, with pretty sunset views.

From the theatre a path continues up to the **Acropolis,** spread out across three summits. On the first hill stands a Genoese fortress built out of the temple of Pythian Apollo. The museum's *Kriophoros* was discovered embedded in its walls, and a fine relief of a funerary feast (4th century BC) can still be seen near the guardroom. The second hill had a **Temple of Athena Paliouchos** (5th century BC), but the Genoese treated her no better than Apollo, leaving only the foundations. The third and highest summit of the acropolis is believed to have been a **Sanctuary of Pan,** from the Hellenistic relief of Pan piping to his goats. Again, the view more than anything else survives; on a clear day you can see from Mount Áthos to Samothráki, while inland the most prominent sight is the marble mountain eaten away by quarrying, these days mostly for Saudi clients. A curious exedra resembling a stone sofa is carved below the sanctuary, and around the back the vertiginous **Secret Stair,** carved into the rock in the 6th century BC, descends precipitously down to the remaining walls and gates (be very careful if you attempt it: the stair-rail is rusted away in many places and there are some scary gaps between the steps). Here you'll find the watchful stone eyes of the **Apotropaion** (to protect Thássos from the Evil Eye), the well-preserved **Gate of Parmenon,** and, best of all, the large **Gate of Silenus,** where the vigorous bas-relief of the phallic god (6th century BC) has lost its most prominent appendage to a 'moral cleansing' of the 20th century. Continuing back towards the modern town are, respectively, the **Gate of Dionysos and Hercules** with an inscription, and the **Gate of Zeus and Hera** with an Archaic relief; this last one is just beyond the Venus Hotel if you gave the Secret Stair a miss.

The sandy town beach is small and shaded with tamarisks and plane trees, but also tends to be the most crowded on the island. **Makryámmos,** 3km to the east, is lovely but has become a hyper chi-chi tourist beach with an entrance fee for use of its facilities; just west, buses or boats wait to take you to **Chrysí Ámmos, Glyfáda** and **Papalimáni** beaches, endowed with bars and tavernas, the latter with windsurfing.

Liménas ✉ *64004,* ☎ *(0593–)*   **Where to Stay**

The poshest place to stay on the island is the very modern **Makryámmos Bungalows,** ☎ 22 101, ◉ 22 761, *makryamo@otenet.gr* (*A; exp*), on the soft sandy beach of the same name, with watersports, tennis, pool, a small deer park and a nightclub. *Open Apr–Oct.* On the edge of Liménas, **Ethira,** ☎ 23 310, ◉ 23 555 (*B; exp–mod*), offers bright white bungalows, green lawns and a pool. One street back from the waterfront is the spacious **Amfipolis,** ☎ 23 101, ◉ 22 110 (*A; exp*), converted from a tobacco warehouse, with a pool. **Akti Vournelis** on the beach just outside town along the Prínos road, ☎ 22 411, ◉ 23 211 (*C; exp–mod*), is a good choice, and the bar nearby has live Greek music in the evenings. A green lawn and olive groves surround **Garden Studios,** ☎ 22 184, ◉ 22 612 (*mod*), 80m from the sea; in the centre **Timoleon,** ☎ 22 177, ◉ 23 277 (*B; mod*), is a pleasant, spacious option, but it's best to phone ahead in season. **Filoxenia Inn** is an old white villa near the port with a petite pool, ☎ 23 331, ◉ 22 231 (*C; mod*). The **Akropolis,** ☎ 22 488, is in another traditional building; some rooms can be noisy. **Villa Molos**, ✆ 22 053 (*mod–inexp*), is a pleasant bed and breakfast near the sea in a quiet garden setting. **Alkyon**, ✆ 22 148, ✉ 23 662 (*C; mod–inexp*), is a welcoming, airy place by the harbour. **Lena**, ✆ 23 565, ✉ 22 123 (*E; inexp*), is a good cheaper choice, and there are plenty of rooms in the backstreets of town. There is also **Camping Nysteri**, under the trees near Glyfáda, ✆ 23 327.

Liménas ✆ *(0593–)*   **Eating Out**

While *Wiener schnitzel*, baked beans on toast and English tea and cakes (at the Alkyon on the waterfront) are widely available in Liménas, you can find traditional Greek specialities at **Ipigi** in the centre. One street back from the main seafront, **Asteria** has been in business since 1962 and has lots to offer from the spit including revolving goats' heads sporting lascivious grins. At the eastern end of the harbour, towards the town beach, the touristy **Platanakia** serves fish at the appropriate prices, and just beyond, the **New York Pizza Restaurant** covers all options with traditional Greek food, giant pizza for five (*about 4,000dr*), various pasta dishes and occasionally fresh mussels. Nearby **Syntaki** has home-grown vegetables and good fish. In the evening Liménas is a bopping place and the long-established, British-owned **Marina's bar** right on the waterfront is a friendly jam-packed place to begin and end the evening. In between, you could try out **Full Moon** or nearby **Café Anonymous**, with a broad selection of beers.

Clockwise Round the Island: Beaches and More Beaches

Thássos has one main road encircling the island. Directly south of Liménas, it ascends to **Panagía** (ΠΑΝΑΓΙΑ), one of the most charming villages of Thássos. Its old whitewashed Macedonian houses, decorated with carved wood and slate roofs, overlook the sea, with their high-walled gardens, watered by a network of mountain streams, some flowing directly under their ground floor; the church **Panagías** has an underground spring. Down by the sea, the lovely town beach **Chrysí Ammoudiá** has many tavernas.

To the south of Panagía is another large, well-watered mountain village, **Potamiá**, which has two museums: a small **folk art museum** (*closed Tues*) and the **Polýgnotos Vages Museum** (*open Tues–Sat 9–1 and 6–9, Sun 10–2*), dedicated to the locally born sculptor (d. 1965) who made it big in New York. A marked path from Potamiá leads to the summit of marbly Mount Ipsárion, while below stretches the excellent beach of **Chrysí Aktí** (or **Skála Potamiás**), lined with tavernas and rooms. Quiet **Kínira** has a small shingly beach closed off by an islet of the same name; only a kilometre south are the white sands of **Paradise Beach**, folded in the pine-clad hills; clothing optional.

The little slate-roofed hamlet of **Alikí** is beautifully set on a tiny headland overlooking twin beaches. It was an ancient town that thrived on marble exports, and ruins are strewn about its sandy shore—especially an Archaic Doric double sanctuary. Another ancient settlement was at **Thimoniá** nearby, where part of a Hellenistic tower still stands. Further along, the **Monastery Archángelou** with its handsome slate roof is perched high over the sea on arid chromatic cliffs, with beaches tucked in pockets here and there. Its cloistered nuns are in charge of a sliver of the True Cross, and the pretty courtyard and church may be visited (*proper attire, even long sleeves, required*); paradoxically, the pebble beach nestling in the cliffs below is frequented by nudists. The lovely beach of **Astrís**, above pretty Cape Sapúni, is still defended by its medieval towers, and is one of a score of places in the Mediterranean that claims the sweet singing Sirens. Continuing clockwise round the island, much of Thássos' resort hotel development (and worst forest fires in 1985) has happened above the excellent sandy beaches around **Potós** (ΠΟΤΟΣ), golden **Pefkári** and lovely white **Psilí Ámmos**, with plenty of olive groves in beween. Potós is a good place for an evening drink over the sunset (although pretty packaged), and for exploring inland; a handful of buses each day make the 10km trip up to the handsome slate-roofed village of **Theológos** (ΘΕΟΛΟΓΟΣ), one of Thássos' greenest spots and the capital of the island until the 19th century, with the ruins of the Genoese castle **Kourókastro**. The church Ag. Dimítrios has 12th-century icons.

Limenária (ΛΙΜΕΝΑΡΙΑ), the second largest town on Thássos, draws a fair crowd of tourists in the summer. It has a bit more of a village atmosphere than Liménas, surrounded by trees and endowed with a huge stretch of shady beach. In 1903 the German Spiedel Company arrived in Limenária to mine the ores in the vicinity—its plant can still be seen south of town, while the company's grand offices, locally called the **Palatáki**, 'Little Palace', stand alone in a garden on the headland. From Limenária excursion boats tour the coast of Mount Áthos—the closest women can get to the monastic site—or you can hire a little boat for a swim off the islet of Panagía. **Kalývia** just inland has some reliefs embedded in the wall of its church, while 15km further up on a dirt track **Kástro** sits high on a sheer precipice and was the refuge of the Limenarians in the days of piracy. Although completely abandoned in the 19th century, in the last decade most of its old houses have been restored as holiday homes; there's a taverna in the summer but no public transport.

The less dramatic west coast of Thássos is farm country, lined with beaches, usually less frequented than those on the east coast. **Tripití** has a fine sandy beach near **Skála Marión**, which is a somewhat ramshackle little port, while **Mariés** proper, 10km inland, is perhaps the least changed of the island's traditional villages. Just along the road, a sign points the way to the remains of an Archaic era pottery workshop. **Kallioráchis** and **Skála Sotíras** have rocky beaches, not up to Thássos' usual standard, while **Skála Prínos** (ΣΚΑΛΑ ΠΡΙΝΟΣ) enjoys views of Greece's oil platform. There's just enough black gold in the Northeastern Aegean to cause friction with Turkey; the military presence at Kaválca accounts for the strict limits on commercial flights to its airport. Skála Prínos has the main ferry connections to Kaválca. Inland from here is the village of **Prínos**, beyond which lie the two smaller villages of **Megálo** and **Mikró Kasaváti** (otherwise known as Megálo and Mikró Prínos—worth a visit for their lovely setting, beehives and charming old houses, many of which have been bought up and renovated by Germans. **Rachóni** and **Ag. Geórgios** are two quiet inland villages. A small islet off the north coast, **Thassopoúla**, is pretty and wooded but full of snakes, according to the locals.

Thássos ✆ (0593–)　　　　　　　　　　　　　　**Where to Stay and Eating Out**

There are excellent campsites by the sea and pines all around Thássos: at **Prínos** (Príno, ✆ 71 170), **Pefkári** (Pefkári, ✆ 51 190), **Potós** (Paradisos, ✆ 51 950), **Skála Rachóni** (Perseus, ✆ 82 242), **Skála Sotíros** (Daedalos, ✆ 71 365), **Skála Panagías** (Chrysí Ammoudiá, ✆ 61 207) and **Nysteri** (Nysteri, ✆ 23 327).

Panagía ✉ 64004

The **Thassos Inn**, ✆ 61 612, 🖷 61 027 (*C; mod*), is a charming place to relax, while the small **Helvetia**, ✆ 61 231 (*E; inexp*), is also perfectly reasonable. Panagía contains one of the island's most popular tavernas, **Kosta**, packed on Sunday afternoons with locals (*3,000dr*). Next to the church, **Tris Piges Taverna** has bouzouki nights with dancing on Friday, Saturday, Sunday and Monday nights.

Skála Potamiás/Kínira ✉ 64001

Miramare, ✆ 61 040, ✉ 61 043 (*B; exp–mod*), is moderate-sized, with a restaurant and pool close to the sea, but the **Blue Sea**, ✆ 61 482, ✉ 41 278 (*C; mod*), is better if you can nab one of its 12 rooms. At Kínira, **Sylvia**, by the sea, ✆ 41 246, ✉ 41 247 (*C; mod*), is quiet, medium-sized and modern, with a pool and playground; **Athina**, ✆ 41 214 (*E; inexp*), is adequate but only open from June to August, and there are plenty of other rooms on offer in the surrounding olive groves. For a bite to eat, try **Faros** taverna.

Limenária/Pefkári/Potós ✉ 64002

Rooms are very plentiful and relatively cheap, if not picturesque, in Limenária; for a studio with a pool, try reasonably priced **Garden**, ✆ 52 650, ✉ 52 660 (*C; inexp*). *Open all year.* The **Thássos**, at Pefkári, ✆ 51 596, ✉ 51 794 (*C; exp*), has a pool and tennis. The handsome air-conditioned **Alexandra Beach** in Potós, ✆ 52 391, ✉ 51 185, *alexandra@tha.forthnet.gr* (*A; exp*), has nearly every imaginable watersport on offer, as well as tennis and a pool; **Coral Beach**, right on the sea on the south end of Potós, ✆ 52 402, ✉ 52 121 (*B; exp*), is cheaper but still has all kinds of mod cons and pool. **Io**, ✆ 51 216 (*D; inexp*), is an OK cheapie. **Iy Mouria** taverna is a good Potós bet.

Skála Prínos/Skála Rachóni ✉ 64004

Xanthi, ✆ 71 303 (*C; inexp*), is a good pension on the edge of town; the smaller **Europa** ✆ 71 212, ✉ 71 017 (*C; inexp*), is also decent, with wheelchair access. As you step off the boat at Prínos, **Kyriakos Taverna**, in front of you, has good fresh food and a wider than average selection. Next door, **Zorba's** is just as popular, and an added treat is the traffic policemen assailing your eardrums with their whistles. In Skála Rachóni, the **Coral**, ✆ 81 247, ✉ 81 190 (*C; mod*), is a well-scrubbed, stylish place to stay with a pool amid the olives, and there's a row of beach tavernas.

Zákynthos/Zante (ΖΑΚΥΝΘΟΣ)

Of all their Ionian possessions the Venetians loved Zákynthos the most for its charm and natural beauty. *Zante, fiore di Levante*—'the flower of the East'—they called it, and built a city even more splendid than Corfu town on its great semi-circular bay, all turned to rubble by the earthquake of 1953. Nevertheless, the disaster did nothing to diminish the soft, luxuriant charm of the landscape and its fertile green hills and mountainsides, the valleys planted with vineyards and currant vines, olive and almond groves and orchards, or the brilliant garlands of flowers and beautiful beaches (the flowers are best in spring and autumn, a time when few foreigners visit the island). And if the buildings are gone, the Venetians left a lasting impression—many islanders have Venetian blood, which shows up not only in their names, but in their love of singing. The flip side of the coin is that the once politically progressive Zákynthos has bellied up to the trough of grab-the-money-and-run tourism that doesn't do the island justice, to the extent of sabotaging efforts to preserve the beaches where the loggerhead turtles breed.

Zákynthos

History

According to tradition, Zákynthos was named for its first settler, a son of Dardanus from Arcadia. The Arcadians were famous from earliest antiquity for their love of music and festivals, and passed the trait on to their colony. According to Homer, Zákynthos' troops fought under the command of Odysseus in the Trojan War, although when he returned home and shot 20 local nobles—Penelope's suitors—the island rebelled and became an independent, coin-minting state. It set up colonies throughout the Mediterranean, especially Saguntum in Spain, a city later to be besieged and demolished by Hannibal. Levinus took the island for Rome in 214 BC, and when the inhabitants rebelled, he burnt all the buildings on Zákynthos. Uniting with the Aeolians, the islanders forced the Romans out, although in 150 BC Flavius finally brought them under control.

In 844 the Saracens captured the island from their base in Crete, but the Byzantines were strong enough to expel them. The Norman-Sicilian pirate Margaritone took Zákynthos in 1182, and three years later made it part of his County Palatine of Kefaloniá. One of his successors ceded the island to the Venetians in 1209, who held on to it for almost 350 years, with a Turkish interval between 1479 and 1484. The aristocratic privileges of the Venetians and wealthy Zantiotes caused so much resentment among the commoners that they rose up in 'the Rebellion of the Popolari' and seized control of the island for four years. The influx of artists escaping Crete after the fall of Herákleon in 1669 made Zákynthos an art centre, and led to the founding of the Cretan-Venetian Ionian school of painting. The Cretans also influenced local music, although the most obvious influence in the island's special serenades, the *kantádes*, is Italian. Like Lefkáda, Zákynthos has also been a cradle of poets, producing the Greek-Italian Ugo Foscolo (*d.* 1827), Andréas Kálvos and Diónysios Solomós.

Enthused by the ideas of the French Revolution, the Zantiots formed their own Jacobin Club and destroyed the rank of nobility, symbolically burning the Venetian Libro d'Oro, the book listing the island aristocracy, in Plateía Ag. Márko. In 1798, the Russians forced the French garrison and the inhabitants to surrender, after a siege of months, and when the Septinsular Republic established an aristocracy of its own in 1801, populist, high-spirited Zákynthos rebelled again. During the War of Independence many rebels on the mainland, notably Kolokotrónis, found asylum on the island before Zákynthos joined Greece with its Ionian sisters in 1864.

© *(0695–)*   **Getting There and Around**

By air: daily flights from Athens; the Olympic office is at Alex. Róma 16, Zákynthos town, © 28 611. There are several charters from major European cities, including flights to various locations in the UK with Monarch, Britannia and jmc. For airport information, call © 28 322. The airport is 5km from town; a taxi will set you back around 1,500dr.

By sea: from Zákynthos town and Alikés, **excursion boats** regularly take tourists to the spectacular west-coast beaches; caiques sail several times a week from Laganás to the deserted Strofádes. There are also regular excursions from Skinári to Kianoún Cave and Kerí around the coast.

By road: all **buses** leave from the central station on Filíta Klavdianú in Zákynthos town (© 22 255 for long-distance buses; © 23 776 for local buses). The main station has buses every hour to Laganás, 10 times daily to Tsiliví, four times a day to Alikés, twice to Volímes and three times to Vassilikiós.

© *(0695–)*   **Tourist Information**

The helpful **tourist police** are at 1 Tzoulati, Zákynthos town, © 27 307. For information in English about island happenings, pick up a free copy of *Zante Moments*, issued every 10 days in the summer. **Friendly Tours**, 5 Foscolos, Zákynthos town, © 28 030, ✉ 23 769, live up to their name and can help with accommodation, excursions and rentals. **Internet** access is available at a bulbous joint known as Top's, by the bus station. The **post office** is on Terseti Street, three roads back from the bus station.

Festivals

A carnival initiated by the Venetians, known for its masked singers and dancing, remains strong in Zákynthos and lasts for **two weeks prior to Lent**. During **Holy Week** the inhabitants also give themselves over to an infectious merriment. In **July** the Zakýnthia takes place, with cultural activities; at the **end of August and beginning of September**, there's the International Meeting of Medieval and Popular Theatre, with daily performances. For the major feast days of Ag. Diónysios on **24 August** and **17 December**, Zákynthos town is strewn with myrtle and there are fireworks at the church. Slightly more modest is Zoodóchos Pigí in the town on **10 November**.

When the time came to rebuild their earthquake-shattered town, the inhabitants gamely tried to incorporate some of the old city's delight and charm into the dull lines of modern Greek architecture. They didn't fully succeed. But Zákynthos town, or Chóra (pop. 10,000), is saved from anonymity by its superb setting—the ancient acropolis hovering above, crowned by a castle, and the graceful sweep of the harbour, punctuated off to the right by the unusual form of Mount Skopós. It is also graced with one-storey, painted clapboard houses, draped to the hilt with bougainvillea and hibiscus. Wrapped along the waterfront, the streets of the long, narrow town are sheltered by arcades (as they were before the earthquake), where a few shops still sell the local speciality, *mandoláto* (white nougat with almonds) amongst the figurines of coupling turtles and other tourist foofaraws.

The rebuilders of Zákynthos failed where they should have done their best, in the town's front parlour, **Plateía Solomoú**, a seaside square with flowerbeds and a statue of the portly Diónysios Solomós, raising a hand in greeting; the square is simply too large and open for comfort, and its pair of small cafés are overwhelmed by the solemn formal buildings: the Town Hall (with another statue of another homegrown poet, Ugo Foscolo, and the inscription 'Liberty Requires Virtue and Daring'), the Cultural Centre, and in one corner the sailors' church, **Ag. Nikólaos tou Mólou** 'of the Mole' (1561), pieced together like a jigsaw after the quake.

The **Neo-Byzantine Museum** (*open 8–2.30, closed Mon; adm; free Sun*) contributes to the sterile formality of the square, but can be forgiven for its contents: lovely paintings by the Ionian school, icons and other works of art salvaged from shattered churches across Zákynthos. The 17th century was a golden age for art, especially after the arrival of refugees from Crete (1669), among them Michael Damaskinós, the great icon painter and teacher of El Greco. Italian influences show up even stronger here than in Crete; by the late 18th and 19th centuries, local painters were producing pure rosy-cheek fluff. But before turning into candy floss, the Ionian School left Zákynthos with some spirited, lovely works: the iconostasis of Ag. Dimitrioú tou Kollás and one from Pantokrátoras (1681), the latter further adorned with intricate wood carvings. There are marble fragments, ancient and Byzantine tombs, and excellent 16th-century frescoes from Ag. Andréa at Volímes, showing Jesus in the cosmic womb in the apse, New Testament scenes, nearly every saint in the Orthodox calendar on the side walls, and a *Last Judgement* on the back wall, with a great tree branch emanating from hell and the empty throne awaiting, cupped by the hand of God. The icons, mostly from the 16th and 17th centuries, are superb, varying between Oriental and Western extremes; there are works by Damaskinós, Ioánnis Kýprios, Emmanuel Zána and Nikólas Kallérgis. The last exhibit is a scale model of Zákynthos town before the earthquake.

Inland from Plateía Solomoú, the smaller, triangular, marble-paved, pizzeria-lined **Plateía Ag. Márkou**—Zákynthos' Piazza San Marco—is as lively as the bigger square is sleepy. The social centre of town since the 15th century, before the earthquake it was the site of the Romianiko Casino, which everyone loved but no one rebuilt. The Catholic church of San Marco, now sadly devoid of all its art, occupies one end, near the **Solomós Museum** (*open 9–2; adm*), with mementoes of the poets and other famous Zantiotes, as well as photographs of the island before 1953. Adjacent are the mausoleums of Diónysos Solomós and Andréas Kálvos; the latter lived in London and Paris for much of his life, but was granted the wish he expressed at the end of his romantic ode *Zante*: 'May Fate not give me a foreign grave, for death is sweet only to him who sleeps in his homeland.'

A Patriotic Perfectionist

Of the two poets, Solomós is the more intriguing character. Born in 1798, he was educated along with other Ionian aristocrats in Italy and wrote his first poems in Italian, when he decided that it was time for Greece to have a Dante of its own: like Dante, he rejected the formal scholarly language of the day (in Dante's day Latin, in Solomós' the purist Greek, or *katharévousa*) but chose the demotic everyday language. Nearly as important, he broke away from the slavery to the 15-syllable line that dominated Greek poetry from the 17th century, and introduced Western-influenced metres and forms. Solomós concentrated on lyrical verse until the War of Independence became an important inspiration, bringing forth deeper, and increasingly more spiritual works, especially in 'The Free Besieged', written after the heroic resistance of Missolóngi. His verse has a degree of beauty, balance and delicacy that rarely has been matched by other Greek poets—that is, whatever fragments have survived; highly strung and hyper-critical, Solomós destroyed nearly everything he wrote in later years while living on Corfu, where he often used his influence with the British to gain more lenient sentences for Greek nationalists on the Ionian islands. The first stanzas of his *Ode to Liberty*, which he composed upon hearing of the death of Lord Byron, are now the lyrics to the Greek national anthem:

> Σε γνωρίζω απο την κοψυ του σπαθιου την τρομερη
> σε γνωρίζω απο την οψη που με βια μετραει τη γη...
>
> *I recognize you by the fierce edge of your sword;*
> *I recognize you by the look that measures the earth...'*

Zákynthos' most important churches were reconstructed after the quake, among them little **Kyrá tou Angeloú**, in Louká Karrer Street, built in 1687; inside are icons by Panagiótis Doxarás of Zákynthos and a pretty carved iconostasis. Near the Basilica tis Análipsis on Alex. Roma Street is the boyhood **home of Ugo Foscolo**, marked by a marble plaque and angel; he used to read by the light of the icon lamp in the shrine across the street. Further south, the restored 15th-century **Faneroméni** church with its pretty campanile (on the corner of Lisgara and Doxarádou Streets) was before the earthquake one of the most beautiful churches in all Greece. At the south end of town a huge **basilica of Ag. Diónysios** was built in 1925 to house the bones of the island's patron saint, stored in a fine silver reliquary. It was one of only three buildings left standing after the earthquake of 1953, thanks in small part to Dionysios' divine influence but in large part to its concrete construction. There are New and Old Testament paintings on the walls, and an array of gold and silver ex-votos are witness to his power that draws throngs of pilgrims every 24 August.

Up to Boch*á*li

Filikóu Street, behind Ag. Márkou, leads up to Bocháli; on the way, you pass the small **Maritime Museum** (*open 9–1.30 and 6–8.30*), luring you in with its imposing torpedo display. Bocháli is a suburb with gorgeous views over town and sea, where the church of Ag. Giórgios Filíkou was the seat of the local revolutionary Friendly Society. One road from the Bocháli crossroads leads to Lófos Stráni, where a bust of Solomós marks the spot where the poet sat and composed the *Ode to Liberty* during the siege of Missolóngi. Another road is sign-posted to the well-preserved Venetian Kástro (*open 8–2.30, closed Mon*), a short taxi ride or 5-minute walk up an old cobbled path from Bocháli. Three gates, the last bearing the Lion of St Mark, guarded the medieval town. Ruins of churches still stand amid the pines up here, but a 16th-century earthquake rent the walls of the ancient acropolis. Various attractive cafés over-look the vista at the foot of the castle (notably the shady Diogenes). Some neglected gardens in Akrotíri (take the north road at the Bocháli crossroads) recall the Venetian villas that once stood here, the centre of Zante society into the period of British rule; the one belonging to Diónysios Solomós' father was the residence of the High Commissioner. At Villa Crob nearby, the British laid out the first tennis court in Greece. Down in the north end of town, a romanti-cally melancholy British cemetery is wedged next to the green cliffs (turn right at Bociari Street from N. Kolíva).

Beaches under Mount Skopós

The town beach isn't all that good—for better, cleaner swimming try the beaches along the beautiful rugged eastern peninsula under Mount Skopós, beyond **Argássi** (ΑΡΓΑΣΙ), a some-what soulless assembly line of hotels and tavernas along its waterfront. Heading further along, there's **Pórto Zóro**, **Banana Beach** (wide and sandy and strewn with sea daffodils, which send such a strong fragrance out to sea that they may have been the origin of the island's nick-name, *Fiore di Levante*), **Ag. Nikólaos**, **Mavrándzi** and the thinnish crescent strand at **Pórto Róma**, all with tavernas and at least minimum facilities. The 16th-century Domenegini tower by the sea was used for covert operations by the *Philikí Hetaireía*, or Friendly Society, espe-cially in sending men and supplies over to the battles on the Peloponnese. To keep busybodies away they spread word that the tower was haunted, and installed a 'devil' at night to holler and throw stones at any passer-by. **Vassilikós** (ΒΑΣΙΛΛΙΚΟΣ) is a tiny village at the end of the bus line, but bear in mind that services are infrequent and you may have to get back to town by taxi. **Gérakas**, at the tip of the peninsula, has another long, lovely stretch of sandy beach, the finest of them all. Although popular with bathers, it's also popular with nesting loggerhead turtles and has been saved from any more hotels by its designation as a conserva-tion area. Roads cross the peninsula for **Daphní** and **Sekánika**, two secluded, undeveloped beaches to the south, facing Laganás Bay, and both equally popular with the turtles.

Loggerheads over Loggerheads

A decade ago Zákynthos became the centre of an international stir when environmentalists themselves went at loggerheads with government ministries and the island tourist industry to protect Laganás Bay, nothing less than the single most important nursery of rare loggerhead turtles (*Caretta caretta*), hosting around 1,000 nests a year on 4km of beach. These sea turtles are among the oldest species on the planet, going back hundreds of millions of years. As long as anyone can remember, they have gathered from all over the Mediterranean on the sands of Zákynthos every June until September, to crawl up on to the beaches at night, dig a deep hole with their back legs, lay between 100 and 120 eggs the size of golf balls and cover them up again before lumbering in exhaustion back to the sea. For 60 days the eggs incubate quietly in the warmth of the sands, and, when they hatch, the tiny baby turtles make a break for the sea. It is *absolutely essential* that the nesting zones remain undisturbed as much as possible—and everyone can help by staying away from the beaches between dusk and dawn, by not poking beach umbrellas in the sand, running any kind of vehicle over it, or leaving litter. Even then the odds for the turtle hatchlings aren't very good: the lights in the bay are liable to distract them from their all-important race to the sea, and they die of exhaustion.

Whether or not the turtles succeed in co-existing with the local tourist economy remains to be seen. At first the going was rough; uncompensated for the beaches they owned, some Zantiotes did all they could to sabatoge the efforts of the marine biologists and even resorted to setting fires on the beaches to keep the turtles away. In 1983, when the steep decline in nests was noticed, the Sea Turtle Protection Society of Greece (STPS) was formed to monitor the loggerheads and mark their nests, and lead the fight for their protection. They have succeeded in improving public awareness, in limiting sea traffic in Laganás Bay, and in general making the loggerheads such a hip issue that the souvenir shops peddle little ceramic models of them. A Marine Park was finally established in December 1999 to protect the turtle rookery. However, opposition remains from some local traders. In July 2000 a Greek turtle project coordinator was beaten up with an iron bar by two men who jet-skiied into the park's protected zone.

Up Mount Skopós

From the edge of Argássi, a road leads up through the wildflowers, including several species of indigenous orchid, to the top of **Mount Skopós** ('Lookout'), the Mount Hellatos of the ancient Greeks and the Mons Nobilis of Pliny, who wrote of a cavern that led straight to the Underworld. On the way note the picturesque ruins of the 11th-century **Ag. Nikólaos Megalomátis**, with a mosaic floor, built on the site of a temple to Artemis. Views from the summit not only take in all of Zákynthos, but the Peloponnese and the Bay of Navarino, where on 20 October 1827 the most famous battle of modern Greece was fought between the Turko-Egyptian navy and the Anglo-Franco-Russian fleet, leading directly to Greek independence. By the rocky lump summit or *toúrla* of Mount Skopós stands the venerable white church of **Panagía Skopiótissa**, believed to replace yet another temple to Artemis. The interior is decorated with frescoes and a carved stone iconostasis; the icon of the Virgin was painted in Constantinople, and there's a double-headed Byzantine eagle mosaic on the floor.

Zákynthos Town ✉ *29100,* ✆ *(0695–)*   **Where to Stay**

Outside August, accommodation in Zákynthos town is usually feasible; if you have any difficulty, the tourist police at 1 Tzoulati have a list of rooms to let. **Hotel Bitzaro**, on the waterfront, ✆ 23 644, 📧 45 506 (*C; exp*), with its glam reception, has smart rooms with balcony and a pleasant veranda. Adjacent **Hotel Reparo**, ✆ 23 578, 📧 45 617 (*B; exp*), is similarly priced and comfortable. The larger but less smart **Strada Marina** at 14 K. Lombárdou Street, ✆ 42 761, 📧 28 733 (*B; exp*), is well located for ferries. *Open all year.* **Lofos Strani**, on Kapodístrias, ✆ 27 122 (*B; mod*), is a peaceful hotel set in greenery with a pool up at Bochále. Cheaper choices include **Ionion**, 18 A. Roma, ✆ 22 511 (*D; inexp*), and **Dessy**, 73 N. Kolíva, ✆ 28 505 (*E; inexp–mod*).

Along the peninsula **Matilda**, at Pórto Zóro, ✆ 35 430, ✉ 35 429 (*B; lux–exp*), 200m above the sea, is a fancypants complex with two pools and sea sports. *Open May–Oct.* **Aquarius**, ✆ 35 300, ✉ 35 303 (*B; exp*), is prettily set in greenery, and advertises itself as 'a place to forget the world'. **Locanda**, ✆ 45 563, ✉ 23 769 (*C; mod*), is a well-run family hotel by the beach at Argássi. Vassilikós houses various decadent complexes, of which **Louis Royal Palac**e, ✆ 35 492, ✉ 35 488, *plus12@ath.forth net.gr* (*A; lux*), offers the air-con works, replete with Watermania for the kids. **Porto Roma**, ✆ 22 781 (*D; inexp*), is small, but perfectly adequate and a mile cheaper.

Zákynthos Town ✆ *(0695–)*   *Eating Out*

There are several expensive places on Plateía Ag. Márkos, although **Restaurant-Pizzeria Corner** is perfectly reasonable. On the road to Argássi, near the basilica of Ag. Diónysos, **Karavomilos** has the name for the best fish on the island; the friendly owner will recommend the best of the day's catch (*4,000dr and up; note the prices are per kilo*). In a similar direction, locals in the know go for lunch at delightful **Malanou**, 38 Athanásou, ✆ 45 936. At night, they head to the **Quartetto di Zante** near Stavros and to **Arekia**, on the coast road north out of town, for live Greek music and traditional Zákynthos *kantádes*, performed by male trios. The **Panorama** is in a lovely spot up by the castle, with live *kantádes* as well as traditional Zantiote dishes such as rabbit casserole and *moskári kokkinistó*, beef in tomato sauce (*4,500dr*). For entertainment, try **Base** bar on Plateía Ag. Márkos, which has a jazzy ensemble.

Laganás Bay and the South

On the map, Zákynthos looks like a piranha with huge gaping jaws, about to devour a pair of crumb-sized fish in Laganás Bay. These small fry are **Marathoníssi** and **Peloúzo**, the former with a sandy beach and a popular excursion destination, the latter colonized in 1473 BC by King Zákynthos. The island's most overripe tourist developments follow the sandy beaches step by step, starting at **Kalamáki**, on the east end of the bay, with a sandy beach under Mount Skopós, at the beginning of currant country. The next town, **Laganás** (ΛΑΓΑΝΑΣ) is Zákynthos' equivalent of Spencer's Blatant Beast, a resort that has long abandoned any sense of proportion and commerical decorum, set on flat hard sand beach that overlooks some curious rock formations by the sea. This brash Las Vegas on the Ionian is a favourite of British and German package tourists and about as un-Greek as it gets anywhere in Greece. At night its 'Golden Mile' of open bars, throbbing with music and flashing kinetic neon lights, are the joy of holiday revellers and ravers, but the dismay of the turtles. A bridge leads out to the pretty islet of **Ag. Sostís**, its limestone cliffs falling abruptly where the earthquake of 1633 cleaved it from the rest of Zákynthos. It's topped with pine trees and, this being Laganás, a disco.

The Belgian on the Beach

Not a few sunbathers at Laganás are keen students of the opposite sex's anatomy, so generously displayed and baked to a T. None, however, are as studiously keen as Vesalius (1514–64), the Renaissance father of anatomy, whose statue stands at the south end of the beach. Born in Brabant, Vesalius studied in Paris, where he edited the 2nd-century AD anatomical works of Galen, the Greek physician to the gladiators and Emperor Marcus Aurelius. Vesalius went on to the medical university of Padua, and made it the leading school of anatomy in Europe, where in 1543 he published his milestone *De humani corporis fabrica*, the first thorough and original study of the human body since Galen's time. In 1555 Vesalius became the personal physician to Philip II of Spain, only to be sentenced to death by the Inquisition for dissecting a dead Spaniard. Philip commuted the sentence to a pilgrimage to the Holy Land, and on the way home the doctor's ship was wrecked off the coast at Laganás. Vesalius, realizing a return to Inquisition-plagued Madrid would mean an end to his studies anyway, decided to spend the rest of his life in the now ruined Franciscan monastery at Faneró, along the road from Laganás to Pantokrátoras; his epitaph is still intact.

A Gently Inclined Plain

Behind Laganás extends the lush plain of Zákynthos, a lovely, fairly flat region to cycle through, dotted with the ruins of old country estates wrapped in greenery. One still happily intact is the **Domaine Agria**, the oldest winery in Greece, run by the Comoutós family since 1638. The Comoutóses made their fortune in raisin and currant exports, and were ennobled in the Libro d'Oro; today their estate is divided between olive groves and vines that yield excellent reds, rosés, whites, and old-fashioned, high-alcohol dessert wines. To visit their tasting room and museum of old winemaking tools, call © (0695) 92 285.

The chief village to aim for is **Pantokrátoras**, near three fine churches: the beautiful **Pantokrátor**, founded by Byzantine Empress Pulcheria, and still retaining a number of Byzantine traits; **Kiliómeno**, restored after the quake, with beautiful icons; and the medieval church of the **Panagía**, with a pretty bell tower and stone carvings. The picturesque ruins of the Villa Loundzis, once one of Zákynthos' most noble estates, are in **Sarakína** nearby. **Lithakiá**, south of Pantokrátoras, has another restored church, the 14th-century Panagía Faneroméni, containing works of art gathered from ruined churches in the vicinity.

From Lithakiá the main road continues south over the Avyssos Gorge—a rift made by the 1633 earthquake—to the coastal swamp known as **Límni Kerióu**. If you look carefully at the roots of the aquatic plants, you can see the black bitumen or natural pitch that once welled up in sufficient quantity to caulk thousands of boats; both Herodotus and Pliny described the phenonemon and more recently an exploratory oil bore was sunk, but with negligible results. There are tavernas by the rather mediocre beach. Just to the south extends a second Mount Skopós.

From the sea (there are caique excursions offered from Kerí Beach) this coast is magnificent, marked by sheer white cliffs, deep dark-blue waters and two towering natural arches at Marathía.

At the end of the road the mountain village of **Kerí** offers fine views, especially from its white lighthouse, and the cheapest rooms on the island. From the main road a secondary road winds westward to one of Zákynthos' more remote villages, **Agalás**, passing by way of the two-storey grotto called **Spiliá Damianoú**, where one formation resembles a horse. The legend goes that a giant named Andronia once lived in the area and pestered the good people of Agalás for food. His appetite was huge, and the people were at their wits' end when an old lady slipped him a poison pie. Down he fell at a place still called Andronia, where you can see twelve 15th-century wells with their old well-heads. His horse was so shocked it turned to stone.

Michelos, ☎ 48 080, one of the best tavernas in Zákynthos (and one of the most crowded), is just along the main Kalamáki–Zákynthos road. There's a convenient bar next door if you have to wait for a table. The **Cave Bar**, also away from the coast, up a little road lined with lights, is a romantic place of various levels, perfect for a troglodyte cocktail, while **Vios** is more of a club, in a panoramic garden.

Heading Northwest

From Zákynthos town the coastal road leads north, past the **Kryonéri Fountain**, built by the Venetians to water their ships. The red rock overhead was used for a suicide leap in a popular Greek novel, *Kókkinos Vráchos*. Beyond, the road turns abruptly west to reach a series of pretty sandy beaches, connected by short access roads and backed by orchards and vineyards. Holiday development is taking off with abandon, although it is still calm when compared to the babylonian crud along Laganás Bay: long and narrow **Tsiliví** (ΤΣΙΛΙΒΙ), a packaged paradise; **Plános** (overlooking **Tragáki Beach**); little **Ámpoula** with golden sand; **Pachiámmos**; **Drossiá**; **Psaroú**; **Ammoúdi**; and **Alikanás**, where a wonderful long stretch of sand sweeps around the bay west to **Alikés** (ΑΛΥΚΕΣ), named for the nearby saltpans, an area popular with windsurfers.

The rich agricultural land inland from the coast is pleasant to explore, if directions can be a bit confusing. **Skoulikádo** rewards visitors with several interesting churches, among them the **Panagía Anafonítria**, decorated outside with stone reliefs and with a lovely interior, and **Ag. Nikólaos Megalomáti**, named for a 16th-century icon painted on stone of St Nicholas, with unusually large eyes. **Ag. Marína**, a rare survivor of the earthquake, has a cell behind the altar where the insane would be chained in hope of a cure. Inland from Alikés, **Katastári** is the island's second-largest town, marking the northern edge of the plain; from here the main road divides, one branch spiralling into the mountains, while a newer offshoot follows the sea all the way to Korithí. In its early stages, this coastline is a sequence of beautiful pebbled beaches, such as **Makri Aloú** and **Makrí Giálos**, becoming more dramatic, volcanic and inaccessible as it wends northwards. The port of **Ag. Nikólaos**, where the little ferry from Kefaloniá calls, nestles in a bay with beautiful views of its eponymous islet; sadly, the architecture doesn't live up to the natural setting. (Note there is no bus and, unless you find one waiting, taxis called in from afar can be pricey.) The white coast around here is pocked with caves, cliffs and natural columns and arches, and most spectacularly of all, one hour by boat from Skinári, **Kianoún Cave**, the local version of Capri's Blue Grotto, glowing with every imaginable shade of blue; the light is best in the morning. Excursions from Ag. Nikólaos also run south to **Xinthia**, with sulphur springs—evidence of the island's volcanic origins—and rocks and sand so hot that you need swimming shoes to protect your toes, and to the cave of **Sklávou**.

Zákynthos ✉ *29100,* ☎ *(0695–)* **Where to Stay and Eating Out**

If you do wish to stay in Tsiliví, it's probably easiest through a tour operator—they occupy most of the hotels and rooms—though you could try the package hotel **Princess**, ☎ 45 642 (*mod*), or **Mayrikos**, ☎ 22 648 (*inexp–mod*). Eat at **The Olive Tree**, the first taverna in town and one of the few playing Greek rather than English music. Another traditional taverna is **Koukos**, just behind Popeye's. There's a plethora of throbbing bars/clubs to see you through the night.

Caravel at Plános, ✆ 45 261, 🖷 45 548 (*A; exp*), sister to the one in Athens, will lighten your wallet, but has all the trimmings. **Louis Plagos Beach**, at Ámpoula Beach, ✆ 62 800, 🖷 62 900 (*A; lux*), is a big white hotel and bungalow complex, a stone's throw from the sea, with a pool, tennis court and babysitting on offer. There's also a good campsite, **Camping Zante**, on Ámpoula Beach, ✆ 61 710. Your best bet for Alikanás is to pre-book a villa or apartment through one of the specialist companies (*see* p.31). A bevy of hotels is set back from the sea by Alikés: try the decent **Montreal**, ✆ 83 241, 🖷 83 342 (*C; mod*). **Mantolina**, in Alikanás, is a family-run taverna offering appetising food; for a quiet post-prandial bar, head for the **Catacombs**. Alikés has ample eateries.

Further north and well away from the block-booked beach resorts, the English-owned **Peligoni Club**, ✆ 31 482 or in the UK ✆ (01243) 511 499, *www.peligoni.com*, is a little surf and sailing holiday haven set into the rugged volcanic coastline. Accommodation is in a sprinkling of villas within driving distance of the friendly club-house; the club caters just as well for watersports beginners and experts as it does for lazybones landlubbers with vast appetites and a talent for Scrabble. It's also possible for some or all of the party to stay nearby at well-equipped **Camping Skinari**, ✆ 31 061, or pristine **Pension Panorama**, ✆ 31 013 (*mod–inexp*), and, for a fee, to use the club's facilities on a more ad hoc basis. On the coast road, not far from Koroní and worth a detour, **Taverna Xikia**, ✆ 31 165, serves tasty Greek food in an idyllic clifftop setting. At Ag. Nikólaos, **Astoria** serves good fish overlooking the beautifully appointed harbour.

Up the Southwest Coast

Unlike the low rolling hills and plain of the east, the west coast of Zákynthos plunges steeply and abruptly into the sea, some 1000ft in places, and is a favourite place for caique excursions either from Zákynthos town or Alikés. The last stop on the plain, taking the pretty road from Zákynthos town, is **Macherádo**, in the centre of a cluster of farming villages. Its church of **Ag. Mávra** has a very ornate interior, with a beautiful old icon of the saint covered with ex-votos and scenes in silver of her life and martyrdom; the Venetian church bells are famous for their clear musical tones. Note the fine reconstructed belfry of the 16th-century church of the Ipapánti. In the nearby wine growing village of **Lagopóda** there is also the pretty crenellated Eleftherias convent, where the nuns do fine needlework.

From Macherádo the road rises to **Koiloménos**, with a handsome stone belltower from 1893, attached to the church of Ag. Nikólaos: unusually for Greece it is carved with Masonic symbols, and if it looks stumpy it's because it lacks its original pyramidal crown. A secondary road from here leads to the wild coast and the **Karakonísi**, a bizarre islet just offshore that looks like a whale and even spouts great plumes of spray when the wind is up. At Ag. Léon (with another striking bell tower, this time converted from a windmill) there's another turn-off to the coast, to the dramatic narrow creek and minute sandy beach at **Limnióna**. Just before Exo Chóra, another road descends to **Kámbi**, where Mycenaean rock-cut tombs were found and two tavernas perched on the 650ft cliffs are spectacular sunset viewing platforms, although in summer you'll probably have to share them with coach parties from Laganás.

The main road continues to Anafonítria, site of the 15th-century **Monastery of the Panagía Anafonítria**, which survived several earthquakes intact along with its time-darkened frescoes and cell of St Dionysios—he was abbot here and his claim to sainthood was that he gave sanctuary to his brother's killer. Below is **Porto Vrómi**, 'Dirty Port' because of the natural tar that blankets the shore, although the water is perfectly clear. Around the corner is a perfect white sandy beach, wedged under sheer white limestone crags set in completely clear azure water—the setting for Zákynthos' notorious '**shipwreck**'. The scene that graces a thousand postcards is a prime destination for excursion boats; although some tour guides let the punters fantasise that the wreck has been there for decades, the boat really belonged to cigarette smugglers in the late 1980s who ran the ship aground and escaped when they were about to be nabbed by the Greek coastguard. When word reached the inhabitants of the small villages above, immediate action was taken, and by the time the coastguard got back to the ship it was empty; the free smokes lasted for years. You can look down at 'shipwreck' beach from the path near the abandoned 16th-century monastery of **Ag. Geórgios sta Kremná**. The path, ever more overgrown, leads to the narrow cave-chapel of **Ag. Gerásimou**.

The road passes through an increasingly dry landscape on route to **Volímes** (ΒΟΛΙΜΕΣ), the largest village on the west coast, permanently festive with billowing, brightly coloured handwoven goods displayed for sale. Seek out the fine church of Ag. Paraskeví and the 15th-century Ag. Theodósios, with its stone carved iconostasis. On the village's main road, Dionysos' taverna is the place for top-notch spit-roast lamb and other excellencies. **Áno Volímes**, just above its sister town, is a pretty little mountain village.

The Strofádes

A couple of times a week caiques from Laganás sail the 37 nautical miles south of Zákynthos to the Strofádes (there are two, **Charpína** and **Stamvránio**), passing over the deepest point in the entire Mediterranean, where you have to dive 4,404m down to reach Davy Jones' locker. Strofádes means 'turning' in Greek: according to myth, the Harpies, those composite female monsters with human heads, hands and feet, winged griffon bodies and bear ears, were playing their usual role as the hired guns of the gods, chasing the prophet Phineas over the little islets, when Zeus changed his mind and ordered them to turn around and come back.

Although little more than flat green pancakes in the sea, the Strofádes offered just the right kind of rigorous isolation Orthodox monks and mystics crave, and accordingly in the 13th century Irene, wife of the Byzantine emperor John Láskaris, founded the **Pantochará** ('All Joy') monastery on Charpína. Pirates soon proved to be a major problem, and in 1440, just before Constantinople itself fell to the Turks, Emperor John Palaeológos sent funds to build high walls around it. As on Mount Áthos, no women or female animals were allowed, and the 40 monks who resided there (among them Ag. Diónysos) spent their days studying rare books. In 1530, however, the Saracens managed to breach the walls, slew all the monks and plundered it; in 1717 the body of Ag. Diónysos was removed to Zákynthos town for safe keeping. The evocative, desolate citadel is now owned by the monstery of Ag. Diónysos, and remains in a fine state of preservation, complete with a new pink tile roof, although the population has been reduced to migratory turtle doves and quails. If you have your own boat and provisions and have been looking for an out-of-the-way, romantic destination, you won't find a better one.

Astypálaia	312
Chíos	315
Ikaría	329
Foúrni	335
Kárpathos	336
Kýthera	344
Léros	351
Límnos	357
Ag. Efstrátios	363

From Athens

Mílos	364
Mýkonos	372
Délos	378
Páros	384
Antíparos	391
Santoríni	392
Skýros	402
Sýros	409

Astypálaia (ΑΣΤΥΠΑΛΑΙΑ)

Butterfly-shaped Astypálaia is the most westerly of the Dodecanese, halfway between Amorgós and Kos, and it offers the perfect transition from the Cyclades—in fact, it would be perfectly at home in the archipelago, with its austere rocky geography and dazzling sugar-cube houses spilling down from the citadel on the hill. Yet there's more here than first meets the eye: the island nurtures a rich, fertile, definitely Dodecanesian valley called Livádia in its bosom, which led Homer to call it 'the Table of the Gods', and equally fertile fishing in the sheltered nooks and crannies of its wildly indented coastline—in antiquity Astypálaia was called Ichthyoessa, 'fishy island'. Besides the lure of seafood, Astypálaia's relative inaccessibility makes it a good place to escape the worst of the summer crowds. It now has a tiny airport, offering the chance to skip the long ferry slog from Piraeus or hops from Kos. Most of all, although it gets busy in August, it remains a friendly, jovial, relaxed island that moseys along at its own pace.

History

The name Astypálaia may mean 'old city', but mythology claims that the name is derived from a sister of Europa, the mother of King Minos. Early on, its inhabitants may have founded another Astypálaia, the ancient capital of Kos. In classical times the island was most famous for its lack of snakes and a tragically short-tempered boxer named Kleomedes, who, when competing in the Olympics, killed his opponent, which even then was enough to merit instant disqualification. Kleomedes returned to Astypálaia seething with rage and took his disappointment out on the local school, knocking it down and killing all the pupils. Pliny says the island's snails have curative powers.

℗ (0243–)   **Getting There and Around**

By air: six flights a week from Athens (four in the winter) on a 50-seater: book early in season. Olympic Airways: ℗ 61 328; **airport**: ℗ 61 665. Buses run between Skála, Chóra and the airport; a taxi costs around 2,500dr.

Excursion boats: from Skála to the south coast beaches of Ag. Konstantínos, Vatsés, and Kaminiakia, and to the islets of Ag. Kyriáki and Koutsomíti. **Port authority**: ℗ 61 208. Astypalea Tours, ℗ 61 571, under Vivamare Hotel, are helpful.

By road: there are two **buses** a day between Skála, Chóra, Livádia and Maltézana. **Taxis** are also available at reasonable rates; fares are posted. Skála has three **car rental** agencies, as well as **bikes** of varying description.

℗ (0243–)   **Tourist Information**

The **Municipal Tourist Office**, run by helpful Kalliopi Mariaki (Pópi), has a booth down by the port that opens when ferries arrive, and otherwise may be found from June to the end of September in one of the windmills at Chóra, ℗ 61 412 (*open 9.30–1 and 6–9*). She has a list of rooms if you find yourself homeless.

Police: ℗ 61 207.

Festivals

21 May, Ag. Konstantínos; **20 July**, Profítis Ilías; **27 July**, Ag. Pantelémonos; **15 August**, Panagía Portaïtíssa in Chóra

N

Skála and Chóra

The capital of the island consists of two parts: **Skála** (or Perigialós), the port, and **Chóra**, the old town, which curls gracefully down from the Venetian castle to a sandy beach. In the morning or evening in Skála you'll see the fishermen's mascots, a pair of pelicans, currently named Iannis and Carlos, although those hoping for romance think Carlos is really a Jenny. Skála has everything you need if you don't want to go any further, including an antique shop selling foreign papers and a new ATM machine. Just above the bus stop, the new **Archaeology Museum** (*open in season Tues–Sun 10–2 and 6–10; adm*) contains finds from Kástro as well as four Mycenaean chamber tombs discovered in the 1970s by shepherds, classical steles, a 6th-century Byzantine chancel screen and the Quirini coat of arms. The best architecture, however, is up character- and thigh-building flights of steps (or more circular road) in the upper town of Chóra, marked by a file of eight restored windmills standing sentinel along the ridge of the butterfly wing. The lanes are lined with appealing whitewashed houses, many sporting Turkish-style painted wooden balconies or *poúndia*. Halfway up, nine little barrel-vaulted chapels are stuck together in a row to hold the bones of Chóra's oldest families.

The winding lanes and steps eventually lead up to the one entrance to the citadel, or **Kástro**, built between 1207 and 1522 by the powerful Venetian Quirini family who ruled the island as the Counts of Stampalia. On either side of the narrow entrance, once locked tight every evening, a pair of new buttresses support the high walls; you can see what a tight corset squeezes Astypálaia's middle, and if it's clear you can make out Amorgós and Santoríni on the horizon. Among the ruined medieval houses built into the walls and surviving Quirini coat-of-arms (a display of pride that would have been much frowned on back in Venice) are two bright white churches: **St George**, on the site of an ancient temple, and the **Panagía Portaïtíssa**, one of the most beautiful in the Dodecanese, topped with a white-tiled dome and lavishly decorated inside with intricate lace-like designs and a carved wooden shrine high-lighted with gold leaf (*unusually open late afternoons in season*). Archaeologists have dug up much of the rest, finding ancient lanes and temple foundations dating back to the 6th century BC, with a sophisticated system of drains. Finish your visit with a drink just under the walls at the pretty Castro bar, with a goat's skull over the entrance.

Around Astypálaia

Set in a wide lush valley, **Livádia** (ΛIBAΔIA) is downhill from the windmills to the west; its shingly, sandy beach can get busy with Greek families in high season. Little roads through farms lead back eventually to the barren mountains, where in 1994 EU funds built a dam to create a rather unexpected little **lake**, and the first thing the locals did when it was finished was plant little trees around it; bring some bread for the ducks. Follow the coast along to the south and you can cast your clothes to the wind on the unofficial nudist beach at **Tzanáki**, or continue along the track to **Ag.Konstantínos**, one of the best beaches on the island; other sandy strands, at **Vatses** (with a stalactite cave, **Negrou**, just behind) and **Kaminiakia** can only be reached by boat. An unpaved road starting at the windmills goes to **Ag. Ioánnis** on the west coast, a lush spot with orchards, a whitewashed church and ruined Byzantine castle, as well as an excellent beach, calling in at the monastery of **Panagía Flevariótissa** en route.

The paved road north of Skála passes a few beaches, all called Mármari. Just over on the north coast, ferries dock at **Ag. Andréas** if the wind is up. The road passes over the waist of the butterfly, or Steno (barely 50 metres wide at its narrowest point) and ends up after 9km near the airport at wannabe resort Análypsi or more commonly, **Maltezána**, once a lair of Maltese pirates and named accordingly. Here the French Captain Bigot died in 1827 when he set fire to his corvette to avoid capture. The cove next door is popular with nudists and on the fringe of the surrounding olive groves look out for the remains of the **Roman baths** with their well-preserved zodiac floor mosaics. On the far wing, the lost lagoon of **Vathí** (BAΘHΣ) is a favourite if lonely summer yachting port, a tiny fishing hamlet with an excellent fish taverna and a handful of rooms to rent, accessible only by sea or path and heading a deep, fjord-like bay. From here it's possible to visit the stalagmite caves of **Drákospilia** by boat, but take a torch; a path leads south to **Kastéllano**, built by the Italians between the wars.

Astypálaia ✉ *61207,* © *(0243–)*   ***Where to Stay***

In past years there was a building spree around the harbour in Perigialós, but the pace has eased and bargains are relatively easy to find. For a traditional house or apartment just under the Kástro up in Chóra, contact **Kostas Vaikousis**, ©/✆ 61 430 (*mod*), usually to be found in the antique shop at the port, or **Titika**, ✆ 61 677 (winter: Athens ✆ (01) 771 1540; *mod*). **Astynea**, ✆ 61 040, 🖷 61 041 (*C; inexp*), has fine, clean rooms with balcony right on the port, or there's **Vivamare**, ✆ 61 292, 🖷 61 328 (*C; inexp*), inland from the harbour, with a kitchen thrown in. **Afroditi Studios**, ✆ 61 478 (*inexp*), are just a bit higher up, with better port and sea views from the verandas. Up in Chóra, **Anatoli Studios**, ✆ 61 680/61 066 (*inexp*), have soaring castle views from higher rooms, whilst kind **Poppy**, ✆ 61 267 (*inexp*), has clean rooms and a panoramic veranda a bit further down, and is happy to practise her English on you. If you're under canvas, **Camping Astypálaia**, ✆ 61 338, is just out of town near the Mármaris; follow the signs (a minibus usually meets ferries).

Astypálaia ✆ (0243–)   *Eating Out*

Good tavernas include simple **Monaxia** (or **Vicki's**), in a small street back from where the ferry docks, with excellent home cooking, and **Akroyiali**, a tourist favourite on the beach at Perigialós, with lovely views up to Chóra after dark when the Kástro is bathed in golden light. **Maistrali** is an attractive place with reasonable food. Up by the windmills, **Pizzeria Aeolos** does all the pizza favourites well plus 'Lenten Pizza' without meat or cheese (only in Greece!); **Meltemi** and **Eva**, in Chóra and on the way down respectively, are known for their sweet things. Livádia has several waterfront eateries which tend to change hands every so often, but **Kalamia** and **Stefanida** are cheap and reliable, or try one of the rustic *ouzeries* in the hinterland. In Maltezána, **Porto Stampalia** is the best place to dine, and the **Glykazytiko** is famous island-wide for its pastries.

Entertainment and Nightlife

Astypálaia is not exactly the place to rave it up, but there are some relaxed bars: try **Panorama** or **Aiyaion** (for backgammon) in Chóra, or **Excite** near the water.

Chíos (ΧΙΟΣ)

Soak me with jars of Chian wine and say 'Enjoy yourself, Hedylus.' I hate living emptily, not drunk with wine.

Hedylus, *c.* 280 BC

Chíos is a fascinating and wealthy island celebrated for its shipowners, friendly good humour and the gum mastic that grows here and nowhere else in the world. It offers the most varied geography in the Northeast Aegean: lush fertile plains, thick pine forests, mainly unspoiled beaches, Mediterranean scrublands and startlingly barren mountains that bring to mind the 'craggy Chíos' of Homer, who may have been born on the island. Its architecture is unique and varied and its church of Néa Moní has some of the finest 11th-century Byzantine mosaics anywhere. Tourism, with charters and package companies, is fairly new to Chíos, and most of the islanders are still at the stage where they want visitors to share their deep love for the island rather than just take their money.

Mythology

 Chíos was an island favoured by Poseidon, and is said to owe its name to the heavy snowfall (*chioni*) that fell when the sea god was born. Vine-growing was introduced to the island by Oenopion, son of Ariadne and Theseus. Oenopion pledged his daughter Merope in marriage to the handsome giant Orion, the mighty hunter who boasted that he could rid the entire world of harmful creatures, on the condition that he rid Chíos of its ferocious beasts, a task the young man easily performed. Rather than give Orion his reward, however, Oenopion kept putting him off (for he loved his daughter himself), and finally Orion took the matter into his own hands and raped Merope. For this the king poked out his eyes. Orion then set out blindly, but the goddess of dawn, Eos, fell in love with him and persuaded Helios the sun god to restore his sight. Before he could avenge himself on Oenopion, however, Orion was killed when Mother Earth, angry at his boasting, sent a giant scorpion after him. Orion fled the scorpion, but his friend Artemis, the goddess of the hunt, killed him by mistake. In mourning, she gave him a belt in the stars.

History

Inhabited from approximately 3000 BC, Chíos was colonized by the mysterious seafaring Pelasgians who left walls near Exo Dídyma and Kouroúnia and a temple of Zeus on top of Mount Pelinaío. The Achaeans followed, and were in turn usurped by the Ionians, who had the longest-lasting influence on the island; one tradition asserts that Homer was born here in the 9th or 8th century BC (although nearby Smyrna/Izmir disputes this). By then Chíos was a thriving, independent kingdom, founding commercial ports or *emporia*, notably Voroniki in Egypt. It was famed for its unique mastic and wine (especially from the medicinal *arioúsios* grapes), and for its sculpture workshop and system of government, studied by Solon and adapted for use in his Athenian reforms. Around 490, a Chiot named Glaucus invented the art of soldering metals; less nobly, Chíos was the first state in Greece to engage in slave-trading. As a member of the famous Ionian confederacy, Chíos joined Athens in the Battle of Lade (494 BC) in an unsuccessful attempt to overthrow the Persian yoke. Fifteen years later, however, after the battle of Plateía, Chíos regained its independence, and held on to it even after Athens subjugated its other allies as tribute-paying dependencies.

Chíos allied itself with Rome and fought the enemy of the Empire, Mithridates of Pontus (83 BC), only to be defeated and destroyed, although it was liberated after two years when Mithridates was defeated by Sulla. A few hundred years later Chíos made the mistake of siding with Galerius against his brother-in-law Constantine the Great. Constantine conquered the island and carried off to his new city of Constantinople many of Chíos' famous ancient sculptures, including the four bronze horses that ended up on the front of St Mark's in Venice in 1204. In 1261 the Emperor Michael Paleológos gave Chíos to the Giustiniani, the noble Genoese family who helped him reconquer Byzantium from Venice and its Frankish allies. In 1344, the Giustiniani chartered a stock company called the Maona (from the Arabic *Maounach*, or trading company) with 12 merchants and ship owners to govern and defend the island, which they did successfully until 1566 when Chíos was lost to the Turks.

The Sultans loved the island, especially its mastic, and they granted Chíos more benefits and privileges than any other island, including a degree of independence. The island became

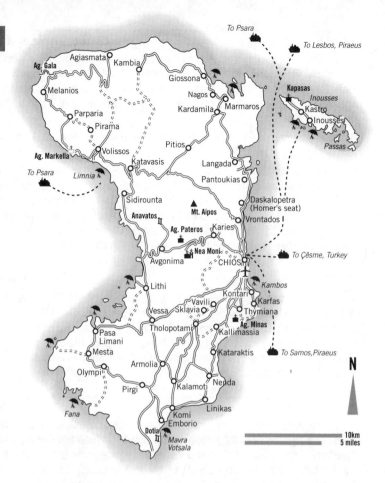

famous for its doctors and chess players; and elsewhere in Greece, where everyone was fairly miserable, the cheerfulness of the Chiots was considered pure foolishness. This came to an abrupt end in 1822. The islanders had already refused to join the Hydriots in the revolt, when a band of 2000 ill-armed Samians disembarked, proclaimed independence and forced the Chiots to join the struggle. The Sultan, furious at this subversion of his favoured island, ordered his admiral Kara Ali to quell the revolt mercilessly and make an example of Chíos that the Greeks would never forget. This led to one of the worst massacres in history. In two weeks an estimated 30,000 Greeks were slaughtered, and another 45,000 taken into slavery, whilst all the vines were uprooted. All who could fled to other islands, especially to Sýros (where they picked up a number of useful lessons about owning ships). News of the massacre deeply moved the rest of Europe; Delacroix painted his stirring canvas of the tragedy (the *Massacre à Hios* in the Louvre) and Victor Hugo sent off reams of rhetoric. On 6 June of the same year, the Greek Admiral Kanáris took revenge on Kara Ali by blowing up his flagship, killing Kara Ali and 2000 men. In 1840 Chíos attained a certain amount of autonomy under a Christian governor, and it was incorporated into Greece in 1912.

By air: four flights a day from Athens with Olympic and Manos, one a week to/from Lésbos and Thessaloníki with Olympic. Olympic: © 24 515; Manos is represented by Ionia Touristiki: © 41 047; **airport:** © 23 998. The 4km journey between Chíos town and runway can be made by taxi (under 1,000dr) or the blue Kondári–Kaifas bus (around 10 a day).

By sea: summer one-day **excursions** to Psará and Inoússes 2–3 times a week (contact Minion's Lines, © 24 670).

By road: blue **buses** (© 23 086) serve Chíos town, the Kámbos area, Karfás beach, and Vrontádos. Green buses depart from next to the Homerium Cultural Centre near Plateía Vounáki (© 24 257) 6–8 times daily to Pirgí, Mestá, Kalamotí, Katavakris and Nenita; four times to Komi, Emborió, Kardamila, Lagada and Ag. Fotia. **Taxi:** © 41 111. **Car**, rather than bike, rental is more appropriate for getting around Chiós; there are a couple of agencies behind the Chandris Hotel in Chíos town.

Very helpful **tourist office**, 11 Kanári St, Chíos town, © 44 389, @ 44 343 (*open Mon–Fri 7am–2.30pm and 7–10pm, Sat 10–1 and Sun 7am–10am; Nov–March Mon–Fri 7–2.30*). The **tourist police**, © 44 427, are at the far end of the quay, next to the regular police and the customs house.The **post office** is at the corner of Omirou and Rodokanaki, with fax service; **OTE telephones** are just back from the port, at Ladis and Kanári (*open 7–7*).

Festivals

Chíos' most important *panegýri*, Ag. Marcéllus, takes place on **22 July** at Ag. Markélla monastery; also **22 July**, Ag. Marcéllus in Volissos and Karyés; **26 July**, Ag. Paraskeví in Kástello and Kalamotí; **27 July**, Ag. Pandeleímon in Kalamotí; **8 August**, Ag. Emilianós; **12 August**, Ag. Fotiní (both in Kallimasía); **15 August**, Panagía in Pirgí, Nénita, Kámbos and Ag. Geórgios. Then there are the **Easter** celebrations in Pirgí, featuring the slaughter of the lambs, if you have the stomach for it.

Excursions on Chíos

1 Meander through the labyrinthine lanes of the Kámbos, flanked by crumbling, delectable villas, and then head southwest to the Mastic villages. At Kalamotí, with its tall stone houses, branch down to Kómi or Emborió for a seaside lunch. Then head on to Pirgí, famous for its bold *xistá* decoration, and Mestá, the most fortified village; beautiful beaches beckon nearby.

2 A homage to Homer: head north past Homer's seat to Langáda for a fishy lunch. Continue up to Kardámila and then turn southwest to scenic Pitiós, birthplace of the bard. A vast, rocky landscape leads from here to fortified Volissós, where Homer picked up his wife; much of the old town remains ruined and there's a fine beach below. Head south to Chíos via spectacular Néa Moní monastery (*open till 8*).

First-time visitors to Chíos arriving by ferry wonder what they've let themselves in for. The long harbour-front of Chíos town (pop. 25,000) doesn't even try to look like a Greek island, with tall buildings holding half a dozen American pool halls, and a score of brightly lit bars and tavernas; throngs saunter and dawdle, and in summer evenings every single table is full. Badly hit by an earthquake in 1881, the town that arose from the rubble is slick and glossy, full of new apartment blocks and high-rise offices and perhaps more fast-food joints run by Greek Americans than strictly necessary. Yet after the first surprise, the town—a sister city of Genoa, for old times' sake—is a very likeable place well worth a few hours' poking about.

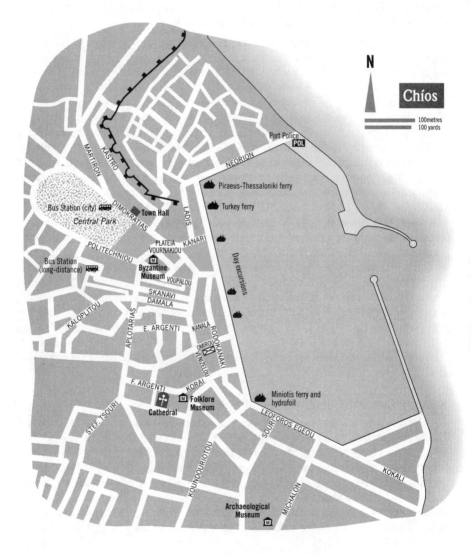

Most of what survives from the Turkish occupation is enclosed within the Byzantine **fortress**, which more or less follows the lines of the Macedonian castle destroyed by Mithridates. The Giustiniani repaired the walls, and after 1599 only Turks and Jews were allowed to live in it, as the Greeks were forced to live outside the walls, and the main gate or **Porta Maggiore** was closed every day at sundown. Within the walls is a ruined **mosque** and in the Turkish cemetery you can see the **tomb of Kara Ali**, 'Black Ali', the same admiral who ordered the massacre of Chíos, its surprisingly unvandalized state perhaps a testimony to the tolerant, easy-going nature of the Chiots, remarked on since antiquity. In a closet-sized **prison** by the gate Bishop Pláto Fragiádis and 75 leading Chiots were incarcerated as hostages in crowded, inhumane conditions before they were all hanged by the Turks in 1822. The **Kastro Justinian Museum**, at the castle entrance in Plateía Frouríou (*open 9–3, closed Mon; adm*), contains detached frescoes, wood carvings and early Christian mosaics.

The town's main square, **Plateía Vournakíou** (or **Plastíra**), with its café and sweet shops under the plane trees, is a few minutes' walk away. On one side stands a statue of Bishop Pláto Fragiádis, and in the municipal gardens behind the square is a statue of Kara Ali's avenging angel, 'Incendiary' Kanáris, a native of Psará. Plateía Vournakíou's crumbling mosque is marked with the *Tugra*, the swirling 'thumbprint of the Sultan' that denotes royal possession. *Tugras*, though common in Istanbul, are rarely seen elsewhere, even in Turkey, and this one is a mark of the special favour that Chíos enjoyed. Today the mosque houses the **Byzantine Museum** (*open 10–1, Sun 10–3, closed Mon, adm*), with a collection of art, tombstones and other old odds and ends too big to fit anywhere else. The new building on the south end of the square is the city cultural centre, or **Homerium**, with frequent art exhibtions and other activities. South of Plateía Vournakíou near the cathedral, the **Koraï Municipal Library** (*open Mon–Thurs 8–2, Fri 8–2 and 5–7.30 and Sat 8–noon*) was founded in 1792 and claims to be the third largest in Greece with 135,000 volumes; the same building houses the **Folklore Museum** (*same hours*), the private collection of London scholar Philip Argéntis, scion of an old Genoese-Chiot family who obviously got tired (with good reason) of looking at his family's portraits. Other displays feature Chiot costumes and handicrafts, bric-à-brac, garish art student copies of Delacroix's 1824 *Massacre à Chíos* and engravings of 18th-century Chíos. The recently reopened **Archaeology Museum**, 5 Michálon Street, near the Chandris hotel (*open 8.45–3, Sun 9.30–2.30, closed Tues; adm*), contains a typical island miscellany of finds, some bearing ancient Chíos' symbol, the sphinx (the same as Thebes); there's also a letter from Alexander the Great addressed to the Chiots. The **Maritime Museum**, 20 Stefanou Tsouri (*open Mon–Sat 10–1*), is a shipping fanatic's fantasy, housed in the Patéras family pile.

Kámbos: Genoese Gentility South of Chíos Town

The Genoese especially favoured the fertile, well-watered plain south of town they called the Campo, or **Kámbos**, where from the 14th-century they and the local Chiot aristocracy built villas and gardens and plantations of citrus fruit, mastic trees and mulberries for silk, an important source of income until the 19th century. Best explored on a pedal bike, Kámbos is an enchanting and evocative mesh of narrow lanes, full of secret orchards and gardens enclosed by tall stone walls, with the gates bearing some long forgotten coat-of-arms or the telltale stripes of the Genoese nobility. Many of the remaining large medieval houses (unfor-tunately many were hit by the earthquake) have their own slowly turning water wheels, while outside the walls the flowering meadows, wooden bridges and ancient trees create a scene of elegaic rural serenity unique on the Greek islands, especially in the golden light near the end of day. Mastodon bones were discovered at **Thymianá**, which was also the source of Kámbos's golden building stone and is now home to a women's cooperative producing rugs, towels and other woven goods. **Sklaviá** is especially lush, although its name is derived from the Greeks forced to work as slaves for the Genoese nobility. Towards the modern village of **Vavíli**, the octagonal domed church **Panagía Krína** (1287) contains fine frescoes by the Cretan school.

The nearest beach to Chíos town and Kámbos is at **Karfás**, reached by frequent blue buses, and so far the only major concession to mass tourism on Chíos. The sand may be 'as soft as flour' but there's less of it to go around all the time as more and more new hotels and flats sprout up like concrete kudzu. If you're after a lower-key beach, continue to **Komi**. Near here is **Ag. Minás monastery** (*closed afternoons until 6*), built in 1590. In the 1822 massacre, women and children from the surrounding villages took refuge there; a small, hopeless battle took place before Ag. Minás was overrun and all 3000 were slain, their bodies thrown down the well. Their bones are now in an ossuary; blood still stains the church floor.

✉ *82100,* ✆ *(0271–)*   *Where to Stay*

Chíos Town

The shipowners hobnob in the large harbourfront landmark, the **Chíos Chandris**, E. Handrí, ✆ 44 401, 📠 25 768 (*B; exp*), light and airy downstairs, with marble floors, but charmlessly comfortable upstairs, many of the balconied, air-con rooms overlooking the port. Opposite the entrance to the Chandris is the more convivial **Hotel Kyma**, ✆ 44 500, 📠 44 600 (*C; exp; discounts available if booked through Sunvil or Greek Sun, see p.32*), owned by friendly Theodore Spordilis, who knows all there is to know about Chíos and can help you plan tailor-made day trips and overnight stays in other worthwhile spots. The main body of his hotel was built by a local shipowner in the style of an Italian villa, with a fine painted ceiling adorning the lobby. Try to stay in this older part for the sea view and atmosphere. All rooms have bathrooms and luscious buffet breakfast is included, as is an all-day supply of orange juice and coffee.

Chíos Rooms, 1 Kokáli, ✆ 26 743 (*mod*), is a renovated neoclassical shipowner's house. **Diana**, 92 Venizélou, ✆ 44 180 (*C; mod*), is modern and utilitarian, but well-kept and friendly. Rooms at the back are much quieter and the bathrooms are better than most. **Faidra**, 13 M. Livanoú, ✆ 41 130 (*mod*), is a stylish pension with handsome (if somewhat noisy) rooms, but no views. **Alex Rooms**, M. Livanoú, ✆ 26 054 (*inexp*), is a colourful pension with a terrace; its owner speaks English. This is not to be confused with nearby **Alexios**, 34 Rodokanaki, ✆ 21 113 (*inexp*), which is less friendly, with high-ceilinged but small-windowed rooms. **Filoxenia**, Roidou, ✆ 22 813 (*D; inexp*), is clean, simple and cheap.

Kámbos

Villa La Favorita, ✆/📠 32 265, or book in Athens ✆ (01) 428 4266 (*exp–mod*), is a charming Genoese villa with 13 beautifully furnished air-conditioned rooms with minibars and a waterwheel in the courtyard. **Perivoli**, 11 Argénti, ✆ 31 513, 📠 32 042 (*A; mod*), a quiet and serene traditional pension with nine rooms, and a good, popular restaurant, has music and dancing on Friday nights. **Villa Clio**, ☎ 43 755 (*mod*), is another renovated traditional place with studios surrounded by banana and palm trees. For something cheaper, ask at the Chiós Tourist Office, ☎ 44 389, about rooms.

Karfás

Near to the airport, Chíos Town and the beach, Karfás has become the island's chief resort and the only place to have succumbed, unashamedly, to the dubious delights of mass tourism. On the road to Karfás, the Korean-run **Golden Odyssey**, ☎ 41 500, 🖼 41 715 (*B; exp*), wouldn't look out of place in the States; rooms have air-conditioning, satellite TV and balconies overlooking the pools, and there's an excellent Chinese restaurant. *Open all year.* On the beach, **Golden Sand**, ☎ 32 080, 🖼 31 700, *goldsand@compulink.gr* (*A; exp*), boasts a large pool in a complex overlooking the sea; try for a room with sea view. **Benovias**, ☎ 31 457 (*mod*), uphill from the beach, has eight one- or two-bedroom apartments. For an altogether atmospheric and restful stay, try **Markos' Place**, in an ex-monastery just south, ☎ 31 990 (*inexp*); booking is advisable.

Chíos Town ☎ (0271–)   *Eating Out*

Besides mastic to masticate, Chíos has two specialities, Greek blue cheese, called *kopanistí*, and a unique brown, wrinkly, nutty kind of olive called *chourmádes*, the Greek word for dates. Try not to miss Chíos' oldest taverna, the **Hotzas**, a 15-minute walk from the harbourfront at 74 Stefánou Tsoúri and worth asking for directions to; the food's excellent, from the *mezédes* to aubergine simmered with tomatoes, delicious whitebait, and other standard Greek dishes, topped off with good barrelled retsina, a rare find on any island (*3,000dr*).

Chíos town's lack of superficial cutesy charm means that, despite a smattering of fast-food yuck on the waterfront, it hasn't been overrun by below-par, overpriced eateries; you can be sure of a good Greek lunch bang in the middle of Prokyméa at **Dolphins**. Of the many waterfront restaurants, the best is **Theodosius**, at the far northern end of the port, at 33 Neoreiou. It relies on good food rather than designer décor for its loyal clientèle.

On the southernmost quay, beyond hotels Chandris and Kyma, **Nox** (Nautical Club of Chíos) is well liked by locals for its simple oven dishes, grilled meats and fish. Twenty yards further on is the **Tassos Taverna**, with tables set in a large, shady garden (but alas no sea views); good for long, lazy lunches away from the frenetic portside strip. For a change of scene as well as a good lunch, wander into town to the only taverna overlooking the big public gardens on Dimokratias.

Out in Karfás, **Aeriko** café, just uphill from the beach, is a pleasant spot, and the **Karatza** on Karfás Street, ☎ 31 221 (*inexp*), has a terrace where you can look out over the sea to Turkey while feasting on grilled or ready-prepared food for around *3,000dr*. Nearby **Fakiris** is also recommended. **Votsalakia**, at Kontári, ☎ 41 181, serves some of the best food on Chíos.

Entertainment and Nightlife

Loafing around the waterfront after the obligatory *vólta* takes up most evenings in Chíos town: **Kavos**, **Remezzo** and **La Loca** are currently the bars to see and be seen in. The best ice-cream in Chíos is scooped out till the small hours at **Kronos**, 2F Argénti Street; **Nifada**, at Prokyméa, serves tasty croissants in a variety of forms. For a drink and disco try **Graffiti**, on Enóseos Ave, or **En Plo Rock Club** on Prokyméa, **B 52** or **Xandres** out at Kontári or **Club Base** (Jungle) on the road to the airport. **Stasis** bar in Karfás is another popular drinking haunt. If you wish to bowl the night away, head for the waterfront alley at 120 Aegeou; alternatively check out upmarket summer **Cine Kipos**.

The Mastikochória, or Mastic Towns of the Southwest

Southwest of green Kámbos stretch the drier hills and vales of mastic land, where it often seems that time stands still. It must have special magic or secret virtue, for the bushy little mastic trees (*Pistacia lentiscus*, a relative of the pistachio) refuse to be transplanted anywhere else in the world—even northern Chíos won't do; the bushes might grow, but not a drop of mastic will they yield. The bark is 'needled' three times a year between July and September, allowing the sweet sap to ooze from the fine wounds, glistening like liquid diamonds in the sun. Some 300 tons of gum mastic are produced annually, although since the advent of synthetics the mastic market just isn't what it used to be. Considered a panacea in antiquity, good for everything from snake bite and rabies in mules to bladder ailments, mastic puts the chew in gum and the jelly in the beans that kept the bored inmates delicately chomping in the Turkish harems; Roman women used toothpicks made of the wood to sweeten their breath. In the more mundane West mastic was used in paint varnish; the Syrians buy it as an ingredient in perfume. On Chíos they use it to flavour a devilishly sweet sticky liqueur, spoon sweets, chewing gum and MasticDent toothpaste, the perfect Chíos souvenir. Nearly all the 20 villages where mastic is grown, known as the Mastikochória, date from the Middle Ages, and were carefully spared by the Turks in 1822. They were designed by the Genoese as tight-knit little labyrinths for defence, the houses sharing a common outer wall with few entrances; if that were breached, the villagers could take refuge in a central keep. Heading south from Chíos town, the first of the Mastikochória is **Armoliá**, which also makes pottery, although not particularly the kind you'll have room for in your luggage. It is defended by the Byzantine **Kástro tis Oréas** (1440), a castle named for the beautiful châtelaine who seduced men only to have them executed. **Kalamotí**, once one of the most thriving villages, has tall stone houses on its narrow cobbled streets and a pretty Byzantine church, Ag. Paraskeví, and isn't far from the 12th-century church **Panagía Sikelia**. The closest beach to both towns is **Kómi**, a darkish stretch of sand, reachable by bus and with tavernas on the beach and rooms to rent. If Kómi gets too busy, **Lilikas** is a good pebbled alternative two kilometres further east.

Pirgí (ΠΥΡΓΙ) is the largest mastic village and an architectural gem, founded in the 13th century and beautifully decorated with *xistá*, the local word for *sgrafitto* decoration taught to the locals by the Genoese; walls are first covered with mortar containing black sand from Emborió, then coated with white plaster, which the artist scrapes off into geometric, floral or animal-based designs. While the decoration is seen here and there elsewhere in Greece, Pirgí is unique in that nearly every house is decorated with *xistá*; in the main square of the village they are particularly lavish. Of the equally adorned churches, the 12th-century **Ag. Apóstoli**, a miniature version of Néa Moní, has frescoes from 1655 (*open most mornings*).

One of Chíos' ancient cities was Levkonion, a rival of Troy that was later mentioned by Thucydides. Near the old mastic-exporting port of **Emborió** (ΕΜΠΟΡΕΙΟΣ), 5km from Pirgí and round the hill from Kómi, archaeologists discovered signs of a settlement that may well fit the bill, dating from 3000 BC. East of the port, under the chapel of Profítis Ilías are ruins of the 7th–4th century BC **temple of Athena Polias** and the enceinte of an ancient acropolis. The wealth of amphorae found underwater here hint at the extent of Chíos' wine trade (Aristophanes wrote that the ancient Chiots were terrible tipplers; these days most of their grapes go into ouzo or a raisin wine not unlike Tuscan *vinsanto*). **Mávra Vótsala** beach, five minutes from Emborió, is made of black volcanic pebbles, but the effect is somewhat spoiled by the DEH's new power lines; around the headland is a second, better black beach which seems to have five or six names, but is usually called Mávra Vótsala too. Some way from the shore near Emborió are the ruins of a 6th-century **Christian basilica** with a marble cross-shaped font and a few mosaics.

Two other medieval mastic villages have impressive defences: **Olýmpi** (ΟΛΥΜΠΟΙ) and **Mestá** (ΜΕΣΤΑ). Olýmpi is built around a 20m tower, and originally had only one gate. Mestá is the ultimate fortress or *kástro* village, with no ground floor windows facing out of the village and only one entrance into its maze of lanes and flower-filled yards much beloved of film crews; most of the time you can almost hear the silence. Two churches are worth a look: the medieval **Ag. Paraskeví** and the 18th-century **Mikrós Taxiárchis**, with a beautifully carved iconostasis. As is usual in Greece, Mestá's two main *kafeneíons* are strictly divided, one for socialists, one for conservatives. The southwest coast is dotted with exquisite wild beaches; **Fana**, to the south, owes its name to the ruins of a fountain recalling the Great Temple of Phaneo Apollo (6th century BC) that stood nearby. Alexander the Great once stopped to consult its oracle; several of its Ionic columns are displayed in the Chíos archaeology museum. The road north from Mestá to Chíos town passes Mestá's old working port of **Liménas** (or **Pasá-Limáni**) and picturesque medieval **Véssa,** deep on the valley floor and worth exploring on foot. From here, another road leads north to **Lithí** (4½km), a pretty village with a so-so sandy beach below, tavernas and a few places to stay. Further up the west coast you can swim at the pebble coves near Elínda and circle back to Chíos town by way of Avgónima and Néa Moní.

✉ *82102* **Where to Stay and Eating Out**

The Mastic Villages ✆ (0271–)

The rather formidable title of the **Women's Agrotourist Cooperative of Chíos**, ✆ 72 496, may put some people off staying in their charming, traditional village rooms in Mestá, Armólia, Pirgí and Olýmpi (*around 7,000dr*). Although run (and beautifully maintained) by women, both men and women are equally welcome as guests. Each room is different, but they tend to be well located, handsomely restored and furnished, with their own bathroom and often kitchen. If you want to get more involved in village life, you can even help the women gather the mastic sap. In Mestá, Despina Syrimis not only runs the Cooperative, but owns one of three excellent tavernas in the main square, and is a mine of information. For cheaper, non-Agrotourist rooms try **Nikos**, ✆ 72 425 (*inexp*), on the edge of Pirgí, or **Argiro**, ✆ 72 226 (*inexp*), in the centre. The main square of Pirgí is a must for people-watching, especially when flashy

Harley Davidsons rev round; unostentatious, family-run **Taverna Nikolaos**, on the corner, will fill you with nourishing traditional fare.

Kómi ✆ (0271–)

For rooms try friendly, family-run **Bella Mare**, ✆ 71 226 (*inexp*), above Pandesia restaurant on the beach, with own bathroom and a free supply of sun loungers and umbrellas, or **Mika's**, just south of town, ✆ 71 335 (*inexp*). For fresh fish and lobster on the strand, eat at **Nostalgia**, ✆ 70 070, which proudly advertises its 'free umprellas'; after dark everyone heads for a drink at beach bars **Kochili** or hip **Onar**, or out to **Blue** for a boogie.

Emborió ✆ (0272–)

Vassiliki, ✆ 71 422 (*inexp*), has apartments set back from the harbour in flowers. **Themis Studios**, ✆ 71 810 (*inexp*), are just above the portlet. The highly recommended **Volcano**, ✆ 71 136, has not only delicious food but a shady terrace and interior containing a wedding chest, photos, plates and the prettiest loos in Greece.

Líthi ✆ (0272–)

Medusa Rooms, ✆ 73 289, ✉ 23 634 (*inexp*), are traditionally furnished, while **Kira Despina Murina** is on the beach, ✆ 73 373 (*inexp*), with a handful of rooms and great fish, fish soup and big breakfasts.

Inland from Chíos Town: Néa Moní (NEA MONH)

A trip to **Néa Moní** (*open 8–1 and 4–8; women should wear knee-length skirts*) is the most beautiful excursion on Chíos, and perhaps easiest made by taxi if you don't have a car; most blue buses only go as far as **Karyés**, a mountain village flowing with fresh springs, a long 7km walk from the monastery. Beautifully perched high in the pines, Néa Moní was 'new' back in 1042, when Emperor Constantine VIII Monomachos ('the single-handed fighter') and his wife Zoë had it built to replace an older monastery, where the monks had found a miraculous icon of the Virgin in a bush; not the least of its miracles was its prophecy that Constantine would return from exile and gain the throne of the Byzantine Empire. In gratitude, the emperor sent money, architects and artists from Constantinople to build a new monastery. The church has a sumptuous double narthex and subtle, complex design of pilasters, niches and pendentives that support its great dome atop an octagonal drum. Its richly coloured 11th-century mosaics shimmer in the penumbra: the *Washing of the Feet*, *The Saints of Chíos* and *Judas' Kiss* in the narthex and *The Life of Christ* in the dome, stylistically similar to those at Dáfni in Athens and among the most beautiful examples of Byzantine art anywhere—even though they had to be pieced back together after the earthquake of 1881 brought down the great dome. A chapel displays the bones of some of the 5000 victims of Kara Ali's massacre who sought sanctuary here (among them, the 600 monks).

From here, a rough road leads to the monastery **Ag. Patéras**, built in honour of the three monks who founded Néa Moní and rebuilt in 1890. Further up, **Avgónima**, a once nearly abandoned village, now has three tavernas and is increasingly full of holiday homes for Greeks. More interestingly, a road zigzags up a granite mountain to the 'Mystrás of Chíos', the striking medieval village and castle of **Anávatos**. It saw horrific scenes in 1822; most of the villagers threw themselves off the 1000ft cliff rather than be captured by the Turks, and ever since then the place has been haunted. There are now only a handful of residents.

North of Chíos Town

Northern Chíos is the island's wild side, mountainous, stark and barren, its forests decimated by shipbuilders, and in the 1980s by fires. Many of its villages are nearly deserted outside of the summer. **Vrontádos** (BPONTAΔOΣ) 4½km north of Chíos town is an exception, a kind of bedroom satellite village, where most of the island's shipowners have their homes, overlooking a pebbly beach and ruined windmills. The locals are proudest of the **Daskalópetra** (the Teacher's Stone), a rather uncomfortable rock throne on a natural terrace over the sea where Homer is said to have sung and taught and where his disciples would gather to learn his poetry, although killjoy archaeologists say it was part of an ancient altar dedicated to the local version of Cybele. A curious legend relates that the most famous Genoese of all, Christopher Columbus, stopped and sat here before going on to America. The headquarters of the International Society of Homeric Studies is aptly in Vrontádos, and there's a small **folklore museum** (*open daily 5–7pm*); the 19th-century **Monastery of Panagía Myrtidiótissa** nearby has the robes of Gregory V, Patriarch of Constantinople.

Near Vrontádos stood Chíos' first church **Ag. Isídoros**, founded in the 3rd century on the spot where the saint was martyred. A later church to house the relics of St Isídoros (whose feast day only happens every four years, on 29 February) was built by Emperor Constantine, but it fell in an earthquake and was replaced by three successive structures, the last ruined by the Turks in 1822; mosaics from the 7th-century version are in the Byzantine museum in Chiós town. The church was never rebuilt, perhaps because the Venetians snatched Isídoros' relics in the 12th century and installed them in a special chapel in St Mark's. In 1967 Pope Paul IV ordered them to return one of Isídoros' bones, now kept in Chíos cathedral.

Further north is **Langáda,** an attractive fishing village, popular with Greek tourists in July and August, and sporting an array of bars, cafés and fish tavernas. Jagged rocks surround **Kardámila** (KAPΔAMΥΛA), the largest village of northern Chíos and cradle of the island's shipowners. Kardámila is actually two villages, 2km from one another: the picturesque upper town and the seaside **Mármaros**, blessed with many philanthropic gifts from wealthy Chiot shipowners, including a statue of the Kardámila sailor on the beach. To the north, **Nagós beach** is set in a green amphitheatre and slowly succumbing to tourism; its name is a corruption of *naos*, or temple, for there used to be one here, dedicated to Poseidon. At nearby **Gióssona**, named after Jason of the Argonauts, there's another pebble beach, longer and more exposed than Nagos, but with fabulous turquoise water and a taverna.

Taxis have a monopoly on transport to the striking and unspoiled mountain village **Pitiós**, which claims to be the birthplace of Homer; you can still see his 'house' and olive grove. A 12th-century tower dominates the village and there's usually something to eat at the café or try O Makellos, under an enourmous plane tree on the edge of town. The landscape from Pitiós towards Chíos town is lunar in its burnt emptiness, but just above the village is a lovely pine forest, filled with fire warnings.

Further to the west, the 13th-century **Moní Moúdon** is strikingly set in the barren hills near Katávasis. Byzantine nobles out of favour were exiled in the medieval fortress at **Volissós** (BOΛIΣΣOΣ), founded by Belisarius, Justinian's great general, although what you see was rebuilt by the Genoese. The popular 16th-century saint Markélla hailed from the little white village, which also lays claim to Homer; in ancient times it was the chief town of the Homeridai, who claimed descent from him. One tradition says Homer met a shepherd named Glaukos in Volissós, and Glaukos introduced him to his master, who hired the poet as a teacher. Soon after Homer married a Volissós girl, had two daughters, wrote the *Odyssey* and decided to sail to Athens, the rising centre of Ionian culture, but he died on the way on Íos. Although renovation is under way, much of the old town up by the Kastro remains evocatively in ruins. The sandy beach below the town, **Skála Volissoú** or **Limniá**, is one of the island's finest and has two good traditional tavernas and a few rooms to let. From nearby, caiques go several times a week to Psará (the shortest way of getting there). There are other excellent beaches near here, just as minimally developed: pebbly **Chóri** just south, the unofficial nudist beach, and **Límnos**, on the road to **Ag. Markélla**, these days the island's favourite pilgrimage destination.

Twice a week or so, buses brave the deserted roads north of Volissós. The westerly one climbs to little **Piramá**, with a medieval tower and the church of Ag. Ioánnis with old icons. **Parpariá** to the north is a medieval hamlet of shepherds, and at **Melaniós** many Chiots were slain before they could flee to Psará in 1822. On the northwest shore stands the 14th-century Byzantine church **Ag. Gála**, by a cave which drips whitish deposits, or milk (*gála* in Greek), said to be the milk of the Virgin. For more strange terrestrial secretions, make your way along the rough coastal road east to **Agiásmata** where Chiots come in the summer to soak in the magic baths.

Where to Stay and Eating Out

Vrontádos ✉ 82100, ✆ (0271–)

Kyveli Apartments at Daskalópetra, ✆ 94 300, 🖅 94 303 (*exp*), has large, bland apartments with pool; try for an upstairs one for the harbour view; alternatively, there's the quirky **Ag. Markella**, ✆ 93 763 (*B; mod*), with dinky pool, in Vrontádos proper. Quite a few places rent rooms, including **Velonas**, ✆ 93 656, *velonas@ compulink.gr* (*inexp*), with clean petite studios just up from the sea. To Limanaki, ✆ 93 647, serves delicious fresh fish, and a short drive north in Pantoukias the imaginatively named **Pantoukios**, ✆ 74 262, is outstanding for lobster. In Daskalópetra, **Omiros** is quite reasonable. Chíos' only official, if inconvenient, campsite, **Camping Chíos**, is at the stony coved beach of Ag. Isídoros at Sikíada, ✆ 74 111.

Langáda ✉ 82300 ✆ (0272–)

Langáda has about a dozen waterside tavernas from which to choose, but steer in the direction of **Stellios**, ✆ 74 813, for excellent octopus, and the popular **O Passos**, next door, for the best food. Later, traipse along to **Timoniera Club** for the obligatory waterfront drink.

Kardámila ✉ 82300, ✆ (0272–)

A good base for exploring the unspoiled north of the island, **Hotel Kardamyla**, ✆ 23 353, 🖅 23 354 (*B; exp*), is on its own shady beach with watersports available. Although in a rather unprepossessing 1960s institutional block, the hotel is brought to life by its owner, the ever genial and helpful Theodore Spordilis. There is a restaurant and, as at his Hotel Kyma in Chíos, an endless free supply of orange juice and coffee. There are several tavernas and bars along the harbour at Mármaros, among which **Ioánnis** is popular.

Volissós ✉ 82300, ✆ (0274–)

English-speaking **Stella Tsakiri** has stylish, well-equipped houses for rent in the village, ✆ 21 421, 📠 21 521 (*inexp*). Near the *plateía* are shady **Taverna Anemi** and an adjacent bar with remarkably good music.

East of Chíos: Inoússes (ΟΙΝΟΥΣΣΕΣ)

Caiques leave Chíos town two to three times a week for Inoússes, 'the wine islands', an archipelago of nine islets to the northeast. Only the largest, all of three by 10km, is inhabited, but per capita it's the richest island in Greece: the Inoussans comprise some 60 of the 180 Greek shipowning families, including the Lemnos clan, the richest of them all. It's not for nothing that the Inoussians have a reputation for being tough and thrifty; most families began as goatherds or wine makers who had to spend centuries in Kardámila, Chíos, until it was safe to return to their defenceless rock pile. After losing everything in the Second World War they cannily parlayed a handful of wartime Liberty ships into a fleet of 500 ships and tankers, not to mention some of the fanciest yachts in Greece that congregate in its little port every summer. The rest of the year they divide between Geneva, London and Athens.

For all that, the island's one town is surprisingly unpretentious, if extremely well kept. Near the village is a medieval fort and there are a few small, clean undeveloped beaches, the furthest a 30-minute walk away. The one road on the island crosses to the western cliffs, where in the 1960s Katíngo Patéras, from one of the most prominent shipowning dynasties, built the multi-million-dollar convent of the **Evanglismós** (*adm only to women with long sleeves, headscarves and long skirts*) after her pious 20-year-old daughter Iríni died of Hodgkinson's disease, having prayed to take the illness from her afflicted father and become a nun. When, as custom has it, her body was exhumed after three years, she was found to be mummified. Her failure to decompose convinced her bereaved mother that she was a saint and, like Sleeping Beauty, she is kept in a glass case on display with the remains of her ship-owning father, who died shortly after, in spite of Irini's efforts. Inoússes has a pair of tavernas and one simple place to stay: **Hotel Thalassoporos**, ✆ (0272) 51 475 (*D; inexp*). *Open all year.*

West of Chíos: Psará (ΨΑΡΑ)

Psará is much further away than Inoússes: 44 nautical miles northwest of Chíos and connected only a few times a week with the larger island—a good 4-hour journey unless you depart from the port of Limniá below Volissós. Archaeologists have discovered signs of a 13th-century BC Achaean settlement near Paliókastro, a town founded by Chiot refugees during Turkish rule. They knew this tiny, remote rock of an islet was generally ignored by the Sultan and over the years developed one of Greece's most important commercial fleets here, rivalled only by the ships of Hýdra and Spétses. During the War of Independence (especially after the 1822 massacre on Chíos, which swelled the islet's population with refugees), Psará enthusiastically contributed its ships and one of the war's heroes, Admiral Kanáris, to the cause. Psará even invented a new weapon, the *bourléta*, which its captains used to destroy the Turkish fleet.

Psará became such a thorn in the side of the Turks that the Sultan finally demanded vengeance, and on 20 June 1824 he sent 25,000 troops to wipe Psará off the map. In the subsequent slaughter only 3000 of the 30,000 men, women and children managed to escape to Erétria, Évia. Most of the rest were blown to bits with the Turks on the famous 'Black Ridge of Psará' when they set their powder stores alight. The heroic little island has never recovered: today only 500 people live on Psará, mostly fishermen and beekeepers. A few old sea captains' mansions survive among the newer houses; the site of the house of Admiral Apostolis, a shipowner who fought in the war, is now a memorial square to the massacre. Your feet are your main transport to the island's fine beaches: the best is **Límnos**, a dandy sandy strand 20 minutes' walk away.

Psará ✉ *82104, ✆(0272–)*　　　　　　　　**Where to Stay and Eating Out**

EOT's **Xenon Psaron**, ✆ 61 293, or contact the main office in Mytilíni, Lésbos, ✆ (0251) 27 908 (*A; mod*), offers unusual accommodation in the 17th-century parliament building at Ag. Nikolaos; the restaurant occupies the old naval quarantine hospital. For something cheaper, there are rooms available; try **Bernardis**, ✆ 61 051 (*inexp*), or **Papas**, ✆ 61 247 (*inexp*), who each offer three rooms.

Ikaría (IKAPIA)

Long, narrow Ikaría is divided by a dorsal spine of mountains, many over 1,000m high and often lost in billowing clouds. It looks like a giant sea cucumber on the map and presents a forbidding, rocky, ungainly face to the world, and much of it is inaccessible except on foot. Yet both the wooded north and more rugged south coast villages are watered by mountain springs that keep them cool and green under oak and plane trees, with added natural air-conditioning from the wind. The Ikarían sea is one of the wildest corners of the Aegean; if it's calm on one side, it's often blustery on the other, whipping up rainbows of sea mist. Forget the myth: it was the wind that downed Icarus here, not the sun. It certainly abetted the fire that began in a roadworks tar pot and incinerated much of the south in 1993, causing 15 deaths.

Ever since Lawrence Durrell slagged off Ikaría so unkindly in his *Greek Islands*, it has been fashionable among British travel writers to spill their poison ink all over its wild rocky shores;

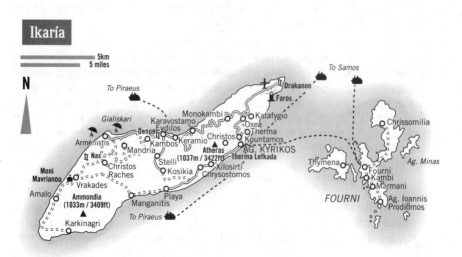

Ikaría

recently, one British newspaper, rating the islands as holiday material, put quirky, slow-paced Ikaría dead last. Well, they make my hot Ikarian blood boil, but just for a moment; let them be as nasty as they like if it helps to ward off the package companies, the twee-totallers, the pubs and lager louts. The truth is few islands have so stubbornly clung to their identity, or indeed their very soul: tourism is irrelevant to 95% of the inhabitants. Granted, Ikaría has little besides a few beaches to charm the hurried island-hopper, but more than tongue can tell if you take the time to stick around. And that's that! (Well, besides the obvious injunction to 'Eat at ΦΑΚΑΡΟΣ's' when you come...)

Mythology

After Theseus entered the Labyrinth at Knossos and killed the Minotaur with the aid of Ariadne's thread, Minos was furious at the inventor Daedalus, who gave Ariadne the yarn. Daedalus fled, but Minos ordered all outgoing ships watched to keep Daedalus on Crete. Unable to flee by land or sea, Daedalus made wings of feathers and wax for himself and his young son Icarus. Off they flew, but the boy, enchanted by flight, forgot the warning and flew too near the sun; the wax binding the feathers melted and the boy plummeted to his death off the south coast of an island thereafter known as Ikaría. In the 2nd century AD, Pausanius mentions that his grave could still be seen.

History

Ikaría has had more names than history, beginning with Dolichi; others were Ichthyoessa, for its fish, or Oenoe, for its wine. So much wine was produced that some writers made it the birthplace of Dionysos, the god of wine; an inscription found on Athens' acropolis describes one Oenoe as being second only to Athens in sending the yearly contributions to Apollo on Délos.

Under the Byzantines the island took on an extra N (many locals, in fact, still call it Nikaria) and was used to exile court officials who had fallen from grace. Kámbos was one of their centres; another Byzantine settlement existed by the hot springs at Thérma. Over time the entire population of Ikaría began to take their airs and claimed to 'have been born in the purple.' To this day Ikarians have a reputation for laid-back eccentricity.

In July 1912 during the Balkan War, the local doctor and priest led the inhabitants in liberating the island (a velvet revolution: they put the handful of Turkish administrators on a boat and said goodbye) and for five proud months Ikaría was an independent state with its own flag and stamps. When it joined Greece, the government promptly forgot about it, and many Ikarians emigrated, mostly to the States. The Colonels used Ikaría as a dumping ground for political dissidents and Communists (who at one point numbered 15,000, twice the number of natives). Like the Byzantine exiles, their presence changed the locals; even today 'Red' Ikaría is one of the most left-wing islands in Greece, although whoever used to paint Maoist slogans on the roads has given up.

© (0275–)   *Getting There and Around*

By air: the **airport** is at Fanári, © 22 981, 13km from Ag. Kýrikos on the far eastern tip of the island; because of the wind, it has a unique north–south runway that can be approached from either direction. There are connections four times weekly with

Athens, six times in the summer (tickets © 22 214). A bus (*1,000dr*) links Ag. Kýrikos to flights.

By sea: small tourist **excursion boats** from Ag. Kýrikos to Foúrni daily. Summer **hydrofoils** run four times a week to Pátmos, which can be visited as a day trip, and three times to Sámos. **Port authority,** © 22 207 in Ag. Kýrikos; © 31 007 in Évdilos.

By road: Ikarian transport is kept to an absolute minimum and you may want to hire a jeep or sturdy bike (in Ag. Kýrikos, Évdilos or Armenestís). **Buses** run once or twice a day to villages on the main roads, and across the island from Ag. Kýrikos to Évdilos and Armenistís (the trip takes over an hour) coinciding with the Piraeus ferries (but don't bet your life on it). **Taxis**, however, are used to making long-haul trips and will estimate fares before setting out; sharing is common.

© *(0275–)* **Tourist Information**

No EOT, but try Dolichi Tours, © 22 346, or Ikariada Travel, © 23 322, both in Ag. Kýrikos, or Blue Nice, © 31 990, in Évdilos. **Police:** © 22 222, in Ag. Kýrikos, or © 31 222, in Évdilos.

Post office: by the central square (*open 7.30–2.30 weekdays*). **OTE:** by post office.

Festivals

In the **summer**, *panegýria* occupy the attention of the whole island and many Ikarians who live abroad come home just to make merry. These feasts are run in the old style: guests order a *próthesi*—a kilo of wild goat meat, a bottle of wine, a huge bowl of soup and a loaf of bread—enough to feed four, and provide enough energy to dance until dawn. However, the biggest festival of all is on **17 July**, in honour of the defeat of the Turks and Ikaría's fling with independence in 1912. Feasts, speeches, music and folk-dancing in costume are part of the day's agenda. Other festivals are: **8th Sun after Easter**, Ag. Pándas in Karavastómos; **26 July**, Ag. Paraskeví in Xilosírti; **27 July**, in Ag. Panteleímonos; **6 August**, in Christós; **15 August**, in Akamátra and Chrissóstomos; **8 September**, in Plagiá and Mananítis; **17 September**, Ag. Sofía in Mesokámbos. As the place synonymous with the world's first hang-glider, Ikaría has been deeply involved since 1990 in setting up the **Ikaríad**, the Olympics of air-sports, to be held every four years in different parts of the world.

Ag. Kýrikos and Thérma

Ag. Kýrikos (ΑΓ. ΚΗΡΥΚΟΣ) or just plain 'Ágios' as everyone calls it, is the capital and largest town, 'obviously designed by a drunken postman' according to Mr Durrell. Well! Its tiny centre of shops, banks, travel agents and a lovely old bakery unchanged since the 1930s has more trees than buildings or people. Like Candide, every Ikarian must cultivate his or her own garden and orchard, so forget urban density; in greater Ágios, it's hard to tell where one village ends and another begins in the great mountain amphitheatre.

The breakwater has been extended to ensure safer landings at the gale-ridden port, and the enormous 'Welcome to the Island of Radiation' once painted there that gave pause to many travellers has been whitewashed to the more benign WELCOME TO THE ISLAND OF IKAROS. The statue on the breakwater—by local sculptor Ikaros—honours the first Icarus, who doesn't seem very airworthy even here, although supported on either side by two tall girder thingamabobs. The string of *kafeneía* along the waterfront see most of the social life, and shops in 'Ágios' sell Ikaría's sweets and honey made from thyme or *koumaro* bush blossoms; a small **archaeology museum** (*generally open 10–1*) has a room of local finds from the Neolithic to Roman periods. Another scupture by Ikaros, called the *Sképsi*, or 'Thinking Woman' (it does happen), is near the road on the west end of Ágios, and he also has to answer for the 'sphinx' by the sea.

For decades tourism on Ikaría has meant **Thérma** (ΘΕΡΜΑ), a short boat taxi or bus ride from Ágios, where natural radioactive springs bubble up from the earth at 33–55°C to treat chronic rheumatism, arthritis, gout and spondylitis; there's also a sauna (℗ 22 202). The springs are the most radioactive in Europe; one, Artemidas, is so strong (790 degrees of radiation) that it's closed to the public. There are a few rough pebble beaches here; for a long sandy strand, take the new road east out to the Fáros or **Fanári**, by the airport. On the very end of the cape stands a round whitish tower from the 3rd or 4th century BC—one of the best preserved Hellenistic towers in Greece; in fact, an entire castle survived until the War of Independence, when Admiral Miaoúlis sailed by and used it for target practice. It stood over the ancient town of **Drakanón**, sacred to Dionysos; only a few 5th-century BC walls survive on the acropolis. Between Thérma and Drakanón lies the hamlet of **Katafýgio**, which means 'shelter' and refers to an underground passageway beneath the church. One day Turkish raiders came to Katafýgio, but as it was Sunday all the villagers were at church. The Turks decided to wait outside and capture the people as they came out. They waited and waited, then impatiently broke into the church—to find it empty. The priest had opened the secret trapdoor in the floor, and everyone had escaped.

The forbidding cliff-bound coast west of Ag. Kýrikos (now green again, with a few charred trunks to recall the 1993 fire) has several more springs; one, **Thérma Lefkáda**, just bubbles out of the sea so hot that villagers on picnics use it to boil their eggs, and Athanatós Neró (the 'deathless water' or fountain of youth: fill up a bottle) runs near the neo-Byzantine **Evangelístrias** monastery (1775), with a pretty schist-roofed church and exactly one nun; just below you'll find the new retirement home. **Xilosírti**, the next village along the coast, is where Icarus plummeted into the sea, off a clean, if occasionally windswept, pebble beach; if you go out in a caique, the locals can point out the exact spot. Xilosírti has black schist roofs (with the wind, even the stones are held down by more stones), spread out among olive and apricot trees, which produce some of the tastiest apricot preserves in Greece. Above, **Chrysóstomos** is large, fairly prosperous and traditional. To the west, the road continues to **Playa**, with a handful of houses and fishboats, but to continue you need a jeep or strong bike, either to head inland to Kosíkia or to continue west along the coast through a long tunnel (paid for by Ikarians in the USA) before linking up to **Manganítis**, the westernmost village on the south shore; most people still make the trip by caique from Ágios. Built on a steep hillside with a pocket-sized port, its lonely position belies the fact that it can be one of the liveliest spots on Ikaría in the summer.

Ikaría ✉ *83000*, ℗ *(0275–)*   **Where to Stay and Eating Out**

The Ikarians are busily reviving their vinous past, and are currently trying out a wide variety of grapes in tiny vineyards, tucked away in any spare corner: the result may often be curiously brown in tone but goes down nicely and it gives quite a buzz, too.

The islanders also make their own cheese, *kathoúra*. Other local products are sweet: honey, fruit preserves (*Ikariaká glyká*), Turkish delight (*loukoúmia*), and ouzo.

Ag. Kýrikos

No frills here, but pristine, pleasant **Maria Elena**, ✆ 22 835, ✉ 22 223 (*B pension; mod*), is on a slope just above town, with 16 simple airy rooms and seven studios, all with balcony and bath. Other places are smaller: for similar comfort and prices try the tastefully kitted out **Kastro**, ✆ 22 474, ✉ 23 700 (*C; mod*), or **Adam's**, ✆ 22 418 (*C; mod; open all year*). **Isabella's**, ✆ 22 839 (*E; inexp*), right in the centre, has a restaurant and pool; **Hotel Akti**, ✆ 22 694 (*E; inexp*), is clean and welcoming with a panoramic garden. Isolated to the west near the sea in Thérma Lefkáda, **Galini**, ✆ 22 530 (*E; mod–inexp*), is closer to the bubbles but open only in July, August and September. The island's best pizzas and now other dishes as well are served at **Filoti**, just off the waterfront, and the *zacharoplasteíon* next door is a good place for snacks and sugary little cakes. **Klimataria** is a basic and good taverna, open all year, and **Pascali's** on the waterfront is reliable. **Kazalas**, in Glarédou, high above Ágios (take a taxi), is known for its authenticity.

Thérma

The hotels and pensions just east of Ágios in Thérma are primarily geared towards the arthritic. Still, you may want to try the airy white **Marina**, ✆ 22 188 (*B; mod*), in a handsome traditional building, or the recently renovated **Ikarion**, ✆ 22 481 (*D; inexp*). The **Radion**, ✆ 22 381 (*D; mod–inexp*), also offers some sea sports.

The North Coast

Ikaría's northern half atttracts far more tourists with its pine forests, stream beds lined thick with shady plane trees, vineyards, sandy beaches and excellent roads and guesthouses. From Ag. Kýrikos a long, winding, breathtaking road climbs up to the barren mountain pass, taking in views of Foúrni, Sámos, Pátmos, Turkey and Náxos, along with a few bored soldiers and power-generating windmills.

After passing above small villages immersed in the trees—Monokámbi, **Karavóstamo** (with a 17th-century church, **Ag. Pántas** and a dinky port) and Keramío—the road descends to the port of **Évdilos** (ΕΥΔΗΛΟΣ), the metropolis of the north coast, a pleasant little place with stone-paved lanes, and a port linked several times a week by ferry to Piraeus and Sámos. It has a good town beach just to the east. From Évdilos the road above winds up past several leafy hamlets on the way to **Kosíkia** (or Messariá),where the mountain pass is guarded by the ruined 10th-century Byzantine **Nikariás castle**, with an old stone church inside. There is an even nicer one further west, at **Kámbos**. Oenoe, the ancient capital of Ikaría, was here, and later Byzantine princelings in exile installed themselves nearby; the columns and arches of their palace remain, as well as their church **Ag. Iríni** with a slate roof. The adjacent local **museum** (ask at Vasilis Dionysos' shop for the key; the owner is pleased to enthuse about the region) houses finds mostly from Oenoe—pottery, clay figurines, coins, tools etc. In the nearby village of **Pygí**, the slate-roofed **Moní Theoktisti** has Ikaría's finest frescoes, by the Mount Áthos school.

Further west along the coast, sandy **Gialiskári** is Ikaría's finest and most beautiful beach with a tiny blue-domed chapel set out on the rocks offshore. There are summer *cantinas* and a few rooms, but these always fill up in the summer; many people freelance-camp here and at **Livádi**, the other great stretch of sand on the opposite side of **Armenistís** (ΑΡΜΕΝΙΣΤΗΣ), an attractive traditional fishing village as well as Ikaría's biggest tourist resort—big by Ikarian standards at any rate. You can 'see' it all in about five minutes, but you can sit here for hours.

Armenistís is the point of departure for two of the island's beauty spots: the wooded mountain village of **Christós Rachés**, the 'Little Switzerland of Ikaría', a bucolic place with orchards and vineyards, and as of 1994, that rarest of island commodities, a little **lake** (artificial, but it looks more natural than most in Greece); Christós' 13th-century convent at **Mounté** has some wall paintings and icons. The second place is the ancient city of **Nas** (from *naos*, or temple), 10 minutes west along an unpaved road. On the bluff above, there's a pair of tavernas and a few rooms, and a path to shimmy down over the rocks to a small naturalist beach in the ancient harbour (don't swim beyond the sheltered bay). Behind, over an old river channel, are the platform and foundations of the 5th-century BC **temple of Artemis Taurópoulos**. A marvellous statue of the goddess was discovered in the 19th century, with eyes that followed the viewer from every angle. The local priest decided at once that it was the work of heathen if not of the devil himself and had it thrown in the nearest lime kiln. Thus perished the *Artemis of Ikaría*, never to hold its place in the Louvre with the *Venus de Milo* or *Victory of Samothrace*.

The road doesn't improve (or get much worse) if you continue southwest to the sweet little whitewashed, slate-roofed **Monastery of Mavrianoú**, next to an old threshing floor; the village above, **Vrakádes**, has a pair of cafés and pretty views. A few kilometres further on **Amálo** has summer tavernas (try the one back at verdant Lagáda). If you're feeling especially adventurous, carry on south to **Karkinágri**, Ikaría's most isolated village, with a tiny port, a summer taverna, a few rooms and not much else; the last 5km of the road are a bit rough.

Ikaría ✆ (0275–) **Where to Stay and Eating Out**

Évdilos ✉ 83302

Most comfortable here is the **Atheras-Kerame**, a hotel and apartment complex, partly in a 19th-century building, ✆ 31 434 , ✆ 31 926, winter in Athens ✆ (01) 685 8096 (*B; exp–mod*), 50m from the sea, with a restaurant and bar, sea-water pool, gym, playground and other comforts. *Open May–Oct.* Further up, overlooking the port, **Evdoxia**, ✆ 31 502, ✆ 31 571 (*C; mod–inexp*), has 10 simple rooms, all with balcony, mini bar and TV; the hotel also has a resturant and a useful laundry. Alternatively, stay out by ancient Oenoe, in Kámbos, where the irrepressible **Vasilis** has comfortable rooms, ✆ 31 300 (*inexp*), with a family ambience and mega breakfasts. Down by the port, the *ouzerie* **To Steki** is also the place to go for fish; for grilled meats, try **Kokos**. Towards Kámbos, on Fitema beach, taverna **Kalypso** is handy for a day on the strand.

Armenistís and Points West ✉ 83301

Ikaría's fanciest hotel, **Messakti Village**, 2km west at Gialiskári, ✆ 71 331, ✆ 71 330, in Athens ✆ (01) 621 9112, ✆ 621 6684 (*B; exp–mod*), was built using traditional island materials and architecture, including slate floors; rooms have kitchenettes and overlook the pool and sandy beach; very friendly management. **Daidalos**, ✆ 71 390, 🖷 71 393, in Athens ✆ (01) 922 9034, 🖷 (01) 923 5453 (C; mod), is another handsome place, traditionally furnished and set among the cedars overlooking the sea (charmingly described in its publicity as 'erected on the wave'), with a pool, children's pool, large garden and restaurant. Or there's the modern **Cavos Bay**, ✆ 71 381, 🖷 71 380 (C; exp), with a pool, restaurant and sea views. There are plenty of rooms—the **Armena**, ✆ 71 320 (inexp), has studios with views, and **Dimitris Ioannidopoulos**, ✆ 71 310 (inexp), has reasonably priced hillside studios and apartments amongst a forest of flowers. **Raches**, up in Christós Rachés, ✆ 41 269 (B; mod), offers peace and quiet and meals in the evening. *Open June–Oct.*

The best food in the village comes from the portside kitchen of **Paskalia**, ✆ 71 302 (although the locals call it **Vlachos**, after the owner); it also has good-value rooms above. **Delfini** is known for fish, while on the other end of the waterfront **Symposio** does vegetarian dishes, fish and mushrooms (one of Ikaría's secrets). Cousin **Charley Facaros' Pub**, ✆ 71 208, on the waterfront, has some rooms and serves drinks and snacks. Taverna **Kelari**, overlooking the fishing boats at Gialiskári, has good seafood. In Nas, there are a score of rooms and the excellent **Taverna Astra**, ✆ 71 255, serving delicious, very reasonably priced seafood (including some of the most tender octopus in Greece), courgette beignets and other dishes prepared in the traditional Ikarian style, with local wine (around 3,000dr).

If you have energy to spare, make for the Pleiades Club, Armenistís, a spacious alfresco space playing Greek and international music.

Foúrni (ΦΟΥΡΝΟΥΣ)

If Ikaría is too cosmopolitan for your taste, turn the clock back a couple of decades and head out to Foúrni (or Foúrnous), quiet islets in their own mini archipelago just about midway between two larger sisters, Sámos and Ikaría. The larger, hook-shaped islet embraces a size-able sheltered cove that long hid a band of Algerian pirates, from where they would pounce on passing ships. Today the waters around the islands are better known as η φωλια των ψαριων, 'the lair of fish', especially the much-loved *barboúnia* (red mullet) and clawless Mediterranean lobster (*astakós*), which, although plentiful, isn't cheap; the surprisingly large fishing fleet, maintained in Foúrni's busy boatyards, sends most of the catch to Athens. Many fish by night, using bright lamps that set the sea aglitter.

✆ (0271–)   *Getting There and Around*

Connected at midday at least three times a week by shopping **caique** from Ag. Kýrikos, Ikaría (buy tickets on board); summer **hydrofoils** connect Ikaría and Foúrni three times a week, enabling day trips from Kámbi. **Caiques** will ferry you to coves and beaches. **Port authority**: ✆ 51 207.

Festivals

The two big holidays on Foúrni are **15 August**, for the Panagía, and Ag. Ioánni tou Thermastí, **29 August.**

Foúrni's Villages

About half of Foúrni's 1600 souls live around the port, also called **Foúrni**, where the action happens along the waterfront or in the lovely plane-shaded square. Just north, up the steps, a path leads to the beaches of **Psilí Ammo**, and **Kálamos**. Further north, the new road ends up at **Chrissomiliá**; if you've been looking for a retreat to write your next novel, this might be it, with beaches, a few rooms and a couple of simple tavernas.

A 15-minute walk south of the port will bring you to **Kámbi**, the 'capital', a pleasant little place scattered Ikarian-style under the trees, with a few rooms, a tamarisk-lined beach and a little cove full of yachts in the summer. From here you can arrange boat trips to **Marmári**, a cove just south, where the ancients quarried marble to build Ephesus, or sail further south to Vlycháda beach. If Foúrni is too cosmopolitan, try its baby islet **Thýmena**, where you'll be stared at if you disembark; bring your own food and be prepared to sleep under the stars.

Foúrni ✉ *83400,* ✆ *(0271–)*　　　　　　　　　　　　　　*Where to Stay and Eat*

Outside August, finding a room in the port is usually no problem, and you may well be met as you disembark. Just back from the sea, **Spyrakos Rooms**, ✆/✉ 51 235, in Athens ✆ (01) 261 9010 (*mod*), are very nice and come with mini-fridges as well as private bath. The **Markakis'** rooms, in a renovated pile by the port, are a pleasant alternative, ✆ 51 268 (*inexp*); for modern rooms, seek out **Eftychia Amorgiannou**, just inland, ✆ 51 364, ✉ 51 290 (*inexp*), and there are about 40 others in the houses. Among the tavernas near the port, **Nikos** is the best for lobster and fresh fish. The two traditional *kafeneía* are shaded by a plane tree apiece on the square.

Kárpathos (ΚΑΡΠΑΘΟΣ)

Halfway between Crete and Rhodes, on the same latitude as Malta and Casablanca, Kárpathos has for decades been an island-hopper's best-kept secret: hard to reach, with a number of beauty spots and a very distinct character, most strongly marked by the affection it inspires in its inhabitants; although many have been forced to go abroad to make a living, they come back as often as possible, and ship their bodies home to be buried on the island if fate decrees they die elsewhere. They have the money: Kárpathos' sons and daughters have one of the highest rates of university education in Europe. And the climate gets a gold star, too, for people suffering from respiratory diseases.

Kárpathos offers two islands for the price of one: long and thin, austere and ruggedly mountainous in the north, and fertile, softer beach-fringed and 'European' in the south, the two linked by a giant's vertebra of cliffs which culminates in two wild mountains over 1,000m in height. These two distinct geographical personalities extend to the population; the northerners and southerners may have originally belonged to different ancient races. For long generations the little contact they had with one another was by caique. The centuries of isolation of the north left it a goldmine of traditions lost a century ago in the rest of Greece. Even today songs, dances and celebrations like Easter remain unchanged; in the village of Ólympos, women still bake their bread in outdoor ovens, and dress every day in their striking, traditional costumes—outfits that are among the most beautiful in Greece. A rough road connecting the south to Ólympos was finished in 1979. Once limited to jeeps, now taxis ply it, and sadly buses, too, and every year they somehow find more 'handicrafts' to sell to tourists.

History

One ancient name of Kárpathos was Porfiris, or 'Red', after a red dye once manufactured on the island and used to colour the clothes of kings; another was Tetrapolis, describing its four ancient cities of Vrykous, Possidion, Arkessia and Nissyros. In Homer the island is called Kárpathos, some believe from *Arpaktos*, or 'robbery', from the earliest days of piracy, when Vróntis Bay hid pirate ships that darted out to plunder passing vessels. The Venetians slurred it into 'Scarpanto', a name you may occasionally spot on maps.

Off the coasts, the prized *scarus* (or parrot fish, which, as Aristotle noted, ruminates its food) was so abundant that the Roman emperors hired special fleets to bring them back for the imperial table. Any signs of prosperity, however, had long ended by the time the pirates made the island their headquarters and one town, Arkássa, their chief slave market. Things were so rough that even the Turks didn't really want Kárpathos, and sent only a *cadi*, or judge, to the island a few times a year; he never stayed longer than a few days, and depended entirely on the Greeks to protect him. The bays at Vróntis and Arkássa are said to be riddled with sunken treasure, although if any has been found it's been kept very hush-hush. In the last war, 6,000 Italians were based on Kárpathos, which they used as a base to attack Egypt.

Kárpathos has a strong tradition of delicately lyrical poetry of its very own, and, as in Crete, people like to compete in impromptu singing contests of *mantinades*, or 15-syllable couplets. Two Austrians, Rudolph Maria Brandl and Diether Reinsch, spent 10 years on the island studying its songs, and wrote the monumental *Die Volksmusik der Insel Kárpathos* (Edition Re 1992), several volumes long, with transcribed songs and cassettes. One of the prettiest old songs was collected in the 19th century:

> *A little bird was singing high up on the rough hillside,*
> *And a king's daughter listened from her window,*
> *'Ah, bird, that I had thy beauty, and would I had thy song,*
> *And would I had such golden plumes for hair upon my head!'*
> *'Why dost thou crave my beauty? why dost thou crave my song?*
> *Why dost thou crave my golden plumes for hair upon thy head?*
> *For thou hast cakes to feed on, as many as thou wilt,*
> *I eat my scanty portion from herbage in the fields;*
> *Thou sleepest on a lofty couch, with sheets of thread of gold,*
> *But I lie out in solitude among the dews and snows;*
> *And when thou drinkest water thou hast a gleaming cup,*
> *But I must drink my water from the spring thou bathest in;*
> *Thou waitest for the priest to come thy way to bless thee,*
> *But I await the huntsman, who comes to shoot me down.'*

✆ *(0245–)*   ***Getting There and Around***

By air: two daily connections with Rhodes, five times a week with Athens and three times with Kássos (the shortest scheduled flight in the world: it takes 5 minutes); also charters—many from Slovenia! There's an Olympic Airways office in town, run by the very helpful Kostis Frangos, by the main square, ✆ 22 150. **Airport information**: ✆ 22 058. Taxis to the airport cost around 4,000dr.

By sea: small **boats** daily in the summer connect the island's two ports, Diafáni and Pigádia, leaving Pigádia at 8.30am and at weekends there's a **caique** from Finíki to Kássos. A pair of excursion boats make beach and picnic outings to Kýra Panagía, Apélla, Acháta and Kató Lata. For information, ring the **port authority**: © 22 227.

By road: not always easy. The often appalling state of the roads makes car and motorbike hire dear, the only petrol pumps are in Pigádia, and the bus service seems like an afterthought, although there are regular services from Pigádia to Ammopí, and Pilés by way of Apéri, Voláda and Óthos, and one or two go on to Finíki and Arkássa and Lefkós.

Tourist Police

© (0245) 22 218, on Eth. Anastasis in Pigádia.

Festivals

25 March, Evangelismós in Pigádia; **Easter** in Ólympos, one of the most ancient in Greece; **1 July**, Ag. Marínas near Menetés; **15 August**, in Apéri and Menetés; **22–23 August**, Kyrá Panagía and Myrtónas; **27–29 August**, Ag. Ioánnis in Vourgounda; **6 September**, Larniotisa in Pigádia; **8 September**, Panagías in Messóchorio.

Kárpathos Town (Pigádia)

The island capital and southern port, Kárpathos or more properly **Pigádia** (ΠΥΓΑΔΙΑ) is attractively sheltered in that old pirate cove, mountain-ringed Vróntis Bay. Once the ancient city of Possidion, it was abandoned in the Byzantine era, and all that remains of its predecessor is a clutch of Mycenaean tombs and a few stones of a temple to Lindian Athena on the rocky outcrop to the east. The modern town is just that—modern, and ungainly, but it's no accident that the local National Bank branch has such an air of prosperity: Kárpathos receives more money from its emigrants than any other island in Greece. New hotels and apartments are mushrooming up in Pigádia and along the sands outside town, and although German and Scandinavian holiday companies seem to be thriving, the town still has a relaxed, friendly feel to it; with all those bucks from Pittsburgh and Baltimore in the bank, the islanders don't have to be obsequious towards tourists.

Beyond the pretty Mussolini port authority building, it's a short walk to the 3km stretch of fairly good beach that rims **Vróntis Bay**, lined with trees, a few new hotels, and dotted with pleasant tavernas specializing in grilled fish. Within an enclosure on the sands several columns have been re-erected of a 5th-century basilica, **Ag. Fotiní**. Across the bay stands the chapel of **Ag. Nikólaos**, the saint who replaced Poseidon as the protector of sailors; a once sacred cave nearby called Poseidona has sweet water. On the south side of Vróntis Bay, another ancient site, **Ag. Kiriakí** (the track is signposted from the road) had a 7th-century BC Geometric-era sanctuary dedicated to Demeter; a few years back one of the tombs hewn in the rock yielded a golden statuette.

Around the South and up the West Coast

South of Pigádia, the land is flat and desolate and vegetation is sparse, the few trees bent over from the wind. The wild coast softens after 7km at **Ammopí**, a pair of sandy coves decorated with great rocks and a popular family resort. Further south, a forlorn ship that ran aground in

1985 is like an advertisement for Kárpathos' windblasted windsurfing 'paradise', **Afiárti**, with accommodation and rentals duly springing up; Homer, after all, called the island, Anemoussa, the 'windy one'. The airport is further south, by the desolate site of the ancient city of Thaetho.

Colourful **Menetés** (ΜΕΝΕΤΕΣ), set in gardens on the flanks of Mount Profítis Ilías above Ammopí, has a small ethnographic museum (ask at Taverna Manolis to visit) and a church in a dramatic setting. Beyond, the road continues down to the west coast and **Arkássa** (ΑΡΚΑΣΑ), with its little beaches and big hotels in a picturesque setting at the mouth of a jagged ravine, cliffs riddled with caves that once sheltered shepherds. A paved road will take you south in a few minutes to the ruins of its - predecessor, ancient **Arkessia**, where the Mycenaean acropolis with Cyclopean walls stands on the rocky headland of Paleokástro. The city was inhabited into late Byzantine times; the coloured geometric mosaic floor of a 5th-century church **Ag. Anastásia** is just under a fine layer of weeds and dirt, although the best sections have been moved to Rhodes.

Just north, **Finíki** is a bijou little fishing harbour with a good, inexpensive restaurant and sandy beach nearby; the sponge divers of Kálymnos call here, and caiques depart for Kássos, if the sea isn't too rough. The asphalted road north passes several tempting strands and mini fjords far, far below in the pines (one spot, **Adia**, has an excellent taverna) en route to **Lefkós** (ΛΕΥΚΟΣ), the nicest beach on the west coast—there's one bus a day from Pigádia. Tucked in the rocks, Lefkós has white sandy beaches, a wealth of pine trees and a scattering of antiquities, including a large stone that resembles

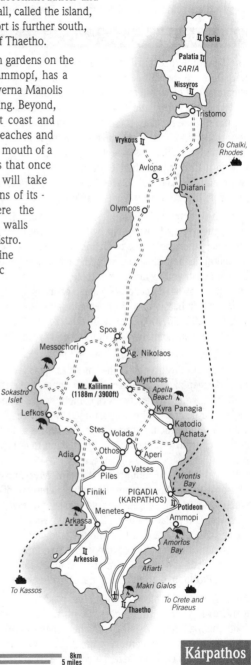

Kárpathos

a menhir. Lefkós is being developed and packages have arrived, but so far nothing too drastic; there are a few small pensions, tavernas and villas owned by the Karpathiots. A short walk away are the ruins of a medieval fort; there was another on the offshore islet of **Sokástro**.

Inland Villages and the East Coast

The beautiful road north of Pigádia rises first to opulent **Apéri** (ΑΠΕΡΙ). The capital of Kárpathos up to 1896, it is reputed to be the richest village in Greece per capita; nearly everyone (90 of whom are said to be doctors) has lived in New Jersey, including the family that gave the world the late Telly 'Kojak' Savalas. One *kafeneíon* still proudly displays a picture of Roosevelt. In the new cathedral built over the Byzantine cemetery, you can pay your respects to Kárpathos' miracle-working icon, and if you have a chance to peek in a house don't miss it; unlike most Greek islanders, the Karpathiots have lavish tastes, and traditionally furnish their homes with colourful carpets, lace, mirrors, portraits, antiques from around the world and elevated carved wood beds, or *souphas*; if you don't get inside, you can glean an idea from the exquisitely tended gardens.

The other central villages are just as houseproud. Delightful whitewashed **Voláda** has pretty lanes, and a ruined castle built by the Cornaros of Venice, who owned the island until 1538. From here the road climbs to **Óthos**, at 650m the highest village of Kárpathos and also one of the oldest, its houses decorated with carved wooden balconies; you may need a pullover, even in summer. If you're game for a tipple, try the fine local red wine, *othitikó krasí*. A 150-year-old house has been opened as a small **ethnographic museum**, run by the excellent Ioannis T. Hapsis, ex-barber and ex-shoemaker and *lýra* player, who now paints pictures, which he sells for 2000–20,000dr, solely by the size. To the west coast, the pretty village of ΠΥΛΕΣ, whose name in Roman letters unfortunately reads **Pilés**, has fine views over Kássos, with the profile of Crete as a backdrop and tasty honey.

Caiques from Pigádia call at the east coast beaches, although you can brave some of them by road. A steep zigzag from Apéri leads down to **Acháta**, a lovely, empty white pebbly beach with fresh water, closed in a rocky amphitheatre. The road north of Apéri takes in the increasingly majestic coast, with a serpentine paved by-road winding from Katodio to **Kyrá Panagía**, a lovely wide beach, varying from fine white sand to large pebbles and with a pretty red-domed church for a landmark. Rooms and tavernas are sprouting apace and fill up in the summer; an easier way to get there is by a 45-minute walk down through the lush greenery and trees from the mountain village of **Myrtónas**. Another rotten road descends from Myrtónas to **Apélla**, the most beautiful, a crescent of fine sand, turquoise water and dramatic scenery, set in boulders and rocks furiously rift, ravaged and rolled in the Clash of the Titans. Myrtónas is the place to be on 22 August, when it hosts the best *panegýri* on the island with music and folk-dancing lasting into the following day. The east coast road ends at **Spóa**, at the crossroads of the road to Ólympos; massive forest fires in the 1980s have left large patches between Spóa and Diafáni denuded and melancholy. A track from Spóa descends to the beach of **Ag. Nikólaos**, with too much new building, and in summer too many people.

Another unpaved, narrow Wild West road from Spóa circles Kárpathos' tallest mountain, **Kalílimni** (1188m), the highest point in the Dodecanese. Continuing anticlockwise from Spóa, the road descends on a corniche to **Messochóri**, set in an amphitheatre facing the sea, with the pretty 17th-century church of Ag. Ioánnis, with a carved iconostasis and well preserved frescoes. From here a road descends to Lefkós (*see* above).

Out of season a few room-owners meet ferries; if you get stuck, ring the **Association of Hotel Owners**, ✆ 22 483.

Kárpathos Town (Pigádia)

Possirama Bay, ✆ 22 916, @ 22 919 (*A; exp*), is 400m from the town centre, on the sandy beach of Affoti, offering air-conditioned apartments for 2–4 people and large balconies overlooking the sea. *Open Apr–Oct.* In the same area **Miramare Bay**, ✆ 22 345, @ 22 631 (*B; exp*), is another new operation, with pool, sea views and good breakfast included. **Romantica**, ✆ 22 460, @ 22 461(*C; mod*), is the most charming place to stay, with 49 studios, half-hidden in a grove of citrus trees, and a short walk from the beach; it serves delicious breakfasts. Up in town, the **Pavillion**, ✆ 22 059 (*C; mod*), is a favourite of Americans, with cocktails served in the roof garden. Newer, moderate-sized **Oasis**, ✆/@ 22 915 (*C; mod*), has flowery and welcoming studios. **Blue Bay**, by the beach, ✆ 22 479, @ 22 391 (*C; mod*), has rooms (some with disabled access), a pool, bar and children's playground. The **Kárpathos** is an older, cheaper choice, ✆ 22 347 (*D; inexp*). *Open all year.* There are also quite a few studios and rooms for rent in this price range; try **Rose**'s well-maintained studios on the hillside, ✆/@ 22 284 (*inexp*), the friendly, pleasantly furnished **Mertonas** studios, ✆ 23 079 (*inexp*), or **Fotoula Georgiadou's**, ✆ 22 519, up at the top of town and among the cheapest and quietest.

Kárpathos' restaurants are beginning to revive traditional recipes and serve wine from Óthos—although it's rare to find it in bottles. Old favourites like **Mike's** in a narrow lane in the centre and **Kali Kardia** (for fish) towards the beach aren't expensive. **Oraia Kárpathos** on the waterfront serves the best *makarounes* (handmade pasta with fried onions and cheese) south of Ólympos. New restaurants include **Aeraki**, on the waterfront, which serves island specialities—pumpkin fritters, stuffed mushrooms, onion pies, chicken stuffed with feta and bacon, local sausages and mild *manouli* cheese; the same owners run **Anemoussa** upstairs, with good Italian dishes. The **kafeneío** is a popular place to survey the scenery, with hearty evening fare accompanied by live music. Little old **Café Kárpathos**, just off the waterfront towards the ferry, is a good cheap place for breakfast or a snack.

Ammopí

Long Beach, ✆ 23 076, @ 22 095 (*C; mod*), has a pool and tennis; **Argo**, ✆ 22 589 (*C; mod*), is a newer beach addition. For windsurfers, there's the traditional styled **Poseidon**, south of Ammopí, ✆/@ 22 020 (*C; mod*), with a lovely garden terrace. **Ammopi Beach**, ✆ 22 723 (*inexp*), has simple, remarkably cheap rooms—help yourself to figs.

Arkássa

The **Arkesia**, ✆ 61 290, @ 61 307 (*B; mod*), is the plush choice here, with all mod cons, pool and kiddies' playground. **Dimitrios**, ✆ 61 313 (*B; mod*), is also comfortable, but with fewer facilities. For something cheaper try **Johnny's**, ✆ 61 310.

Finíki/Lefkós

Fay's Paradise, ℃ 61 308 (*inexp*), has lovely rooms near the harbour. There are three or four good fish tavernas (notably **Dimitrios'**), and the **Cuckoo's Nest** *ouzerie* with an all-blue interior for pre-dinner imbibing. North in Adia, eat at the **Pine Tree,** with great pasta, chick pea soup and fresh-baked bread. In Lefkós, the **Small Paradise,** ℃ 71 171, serves good food; ask about their beach-side studios.

Kyrá Panagía

Book to have a chance at any of these. Since 1976, **Sofia's Paradise Taverna,** ℃ 31 300, ✉ 31 099 (run by a former New Yorker), has offered good home cooking, cheap fish, and figs drowned in raki to go with your coffee; also pleasant rooms with bath and breakfast; she has a boat for private or group outings. If you want to go upscale, there's the new **Kyra Panagia Studios,** ℃ 31 473 (*B; exp*), with a bar, and the popular **Studios Acropolis,** ℃ 31 503 (*mod*), with lovely views. Up in Voláda, the **Klimateria** has traditional good taverna food under a pergola.

Entertainment and Nightlife

There's live impromptu Karpathian *lýra* of variable quality on summer nights under the pergola at the **Kafenion,** on Apodi Kárpathos street. On the town waterfront, **Symposeio** is a popular music bar, or there's the **Yuppy** bar near the church, in the skeleton of an unfinished building playing a mix of Greek and rave, or head up to one of the bars perched panoramically over the bay. **Filagri**, between Pigádia and Ammopí, is where locals and returned Karpathians dance the summer nights away. Every Wednesday night the locals get together and play traditional music in the *kafeneíon* in **Finíki.** In Apéri, the popular **Platania Bar** is in a restored old house, and plays Greek music and international hits.

Ólympos and Northern Kárpathos

The easiest and least expensive way to reach Ólympos (ΟΛΥΜΠΟΣ) from Kárpathos is by caique to **Diafáni,** the village's laid-back little port, from where a minibus makes the connection to Ólympos. The harbour improvements enable big ferries to dock. There's a beach with flat rocks nearby, and several others within walking distance; boats make excursions to ones further afield.

Ólympos, one of the most striking villages on the Greek islands, is draped over a stark mountain ridge, topped by a long line of ruined windmills running like teeth. To the west are magnificent views of mountains plunging headlong into the sea. Decorative painted balconies, many incorporating two-headed Byzantine eagles (one head Rome, one Constantinople), adorn the houses which in many places are literally stacked one on top of another and opened with wooden locks and keys that Homer himself might have recognized. The frescoes and recently cleaned iconastasis in the church date back to the 18th-century.

As the ability of the Byzantines to defend the seas declined, Ólympos became the refuge for the inhabitants of all the abandoned coastal towns in the north, themselves isolated for so long that linguists were amazed to find people here using pronunciations and expressions that could be traced back to ancient Doric and Phrygian dialects. Women are more visible than men, because of emigration; many of those who remain are noted musicians, playing the *lýra* with a bell-covered bow, the *laoúto*, and *tsamboúna* (goatskin bagpipes). Likewise, a mother's property all goes to the eldest daughter, the *kanakára*; if you're lucky enough to be in Ólympos during a *panegýri* or wedding, you can recognize a *kanakára* by the gold coins she wears on chains—coins that her forefathers will have earned while working abroad. Twenty years ago all the women wore their traditional costumes every day: black scarves printed with flowers, baggy white trousers, a dark skirt and apron, a loose embroidered chemise, and fine goatskin boots for special protection (snakes hate the smell of goat) which last for years. One cobbler still makes them for around 50,000dr a pair, but they last a lifetime. Women bake bread in outdoor ovens, even using wheat and barley ground in the two remaining working windmills, out of 40 that turned a few decades ago.

Ólympos, pop. 1,800 in 1951 is down to 340 today, but, where even 20 years ago visitors were so few that they had no effect on the village's traditional life, tens of thousands a year are another story. To see Ólympos as it was stay overnight, or come in the off-season. On weekend evenings the *kafeneíons* still fill with live music. One *kafeneíon* displays a certificate from the Governor of Alabama, thanking him for his service in the state militia.

From Ólympos you can drive most of the way to **Avlóna**, a village that wouldn't look too out of place in Tibet, inhabited only during the harvest season by farmers from Ólympos, who work the surrounding valley; some of the tools they use are more commonly seen in museums. From Avlóna it is a rough walk down to **Vrykoús**, the ancient Phrygian city of Vourkóunda, remembered today by a stair, a breakwater, rock-cut burial chambers and walls; a tiny chapel sits out on the rocks. In a cavern in Vrykoús the chapel of **Ag. Ioánnis** hosts the largest *panegýri* in north Kárpathos, a two-day event where everyone sleeps out, roasts meat over an open fire and dances to the haunting music. Another two hours north of Avlóna, in the bay of the 'three-mouthed' **Tristomo**, are the submerged remains of the ancient city of Níssyros, colonized by the island of Níssyros to exploit the iron and silver mines at Assimovorni; according to the inscriptions, there was a temple of Apollo here. Boats from Diafáni sail to **Sariá**, the islet that dots the 'i' of long, narrow Kárpathos. The ruins known as **Ta Palátia** (the palaces), are actually a post-Byzantine pirate base, with dolmus-style houses under barrel-vaulted roofs. It is a good walk up from the landing place, so wear sturdy shoes.

Kárpathos ✉ *84700*, ✆ *(0245–)*   **Where to Stay and Eating Out**

Diafáni

Chryssi Akti, ✆ 51 215 (*E; inexp*), opposite the quay, is clean and basic; **Nikos**, ✆ 51 289, owned by Orfanos Travel (*inexp*), has decent rooms, and friendly **Delfini**, ✆ 51 391 (*inexp*), a bit further back, is quieter. There is a slightly crazed unofficial campsite at Vanánda Beach, north of Diafáni. **Taverna Anatoli** is a popular waterfront eatery.

Ólympos

Taverna Olympos, ✆ 51 252 (*inexp*), has three traditional rooms with en suite baths and is highly recommended, also with great views. **Aphrodite**, ✆ 51 307 (*inexp*), too has lovely views; if they're full try **Mike's**, ✆ 51 304, or **Astro**, ✆ 51 378. The windmill has a restaurant that serves good pasta stuffed with cheese and spinach.

Kýthera (ΚΥΘΗΡΑ)

Tucked under the great dangling paw of the Peloponnese, Kýthera, the isle of the goddess of love, is on the way to nowhere, and owes a good part of its attraction to that fact. The opening of the Corinth canal doomed even the minor commercial importance Kýthera once had by virtue of its position between the Ionian and Aegean Seas; even today, unless you take the small plane from Athens, getting there is awkward, time-consuming and expensive, requiring a long overland drive and ferry or a long hydrofoil ride. Although sentimentally it continues to be one of the Eptánissa, or Seven Ionian Islands, with whom it shares a common history of Venetian and British occupation, politically it now belongs to Attica and is administered from Piraeus. In this century Kýthera's population has decreased dramatically, most emigrating to the other side of the world; some 100,000 people of Kýtheran origin now live in Australia or 'Big Kýthera' as the 2,500 who still live on Kýthera call it. All the emigrants who possibly can return each summer, constituting its main tourist rush. Nor are many of them interested in developing the island's tourist potential; they like it fine the way it is. The non-Aussies who do visit are usually Italians or hardy Hellenophiles anxious to escape their own countrymen, or the wealthy who have scattered their villas all over Kýthera.

The tourist season is unusually short for a Greek island—mid-July to mid-September—and off season the island is uncannily quiet and shut down. Whatever the time of year, Kýthera is certainly not without its charms, although it can hardly hope to match the shimmering luxuriance of Watteau's sumptuous painting, *Pèlerinage à l'Ile de Cythère*. Much of the landscape has the look of abandoned farms and orchards, but in summer it is lent a golden sheen by the *sempreviva*, which when dried keeps 'forever', or at least a few years, rather like love itself.

History

When Zeus took his golden sickle and castrated his father, Cronos, then ruler of the world, he cast the bloody member into the sea. This gave birth to Aphrodite, the goddess of love, who rose out of the foam on her scallop shell at Kýthera. She found it far too puny for her taste and moved to Paphos, Cyprus, hence her two names in antiquity, the Cypriot or the Kytherian. An ancient sanctuary dedicated to Aphrodite on Kýthera was the most sacred of all such temples in Greece according to Pausanius, but scarcely a trace of it remains today.

Aphrodite was called Astarte by Kýthera's first settlers, the Phoenicians, who came for its murex shells, the source of a reddish purple dye for royal garments—hence the island's other early name, Porphyrousa. The Minoans, the first in Greece to worship Aphrodite, made Kýthera a central trading station for its location at the crossroads between Crete and the mainland, and the Aegean and Ionian Seas. It was a spot on the map in great demand: Kýthera was invaded 80 times in recorded history. Particularly frightful were the visits of the Saracens from Crete, so ferocious in the 10th century that the island was abandoned altogether until Nikephóros Phokás reconquered Crete for Byzantium.

The rulers of Kýthera in the Middle Ages were the Eudhaemonoyánnis family from Monemvássia. The Venetians occupied the island in 1204, but with the help of Emperor Michael Palaeológos, Kýthera was regained for the Eudhaemonoyánnis, and for long years it served as a refuge for Byzantine nobles until in 1537 Barbarossa stopped on his way home from his unsuccessful siege of Corfu and destroyed the island. The Venetians took over again in the 16th century and called the island 'Cerigo', the name you'll see in old history books. In 1864 it was ceded to Greece by the British with the rest of the Ionian islands.

By air: one flight a day from Athens; **airport information:** © 33 292; tickets from the Olympic Airways office at 49 El. Venizélou, Pótamos, © 33 362, or try Porfyra Travel in Livádi (*see* below).

By road: buses essentially operate to deposit schoolchildren at school and take them home again; expect to rely heavily on **taxis**, which charge set fees. At Ag. Pelagía, Pótamos and Kapsáli there are cars and mopeds to **hire**.

For **tourist police** see regular police, © 31 206. In **Ag. Pelagía**, hotels and rooms are listed on a large noticeboard near where the ferry docks. For help with accommodation

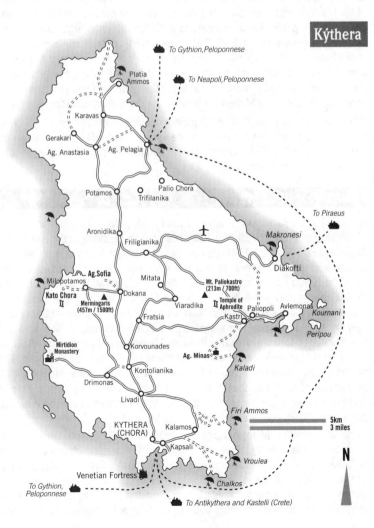

Kýthera

To Gythion, Peloponnese

To Neapoli, Peloponnese

Platia Ammos

Karavas

Gerakari

Ag. Anastasia   Ag. Pelagia

Potamos   Palio Chora   Trifilanika

To Piraeus

Aronidika

Friligianika   Makronesi

Diakofti

Ag. Sofia

Milopotamos   Mitata   Mt. Paliokastro (213m / 700ft)

Kato Chora

Dokana

Mermingaris (457m / 1500ft)   Viaradika   Temple of Aphrodite   Paliopoli   Avlemonas   Kournani

Fratsia   Kastri

Peripou

Mirtidion Monastery

Korvounades   Ag. Minas   Kaladi

Kontolianika

Drimonas

Livadi

Firi Ammos

KYTHERA (CHORA)   Kalamos

5km / 3 miles

Kapsali

N

Vroulea

Venetian Fortress

To Gythion, Peloponnese   Chalkos

To Antikythera and Kastelli (Crete)

in the south of the island try Yannis Fatseas at **Kytheros International**, ℭ 31 790, 🖹 31 688, or **Porfyra Travel**, ℭ 31 888, *porfyra@kythira.com*, both in Livádi. The tourist guide *Kythera* is freely available and full of interesting titbits.

Festivals

29–30 May, Ag. Trias in Mitáta; **15 August**, Panagías Mirtidíon; **24 September** Mirtidión Monastery.

Chóra (Kýthera Town)

Chóra (XΩPA), the capital of the island, is a pretty-as-a-picture-postcard blue and white Greek village, 275m above the port of Kapsáli, and guarded by a mighty if ruined fortress furnished by the Venetians in 1503. Its location was supposedly selected by pigeons, who took the tools of the builders from a less protected site; the views of the sea and surroundings are worth the climb up. Ten old **Venetian mansions** in Chóra still retain their coats-of-arms, and a small two-room **museum** (*open 8.30–2.30, closed Mon*) contains artefacts dating back to Minoan times. Below, a 20-minute walk down the hill, the port mini-resort of **Kapsáli** (KAΨAΛI) has a few restaurants and two picturesque pebble and sand beaches, one very sheltered and boaty, the other only a tiny bit more exposed; pedaloes will take you to other pebbly strands. The little 'egg islet', Avgó, offshore here is said to be the spot where Aphrodite was born.

Kálamos, just east, is within walking distance. One of its churches, Ag. Nikítas, has a pretty bell tower, and there is a *kafeneíon* by the square. Dirt roads continue across the rugged landscape to various beaches; nearest is pebbly **Chalkos**, set in a beautiful, almost enclosed bay, with a small summer snackbar.

Northwest of Chóra

From Chóra, the paved road heads north to **Livádi** (ΛIBAΔI), where there's a stone bridge of 13 arches, built by the British in 1822 and proudly heralded as the largest in Greece. If you ring ahead (ℭ (0735) 31 124) you can visit the Roússos family ceramic workshop, where the ancient tradition of Kýthera pottery is kept alive, now into the fourth generation. Heading east from Livádi, you'll come across a good collection of Byzantine and subsequent pieces in **Káto Livádi**'s museum (*open 8.30–2.30, closed Mon*). A 4km dirt road leads on to the dramatic beach and tiny snack shack of **Fíri Ámmos** ('red sands'), popular with snorkellers; in an ordinary car, the final descent is manageable, if a little hair-raising. West of Livádi via Drimónas is the important **Monastery of the Panagía Mirtidíon** with a tall carved bell tower, magnificently set on the wild west coast among cypresses, flowers and peacocks. The monastery is named after a gold-plated icon of the Virgin and Child, whose faces have blackened with age—a sign of special holiness that attracts huge numbers of pilgrims. Two small islets just offshore are said to be pirate ships that the Virgin turned to stone for daring to attack the monastery. Pilgrims can stay in the very simple hostel.

North of Drimónas, **Milopótamos** (MYΛOΠOTAMOΣ) is the closest thing to Watteau's vision of Kýthera, a pretty village criss-crossed by tiny canals of clear water—so much water, in fact, that the toilet in the valley is in a constant state of flush. The stream valley through the middle of town is called the Neraída, or Nymph; an old watermill lies along the somewhat overgrown path to the waterfall at Foníssa, surrounded by the ancient plane trees, flowers and banana palms; on quiet evenings you can hear the nightingales sing. The ghost town **Káto**

Chóra lies just below Milopótamos, within the walls of a Venetian fortress built in 1560. Above the gate there's a bas-relief of the lion of St Mark gripping his open book reading the angelic words '*Pax Tibi, Marce, Evangelista Meus*' that gave the Venetians a certain celestial legitimacy, at least in their own eyes. It welcomes you to a desolation of empty 16th-century stone houses and churches, although some are slowly being restored. A road descends steeply down to one of the island's best secluded beaches, white sandy **Limiónas**. Signs from Milopótamos lead down to the cave **Ag. Sofía**, Kýthera's most impressive, at the end of a rugged, declining track (*usually open Mon–Fri 3–8 in summer, weekends 11–5, but check in the village or call © (0735) 34 062*). In the past, the cave was used as a church, and inside there are frescoes and mosaics, as well as stalactites and stalagmites and small lakes that go on and on; some say it tunnels all the way under Kýthera to Ag. Pelagía. And at Ag. Pelagía a sign does indeed point down a rocky hill to a mysterious Ag. Sofía.

The East Coast

From both Fratsiá and Frilingianiká, roads branches east to **Paliópoli** (ΠΑΛΑΙΟΠΟΛΙΣ), a tiny village on the site of **Skandeia**, the port mentioned by Thucydides. The Minoan trading settlement was here, from 2000 BC until the rise of the Mycenaeans; their long-ago presence (ruins of the settlement may be seen at a place called **Kastrí**) has bestowed archaeological status on the long and lovely beach, which has kept it pristine except for a good taverna.

In ancient times, devotees would climb to the temple of Urania Aphrodite, 'Queen of the Heavens', to pay their respects to the goddess. Urania Aphrodite was often known as the 'eldest of the Fates', the daughter of the Great Goddess Necessity, whom even the great Zeus could not control. Pausanius wrote that her temple was one of the most splendid in all Greece, but the Christians destroyed it and built the church of Ag. Kosmás (with the temple's Doric columns); now only the acropolis walls remain at the site, called **Paliokástro**. From Paliópoli the coastal road descends to **Avlémonas** (ΑΒΛΕΜΟΝΑΣ), a fishing village with good restaurants. By the sea is a small octagonal fortress built by the Venetians, who left a coat-of-arms and a few rusting cannon inside. A short drive and walk from the village is one of the island's finest beaches, **Kaladí**, featured on many a tourist office poster. Follow signs marked ΠΡΟΣ ΚΑΛΑΔΙ along 2km of dirt road which leads past a blissful little chapel and abruptly stops; from here there's a steep, but mercifully short, climb down to the glorious double-coved pebbly beach—definitely not for the faint-hearted, but well worth it in the end. Another dirt road leads north of Avlémonas, 7 km to **Diakófti** (ΔΙΑΚΟΦΤΙ), a scrap of a resort popular with Greek families, which has taken over as the island's main port and has a strip of white sand, protected by a pair of islets, Makronísi and Prasonísi. The main road from Diakófti passes the airport; to the south, near the centre of Kýthera, **Mitáta** is a great place for picnics, surrounded by lovely green countryside and lemon trees; the cool clear water of its spring is delicious. It's also a good spot to purchase delicious thyme honey, at about half the price of the rest of Greece; one source is George and John Protopsáltis, © (0735) 33 614.

Palio Chóra and the North

Palio Chóra (or Ag. Dimitríou), is Kýthera's Byzantine ghost town, founded by the noble Eudhaemonoyánnis clan in the Monemvassian style. Set high on the rocks, it was carefully hidden from the sea in a magnificent gorge—according to legend, the terrible Barbarossa found it only by capturing the inhabitants and torturing them until they told him where it was.

Beside the ruins of the fort is a terrible 330ft abyss, where mothers threw their children before leaping themselves, to avoid being sold into slavery by Barbarossa. Most of the island's ghost stories and legends are set here. The dirt road drive and the scramble up are rewarded not only by views over the precipice, but a few frescoes in the haunted churches.

Palio Chóra is near **Potamós** (ΠΟΤΑΜΟΣ), which, despite its name, has no river. It is the largest village in the north, all blue and white like the new Chóra. It has a bank and an Olympic Airways office, but the largest building at the edge of town is Kythera's retirement home. Come on Sunday if you can, when the village hosts the island's biggest market. West of Potamós, **Ag. Elefthérios** is a lovely secluded beach, and a pretty place to watch the sunset.

At **Gerakári** to the northwest you can see yet another tower, this time built by the Turks in the early 18th century. From the pretty village of **Karavás**, the road continues to the fine beach and good taverna at **Platiá Ámmos. Ag. Pelagía** (ΑΓ. ΠΕΛΑΓΙΑ), Kýthera's northern port, also has a long pebble beach and a few more facilities, if not a lot of soul, nor even a lot of boats, since many have diverted to Diakófti's big, new harbour. There are some excellent beaches to the south including another by the name of **Fíri Ámmos**.

Kýthera ✉ *80100,* ✆ *(0735–)*　　　　　　**Where to Stay and Eating Out**

When it comes to finding a place to stay on Kýthera you may be hard pressed to locate anything luxurious.

Chóra (Kýthera)

Margarita, tucked away off the main street, ✆ 31 711, ✆ 31 325 (*C; exp–mod*), is an attractive blue and white hotel in a building that was once a bank, with an impressive wooden spiral staircase. **Castello**, ✆ 31 069, ✆ 31 869, has three studios and six rooms leading off a walled garden near the fortress; immaculate and well-designed, rooms all have telephone, fridge and overhead fans. **Ta Kythera**, just inland at Manitochóri, ✆ 31 563 (*B; mod–inexp*), has clean, pleasant double rooms. *Open June–Aug only*. There are a number of typical, simple tavernas offering straightforward Greek food up in Chóra, notably **Zorba's**, in the main street. Chóra is also well endowed with shops selling local arts and crafts; at **Nikolaou**, on the road coming into town from the north, you can see rugs being woven and a fine selection of ceramics, gifts and ethnic-style jewellery. **Stavros** is known the island over for stocking well-presented local produce—wine, jam, honey, chutneys, oils, vinegars, freshly baked sweets and an eclectic selection of books.

Kapsáli

One of the nicest places to stay on Kýthera, Kapsáli is the chosen spot for **Greek Islands Club's** fine selection of villas and apartments (*see* p.32), in the UK ✆ (01932) 220 477, ✆ 229 346. Also here, the **Raikos** hotel, ✆ 31 629, ✆ 31 801 (*B; exp*), is one of the island's posher places, with a pool. *Open May–Sept*. **Kalokerines Katikies**, ✆/✆ 31 265 (*C; exp*), are upmarket furnished apartments. At the other end of the price range, **Poulmendis Rooms**, ✆ 31 451 (*mod–inexp*), are perfectly clean and comfortable. Taverna **Magos**, ✆ 31 407, and the lone taverna at the far western end of the beach, have lovely views of Kapsáli, and serve all the usual Greek specialities.

Livádi

In Livádi itself, **Aposperides**, ✆ 31 656, ✆ 31 688 (*C; exp*), is a pristine hotel (*open all year*), while **Rousos**, in Káto Livádi, ✆ 31 124, offers apartments. **Taverna**

Pierros is probably the oldest and most traditional taverna on Kýthera, with authentic home cooking and kind prices. **Eleni**, near the 'British bridge', is a favourite for *mezédes*. Three kilometres north, the **Lokanda** in Karvoynádes is a good place for a pizza or snack.

Avlémonas

There are plenty of self-catering apartments here: give **Poppy's**, ✆ 33 735; **Roulas**, ✆ 33 060; **Christoforos**, ✆ 33 057; **Manolis Stathis**, ✆ 33 732; or **Mandy's**, ✆ 33 739, a try (*all mod*). **Taverna Sotiris**, ✆ 33 722, prettily set in a small square over-looking the sea, prepares excellent seafood as fresh as can be, caught by the owners themselves. Just outside nearby Paliópoli, try the **Skandia**, serving Greek specialities served under an enormous elm tree—a great place for lunch.

Diakófti

For peace and quiet you can't beat **Sirene Apartments**, right on the sea, ✆ 33 900, or winter in Athens ✆ (01) 481 1185 (*A; exp*), with their big verandas and kitchens. Also try **Kythera Beach Apartments**, ✆ 33 750, ✉ 33 054 (*C; exp*), within spitting distance of the sea. *Open Apr–Oct.*

Mitáta

People come from across Kýthera to eat at **Michalis** (ΜΙΧΑΛΗΣ), an informal taverna in the village's main square, with panoramic views of the surrounding hills and valleys; Michális' wife cooks a number of island specialities, including cockerel and rabbit, prepared with vegetables from their own garden.

Ag. Pelagía

Filoxenia, ✆ 33 800, ✉ 33 610 (*B; exp*), has 27 well-furnished apartments and a pool. The 10-roomed **Kytheria** pension, ✆ 33 321, ✉ 33 825 (*D; mod*), is nearest the pier, comfortable and serves breakfast. The **Romantica**, ✆ 33 834, ✉ 33 915 (*exp*), has nine well-laid-out apartments for two or four, as well as a pool. There's a limited selection of tavernas: the popular **Kaleris**, ✆ 33 461, has tables right on the sand. In the evening a lot of people end up inland at Karavás, at the **Amir Ali** piano bar, named after a Turk, but no one knows why.

Elafónissos (ΕΛΑΦΟΝΗΣΟΣ) and Antikýthera (ΑΝΤΙΚΥΘΗΡΑ)

From Ag. Pelagía you can look out across the Lakonian Sea to the islet of **Elafónissos**, which until the 17th century was part of the Peloponnese, and is now connected daily in the summer by caique every 40 minutes from Neápolis (July–September) or less often from Ag. Pelagía (call ✆ (0734) 61177 for info). The one village is mostly inhabited by fishermen and sailors, but the main reason for visiting is 5km south of the village, **Katá Nísso**, a twin bay endowed with two gorgeous white sandy beaches that go on and on, as yet hardly discovered by tourists (a caique from the 'capital' makes the trip). There are two tavernas and two small B-class pensions in the village (*open June to September*) if you want to escape it all: **Asteri tis Elafonissou**, ✆ (0734) 61 271 and **Elafónissos**, ✆ 61 268; rough camping on the beach is another possibility.

Another islet, the utterly remote **Antikýthera**, lies far to the south of Kapsáli, midway between Kýthera and Kastélli, Crete. If the *meltémi* isn't up, as it often is, ships call twice a week en route between Kýthera and Crete. Fewer than 100 people live in Antikýthera's two villages, **Potamós** and **Sochória**, and the rest is very rocky with few trees; curiously, like west Crete, the island is slowly rising. By Potamós, ancient **Aígilia** has walls dating back to the 5th century BC. There's a small beach at **Xeropótamo**, 5 minutes from Potamós by boat, or 30 minutes on foot. Water is a luxury, and the few rooms available are quite primitive; running water and toilets are rare. Potamós has a taverna, but food can also be scarce.

The World's Oldest Computer

Antikýthera is just a tiny smudge on the map, but thanks to the wild winds that churn the surrounding sea it is also a name familiar to any student of ancient Greek art. For on the 22nd day of the ancient Greek month of Mounichon, in the first year of the 180th Olympiad (5 May, 59 BC), a Roman ship sailing from Rhodes, laden with booty that included the magnificent 4th-century BC bronze statue known as the *Ephebe of Antikýthera* (one of the celebrities of the National Archaeology Musem in Athens), went down off the coast of Antikýthera. Now you might ask: how is it that anyone could even begin to know the precise date of a 2,000-year-old shipwreck? Pinpointing even the century of ancient finds is more often than not just an archaeological guessing game. The answer is that part of the booty from Rhodes included the world's first computer, and its timekeeping mechanism was stopped forever on the day the ship went down.

The wreck was discovered by chance in 1900 by sponge divers from Sými, who in a storm sheltered off the inaccessible coast of Antikýthera. After the storm, a few divers donned their weighted belts and went down to see if this remote seabed might in fact shelter a sponge or two. Instead they were startled to see a man beckoning to them—the famous Ephebe. The Greek archaeological service was notified, and sent down a small warship to haul up the bronze and marble statues, vases, and glass—the world's first underwater archaeological dig. One of the items was a lump; as the months passed and the sea mud dried, a wooden cabinet about a foot high was revealed. This quickly deteriorated on contact with the air, leaving a calcified hunk of metal that broke into four bits. Archaeologists were astonished to see that they belonged to a mechanical device inscribed with ancient Greek script.

At first dismissed as a primitive astrolabe, the Antikýthera Mechanism, as it was known, soon proved to be much more complex. In 1958, a young British historian of science, Derek de Solla Price, was allowed to examine it and was the first to recognize it as an astronomical computer, which, by its setting, was made on the island of Rhodes in 82 BC. The days of the month and the signs of the zodiac were inscribed on bronze dials, with pointers to indicate the phases of the moon and position of the planets at any given time, operated within by a complex mass of clockwork: bronze cog wheels with triangular teeth, connected to a large four-spoke wheel (the most prominent part visible at the National Archaeology Museum in Athens) driven by a crown gear and shaft, which probably had some kind of key for winding. A moveable slip ring allowed for Leap Year adjustments and alignments. As far as anyone can judge, it was last set by the Roman sea captain on the day his vessel went down. He may have been bringing it to Rome on the special order of Cicero, who knew of the 'future-telling astronomical device' from his school days at Rhodes' famous School of Rhetoric. 'It is a bit frightening to know,' concluded Derek Price, 'that just before the fall of their great civilization, the Ancient Greeks had come so close to our age, not only in their thought, but also in their scientific knowledge.' The next similar device to be noted anywhere was in 11th-century India, by the Iranian traveller al-Biruni. (For all the details, pick up a copy of Victor Kean's *The Ancient Greek Computer from Rhodes*, Efstathiadis Group, 1991.)

Léros (ΛΕΡΟΣ)

With its wildly serrated coastline like an intricate jigsaw puzzle piece, sweeping hills, tree-fringed beaches and unspoiled villages, Léros is a beautiful, underrated and much misunderstood island. Few places have had such a bad press, both as an isle of exile and home to Greece's most notorious mental institutions. Perhaps to make amends, the people are welcoming and friendly, and visitors who discover the island's charms are often hooked.

Léros has long been the butt of ignorant jokes in Greece, where its name evokes the same reaction as 'Bedlam' in Britain; to make matters worse, Léros sounds like *léra*, 'filth' or 'rogue'. The 1989 Channel 4 documentary exposing the grim conditions in the hospitals was another blow, but at the same time it prodded the authorities to get their act together. Dutch medical teams have been working to improve conditions; a care-in-the-community scheme was set up and you might see patients in the villages. But they are not intrusive, and, to be frank, you're likely to see more lost souls wandering the streets back home.

Léros is not a dreary or downbeat island. Green and pretty, its indented coastline offers little strands of shingly sand, very clear waters, excellent fish tavernas, and a lively but very Greek nightlife. It is an exceptionally musical place, home of the famous Hajiadákis dynasty whose folk songs have influenced Greece's leading composers; it's not at all rare to hear the hammer dulcimer (*sandoúri*), or the bagpipes (*tsamboúna*), as well as the more usual instruments playing dances such as the Issós Lérikos, Soústa, Stavrotos, Passoumáki and the ancient Dance of the Broom. The ancient island of Artemis, Léros has a special atmosphere you either love or hate; and the bad press shields the island from the masses which might help preserve its charm.

History

On the death of the hero Meleager (of Chalydonian boar hunt fame), his sisters mourned him so passionately that Artemis turned them into guinea fowl and put them in her temple on Léros. This worship of the goddess of the chase and guinea fowl might be traced back to Ionians from Miletus who colonized Léros; Robert Graves notes that, because of their religious conservatism and refusal to adopt the patriarchal state religion of Olympos, the Greeks called the Leriots 'evil-livers' (an epigram went, 'The Lerians are all bad, not merely some Lerians, but every one of them—all except Prokles, and of course he is a Lerian too'). Fittingly for an island dedicated to Artemis, property has been passed down through the female line, to the extent that most of Léros is owned at least on paper by women.

Homer included Léros with Kálymnos as the 'Kalydian isles' in his Catalogue of Ships. The island sided with Sparta in the Peloponnesian War, despite its Ionian ancestry. Under the Romans, pirates preyed among the islets that surround Léros; some nabbed a handsome young lawyer named Julius Caesar on his way back to Rome from Bithynia, where according to rumour, he had a dissolute affair with the governor; released after a month when his ransom

was paid, Caesar later took his revenge by capturing and crucifying every brigand around Léros. Under the Byzantines, the island was controlled by Sámos, but in 1316 it was sold to the Knights of St John and governed by the Duke of Náxos as part of the monastic state of Pátmos.

Léros paid a high price for its excellent anchorages in the Second World War. After 1912, the occupying Italians built their main air and naval ordnance bases at Lépida. Their Eastern Mediterranean fleet was based in Lakkí Bay; when Churchill sent the British to occupy the island after the Italian surrender in 1943, Hitler sent in an overwhelming force of paratroopers to take it back, causing a good deal of damage in the Battle of Léros (12–16 November); see the photos displayed in the Kastis Travel Agency. The Allies in turn bombed the German fleet at Lakkí, and for three years after the War the British fleet held fort. When the *junta* took power in 1967, Communist dissidents were imprisoned in the notorious camp in Parthéni; during the later Cyprus dispute the Greek government dismantled its military installations to show that it had no warlike intentions against Turkey. One of the brightest lights in Australian poetry, Dimítris Tsaloúmas, was born on Léros and emigrated with his family to Melbourne in 1952; his work explores the bittersweet feelings of emigrants in the Greek diaspora and explains why so many hotels, bars and restaurants are named *Nostos*, a longing for home.

Getting There and Around

By air: daily from Athens with Olympic, © 22 844; three times a week with Hellenic Star (contact Kastis Travel in Lakkí, © 22 500, @ 23 500; also offices in Ag. Marína and Alínda). **Airport:** © 22 777; it is best reached by taxi.

Excursion boats: from Ag. Marína to Lipsí, Arki, Marathi, Tiganakia and Pátmos (contact Lipsos Travel, © 41 225). **Caique** once a day in high season from Xirókambos to Myrtiés, Kálymnos. **Port authority:** Lakkí, © 22 234.

By road: taxi ranks: Lakkí © 22 550, Ag. Marína © 23 340, Plátanos © 23 070 (prices are more or less fixed and reasonable). Buses run five times daily in season between Plefouti, Partheni, Alínda, Plátanos, Lakkí and Xirocampos; alternatively, rent a scooter in any of the main towns.

Tourist Information

There's a helpful **Municipal Tourist Office** at the quay in Ag. Marína (*open daily 8.30–noon and 3–4.30, Weds 2.30–3.30*).

Festivals

During the **pre-Lent** Carnival children don monks' robes and visit the homes of the newly married, reciting verses made up by their elders; **16–17 July**, Ag. Marínas in Ag. Marína; **first 10 days of August** in Alínda, the Alintia regatta run since 1907 with sailing races; **6 August**, Sotíris in Plátanos; **15 August**, Panagías at the Kástro (Plátanos); **20 August**, foreign tourist day in Alínda; **24–25 September**, Ag. Ioánnis Theológos in Lakkí. Starting on **26 September**, three days of memorial services are held for those who lost their lives on the *Queen Olga*; Greek naval vessels always attend this annual commemoration; **20 October**, Ag. Kýras in Parthéni.

Lakkí and South Léros

Arriving at **Lakkí** (ΛΑΚΚΙ), by ferry, usually at night, is quite an experience, its extraordinary *Fascisti* Art Deco buildings reflected in the gulf. If Fellini had been Greek, Lakkí would have been one of his favourite sets. The streets are perfectly paved and wide enough to accommodate several lanes of traffic, although they're usually empty except for a few lone bikers rumbling through, while what remains of Mussolini's dream town, a tribute to Italian Rationalism and the International Style, crumbles away, forlorn, dilapidated but still weirdly compelling, a proper De Chirico ghost town. The grandiose cinema and school are defunct, as is the old Hotel Roma, later the **Leros Palace** (where this writer was once led down a mile of huge white halls, hypnotically lit by swaying bare bulbs, to a room the size of a bus station, completely untouched since its last clients pounded a flock of mosquitoes into the walls. The son of the owner, seeing my reluctant glances at the rumpled bed, rolled his eyes and exclaimed in disgust, 'Oh, and I suppose you want clean sheets, too!'). Now it's stuffed with litter. Lakkí's style was dubbed 'Ignored Internationalism' by Greek scholars when the Lerians decided to abandon the town and make the more convivial Plátanos the capital. Many islanders commute to Lakkí to work in the three mental hospitals, set up during the Italian occupation across the bay. These days the park around the institutions is open to visitors; one building here was intended to host Mussolini—the Duce's summer retreat.

Near the waterfront there's a monument to the many who perished in 1943 when a Greek ship, the *Queen Olga*, was bombed by German planes and sank in Lakkí's harbour. A path leading up from the jetty goes to the nearest beach at **Kouloúki**, with a taverna and unofficial camping under the pines. At **Lépida**, across the harbour, the **Moní Panagía** is built on the ruins of an old lighthouse, and further south, overlooking **Xirókambos** (ΞΗΡΟΚΑΜΠΟΣ), is the fort **Paliokástro**, built near an older fortification dating back to the 3rd century BC. The church inside has mosaics and Xirókambos itself, a simple fishing village, has a pleasant sandy beach to the west. In summer the caique goes over to Myrtiés on Kálymnos once a day. There are also secluded pebbly coves accessible from a track beside the chapel.

Pantéli, Plátanos and Ag. Marína

Up the tree-lined hill from Lakkí, it's only 3km to the very popular coarse sandy beach of **Vromólithos** ('Dirty Rock'), with sunbeds and tavernas, prettily closed in by deeply wooded hills. There are more places to stay just around the bay at **Pantéli** (ΠΑΝΤΕΛΙ), a working fishing village by day with its little harbour full of caiques and passing yachts, and by night the rendezvous of Léros' seafood-lovers, with tables spilling on to the the small, tree-fringed beach.

Up hill, the capital **Plátanos** (ΠΛΑΤΑΝΟΣ) is as near the centre of Léros as possible. With a smattering of neoclassical houses mixed in with more traditional ones it's a pretty place, especially at night with stunning views over Pantéli. The main square is the focus of local hubbub and transport. Overhead the ancient acropolis is occupied by the **Kástro**, a Byzantine fortress renovated by the Venetians, the Knights and the Greek military, who have recently upped sticks for another hill. A winding, rough asphalt road rises to the top, but the alternative 370 steps, lined by houses with fragrant flower gardens, will make you feel more righteous. From the top, the 'four seas' of Léros are spread at your feet: the bays of Pantéli, Ag. Marína, Gournás and Lakkí. Within the walls, the church of the **Megalóchari Kyrás Kástrou** (*open 8.30–12.30 and Wed, Sat and Sun 3.30–7.30*) houses a miraculous icon of the Virgin and small display of religious relics. The story goes that during the Turkish occupation the icon set sail from Constantinople on board a boat lit by a sacred candle, and turned up on Léros. The inhabitants, led by the bishop, carried it in great procession to the cathedral. The next day, however, the icon had vanished and the Turkish captain of the Kástro found it, candle dangerously blazing, in the fortress gunpowder store, even though the door had been firmly locked. The icon was taken back to the cathedral, but the following nights decamped to the arsenal again and again, until the Turkish governor was convinced it was a miracle and gave the powder storeroom to the Christians. They cleaned it up, and the wilful icon has been happy to stay put ever since.

Ag. Marína (ΑΓ. MAPINA), the seaside extension of Plátanos, is easily reached by the main street, Ódos Xarami, but if you want to avoid the motorbike Grand Prix, take the quiet lane that runs parallel down to the pottery. Ag. Marína is a windswept harbour, again full of fishermen at work and excursion boats from Lípsi and Pátmos; there are plenty of tavernas, and accommodation up the road by the beach and coves at **Krithóni**.

Álinda and the North

Álinda (ΑΛΙΝΤΑ), once the old commercial port of Léros on the north end of the same bay, is the island's oldest resort and principal package holiday destination, although still low-key by Kos standards. There's a long sandy beach, with water sports, and plenty of seafront cafés and tavernas. The pretty mosaics of an Early Christian basilica, **Panagía Galatiani**, may be seen in the forecourt of the town hospice, while nearby the immaculate **British War Cemetery** where 183 servicemen lie at rest looks out over the crystal bay—next to a motorbike rental shop, where lads the age that they died are known as the *kamikazi*. Léros has strong links with Egypt as many notables fled to Cairo in the twenties, and Álinda's folly, the **Bellini Tower**, was built by one of them, Paríssis Bellínis, and now houses a more interesting than average **Historic and Folk Museum** (*open daily 10–1 and 6–9; adm*). North of Alínda, a track leads to the secluded beaches at **Panagíes** and sandy **Kryfós**, where you can skinny-dip. There's a large sandy beach just over the isthmus at **Gourná**, although it tends to be windblown; you're better off seeking out one of the small coves leading to Léros's answer to Corfu's Mouse Island, **Ag. Isidóros**, a white chapel perched on an islet reached by a causeway. If you fancy a long walk off the road there are sandy beaches at **Ag. Nikólaos** further along the coast.

From Alínda there's a road lined with eucalyptus trees north to **Panthéni** ('the Virgins'), former centre of guinea fowl worship, now a very masculine military base and used in the 60s as a detention centre for political dissidents. Above, only a few ruins remain of the ancient **Temple of Artemis** (near the present church of Ag. Kyrás) but they still enjoy a superb setting; linger under a sacred myrtle tree and look at the airport next door. Further north there's a popular family beach and taverna at **Plefoúti**, in a lake-like bay, while over the headland at **Kioúra** there are quiet pebble coves reached via the chapel gates. You can easily do a round-island trip by car past **Drymónas** with lovely coves, an oleander gorge and **Sotos** fish taverna, then over the mountain back to Lakkí.

Léros ✉ *85400,* ✆ *(0247–)*   **Where to Stay and Eating Out**

The lushness of Léros translates into an extra airborne division of Lilliputian vampires by night so bring big bug-goo, especially if you sleep under the stars.

Lakkí/Xirókambos

Katikíes, ✆ 23 624, @ 24 645 (*A; exp*), has lovely studios and apartments in traditional style, set away from the road and sleeping up to six. **Miramare**, ✆ 22 053, @ 22 469 (*D; inexp*), gilds the lily with its gold cornicing and is both central and comfortable; **Katerina**, ✆ 22 460, @ 23 038 (*E; inexp*), is all cool marble nearby. Food is generally limited to fast food and pizza, a notable exception being classy **Petrinos**, ✆ 24 807, specializing in refined meat dishes influenced by the time owner-chef Giorgos spent in Belgium; Lerians flock here all year. Just out of town, **Merikia** taverna, at the eponymous beach just past the Koulouki strands, is a good fish bet. In Xirókambos, **Efstathia**, ✆/@ 24 199 (*C; mod*), has roomy studios and apartments with pool, while **Villa Maria**, ✆ 22 827 (*inexp*), is also comfortable, and **Camping Leros**, ✆ 23 372, is up the road.

Vromólithos/Pantéli

Tony's Beach, ✆ 24 742, @ 24 743 (*C; inexp*), often has rooms in Vromólithos, although the rest tends to be block-booked. Slap on the beach, **Frangos** is legendary for traditional food, while the **Taverna Paradisos** also has a good menu but slow service in high season. Several good inexpensive pensions overlook the picture-postcard harbour at Pantéli, including the cheaper but perfectly reasonable **Rosa**, ✆ 22 798 (*inexp*), and the marginally preferable **Cavos**, ✆ 23 247 (*inexp*), with rooms and studios (the same family also owns Pension Anastasios, in Vromólithos). Up the lane back towards Plátanos, **Rena** near the church is set in flowers; neighbouring **Aegean Sky Apartments**, ✆ 24 722 (*inexp*), are another decent, friendly possibility, while **Pension Afroditi**, ✆ 22 031 (*inexp*), has rooms and studios, some with pretty sea views. On the beach, **Zorba's** is popular and **Patimenos** has good food and frappés; **Drossia**, opposite Pension Rosa, is less touristy than some, with fish almost leaping from the family nets; **Taverna Maria** at the eastern end of the strand is the best for atmosphere and popular with the local fishermen. Gold-toothed Maria will rustle you up a huge dish of small whitebait-style *marídes* or *kalamári* fresh from their caiques.

Plátanos/Ag. Marína/Krithóni

In Plátanos, the pleasant and quiet **Eleftheria**, ✆ 23 550 (*C; mod*), has family apartments as well as decent doubles, owned by Antónis Kanáris of the local Laskarina Travel agency, confusingly unconnected with the British holiday company. Food choices here run the gamut from **Funny Bunny Fast Food** to traditional *tavli* ouzeries.

Down in Ag. Marína, **Kapaniri** is the place to sample a selection of *mezédes* with your ouzo, while **Glaros** corners the pizza market. Just outside town, newly opened **Neromylos** is popular with locals and tourists alike for its traditional food. Further up the bay in Krithóni, **Krithoni Paradise**, ✆ 25 120, ✉ 24 680 (*B; exp*), is a swish complex with a pool and piano bar. **Nefeli Apartments**, ✆ 24 611, ✉ 22 375 (*C; mod*), is another tasteful, upmarket establishment designed by a woman architect. Next to the Paradise is the tasty **Esperides** taverna.

Álinda

Set in a cool, flowery garden, **Archonitkó Angelou**, ✆ 22 749, ✉ 24 403 (*C; mod*), built in 1895, was lovingly restored by the friendly owners. **Boulafendis Bunglalows**, ✆ 23 515, ✉ 24 533 (*C; mod*), is a pleasant, spacious studio development around a traditional mansion and pool-bar area. **Chryssoula**, ✆ 22 451 (*C; mod*), has bright white studios overlooking a pool and the sea, 300m away; **Ara**, set up high with lofty views of both 'seas', ✆ 24 140, ✉ 24 194 (*C; mod*), has studios and apartments, restaurant, pool and Internet access; **Marilen**, ✆ 24 100, ✉ 22 531, *marilen@otenet.gr* (*C; mod*), also has studios overlooking a pool-bar area (but lacking Ara's vistas), with a convenient mini-market. Friendly **Papafotis**, ✆ 22 247 (*inexp*), has cheaper, clean rooms and studios; the ones facing the mountains are fanned by the *meltémi*, thus cooler when it swelters. Amongst the tavernas, **Alinda** is the best for traditional fare; seaside **Finikas** is an old favourite.

Entertainment and Nightlife

There are a number of cultural events during the summer, including performances by the **Léros Theatre Group** and **Artemis**, a society dedicated to the revival of the island dances in traditional costume. There is a **bouzouki club** on the road up to Plefoútis; otherwise Pantéli has a disco and the cool **Savanna** bar at the end of the harbour; **Nectar** and **Café Continent** are also decent watering-holes. In Ag. Marína, **Apothiki** and **Apokalipsi** are happening places and the **Faros** plays great world music. **Seagull** café/bar is a mellow place with marble tables on the port and good frappés. Alínda's waterfront bars cater for a range of musical predilections. Succumb to a sundae at **Palatino**, with good music and the live Greek variety on summer weekends. **Cosmopolitan** also offers live music and international DJs in season. For a bit of a dance, locals and tourists head for **Puerto Kinesos** in Lakkí.

Límnos (ΛΗΜΝΟΣ)

Límnos hardly fits any Greek island stereotypes. It lies low, with gently rolling hills: a lush green carpet in the spring that becomes crackling yellow-brown in the summer, when water is in short supply. The landscape is dotted with fields of grain, quirky scarecrows and beehives (the island's thyme honey was favoured by the gods); it takes pride in being one of the few islands to support a herd of deer. But the main occupation of Límnos has long been military: its magnificent natural harbour near the mouth of the Dardenelles has ensured that the island has always been of strategic importance. It was the holy island of the smithy god Hephaistos (Vulcan), who was worshipped on Mount Móschylus, which in ancient times emitted a fiery jet of asphaltic gas; today Límnos' volcanic past is manifest in its astringent hot springs and the highly sulphuric 'Limnian earth', found near Repanídi, used from ancient times until the Turkish occupation for healing wounds and stomach aches.

Mythology

 The smithy god Hephaistos (in Latin, Vulcan) was so weakly when he was born that his mother Hera hurled him off Mount Olympos. He survived by falling in the sea, near Límnos, where the sea goddesses Thetis and Eurynome cared for him. Years later, when Hera found Thetis wearing a magnificent brooch made by Hephaistos, she had a change of heart about her son, brought him back to Olympos and married him to the lovely Aphrodite. Hephaistos became so fond of his mother that he attempted to rescue her when Zeus hung Hera by the wrists from the sky for rebelling against him. Zeus in his fury picked up the upstart and hurled him again from Mount Olympos and this time he fell smack on Límnos, a fall that crippled Hephaistos for life, despite all the care lavished on him by the islanders. (In the early days of metallurgy, the magic powers of the smith were so valued in many cultures that he was hobbled like a partridge to keep him from running away or joining an enemy.)

Hephaistos was so beloved on Límnos that when his wife Aphrodite betrayed him with the war-god Ares, the women of Límnos stopped worshipping her and tossed her cult statue into the sea. Aphrodite retaliated by making their breath and underarms stink (Robert Graves suggests this may have been because they worked with woad, a putrid-smelling blue dye used in the manufacture of tattoo ink). This led the men of Límnos to prefer the company of captive Thracian women to that of their own wives. The smelly women of Límnos were having none of this: they doctored their husbands' wine to make them sleep, slit their throats, threw their bodies into the sea and lived as Amazons, warlike and independent. When Jason and the Argonauts appeared on the horizon, the women would have attacked had not one of them realized that a shipload of Greek sailors was just what they needed to continue the Limnian race. So the Argonauts met only the kindest courtesy, and a son born to Jason, Euneus, went on to become King of Límnos during the Trojan War, supplying the Achaeans with wine.

Another figure associated with Límnos was Philoctetes, the son of Heracles. Philoctetes had inherited his father's famous bow when Heracles was dying in torment from Nessus' poisoned shirt, as Philoctetes was the only one who would light the pyre to put him out of his misery. When Zeus made Heracles an immortal, Hera, who never liked him, took out her pique on his son, sending a poisoned snake after Philoctetes when the Troy-bound Achaeans landed on Límnos. Bitten on the ankle, Philoctetes lingered behind in pain—his comrades could not stomach the stench of his gangrenous wound—and he lived in an island cave, with only his bow for comfort. After the death of Achilles, an oracle declared that Achaeans could only capture Troy with Philoctetes' bow. Odysseus and Neoptolemos, the son of Achilles, tried to take it from him by trickery (in Sophocles' *Philoctetes*), but in the end, according to most accounts, Philoctetes himself took his bow to Troy, where he slew Paris.

History

Límnos' highly intriguing past also bucks the stereotypes. Homer wrote that the first islanders hailed from Thrace, but Herodotus says they were Tyrrhenian—related to the mysterious, sophisticated Etruscans of Rome and Tuscany. This remarkable claim has been given substance by pre-6th century BC non-Greek inscriptions found on Límnos that show linguistic similarities to the Etruscans, as do some of the ancient burials. The Etruscans themselves claimed to have originally immigrated to Italy from Asia Minor.

But Límnos was exceptional from the start. Excavations at Polióchne have uncovered a settlement of oval huts dating back to 4000 BC—the most advanced Neolithic civilization yet discovered in the Aegean. These precocious ancient Limnians may have been the first to colonize Troy; the dates coincide and there were certainly close cultural contacts between the two into the Mycenaean era. Whoever they were, the ancient Limnians were not Greek and held on to their autonomy until 490 BC, as Herodotus tells in his account of the Persian Wars: years previously the Limnians had captured some Athenian women and had children by them. When these mixed race children they bore began putting on airs, the Limnians were so outraged that they slaughtered them and their mothers, giving rise to the expression 'Limnian deeds', synonymous in classical times with especially atrocious acts. The gods punished them by making their wives and animals barren. In dismay the Limnians went to Delphi, where the oracle said the only cure for it was to promise to surrender their independence to Athens if the Athenians ever sailed to Límnos in one day. It seemed a fair hedge, until Athens conquered some territory near Mount Áthos, and General Miltiades appeared on Límnos to claim what was promised by the oracle.

The Venetians took Límnos in the 13th century, but it was soon regained by the Byzantines. In 1475 Mohammed the Conqueror sent troops to conquer Límnos, only to be repelled by the heroine Maroúla, who seized her dying father's weapons and shouted a blood-curdling battle cry. In 1478, however, Mohammed came in person and took the island. The Turks held it until 1912; later, Moúdros Bay became the naval base of the Allies in the Gallipoli campaign.

© (0254–)   ***Getting There and Around***

By air: thrice daily with Athens, daily except Thursday with Thessaloníki, thrice weekly with Lésbos. Olympic Airways, © 22 214, is opposite Hotel Paris; for **airport**

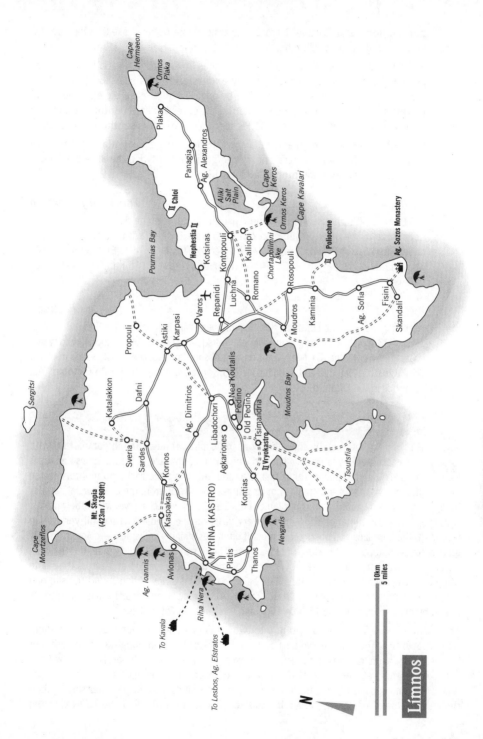

Límnos

information, call ✆ 31 204. To reach the airport from Mýrina, take the Olympic bus, or taxi (but it's a hefty 22km trip).

By sea: four **ferries** a week and day excursions in season run to Ag. Efstrátios (*see* pp.363–4). In summer, there's a weekly **excursion** to Mount Áthos. Some of the island's best beaches are only accessible by boat. Caiques make the excursion from Mýrina's north harbour to beaches and the sea caves at Skála. **Motorboats** can be hired at other nearby beaches, such as Rihanera, ✆ 24 617. **Port authority**: ✆ 22 225.

By road: buses (✆ 22 464) around Límnos are not very frequent. Many villages have only one service a day, so there's no way to get back to Mýrina the same day, hence the town's many **taxis** and **moped and car hire** firms.

✆ *(0254–)*   *Tourist Information*

EOT: ✆ 22 996, housed in the municipal buildings near the port; look out for the little kiosk on the quay. In summer, call in advance for help with travel or accommodation: try Alex at **Pravlis Travel**, Mýrina, ✆ 24 617, ✉ 22 471; **El Travel**, 11 Ralli Kopsidi Street, ✆ 24 988, ✉ 22 697; or **Petridou Travel**, 116 Karatsa Street, ✆ 22 998, ✉ 22 129.

Festivals

At their *panegýria*, the Limnians still do a number of ancient dances, such as the *kechagiátikos*. **23 April**, Ag. Geórgios in Kalliópi—horse-races are run by the locals, who wager goats on the outcome; **21 May**, Ag. Konstantínos in Romanó; **6 August**, Sotíris in Pláka; **15 August**, in Kamínia and Tsimántria; **7–8 September**, Ag. Sózos; **26 October**, Ag. Dimítrios in Ag. Dimítrios.

Mýrina

Mýrina (MYPINA), the island's appealing port and capital, though tiny in comparison with most Northeastern Aegean capitals, is Límnos' only town of any size. It is sometimes known as Kástro for its striking landmark, the romantic castle built over the rocky promontory in the midst of the sandy shore. A long main shopping street noodles up from the commercial harbour in the south, lined by houses and shops built in the Turkish or Thracian style with little gardens. Although a new boutique or shop opens every year, on the whole Mýrina still very much belongs to the Límnians and offers the distinct if often dusty sights and smells—cologne, freshly ground coffee, and pungent herbs—of old Greece. There isn't much to see inside, but the walk up to the **kástro** offers a fine view over much of the low rolling island and across the sea to Mount Áthos. The castle foundations date back to classical times, when it was the site of a temple of Artemis; the walls were built in 1186 by Andronicus Comnenus I, then substantially rebuilt by the Venetians in the 15th century, and the Turks a century later.

The Kástro divides Mýrina's waterfront into two: a 'Turkish' or harbour beach on the south side of town near the commercial port and, to the north, the main long sandy Romaïkos or 'Greek beach', with tavernas and much of Mýrina's night life. The north port is closed by Cape Petassós and the pretty beach of **Aktí Mýrina**, with its exclusive bungalow hotel, on the spot where the Amazons of Límnos hurled their hapless husbands into the sea after slitting their throats. Off Romaïkos Beach, the **Archaeological Museum** (*open 9–3, closed Mon; adm*) has been renovated to show off its superb collection, filling 10 rooms with Limnian finds. Upstairs are prehistoric relics from Polióchne, divided into four different periods by colour, beginning with the 'Black' period, from 4000 BC. Downstairs are more recent discoveries from Hephestía, Chloï and Mýrina.

Around Límnos

There are beaches to try both north and south of Mýrina, where discreet freelance camping is usually tolerated. North of Mýrina the beaches are pebbly but safe for children, especially **Riha Nera**, with tavernas and watersports, **Avlónas**, with a bungalow development, and **Ag. Ioánnis**, again with tavernas. North of **Ag. Ioánnis**, the road deteriorates rapidly, but with a jeep, head up the coast for about fifteen minutes until you reach a promontory with a three-pronged rock. The sunset is to die for.

The more popular beaches are past the army base to the south of Mýrina, on the beautiful buxom bays below **Platís** and **Thános** (a particularly beautiful, golden stretch of sand), both with good tavernas. Others with no facilities at all are scattered here and there all the way to Kontiás: aim for **Nevgatis**, a kilometre of fine sand kissed by a crystal, shallow sea. **Kontiás** is the island's liveliest and prettiest red-tiled village, home of Kontiás ouzo. In the summer it fills up with returned immigrants from South Africa and Australia. Just south is an old Mycenaean tower called the **Vryókastro**; **Evgáti** is a decent sandy beach.

East of Kontiás, **Néa Koutális beach** with pine trees and restaurants is the finest on **Moúdros Bay**, one of the biggest natural harbours in the Mediterranean. In April 1915, the Anglo-French fleet launched its ill-fated attack on the Dardanelles from here, a campaign planned partly on Límnos by the then Lord of the Admiralty, Winston Churchill; in 1918, after leaving over 30,000 dead at Gallipoli, an armistice with the Turks was signed on board a ship in the bay where it had all begun. East of gloomy **Moúdros** (ΜΟΥΔΡΟΣ), the island's second largest town and even today dependent on its sizeable military presence, is the immaculately kept lawn of the **British Commonwealth war cemetery**; the 800 graves belong to wounded personnel brought back to Moúdros, only to die in hospital. Límnos' airport (civil and military) is at the north end of the bay, where the island is only a few kilometres wide. Most of the beaches around the bay are on the muddy side.

The ancient Limnians preferred living on the island's easterly wings. Northeast of the airport on Pournías Bay, **Kótsinas** was the walled medieval capital of Límnos. A statue of the heroine Maroúla stands here and a spring with good water flows down a long stairway by the church, **Zoodóchos Pigí**. A couple of pleasant, sleepy bars overlook the tiny fishing port, while from the top of the village there are views east across the island to **Ormos Kéros**. This sandy stretch of beach is the most popular on the island with both swimmers and (experienced) windsurfers, filling the inner curves of Pournías Bay with dunes all the way to **Kontopoúli** (ΚΟΝΤΟΠΟΥΛΙ). Also by the sea here is ancient Mýrina's rival, **Hephestía**, named after the god who crash-landed in the lagoon below. Mostly unexcavated, part of the theatre remains, and you can make out a few ancient houses, and bits of the acropolis and tombs.

Across little Tigáni Bay from Hephestía, **Chloï** (*open 9.30–3.30*) is better known these days as **Kavírio** after the earliest-known sanctuary of the Underworld deities of fertility, the Cabiri, before the cult was transferred to Samothrace. Guided tours are offered of the Archaic foundations of the sanctuary, built around a 6th–7th century BC temple of initiation, dedicated to

Thracian Aphrodite, with the bases of 12 Doric columns intact, but not much more besides the usual graceful setting. There is a beach below, and a bungalow hotel. Under the sanctuary a trail at the end of the ledge leads to the **cave of Philoktétis**, the miserable archer. Another Trojan War site is beyond the large, pleasant village of **Pláka** at the tip of Cape Hermaeon, where a beacon was lit by order of Agamemnon to signal the end of the Trojan War—a signal relayed over the islands back to Mycenae. About 30m off the shore of Pláka are the ruins of **Chryse**, an ancient city submerged by an earthquake. A temple of Apollo was discovered in a reef; on a calm day you can see its marble blocks from a boat. Pláka has good beaches, Ag. Stéfanos and Mandrí, but little in the way of tourist facilities.

Polióchne (ΠΟΛΙΟΧΝΗ), the island's most important archaeological site (*open 9.30–5.30*), is signposted from **Kamínia**, on Límnos' southeast wing. Here Italian archaeologists discovered seven different layers of civilization, one on top of the other, dating back to the very dawn of time. The Neolithic town predates the Egyptian dynasties, the Minoan kingdoms of Crete, and even the earliest level of Troy; walls and houses remain of the next oldest town (2000 BC) which was probably destroyed suddenly by an earthquake but could claim the oldest known baths in the Aegean; the third city dates back to the Copper Age, while the top Bronze Age settlement was contemporary with the Mycenaeans—the Límnos of Homer—dating from 1500 to 100 BC. There's little to see other than the walls of the second city and the foundations of houses, but the explanations in English help bring them to life. Between Polióchne and the abandoned monastery of **Ag. Sózos** to the south stretches the sandy expanse known as the 'Sahara of Límnos'. Ag. Sózos overlooks the sea from a high cliff and on 8 September each year it is the focus of a small religious festival.

The Perfect Christmas Wine?

Although now mostly devoted to grains and cotton, Límnos was famous since antiquity for its vineyards; Aristotle wrote about the traditional red wine of the island, produced from a very ancient and unique variety of grape that he called Limnio (locally referred to as Kalambáki). No other wine tastes anything like it; wine experts, grasping for a description of its bouquet, have hit upon sage and bay leaf, rather like turkey stuffing. The variety has been transplanted in Chalkidikí, near Mount Áthos, where the Domaine Carrás produces a sophisticated Limnio, blended with 10 per cent Cabernet Sauvignon. White grapes grown on Límnos are usually Moscháto Alexándrias, which yields a dry white wine with a light muscat fragrance.

Límnos ✆ *(0254–)*   ***Where to Stay and Eating Out***

Accommodation on Límnos is limited and surprisingly upmarket; don't arrive in July and August without a booking or a sleeping bag.

Mýrina ✉ 81400

The posh deluxe bungalow complex on the beach in Mýrina is known as the **Akti Myrina**, ✆ 22 681, ✆ 22 352 (*L; lux*). It has three bars, four restaurants, three tennis courts, its own nightclub, private beach, caique and, after all that, a rather disappointing swimming pool. Wooden chalets house 125 rooms. The complex is famous throughout Greece, for its prices alone: a bungalow for two in high season will set you back at least £180 (half-board), and there are some for triple that figure; however, booking through a UK holiday agent or out of season should ease the pain. *Open May–Oct.* **Portomyrina Palace** is nearby, ✆ 24 805, 🖳 24 858 (*L; lux*), built in 1995; clad in marble, it boasts an Olympic outdoor pool and an indoor one, as well as all mod cons. *Open May–Oct.* **Kastro Beach**, ✆ 22 772, 🖳 22 704 (*B; exp*), is large and comfortable, near the post office. **Astron**, ✆ 24 392, 🖳 24 396 (*A; exp*), has nicely furnished apartments, and is fairly centrally located. *Open all year.* **Nefeli**, ✆ 23 415, 🖳 24 041 (*B; exp*), is in a lovely position just off Romaíkos Beach, under the castle, but can be noisy from the nearby bars. **Villa Afrodite**, ✆ 24 795, 🖳 25 031 (*C; mod*), is just outside the centre near Platís beach, with a pool and pleasant gardens. **Afrodite Apartments**, ✆ 23 489, 🖳 25 031 (*mod*), are run by the same family, near Riha Nera; set amongst greenery, they are ideal for self catering. Nearby, the **Ifestos**, 17 Eth. Antistasseos, ✆ 24 960, 🖳 23 623 (*C; exp–mod; cheaper if booked through Sunvil, see p.32*), is a friendly, well-designed, new hotel 100m from Platís beach; all rooms come with a fridge and balcony. **Hotel Lemnos**, ✆ 22 153, 🖳 23 329 (*C; mod–inexp*), is a good waterfront bet. *Open all year.* For peace and quiet, there's **Sunset**, 2km north at Ag. Ioánnis beach, ✆ 61 555 (*D; mod*). There's a selection of tavernas and grills along the Mýrina waterfront, including five fish tavernas in the north harbour. **Avra**, where the boat docks, is undoubtedly the best deal in town, and **O Platanos**, suitably situated by a pair of massive plane trees in a quaint squarelet, has excellent traditional fare. If you fancy a spectacle, ask at EOT about the **Limnian dances** put on by the Kehayiades Folklore Association. For more active involvement, head for **Avlonas Club**, just out of town.

Kontiás/Tsimántria ✉ 81400

There are about 20 rooms to rent in Kontiás, and good tavernas; in Tsimántria, **Nasos Kotsinadelis' Taverna** is famous for its chicken grilled over coals. Mr Kotsinadélis is the island's foremost lyra player, and on 15 August he serenades his customers.

Moúdros ✉ 81401

To Kyma, ✆ 71 333, 🖳 71 484 (*B; exp*), is a tranquil place to stay, with a reasonable restaurant and bar. *Open all year.*

Ag. Efstrátios (ΑΓ. ΕΥΣΤΡΑΤΙΟΣ)

The remote, partly dry, partly green little volcanic triangle of **Ag. Efstrátios** (locally known as **t'Aïstratí**) lies 21 nautical miles southwest of its big sister Límnos. It is linked by ferry four times a week from Límnos; the port (✆ (0254) 93 333) is too shallow for the big boats, so be prepared to transfer into caiques. Rich in minerals (including petroleum), the islet has been inhabited from Mycenaean times, and on the north coast stand the walls and ruins of the ancient settlement, which endured into the Middle Ages. In 1968 an earthquake wreaked havoc on Ag. Efstrátios' port and major village, and now nearly all of the island's 250 inhabitants live next to a wide, sandy beach in a rather dreary village of concrete huts thrown up by the junta after the disaster; as on Alónnisos, the inhabitants weren't allowed to repair their homes. The sea—the surrounding waters are transparent and rich in fish—brings in most of their income. Besides the village beach, which is really quite pleasant, there are several others scattered about that are perfect for playing Robinson Crusoe, but you will need to hike for at least an hour or hire a caique to reach them; for real isolation try the long sandy beach at Ag. Efstrátios' baby islet, **Vélia**. Between 1936 and 1962 Ag. Efstrátios played Alcatraz to scores of Greek Communists. Today it receives very few visitors, but if you want to stay, the **Xenonas Aï-Strati** pension, © (0254) 93 329 (*inexp*), is a good bet and occupies one of the very few houses to survive the quake; there are also quite a few rooms, tolerated free camping on any beach, a small shop or two and a couple of tavernas with very limited menus.

Mílos (ΜΗΛΟΣ)

Like Santoríni, Mílos, the most westerly of the Cyclades, is a volcanic island. But where the former is a glamorous beauty associated with misty tales of Atlantis, Mílos is a sturdy fellow who has made his fiery origins work for a living. Few places can boast such a catalogue of geological eccentricities: hot springs bubble in its low rolling hills, rocks startle with their Fauvist colours and fantastic shapes, and the landscape is gashed with obsidian, sulphur, kaolin, barium, alum, bensonite and perlite quarries begun in the Neolithic era. In a beach beauty contest Mílos would score over Santoríni hands-down with miles of pale golden sands, among the finest in Greece; long strands and weird fjord-like inlets all lapped by deep turquoise waters, some bubbling with the geothermal springs. It seems an odd trick of Mother Nature to so endow such an out-of-the-way island with this mineral cornucopia. Yet in spite of all its strange and wonderful rocks, Mílos still mourns for the one it lost—the renowned Venus, now in the Louvre.

Walks through the gently undulating countryside will bring you down to tiny whitewashed chapels at the water's edge, or unique little settlements that sit on the water, with brightly painted boat garages beneath their balconies. Not surprisingly, Mílos receives more tourists every year (especially Italians and Germans), numbers that will only increase once the new jet runways are complete and the yacht marina is in place in the island's magnificent harbour.

History

But Mílos has long been a popular place. In the early Neolithic era, people braved the Aegean in papyrus boats to mine Mílos's abundant veins of obsidian, the petroleum of its day, hard black volcanic glass prized for the manufacture of tools. Until the recent discovery of the Mesolithic settlement in Kýthnos, Mílos laid claim to the oldest town in the Cyclades, at Phylakope, settled by either Phoenicians or Cypriots; under Minoan and later Mycenaean rule the island became rich from trading obsidian all over the Mediterranean.

As the inhabitants of Mílos in later years were predominately Dorian like the Spartans, they declared themselves neutral in the Peloponnesian War. In 415 BC, Athens sent envoys to change their minds. Their famous 'might makes right' discussion, known as 'the Milian Dialogue', in the fifth chapter of Thucydides, is one of the most moving passages in classical history. When Mílos, unconvinced, still refused to cooperate, the Athenians besieged the island, and when the Milians unconditionally surrendered they massacred all the men of fighting age, enslaved all the women and children, and resettled the island with colonists from Athens. They were famous in antiquity for raising the best, toughest roosters—for cock fights.

Christianity came early to Mílos in the 1st century, and the faithful built a great series of cata-combs—the only ones in Greece. Marco and his brother Angelo Sanudo captured Mílos, and

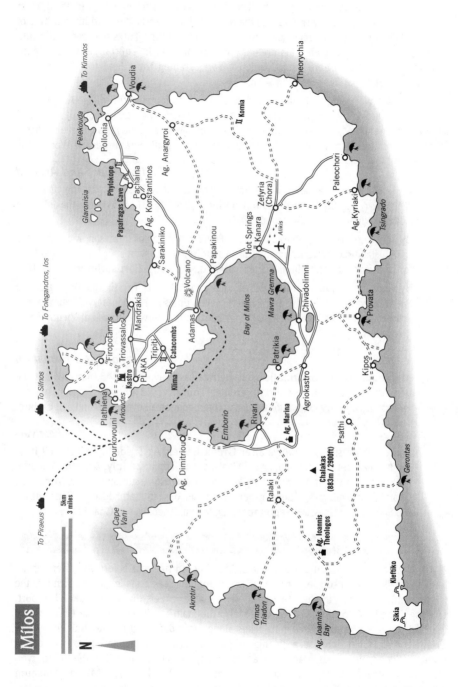

Mílos

N

5km
3 miles

To Piraeus
To Sifnos
To Folegandros, Ios
To Kimolos

Pelekouda
Voudia
Pollonia
Phylokope
Papafragas Cave
Pachaina
Ag. Konstantinos
Glaronisia
Ag. Anargyroi
Komia
Theonychia
Sarakiniko
Paleochori
Zefyria (Chora)
Ag.Kyriaki
Tsingrado
Kanara
Hot Springs
Alikis
Papakinou
Volcano
Firopotamos
Mandrakia
Triovassalos
Tripiti
Plathiena
Kastro
PLAKA
Klima
Catacombs
Adamas
Bay of Mílos
Mavra Gremna
Chivadolimni
Provata
Kipos
Arkoudes
Fourkovouni
Patrikia
Agriokastro
Psathi
Gerontas
Emborio
Rivari
Ag. Marina
Ag. Dimitriou
Ralaki
Chalakas
(883m / 2900ft)
Cape Vani
Ag. Ioannis
Theologos
Akrotiri
Ormos Triadon
Ag. Ioannis Bay
Sikia
Kleftiko

later placed it under the Crispi dynasty. The Turks laid claim to the island in 1580, even though Mílos was infested with pirates. One of them, John Kapsís, declared himself King of Mílos, a claim which Venice recognized for three years, until the Turks flattered Kapsís into coming to Istanbul, and ended his pretensions with an axe. In 1680 a party from Mílos emigrated to London, where James, Duke of York, granted them land to build a Greek church—the origin of Greek Street in Soho.

In 1836 Cretan war refugees from Sfakiá fled to Mílos and founded the village Adámas, the present port. During the Crimean War the French navy docked at the harbour of Mílos and left many monuments, as they did during the First World War; at Korfos you can see the bases of the anti-aircraft batteries installed during the German occupation in the Second World War.

© *(0287–)*   **Getting There and Around**

By air: at least one daily from Athens. Olympic Airways is just past the *plateía* in Adámas, © 22 380; for **airport information**, call © 22 381. A taxi from the airport to Adámas will set you back around 2,000dr.

By sea: taxi boat five times a day from Pollónia to Kímolos in season; recommended round-island **excursion boats,**with stops for lunch and swims, or hire the *Apollonia* for your own excursion from Manolis Galanos, © 51 385. **Port authority**: © 22 100.

By road: hourly **buses** from Adámas square to Pláka, via Tripití; nine times a day to Pollónia by way of Filikopi and Pachera; seven times to Paleóchora via Zephyria and Provatás. For a **taxi**, call © 22 219. Or **rent** your own wheels: ask at Vichos Tours (*see* below).

© *(0287–)*   **Tourist Information**

Municipal tourist information, on the Adámas quay, © 22 445, has accommodation lists (only open in season). **Vichos Tours**, © 22 286, ✉ 22 396, on the waterfront, are very helpful for tickets, accommodation all over the island and car hire.

Festivals

Easter, Triovassálos; **50 days after Greek Easter**, Ag Triáda in Adámas; **19 July**, Profítis Ilías on the mountain, and in Chalákas and Tripití; **26 July**, Ag. Panteleímonos in Plakotá; **5 August**, Sotíris in Paraskópou; **15 August**, Assumption of the Virgin, Ag. Charálambos, Adámas; **7 September**, Panagía Eleoúsa in Psathádika; **16 September**, Ag. Sofía in Chalákas; **25 September**, Ag. Ioánnis Theológos in Chalákas.

Adámas and the Beaches around the Bay

If you arrive by sea, you can see a sample of Mílos' eccentric rocks before you disembark: a formation called the **Arkoúdes**, or bears, rises up from the sea on the left as you turn into the largest natural harbour in the Mediterranean–so large it feels like a vast lake. The port, bustling, friendly **Adámas** (ΑΔΑΜΑΣ), is also the main tourist centre. The Cretans who founded the town brought their holy icons along, now displayed in the churches of **Ag. Tríada** and **Ag. Charálambos**, at the highest point in town; in the latter, one ex-voto, dating from 1576, portrays a boat attacked by a raging fish; the captain prayed to the Virgin, who resolved the struggle by snipping off the fish's nose. There's also a new **Mining Museum** (*open daily 9.30–1 and 5–8*), heading south along the waterfront, illustrating Milos' geological and mining history. West of town you can ease your aches and pains wallowing in the warm sulphurous mineral waters of the municipal **spa baths**, in an old cave divided into three bathrooms (*open daily 8–1; take a towel; adm*). Beyond is small **Lagáda Beach**, popular with families; a monument at Bombarda commemorates the French who died there during the Crimean War. Further along the track, reed-beds with gurgling hot mud pools mark the route to the **'Volcano'**, really a glorified steaming fissure in the rock.

The vast, sandy **Bay of Mílos** is fringed with a succession of beaches like **Papikinoú**, backed by hotels and apartments. There's a quieter beach at **Alýkes**, the salt marshes before the Mávra Gremná, or the black cliffs, with fantastical rock formations; at several places out in the bay the sea bubbles from the hot springs released below. The generous spring near the Kanava junction supposedly is a sure cure for sterility in women. Past the salt-beds and the industrial and airport clutter stretches the spectacular sandy beach at **Chivadólimni**, the island's longest, with a deep turquoise sea in front and a saltwater lake behind, named after the clams who live there; it also hosts the island's official campsite. Continuing along the coast, other pale golden beaches are **Patrikia** and **Rivári**, the latter backed by a lagoon once used as a vivarium by the monks at up at **Ag. Marína Monastery**, and **Emboriós** with rooms to let and a quaint taverna. Further north, **Ag. Dimitríou** is often battered by winds.

Pláka: Ancient Melos and its Catacombs

Buses leaves frequently for **Pláka** (ΠΛΑΚΑ) the labyrinthine, sugar-cube capital, 4km uphill from Adámas, blending into the windmill-topped suburb of **Tripití** (ΤΡΥΠΗΤΗ). Next to the bus stop is the **Archaeology Museum** (℗ 21 620, *open 8.30–3, closed Mon; adm*). Just inside is a plaster copy of Venus, a thoughtful consolation prize from Paris, but the real finds are from the Neolithic era: terracotta objects and lily-painted ceramics from Phylakope, including the famous *Lady of Phylakope*, a decorated Minoan-style goddess. There are Hellenistic artefacts from Kímolos and several statues, but like Venus, the famous marble *Poseidon* and the *Kouros of Mílos* are not at home (this time in the National Archaeological Museum in Athens). Signs point the way to the **Historical and Folklore Museum** (℗ 21 292, *open Tues–Sat 10–1 and 6–8, and Sun 10–1; adm*), housed in a 19th-century mansion; it's especially fun if you can find someone to tell you the stories behind the exhibits, which include everything down to the kitchen sink.

Steps lead up to the Venetian **Kástro** set high on a volcanic plug. Houses formed the outer walls of the fortress. Perched on top was an old church, Mésa Panagía, blown up by the Germans during the Second World War. After liberation, a new church was built lower down, but the old icon of the Virgin reappeared in a bush on top of the Kástro. Every time they moved the icon it returned to the bushes so they gave in and built another church, **Panagía Skiniótissa**, 'Our Lady of the Bushes'. There are stunning views from here, and on the way up from **Panagía Thalassítras**, 'Our Lady of the Sea' (1228), where the lintel bears the arms of the Crispi family, who overthrew the Sanudi as dukes of Náxos. The church houses fine icons by Emmanuel Skordílis. **Panagía Rosaria** is the Roman Catholic church built by the French consul Louis Brest, and **Panagía Korfiátissa** on the edge of a sheer cliff to the west of the village has Byzantine and Cretan icons rescued from the ruined city of Zefyría.

Pláka itself is built over the acropolis of ancient **Melos**, the town destroyed by the Athenians and resettled by the Romans. In the 1890s the British school excavated the site at **Klíma**, a short walk below Pláka (if you take the bus, ask to be let off at Tripití), where you can visit a termitiary of **Catacombs** (✆ 21 625, *open 8–2, closed Mon*), dating from the 1st century AD. One of the best-preserved Early Christian monuments in Greece, it has long corridors of arched niches carved in the rock. When first discovered, the tombs were still full of bones, but contact with the fresh air quickly turned them to dust. Some held five or six bodies; other cadavers were buried in the floor. On various tombs, inscriptions in red remain, as well as later black graffiti. The habit of building underground necropoli (besides the many at Rome, there are catacombs in Naples, Sicily and Malta) coincides with the presence of soft volcanic tufa more than with romantic notions of persecution and secret underground rites; interring the dead underground saved valuable land. (Curiously, the modern cemetery near Pláka resembles a row of catacombs above ground, the more posh ones even done out with carpets.) A path from the catacombs leads to the spot where Venus was discovered—there's a marker by the fig tree.

The Venus de Milo, or Unclear Disarmament

 On 8 April 1820, farmer Geórgios Kentrotás was ploughing a field when he discovered a cave containing half of a statue of the goddess Aphrodite. A French officer, Olivier Voutier, who just happened to be visiting Mílos at the time, urged the farmer to look for the other half. He soon found it, along with a 6th-century BC statue of young Hermes and Hercules as an old man—an ancient art lover's secret cache, hidden from the Christians. Voutier sketched the Aphrodite for Louis Brest, the French vice consul for Mílos. Brest sent this on to the French consul in Constantinople, who decided to obtain Aphrodite for France, and immediately sent an envoy over to complete the deal. But meanwhile Kentrotás, persuaded by the island's elders, had sold the statue to another man on behalf of the translator of the Turkish fleet, the Prince of Moldavia, Nichólas Mouroúzis. The statue was in a caique, ready to be placed aboard a ship for Romania just when the French ship sailed into Adámas. Eventually, after some brisk bargaining, the envoy and Brest managed to buy the Aphrodite as a gift for Louis XVIII (although some say the French sailors attacked the caique and grabbed her by force). On 1 March 1821 she made her début in the Louvre. Somewhere along the line—in the caique battle?—she lost her arms and pedestal with the inscription *Aphrodites Nikiforos* 'Victory-bringing Aphrodite'. The French cadet's sketch showed the arms, one hand holding an apple.

The path continues past the ancient Cyclopean city walls to the well-preserved **Roman Theatre**, where spectators looked out over the sea, excavated and reconstructed to something approaching its former glory; a company from Athens sometimes performs in the theatre in August (ask at the tourist office for details). Remains of a **temple** are on the path back to the main road. From there you can take the road or an old *kalderími* pathway down to the picturesque fishing hamlet of **Klíma**, with its brightly painted boat garages, *syrmata*, carved into the soft volcanic tufa, with rickety balconies above and ducks waddling on the beach below. A museum-style reconstruction shows how the fishing families once lived around their caiques.

Around Pláka

Near Pláka, the market village **Triovassálos** merges into **Péra Triovassálos**. The churches in Triovassálos contain icons from the island's original capital Zefyría. The great rivalry between the two villages expresses itself on Easter Sunday, when after burning an effigy of Judas, the young bloods of Triovassálos and Péra Triovassálos hold a dynamite-throwing contest on the dividing line between the villages; the most ear-splitting performance wins. Tracks lead down to a wide selection of beaches, some adorned with wonderfully coloured rocks. One of the best beaches is **Pláthíena** near the Arkoúdes, with dazzling orange and white rock formations; it's also the best place on Mílos to watch the sun set. The old path from Pláka leads past **Fourkovoúni** with picturesque *syrmata* hewn into the cliffs. **Mandrákia**, under Triovassálos, is one of the island's most outstanding beauty spots, a stunning little cove studded with garages and topped by a white chapel. Further north, **Firopótamos** is another pretty fishing hamlet.

The North Coast: Phylakope and Pollónia

The road from Adámas or Pláka to Pollónia offers a pair of very tempting stops along the north coast. A side road descends into the bleached moonscape of **Sarakíniko**, of huge rounded rocks and pointed peaks whipped by the winds into giant white petrified drifts, with a tiny beach and inlet carved in its bosom. To the east the fishing hamlets of **Pachaina** and **Ag. Konstantínos** have more *syrmata*; from the latter it's a short walk to **Papafrángas Cave**, actually three sea caves, where the brilliant turquoise water is enclosed by the white cliffs of a mini fjord, once used by trading boats as a hiding place from pirates. Bring an air mattress to paddle about on.

On the other side of Papafrángas, **Phylakope** (ΦΥΛΑΚΩΠΗ) is easy to miss but was one of the great centres of Cycladic civilization, excavated by the British in the 1890s. The dig yielded three successive levels of habitation: early Cycladic (3500 BC), Middle Cycladic (to around 1600 BC) and Late Cycladic/Mycenaean. Even in Early Cycladic days Mílos traded in obsidian far and wide—pottery found in the lowest levels showed an Early Minoan influence. Grand urban improvements characterize the Middle Cycladic period: a wall was built around the more spacious and elegant houses, some with frescoes—one depicts a flying fish, that in the absence of Venus has become the artistic symbol of Mílos. A Minoan-style palace contained fine ceramics imported from Knossós, and there was trade with the coasts of Asia Minor. In this period Mílos, like the rest of the Cyclades, may have come under the direct rule of the Minoans; a tablet found on the site is written in a script similar to Linear A. During the Late Cycladic age, the Mycenaeans built their own shrine, added a wall around the palace, and left behind figurines and ceramics. Phylakope declined when metals replaced the need for obsidian. For all its history the actual remains at the site are overgrown and inexplicable.

The bus ends up at Apollo's old town, **Pollónia** (ΠΟΛΛΩΝΙΑ) on the east coast, a popular resort with a tree-fringed beach, fishing boats, and tavernas. There's quite a bit of new holiday development with apartments and bars on the **Pelekóuda** cape, popular as it is with windsurfers and those who enjoy a good buffeting. Water taxis leave Pollónia harbour for Kímolos five times a day, weather permitting. **Voúdia** beach to the south has a unique view of the island's mining activities.

In the Centre: Zefýria, Paleochóri and Around

Buses cross the island to **Zefýria** or Chóra, the capital of Mílos from 800 to 1793. **Panagía Portianí** was the principal church of the village; its priest was accused of fornication by the inhabitants, and although he steadfastly denied it, the villagers refused to believe him. With that the priest angrily cursed the people, a plague fell on the town, and everyone moved down to Pláka. Today Zefýria is a very quiet village of old crumbling houses, surrounded by olive trees. A paved road and the bus continues to popular sandy **Paleochóri Beach**; quieter **Ag. Kyriakí** to the west has rooms and tavernas. **Kómia**, east of Zefýria, has ruined Byzantine churches and nearby at **Demenayáki** are some of Mílos' obsidian mines.

South and West Mílos

If eastern Mílos is fairly low and green, the south and west are mountainous and dry. Just south of Chivadólimni, **Provatás** has another sandy beauty and hot springs, **Loutrá Provatá,** where you can examine remains of Roman mosaics, followed by a natural sauna to ease your rhematism, recommended by no less than Hippocrates himself. **Kípos**, further along the coast, has two churches: one, the 5th-century **Panagía tou Kipou**, is the oldest in Mílos. To the west, in the wild **Chalákas** region, where small woods of rare snake root and cedars survive in little canyons, the old monastery at **Ag. Marína** is worth a trip; from here you can climb to the top of **Profítis Ilías**, with a gods' eye view over Mílos and neighbouring islands.

Down in the southwest, at the famous monastery of **Ag. Ioánnis Theológos Siderianós**, St John is nicknamed the Iron Saint—once during his festival, revellers were attacked by pirates and took refuge in the church. In response to their prayers, the saint saved them by turning the church door to iron (you can still see a scrap of a dress caught in the door as the last woman entered). The pirates could not break in, and when one of them tried to shoot through a hole in the church dome, Ag. Ioánnis made his hand wither and fall off, still holding the pistol. Another miraculous story from April 1945 tells of a shell from an English warship zapping through the church door and embedding itself in the wall without exploding. Ask if you can camp on the beach below; the warden usually says yes.

A Geological Mystery Tour

From Adámas excursion boats tour the island's fascinating rock formations from sea. Highlights include the **Glaroníssia**, four cave-pocked basalt islets shaped like organ pipes, off the north coast; **Paleoréma** on the east coast with a disused sulphur mine which turns the water emerald-green; and on the southwest corner, the sea caves of **Sikía** where the sun's rays slant through the roof to create dramatic colours in the water, and next door **Kléftiko**, the pirates' hideaway with another set of fantastic cream and white rocks rising from the sea. You can also sail near **Andímilos** to the northwest, a reserve for the rare Cretan chamois goat, or *kri-kri*.

Mílos ✉ *84800,* ✆ *(0287–)*　　　　　　　*Where to Stay and Eating Out*

Mílos fills up to the brim from 15 July to 15 September, so be sure to book then. If you get stuck call the **Rooms to Let Association,** ✆ 23 429.

Adámas

Kapetan Georgadas, ✆ 23 215, ✆ 23 219 (*C; exp*), are re-vamped traditional style apartments, small but exclusive, with satellite TV, mini bars, air-con and pool. *Open all year.* **Santa Maria Village** is set back from the beach, ✆ 22 015, ✆ 22 880 (*C; exp*), with a smart mix of rooms, studios and apartments; wheelchair access. On the other side of town, **Popi's,** ✆ 22 286, ✆ 22 396, in Athens ✆ (01) 361 3198 (*C; exp*), is comfortable with very helpful management and by the water. *Open all year.* **Delfini,** ✆ 22 001, ✆ 22 688 (*D; mod*), is a friendly family-run hotel with a nice breakfast terrace; the same family also runs the smart new **Seagull Apartments,**

© 23 183/193 (*lux–exp*). **Semiramis**, © 22 118, ✆ 22 117 (*D; mod*), is excellent with a pretty vine-clad terrace—help yourself to grapes—bar, transfer minibus and rent-a-bike service. *Open all year.* **Adamas**, © 22 322/581, ✆ 22 580 (*C; mod*), has well-equipped air-conditioned rooms perched above the harbour. White and quiet **Mílos**, © 22 087, ✆ 22 306 (*C; mod*), on the seafront, doesn't look much but has an excellent restaurant popular with Greeks.

Adámas has most of the island's restaurants; if you come in the right season, look for clams from Chivadólimni. On the waterfront the best bet for fair-priced Greek home cooking is **Barko**, with good barrel wine. Friendly **Flisvos** has the usual fish and oven-ready dishes; next door **Kynigos** serves good, standard fare in unpretentious but pleasant surroundings. **Vedema** above the ferry port serves tasty Greek and Middle Eastern dishes. Fish come up to feed beneath the terrace at **Trapatseli's**, which has an excellent menu, especially for fish dishes. The *spetsofái* fish stew and *soupiés*, cuttlefish *stifádo*, are good as well as the local *dópio* hard cheese; next door, good-value **Navayio** also has fresh fish and local *mezédes*. **Ta Pitsounakia** spitroasts all kinds of meats and *kokorétsi*.

Pláka/Tripití/Klíma

In Pláka, the **Plakiotiki Gonia**, is a sweet little taverna with local dishes like cheese pies and country bread with tomatoes; **Kastro**, in Pláka's square, is also popular, with views up to the castle, and **Arhondoula**, nearby, is recommended. At Tripití, **Popi's Windmill**, © 22 287, ✆ 22 396 (*exp*), has rooms that sleep 4–5 in two beautifully converted mills. *Open June–Sept.* **Sophia Apartments**, © 22 039, ✆ 21 980 (*mod*), are traditionally furnished and overflowing with arches. *Open all year.* There are lots of new tavernas here; **Mayeriko** is the best, with superb views. The *ouzerie* **Methismeni Politia**, the 'Drunken State', is pricier, specializing in *mezédes*, wines and ouzo in a romantic garden setting with views across the gulf. In Klíma the **Hotel/Restaurant Panorama**, © 21 623, ✆ 22 112 (*C; mod*), has rooms with private bath and dining terrace with great views; a good bet for lunch.

Pollónia

Kapetan Tassos, 100m from the beach, © 41 287, ✆ 41 322 (*A; exp*), has smart Cycladic-style apartments. **Apollon** apartments and studios, © 41 347 (*exp*), have views over Kímolos and home-cooking at the family taverna. Other local favourites are **Araxovoli** and **Kapetan Nikolas**.

Paleochóri /Ag. Kyriakí

At Paleochóri, the **Artemis Restaurant** has bungalows near the beach, © 31 221, and the **Pelagos** taverna has great food. **Thirios Restaurant** at Ag. Kyriakí has rooms, © 22 779/058.

Entertainment and Nightlife

Mílos has quite a sophisticated nightlife with scores of dancing bars and discos; there's even a roller-skating rink in Adámas. Locals hang out at **Yanko's**, near the bus stop, **To Ouzerie** on the front or **To Kafeneion**, for cocktails and Greek music in a flower-filled courtyard. Other Adámas hot spots are **Notos Club** on the north end of town;

Milo Milo disco at Langáda beach, and **Viagra**, which just doesn't stop (at the end of the sand); or else try **Vipera Libertina Bar**, and **Puerto** for Greek music.

In Pollónia head to **8 Bofor** (8 ΜΠΩΦΟΡ), at Pelekoúda for jazz, blues and rock.

Mýkonos (ΜΥΚΟΝΟΣ)

This dry, barren island frequently plagued by high winds, but graced with excellent beaches and a beautiful, colourful, cosmopolitan town, has the most exciting and sophisticated nightlife in Greece. This, and its proximity to ancient Délos, has made Mýkonos the most popular island in the Cyclades. If the surge in tourism in recent years caught the other islands unawares, Mýkonos didn't bat a mascaraed eyelid, having made the transformation long ago from a traditional economy to one dedicated to every which whim of the international set. If you seek the simple, the unadorned, the distinctly Greek—avoid Mýkonos like the plague. But the party will go on without you; Mýkonos' streets are jammed with some of the zaniest, wildest, raunchiest and Most Beautiful People in Greece. It also has the distinction of being one of the most expensive islands, and the first officially to sanction nudism on some of its beaches, as well as being the Mediterranean's leading gay resort.

History

The Ionians built three cities on Mýkonos: one on the isthmus south of Chóra, the second at Dimastos, dating back to 2000 BC and the third at Pánormos near Paliókastro. During the war between the Romans and Mithridates of Pontus, all three were destroyed. Chóra was rebuilt during the Byzantine period, and the Venetians surrounded it with a wall that no longer exists; however, at Paliókastro a fort built by the Gizzi rulers still remains. In 1537 Mýkonos fell without resistance to Barbarossa, and came into its own as a pirate island, settled with pirate families who ran a very profitable plunder market, fencing goods to European merchants; even so, it was on the front lines in the War of Independence, its fleet of 22 ships led by Manto Mavrogenous, the local heroine, who donated all of her considerable fortune to the cause.

Mythology

In myth Mýkonos is best known as a graveyard, site of the rock tombs of the giants slain by Hercules and that of Ajax the Lokrian, one of the heroes of the Trojan War. This Ajax was known as Little Ajax to differentiate him from Big Ajax, who committed suicide when the weapons of the dead Achilles were given to Odysseus rather than him. After the capture of Troy, Little Ajax proved himself just as pathetic a hero when he raped Priam's daughter Cassandra, who had sought protection in a temple of Athena. Athena avenged this blasphemy by wrecking Ajax's ship off the coast of Mýkonos. Poseidon saved him in a sea storm but, defiant as ever, Ajax declared that he would have been perfectly able to save himself without the god's assistance. Poseidon's trident finished Ajax then and there, and his Mycenaean tomb can still be seen at Pórtes.

✆ *(0289–)*   ***Getting There and Around***

By air: several connections daily with Athens, several a week with Thessaloníki, Santoríni, Rhodes and Herákleon (Crete). The Olympic Airways office is on the edge of

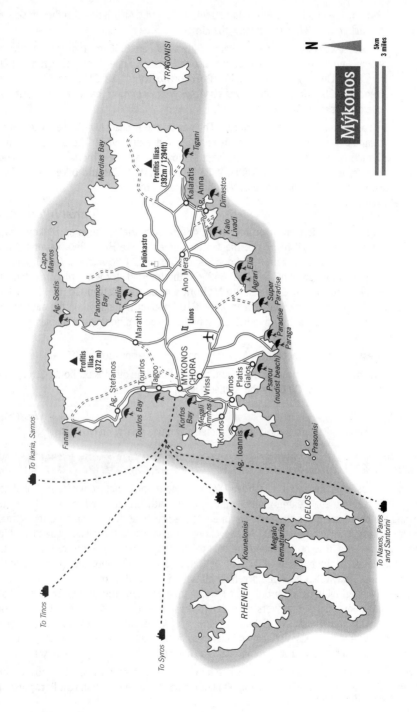

Mýkonos

5km
3 miles

N

TRAGONISI

Merdias Bay

Profitis Ilias
(392m / 1294ft)

Tigani

Kalafatis

Ag. Anna

Dimastos

Kalo
Livadi

Paliokastro

Ano Mera

Elia

Agrari

Super
Paradise

Paradise

Cape
Mavros

Ag. Sostis

Panormos
Bay

Ftelia

Marathi

Linos

Paraga

Profitis
Ilias
(372 m)

Ag. Stefanos

Tourlos

Tagoo

MYKONOS
CHORA

Vrissi

Platis
Gialos

Psarou
(nudist beach)

Fanari

Tourlos Bay

Korfos
Bay

Megali
Ammos

Ornos

Korfos

Ag. Ioannis

Prasonisi

To Ikaria, Samos

To Tinos

To Syros

Kounelonisi

Megalo
Remmatiarisi

DELOS

RHENEIA

To Naxos, Paros
and Santorini

373

town, at the end of Ag. Efthimiou street, ✆ 22 490. Air Manos also flies in season. **Airport**: ✆ 22 327. Buses stop by the airport.

By sea: excursion boats to Délos daily between 8.30am and 1pm, returning between noon and 3, except Monday; also to Paradise, Super Paradise, Agrari and Eliá from both Chóra and Platís Gialós, **Port authority**: ✆ 22 218. Sea & Sky Travel Agency, ✆ 28 240, ✉ 24 582, *sea-sky@myk.forthnet.gr*, on the waterfront near 'taxi square', is friendly and helpful.

By road: there are two **bus** stations. The one by the Archaeology Museum serves Ag. Stefanos, Tourlos, Áno Merá, Eliá, Kalafátis and Kaló Livádi. The one by Olympic Airways is for Ornós, Ag. Ioánnis, Platís Gialós, Psaroú, the airport and Kalamopodi. For information, ✆ 23 360. **Taxis**: ✆ 23 700 or 22 400. **Car and bike rental** places abound around the bus stations, but don't expect a bargain.

✆ *(0289–)*   *Tourist Information*

On the quay, the **tourist police**, ✆ 22 482 (run by the one man on Mýkonos who doesn't speak English!), share the same complex as the Hotel Reservations Office, ✆ 24 540; the Association of Rooms and Flats, ✆ 24 860 (*open 10–6*); and the camping information office, ✆ 22 852. On the Internet, try *www.mykonos.forthnet .gr/skaphp1.htm*. The Belgian-run **Mýkonos Accommodation Centre**, ✆ 23 160, ✉ 24 137, *mac@mac.myk.forthnet.gr*, at 10 Enoplon Dynameon, in the old town, is also very helpful, taking an individual approach to accommodation and able to arrange it all by email.

Internet: a pricey medium in Mýkonos, on offer in various town cafés.

Post office: one is near Ag. Anna and 'taxi square', the other is on Koutsi Street, near Olympic Airways. **OTE**: by the Archaeological Museum.

Festivals

15 August, Panagía Tourliani. But then every day's a party on Mýkonos.

Chóra

Prosperity has kept the homes of **Chóra** (ΧΩΡΑ), the island's picture-postcard capital and port, well maintained, gleaming and whitewashed, with brightly painted wooden trims. During the day it is a quiet place as everyone hits the beach; at night it vibrates. In the main square a bust of war heroine Mantó Mavrogenous once served as the island's guardian of left luggage; now dire little notices keep the backpacks away. Further up the waterfront is the departure quay for the boats to Délos. The pelican mascot of Mýkonos, the successor of the original Pétros, may often be found preening himself in the shadow of the small church here. On the hill overlooking the harbour are several thatched **windmills**; one from the 16th century has been restored to working order (*open June–Sept, 4–6*). They are a favourite subject for the students at the School of Fine Arts, as-is **Little Venice**, the quarter of Alefkándra, where the houses are tall and picturesque and built directly on the sea, just below the windmills; each abode now accommodates a cocktail bar for trendy sunset views.

Mýkonos claims to have 400 churches, some no bigger than bathrooms, and the most famous of these, just beyond Little Venice, is the oft-photographed snow-white **Panagía Paraportianí**, an asymmetrical masterpiece of four churches melted into one. Just opposite, the **Folklore Museum** (*open Mon–Sat 4–8pm, Sun 5–8pm*), houses old curiosities, a traditional bedroom and kitchen, and a gallery of 19th-century prints of sensuous Greek odalisques gazing dreamily into space; downstairs is an exhibition, 'Mýkonos and the Sea'. The **Nautical Museum** (*℗ (0289) 22 700; open summer 10.30am–1pm and 6.30–9.30pm; adm*), in the centre at Tria Pigádia, has rooms containing ships' models from ancient times and a collection of paintings, prints and coins. Old anchors, ships' wheels, cannons, and copies of ancient tombstones of shipwrecked sailors fill the garden. Nearby, **Lena's House** (*℗ (0289) 22 591; open April–end Oct, 7–9pm*), is a branch of the Folklore museum: the 19th-century middle-class home of Léna Sakrivanoú, preserved as she left it, with everything from her needlework to chamber pot. Towards the ferry quay, beyond the ducks and geese on Ag. Anna beach, the **Archaeology Museum** (*℗ (0289) 22 325; open 9–3.30, Sun and holidays 10–3, closed Tues; adm*) was built in 1905 in the jailhouse style to imprison ceramics, many boldly decorated with sphinxes, lions, birds and horses, from the necropolis islet of Rhéneia (*see* Délos, pp.378–83). But the finest single item was found on Tínos: a red 7th-century BC funeral pithos with relief scenes from the Fall of Troy, like comic book strips, showing the death of Hector's son and a delightful warrior-stuffed Trojan horse, fitted with airplane windows.

Around Mýkonos: Inside and Around the Edges

In ancient times Mýkonos was the butt of many jokes and had the dubious distinction of being famous for the baldness of its men, and even today the old fishermen of the island never take off their distinctive caps. Despite all the changes, they have kept their sense of humour, and if you speak a little Greek they'll regale you with stories of the good old days—before all the tourist girls (and boys) began chasing them around. You may find a few old fellows to chat up at **Áno Merá** (ΑΝΩ ΜΕΡΑ), Mýkonos' other town, where the 16th-century **Panagía Tourlianí Monastery** with its sculpted marble steeple protects Mýkonos from harm; it has a carved Florentine altarpiece, fine Cretan icons, an ecclesiastical museum and farm tool museum (*to visit, ring ahead, ℗ (0289) 71 249*). Below, sandy windswept **Pánormos Bay** was the site of one of Mýkonos' three ancient cities; here **Fteliá** and **Ag. Sostis** are wild beaches favoured by windsurfers. At **Linos**, by the airport, are the remains of a Hellenistic tower and walls.

North of Chóra, the beaches at **Tagoo, Toúrlos** and **Ag. Stefanós** have a lot of accommodation and a lot of people to fill it: **Fanári** to the north is considerably quieter. The nearest beaches south of Chóra are **Megáli Ámmos, Kórfos** and **Ornós**, all of which are built up, especially Ornós, with its cute little port. The biggest resort, however, is **Platís Gialós**, to the east, with its own system of boat excursions to the other beaches and Délos, while jet setters like to jet-ski at **Psaroú**, just before Platís Gialós. **Paradise** with its campsite, diving school, and Cavo Paradiso (a pool-bar-restaurant Hard Rock Café clone) and **Super Paradise** are the once notorious nudist beaches on the island, both much less notorious now; little **Agrári**, just east of Super Paradise, has somehow missed out on the exploitation. **Eliá**, a once quiet beach accessible by bus, is divided into straight and gay precincts; just inland sprawls **Watermania**, ℗ (0289) 71 685, the answer to all your aquatic desires (*open Apr–Oct*). **Ag. Ánna** is a quieter beach, and there's the fishing hamlet and the family beach at **Kalafátis**, also worth a trip. At **Pórtes** you can spit on the 'tomb' of Ajax the troublemaker. **Tragonísi**, the islet off the east coast of Mýkonos, has numerous caves, and if you're very lucky you may see a rare monk seal in one of them.

There's certainly no lack of places to stay on Mýkonos, although prices tend to be higher than almost anywhere else in Greece and you should book from June on. Sleek new hotels, many incorporating elements of the local architecture, occupy every feasible spot on the coast, especially along the road to Platís Gialós. When you step off the ferry you'll be inundated with people offering rooms, but beware that many of these are up the hill above Chóra, in a barren, isolated and ugly area of holiday apartments. You'll probably do better using the accommodation-finding desks just beyond or making your way to Mýkonos Accommodation Centre in town. Many places provide free transfer to and from the airport.

Chóra (Mýkonos Town)

Hotel Leto, ✆ 22 207, ✉ 24 365, *leto@leto.myk.forthnet.gr* (*A; lux*), has a wonderful view over the harbour and town, and was for many years the classiest place to stay on the island. **Adonis,** ✆ 24 202, ✉ 23 449 (*C; exp*), is comfortable and central. Overlooking town, **Elysium,** ✆ 23 952, ✉ 23 747 (*C; exp*), is exclusively gay and adds a fitness centre, Jacuzzi and pretty pool to the views from its bungalows. The **Veranda** is also above town, ✆ 23 670, ✉ 25 133 (*exp*), with panoramic views and pool. **Rania,** ✆ 22 315, ✉ 22 370, *rania-ap@otenet.gr* (*mod*), has tasteful, quiet rooms and studios above taxi square; the owners are very helpful. **Pension Marina,** ✆/✉ 24 960 (*mod*), is another good choice. **Manto,** 1 Evangelístrias, ✆ 22 330 (*C; mod*), is convenient for connoisseurs of the night scene. The delightful **Philippi,** ✆ 22 294, ✉ 24 680 (*D; mod*), in the heart of Chóra at 32 Kalogéra Street, has rooms scented by the hotel's lovely garden. **Hotel Lefteris,** ✆ 23 128, ✉ 27 117, *lefteris hot@yahoo.com* (*E; mod*), is more modest, with a great roof terrace, kitchen facilities and the wonderfully laid-back Costas.

Chóra has food for every pocket and appetite. **Philippi** (*see* above; ✆ 22 295 to book) has a good reputation in town for international and Greek cuisine, served in the garden (*count on 9,000dr*). **Edem,** ✆ 22 855, offers a varied international menu around a courtyard pool by Panachrandou church. Centrally placed **Katrin's,** again pretty expensive, has many good French specialities. **Yves Klein Blue,** ✆ 27 391, offers pricey but good Italian dishes. If you need to be reminded that you're in Greece, head for **Niko's Taverna,** behind the town hall, with good dinners in the *3,000dr* range. A notable exception to the rule that the back streets hide the best, secret tavernas is **Antonini's,** slap in the middle of the activity on taxi square; genuine Greek food at fair prices: varied and excellent *mezédes*, shrimp salad and very tasty veal or lamb casserole (*3,000dr*). For fish, dine out at **Kounelas,** at the end of the waterfront, where the owner, a colourful character, promises consistently fresh seafood (*5,000dr*). English-run **Sesame Kitchen,** ✆ 24 710, is a vegetarian's haven; meanwhile, many Greeks seeking a night off from the moussaka head for **Appaloosa**'s Mexican fare and good salads in Mavrogenous Street. If you take the free shuttle bus out of Chóra, there's even a (real) **Hard Rock Café** where you can eat expensive fast food and lounge by a pool.

North of Chóra

On the beach, within walking distance of town at Tagoo is the award-winning Cubist beauty **Cavo Tagoo,** ✆ 23 692, ✉ 24 923 (*A; lux*), 'pour les lucky few', with seawater pool, beautiful view of Mýkonos, and the chance to rub shoulders with the stars. **Aegean**, in Tagoo, ☎ 22 869, 🖷 24 927 (*B; exp*), is well-appointed but still family run and friendly; **Spanelis**, ☎ 23 081 (*D; exp*), and **Madalena**, ☎ 22 954, 🖷 24 302 (*C; exp*), are lesser options, the latter with a pool. Toúrlos Beach has the **Rhenia**, ☎ 22 300, 🖷 23 152, *rhenia@otenet.gr* (*B; exp*), with tranquil, sheltered bungalows and pool, overlooking Chóra and Délos, and **Hotel Olia**, ☎ 23 123, 🖷 23 824 (*B; exp*), with pleasing, traditionally styled rooms and pool nearer the water; the smaller **Sunset Hotel**, ☎ 23 013, 🖷 23 931 (D; exp-mod), has a terrace café where they will cook to your order. **Matthew Taverna** is slick and well patronized.

Favourite of Jane Fonda is the **Princess of Mýkonos**, ☎ 23 806, 🖷 23 031 (*B; lux*), at Ag. Stefanós, with pool, sauna, Jacuzzi and the works. It isn't in the heart of the action, but only a taxi-ride away; nearby, the **Hotel Artemis**, ☎ 22 345, 🖷 23 865 (*C; exp-mod*), has clean if uninspiring rooms with big balcony; there are various tavernas along the beach.

Further north, just before Fanári at Choulakia beach, little **Vaggeli**, ☎ 22 458, 🖷 25 558 (*mod*), is quiet, small and very Greek, with a good restaurant.

South Coast Beaches

At Ag. Ioannis beach, **Manoula's Beach**, ☎ 22 900, 🖷 24 314 (*C; exp–mod*), is the pretty bungalow complex where they filmed *Shirley Valentine*. There are also a couple of tavernas, with boat trips and beach parties on the menu. At Ornós, the **Ornós Beach Hotel**, ☎ 23 216, 🖷 22 243 (*B; lux-exp*), has stylish, traditionally designed rooms, pool and private beach, while **Kivotos**, ☎ 24 094, 🖷 22 844 (*C; lux*), is one of the 'Small Luxury Hotels of the World' with Olympic squash courts, antique shops and a wet bar in the seawater pool; another choice, **Yannaki**, ☎ 23 393, 🖷 24 628 (*C; exp*), is away from Ornós centre, with a tranquil pool and mod cons. At Platís Gialós, the Petinos Group offers various levels of luxury: the ritzy **Petinos Beach**, ☎ 24 310, 🖷 23 680, *george55@otenet.gr* (*A; lux–exp*), is a pastel paradise with every facility, including pool, and water sports; **Hotel Argo**, ☎ 23 405, 🖷 24 936 (*E; exp*), is friendly, clean and the owner swears there will be a pool before long; **Studios Katerina**, ☎ 24 086, 🖷 27 486 (*mod*), offer pleasant self-catering facilities set back from the beach.

In Parága, the classy **San Giorgio**, ☎ 27 474, 🖷 27 481 (*A; lux*), has a sea-water pool and all comforts, including mini-bars, while **Zephyros**, ☎ 23 928, 🖷 24 902 (*C; exp*), has a pool at more manageable prices. At Kalafatis, **Anemoessa**, ☎/🖷 71 420 (*exp*), is built in the Cycladic style, with pool and Jacuzzi, and serves a big American buffet breakfast. The Italian seafood restaurant **Marcos** is an old standby. In nearby Ag. Ánna, at the end of the road that crosses the island, **Nikola's** is authentic and a local favourite. The **Ano Mera** at Áno Merá, ☎ 71 113, 🖷 71 276 (*A; mod*), is a cavernous building offering remarkable value given its Olympic-size pool, restaurant and disco. The Stavrokopóulos family has two Áno Merá eateries: **Stavros**, on the square, is recommended, while **Vangelis Taverna** is set back and more of a grill house. All campers are referred to the barracks-like **Paradise Beach**, ☎ 22 582, 🖷 24 350, and nearby the preferable **Mykonos Camping**, Parága Beach, ☎ 24 578. Both have good facilities, minibuses and continuous boat service from Platís Gialós.

Plunge into the old town's labyrinth for no end of quaint café/bars for that evening drink or ice cream; **L'Unico** is one, opposite Ag. Kyriaki. An open-air cinema also operates in season. The international and gay set still bop the night away in venues ranging from the cosy to the crazy. The waterfront from Cathedral Square to Paraportiani is lined with inviting places for sunset conoisseurs, amongst which **Veranda Bar** in a converted mansion is a place to relax with a pleasant view of the windmills too, and **Kastro's** in Little Venice will be forever famous for its sunset views, classical sounds and strawberry daiquiris; if you prefer piña coladas, try **Katerina's** next door. **Bolero**, in the centre of town, has good music and cocktails; Live music and snazzy cocktails can be had at the **Piano Bar** above taxi square, but get there early for a seat; **Monna Lisa**, also here, plays lots of salsa and other Latin numbers. High-tech **Astra Bar** is a cool place to be seen, along with **Aígli**, opposite. The **City Club** has a nightly transvestite show, although the sexiest stuff provocatively struts its way along the bar at **Icarus**, above Pierro's (*see* below). The perennial favourite, **Mykonos Dancing Bar**, plays Greek music, while **Zorba's** has live *rembétika*. **Mud Club**, in taxi square, is good for shakin' your thang, but **Pierro's**, just back from the main waterfront, remains the most frenzied of the lot, where hordes gyrate to the loud, lively music and spill out into the square.

Délos (ΔΗΛΟΣ)

Délos, holy island of the ancient Greeks, centre of the great maritime alliance of the Athenian golden age, and hub of the Cyclades, is now a vast open-air museum. A major free port in Hellenistic and Roman times that controlled much of the east–west trade in the Mediterranean, today it is completely deserted except for the lonely guardian of the ruins—and the boatloads of day-trippers. Even though the ancients allowed no burials on Délos, the islet is haunted by memories of the 'splendour that was Greece'; the Delians themselves seem to have been reincarnated as little lizards, darting among the poppies and pieces of broken marble.

Mythology

Zeus, they say, once fancied a very ancient moon goddess named Asteria. Asteria fled him in the form of a quail, and Zeus turned himself into an eagle the better to pursue her. The pursuit proved so hot that Asteria the quail turned into a rock and fell into the sea. But Asteria, in an older version of the story, was actually the sacred ship of the sky, crewed by the first Hyperborians, who after thousands of years alighted in Egypt and sailed up the Nile to this spot. The ship-rock was called Ortygia ('quail') or Adélos, 'the invisible', as it floated all over Greece like a submarine just below the sea's surface.

Zeus subsequently fell in love with Asteria's sister Leto, and, despite the previous failure of the bird motif, succeeded in making love to her in the form of a swan—the subject of some of the most erotic fancies produced by Michelangelo and other artists in the Renaissance. But Zeus' humourless, jealous, Thurberesque wife Hera soon got wind of the affair and begged Mother Earth not to allow Leto to give birth anywhere under the sun. All over the world wandered poor, suffering, overripe Leto, unable to find a rock to stand on, as all feared the wrath of Hera. Finally in pity Zeus turned to his brother Poseidon and asked him to lend a hand. Poseidon thereupon ordered Ortygia to halt, and anchored the islet with four columns of diamond. Thus Adélos the Invisible, not under the sun but under the sea, became Délos, or 'visible'. Délos, however, was still reluctant to host Leto, fearing her divine offspring would give the island a resounding kick back into the sea. But Leto promised the islet that no such thing would happen; indeed, her son would make Délos the richest sanctuary in Greece. The island conceded, and Leto gave birth first to Artemis, goddess of the hunt and virginity, and then nine days later to Apollo, the god of reason and light.

History

In the 3rd millennium BC Délos was settled by people from Caria in Asia Minor. By 1000 BC the Ionians had made it their religious capital, centred around the cult of Apollo, the father of Ion, the founder of their race—a cult first mentioned in a Homeric hymn of the 7th century BC. Games and pilgrimages took place, and Délos was probably the centre of the Amphictyonic maritime league of the Ionians. In 550 BC Polycrates, the Tyrant of Samos, conquered the Cyclades but respected the sanctity of Délos, putting the islet Rheneia under its control, and symbolically binding it to Délos with a chain. With the rise of Athens, notably under Pisistratos, Délos knew its greatest glory and biggest headaches. What was once sacred became political as the Athenians invented stories to connect themselves to the islet—did not Erechtheus, the King of Athens, lead the first delegation to Délos? After slaying the Minotaur on Crete did not Theseus stop at Délos and dance around the altar of Apollo? In 543 BC the Athenians even managed to trick (or bribe) the oracle at Delphi into ordering the purification of the island, which meant removing the old tombs, a manoeuvre designed to alienate the Delians from their past and diminish the island's importance in comparison to Athens.

In 490 BC the population of Délos fled to Tínos before the Persian king of kings, Darius, who, according to Herodotus, not only respected the sacred site and sacrificed 300 talents' worth of incense to Apollo, but allowed the Delians to return home in safety. After the Persian defeat at the Battle of Salamis the Athenians, to counter further invasions, organized a new Amphictyonic league, again centred at Délos. Only the Athenian fleet could guarantee protection to the islands, who in return were required to contribute a yearly sum and ships to support the navy; Athenian archons administered the funds. The Delian alliance was effective, despite resentment amongst islanders who disliked being bossed around by the Athenians. No one was fooled in 454 BC when Pericles, in order better to 'protect' the league's treasury, removed it to Athens' acropolis; the money went not only to repair damage incurred during the previous Persian invasion, but to beautify Athens generally. Shortly afterwards, divine retribution hit Athens in the form of a terrible plague, and as it was determined to have been caused by the wrath of Apollo, a second purification of Délos (not Athens, mind) was called for in 426 BC. This time, not only did the Athenians remove all the old tombs, but they forbade both birth and death on Délos, forcing the pregnant and the dying to go to Rheneia and completing the alienation of the Delians. When the people turned to Sparta for aid during the Peloponnesian War,

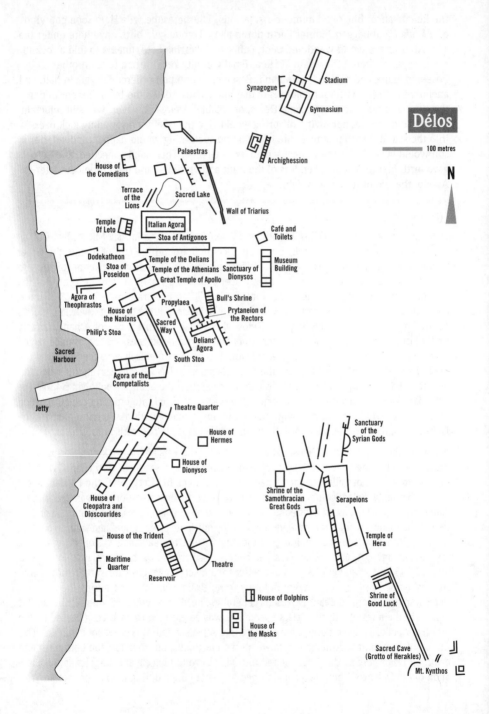

Délos

100 metres

N

Stadium
Synagogue
Gymnasium
Archighession
Palaestras
House of
the Comedians
Terrace
of the
Lions
Sacred Lake
Wall of Triarius
Temple
Of Leto
Italian Agora
Café and
Toilets
Stoa of Antigonos
Dodekatheon
Museum
Building
Stoa of
Poseidon
Temple of the Delians
Temple of the Athenians
Sanctuary of
Great Temple of Apollo
Dionysos
Agora of
Theophrastos
Propylaea
Bull's Shrine
House of
the Naxians
Prytaneion of
the Rectors
Sacred
Way
Philip's Stoa
Delians'
Agora
Sacred
Harbour
South Stoa
Agora of the
Competalists
Jetty
Theatre Quarter
Sanctuary
of the
Syrian Gods
House of
Hermes
House of
Dionysos
Shrine of the
Samothracian
Great Gods
Serapeions
House of
Cleopatra and
Dioscourides
House of the Trident
Temple of
Hera
Maritime
Quarter
Theatre
Reservoir
House of Dolphins
Shrine of
Good Luck
House of
the Masks
Sacred Cave
(Grotto of Herakles)
Mt. Kynthos

380

the Spartans remained unmoved: since the inhabitants couldn't be born or die on the island, they reasoned that Délos wasn't really their homeland, and why should they help a group of foreigners? In 422 BC Athens punished Délos for courting Sparta by exiling the entire population (for being 'impure') to Asia Minor, where all the leaders were slain by cunning. Athenian settlers moved in to take the Delians' place, but Athens herself was punished by the gods for her greed and suffered many setbacks against Sparta. After a year, hoping to regain divine favour, Athens allowed the Delians to return. In 403 BC, when Sparta defeated Athens, Délos had a breath of freedom for 10 years before Athens formed its second Delian alliance. It was far less forceful, and 50 years later the Delians had plucked up the courage to ask the league to oust the Athenians altogether. But the head of the league at the time, Philip II of Macedon, refused the request, wishing to stay in the good graces of the city that hated him most.

In the confusion following the death of Philip's son, Alexander the Great, Délos became free and prosperous, supported by the pious Macedonian general-kings. New buildings and shrines were constructed and by 250 BC Délos was a flourishing cosmopolitan commercial port, inhabited by merchants from all over the Mediterranean. When the Romans defeated the Macedonians in 166 BC they returned the island to Athens, which once again exiled the Delians. But by 146 BC and the fall of Corinth, Délos was the centre of all east–west trade, and declared a free port by the Romans in order to undermine the competition at Rhodes. People came from all over the world to settle in this ancient Greek Hong Kong, and set up their own cults in complete tolerance. Roman trade guilds centred on the Italian Agora. New quays and piers were constructed in order to deal with the heavy flow of vessels. The slave markets thrived.

In the battle of the Romans against Mithridates of Pontus in 88 BC, Délos was robbed of many of her treasures; 20,000 people were killed, and the women and children carried off as slaves. This was the beginning of the end. Sulla regained the island, but 19 years later Délos was again pillaged by pirates allied to Mithradates, who once more sold the population into slavery. General Triarius retook the island and fortified it with walls, and Hadrian attempted to revive the waning cult of Apollo with new festivities, but by this time wretched Délos had fallen into such a decline that, when Athens tried to sell it, no one offered to buy. In AD 363, Emperor Julian the Apostate tried to jumpstart paganism one last time on Délos until the oracles warned: 'Délos shall become Adélos.' Later Theodosius the Great banned heathen ceremonies altogether. A small Christian community survived until the 6th century, when it was given over to the rule of pirates. House-builders on Tínos and Mýkonos used Délos for a marble quarry, and its once busy markets became a pasture.

After the War of Independence, Délos and Rhéneia were placed in the municipality of Mýkonos. Major archaeological excavations were begun in 1872 by the French School of Archaeology in Athens under Dr Lebeque, and work continues to this day.

Getting There and Around

By sea: tourist boats from Mýkonos leave between 8.30am and 1pm daily (except on Mon), returning between 12noon and 3pm, for around 1,900dr return. Guided tours (*4,500dr*) are available from agencies, or alternatively hire a **private boat** at the main harbour.

The Excavations

*A trip to **Délos** (© (0289) 22 259, open Tues–Sun 8.30–3 begins as you clamber out of the caique and pay the 1,500dr entrance fee. Sensible shoes, sunhat, and water are essential. The quality of 'official' guides varies, and you have to fit in with their timetables. Major sites are labelled, badly translated guidebooks are on sale, and everything of interest can be seen in two or three hours. The site can be overrun in the summer. To get your bearings head up the hill, **Mount Kýthnos**, which has a great view over the site and the neighbouring islands of Mýkonos, Tínos and Sýros.*

To your left from the landing stage is the **Agora of the Competalists**. *Compita* were Roman citizens or freed slaves who worshipped the Lares Competales, or crossroads gods. These Lares gods were the patrons of Roman trade guilds, while others came under the protection of Hermes, Apollo or Zeus; many of the remains in the Agora were votive offerings built to them. A road, once lined with statues, leads from here to the sanctuary of Apollo. To the left of the road stood a tall and splendid Doric colonnade called **Philip's Stoa**, built by Philip V of Macedon in 210 BC, and now marked only by its foundations; it once held a votive statue dedicated by Sulla after his victory over Mithridates. The kings of Pergamon built the **Southern Stoa** in the 3rd century BC, and you can also make out the remains of the **Delians' Agora**, the local marketplace in the area.

The **Sanctuary of Apollo** is announced by the **Propylaea**, a gateway built of white marble in the 2nd century BC. Little remains of the sanctuary itself, once crowded with temples, votive offerings and statues. Next door is the **House of the Naxians** (6th century BC). A huge *kouros*, or statue of Apollo as a young man, originally stood here, of which only the pedestal remains. According to Plutarch, the *kouros* was crushed when a nearby bronze palm donated by Athens (symbolic of the tree clutched by Leto in giving birth) toppled over in the wind.

Next are three temples in a row. The first and largest, the **Great Temple of Apollo**, was begun by the Delians in 476 BC. The second was an **Athenian Temple** of Pentelic marble, built during the Second Purification, and the smallest, of porous stone, the **Temple of the Delians**, was made by the 6th-century Athenian tyrant Pisistratos to house the sacred *Asteria*, the 'ship of the sky', represented by a moon setting in the sea. Dimitrios the Besieger contributed the nearby **Bull's Shrine**, which held a model of another ship, a trireme in honour of the sacred Athenian delegation ship—the one Theseus sailed in on his return to Athens after slaying the Minotaur, and whose departure put off executions (most famously that of Socrates) until its return to Athens. Other buildings in the area were of an official nature—the **Prytaneion of the Rectors** and the **Councillor's House**. Towards the museum is the **Sanctuary of Dionysos** (4th century BC), flanked by lucky marble phalli. The **Stoa of Antigonos** was built by a Macedonian king of that name in the 3rd century BC. Outside is the **Tomb of the Hyperborean Virgins,** who came to help Leto give birth to Apollo and Artemis, a sacred tomb and thus the only one to stay put during the purifications.

On the opposite side of the Stoa stood the **Abaton**, the holy of holies, where only the priests could enter. The **Minoan Fountain** nearby is from the 6th century BC. Through the **Italian Agora** you can reach the **Temple of Leto** (6th century) and the **Dodekatheon**, dedicated to the 12 gods of Olympos in the 3rd century BC. Beyond, where the **Sacred Lake** once hosted a flock of swans, is the famous **Terrace of the Lions**, ex-votos made from Naxian marble in the 7th century BC; originally nine, one now sits by the arsenal in Venice and three have permanently gone missing. The site of the lake, sacred for having witnessed the birth of Apollo, is marked by a small wall. When Délos' torrent Inopos stopped flowing, the water evaporated. Along the shore are two **Palaestras** (for exercises and lessons) along with the foundation of the **Archigession**, or temple to the first mythical settler on Délos, worshipped only here. Besides the **Gymnasium** and **Stadium** are remains of a few houses and a **synagogue** built by the Phoenician Jews in the 2nd century BC.

A dirt path leads from the tourist pavilion to Mount Kýthnos. Along the way stand the ruins of the **Sanctuary of the Syrian Gods** of 100 BC, with a small religious theatre inside. Next is the first of three 2nd-century BC **Serapeions**, all temples dedicated to Serapis, the first and only successful god purposely invented by man—Ptolemy I of Egypt, who combined Osiris with Dionysos to create a synthetic deity to please both Hellenistic Greeks and Egyptians; syncretic Délos was one of the chief centres of his worship. Between the first and second Serapeions is the **Shrine to the Samothracian Great Gods**, the Cabiri or underworld deities. The third Serapeion (still housing half a statue) was perhaps the main sanctuary, with temples to both Serapis and Isis. In the region are houses with mosaic floors, and a **Temple to Hera** from 500 BC. The **Sacred Cave**, where Apollo ran one of his many oracles, is en route to the top of Mount Kýthnos, later it was dedicated to Heracles. On the mountain itself is the **Shrine of Good Luck**, built by Arsinoë Philadelphos, wife of her brother, the King of Egypt. On the 113m summit signs of a settlement dating back to 3000 BC have been discovered, but better yet is the view, encompassing nearly all the Cyclades.

The exclusive **Theatre Quarter** surrounded the 2nd-century BC **Theatre of Délos**, with a 5500 capacity; beside it is a lovely eight-arched **reservoir**. The houses here date from the Hellenistic and Roman ages and many have mosaics, some beautifully preserved, such as in the **House of the Dolphins** and the **House of the Masks**. All have a cistern beneath the floor, spaces for oil lamps and sewage systems. Some are built in the peristyle 'style of Rhodes', with a high-ceilinged guest room and colonnades surrounding the central courts, which are left open to the sun. Seek out the **House of the Trident** and the **House of Dionysos**, both with mosaics, and the **House of Cleopatra and Dioscourides**, where the statues stand a headless guard over the once-great town.

Surrounding Délos are the islets **Ag. Geórgios** (named after its monastery), **Karavoníssi**, **Mikró** and **Megálo Rematiáris**, the last consecrated to Hecate, the Queen of the Night. **Rhéneia**, also known as Greater Délos, lies just west of Délos and is just as uninhabited. Here came the pregnant or dying Delians—a large number of little rooms were excavated in the rock to receive them, before they moved into the realm of tombs and sepulchral altars. A necropolis near the shore was the repository of the coffins which the Athenians exhumed in the second purification. On the other side of Rhéneia are the ruins of a lazaretto (leprosy hospital), once used by Sýros-bound ships sent into quarantine.

Where to Stay and Eating Out

You can't. Near the museum there's an overpriced café for the tourists. Don't be caught out; bring snacks and plenty of water with you.

Páros (ΠΑΡΟΣ)

Despite the tens of thousands who descend on Páros each summer, the Cycladic houses, narrow alleys, little bridges and balconies overflowing with potted plants seem to dilute their presence. The Parians have approached the boom in tourism with less fervour than their neighbours on Mýkonos, managing, against overwhelming odds, to maintain a Greek island atmosphere. The inhabitants have, for the most part, remained fun-loving and hospitable and, if you can find a place to stay, it's a fine spot to while away a few days on golden beaches and charming villages, whose main building material comes from Páros' gentle mountain, Profítis Ilías (771m)—some of the finest, most translucent marble in the world, prized by classical sculptors and architects. Páros is one of the larger and more fertile Cyclades, with vineyards, wheat and barley fields, citrus and olive groves, and—an unusual sight in the archipelago—pastures of grazing cattle and sheep. Apart from its beaches, the island has several other attractions, including a famous Byzantine cathedral and a valley filled with butterflies.

History

With the trade in Parian marble, the island of Páros prospered early on. Its thriving Early Cycladic town was connected with Knossós and then with the Mycenaeans in the Late Cycladic period (1100 BC). In the 8th century BC Ionians moved in and brought about a second wave of prosperity. The 7th-century BC soldier poet Archilochos, the first to write in iambic

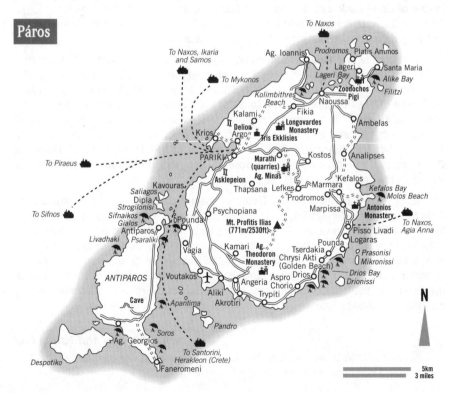

meter and whose ironic detachment inspired Horace, was a son of Páros. During the Persian Wars, Páros supported the Persians at both Marathon and Salamis; when Athens' proud General Miltiades came to punish them after Marathon, they withstood his month-long siege, forcing Miltiades to retire with a broken leg that developed into the gangrene that killed him. During the Peloponnesian Wars Páros remained neutral until forced to join the second Delian league in 378 BC. The island produced the great sculptor Skopas in the Hellenistic period and did well until Roman times, exporting marble to make the Temple of Solomon, the *Venus de Milo*, the temples on Délos and, much later, part of Napoleon's tomb. When the Romans took over Páros, their main concern was to take over the marble business.

Later invasions and destructions left the island practically deserted, and after 1207 the Venetian Sanudos ruled Páros from Náxos. Barbarossa captured the island in 1536, and from then on the Turks ruled by way of their proxy, the duke of Náxos, although his control was often shaky, especially in the 1670s, when Páros was the base of Hugues Chevaliers, the inspiration for Byron's *Corsair*. In 1770, the Parians had to put up with more unlikely visitors when the Russian fleet wintered on the island. During the War of Independence Mandó Mavroyénous, whose parents were from Páros and Mýkonos, led guerrilla attacks against the Turks throughout Greece; after the war she returned to Páros and died there.

℗ (0284–) **Getting There**

By air: two to seven flights daily in season from Athens with Olympic, ℗ 21 900; flights most days withh Hellenic Star, Avant Travel, ℗ 22 302. **Airport**: ℗ 91 256; bus to and from Parikiá seven times daily.

By sea: frequent boats to Antipáros from Parikiá and Poúnda. **Port authority**: ℗ 21 240. Vacances Horizon International, ℗ 24 968, @ 24 969, *vhigr@yahoo.com*, offers cruises around Antipáros and neighbouring islets, as well as boat rental.

By road: frequent **buses** depart from the portside to all the towns and villages, and connect Náoussa and Dríos, ℗ 21 395. Beware that if you want to **hire a car or bike**, some places are ripe rip-offs; Cyclades, on the waterfront towards Livádi, ℗ 21 057, and Páros Europecar, by the port, ℗ 24 408, @ 22 544, are among the more reliable.

℗ (0284–) **Tourist Information**

Tourist police: Plateía Mandó Mavroyénous, Parikiá, ℗ 23 333. **Information offices**: by the bus station in Náoussa, ℗ 52 158, @ 51 190 (*open 10.30–2.30 and 5–9 but potentially all day soon*). The Parikiá branch (by the windmill) is invariably closed. For up-to-date details of events, bus schedules and ex-pat chit-chat, pick up a copy of *The Foreigner.*

Internet: costly on Páros, but offered by several Parikiá waterfront joints and Calypso Café in Náoussa.

Post office: on the waterfront, between the port and Lividia. **OTE**: surrounded by card phones on the main square.

Ecology/Diving: diver/oceanographer Peter Nicolaides runs the Aegean Diving College from Chryssi Akti, ℗ (0932) 289 649, *aegeandive@otenet.gr*, offering a plethora of courses, from snorkelling to scuba to marine ecology, as well as dive expeditions. He also does terrestrial ecology courses and walks exploring Páros' bio-diversity and geological structures, meals included.

Riding: offered in Parikiá (*see* below) and by Kokou Riding, ✆ 51 818, in Náoussa.

Festivals
23 April, Ag. Geórgios in Agkairia; **21 May**, Ag. Konstantínos in Parikiá; **Good Friday–Easter**, in Marpissa, with re-enactments of the Crucifixion; **40 days after Orthodox Easter**, Análypsis in Píso Livádi; **15 August**, Ekatontapylianí in Parikiá; **23 August** Náoussa sea battle; **29 August**, Ag. Ioánnis in Léfkas.

Parikiá

Parikiá (ΠΑΡΟΙΚΙΑ), the island's chief town and main port, still greets arrivals with its old, now empty windmill. Behind it, however, the town has quintupled in size in the last couple of decades, so obscuring the original version that it's almost been forgotten; the locals have put up signs pointing the way to the 'Traditional Settlement'. Once you've found it, Parikiá shows itself to be a Cycladic beauty, traversed by a long, winding main street that invites leisurely exploration, without having to trudge up a single stair. The centrepiece in the heart of town are the walls of the **Venetian Kástro**, built wholesale out of the white marble temples of Apollo and Demeter into an attractive collage of columns and pediments; a tiny white chapel tucked underneath adds to the effect. Three more windmills close off the waterfront on the south end of town, where the ouzeries are a popular evening rendezvous.

Most of Parikiá's sprawling, in the form of hotels, bars and restaurants, has happened in the direction of **Livádia** and its tamarisk-lined beach, although if you continue along the strand past the main tourist ghetto to Argo, café life becomes much more relaxed. While digging here in 1983, part of the **ancient cemetery** was uncovered, in use from the 8th century BC to the 3rd AD; it lies below sea level and has to be constantly drained. More recently, in the course of building a new pier, a Doric-style temple with foundations the size of the Parthenon has been unearthed. If you get fed up with the crowds you can ride away; there's a riding stable nearby (ask at the Scouna restaurant, ✆ (0284) 570 981).

The Church of a Hundred Doors and the Archaeology Museum
Set back between Livádi and the 'Traditional Settlement' is Páros' chief monument, the cathedral **Ekatontapylianí** or 'Church of a Hundred Doors', hidden behind a modern wall (*open 8–1 and 4–9, additional clothing provided for the scantily clad*). In 326, St Helen, mother of the Emperor Constantine, was sailing from Rome to the Holy Land when her ship put into Páros during a storm. She prayed that if her journey was a success and she found the True Cross she was seeking, she would build a church on Páros. She did, and told Constantine her promise, and he dutifully built a church. What stands today is a 6th-century building by the Byzantine Emperor Justinian. The story goes that he hired an architect named Ignatius, an apprentice of the master builder of Ag. Sophia in Constantinople, and when the master came to view his pupil's work, he was consumed by jealousy and pushed Ignatius off the roof—but not before Ignatius had seized his foot and dragged him down as well. They are represented by two bizarre figures under the columns of the marble gate to the north of the church, one holding his head and the other covering his mouth; some say they are really satyrs taken from an old temple of Dionysos that originally stood here.

In 1966, the church, more human in scale by far than Ag. Sophia, was restored to approximately its 6th-century appearance, with its dome on pendentives and a women's gallery running along the nave. Originally the interior was entirely covered with gleaming white marble. Another story says that only 99 entrances (anything a mouse could squeeze in apparently counts) have ever been found but once the 100th is discovered, Constantinople will return to the Greeks. In fact, the name itself is a 17th-century Greek fantasy; the original was probably *Katapoliani*, 'towards the ancient city'.

The marble iconostasis has an especially venerated icon of the black Virgin, silver-plated and worked all around with intricate little scenes (all made in Bucharest, in 1788); you can see frescoes and a marble ciborium, with a little marble amphitheatre behind it, known as a *synthronon*—in the earliest churches, before the iconostasis totally blocked the view of the sacred area, the high priest and clergy used to stand and sit here. In an alcove in the north wall is the tomb of the 9th-century Ag. Theóktisti. A nun captured by pirates on Lésbos, Theóktisti managed to flee into the forests of Páros, when the ship landed for water. For 35 years she lived a pious existence in the wilderness. A hunter finally found her, and when he brought her the communion bread she requested, she lay down and died. Unable to resist a free saintly relic, the hunter cut off her hand and made to sail away, but he was unable to depart until he had returned it to the saint's body. The **Baptistry** to the right of the church has a 4th-century sunken cruciform font—the oldest one in Orthodoxy—adult-size, with steps leading down, and a column for the priest to stand on; baptism of children only began in the reign of Justinian.

Off the courtyard in front of the church is the little **Byzantine Museum** (*open 9–1 and 5–9; adm*); behind the church and next to the school, a row of sarcophagi marks the **Archaeology Museum** (*open Tues–Sun 8.30–2.30; adm*), containing a section of the renowned 'Parian Chronicles'—an art-orientated history of Greece from Kerkops (*c.* 1500 BC) to Diognetos (264 BC) carved in marble tablets and discovered in the 17th century; to read the rest you'll have to go to the Ashmolean in Oxford. There are finds from the temple of Apollo, a mosaic of the Labours of Hercules, found under the Ekatontapylianí, a 5th-century BC Winged Victory, a 7th-century BC amphora with the Judgement of Paris and swastikas (ancient solar symbols) going every which way and a segment of a monument dedicated to Archilochos, who took part in the colonization of Thássos by Páros before he turned to lyric poetry.

Archilochos was buried along the road to Náoussa; in the 4th-century BC a *heröon*, or tomb-shrine of a hero or notable, was erected over his tomb, and in turn, in the 7th-century, the basilica **Tris Ekklisíes** (or Ag. Charálambos) was built over the site. Northeast of Parikiá the marble foundation and altar mark the **Temple of Delian Apollo**. Together with temples to Apollo on Délos and Náxos, it forms part of a perfect equilateral triangle. One of the triangle's altitudes extends to Mycenae and Rhodes town, site of the Colossus—the biggest of all the statues of Apollo. Another heads up to holy Mount Áthos.

Náoussa

Frequent buses connect Parikiá with the island's second port, the lovely fishing village turned jet-set hang-out of **Náoussa** (ΝΑΟΥΣΑ). In 1997 it made history as the first place where the Greek government at last clamped down on shoddy indiscriminate building. Near the harbour stand the half-submerged ruins of the Venetian castle, with colourful caiques bobbing below and octopus hung out the dry for later scorching into chewy titbits to accompany ouzo. West of town is a winter flamingo haven. On the night of 23 August 100 boats lit by torches re-enact the islanders' battle against the pirate Barbarossa, storming the harbour, but all ends in merriment, music and dance. Náoussa's church **Ag. Nikólaos Mostrátos** has an excellent collection of icons.

There are beaches within walking distance of Náoussa, or you can make sea excursions to others, notably **Kolimbíthres,** with its bizarre, wind-sculpted rocks; other sands nearby are at **Ag. Ioannis** (known as Monastiri beach) and **Lágeri** (take the caique from Náoussa harbour, then walk to the right for about 10 minutes). Lágeri is nudist, a relaxed mix of gay and straight. **Santa Maria** is even further around the coast, with a good windsurfing beach; the fishing village of **Ambelás** has sandy coves, an ancient tower, a taverna and three hotels. Páros' main wine growing area is just south.

Into the Land of Marble

From Parikiá, the main road east leads to Páros' ancient marble quarries at **Maráthi,** not far from the fortified but abandoned monastery of Ag. Mínas. The quarries, re-opened in modern times for the makings of statues and decorations around Napoleon's tomb in the Invalides, are still in use—the longest tunnel stretches 90m underground. It produces the finest of all white marble, called 'Lychnites' by the ancients, or 'candlelit marble', for its translucent quality, admitting light 3.5cm into the stone (light penetrates the second most translucent Carrara marble only 2.5cm). The Venus de Milo, the Victory of Samothrace and the Hermes of Praxiteles are all made of the stuff. Blocks and galleries, some with ancient inscriptions, lie off the road.

The road continues to Páros' attractive medieval capital **Léfkes,** with churches from the 15th century and one made of marble: Ag. Triáda. There's also a small museum (*open in season*) dedicated to another local speciality, here and in nearby Kostos—ceramics—and good walks to be had along the Byzantine road. East of Léfkes, **Pródromos** is an old farming village; **Mármara,** another village, lives up to its name ('marble')—even some of the streets are paved with it. Prettiest of the three, though, is shiny white **Márpissa,** laid out in an amphitheatre. Above its windmills are the ruins of a 15th-century Venetian fortress and the 16th-century **monastery of Ag. Antónios,** constructed out of ancient marbles and containing lovely frescoes (note the 17th-century *Second Coming,* which seems a bit out of place in *bon-vivant* Páros). The ancient city of Páros stood somewhere nearby.

Down on the east coast **Písso Livádi** served as the port for these villages and the marble quarries, and now has excursion boats to Náxos, Mýkonos and Santoríni. It is the centre of Páros' beach colonies: at **Mólos,** just north, luxurious villas line the bay where the Turkish fleet used to put in on its annual tax-collecting tour of the Aegean, while just south at **Poúnda** (not to be confused with the ferry port for Páros) beautiful people flock to a nightclub even bigger than the beach, the hip place for Athenians and foreigners to chill out and pick up. The winds on Páros blow fiercely in July and August, and the next beach, **Tserdakia** (or **Néa Chrysí Aktí**) in particular has become a Mecca for serious windsurfers; early every August since 1993 it has hosted the Professional Windsurfers' World Cup as well as the 'Odyssey' (a windsurfing relay race) which is due to recommence. Just to the south, the island's best beach, **Chrysí Aktí,** 'Golden Beach' stretches 700m. Further south, **Driós** is a pretty green place with a duck-pond, tavernas and sandy coves, and the remains of ancient shipyards.

Southwest of Parikiá

Just south of Parikiá, by a spring, are the ruins of a small classical-era **Asklepeion** (dedicated to the god of healing); originally a temple to Pythian Apollo stood nearby. The road south continues 6km to **Psychopianá** ('Valley of the Butterflies'), where swarms of tiger moths set up housekeeping in July and August and fly up in clouds as you walk by (*open June–Sept 9–8; adm*). Petaloúdes/Psychopianí has the ruins of a Venetian tower, while just outside the village stands the convent of Páros' second patron saint, **Ag. Arsénios**, the schoolteacher, abbot and prophet who was canonized in 1967. The saint is buried in the convent, but this time men are not allowed in. At **Poúnda** there is a beach and the small boat that crosses to Páros. There's another beach at **Alikí** which has some facilities—and the airport, and now, perhaps inevitably, a roadside attraction, the **Historical Museum Scorpios**, with 'animated hand-made miniatures' depicting the old days on Páros (*open 10–2 and 6–8; adm*).

Páros ✆ (0284–)   **Where to Stay and Eating Out**

Páros is packed in the summer, and it may be hard to find a place if you just drop in, although the various well-organized reservations desks on the quay will do their darnedest to find you a place to flop (Rooms Association, ✆/✉ 24 528; Hotels, ✆ 24 555). Beware—in season prices are high. At some point, try Páros' dry white, red or rosé labelled KAVARNIS.

Parikiá ✉ 84400

Fanciest here is **Iria**, 3km from the centre on Parasporos Beach, ✆ 24 154, ✉ 21 167 (*A; exp*), a good family choice with air-conditioned bungalows, playground, tennis, pool and big American breakfasts. If you want a cheaper pool, with billiards thrown in, try **Argo**, on Livadia beach, ✆ 21 367, ✉ 21 207 (*C; exp*). **Argonauta**, ✆ 21 440, ✉ 23 442, *hotel@argonauta.gr* (*C; mod*), just back from the waterfront, is pleasant, with a lovely first-floor courtyard littered with amphorae. **Bayia**, ✆ 21 068 (*C; mod*), is a small family-run hotel, set back on the Náoussa road, surrounded by olive trees. In the old town, **Dina**, ✆ 21 325 (*mod*), is a more modest, charming place with simple rooms. **Kapetan Manolis**, ✆ 21 244, ✉ 25 264 (*C; mod*), is another old-town option, while **Eleni**, ✆ 22 714, ✉ 24 170 (*mod*), has attractive double-balconied rooms near the beach. **Hotel Helliniko**, ✆ 21 429, ✉ 22 743 (*C; mod*), is another reasonable Livádia establishment. Cheaper is **Pension Antoine**, ✆ 24 435 (*inexp*), in the old town near the port, run by a very helpful architect. **Katerina Restaurant** in Livadia, ✆ 22 035 (*inexp*), also has rooms. Páros is especially popular among campers: **Camping Koula**, ✆ 22 082, and friendly **Parasporos**, ✆ 21 100, for the laid back, are near Parikiá, and **Krios Camping**, ✆ 21 705, is at Kríos Beach, opposite the port. Most have minibuses that meet ferries.

To Tamarisko (*mod*), offers good international cuisine in the secluded garden at reasonable prices. **Argonauta**, ✆ 23 303, in the big square by the National Bank, is well known for its fresh fresh food and grills; vegetarians can find sustenance, including good falafel, just behind at the **Happy Green Cow**. The **Levanti** (*exp*), back from the harbour to the right of the Venetian castle walls, has good Greek, French and Lebanese dishes like *tabouleh* and *falafel*. The **Páros**, signposted from Ekatoapylani, serves simple homecooking and seafood under a trellis. **Distrato** bar offers crêpes accompanied by jazz in a shady, old-town square. Alternatively, follow the road round through Livádia to Argo for relaxed beach taverna/bars.

Náoussa and Around ✉ 84401

The island's most luxurious hotel is the **Astir of Páros**, ✆ 51 976, ✉ 51 985 (*A; lux*), on Kolymbíthres beach, with all your heart's desires plus VIP suites and gourmet restaurant. Neo-monastic **Antrides**, ✆ 51 711, ✉ 52 079 (*B; exp*), is comfortably constructed around a pool. **Atlantis**, ✆ 51 340, ✉ 52 087 (*C; exp*), has rooms with verandas facing on to a quiet pool and Jacuzzi. **Kalypso**, on Ag. Anargiri beach, ✆ 51 488, ✉ 51 607, *kalypso@otenet.gr* (*C; exp*), has rooms, studios and suites; **Lilly Apartments**, ✆/✉ 51 377 (*exp*), are nearby and airy. **Petres**, ✆ 52 467, ✉ 52 759 (*C; mod*), is 2km out of town, with comfy air-conditioned rooms, and a pool. **Stella**, ✆/✉ 51 317, *stellaa@otenet.gr* (*D; mod*), has plain, clean rooms in the old town round a shady courtyard, while **Senia Apartments**, ✆ 51 971 (*mod*), are new and airy, with large balconies. Just east in Ambelas, **Miltiadis**, ✆/✉ 52 020 (*mod*), has rooms and apartments in a lush garden. **Galini**, ✆ 51 210 (*C; inexp*), has plain rooms with balcony; **Flora and Maria Pouliou**'s rooms, ✆ 51 118 (*inexp*), have fridge and balcony; also apartments. Náoussa is one of the most picturesque places to eat in all Greece with *ouzeries* chockablock by the water. **Papadakis**, ✆ 51 047, is a wonderful waterfront fish restaurant (book in season). **Barbarossa** also serves tasty fresh fish. **Diamantis** just up the hill serves good food at good prices, with draught wine. Ritzy **Christos** offers seafood and elegant Greek cuisine.

Písso Livádi and East Coast Beaches ✉ 84400

Perantinos Travel, Pisso Livádi, ✆/✉ 41 135, can help with accommodation and other travel queries. *Open Easter–mid-Sept.* **Hotel Aloni**, ✆/✉ 42 438 (*C; exp*), is a nicely done complex with cool blue rooms and some bird's-eye views. **Elena Studios & Apartments**, ✆ 41 082, ✉ 42 363 (*exp*), is another nice set-up, with playground, above town. **Elina Residence**, in the UK contact ✆ (01274) 832771 (*mod*), is a lovely British-owned apartment overlooking the bay with views of Náxos. **Anna Agourou**, ✆ 41 320, ✉ 43 327 (*mod*), has rooms and apartments with good watery views; **Vrohaki** rooms and studios are attractive and quiet, just up the hill, ✆ 41 423 (*mod*). Captain Kafkis has his **Camping** on the way into town, ✆ 41 479. **Mouraghio** is the place to eat fish (*exp*), while **Stavros Taverna** and **Vrochas** are old favourites. Just south in Logarás, **Albatross**, ✆ 41 157, ✉ 41 940 (*C; exp*), has a family-oriented bungalow complex with pool. More modest accommodation is provided by **Free Sun**, ✆ 42 808, ✉ 42 809, and **Stavros** opposite, flanked by storks and with kitchenettes (*both mod*). **Fisilani's** is a good bet for food. Up in Márpissa, **Afendakis Apartments**, ✆/✉ 41 141 (*C; mod*), are beautifully appointed, and dining at **Haroula's**, in the old town, is a joy; **Laini**, just off the main road, has grills, and often live Greek music.

Paros Philoxenia, ✆ 41 778, ✉ 41 978 (*B; exp*), is a hotel-bungalow complex at Tserdakia beach, with surf club, sea sports, and pool. Nearby is **Silver Rocks**, ✆ 41 244, ✉ 41 944, *silverrocks@email.com* (*C; exp*), with similar facilities and kiddies' playground. ΘΕΑ family taverna, nearby in Messadha, will feed you on home-grown fare. **Poseidon**, ✆ 42 650, ✉ 42 649, *poseidon@otenet.gr* (*lux*), is a luxurious apartment complex set in spacious grounds in Chryssí Aktí. Driós has plenty of Cycladic-style rooms, a good taverna on the beach, and the **Anezina**, © 41 037, @ 41 557 (*C; mod*), with a romantic garden restaurant.

Entertainment and Nightlife

Páros has something for everyone, from the rowdy waterfront bars at Parikiá to the sophisticated haunts of Náoussa. Parikiá has an outdoor cinema, **Cine Paros**, set back from the waterfront, as well as the **Rex**; **Black Barts** and the **Salon d'Or** for cocktails on the strip; **Pirate's** for jazz (*open all day and year*); and a quad complex of four disco bars of the **Paros Rock** complex including the **Dubliner**. The music is altogether gentler and more classical at **Pebbles** and **Evinos**, on the waterfront. In the old town, **Simposium** is an august setting for a late ice cream. Along Náoussa's covered-up torrent bed you'll find one of the trendiest nightclub strips in Greece, with **Varrelathiko**, summer headquarters of the hippest club in Athens. Café del Mar, on the waterfront, is a popular drinking hole. The **Golden Garden** at Chryssí Aktí is a popular, laid-back garden bar with a wide range of international sounds; in Písso Livádi **Remezzo** is a favoured watering hole, while **Captain Yannis** offers endless sea views.

Antíparos (ΑΝΤΙΠΑΡΟΣ)

Just a mile to the west, mountainous little Antíparos (the name means 'opposite Páros'), was known as Oliaros when it was first mentioned as a base of Phoenician merchants of Sidon. A deep cave full of stalactites was discovered on Antíparos in antiquity (tradition has it that Antilochos himself was the first to carve his name on a stalactite in the 6th century BC) and ever since it has been a must stop for every traveller in the region. Antíparos is the octopus capital of Greece, and it just may be that the tasty eight-legged, sucker-bedecked mollusc is an unsung aphrodisiac, considering the little island's current reputation. Even the local year-round population is rising, and that, in the Cylcades, is rare.

Getting There and Around

Every two hours or so by **caique** from Parikiá, Páros, and hourly **car ferry** from Pounda, Páros. Buses link the port with the cave. **Port authority**, © (0284) 21 240. Vacances Horizon International cruises around the island (*see* p.385).

Tourist Police

See regular police in town: © (0284) 23 333.

Festivals

23 April, Ag. Geórgios; **8 May**, Ag. Ioánnis Theológos.

Kástro and the Cave

Lacking any defences, Antíparos was uninhabited after the fall of Rome until the Venetians, under Leonardo Lorentani, built a small castle, its thick walls doubling as the outer walls of the houses; **Kástro** is the alternative name of the main settlement. Everyone tos and fros down the Kampiara, the wide street linking the port to the charming square, lined with *ouzeries* and bars. Kástro has a good beach, **Psaralíki**, just south, and another one for skinny-dippers a 5-minute walk north by the campsite. In the late afternoon everyone wanders over to **Sifnaíkos Gialós**, also known as Sunset Beach. The best beach, **Ag. Geórgios,** just south of the cave, is being developed as a resort.

The **cave** (*open daily 10.45–3.45; adm*) remains Antíparos' star attraction, and buses now do the old donkey work of getting you there from the village. Some 400 steps descend 210ft into the fantastic, spooky chamber. The cave is really about twice as deep, but the rest has been closed as too dangerous for visits. Perhaps to make up for breaking off the stalactites, famous visitors of the past have smoked and carved their names on the walls, including Lord Byron and King Otho of Greece (1840). One stalagmite attests in Latin to a Christmas mass celebrated in the cavern by the French ambassador Count Novandel in 1673, attended by 500 (paid) locals. Many inscriptions were lost in 1774, when Russian officers chopped off stalactites as souvenirs, and in the last war, when the Italians and Germans shot up the cave, including one of the oldest, in which its several authors declared that they were hiding in the cave from Alexander the Great, who had accused them of plotting an assassination attempt. The church by the entrance of the cave, **Ag. Ioánnis**, was built in 1774.

Of the islets off Antíparos, **Strogilónisi** and **Despotikó** are rabbit-hunting reserves. On **Sáliagos**, a fishing village from the 5th millennium BC has been excavated by John Evans and Colin Renfrew, the first Neolithic site discovered in the Cyclades.

Antíparos ✉ *84007,* ✆ *(0284–)*   ***Where to Stay and Eating Out***

Antíparos has a desk at Parikiá port, so you can book accommodation before you go, but beware—prices have now risen to match big sister Páros. **Artemis**, ✆ 61 460, 🖷 61 472 (*C; mod–inexp*), is relatively new, 500 yards from the port, and all rooms have fridges and sea-view balconies. Little **Chryssi Akti**, ✆ 61 220 (*C; mod*), is an elegant hotel on the beach; attractive **Mantalena**, ✆ 61 206, 🖷 61 550 (*C; mod*), on the waterfront has tidy rooms, all with bath; just in from the beach, **Bergleri**, ✆ 61 378, 🖷 61 452 (*D; mod*), is similar, with a decent taverna and library of bestsellers. **Antíparos**, ✆ 61 358, 🖷 61 340 (*E; mod–inexp*), all rooms with shower, is simple, with a restaurant and bar. **Korali**, ✆ 61 205 (*E; inexp*), is about the cheapest pension, with a restaurant. There's also a famously laid-back campsite, **Antíparos**, ✆ 61 221, clothes optional; freelancers are tolerated away from town. The **Garden** and **Anargyros** have good food, and the **Time Marine Beach Bar** and **Café Yam** are popular hang outs. Soros and Ag. Georgios beaches also have summer tavernas, of which **Captain Pipinos**, facing Despotikó, is a good bet.

Santoríni/Thíra (ΣΑΝΤΟΡΙΝΙΗ/ΘΗΡΑ)

> *…We found ourselves naked on the pumice stone*
> *watching the rising islands*
> *watching the red islands sink*
> *into their sleep, into our sleep.*
>
> George Seféris, *Santoríni*

As many people's favourite Greek island, the pressure is on Santoríni to come up with the goods. And it does. The awesome mixture of sinister multi-coloured volcanic precipices,

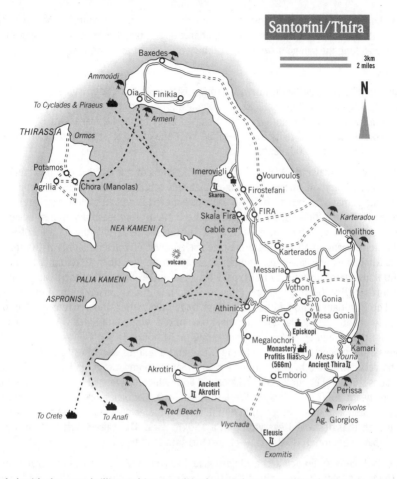

3km
2 miles

N

Baxedes
Ammoúdi
Oia Finikia
To Cyclades & Piraeus
Armeni
THIRASSIA Ormos
Potamos
Agrilia Chora (Manolas)
Imerovigli Vourvoulos
Skaros Firostefani
FIRA
Skala Fira Karteradou
NEA KAMENI Cable car Monolithos
volcano Karterados
PALIA KAMENI Messaria
Vothon
ASPRONISI Exo Gonia
Athinios Mesa Gonia
Pirgos
Episkopi
Megalochori
Monastery Kamari
Profitis Ilias Mesa Vouna
(566m) Ancient Thira
Akrotiri Emborio
Ancient Perissa
Akrotiri
Perivolos
To Crete Red Beach Ag. Giorgios
To Anafi Vlychada
Eleusis
Exomitis

dappled with the most brilliant-white, trendiest bars and restaurants in the country, gives the island a splendid kind of schizophrenia; forget *Under the Volcano*, here you're teetering on the edge. Usually bathed in glorious sunshine, but occasionally lashed by high winds and rain, everything seems more intense here, especially daily life. Some call it Devil's Island, and find a stay here both exhilarating and disturbing. And it's the honeymoon capital of Greece.

There are plenty of flights, but there's nothing like arriving by sea. As your fragile ship sails into the caldera, Santoríni looms like a chocolate layer cake with an enormous bite taken out of it, frosted with coconut cream towns slipping over the edge, while the charred islands opposite look suitably infernal. All of this little archipelago has, literally, had its ups and downs: throughout history parts have seismatically appeared and disappeared under the waves. Human endeavours have fared similarly: you can visit no fewer than three former 'capitals'— the Minoan centre of Akrotíri, a favourite candidate for Metropolis, the capital of Atlantis; the classical capital Thíra at Mésa Vouná; and the medieval Skáros, as well as the picturesque modern town of Firá, perched on the rim. But this, too, was flattened by an earthquake in 1956. Although the island is now a must on the cruise ship itinerary, older inhabitants can remember still when Santoríni hosted more political prisoners than tourists, and nights were filled with the rumour of vampires rather than the chatter of café society sipping Bloody Marys, watching the sun go down in one of the world's most enchanting settings.

History

In the long-distant past Santoríni was a round island, with a crater called Strogyle in the centre. Its regular eruptions created a rich, volcanic soil, which attracted inhabitants early on—from Karia originally, until they were chased away by the Minoans. One of the Cretan towns was at Akrotíri. Its rediscovery resulted from one of the most intriguing archaeological detective stories of the 20th century.

In 1939, while excavating Amnisós, the port of Knossós on the north coast of Crete, Greek archaeologist Spirýdon Marinátos realized that only a massive natural disaster could have caused the damage he found. At first Marinátos believed it was an earthquake, but over the years evidence of a different kind of catastrophe came in: southeast of Santoríni oceanographers discovered volcanic ash from Strogyle on the sea bed, covering an area of 900 by 300km; on nearby Anáfi and Eastern Crete itself a layer of volcanic tephra 3–20mm thick covers Minoan New Palace sites. Another clue came from the Athenian reformer Solon, who in 600 BC wrote of his journey to Egypt, where the scribes told him of the disappearance of Kreftia (Crete?) 9000 years before, a figure Solon might have mistaken for a more correct 900. The Egyptians, who had had important trade links with Minoan Crete and Santoríni, told Solon about the lost land of Atlantis, made of red, white and black volcanic rock (like Santoríni today) and spoke of a city vanishing in 24 hours. In his *Critias*, Plato described Atlantis as being composed of one round island and one long island, a sweet country of art and flowers connected by one culture and rule (Santoríni and Crete, under Minos?). Lastly, Marinátos studied the eruption of Krakatoa in 1883, which blew its lid with such force that it could be heard 3000 miles away in Western Australia. Krakatoa's volcano formed a caldera of 8.3sq km, and as the sea rushed in to fill the caldera, it created a *tsunami* or tidal wave over 200m high that destroyed everything in a 150km path. The caldera left by Strogyle (the present bay of Santoríni) is 22sq km—almost three times as big.

In the 19th century French archaeologists had discovered Minoan vases at Akrotíri, and it was there that Marinátos began to dig in 1967, seeking to prove the chronology of his theory: that Minoan civilization owed its sudden decline to the eruption, earthquakes, and tidal waves caused by the explosion of Santoríni in *c.* 1450 BC. Marinátos hoped to unearth a few vases. Instead he found something beyond his wildest dreams: an entire Minoan colony buried in tephra, complete with dazzling frescoes.

The rest of the island's history has been fairly calm by comparison. In the 8th century BC the Dorians settled the island, naming it Thíra, building their capital at Mésa Vouná, and colonizing the city of Cyrene in Libya. The Byzantines covered the island with castles, but the Venetians under the Crispi got it anyway. Skáros near Imerovígli was their capital and Irene their patron saint, hence the island's second name, Santoríni, which has stuck as hard as officialdom tries to change it back to the classical era Thíra.

© *(0286–)*   ***Getting There and Around***

By air: daily flights from Athens; four a week from Mýkonos; three a week from Thessaloníki; two a week in season from Herákleon (Crete) and Rhodes. The Olympic

Airways office is at Fíra, ✆ 22 493; **airport**: ✆ 31 525. There are regular buses from the airport to Firá, or take a taxi for 2,000dr.

By road: Santoríni has an astonishingly efficient if often crowded bus service, given its size. **Taxis:** ✆ 22 555. Alternatively, rent a scooter and you'll be spoilt for choice.

✆ (0286–)   Tourist Information

For tourist police, see the regular **police**: 25 Martíou Street, ✆ 22 649.

Kamari Tours, based, oddly enough, in Kamari, ✆ 31 390, ✉ 31 491, *kamaritours@ san.forthnet.gr*), but with offices in every village on the island, is helpful and can arrange accommodation, tours and cruises. **Nomikos Travel** (also with various offices; in Fíra, ✆ 23 660) are also helpful.

OTE: on the main street to the north of town (*open 7.30–3*). **Post office:** opposite the police (*open 8–2*). **Internet:** PC World, in the main square in Fíra, offers the usual (*open 9–9*); Ecorama in Oía (*see* p.402) also has access.

Walking: there are wonderful walks along the northern coast; for more details, consult Ecorama in Oía. **Diving:** Paul Stefanidis runs the Mediterranean Dive Club from Perissa Camping, ✆ 83 080, ✉ 83 081, *www.diveclub.gr*, and offers all sorts of volcano and wreck dives, as well as courses.

Festivals

19 and **20 July**, in Profítis Ilías; **15 August**, Panagía in Mésa Goniá and Firá; **September**, Santoríni Music Festival, in Fíra, with Greek and international music. **20 October**, Ag. Artemiou in Fíra; **26 October**, Ag. Dimítríou in Karteráthos.

Firá (ΦΗΡΑ)

Most visitors' first taste of the city is a rather zoo-like modern square where tourists are processed and fattened on fast food before being sacrificed to the volcano god. Cruise ships rather more pleasantly anchor beneath the towering cliffs at Firá, where motor launches ferry passengers to the tiny port of **Skála Firá**; there, donkeys wait to bear them up the winding path to town 885ft above. An Austrian-built **cable car** (*every 15 minutes from 6.45am to 8.15pm; 800dr*), donated to the island by ship-owner Evángelos Nomikós does the donkey-work in two minutes. Profits go to a community fund—and to the donkey drivers.

Those who remember Firá before 1956 say that the present town can't compare to its original, although it's pleasant enough—perfectly Cycladically white, spilling over the volcano's rim on several terraces, adorned with pretty blue-domed churches, all boasting one of the world's most magnificent views. Understandably, the families who sold their damaged caldera-front properties for peanuts after the big quake have been kicking themselves ever since; the little lanes are now chock-a-block with shops, bars, hotels and restaurants. Firá now blends into quieter **Firostefáni**, a kilometre to the north; here are some magnificent old *skaftá*, barrel-roofed cave houses, Santoríni's speciality, now equipped with all mod cons.

The **Archaeological Museum** (✆ (0286) 22 217; *open Tues–Sun, 8.30–3; adm*), not to be confused with the Museum of Prehistoric Thíra (✆ (0286) 23 217; *same hours*), is near the cable car on the north side of town and houses finds from Akrotíri, Mésa Vouná and Early Cycladic figurines found in the local pumice mines. The famous Santoríni frescoes are still in the National Museum in Athens, although there are rumours that a new museum will be built in Firá to bring them home; at present, you'll have to settle for the exhibition of reproductions in the Nomikos Conference Center (© (0286) 23 016; *open daily 10–9*). The handicraft workshop founded by Queen Frederíka, where women weave large carpets on looms, is also worth a visit. The **Mégaron Gýzi Museum** (© (0286) 22 244; *open daily 10.30–1.30 and 5–8pm, Sun 10.30–4; adm*), located in a beautiful 17th-century mansion, houses exhibits on the island's history—manuscripts from the 16th to 19th centuries, costumes, old maps of the Cyclades, and photographs of Santoríni before the 1956 quake. Another, privately run **Folklore Museum** (© (0286) 22 792; *open 10–2 and 6–8; adm*) occupies an 1861 cave house, with all of the owner's uncle's belongings on display.

Firá ✉ *84700,* © *(0286–)*   **Where to Stay**

Firá isn't the only village with hotels spilling over the caldera rim, but it's the most expensive. Just out of season, in early July even, you can wheel and deal with the room owners who mug you as the Athiniós bus pulls into town.

Top of the list for luxury is the **Santoríni Palace**, © 22 771, ✆ 23 705 (*A; lux*), followed by the classy **Atlantis**, © 22 232, ✆ 22 821, *atlantissa@otenet.gr* (*A; lux*), overlooking the volcano. For all the mod cons (including a counter swim unit in the pool) in a traditional, antique furnished cliff side *skaftá*, there's **Aigialos**, © 25 191, ✆ 22 856 (*A; lux*). **Kavalari**, © 22 455, ✆ 22 603 (*C; lux*), has attractive rooms dug out of the cliff, as has **Lucas**, © 22 480, ✆ 24 882 (*B; exp*). **Porto Carra**, © 22 979, ✆ 24 979 (*C; exp*), also faces the volcano from the central square. The air-conditioned **Pelican**, © 23 113, ✆ 23 514 (*C; exp*), has a tank of odd fish in the lounge (*open all year*). Just north along the cliff edge at Firostefáni, **Sun Rocks**, © 23 241, ✆ 23 991, *info@sunrocks.gr* (*B; lux*), is a stylish, couples-only place; **Efterpi Villas**, © 22 541, ✆ 22 542 (*D; lux*), provide more affordable luxury in traditional apartments. **Galini**, © 22 095, ✆ 23 097, *galini-htl@otenet.gr* (*C; exp*), offers nice rooms with caldera views, and transfers to the port. **Kafieris Apartments**, ©/✆ 24 186 (*C; exp*), are also fully equipped. Cheaper, view-less places in Firá include bohemian **Tataki**, in the centre, © 22 389 (*D; mod; open year-round*); **Argonaftis**, © 22 055 (*mod*), friendly with breakfast served in the garden; and the pleasant, quiet rooms by the Villa Popi sign, on the road to Firostefani, © 23 497 (*inexp*). **Stella**'s rooms in Firostefani, © 23 464 (*inexp*), are plain but with kitchen and views to the other side of the island. The **International Youth Hostel**, © 22 387, 5 minutes' walk from Firá centre, has doubles and dorms. Nearby **Camping Santoríni**, © 22 944, is a superb site with pool.

Eating Out

Besides wine, Santoríni is famous for its fava bean soup (puréed, with onions and lemon) and *pseftokeftédes*, 'false meatballs', made of deep-fried tomatoes, onion and mint; the tiny tomatoes of the island are said to be the tastiest in Greece. The owner and chef of one of Athens' most innovative restaurants, Vitrina, spends the summer serving up similar refined fare at **Tomates** (*exp*). *Open mid Apr–10 Oct.* Up on top of the Fabrica Shopping Centre, **Meridiana**, © 23 247, claims to be the only restaurant on the island with views of both sides of the island, as well as gourmet and Thai cuisine and live jazz most evenings. *Open from lunch until 3am.*

Kastro with big views near the cable car will set you back a bit for one of its lavish international spreads. On the main street, try and squeeze in at **The Roosters**, a fun little restaurant with tasty Greek dishes, and an inquisitive owner; **Nikolas** is another good place for traditional food. **Alexandria** on the caldera is very expensive but even serves up ancient Greek specialities. Italians flock to **Bella Thira** for freshly made pasta and pizzas. The 24-hour diner, **Poseidon**, under the bus stop has reasonable priced filling food. If tacos tickle your fancy, mosey on down to **Señor Zorba's** for Mexican fare, on the caldera south of town.

Entertainment and Nightlife

Café and bar life takes up as much time as eating in Santoríni. **Bebis** is the watering hole for a pleasantly loony young crowd. **Two Brothers** draws the backpackers and is a hot spot for rock; **Kira Thira** appeals to all ages for jazz, blues and *sangria*, while **Alexandria** is more sedate and attracts an older set. **Franco's**, playing gentle classical music, is still *the* place to laze in deckchairs for sunset, even if the price of a coffee is sky-high. Cocktails are works of art, but a bottle of wine and *mezédes* are the best deal. **Enigma** bar, on the rim, is a pleasant place to contemplate volcanoes, while **Enigma** the club is the hippest place to dance through the night; the adjacent **Koo Club** is also big, central and packed; lively **Mamounia Club** plays Greek hits, or rock away at **Tithora Club** in the main square.

Way Down South: Minoan Akrotíri

Akrotíri (ΑΚΡΩΤΗΡΙ), a pleasant wine village on the south tip of the island, was a Venetian stronghold, and although damaged in the earthquake the fort still stands at the top of the town. There are beaches nearby on either coast, and a pretty walking path along the caldera rim. The first clues indicating that something else may have once been here came in the 1860s during the excavation of pumice for the rebuilding of Port Said during the Suez Canal project: cut stone blocks belonging to ancient walls kept getting in the way. A French geologist named Fouqué, who came to study Thíra's eruption of 1866, began digging and with later French archaeologists he unearthed carbonized food, vases, frescoes and a pure copper saw. In 1967 Spyrídon Marinátos, following his hunch about the destruction of Minoan Crete through a volcanic eruption, led a team back to the site. The trenches were disappointing until they reached the level of volcanic ash 15ft below the surface, when suddenly they broke through into rooms full of huge storage vases, or *pithoi*. Excavations are still under way.

The **Minoan city**, buried in *c.* 1550 BC (*buses from Firá end up here;* © *(0286) 81 366; open Tues–Sun 8.30–3; adm*) laboriously revealed beneath its thick sepulchral shell of volcanic tephra—a material so hard that it's used to make cement for tombstones—is wonderful and strange, made even more uncanny by its huge modern protective roof. A carpet of volcanic dust silences all footsteps on paved lanes uncovered after 3500 years, amid houses up to three storeys high, many still containing their *pithoi* and linked up to a sophisticated drainage system. The residents must have had ample warning that their island was about to blow: no jewellery or other valuables were found, and the only skeleton found so far belonged to a pig. As they escaped they must have shed more than a few tears, for life at Akrotíri was sweet judging by the ash imprints of their elaborate wooden furniture, their beautiful ceramics and the famous frescoes full of colour and life—every house had a least one frescoed room; one, unique in peace-loving Minoan art, shows a sea battle. The size of the storage areas and cooking pots suggests a strong communal life and collective economy. In one of the houses is the grave of Marinátos, who died after a fall on the site and requested to be buried by his life's work. For more details, pick up *Art and Religion in Thira: Reconstructing a Bronze Age Society*, by his son, Dr Nannó Marinátos. Below the site, the road continues to Mávro Rachidi, where cliffs as black as charcoal offer a stark contrast to the white chapel of Ag. Nikólaos; a path over the headland leads to **Kókkino Paralía** or Red Beach, with sun beds under startling blood-red cliffs.

The Southeast: Embório, Períssa and Ancient Thira

East of Akrotíri, farming villages encircle Mount Profítis Ilías. **Megalochóri,**'big village', actually has a tiny, resolutely old Greek core, with a tiny outdoor taverna. **Embório** (ΕΜΠΟΡΕΙΟ) still has its Venetian *goulas*, or fort; with its lone palm, like something out of the Sahara. A modern church replaces the Byzantine St Irene, the island's namesake and patroness of the Greek police. Another 3km east of Embório, in a pretty setting under the seaside mountain Mésa Vouna, the black sands of **Períssa** (ΠΕΡΙΣΣΑ) have attracted a good deal of development, and can be pleasant at either end of the season because the sand warms quickly in the sun. Eucalyptus groves provide shade; bars and clubs provide for plenty of nightlife; and a Byzantine church is being excavated on the edge of town.The coastal road south of Períssa leads around to **Cape Exomítis**, past Perivolos beach, guarded by one of the best-preserved Byzantine fortresses of the Cyclades; submerged nearby are the ruins of the ancient **Eleusis**. The road ends by the wild cliffs and often big waves at **Vlycháda**, with a pretty beach, snack bar and world's end air, in spite of nearby smokestacks.

Pírgos (ΠΥΡΓΟΣ) shares with Embório the title of the oldest surviving village on the island, with interesting old barrel-roofed houses, Byzantine walls, and a Venetian fort. Much of the surrounding country is covered in vineyards, which swirl up the white flanks of **Mount Profítis Ilías**, Santoríni's highest point (566m). On a clear day you can see Crete from here, and on an exceptionally clear day, it is said, even Rhodes hovers faintly on the horizon. The locals say the monastery, built in 1712, is the only place that will protrude above sea level when the rest of Santoríni sinks into the sea to join its other half. Don't miss the scenes at the entrance, of the narrow road to heaven and the considerably wider one to hell, where the devil whiles away time playing the *laouto*; if you have bare knees, the monks won't let you any further. The monastery also has an interesting little museum. At the foot of Profítis Ilías, by the village of Mésa Goniá, the 11th-century **Panagía Episkopí** has fine Byzantine icons, although 26 that managed to miraculously survive earthquakes and fires were stolen in 1982. On 15 August the church holds the biggest *panegýri* on the island (note how all the churches on Santoríni proudly fly the Greek flag).

North, another black beach and a million sun beds and umbrellas announces **Kamári** (ΚΑΜΑΡΙ), with 300 hotels and pensions, and just as many tavernas, bars, and tourist shops, while a mile away women thresh fava beans in the field. Above, on the rocky headland of Mésa Vouna, **Ancient Thíra** (ΠΑΛΑΙΑ ΘΗΡΑ), accessible by tour bus or cobbled path from Kamári) is spread over its great terraces (*open Tues–Sun 9–3*). Excavated by German archaeologist Hiller von Gortringen in the late 19th century, the site produced the fine 'Santoríni vases' in the museum. Most of what you see today dates from the Ptolemies, who used the city as a base for their enterprises further north and adorned it with temples to the Egyptian gods, Dionysos, Apollo, to their semi-divine selves and to the mythical founding father Thira. There are impressive remains of the *agora* and theatre, with a dizzying view down to the sea, several cemeteries and a gymnasium. Numerous houses still have mosaics; graffiti dating from 800 BC may be seen on the Terrace of Celebrations, recording the names of competitors and naked dancers of the *gymno paidiai*; note the enormous Cyclopean walls. The church by the entrance, **Ag. Stefanos**, is the island's oldest, founded in the 5th century.

The coastal road north leads past the airport to **Monólithos**, a soft grey sandy beach, with a big isolated lump of rock draped with a few ruins, tamarisks along the shore, windsurfers to hire and a few places to stay and eat. **Messariá**, an important wine and market village, has the **Archontiko Argyrou Museum**, in a 19th-century neoclassical mansion owned by a wealthy vintner, with murals and traditional furnishings (℅ (0286) 31 669; *guided tours April–Oct at 11, 12, 1, 5, 6, and 7; adm*); you can stay there, too.

Santoríni in a Glass

 Santoríni is one of Greece's premier white wine producers. Because of its exclusively volcanic soil, its vines were among the few in Europe to be spared the deadly plant lice *phylloxera*, so the original rootstock remains intact; the average age of an *assyrtiko* vine, the main variety of white grape on the island, is 70 years; the oldest vines, near Akrotíri, are estimated at over 150 years. *Assyrtiko* yields everything from a bone dry light wine to a sweet aged Vinsanto made from sun-dried grapes; a second rare variety, Aidani, is known for its jasmine bouquet. Because of the wind the vines are kept low and often protected by woven cane; some fields look as if they're growing baskets. Moribund for many years, churning out high-alcohol, low-quality wine, the Santoríni wine industry has recently had a shot in the arm from the forward-thinking national winemaker Boutari, who in 1988 built a new domed winery, restaurant, and accessory shop at Megalochóri, towards Akrotíri (℅ 81 011). A second winery, Koutsoyanópoulos (℅ 31 322), on the road to Kamári, also offers tastings. While connoisseurs are most welcome, they still insist you have a good time.

Santoríni ℅ *(0286–)*   ***Where to Stay and Eating Out***

Akrotíri/Megalochóri ✉ 84700

Friendly and comfortable **Villa Mathios**, ℅ 81 152, ✆ 81 704, *vmathios@otenet.gr* (*exp August; otherwise quite good value*), has a pool overlooking the island, air-conditioning and colour TVs in the rooms, and a travel agency in reception to organize your whole holiday. Similarly priced, but offering slightly less, **Villa Kalimera**, ℅ 81 855, ✆ 81 915 (*exp*), is next door. **Pension Karlos**, ℅ 81 370, ✆ 81 095 (*mod*), offers clean rooms with bathroom and balcony. For sunset views over all Santoríni, dine at the cliffside **Panorama**; **Glaros** down towards the Red Beach has good fish, and **Villa Mathios** has a reasonable menu and home-made wine. In Megalochóri, a former winery has been converted into **Vedema**, ℅ 81 796, ✆ 81 798, one of the 'Small Luxury Hotels of the World' (*A; lux*), offering every amenity, art gallery, marble baths, in-house movies and a private beach 3km away with minibus service. Nearby in

Pirgos, the **Pyrgos** taverna, ℭ 31 346, occupies a huge panoramic terrace just below town, a favourite for Greek parties and weddings. *Open year-round.*

Períssa ✉ 84700

A gentle swathe of tavernas, bars and accommodation lines Períssa's strand. Right on the black sands, **Veggera**, ℭ 82 060, ✉ 82 608 (*lux*), offers comfortable, fully equipped rooms with a neoclassical touch, pool and laundry. **Sellada Beach** next door, ℭ 81 859, ✉ 81 492 (*exp*), offers handsome traditional rooms and flats with pool. **Ostria**, ℭ/✉ 82 607 (*mod*), has good-value apartments by the sea, as does **Blue Albacor** next door, ℭ 81 654 (*mod*); both are cheap out of season. **Perissa Camping** is also near the beach. Shady **Taverna Markos** corners one end of the strand, while at **Yazz Club**, you can contemplate beach life from a hammock.

Messariá ✉ 84700

Archontiko Argyrou, ℭ 31 669, ✉ 33 064 (*A; exp*), occupies a lovely 1860s mansion with rooms on the ground floor.

Kamári ✉ 84700

The beachfront is lined with hotels and pools. **Kamari Beach**, ℭ 31 243, ✉ 32 120 (*C; exp*), is smack on the black sands, with a large pool; all rooms have big verandas. The **Matina**, ℭ 31 491, ✉ 31 860 (*C; exp*), is comfortable, as is the **Sunshine**, ℭ 31 394, ✉ 32 240 (*C; mod*), next to the sea. Modest **Andreas**, ℭ 31 692, ✉ 31 314 (*D; mod*), has a lush garden. Quiet **Sigalas**, ℭ 31 260, ✉ 31 480 (*D; mod*), is at the end of the beach, with a shady garden and taverna. **Kamari Camping**, ℭ 31 453, is up the main road from the beach.

Camille Stefani on the beach is one of the island's best restaurants with a French-influenced Greek menu and its own wine label; **Kamari** is a good, inexpensive family-run taverna, serving *fáva* soup. Next to the sea, **Almira** has a good selection of starters and lemon chicken. The locals drive out to Monolithos and the seaside **Taverna Galini** for good cheap home cooking, fish and *pseftokeftédes*. Kamári throbs with bars. **Hook**'s tangerine chairs are a pleasant place to sit with mellow music; the **Sail Inn** has loud music, fun evenings and glamorous bar girls, and **Valentino's** always has a large crowd. Strut your stuff at **Dom Club** or drop in at the **Yellow Donkey** and dance till dawn—there's very little point in trying to get an early night anyway.

North of Firá to Oía

Imerovígli is on the verge of merging into Firostefáni and can be a good base if you prefer your caldera minus the crowds and daytripper paraphernalia. A traditionally Catholic village, it has views as magnificent as Firá or Oía, this time over a startling great big lump of volcanic crud with a knob on top in the foreground. This, incredibly, was the site of **Skáros**, the medieval capital of Santoríni, once defended below by an impregnable castle of 1207 built by Marco Sanudo; another fortress, the Rocca, sat on the top of the rock until a volcanic eruption in 1650 destroyed the town. A path (do it first thing in the morning, before it gets too hot, and not if you're subject to vertigo) leads in about half an hour to the site of the Rocca, now occupied by a little white chapel. The views are sublime, awe-inspiring, terrifying. Other ruins belong to a Catholic convent, built after a young girl's vision in 1596. The nuns stuck it out in extreme hardship until 1818 when they moved to the new **Ag. Nikólaos**. In the 19th century it was one of the biggest convents in Greece, and has a fine collection of bishops' portraits.

The road north continues to that trendy mouthful of vowels called **Oía**, or **Ía** (OIA), the third port of Santoríni, although these days only yachts and caiques to Thirassía call here. In 1900, 9000 people lived here, mostly seamen; today most are in Pireaus. The 500 who remain are fiercely independent of Firá although, ironically, vastly outnumbered in season by Athenians milking the tourist trade. Half-ruined by the earthquake, its houses, painted in rich, Fauvist colours are nearly all restored now (beautifully enough to have won major international restoration prizes) and piled on top of one another over the jumble of broken red and white cliffs; the roofs of the lower houses are courtyards for their neighbours above. There's a half-ruined Venetian lookout fort and working windmills; if you want the sea, it's 286 steps down to **Arméni** beach with a little clutch of houses, or 214 steps down to **Ammoúdi** beach with tavernas and one hotel run by Ecorama (*see* p.402), where you can fill your pockets with pumice-stone souvenirs, or 3km by bus to **Baxédes**, with coarse blackish sand and shade. An old mansion houses the **Nautical Museum** (✆ (0286) 71 156; *open 12.30–4 and 5–8.30, closed Tues; adm*), created by an old sea captain; it has ships' models and figureheads, and rare instruments. Oía is reputedly haunted, but most of the spirits these days seem to come out of bottles, especially when everyone gathers down on the tip by the Kástro to watch the sun call it a day.

Islets Around the Caldera

Santoríni's caldera is 10km wide and 380m deep. Curving around the northwestern rim, the islet **Thirassía** was part of Santoríni until another eruption-earthquake in 236 BC blasted them apart. In one of the quarries a Middle Cycladic settlement was discovered, pre-dating Akrotíri, though there are no traces of it now. The main business on rural Thirassía, pop.245, is growing tomatoes and beans on the fertile plateau; the largest village, **Manolás**, has tavernas and rooms to rent by the sea. Excursion boats from Oía also make trips out to the 'burnt isles', **Palía Kaméni** (appeared in AD 157) and **Néa Kaméni** (born in 1720), both still volcanically active, especially the Metaxá crater on Néa Kaméni, which last erupted in 1950 and still spews steam. However, even though a local brochure refers to it as 'the strange volcano which cause you greatness', be forewarned that most people come away disappointed. The tourist trail up the mountain is rubbish-strewn, stinks of sulphur, and there's plenty of black ash to look at. There are also tourist excursion boats taking people to swim in the 'healthy' sulphurous mud nearby and hot volcanic waters around Palía Kaméni, which, if nothing else, makes an unusual chat-up line ('Gosh, you stink!') in the bars.

Santoríni ✆ *(0286–)*   **Where to Stay and Eating Out**

Imerovigli ✉ 87400

> **Heliotopos**, ✆ 23 670, ✉ 23 672, *helio@hol.gr* (*A; lux*), is an intimate, elegant Cycladic hideaway, with a restaurant and grand views. **Villa Spiliotica**, ✆ 22 637, ✉ 23 590 (*exp*), has similar views, lower prices for its apartments and studios, and publicizes the mirrors on the ceilings of honeymoon suites. **Tholos Villas**, ✆ 23 967, ✉ 24 549 (*B; mod*), offers more of the traditional architecture and views, minus pool, while **Katerina's Castle**, ✆ 22 708, ✉ 23 398 (*E; mod*), offers simple rooms on the

caldera. **Blue Note** is a good bet for dinner with grand views, or for something Greek, simple, and much cheaper, **Marilos**, near the car park, has no views at all but is run by a kindly old gent. **Skaros Fish Taverna** is also excellent.

Oía ✉ 84702

The swishest place to stay is the luxury *skaftá* of **Fanari Villas**, ✆ 71 008, ✆ 71 235 (*exp*), below the windmill, with small bar, and steps down to Ammoúdi Bay. **Zoe-Aegeas Traditional Houses**, ✆/✆ 71 466 (*B; exp*), are four caldera-rim double studios and four flats sleeping up to six. Just out of town, **Katikies**, ✆ 71 401, ✆ 71 129 (*exp*), are beautifully decorated rooms and apartments with great views, a spectacular pool and homemade breakfasts on the terraces, and **Perivolas**, ✆ 71 308 (*A; exp*), has 14 lovely traditional houses, with a unique pool. Helpful Ecorama travel agency, by the bus stop, ✆ 71 507, fax 71 509, *ecorama@otenet.gr*, has a range of accommodation, from the highly recommended, tranquil **Ammoudi Villas** (*exp*), offering all mod cons in traditional apartments with verandas and a café providing breakfast and excellent hand-made ice cream, to maisonettes and cheaper rooms in Oía proper. The good **youth hostel**, ✆ 71 465, offers cheap dorm beds, breakfast and a pleasant terrace.

For a romantic dinner by candlelight, **1800**, in a shipowner's house on the main street, ✆ 71 485, serves imaginative international cuisine; the **Blue Sky Taverna**, a bit further down, is reasonable and deservedly popular; **Neptune** and **Thalami** are good for fish in town, or descend to Ammoudi for excellent fresh catch at **Kyma** or **Katina** tavernas. If you want to have aperitifs and dinner by the famous Oía sunset, arrive early to get a table at **Kastro**, or escape the tourist throng a bit by heading for a better view at **Palea Orihia** (or Old Mines) or **Ether Club** (on the road to Ammoudi). **Pelecanos Café** is a popular drinking haunt; its terrace overlooks *that* crater.

Skýros (ΣΚΥΡΟΣ)

Skýros, with a permanent population of 2,750 souls, is an exceptional island in many respects. It has two distinct geological regions, squeezed in the middle by a girdle where nearly everybody lives in either the port or town; the southern half is barren, rugged and ringed with cliffs, the northern half is fertile and pine-forested. A native race of tiny ponies called the Pikermies roams the southern part undisturbed, except when rounded up to help with the chores or to give the kids a ride; a five-year-old can look them right in the eye.

Throughout history Skýros was uncommonly remote. Even today, under ideal conditions it takes about seven hours by land and sea to get there from Athens; connections from nearby Kými on Évia were so limited a few decades ago that the Skyriots purchased their own ferry to get about. These long years of isolation account in part for the island's distinctive charm and character and the staying power of its old customs. The oldest men still don their baggy blue trousers, black caps and flat leather sandals with many straps or *trohádhia*, and the older women can sometimes be seen in their long headscarves; the interiors of their tidy houses remain resolutely traditional (*see* below) while incorporating such novelties as digitally controlled American refrigerators. In other words, the outside world has arrived, but the Skyriots are determined to set the rules by which it operates on their island.

Mythology

 When it was prophesied that Achilles, son of the sea goddess Thetis and Peleus, would either win great glory at Troy and die young, or live peacefully at home to a ripe old age, his doting mother thought to hide him from the Achaeans by disguising him as a girl and sending him to live among the women at King Lykomedes' palace in Skýros. Achilles didn't mind, and, apparently adopting the name of Pyrrha, or 'Goldie', for the colour of his hair, took advantage of his stay in the harem by fathering a son, Neoptolemis. All would have been well had not another oracle declared that the Achaeans would never win the Trojan War without Achilles, and crafty Odysseus was sent in search of the young hero. Odysseus brought a chest full of gifts for the women when he called on King Lykomedes—perfumes, jewellery, finery—and a sword, which the young transvestite in the crowd seized joyfully for his own, just as Odysseus had anticipated. Once discovered, Achilles willingly joined the Achaeans. When an arrow in his heel ended his life, Odysseus returned to Skýros to fetch his son Neoptolemis to Troy, and the war was eventually won.

King Lykomedes of Skýros plays a less benign role in another story: when the hero Theseus returned to Athens after spending four years glued to the Chair of Forgetfulness in Hades (his punishment for trying to help a friend abduct Persephone, the Queen of Hell), he found Athens corrupt and divided into factions against him. Theseus laid a curse on his native city and sought asylum in Crete, but was blown off course to Skýros, where he was received with such honour by Lykomedes that Theseus announced that he meant to retire on an estate his family owned on Skýros—an estate coveted by Lykomedes himself. After a drinking party Lykomedes led Theseus to the pinnacle of Skýros' acropolis and gave him a push, hurling him to his death on the rocks below.

History

Theseus was buried on Skýros and his memory neglected by the Athenians until his spirit was seen at Marathon, rising out of the earth to lead the Athenians to victory over the Persians. The Delphic oracle then charged the Athenians to bring Theseus' bones back to Athens—just the excuse the Athenians needed to nab Skýros for themselves. In 476 BC Kimon captured it, enslaved the inhabitants and, guided by a she-eagle, which scratched at the ground with her beak, was led to the grave of a tall skeleton buried with his weapons. Certain that it was Theseus, Kimon exhumed the coffin, carried it back to Athens, and enshrined it in the Theseion.

So many Athenians then came to settle the island that Athens treated Skýros as an equal and demanded no tribute. The Athenian Dionysia was made the biggest festival, and the tallest mountain was re-named Olympos by the settlers, who adopted the island's local cult of the sky god into their own state religion of Zeus. Under Byzantine rule, so many important people were exiled to Skýros from Constantinople that they created a tyrannical and much resented upper class, one remembered in the double-headed eagle and other folk motifs in the local art. In this century, Skýros is best known as the last resting place of the young First World War poet Rupert Brooke, and more recently, among British New Agers, as the home of the Skyros Centre, where you can get in harmony with your inner space, or perfect your water sports or writing skills (see p.407).

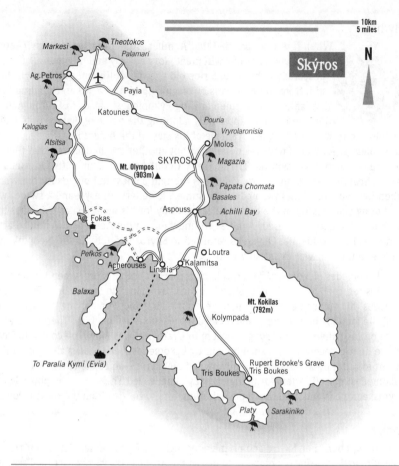

Markesi
Theotokos
Palamari
Ag.Petros
Payia
Katounes
Pouria
Kalogias
Vryrolaronisia
Atsitsa
Molos
SKYROS
Mt. Olympos
(903m)
Magazia
Papata Chomata
Basales
Aspouss
Achilli Bay
Ag. Fokas
Pefkos
Loutra
Acherouses
Linaria
Kalamitsa
Balaxa
Mt. Kokilas
(792m)
Kolympada
To Paralia Kymi (Evia)
Rupert Brooke's Grave
Tris Boukes
Tris Boukes
Platy
Sarakiniko

© (0222–)   **Getting There and Around**

By air: two flights a week from Athens; Olympic Airways, *©* 91 600 or 91 123; **airport information**: *©* 91 625. Alternatively, if it's all booked up, fly to Skiáthos and connect with a hydrofoil on the appropriate day.

By sea: From Linariá, **caiques** travel to Skyropoúla islet; from Kalamitsa, they head for Tris Boukés. There are also excursions further south; ask at Skyros Travel. Pappas Travel, *©* 96 472, has caiques to hire. **Port authority**: *©* 96 475.

By bus: five buses daily reach Linariá and Molos; other services are less reliable.

By road: car, motorbike and bicycle hire is available from agencies near the main square; the perenially helpful Skyros Travel will also be happy to oblige.

© (0222–)   **Tourist Information**

Tourist police: see regular police, Skýros town, *©* 91 274. Leftéris Trákes at Skýros Travel, in the centre of town, *©* 91 123, *✉* 91 123, is helpful, whether you need a villa, a boat ticket or information on island excursions.

Post office: in Skýros town, turn right after the bus terminal. **OTE**: in Skýros town, opposite the police.

Festivals

Skýros preserves some fascinating vestiges of the ancient Mediterranean goat and cattle cults during its **Carnival**, when three characters dance down the street: a man in a goatskin costume and mask and sheep bells called the Old Man, with a humpback made of rags, followed by the Frángos (the Frank, or foreigner), dressed in motley clothes and long trousers, with a mask and bell hanging behind and blowing a conch shell to scare children, and the Koréla, a man dressed up as a woman. These perform the Horós tou Trágou, or the Goat Dance, possibly a relic of the ancient rite that gave us the word 'tragedy' (from *tragoudía*, or 'goat song'). Every day during carnival the Old Man, the Frángos and the Koréla make their rollicking way through town, joining in satires (another goatish word, derived from the mischievous half-goat Satyrs) until they end up at the monastery of Ag. Geórgios.

Other festivals include: **12 March**, in town; **23 April**, Ag. Geórgios; **27 July**, Ag. Panteleímon, near Péfkos. A new outdoor theatre hosts a festival in **late July and early August**; **15 August**, children's pony races; **2 September**, Ag. Máma (Ag. Máma is the patron of shepherds, and like Carnival, the festival also includes traces of ancient rites).

Skýros Town

Skýros, or Chóra, is a striking town that wouldn't look out of place in the Cyclades, its white houses stacked one on top of the other along the steep, narrow pedestrian-only lanes and steps. From the distance it sweeps like a full skirt around the massive rocky precipice of the ancient acropolis, looming high over the sea. The main street curls past a pleasant mix of hardware stores and trendy boutiques, rimmed by the terraces of a dozen cafés, tavernas, and cocktail bars; few islands manage such a harmonious balance between the needs and desires of the locals and visitors.

Signs near the market point the way up to the **Kástro**, a 15-minute walk up, passing by way of the usually open church of **Ag. Triáda** (with frescoes) and the white monastery of **Ag. Geórgios**, founded in 962 by Emperor Nikephóros Phókas, himself known as 'the Pale Death of the Saracens' after his liberation of Crete. The emperor gave Ag. Geórgios to his saintly friend Athanásios, who went on to found the Great Lavra monastery on Mount Áthos; Ag. Geórgios, and a good chunk of land on Skýros, belong to the Great Lavra to this day. The church (restored in 1984 after earthquake damage) holds a fine painting of St George slaying the dragon and the old icon of St George with a black face, brought over from Constantinople during the iconoclasm. A crusty lion of St Mark (1354) marks the gate of the Byzantine-Venetian citadel, built in on the site of the classical fortifications, of which a few blocks survive at the base. It was from here that Lykomedes gave Theseus his mortal shove. On one side are fine views over the rooftops; on the other the escarpment plunges abruptly towards the sea.

Brooke Square, on a terrace at the far end of town, has been wearing a rather neglected air of late, although the willy of the gormless bronze nude *Statue of Immortal Poetry* by sculptor M. Tómbros (1931) commemorating Rupert Brooke is administered to weekly by local spray painters. The **archaeology museum** is just under Brooke Square, along the steps leading down to Magaziá (*open 8.30–3, closed Mon; adm*); grave offerings and goods from copper-age Palamári (2500–1900 BC) on the extreme northern tip of the island and from proto-geometric Thémis (950–800 BC) are among the highlights; from the latter note the ritual vase, decorated with eight ducks and two bird-swallowing snakes. Amongst the relics of ancient times, you'll find a traditionally furnished Skyriot home, 35sq m in size—the average living space per family.

Small but Perfectly Formed—Skyriot Houses

 Few houses combine so much function and beauty in such small spaces, dictated by the necessity of living crammed together on the slope, within easy distance of the Kástro should a pirate sail appear on the horizon. Because most of the older houses back into the steep hill and have shared walls, the *xóporto*, an outer half-door flap, was developed to allow light and air to enter while retaining privacy. The central living area is called the *alóni*, a Greek word that recalls the circular disc of the sun, since the walls and possessions on display are seen 'all around'. Focus, however, naturally fell on the chubby, conical fireplace, or *fgou*, with two little ledges for children to sit on in the winter. Some *fgous* have a pair of breasts in bas-relief to symbolize motherhood. An embroidered cloth over the upper mouth of the hearth protected the room from smoke, while shelves across the front of the *fgou* displayed rows of colourful porcelain plates and jugs. Crockery has been a Skyriot obsession and status symbol since the 16th century, when the Turkish conquest forced the island's aristocratic Byzantine exiles into such poverty that they had to sell off their dinnerware. Pirates who looted cargoes of plates would sell them on Skýros, or the pirates themselves would be looted by the plate-crazed islanders if they pulled into a bay to shelter from a storm. A Skyriot sailor never has to think twice about the perfect gift for his wife or mother: some examples come from as far away as China.

Furniture, often beautifully carved with folk motifs, is simple and functional. An intriguing variety of benches and settees double as chests for clothes, or have hollows in fronts of them to slide in pots, pans or bottles; other objects were stored in baskets suspended from the ceiling and reached by long forked poles. Niches in the walls were used to store jugs filled with water. Food would be served on a low table, which in the old days had a removable top, a large engraved copper plate called a sinía. These are now mostly used for decoration.

An ornate latticework partition, the *bóulmes*, crowned by a carved wooden parapet, cuts off the back third of the interior while admitting precious light. The kitchen and storage area was on the ground floor, and the bedroom(s), or *sfas* (from the Turkish word 'sofa'), in the loft. A thin beam just below the ceiling of the *sfas* was used to hang large decorative weavings that hide the rolled up mattresses. If there is no room for an external stair to the sfas, access is by way of a steep narrow internal stair and trap door. The roof is made of wooden beams, covered with layers of dried cane, dried seaweed and earth rich in waterproof clay; new layers of clay are added every few years. A broken jar on top of the chimney draws out the smoke from the *fgou*.

You can examine many of the items mentioned above in the charming **Faltaits Museum of Folklore** (*open 10–1 and 6–9 in summer; otherwise 5.30–8*), also just under Brooke Square; a fascinating collection of domestic items, poetry, traditional costumes, and richly coloured embroideries decorated with mermaids, double-headed eagles, Turkish judges, ships, deer, pomegranates and hoopoes (a bird closely identified with Skýros). The museum shop is full of lovely if rather costly handmade goods, including printed patterns of Skyriot designs to make your own embroideries (the ladies of Skýros buy them) and locally made pottery inspired by the examples brought home from the four corners of the world.

A 10-minute walk below Skýros town stretches the long sandy beach of **Magaziá** (ΜΑΓΑΖΙΑ), named after the Venetian powder magazines once stored here, and next to it is **Mólos beach**; most of the island's accommodation and surprisingly jumping nightlife are concentrated here. If these two beaches are too crowded there are others within walking distance; avoid sewage-prone Basáles, but continue south to **Papá ta Chómata** ('Priests' Land'), where no one, not even the priest, minds if you sunbathe in your altogether. From **Órmos Achílli**, further south, Achilles is said to have embarked for Troy; a new marina allows yachties to do the same.

Around the Island

Although buses run regularly between the port of Linariá, Skýros town and Mólos, the only way to visit the rest of the island is by foot, taxi or hired wheels. The pine-wooded northern half of Skýros has better roads (and the army airforce), and there are small beaches just off the road that follows most of the coast. The sandy beach of **Ag. Pétros** near the top of the island (past the airport) is the prettiest, and worth hiring a car and packing a picnic. A walking path (taking about 3 hours and not always easy to find) crosses the island from Skýros town to **Atsítsa**, where a taverna sits on a rocky beach among the pines, near a branch of the Skyros Centre offering courses ranging from sailing to dance and ponytreking to yoga; the very English PRIVATE sign must dent the karma somewhat. A second path (and in parts road) to Atsítsa begins in the port **Linariá** (ΛΙΝΑΡΙΑ), a mostly modern fishing village, built after 1860; it passes by way of **Achérouses** and the pretty beach and summer tavernas at **Péfkos**, site of ancient marble quarries. Even prettier **Ag. Fokás** beach, with white pebbles, is further north but accessible only on foot; it has a very basic taverna and a handful of rooms. From Linariá, caique excursions sail to the islet **Skyropoúla** between Skýros and the mainland. Skyropoúla has two beaches and a cave, **Kávos Spilí**, and a herd of the wild munchkin ponies.

The beaches in the rocky rugged south half of Skýros are less appealing, with the exception of **Kalamítsa**, linked by bus in the summer. The beach is of sand and stones, and fronted by tavernas and a few places to rent rooms. Signs of one of ancient Skýros' three rival towns, Chrission, were found near here, as well as an ancient tomb locally claimed to be Homer's, and traces of an Early Christian basilica. A taxi, a 2-hour walk from Kalamítsa, or caique (by far the most pleasant means if it's a calm day) will take you to **Tris Boukés** and the **grave of Rupert Brooke** at the southernmost point of Skýros. On 23 April 1915, the 28-year-old poet, on his way to fight at Gallipoli, died of blood poisoning aboard a French hospital ship and was buried in this desolate olive grove at dawn the next morning. His well-tended grave—6ft of official British soil—is maintained by the Anglo-Hellenic society. It was only a year before Brooke died that he wrote his famous lines:

If I should die, think only this of me:
That there's some corner of a foreign field
That is for ever England.

Among the boat excursions offered in the summer, the one to the region south of Tris Boukés, to Sarakíno beach and Platý island, and around the cliffs at Renés, is spectacular. Sea caves pierce the cliffs, and the Eleanora falcons sweep across the azure sky as thick as sparrows in London.

Skýros ✉ *34007,* ✆ *(0222–)*   **Where to Stay and Eating Out**

Linariá

King Likomides, ✆ 96 249, 📧 96 412, in Athens ✆ (01) 721 3773 (*mod*), has pleasant rooms right by the port, all with fridge and sea views (*open May–Oct*), while the new **Linaria Bay,** ✆ 96 476, 40m from the sea (*exp–mod*), has air con rooms with TV and phone. *Open all year.* **Philipeo** has the best food in the village, while **Psariotis** is reasonable; at Achérouses, just north, there's a campsite and a simple, friendly taverna where you can dine with your feet in the sea. **Kavos**, a bar just along the road to Skýros, is a lovely place to sit and watch the sun set over an ouzo or cocktail; if you want to live it up, proceed to the **Kastro Club**, playing both disco and Greek music.

Skýros Town

The principal hotel in town, **Nefeli,** ✆ 91 964, 📧 92 061 (*C; exp*), is comfortable and has a roomy pool. *Open all year.* **Pension Nikolas,** ✆ 91 778 (*mod*), has tranquil, comfortable rooms behind Kristina's restaurant. There are scores of rooms to let, many of them in charming traditional houses (just mind you don't break the plates); let yourself be propositioned by the little old ladies at the bus stop. Current rates for a stay of more than two days average at about *8,000dr* per double room per night, but out of season you can bargain for a lot less. There's also a friendly, pleasant campsite, located two-thirds of the way down the road to Magaziá beach.

Skýros is well endowed with good restaurants. One of the oldest, little **Margetis**, is on the main street, serving good meat and especially fish dishes in an ideal location to watch the bustling pedestrian traffic (*around 3,000dr*). **Sisyphos**, at the bottom of the main street, serves good-quality Greek dishes, including a selection for vegetarians. **Pegasos**, an elegant restaurant in a 19th-century mansion 20m below Skyros Travel, serves prepared Italian dishes, kid casseroles, and tasty moussaka. **Kristina's,** ✆ 91 778, which has tables out in a garden courtyard, is run by Greek-Australian Kristina Tsalapatani, with a delicious change-of-pace menu and warm herb breads (she also runs Greek cookery courses out of season). Tiny **Trypa**, on the main street, will ply you with good, cheap coffee, snacks and pizza all day.

By the Sea: Magaziá, Gialós and Mólos

The **Skýros Palace**, 50m from the beach at Grismata, ✆ 91 994, 📧 92 070, winter 📧 in Athens (01) 275 2094 (*A; exp*), is the most sophisticated place to stay; built in the traditional Skýros-Cyclades style, it has a lovely sea-water pool, restaurant, superior rooms and a relaxed atmosphere. *Open mid-May–Sept.* **Xenia**, smack on the beach at Magaziá, ✆ 91 209, 📧 92 062 (*B; exp*), is older but comfortable with 22 rooms and a restaurant and water sports. *Open Apr–Oct.* **Aegeolis**, a stone's throw from the sea at Magaziá, ✆ 91 113, 📧 92 482, winter 📧 (01) 418 2466 (*C; mod*), is a set of 11 apartments with veranda, built in 1992. *Open all year*. Set in a large garden, **Skýros Studios**, near the sea in Mólos, ✆ 91 376, in Athens in winter ✆ (01) 723 0871, 📧 723 0957 (*B; exp–mod*), are built and furnished in the traditional style; the nearby **Molos**, ✆ 91 381, in winter in Athens ✆ (01) 262 7513 (*mod–inexp*), offers further garden studios, pleasant but cheaper, with big discounts in May and June. *Open May–Sept*. There's also a handful of studios and rooms circling a luscious garden at the well-kept **Perigali**, set back from the sea in Magaziá, ✆ 91 880, 📧 92 770 (*mod*). *Open May–Oct*. **Efrosýni Varsámon**, in Magaziá, ✆ 91 142 (*mod*), are charmingly decorated rooms above the family's pottery shop.

If you get peckish, head for **Mylos Taverna**, in Molos, ideal for those Aegean sunsets, or fishy **Thoma to Magazi**, by the water. In Magaziá, **Koufari**, near Xenia Hotel, has fine, albeit not cheap, fare.

Sýros (ΣΥΡΟΣ/ΣΥΡΑ)

Inhabitants of Sýros (locally known as Sýra) affectionately call their island home 'Our rock', and it's as dry and barren a piece of real estate as you can find. But at the beginning of the Greek War of Independence in 1821 it was blessed with three important qualities: a large natural harbour, the protection of the King of France, and a hardworking population. The result is Sýros' capital, Ermoúpolis, once the premier port in Greece, and today the largest city and capital of the Cyclades. Don't come here looking for Cycladic sugar cubism: Ermoúpolis is the best-preserved 19th-century neoclassical town in the whole of Greece.

A sophisticated island, with many Athenians working there in law or local government, Sýros can afford to snap its fingers at tourism, but it's booming nonetheless. However, it remains very Greek and tourists are treated more like guests rather than customers—except when it comes to *loukoúmia*, better known as Turkish Delight (both Greeks and Turks claim to have invented it; no one really knows). These sweet, gummy squares, flavoured with roses, quinces or pistachios, smothered in icing sugar, are an island speciality, and vendors stream aboard the ferries to peddle it. The other Sýros sweetmeats are *halvadópittes*, rather like nougat.

History

Homer's swineherd Eumaeus, who helped Odysseus when he finally returned to Ithaca, was actually a prince of Sýros who had been captured by Phoenician pirates, and he described his native island as a rich, fertile place where famine and disease were strangers, and inhabitants died only when they were struck by the gentle arrows of Apollo or Artemis after living long, happy lives. The first inhabitants, who may have been the same Phoenicians who made off with Eumaeus, settled at Dellagrácia and at Fínikas. Poseidon was the chief god of Sýros, and in connection with his cult one of the first observatories in Europe, a heliotrope (a kind of sundial), was constructed in the 6th century BC by Sýros' own philosopher, Ferekides. Ferekides was a keen student of ancient Chaldaean and Egyptian mysteries, and spent two years in Egypt being initiated into secret cults; on his return to Greece, he became Pythagoras' teacher, imparting a mix of astrology and philosophy, and beliefs in reincarnation and the immortality of the soul; he was also the first Greek to write in prose. In Roman times the population emigrated to the site of present-day Ermoúpolis, at that time known as 'the Happy' with its splendid natural harbour

Megaslakkos
Grammata
Bay
Kambos
Lia
Kastri
Necropolis
Chalandriani
Aetou
Bay
Ferekides' Cave
Varvarousa
Islet
Mytakas
Platos
Koraki Bay
Delfini
Bay
Pyrgos
(411m / 1350ft)
Ano Syra
Dili
Ag. Dimitrios
To Piraeus,
Rafina
Kini
ERMOUPOLIS
Ag. Barbara
Danakos
Episkopio
Lazaretta
GAIDAROS
Strogulo
To Tinos and
Mykonos
To Paros
and Naxos
Armeos
Cape
Ag. Stefanos
Galissas
Pagos
Manna
Messaria
Ano Manna
Azolimnos
Faneromeni
Vissas
Chroussa
Finikas
Adiata
Kabrika
Agathopes
Posidonia
(Dellagracia)
Komito
Vari
Varis
Bay
Megas Gialos
Ambela
Bay

N

Sýros

5km
3 miles

and two prominent hills. After the collapse of the *pax Romana*, Sýros was abandoned until the 13th century, when Venetians founded the hilltop town of Áno Sýros.

Because Áno Sýros was Catholic, the island enjoyed the protection of the French, and remained neutral at the outbreak of the War of Independence in 1821. War refugees from Chíos, Psará and Smyrna brought their Orthodox faith with them and founded settlements on the other hill, Vrondádo, and down at Sýros' harbour. This new port town boomed from the start, as the premier 'warehouse' of the new Greek state where cotton from Egypt and spices from the East were stored, and as the central coaling station for the entire eastern Mediterranean. When the time came to name the new town, Ermoúpolis—'the city of Hermes' (the god of commerce)—was the natural choice. For 50 years Sýros ran much of the Greek economy, and great fortunes were made and spent not only on elegant mansions, but also on schools, public buildings and streets. Ermoúpolis built the first theatre in modern Greece and the first high school, financed by the citizens and government; and when the Syriani died they were so pleased with themselves that the most extravagant monuments to be seen in any Greek cemetery were erected in their memory. By the 1890s, however, oil replaced coal and Piraeus, with the building of the Corinth Canal, replaced Ermoúpolis as Greece's major port; Sýros declined, but always dominated the Cyclades, supporting itself with shipyards and various industries, prospering just enough to keep its grand old buildings occupied, but not enough to tear them down to build new concrete blocks. Today Ermoúpolis is a National Historical Landmark.

✆ (0281–)   *Getting There and Around*

By air: at least three daily flights from Athens with Olympic and up to two with Hellenic Star; also Paros–Sýros (but not vice versa). Olympic's office is at 52 Andistasios, on the harbour, ✆ 82 634; Hellenic Star is at Galera Travel Agency, ✆ 87 666. **Airport:** ✆ 87 025. Taxis into town cost around 1,000dr.

By sea: day excursions to Délos. Doudouris, ✆ 83 400, has caiques to hire. **Port authority:** ✆ 88 888.

By road: good **bus** service around the island, ✆ 82 575, departing from by the ferry port; every hour or so a bus circles the island, by way of Azólimnos, and there are regular departures for Kíni. **Taxi rank:** ✆ 86 222.

✆ (0281–)   *Tourist Information*

Friendly **EOT** information office on Dodekanesou St, by the port and bus station, ✆ 86 725, ✆ 82 375 (*open weekdays 7.30am–2.30pm*). **Police:** ✆ 82 620. The **Teamwork** travel office in the port, ✆ 83 400, ✆ 83 508, *teamwork@otenet.gr*, organizes accommodation, travel and guided tours of Ermoúpolis.

Internet: Net Café, by the town hall, has smart surfing facilities. **Post office:** between the port and main square, on Proto Papadhaki.

Festivals

Carnival, with dancing to the ancient *tasmbouna* and *toubi*, in Áno Sýra. The **last Sunday in May**, celebrating the finding of the icon at Ag. Dimitríou. In **June**, a folklore festival is held in Azólimnos with three days of dancing, wine and song. **Late July/August**, the Ermoupoleia Arts Festival. **24 September**, an Orthodox and Catholic celebration in Faneroméni. **26 October**, also in Ag. Dimitríou; **6 December**, Ag. Nikólaos in Ermoúpolis.

Ermoúpolis

Greece was reborn in Ermoúpolis.

Elefthérios Venizélos

As you sail into the **commercial port**, Ermoúpolis (ΕΡΜΟΥΠΟΛΗ), pop. 12,000, presents an imposing, unexpected sight much commented on by early travellers: a sweeping crescent meringue rising in twin peaks, one for each religion; older Catholic **Áno Sýros** to your left (or north), and **Vrondádo**, on the right, the Orthodox quarter. The whole wears a stately elegance, especially now that the buildings have been restored to their original soft colours; in the evening, horse-drawn carriages clopping down the marble lanes, softly illuminated with old street lamps, with the silhouettes of palms outlined against the moon, creates a rare urban idyll— 'Who could ever imagine finding such a city on a rocky island of the Aegean sea!' Gautier marvelled, when he visited it back when it was new. Yet at the same time there's no doubt that the city works for a living; prominent on the harbour are the Neórion shipyards, now back in business under new management.

Ermoúpolis' central square, **Plateía Miaoúlis**, is the most elegant in Greece, with its marble band stand and palms, its worn, lustrous marble pavement, and its cafés and statue of Admiral Miaoulis, revolutionary hero and old sea-dog, looking down to the port, the whole embraced by fine neoclassical buildings and wrought-iron balconies. In *Aegean Greece*, Robert Liddell wrote that he could think of no square 'except St Mark's that more gives the effect of a huge ballroom, open by accident to the sky.' Grandest of all is the neoclassical **town hall**, designed in 1876 by the German architect Ziller; you can pop inside for a coffee and have a look at the old fire engine in the courtyard. The **Archaeology Museum** (© 88 487, *open 8.30–3, closed Mon*) up the steps to the left, contains proto-Cycladic to Roman era finds from Sýros and other islands: note the Hellenistic era 'Votive relief to a hero rider from Amorgos' with a snake crawling on the altar as a sheep is led to sacrifice, and more snakes on a marble plaque referring to Homer, from Íos. The **Historical Archives**, on the same side of the town hall, host the Ermoúpoulis Seminars in summer, when the archives are on show (*same hours*). To the right, behind the square, the **Apóllon Theatre**, a copy of La Scala, Milan, was the first ever opera house in Greece; until 1914 it supported a regular Italian opera season, and has now been restored after a botched repair that wrecked more than it fixed in 1970. Up the street a little way from here, the **Velissarópoulos Mansion**, now housing the **Labour Union**, is one of the few places you can get in to see the elaborate ceiling and wall murals characteristic of old Ermoúpolis. In the lanes above the square, the **Metamórphosis** is the Orthodox cathedral, with a pretty *choklakía* courtyard and ornate Baroque interior—rare in Orthodoxy. Chíos Street, descending towards the port, has the town's bustling **market**. Down towards the port, just up from the bus terminal, the church of the Annunciation, built by refugees from Psára, contains the rare icon of the *Assumption* painted and signed by Doménicos Theotokópoulos (*aka* El Greco) after he left for Venice. Nearby the old Europa hotel with another lovely *choklakía* courtyard is now part of Sýros' new **Casino**.

The elegant **Vapória** quarter of fantastic old shipowners' mansions with marble façades, lavishly decorated inside with frescoes and painted ceilings, stretches off to the northeast. The main square here has one of the town's best churches, blue and golden-domed **Ag. Nikólaos**, dedicated to the patron saint of the city and boasting a carved marble iconostasis by the 19th-century sculptor Vitális of Tínos. In front of the church, a memorial topped by a stone lion, also by Vitális, is the world's first **Monument to the Unknown Soldier**. Vapória's grand houses hug the coastline above the town beaches of **Ag Nikólaos**, **Tálliro** and **Evangelídis** which have marble steps down from the street.

Crowning **Vrondádo Hill** (take the main street up from behind Plateía Miaoúlis), the Byzantine church **Anástasis** has a few old icons and superb views stretching to Tínos and Mýkonos. Vrondádo has some excellent local tavernas spread out in its steps at night—follow your nose. More remote—870 cobbled steps, or a hop on the bus—is its twin, the medieval quarter of **Áno Sýros** (Apáno Chóra), a Cycladic enclave on top of Ermoúpolis and a pretty pedestrian-only labyrinth of whitewashed lanes and archways forming a close-knit community where public and private spaces meld. Herman Melville, who visited in 1856, wrote that 'the houses seemed clinging around its top as if desperate for security, like shipwrecked men about a rock beaten by billows.' Since the Crusades, most of the families in Áno Sýros have been Catholic, and some have lived in the same mansions for generations and attended the **Catholic Cathedral of St George**, known as **Ai-Giórgi**, on top of the rock. The main entrance, the **Kámara**, is an ancient arched passageway which leads past tavernas and little shops to the main street or **Piátsa**. There's a town hall, the **Women's Association of**

Handicraft **Workers** with a folklore collection and workshop, the **Cultural Centre** and local radio station.The large, handsome **Capuchin Convent of St Jean** was founded there in 1635 by France's Louis XIII as a poorhouse and contains archives dating from the 1400s; the Jesuits, just above at 16th-century **Panagía Karmílou**, have a cloister from 1744 with an important library. Áno Sýros was also the birthplace of the famous *rembetiko* composer Márkos Vamvakáris whose bust graces the square named after him. On your way up or down the hill, don't miss the **Orthodox cemetery of Ag. Geórgios**, with its elaborate marble mausoleums and dolorous decorous damsels pining over wealthy shipowners and merchants.

A 45-minute walk from Ermoúpolis leads to the pretty seaside church of **Ag. Dimítrios**, founded after the discovery of an icon there in 1936. All ships coming into port hoot as they pass and a bell is rung in reply—cup your hand and you'll hear it. In **Díli**, just above, are the remains of a **Temple of Isis** built in 200 BC. Across the harbour at **Lazarétta** stood a 5th-century BC temple of Poseidon, although the only traces of it are a few artefacts in the museum; it may have been the Poseidonia mentioned in the *Odyssey*.

Around Sýros

'Our Rock' is a pretty wild place on the whole but it isn't quite as barren as it sounds; olives, pistachios and citrus fruit grow here, and the bees make an excellent thyme honey. Other ancient sites are in the quiet, seldom visited north side of the island. At lagoon-like **Grámmata Bay** (reached only by boat), sailors from classical to Byzantine times who found shelter from storms engraved epigrams of gratitude, still legible on the rocks. If you want a beach away from it all this is the place; sea-lilies grow here and on the beaches of **Lía** and **Mégas Lakkos**. Towards the east coast, the wealth of grave-goods discovered in 1898, in the 500 tombs at the Bronze Age necropolis of **Chalandrianí** (2600–2300 BC) contributed much to the understanding of Early Cycladic civilization. **Kástri**, an hour's walk north, was their citadel: its walls, six towers, and foundations of houses remain in the undergrowth. The **cave** where philosopher Ferekides whiled away the summer may be seen just south of Chalandrianí.

Buses from Ermoúpolis travel to the main seaside resorts: **Kíni** (KINI), a small west coast fishing village with two sandy beaches, is a popular rendezvous for sunset-watching, and home to a famous singing family who play authentic bouzouki music at their beachside taverna. North over the headland is **Delfíni Beach** for that all-over tan. In the middle of the island, **Episkópio** boasts the oldest Byzantine church on Sýros, **Profítis Ilías**, prettily set in the pine-covered hills. The Orthodox convent **Ag. Barbára**, inland from Kíni, has a school of arts and crafts with needlework on sale. The walls of the church are decorated with frescoes depicting Barbára's martyrdom—her father locked her in a tower and put her to death, but immediately afterwards was struck down by a thunderbolt, making her the patron saint of bombardiers.

The foreign tourists who come to Sýros concentrate in lively **Galissás** (ΓΑΛΗΣΣΑΣ), which has the best sheltered beach on the island, a sweeping crescent of sand fringed by tamarisks, with the island's two campsites. You can hire sail boats; on shore, however, it's all mini-markets and heavy metal, backpackers and bikers in high season. Nearby **Arméos** is for nudists. Further south, **Fínikas** (ΦΟΙΝΙΚΑΣ), 'Phoenix', originally settled by the Phoenicians and mentioned in Homer, is another popular resort with a gritty roadside beach.

The grandees of Ermoúpolis built their ornate summer houses at **Dellagrácia** or **Posidonía** (ΠΟΣΕΙΔΩΝΙΑ), a genteel resort with a serene film-set atmosphere of ornate Italianate mansions and pseudo castles, and a blue church. Further south, quieter **Agathopés** has a sandy beach and islet opposite and you can take the track from here to **Kómito**, a stony stretch in front of an olive grove. **Mégas Gialós** (ΜΕΓΑΣ ΓΙΑΛΟΣ) is a pretty family resort, with shaded sands. **Vári** (ΒΑΡΗ) to the east, first settled in the Neolithic era, is now a major resort, but still has its fishing fleet. **Azólimnos** is particularly popular with the Syriani for its *ouzeries* and cafés, and has three hotels and some rooms. Inland, **Chroússa** is a pleasant, pine-shaded village, home to more shipowners' villas, while nearby **Faneroméni** ('can be seen from everywhere') itself has panoramic views of the island.

Sýros ✉ *84100,* ✆ *(0281–)*   ***Where to Stay and Eating Out***

Sýros has some refined, stylish new hotels in restored neoclassical buildings. The **Rooms and Apartments Association**, ✆ 82 252, has a booth at the port and publishes an excellent booklet with a map. Culinary specialities include smoky San Michaeli cheese, *loúza*, salt pork, various sausages and the excellent Vátis wines.

Ermoúpolis

The newly opened **Aegli Hotel**, 17 Kleisthenous, ✆/☏ 79 279, *hotegli@otenet.gr* (*exp*), is swishly neoclassical with panoramic views from the roof terrace, with bar. Gorgeous **Omiros**, 43 Omirou, ✆ 84 910, ☏ 86 266 (*A; exp*), is pick of the pricey places in a 150-year-old neoclassical mansion, the elegantly restored family home of sculptor Vitalis. **Hermes**, ✆ 83 011, ☏ 87 412 (*C; exp*), on the harbour, has smart rooms with bath and balconies right over the sea. The stylish **Palladian**, Stamatoú Proioú, ✆ 86 400, ☏ 86 436 (*C; exp*), is a little less, with a quiet internal courtyard terrace. By the beach just north of town, **Sea Colours Apartments**, ✆ 88 716, ☏ 83 508 (*A; exp*), are luxurious and modern with marble terraces and wonderful views. In the same area the **Ypatia**, 3 Babagiotou, ✆ 83 575 (*B; exp*), is a super neoclassical mansion with brass bedsteads. **Silvia**'s rooms, 42 Omirou, ✆ 81 081 (*mod*), are elegantly furnished, good value and quiet, in yet another old mansion, as is **Villa Nostas**, 2 Spartiaton, ✆ 84 226 (*B; mod*). **Paradise** rooms, 3 Omirou, ✆ 81 754 (*mod*), have a quiet courtyard; even nearer to the port, **Ariadne**, 9 Filini, ✆ 80 245 (*mod*), has clean rooms, convenient if you arrive at an ungodly hour. For tighter budgets, **Villa Nefeli**, 21 Parou, ✆ 87 076 (*inexp*), has six atmospheric rooms in a traditional house close to the water. For a more reclusive holiday you can always stay at the **Capuchin Monastery Guest House** in Áno Sýros, ✆ 82 576, rates on request.

In Áno Sýro, **Lilli's** is famous for its wonderful views, excellent food (try the *louza*, the local sausage) and *rembétika* music at weekends. Opposite the ferry port, **Bouba's**, a fine old island *ouzerie*, has exquisite barbecued octopus, local, smelly *kopanistí* cheese on *paximádia* bread rusks, and the biggest slabs of feta you're likely to find on a Greek salad. The waterfront is heaving with eateries and bars. **Muses**, in the casino, is good, although tables near the water's edge can get a bit whiffy. **Taverna 1935** is smart with international as well as Greek food. For the best roasts and barbecues as well as take-aways there's **Ta Yiannena Psistaria** further along the quay, with *kokorétsi*, chicken and some imaginative vegetable dishes too. In the maze of small alleys just east of the main square lurk many good, small tavernas;

Archotariki is worth a try. By the sea north of town, towards Ag. Dimítrios, **Haravgi** serves excellent fare.

Kíni/Galissás

In Kíni, the little **Sunset**, ✆ 71 211 (*C; mod –inexp*), is right on the sea and has fine views of you know what, while **Harbour Inn**, ✆ 71 377, ✉ 71 378, *tboukas@ otenet.gr*, has six rooms close to the water. The twilight hour can also be enjoyed over delicious stuffed aubergines at **Delfini's**. In Galissás, **Akti Delfiniou**, ✆ 42 924, ✉ 42 843 (*A; exp*), is a complex of apartments with everything from volleyball to disco. The newish **Benois**, ✆/✉ 42 833 (*C; mod*), is open all year; family-run **Semiramis**, ✆ 42 067 (*C; mod*), and **Petros**, ✆ 42 067, ✉ 43 000 (*E; mod–inexp*), are both near the beach. **Two Hearts Camping**, ✆ 42 052/321, has mini-golf, motorbike hire and a minibus to meet ferries. The other site is **Yianna**, ✆ 42 418. The main road is lined with eateries.

Posidonía and Around

Eleana, ✆ 42 601, ✉ 42 644, (*C; mod*), is a very pleasant hotel with lovely grounds right on the beach, while **Willy** has eight rooms, ✆/✉ 42 426 (*mod*). *Open all year.* **Chroussa**, up in the little village of the same name, has the best food on Sýros; the menu changes weekly, and **Acapulco** restaurant on Finika marina is only a 10-minute drive away.

Entertainment and Nightlife

There's no shortage of both on Sýros, from culture at the **Apollon Theatre**, movies at the **Pallas outdoor cinema** near the market (and a winter indoor one) and a huge range of bars from sophisticated to rowdy. The **Aegean Casino** by the ferry port occupies two buildings, the old Europa Hotel and a portside warehouse, and both the games tables and restaurant are the rage. The evening *vólta* up and down Miaoúlis Square is still important; at one time the square was even specially paved so that the unmarried knew on which side to stroll to show they were available!

The waterfront buzzes with bars. **Traffic** is for ex-pats, **Highway** for loud music, and the **Cotton Club** and next-door **Cocoon** good for laid-back drinks. **Kimbara** and **Archaeo** bars at the port are also popular. Trendy Ermoúpolis flocks to the **Rodo Club**, 3 Arcimidous, in a half-ruined, half-beautifully restored building behind the Neorian shipyards, while **Neos Oikos** is the biggest club, near Iroon Square. For *rembétika* music head to **Lilli's** and **Xanthomalis** in Áno Sýros. **Argo Café** in Galissás has live Greek music.

BC

7000–2800	Neolithic Era
4000	Precocious civilization at Palaeochoe, Límnos
3000	Mílos exports obsidian
3000–2000	Early Cycladic civilization
2800–1000	Bronze Age
2600–2000	Early Minoan civilization in Crete
2000–1700	Middle Minoan: Cretan thalassocracy rules the Aegean
1700–1450	Late Minoan
1600–1150	Mycenaean civilization begins with invasion of the Peloponnese
c. 1450	Eruption of Santoríni's volcano decimates the Minoans; Mycenaeans occupy ruined Crete and Rhodes
1180	Traditional date of fall of Troy (4 July)
c. 1150	Beginning of the Dark Ages: Dorian invasion disrupts Mycenaean culture; Ionians settle Asia Minor and islands
1000	Kos and the three cities of Rhodes join Doric Hexapolis
1100–100	Iron Age
1100–700	Geometric Period
700–500	Archaic Period
650	Aegina is first in Greece to mint coins
Late 600s	Sappho born on Lésbos
570–480	Pythagoras of Sámos
500–323	Classical Age
490–479	Persian Wars end with defeat of Persian army and fleet
478	Delos becomes HQ of the Athenian-dominated Maritime League
460–377	Hippocrates of Kos
431–404	Peloponnesian War cripples Athens
378	Second Delian League
338	Philip of Macedon conquers Athens and the rest of Greece
334–323	Conquests of Alexander the Great
323–146	Hellenistic Age
146–AD 410	Roman Age
88	Mithridates of Pontus, enemy of Rome, devastates many islands
86	Romans under Sulla destroy Athens and other Greek rebels who supported Mithridates

AD

58	St Paul visits Líndos, Rhodes
95	St John the Divine writes the Apocalypse on Pátmos
391	Paganism outlawed in Roman Empire
410–1453	Byzantine Era
727–843	Iconoclasm in the Eastern Church
824–861	Saracen/Arab Occupation
961	Emperor Nikephoros Phokas reconquers Crete from the Saracens
1054	Pope excommunicates Patriarch of Constantinople over differences in the creed
1088	Foundation of the Monastery on Pátmos
1204	Venetians lead Fourth Crusade conquest of Contantinople and take the islands as their share of the booty
1261	Greeks retake Constantinople from Latins
1309	Knights of St John, chased out of Jerusalem, established on Rhodes
1453	Turks begin conquest of Greece
1522	Ottomans defeat Knights of St John
1541	El Greco born on Crete
1669	Venetians lose Herákleon, Crete to the Turks after a 20-year siege
1771–74	Catherine the Great sends Russian fleet into the Aegean to harry the Sultan
1796	Napoleon captures Venice and her Ionian islands
1815–64	British rule Ionian islands
1821–27	Greek War of Independence
1823	Aegina made the capital of free Greece
1827	Annihilation of Turkish fleet by the British, French and Russian allies at the Battle of Navarino
1833	Otho of Bavaria becomes the first king of the Greeks
1883–1957	Cretan writer Nikos Kazantzakis
1912–13	Balkan Wars give Greece Macedonia, Crete and the Northeast Aegean islands; the Italians pick up the Dodecanese
1922–23	Greece invades Turkey with catastrophic results
1924	Greece becomes a republic
1935	Restoration of the monarchy

1941	Nazi paratroopers complete first ever invasion by air on Crete	1974	Failure of the Junta's Cyprus adventure leads to the regime's collapse and restoration of democracy
1945	Treaty signed returning Dodecanese islands to Greece	1981	First ever nominally socialist government (PASOK) elected
1948	Dodecanese islands reunite with Greece	1983	Greece joins the EEC
1949	End of civil war between communists and US-backed government	1990	PASOK lose election to conservative Néa Demokratikí (ND)
1953	Earthquake shatters the Ionian islands	1996	Death of Panandréou; PASOK's Kósta Simítis becomes Prime Minister
1967	Colonels' coup establishes a dictatorship		

Glossary of Terms

acropolis — fortified height, usually the site of a city's chief temples

agíos, agía, agii — saint or saints, or holy abbreviated **Ag.**

ágora — market and public area in a city centre

amphora — tall jar for wine or oil, designed to be shipped (the conical end would be embedded in sand

áno/apáno — upper

caique — a small wooden boat, pronounced '*kaEEki*' now mostly used for tourist excursions

cella — innermost holy room of a temple

choklakía (or ***hokalaía***) — black and white pebble mosaic

chóra — simply, 'place'; often what islanders call their 'capital' town, although it usually also has the same name as the island itself

chorió — village

dimarchíon — town hall

EOT — Greek National Tourist Office

epachía — Orthodox diocese; also a political county

exonarthex — outer porch of a church

heroön — a shrine to a hero or demigod, often built over the tomb

iconostasis — in an Orthodox church, the decorated screen between the nave and altar

kalderími — stone-paved pathways

kástro — castle or fort

katholikón — monastery chapel

káto — lower

kore — Archaic statue of a maiden

kouros — Archaic statue of a naked youth

larnax — a Minoan clay sarcophagus resembling a bathtub

límani — port

limenarchíon — port authority

loutrá — hot spring, spa

megaron — Mycenaean palace

metope — sculpted panel on a frieze

meltémi — north wind off the Russian steppe that plagues the Aegean in the summer

moní — monastery or convent

monopáti — footpath

narthex — entrance porch of a church

néa — new

nísos/nísi — island/islands

nomós — Greek province

OTE — Greek national telephone company

paleó — old

panagía — Virgin Mary

panegýri — Saint's feast day

pantocrátor — the 'Almighty'—a figure of the triumphant Christ in Byzantine domes

paralía — waterfront or beach

períptero — street kiosk selling just about everything

pírgos — tower, or residential mansion

pithos (pithoi) — large ceramic storage jar

plateía — square

skála — port

spilio — cave or grotto

stoa — covered walkway, often lined with shops, in an *ágora*

temenos — sacred precinct of a temple

tholos — conical Mycenaean temple

Greek holds a special place as the oldest spoken language in Europe, going back at least 4000 years. From the ancient language, Modern Greek, or Romaíka, developed into two forms: the purist or *katharévousa*, literally 'clean language', and the popular, or Demotic *demotikí*, the language of the people. But while the purist is consciously Classical, the popular is as close to its ancient origins as say, Chaucerian English is to modern English. These days few purist words are spoken but you will see the old *katharévousa* on shop signs and official forms. Even though the bakery is called the *foúrnos* the sign over the door will read ΑΡΤΟΠΟΛΕΙΟΝ, bread-seller, while the general store will be the ΠΑΝΤΟΠΟΛΕΙΟΝ, seller of all. You'll still see the pure form on wine labels as well.

At the end of the 18th century, in the wakening swell of national pride, writers felt the common language wasn't good enough; archaic forms were brought back and foreign ones replaced. Upon independence, this somewhat stilted, artificial construction called *katharévousa* became the official language of books, documents and even newspapers. The more vigorous and natural Demotic soon began to creep back; in 1901 Athens was shaken by riots and the government fell when the New Testament appeared in *demotikí*; in 1903 several students were killed in a fight with the police during a *demotikí* performance of Aeschylus. When the fury subsided, it looked as if the Demotic would win out by popular demand until the Papadópoulos government (1967–74) made it part of its puritan 'moral cleansing' of Greece to revive the purist. *Katharévousa* was the only language allowed in secondary schools and everything from textbooks to matchbook covers had to be written in the pure form. The great language debate was eventually settled in 1978 when Demotic was made the official tongue.

Greeks travel so far and wide that even in the most remote places there's usually someone who speaks English, more likely than not with an American, Australian or even South African drawl. On the other hand, learning a bit of Greek can make your travels more enjoyable. Usually spoken with great velocity, Greek isn't a particularly easy language to pick up by ear. But even if you have no desire to learn Greek, it is helpful to know at least the alphabet— so that you can find your way around—and a few basic words and phrases.

Greekspeak

Sign language is an essential part of Greek life and it helps to know what it all means. Greekspeak for 'no' is usually a click of the tongue, accompanied by raised eyebrows and a tilt of the head backwards. It could be all three or a permutation. 'Yes' is usually indicated by a forward nod, head tilted to the side. If someone doesn't hear you or understand you properly they will often shake their heads from side to side quizzically and say '*Oríste?*' Hands whirl like windmills in conversations and beware the emphatic open hand brought sharply down in anger. A circular movement of the right hand usually implies something very good or in great quantities. Women walking alone might hear hissing like a demented snake emanating from pavement cafés. This will be the local Romeos or *kamákis* trying to attract your attention.

Greeks also use exclamations which sound odd but mean a lot, like *po, po, po!* an expression of disapproval or derision; *brávo* comes in handy for praise while *ópa!* is useful for whoops! look out! or watch it!; *sigá sigá* means slowly, slowly; *éla!*, come or get on with you, *kíta!* look. Other phrases you'll hear all the time but won't find in your dictionary include:

paréa	gang, close friends
pedhiá	guys, the lads
ré, bré	mate, chum, slang for friends
endáxi	OK
malákka	rude, lit. masturbator, used between men as term of endearment
kéfi	high spirits, well-being
kaïmós	the opposite, suffering, sad
lipón	well, now then
hérete	formal greeting
sto kaló	go with God, formal parting
listía	rip-off
alítis	bum, no-good person
palikári	good guy, brave, honourable
pedhí mou/korítsi mou	my boy/my girl
yasoo koúkla/os	Hi doll, hello gorgeous
etsi íne ee zoí	that's life!
ti na kánoume	what can we do!
kaló taxídhi	good trip, Bon Voyage!
kalí órexi	Bon appetit!

The Greek Alphabet (*see* also **Introduction** p.x)

Pronunciation			English Equivalent	Pronunciation			English Equivalent
A	α	*álfa*	short 'a' as in 'father'	N	ν	*ni*	n
B	β	*víta*	v	Ξ	ξ	*ksi*	'x' as in 'ox'
Γ	γ	*gámma*	guttural *g* or *y* sound	O	o	*ómicron*	'o' as in 'cot'
Δ	δ	*délta*	hard *th* as in 'though'	Π	π	*pi*	p
E	ε	*épsilon*	short 'e' as in 'bet'	P	ρ	*ro*	r
Z	ζ	*zíta*	z	Σ	σ	*sígma*	s
H	η	*íta*	long 'e' as in 'bee'	T	τ	*taf*	t

Language

Θ	θ	*thíta*	soft *th* as in 'thin'	Υ	υ	*ípsilon*	long 'e' as in 'bee'
I	ι	*yóta*	long 'e' as in 'bee'; sometimes like 'y' in 'yet'	Φ	φ	*fi*	f
				X	χ	*chi*	German *ch* as in 'doch'
K	κ	*káppa*	k	Ψ	ψ	*psi*	*ps* as in 'stops'
Λ	λ	*lámtha*	l	Ω	ω	*oméga*	'o' as in 'cot'
M	μ	*mi*	m				

Diphthongs and Consonant Combinations

AI	αι	short 'e' as in 'bet'
EI	ει, OI οι	'i' as in 'machine'
OΥ	ου	*oo* as in 'too'
AΥ	αυ	*av* or *af*
EΥ	ευ	*ev* or *ef*
HΥ	ηυ	*iv* or *if*
ΓΓ	γγ	*ng* as in 'angry'
ΓK	γκ	hard 'g'; *ng* within word
NT	ντ	'd'; *nd* within word
MΠ	μπ	'b'; *mp* within word

Useful Phrases

Yes	*né/málista* (formal)	Ναί /Μάλιστα
No	*óchi*	Όχι
I don't know	*then xéro*	Δέν ξέρω
I don't understand... (Greek)	*then katalavéno... (elliniká)*	Δέν καταλαβαίνω... (Ελληνικά)
Does someone speak English?	*milái kanis angliká?*	Μιλάει κανείς αγγλικά?
Go away	*fíyete*	Φύγετε
Help!	*voíthia!*	Βοήθεια!
My friend	*o fílos moo (m)*	Ο φίλος μου
	ee fíli moo (f)	Η φίλη μου
Please	*parakaló*	Παρακαλώ
Thank you (very much)	*evcharistó (pára polí)*	Ευχαριστώ (πάρα πολύ)
You're welcome	*parakaló*	Παρακαλώ
It doesn't matter	*thén pirázi*	Δέν πειράζει
OK, alright	*endaxi*	Εντάξι
Of course	*vevéos*	Βεβαίος
Excuse me, sorry	*signómi*	Συγγνώμη
Pardon? Or, from waiters, what do you want?	*oríste?*	Ορίστε?
Be careful!	*proséchete!*	Προσέχεται!
Nothing	*típota*	Τίποτα
What is your name?	*pos sas léne? (formal)*	Πώς σάς λένε?
	pos se léne?	Πώς σέ λένε?
How are you?	*ti kánete? (formal/pl)*	Τί κάνεται?
	ti kanis?	Τί κάνεις?
Hello	*yásas, hérete (formal/pl)*	Γειάσας, Χέρεται
	yásou	Γειάσου
Goodbye	*yásas, hérete (formal/pl)*	Γειάσας, Χέρεται
	yásou, adío	Γειάσου, Αντίο
Good morning	*kaliméra*	Καλημέρα
Good evening/good night	*kalispéra/kaliníchta*	Καλησπέρα /Καληνύχτα
What is that?	*ti íne aftó?*	Τί είναι αυτό?
What?	*ti?*	Τί?
Who?	*piós? (m), piá? (f)*	Ποιός? Ποιά?
Where?	*poo?*	Ποιός?
When?	*póte?*	Πότε?

why?	yiatí?	Γιατί?
how?	pos?	Πώς?
I am/ You are/He, she, it is	íme/íse/íne	Είμαι /Είσε /Είναι
We are/ You are/They are	ímaste/ísaste/íne	Είμαστε /Είσαστε /Είναι
I am lost	échasa to thrómo	Εχασα το δρόμο
I am hungry/I am thirsty	pinó/thipsó	Πεινώ/Διψώ
I am tired/ill	íme kourasménos/arostos	Είμαι κουρασμένος /άρρωστος
I am poor	íme ftochós	Είμαι φτωχός
I love you	s'agapó	Σ'αγαπώ
good/bad/so-so	kaló/kakó/étsi kétsi	καλό /κακό /έτσι κ'έτσι
slowly/fast/big/small	sigá sigá/grígora/megálo/mikró	σιγά σιγά /γρήγορα /μεγάλο /μικρό
hot/cold	zestó/crío	ζεστό /κρίο

Shops, Services, Sightseeing

I would like...	tha íthela...	Θά ήθελα...
where is...?	poo íne...?	Πού είναι...?
how much is it?	póso káni?	Πόσο κάνει?
bakery	foúrnos/artopoleion	φούρνος /Αρτοπολείον
bank	trápeza	τράπεζα
beach	paralía	παραλία
church	eklisía	εκκλησία
cinema	kinimatográfos	κινηματογράφος
hospital	nosokomío	νοσοκομείο
hotel	xenodochío	ξενοδοχείο
hot water	zestó neró	ζεστό νερό
kiosk	períptero	περίπτερο
money	leftá	λεφτά
museum	moosío	μουσείο
newspaper (foreign)	efimerítha (xéni)	εφημερίδα (ξένη)
pharmacy	farmakío	φαρμακείο
police station	astinomía	αστυνομία
policeman	astifílakas	αστιφύλακας
post office	tachithromío	ταχυδρομείο
plug, electrical	príza	πρίζα
plug, bath	tápa	τάπα
restaurant	estiatório	εστιατόριο
sea	thálassa	θάλασσα
shower	doush	ντούς
student	fititís	φοιτητής
telephone office	Oté	ΟΤΕ
theatre	théatro	θέατρο
toilet	tooaléta	τουαλέττα

Time

What time is it?	ti óra íne?	Τί ώρα είναι
month/week/day	mína/evthomáda/méra	μήνα /εβδομάδα /μέρα
morning/afternoon/evening	proí/apóyevma/vráthi	πρωί /απόγευμα /βράδυ
yesterday/today/tomorrow	chthés/símera/ávrio	χθές /σήμερα /αύριο
now/later	tóra/metá	τώρα /μετά
it is early/late	íne norís/ argá	είναι νωρίς/αργά

Travel Directions

I want to go to …	*thélo na páo sto (m), sti (f)…*	Θέλω νά πάω στό, στη…
How can I get to…?	*pós boró na páo sto (m), sti (f)…?*	Πώς μπορώ νά πάω στό, στη…?
Where is…?	*poo íne …?*	Πού είναι…?
How far is it?	*póso makriá íne?*	Πόσο μακριά είναι
When will the… come?	*póte tha érthi to (n), ee (f), o (m)…?*	Πότε θά έρθη τό, ή, ό…?
When will the… leave?	*póte tha fíyi to (n), ee (f), o (m)…?*	Πότε θά φύγη τό, ή, ό…?
From where do I catch…?	*apó poo pérno…?*	Από πού πέρνω…?
How long does the trip take?	*póso keró pérni to taxíthi?*	Πόσο καιρό πέρνει τό ταξίδι?
Please show me	*parakaló thíkste moo*	Παρακαλώ δείξτε μου
the (nearest) town	*to horió (to pió kondinó)*	Το χωριό (το πιό κοντινό)
here/there/near/far	*ethó/ekí/kondá/makriá*	εδώ/εκεί/κοντά/μακριά
left/right	*aristerá/thexiá*	αριστερά/δεξιά
north/south	*vória/nótia/anatoliká/thitiká*	βόρεια/νότια/ανατολικά/δυτικά

Driving

where can I rent …?	*poo boró na nikiáso …?*	Πού μπορώ νά? νοικιάσω …?
a car	*éna aftokínito*	ένα αυτοκινητο
a motorbike	*éna michanáki*	ένα μηχανάκι
a bicycle	*éna pothílato*	ένα ποδήλατο
where can I buy petrol?	*poo boró nagorásso venzíni?*	Πού μπορώ ν'αγοράσω βενζίνη?
where is a garage?	*poo íne éna garáz?*	Πού είναι ένα γκαράζ?
a mechanic	*énan mihanikó*	έναν μηχανικό
a map	*énan chárti*	έναν χάρτη
where is the road to…?	*poo íne o thrómos yiá…?*	Πού είναι ο δρόμος γιά…?
where does this road lead?	*poo pái aftós o thrómos?*	Πού πάει αυτός ο δρόμος?
is the road good?	*íne kalós o thrómos?*	Είναι καλός ο δρόμος?
EXIT	*éxothos*	ΕΞΟΔΟΣ
ENTRANCE	*ísothos*	ΕΙΣΟΔΟΣ
DANGER	*kínthinos*	ΚΙΝΔΥΝΟΣ
SLOW	*argá*	ΑΡΓΑ
NO PARKING	*apagorévete ee státhmevsis*	ΑΠΑΓΟΡΕΥΕΤΑΙ Η ΣΤΑΘΜΕΥΣΙΣ
KEEP OUT	*apagorévete ee ísothos*	ΑΠΑΓΟΡΕΥΕΤΑΙ Η ΕΙΣΟΔΟΣ

Numbers

one	*énas (m), mía (f), éna (n)*	ένας, μία, ένα
two	*thío*	δύο
three	*tris (m, f), tría (n)*	τρείς, τρία
four	*téseris (m, f), téssera (n)*	τέσσερεις, τέσσερα
five	*pénde*	πέντε
six	*éxi*	έξι

seven/eight/nine/ten	*eptá/ októ/ ennéa/ théka*	επτά/οκτώ/εννέα/δέκα
eleven/twelve/thirteen	*éntheka/ thótheka/ thekatría*	έντεκα/δώδεκα/δεκατρία
twenty	*íkosi*	είκοσι
twenty-one	*íkosi éna* (*m, n*) *mía* (*f*)	είκοσι ένα, μία
thirty/forty/fifty/sixty	*triánda/ saránda/ penínda/ exínda*	τριάντασαράντα/πενήντα/εξήντα
seventy/eighty/ninety	*evthomínda/ ogthónda/ enenínda*	ευδομήντα/ογδόντα/ενενήντα
one hundred	*ekató*	εκατό
one thousand	*chília*	χίλια

Months/Days

January	*Ianooários*	Ιανουάριος
February	*Fevrooários*	Φεβρουάριος
March	*Mártios*	Μάρτιος
April	*Aprílios*	Απρίλιος
May	*Máios*	Μάιος
June	*Ioónios*	Ιούνιος
July	*Ioólios*	Ιούλιος
August	*Avgoostos*	Αύγουστος
September	*Septémvrios*	Σεπτέμβριος
October	*Októvrios*	Οκτώβριος
November	*Noémvrios*	Νοέμβριος
December	*Thekémvrios*	Δεκέμβριος
Sunday	*Kiriakí/*	Κυριακή
Monday	*Theftéra*	Δευτέρα
Tuesday	*Tríti*	Τρίτη
Wednesday	*Tetárti*	Τετάρτη
Thursday	*Pémpti*	Πέμπτη
Friday	*Paraskeví*	Παρασκευή
Saturday	*Sávato*	Σάββατο

Transport

the airport/aeroplane	*to arothrómio/ aropláno*	τό αεροδρόμιο /αεροπλάνο
the bus station/bus	*ee stási leoforíou/leoforío*	ή στάση λεωφορείου /λεωφορείο
the railway station/the train	*o stathmós too trénou/to tréno*	ό σταθμός τού τραίνου/τό τραίνο
the port/port authority	*to limáni/ limenarchío*	τό λιμάνι/λιμεναρχείο
the ship	*to plío, to karávi*	τό πλοίο, τό καράβι
the steamship	*to vapóri*	τό βαπόρι
the car	*to aftokínito*	τό αυτοκίνητο
a ticket	*éna isitírio*	ένα εισιτήριο

Finding your way round a Greek menu, *katálogos*, takes some doing, but there's a basic layout with prices before and after local tax. You begin with Orektiká, ΟΡΕΚΤΙΚΑ; dishes cooked in olive oil are known as Laderá, ΛΑΔΕΡΑ; main courses are Entrádes, ΕΝΤΡΑΔΕΣ; Fish are Psária, ΨΑΡΙΑ; dishes with minced meat, Kimádhes, ΚΥΜΑΔΕΣ and things grilled or barbecued to order are either Psitá, ΨΗΤΑ or Tis Oras, ΤΗΣ ΩΡΑΣ.

Ορεκτικά (Μεζέδες)	Orektiká (Mezéthes)	Appetisers
τζατζίκι	tzatziki	yoghurt and cucumbers
εληές	eliés	olives
κοπανιστι (τυροσαλατα)	kopanistí (tirosaláta)	cheese purée, often spicy
ντολμάδες	dolmáthes	stuffed vine leaves
μελιτζανοσαλατα	melitzanosaláta	eggplant (aubergine) dip
ταραμοσαλάτα	taramosalata	cod's roe dip
σαγανάκη	saganáki	fried cheese with lemon
ποικιλια	pikilía	mixed hors d'œuvres
μπουρεκι	bouréki	cheese and vegetable pie
τυροπιττα	tirópitta	cheese pie
χόρτα	chórta	wild greens
αξινι	eahíni	sea urchin roe (quite salty)

Σούπες	Soópes	Soups
αυγολέμονο	avgolémono	egg and lemon soup
χορτόσουπα	chortósoupa	vegetable soup
ψαρόσουπα	psarósoupa	fish soup
φασολαδα	fasolada	bean soup
μαγειρίτσα	magirítsa	giblets in egg and lemon
πατσας	patsás	tripe and pig's foot soup (for late nights and hangovers

Λαδερά	Latherá	Cooked in Oil
μπαμιες	bámies	okra, ladies' fingers
γιγαντες	yígantes	butter beans in tomato sauce
μπριαμ	briám	aubergines and mixed veg
φασόλακια	fasólakia	fresh green beans
φακή	fakí	lentils

Ζυμαρικά	Zimariká	Pasta and Rice
πιλάφι, ρυζι	piláfi/rizi	pilaf/rice
σπαγκέτι	spagéti	spaghetti
μακαρόνια	macarónia	macaroni
πιγγουρι	pingoúri	bulgar wheat

Ψάρια	Psária	Fish
αστακός	astakós	lobster
αθερινα	atherína	smelt
γαβρος	gávros	mock anchovy
καλαμαρια	kalamaria	squid
κεφαλοσ	kefalos	grey mullet
χταπόδι	chtapóthi	octopus
χριστοψαρο	christópsaro	John Dory

μπαρμπούνι	*barboúni*	red mullet
γαρίδες	*garíthes*	prawns (shrimps)
γοπα	*gópa*	bogue (boops boops)
ξιφιας	*ksifías*	swordfish
μαρίδες	*maríthes*	whitebait
μελανουρι	*melanoúri*	saddled bream
συναγρίδα	*sinagrítha*	sea bream
σουπιες	*soupiés*	cuttlefish
φαγρι	*fangri*	bream
κιδονια	*kidónia*	cherrystone clams
σαρδέλλα	*sardélla*	sardines
μπακαλιάρος (σκορδαλιά)	*bakaliáros (skorthaliá)*	fried hake (with garlic sauce)
σαργος	*sargós*	white bream
σκαθαρι	*skathári*	black bream
σκορπενα	*skorpéna*	scorpion fish?? (scorpaena scrofa)
σκουμβρι	*skoumbri*	mackerel
στρείδια	*stríthia*	oysters
τσιπουρα	*tsipoúra*	gilt head bass
λιθρίνια	*lithrínia*	bass
μιδια	*mídia*	mussels

Αυγά — Avgá — Eggs

ομελέττα μέ ζαμπόν	*omeléta me zambón*	ham omelette
ομελέττα μέ τυρί	*omeléta me tirí*	cheese omelette
αυγά τηγανιτά (μπρουγέ)	*avgá tiganitá (brouyé)*	fried (scrambled) eggs
άυγά και μπεικον	*avgá kai bakón*	egg and bacon

Εντραδεσ — Entrádes — Main Courses

κουνέλι	*kounéli*	rabbit
στιφάδο	*stifádo*	casserole with onions
γιουβέτσι	*yiouvétsi*	veal in a clay bowl
συκώτι	*seekóti*	liver
μοσχάρι	*moschári*	veal
αρνι	*arní*	lamb
λουκάνικο	*lukániko*	sausage
κατσυκι	*katsíki*	kid
κοτόπουλο	*kotópoulo*	(roast) chicken
χοιρινό	*chirinó*	pork

Κυμάδες — Kymadhes — Minced Meat

παστίτσιο	*pastítsio*	mince and macaroni pie
μουσακά	*moussaká*	meat, aubergine with white sauce
μακαρόνια με κυμά	*makarónia me kymá*	spaghetti Bolognese
μπιφτεκι	*biftéki*	hamburger, usually bunless
σουτζουκάκια	*soutzoukákia*	meat balls in sauce
ντομάτες γεμιστές	*tomátes yemistés*	stuffed tomatoes
μελιτζάνες γεμιστές	*melitzánes yemistés*	stuffed aubergines/eggplants
πιπεριές γεμιστές	*piperíes yemistés*	stuffed peppers

Της Ωρας — Tis Oras — Grills to Order

μρισολα	*brisóla*	beefsteak with bone
μπριζόλες χοιρινές	*brizólas chirinés*	pork chops
σουβλάκι	*souvláki*	meat or fish kebabs on a skewer

κοκορετσι	*kokorétsi*	offal kebabs
κοτελέτες	*kotelétes*	veal chops
παιδακια	*paidakia*	lamb chops
κεφτέδες	*keftéthes*	meat balls

Σαλάτες — **Salátes** — **Salads and Vegetables**

ντομάτες	*domátes*	tomatoes
αγγούρι	*angoúri*	cucumber
ρώσσικη σαλάτα	*róssiki saláta*	Russian salad
σπανακι	*spanáki*	spinach
καπαρι	*kápari*	caper leaves
χοριάτικη	*choriátiki*	salad with *Feta* cheese and olives
κολοκυθάκια	*kolokithákia*	courgettes/zucchini
πιπεριεσ	*piperiés*	peppers
κρεμιδι	*kremídi*	onions
πατάτες	*patátes*	potatoes
παντσάρια	*pantsária*	beetroot
μαρούλι	*maroúli*	lettuce
χορτα	*chórta*	wild greens
αγκιναρες	*anginâres*	artichokes
κουκια	*koukiá*	fava beans

Τυρια — **Tiriá** — **Cheeses**

φέτα	*féta*	goat's cheese
κασέρι	*kasséri*	hard buttery cheese
ροκφόρ	*rokfór*	blue cheese (roquefort)
γραβιέρα	*graviéra*	Greek 'Gruyère'
μυζήθρα	*mizíthra*	soft white cheese
προβιο	*próvio*	sheeps' cheese

Γλυκά — **Glyká** — **Sweets**

παγωτό	*pagotó*	ice cream
κουραμπιέδες	*kourabiéthes*	sugared biscuits
λουκουμάδες	*loukoumáthes*	hot honey fritters
χαλβά	*halvá*	sesame seed sweet
μπακλαβά	*baklavá*	nuts and honey in fillo pastry
γαλακτομπούρεκο	*galaktoboúreko*	custard in fillo pastry
γιαούρτι (με μελι)	*yiaoúrti (me méli)*	yoghurt (with honey)
καριδοπιτα	*karidópita*	walnut cake
ρυζόγαλο	*rizógalo*	rice pudding
καταΐφι	*kataífi*	shredded wheat with nuts, honey
μπουγάτσα	*bougátsa*	custard tart
αμιγδαλωτά	*amigthalotá*	soft almond biscuits

Φρούτα — **Froóta** — **Fruit**

αχλάδι	*achláthi*	pear
πορτοκάλι	*portokáli*	orange
ροδι	*ródi*	pomegranite
μήλο	*mílo*	apple
κερασι	*kerási*	cherry
ροδάκινο	*rothákino*	peach
πεπόνι	*pepóni*	melon
καρπούζι	*karpoúzi*	watermelon

ακτινιδι	*aktinídi*	kiwi
κιδονι	*kidóni*	quince
δαμάσκινο	*thamáskino*	plum
σύκα	*síka*	figs
σταφύλια	*stafília*	grapes
μπανάνα	*banána*	banana
βερύκοκο	*veríkoko*	apricot
φραουλες	*fráoules*	strawberries

Miscellaneous

ψωμί	*psomí*	bread
βούτυρο	*voútiro*	butter
μέλι	*méli*	honey
μαρμελάδα	*marmelátha*	jam
αλάτι	*aláti*	salt
πιπέρι	*pipéri*	pepper
ζάχαρη	*záchari*	sugar
λάδι	*láthi*	oil
ξύδι	*xíthi*	vinegar
μουστάρδα	*moostárda*	mustard
λεμόνι	*lemóni*	lemon
πιάτο	*piáto*	plate
μαχαίρι	*mahéri*	knife
πηρούνι	*piroóni*	fork
κουτάλι	*koutáli*	spoon
λογαριασμό	*logariasmó*	the bill/check

Drinks

άσπρο κρασί	*áspro krasí*	wine, white
ασπρο /κοκκινο /κοκκινελι	*áspro/kókkino/kokkinéli*	white/red/rosé
ρετσίνα	*retsína*	wine resinated
νερό (βραστο /μεταλικο)	*neró (vrastó /metalikó)*	water (boiled/mineral)
μπύρα	*bíra*	beer
χυμός πορτοκάλι	*chimós portokáli*	orange juice
γάλα	*gála*	milk
τσάϊ	*tsái*	tea
σοκολάτα	*sokoláta*	chocolate
καφε	*kafé*	coffee
φραππε	*frappé*	iced coffee
παγος	*págos*	ice
ποτίρι	*potíri*	glass
μπουκαλι	*boukáli*	bottle
καραφα	*karáfa*	carafe
στήν γειά σαs!	*stín yásas (formal, pl)*	to your health! Cheers!
στήν γειά σου!	*stín yásou (sing)*	

Further Reading

In addition to following titles, check out the new expanding series of modern Greek fiction translated into English by Kedros in Athens, generally available in bookshops in Greece.

Burkert, Walter, *Greek Religion* (Basil Blackwell, Oxford, and Harvard University Press, 1985)—ancient religion, that is.

Castleden, Rodney, *Minoans: Life in Bronze Age Crete* (Routledge, 1990).

Constantinidou-Partheniadou, Sofia, *A Travelogue in Greece and A Folklore Calendar* (privately published, Athens 1992). A mine of information on modern customs and superstitions.

Clogg, Richard, *A Short History of Modern Greece* (Cambridge University Press). Best, readable account of a messy subject.

De Bernières, Louis, *Captain Corelli's Mandolin,* (Martin Secker & Warburg, London 1994, Pantheon, New York. Gorgeous humane novel about the tragic Italian occupation of Kefalonía in World War II.

Du Boulay, Juliet, *Portrait of a Greek Mountain Village* (Oxford University Press). Life in Ambéli, Évia

Durrell, Gerald, *My Family and Other Animals* (Viking Penguin). Charming account of expat life on Corfu in the 1930s.

Durrell, Lawrence, *The Greek Islands, Prospero's Cell* and *The White House; Reflections on a Marine Venus* (Faber & Faber and Viking/Penguin, London and New York). The latter about Rhodes; the first three about Corfu.

Elytis, Odysseus, *Selected Poems* and *The Axion Esti* (Anvil Press/Viking). Good translations of the Nobel Prize winning poet, whose parents are from Mytilini

Finley, M. I., *The World of Odysseus* (Penguin/Viking). Mycenaean history and myth.

Graves, Robert, *The Greek Myths* (Penguin, 1955, but often reprinted). The classic.

Harrison, Jane Ellen, *Themis: A Study of the Social Origins of Greek Religion* (Meridian Books, Cleveland, 1969) and *Prolegomena to the Study of Greek Religion* (Merlin Press, London, 1980). Reprints of the classics.

Kazantzakis, Nikos, *Zorba the the Greek, Report to Greco, Christ Recrucified, Freedom or Death* (Faber & Faber/Simon & Schuster). The soul of Crete in fiction.

Keeley, Edmund and Philip Sherrard, translators, *A Greek Quintet* (Denis Harvey and Co., Évia, 1981). Fine translations of Cavafy, Sikelianos, Seferis, Elytis and Gatsos.

McKirahan Jr., Richard D., *Philosophy Before Socrates* (Hackett Indianapolis, 1994). Know your pre-Socratics and discover there really isn't anything new under the sun.

Myrivilis, Stratis, *The Mermaid Madonna* and *The Schoolmistress with the Golden Eyes* (Efstathiadis, Athens). Excellent novels that take place on Lésbos, the author's home.

Papadiamantis, Alexandros, *Tales from a Greek Island,* translated by Elizabeth Constantinides (John Hopkins University Press). Skiáthos in the old days, by a prose master.

The Penguin Book of Hippocratic Writings. A selection of ancient medical wisdom from Kos.

Pettifer, James, *The Greeks: The Land and People Since the War* (Penguin, London and New York, 1994).

Renfrew, Colin, *The Cycladic Spirit* (Thames & Hudson). A study of Cycladic art.

Rice, David Talbot, *Art of the Byzantine Era* (Thames & Hudson).

Trypanis, Constantine, *The Penguin Book of Greek Verse* (Penguin, London and New York, 1971). From Homer to modern times, with prose translations.

Storace, Patricia, *Dinner with Persephone,* (Pantheon, New York 1996/Granta, London 1997). New York poet fluent in modern Greek tackles the contradictions of modern Greece.

Walbank, F.W., *The Hellenistic World* (Fontana/Harvard University Press). From Alexander to the Romans, a time when many islands prospered

Ware, Timothy Callistos, *The Orthodox Church* (Penguin). All you've ever wanted to know about the national religion of Greece

Woodhouse, C. M., *Modern Greece: A Short History* (Faber & Faber, 1992).

Main page references are in **bold**. Page references to maps are in *italics*.

accommodation *see* where to stay
Achilles 403
air travel 2–7
  airline offices 6–7
  charter flights 2, 3
  children 5
  from Australasia 4
  from North America 3–4
  from UK and Ireland 2–3
  island-to-island flights 7
Andímilos 370
Antikýthera 349–50
Antikýthera Mechanism 350–1
Antíparos 391–2
Aphrodite 41, 357
Apollo 41, 211
architecture 42–6
  Skyriot houses 406
Ares 41
Ariadne 229
Arion 211
art 42–6
Artemis 41
Asteria 378
Astypálaia 312–15, *313*
Athena 41, 48
Athens 48–70
  Acropolis 55
  Agora 58–60
  airline offices 6–7
  airport 6–7, 65–6
  Altar of the Twelve Gods 59
  Anafiótika 53
  Areópagos 57
  Beulé Gate 55
  bookshops 53
  Bouleuterion 58–9
  Cape Soúnion 55
  Central Market 68
  churches **62–3**
    Ag. Dimítrios 57
    Holy Apostles 59
  Dafní Monastery 63

Athens (*cont'd*)
  Ellinikon Airport *see* airport
  emergencies 52
  entertainment and nightlife 69–70
  Erechtheion 57
  Exárchia 54, 68–9
  festivals 15–16
  getting around 51–2
  Glyfáda 55
  Heliaia 59
  history 48–51
  Internet café 53
  Iróon Square 53
  Kavoúri 55
  Kolonáki 53, 67
  Koukáki 54, 69
  left luggage 52
  Library of Pantainos 59
  lost property 52
  Lykavitós Hill 53
  Makrigiánni 54, 69
  Metroön 59
  Metz 54
  Middle Stoa 59
  Monastiráki 53, 67
  Monument of Lysikrátes 58
  museums **60–2**
    Acropolis Museum 57
    Byzantine Museum 44
    National Archaeology 42, 43, 54, **60**
  National Gardens 53
  Odeon of Agrippa 59
  Odeon of Herodes Atticus 58
  Olympic Stadium 54
  Omónia Square 54, 68
  orientation 53
  Parthenon 49, **56**
  Philopáppos Monument 57–8
  Pláka 53, 66
  Plateía Sýntagma 53
  Pnyx 57
  Propylaia 55

Athens (*cont'd*)
  South Stoa 59
  Stoa of Attalus 59–60
  Stoa of Zeus Eleutherios 59
  Sýntagma 66
  Temple of Apollo 59
  Temple of Athena Nike 56
  Temple of Olympian Zeus 62
  Temple to Ares 59
  Theatre of Diónysos 58
  Theseum 60
  Thissío 54, **58–60**, 67–8
  Tholos 59
  Three Giants 59
  tourist information 52
  University 54
  Valerian's Wall 59
  Várkiza 55
  Voúla 55
  Vouliagménis 55
  where to stay 63–6
  Záppeion Park 53
Balkan Wars 37
banks 23
Barbarossa 150
bars 21
bugs and pests 14
Byzantine Empire
  art and architecture 44–5
  in Crete 77–8
  in Rhodes 240–1
cafés 20–1
camping 30–1
Capodístria, Count John 36
car travel 8
charter flights 2, 3
children 5, 28
Children of the Sea 237
Chíos 43, 44, **315–29**, *317*
  Chíos town *319*, 319–20
  Emborió **324**, 325
  excursions 318
  festivals 318
  getting there and around 318

Dora Stratou Theatre 58
East Stoa 59
eating out 66–9

Psirrí 53, 67
Roman Forum 62
Sanctuary of the Eponymous Heroes of Athens 59

history 316–17
Inoússes 328
Kámbos **320–1**, 321–2

Index

Chíos (cont'd)
Kardámila **326**, 327
Karfás **321**, 322
Kómi **323**, 325
Langáda **326**, 327
Líthi **324**, 325
Mastic Villages 323–5
mythology 316
Néa Moní 325–6
Pirgí 323–4
Psará 328–9
tourist information 318
Volissós **326–7**, 328
Vrontádos **326**, 327
Civil War 38
classical art and architecture 43
climate 14–15
Constantine I 37
Constantine II 39
consulates 15, 153
Corcyra 149–50, 160
Corfu (Kérkyra) 43, 45, **148–73**, *149*
Acharávi 168
Achilleíon 161
Afiónas **169**, 170
Ag. Geórgios (northwest) **169**, 170
Ag. Geórgios (South) 172
Ag. Górdis **171**, 172
Ag. Iássonos and Sosipater 160
Ag. Kérkyra 160
Ag. Mattheos **172**, 173
Ag. Panteléimonos 168
Ag. Spyrídonos 167
Ag. Stéfanos (east) **166**, 167
Ag. Stéfanos (west) 169
Ag. Teodóri 161
Agní **166**, 167
Agnos 168
Almirós 168
Alykés 172
Angelókastro 169–70
Ano Korakiána 164
Aríllas 169
Arkoudílas 172
Asprókavos 172
Astrakéri 168
Avláki 166
Barbáti 165–6
Benítses **171**, 172–3
Canal d'Amour 168
Cape Komméno 164
Chorepískopi 170

Corfu (*cont'd*)
consulates 153
Corcyra 149–50, 160
Corfu town 154–9, *156–7*
Dassiá **164**, 165
Dragotiná 172
Episkepsís 168
Ermónes **170**, 171
excursions 154
festivals 148, **153–4**
Gardíki 172
Gastoúri 161
getting there and around 152–3
Glyfáda **170**, 171
golf 170
Gouviá **164**, 165
history 149–54
Ípsos **164**, 165
Kaiser's Throne 170
Kalamáki 166
Kalámi **166**, 167
Kamináki 166
Kanóni peninsula 160–1
Kardáki 160–1
Karoussádes 168
Kassiópi **166**, 167
Kávos 172
Kerásia 166
Kontókali 165
Kouloúra 166
Koyévinas 166
Lagoúdia 172
Lákones 169
Lefkími 172
Límni Korissíon 172
Linía 172
Marathiás 172
Messónghi **171**, 173
Mirtiótissa 170
Mólos 172
Mon Repos 160
Moraítika **171**, 173
Mount Pantokrátor 166
Nímfes 170
Nissáki 167
Old Perithía 166–7
Paleokastrítsa **169**, 170–1
Panagía Vlacharína 161
Paramónas 172
Pélekas **170**, 171
Pérama 161
Perouládes 168
Pírgi 164

Corfu (*cont'd*)
Plátonas 168
Polylas 168
Pondikonísi 161
Róda 168
Rópa Valley 170
Sidári 168
Sinarádes 171
Skithi 172
Stavrós 171
Temple of Artemis 161
tourist information 153
Tría Avlákia 172
Valanión 170
Zoodóchos Pigí 169
Crete 44, 45, **72–146**, *72*
Afráta 89
Ag. Ánna 99
Ag. Déka 124
Ag. Geórgios 133
Ag. Konstantínos 133
Ag. Marína **87**, 89
Ag. Nikólaos 134–7
Ag. Nikólaos monastery 122
Ag. Pandeleímonos 127
Ag. Pávlos 91
Ag. Pelagía 101
Ag. Roúmeli **91**, 92
Ag. Theódori 87
Ag. Triáda 126
Ag. Varvára 122
Ag. Vasílios 121
agriculture 73
Akrotíri 42, **92–3**
Alikianós 90
Almirída 94
Almyrós 136
Amári 99
Ámmos 136
Ammoudára 116
Ammoúdi 135
Amnisós 116
Anemospiliá 119, 121
Anógia 102
Aperta 94
Archánes 118–19
Arkalochóri 127
Arkoudiótissa 93
Avdoú 132
Axós 101
Balí 101
Cape Drápanon 94–5
Cape Spáda 87–9
caves

Crete (*cont'd*)
Diktean 133
Eileithyia 116
Idean 102
Kamarés 122–3
Milátos 134
St John the Hermit 93
Sendóni 101
Skotinó 128
Chaniá 80–6, *81*
Chaniá nomós 87–98, *88*
Chersónisos **128**, 129
Commonwealth War
Cemetery 93–4
Convent of Kardiótissa 132
culture 73
Diktean Cave 133
Diktyna 89
Drápanos 94
Dreros 134, 137
Eileithyia Cave 116
Eléftherna 101
Eloúnda **137**, 138
Embaros 127
entertainment and nightlife
Ag. Nikólaos 137
Chaniá 86
Herákleon 118
Réthymnon 98
Etiá 142–3
Exópoli 94
festivals 87, 130
Ag. Nikólaos 135
Chaniá 82
Herákleon 106
Réthymnon 95
Sitía 140–2
Fódele 101
food and drink 79–80
Gargardóros 136
Gavalochóri 94
getting there 80
Goniés 102
Górtyn 123–4
Gourniá 139
Goúves 128
Herákleon 42, 44, 103–18,
104–5
Herákleon nomós 118–30,
120
history 75–9
Idean Cave 102
Idzeddin 94
Ierápetra 146

Crete (*cont'd*)
Ístro 139
Itanos 143–4
Kakó Poulí 87
Kalathás 92
Kaló Chório 139
Kalýves 94
Kamarés 122–3
Kanlí Kastélli 121
Karouzaná 127
Karphí 132
Kastélli 127
Kastrí 143
Katholikón 93
Káto Stálos 87
Káto Zákro 145
Kefalás 94
Kerá 132
Kéra Panagía 138–9
Kitroplateía 135
Knossós 110–16, *114*
Kókkino Chóra 94
Kolimbári 87
Koufonísi 146
Koureménos 143
Krási 132
Kritsá 139
Lake Voulisméni 135
Lassíthi nomós 130–46, *131*
Lassíthi plateau 130–3
Lato 139
Lyttos 127
Máleme **87**, 89
Mália 42, **128–30**
Margarítes 101
Maronía 142
Megála Choráphia 94
Meniás 89
Mesará Plain 123–4
Milátos Cave 134
Misiriá 99
Mitrópolis 124
Móchlos 140
Mochós 132
Monastiráki 99
moní
Ag. Nikólaos 122
Ag. Triáda 92
Arkádi 98–9
Asómati 99
Balí 101
Chryssopigí 94
Faneroménis 139
Goniás 87

Crete (*cont'd*)
Gouvernétou 93
Kroustallénia 133
Spiliótissa 121
Toploú 143
Valsamonérou 122
Vrondísi 122
Mount Júktas 121
Mourniés 89–90
Myrtiá 121–2
mythology 74–5
Neápolis 134
Nírou Cháni 128
Nisos Chrisí 146
Olous 137
Omalós **91**, 92
Pachiá Ámmos 140
Palaíkastro **143**, 145
Palianí 122
Panagías 91
Pánormos 99, 101
Paralía Milátou 134
patriotism 73–4
Phaistós 124–6, *125*
Phourní necropolis 119
Pláka 94, 138
Plataniás **87**, 89
Plátanos 140
Potamiés 130, 132
Praisós 142
Prasanó gorge 99
Profítis Ilías 92
Pseíra 140
Psilí Korfí 121
Psilorítis 102
Psychró 133
Réthymnon 95–8
Réthymnon nomós 98–118,
100
Roussolakos 143
St John the Hermit's cave 93
Samariá gorge 90–2
Sendóni cave 101
shopping
Ag. Nikólaos 135–6
Chaniá 84
Herákleon 116
Réthymnon 97
Sideróportes 91
Sísi 133–4
Sitía 140–2
Sklaverochóri 127
Sklavokámbos 102
Skotinó 128

Crete (*cont'd*)
  Soúda 93–4
  Spinalónga 138
  sports and activities 96–7
  Stavrós **92**, 93
  Thérisson Gorge 89–90
  Thrapsanó 127
  Thrónos 99
  Toploú Monastery 143
  Torsanás 92
  tourism 72–3
  Trápeza 132
  Týlisos 102
  Tzermiádon **132**, 133
  Vaï 143
  Vámos 94
  Vasilikí 140
  Vathianó Kambó 128
  Vathýpetro 121
  Veneráto 122
  Viranepiskopí 101
  Vóri 126–7
  Vorízia 122
  when to go 80
  Xerókambos 145
  Xylóskalo 91
  Zákros 42, **144–6**, *145*
  Zarós **122**, 123
  Zonianá 101
Cronos 74, 237
cultural attractions 15–17
Cycladic art and architecture 42
cycling 9
cyclopean walls 42
Cyprus 38–9
Daedalus 74–5
Dafní 44
Darius, King 49
Délos 43, **378–83**, *380*
Delphic Idea 204–5
Deméstika 22
Demeter 41
dictatorship 39
Dimitros Poliorketes 239–40
Dionysos 41, 211, 229
disabled travellers 12
diving 26
doctors 22–3
dogs 14
Dorians 48
  Law Code 123–4
dragon fish 14
drinking water 27
driving on the islands 8

E111 forms 22
El Greco 101
Elafónissos 349
electricity 15
Elgin marbles 50
Ellinikon Airport 6–7
embassies 15
entry formalities 7
Erechtheos, King 48
Eríkousa 168–9
Erotókritos 141–2
estiatória 18–19
Evans, Arthur 75, 111
events 15–17
excursion boats 8
festivals 15–17
  Chíos 318
  Corfu 148, **153–4**
  Crete *see* Crete, festivals
  Foúrni 335
  Ikaría 331
  Kárpathos 338
  Kefaloniá 176
  Kos 190
  Kýthera 346
  Lefkáda 202–3
  Léros 353
  Lésbos 214
  Límnos 360
  Mílos 366
  Mýkonos 374
  Náxos 229–30
  Páros 386
  Rhodes 243
  Sámos 275
  Santoríni 395
  Skiáthos 288
  Skýros 405
  Sými 267
  Sýros 411
  Thássos 294
  Zákynthos 301
food and drink 17–22
  of Crete 79–80
  eating out 18–21
  vegetarians 18
  water 27
  wine *see* wine
  see also under individual
    places (eating out)
Geometric art and architecture
  42–3
George I 37, 152
George II 37

Glaroníssia 370
golf 26
Goths 50
Greek Travel Pages 2
Guiscard, Robert 186–7
Hades 41
Hadzimichális, Theóphilos
  215–16
hasapotavérna 19
health 22–3
  bugs and pests 14
Helios 41, 237–8
Hellenistic art and architecture
  43
Hephaistos 41, 357
Hera 41
Herakles 41
Hermes 41
history 36–41
  see also under individual
    places
hitch-hiking 9
horse riding 26
hotels 28–30
  see also under individual
    places (where to stay)
Ikaría 329–36, *329*
  Ag. Kýrikos **331–2**, 333
  Armenistís 334–5
  Évdilos **333**, 334
  festivals 331
  Foúrni 335–6
  getting there and around
    330–1
  history 330
  mythology 330
  north coast 333–5
  Thérma **332**, 333
  tourist information 331
Independence 36–7
Inoússes 328
insects 14
Internet 2
island flights 7
jellyfish 14
John, Saint 93
junta 39
Justinian, Emperor 50
kafeneíons 20–1
Kámiros (Rhodes) 263–5
Kárpathos 336–43, *339*
  Ammopí **338**, 341
  Apéri 340
  Arkássa **339**, 341

Kárpathos (*cont'd*)
 Diafáni **342**, 343
 east coast 340
 entertainment and nightlife
  342
 festivals 338
 Finíki **339**, 342
 getting there and around
  337–8
 history 337
 inland villages 340
 Kárpathos town **338**, 341
 Kyrá Panagía **340**, 342
 Lefkós **339–40**, 342
 northern villages 343
 Ólympos 342–3
 Voláda 340
 west coast 338–40
Kazantzákis, Níkos 110, 122
Kefaloniá 173–87, *175*
 Ag. Andréas 181
 Ag. Evfimía 184–5
 Ag. Geórgios 179
 Ag. Geórgios Castle 181
 Ag. Gerásimos monastery
  181–2
 Ag. Kiriakí 185
 Ag. Spyrídon 179
 Ag. Theódori lighthouse
  177–8
 Andisámos 184
 Angláki cave 184
 Angónas 185
 Ántipata Erissóu 186
 Argostóli **176–7**, 178–9
 Ássos **187–8**, 189
 Avithos 180
 Chalikéri 186
 Damoulináta 179
 Delaportáta 179
 Divaráta 185
 Domáta 180
 Drákondi Spílio 179
 Drakopouláta 185
 Drogaráti cave 184
 excursions 178
 festivals 176
 Fiskárdo **186**, 187
 getting there and around 176
 history 174–6
 Kaminaráta 179
 Karavádos 182
 Katavóthres 177
 Káto Kateliós 182

Kefaloniá (*cont'd*)
 Kipouríon 179
 Kounópetra 179
 Kourkomeláta 181
 Krani 177
 Lakídra 181
 Lassí Peninsula 177–8
 Lépeda 179
 Livathó 180
 Lixoúri **179**, 180
 Lourdáta **182**, 183–4
 Makris Gialós 178
 Mantzavináta 179
 Markópoulo 183
 Mégas Sóros 182
 Melissáni 184
 Metaxáta 181
 Michalitsáta 179
 Miniés 180
 Mount Aínos 180–2
 Mýtos 185
 Omalós plain 181
 Palikí peninsula 179
 Pástra 183
 Pessáda **182**, 183
 Petáni 179
 Platís Gialós 178
 Sámi **184**, 185
 Síssia monastery 182
 Skála **183**, 184
 Soularí 179
 Spartiá 182
 Svoronáta 180
 Tafíon 179
 tourist information 176
 Trapezáki 182
 Tzanáta 183
 Vardianá islet 179
 Varí 186
 wine **180**, 182
 Xi 179
 Zóla 185
Kérkyra *see* Corfu
Kléftiko 370
Kleisthénes 49
Knights Hospitallers of St John
 240–1
Kornáros, Vincénzo 141
Kos 43, 45, **188–200**, *189*
 Ag. Fokás 194
 Ag. Ioánnis Thimianós 198
 Ag. Stéfanos 198
 Ag. Theológos 198
 Amaníou 197

Kos (*cont'd*)
 Antimácheia 197–8
 Asfendíou 197
 Asklepeion 194–5
 Áspri Pétra cave 198
 Astypálaia 198
 Camel Beach 198
 Charmyleion 197
 Díkaios Christós 197
 Embrós Thermá 194
 festivals 190
 getting there and around 189–
  90
 history 188–9
 Kamári 198
 Kardámena **198**, 199
 Kastri 198
 Kéfalos **198**, 199
 Kos town *193*, 194–7
 Lagáda 198
 Lagoúdi 197
 Lampí 194
 Marmári **197**, 198–9
 Mastichári **198**, 199
 Palaío Pýli 197
 Paradise Beach 198
 Pláka 198
 Platáni 195
 Poléni 198
 Psalídi 194
 Psérimos 199–200
 Pýli 197
 sports 195
 Tingáki **197**, 198–9
 Tolíri 198
 tourist information 190
 Xerokambos 198
 Ziá 197
 Zipári 197
Kraterós 116
Kreipe, General 79, 119
Kýthera 344–51, *345*
 Antikýthera 349–50
 Chóra **346**, 348
 east coast 347
 eating out 348–9
 Elafónissos 349
 festivals 346
 getting there and around 345
 history 344
 north coast 347–8
 Palio Chóra 347–8
 tourist information 345–6
 where to stay 348–9

Labyrinth 110–11
Lefkáda 200–10, *201*
 Ag. Nikítas **208**, 210
 east coast 205–6
 festivals 202–3
 getting there and around 202
 history 200, 202
 inland villages 207–8
 Karyá **207**, 208
 lace industry 207
 Lefkáda town 203–5
 lentil production 207–8
 Meganísi 210
 Nidrí **205–6**, 207
 Nikiána **205**, 206–7
 Póros **206**, 207
 Sívota **206**, 207
 tourist information 202
 Vassilikí **209**, 210
 west coast 208
Lefkándi 43
Léros 351–7, *352*
 Ag. Marína **354**, 356
 Álinda **354–5**, 356
 entetainment and nightlife
 356–7
 festivals 353
 getting there and around 353
 history 351–2
 Krithóni **354**, 356
 Lakkí **353–4**, 355
 Pantéli **354**, 355–6
 Plátanos **354**, 356
 tourist information 353
 Vromólithos **354**, 355–6
 Xirókambos **354**, 355
Lésbos 210–28, *213*
 Ag. Ignatios Limónos 219
 Ag. Paraskeví 219
 Ántissa 223–4
 Eftaloú **220**, 221–2
 entertainment and nightlife
 223
 festivals 214
 getting there and around 212
 history 211–12
 Kalloní 219
 Kápi 219
 Mantamádos 218–9
 Míthymna (Mólyvos) **220**,
 221–2
 mythology 211
 Mytilíni Town 214–18, *216*
 Náxos 221

Lésbos (*cont'd*)
 Neápolis 217
 Pétra **220–1**, 223
 petrified forest 224
 Plomári **227**, 228
 Polichnítos 226–7
 Sígri **224**, 225–6
 Sikaminiá 219
 Skála Eressoú **224**, 225–6
 Skála Kalloní **219**, 221
 Skála Polichnítou 227
 Skála Sikaminiá 219
 Southern villages 226–7
 sports and activities 214
 Thérmi 218
 tourist information 212, 214
 Variá 215–17
 Vaterá 227
Leto 378–9
Límnos 357–64, *359*
 Ag. Efstrátios 363–4
 festivals 360
 getting there and around 358,
 360
 history 358
 Kontiás **361**, 363
 Moúdros **361**, 363
 Mýrina **360–1**, 362–3
 mythology 357–58
 tourist information 360
 Tsimántria 363
 wine 362
Lykomedes of Skýros 403
mageiria 19
Maitland, Sir Thomas 151
Mália 42
Marathon, battle of 49
Mathráki 168–9
measurements 15
Meganísi 210
Melissus 273
Metaxás, General 37–8
mezedopoieíons 21
Mílos 364–72, *365*
 Adámas **366–7**, 370–1
 Ag. Kyriakí **370**, 371
 entertainment and nightlife
 371–2
 excursions 370
 festivals 366
 getting there and around 366
 history 364, 366
 inland villages 369–70
 Klíma **367–8**, 371

Mílos (*cont'd*)
 Melos 367–8
 North coast 369
 Paleochóri **370**, 371
 Pláka **367–68**, 371
 Pollónia **369**, 371
 tourist information 366
 Triptí **367**, 371
Minoans 75–7
 art and architecture 42
 Palace of Zákros 42, **144–6**,
 145
 Týlisos villas 102
Minos 74–5
Monastery of Platýteras 155
money 23
mopeds 8–9
mosquitoes 14
motorbikes 8–9
museum opening hours 23
Mykále, battle of 273
Mýkonos 372–8, *373*
 Chóra **374–5**, 376
 eating out 376–7
 entertainment and nightlife
 378
 festivals 374
 getting there and around 372,
 374
 history 372
 mythology 372
 tourist information 374
 villages and sights 375
 where to stay 376–7
mythology 41
 Chíos 316
 Crete 74–5
 Délos 378–9
 Ikaría 330
 Lésbos 211
 Límnos 357–8
 Mýkonos 372
 Náxos 229
 Rhodes 237–8
 Skýros 403
Mytilíni *see* Lésbos
Napoleon Bonaparte 151
national holidays 24
Náxos 43, 228–36, *231*
 Apíranthos 233–4
 Apóllonas **234**, 236
 Chálki 233
 entertainment and nightlife
 236

Náxos (*cont'd*)
  excursions 230
  festivals 229–30
  Galanádo 232
  getting there and around 229
  history 228–9
  inland villages 232–4
  Kinídaros 234
  Mélanes 234
  Mount Zas 233–4
  mythology 229
  Náxos town 230–2
  Sangrí 232
  tourist information 229
  Tragéa 233–4
  west coast 234
Nazi occupation 38
ND (Néa Demokratikí) 39–40
New Palace period 76
nudism 26
Oenopion 316
Old Palace period 76
opening hours 23, 25
Orion 316
Orpheus 211
Otho, King 36–7
Othoní island 168–9
Ottomans 50
  in Crete 78–9
  in Rhodes 241
ouzeriés 21
Paleoréma 370
Papadiamántis 288–9
Papadópoulos, George 39
Papandréou, Andréas 39–40
Páros 44, **384–91**, *384*
  entertainment and nightlife 391
  festivals 386
  getting there and around 385
  history 384–5
  Náoussa **387–8**, 390
  Parikiá **386–7**, 389–90
  Písso Livádi **388**, 390–1
  tourist information 385–6
  villages and sights 388–9
Pasiphaë 74
PASOK 39–40
passports 7
Paul, King 39
Paul, Saint 50
Peloponnesian War 49, 188
Pericles 49
Persians 49

Phaeacian culture 150
Phaistós 42
Philip II of Macedon 49–50
Philoctetes 358
Pisístratos 48
plane tree (*plátano*) 191–2
Plateía 49
plumbing 27
politics 39–41
Poseidon 41, 74, 237
post offices 25
Post-Palace period 77
Pre-Palatial period 75
pregnant women 5
Proto–Geometric period 77
Psará 328–9
psarotavérnes 19
Psérimos 199–200
psistariá 19
public holidays 24
Pythagoras 278–9
restaurants *see* food and drink
retsina 21
Rhea 74, 237
Rhodes 43, 45, **236–65**, *239*
  Afándou **256**, 257
  Apóllona 264
  Archángelos 256
  Arthípoli 264
  Cape Prassonísi 261
  east coast 255–6
  Embónas 263
  excursions 243
  Faliráki **255**, 257
  Faraklós Castle 256
  festivals 243
  getting there and around 241–2
  history 238–41
  Ialysós 253–4
  Ixiá 253
  Kámiros 263–5
  Kataviá 261
  Kolýmbia 256
  Koskinóu **255**, 257
  Kremastí 264
  Kritiká 253
  Ladiko Bay 255–6
  Líndos 257–61
  Monólithos **262**, 264–5
  Mount Atáviros 263
  Mount Filérimos 254
  mythology 237–38
  Paradíssi 264

Rhodes (*cont'd*)
  Rhodes Town 243–53, *246–7*
  Sálakos 264
  Siána 262–3
  Soroní 264
  southern coast 261–2
  sports and activities 243
  Theológos 264
  tourist information 242–3
  Triánda 253
  Tsambíka 256
  weddings 262
  west coast 262–3
Romans 44, 50, 77–8
rooms and studios 30
Salamis 49
Sammicheli, Michele **109–10**, 151
Sámos 42–3, **271–86**, *273*
  Ag. Konstantínos **283**, 284
  Avlákia **282**, 283–4
  festivals 275
  getting there and around 274
  Heréon 280
  history 272–4
  Karlóvassi **284**, 285
  Kokkári **282**, 283
  Limnionas 285–6
  Malagári **282**, 283
  Manolatés 283–4
  north coast 282–4
  Ormos Márathokámpos 285–6
  Pírgos 281
  Pythagório **277–9**, 281–2
  Sacred Way 279
  Sámos Town 275–7
  Temple of Hera 279–80
  tourist information 274
  Vourliótes 283–4
  western villages 284–6
  wine 282–3
Samothráki 43
Santoríni 392–402, *393*
  Akrotíri **397–8**, 399–400
  caldera islets 401
  festivals 395
  Firá 395–7
  getting there and around 394–5
  history 394
  Imerovígli **400–1**, 401–2
  Kamári **398**, 400
  Megalochóri **398**, 399–400
  Messariá **399**, 400

Santoríni (*cont'd*)
Oía **401**, 402
Perissa **398**, 400
Thíra 398–9
tourist information 395
wine 399
scorpions 14
scuba diving 26
sea turtles 304–5
sea urchins 14
Second World War 37
battle of Crete 79
self-catering holidays 31–3
sheepdogs 14
shopping
opening hours 25
Sikelianós, Angelos 204–5
Sikía 370
Simítis, Kósta 40
Skiáthos **286–92**, *287*
Achládies **290**, 292
Ag. Paraskeví 292
beaches 290–1
Evangelístria 291
festivals 288
getting there and around
286–7
history 286
Kanapítsa **290**, 292
Kástro 291–2
Koukounariés **290–1**, 292
Skiáthos town 288–90
tourist information 287–8
Skýros 402–09, *404*
architecture 406
eating out 408–9
festivals 405
getting there and around 404
history 403
mythology 403
Skýros town **405–7**, 408
tourist information 404–5
villages and sights 407–8
where to stay 408–9
snakes 14
Socrates 49
Solomós, Diónysos 159, **302–3**
specialist holidays 9–11
sports and activities 25–6
Spyrídon, Saint 158
Strofádes 310
students 4–5
studios 30
Suleiman the Magnificent 150

Sými 45, **265–71**, *265*
Chorió **268**, 270–1
eating out 269–71
entertainment and nightlife
271
festivals 267
getting there and around
266–7
Gialós **267**, 270
history 266
Nimborió **267**, 271
Pédi **268**, 271
Sesklí 269
Taxiárchis Michael Panormítis
monastery 268–9
tourist information 267
walking tours 267
where to stay 269–71
Sýros 45, **409–15**, *410*
eating out 414–15
entertainment and nightlife
415
Ermoúpolis **411–13**, 414–15
festivals 411
getting there and around 411
history 409–11
tourist information 411
villages and sights 413–14
where to stay 414–15
tavernas 18–21
Telchines 237
telephones 26–7
temperature chart 14
tennis 26
Thássos 43, **293–9**, *295*
festivals 294
getting there and around 294
history 293–4
Liménas 294–7
villages 297–9
Themistocles 49
Theseus 48, 74, 229
Thíra *see* Santoríni
time 15
toilets 27
Toreador Fresco 111–13
tourist excursion boats 8
tourist information 27–8
travel **2–12**
disabled travellers 12
entry formalities 7
getting there 2–7
Greek Travel Pages 2
specialist holidays 9–11

Web sites 2
see also under individual
places (getting there and
around)
traveller's cheques 23
Turkey 37, 45–6
turtles 304–5
Vathí *see* Sámos
vegetarians 18
Venetians 78–9, 150–1, 202
Venizélos, Elefthérios 37, 92
vipers 14
walking 26
wasps 14
water, drinking 27
watersports 25
Web sites 2
weever fish 14
where to stay 28–33
wine 21–2
Crete 79–80
Kefaloniá **180**, 182
Límnos 362
Sámos 282–3
Santoríni 399
women 5, 33–4
youth hostels 30
youth travel 4–5
zacharoplasteío 19
Zákros 42
Zákynthos 45, **299–310**, *300*
Agalás 307
Argássi 304
caves 308
festivals 301
Gérakas 304
getting there and around 301
history 300–1
Kalamáki **306**, 308
Katastári 308
Kerí 307
Laganás Bay 304–5, 306–7
Límni Kerioú 307
Mount Skopós 305
northwest coast 308–9
Pantokrátoras 307
Skoulikádo 308
southwest coast 309–10
Strofádes 310
tourist information 301
Vassilikós 304
Zákynthos town 302–6
Zeus 41, 74, 237, 378–9
birthplace 130, **133**

Also Available from Cadogan Guides...

Country Guides

Antarctica
Central Asia
China: The Silk Routes
Egypt
France: Southwest France;
    Dordogne, Lot & Bordeaux
France: Southwest France;
    Gascony & the Pyrenees
France: Brittany
France: The Loire
France: The South of France
France: Provence
France: Côte d'Azur
Germany: Bavaria
Greece: The Peloponnese
Holland
Holland: Amsterdam & the Randstad
India
India: South India
India: Goa
Ireland
Ireland: Southwest Ireland
Ireland: Northern Ireland
Italy
Italy: The Bay of Naples and Southern Italy
Italy: Bologna and Emilia Romagna
Italy: Italian Riviera
Italy: Lombardy, Milan and the Italian Lakes
Italy: Rome and the Heart of Italy
Italy: Sardinia
Italy: Tuscany, Umbria and the Marches
Italy: Tuscany
Italy: Umbria
Italy: Venetia and the Dolomites
Japan
Morocco
Portugal
Portugal: The Algarve
Scotland
Scotland: Highlands and Islands
South Africa, Swaziland and Lesotho
Spain
Spain: Southern Spain
Spain: Northern Spain
Syria & Lebanon
Tunisia
Turkey
Yucatán and Southern Mexico
Zimbabwe, Botswana and Namibia

City Guides

Amsterdam
Barcelona
Brussels, Bruges, Ghent & Antwerp
Bruges
Edinburgh
Florence, Siena, Pisa & Lucca
Italy: Three Cities—Rome, Florence, Venice
Italy: Three Cities—Venice, Padua, Verona
Italy: Three Cities—Rome, Naples, Sorrento
Italy: Three Cities—Rome, Padua, Assisi
Japan: Three Cities—Tokyo, Kyoto and
    Ancient Nara
Morocco: Three Cities—Marrakesh, Fez, Rabat
Spain: Three Cities—Granada, Seville,
    Cordoba
Spain: Three Cities—Madrid, Barcelona, Seville
London
London–Paris
London–Brussels
Madrid
Manhattan
Moscow & St Petersburg
Paris
Prague
Rome
St Petersburg
Venice

Island Guides

Caribbean and Bahamas
Jamaica & the Caymans
Greek Islands
Greek Islands By Air
Crete
Mykonos, Santorini & the Cyclades
Rhodes & the Dodecanese
Corfu & the Ionian Islands
Madeira & Porto Santo
Malta
Sardinia
Sicily

Plus...

Bugs, Bites & Bowels
London Markets
Take the Kids Travelling
Take the Kids London
Take the Kids Paris and Disneyland
Take the Kids Amsterdam

Available from good bookshops or via, in the UK, **Grantham Book Services**, Isaac Newton Way, Alma Park Industrial Estate, Grantham NG31 9SD, ℗ (01476) 541 080, ℗ (01476) 541 061; and in North America from **The Globe Pequot Press**, 246 Goose Lane, PO Box 480, Guilford, Connecticut 06437–0480, ℗ (800) 243 0495, ℗ (800) 820 2329.

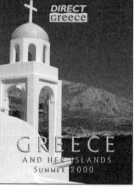